Part 1 English Language Learners: Professional Development Articles

Contents

Resources on Reading Street for English Language Learner Support

All the support you need for your ELL instruction.

The Teacher's Edition has ELL instructional strategies built into the lesson plans at point of use. The lessons provide guidance in using sheltered techniques and routines for teaching academic vocabulary, listening comprehension, phonics, vocabulary, reading comprehension, grammar and conventions, and writing.

Teacher's Edition

ELL Support pages

ELL Posters contain high-quality illustrations and five days of activities to support key oral vocabulary, selection vocabulary, and lesson concepts.

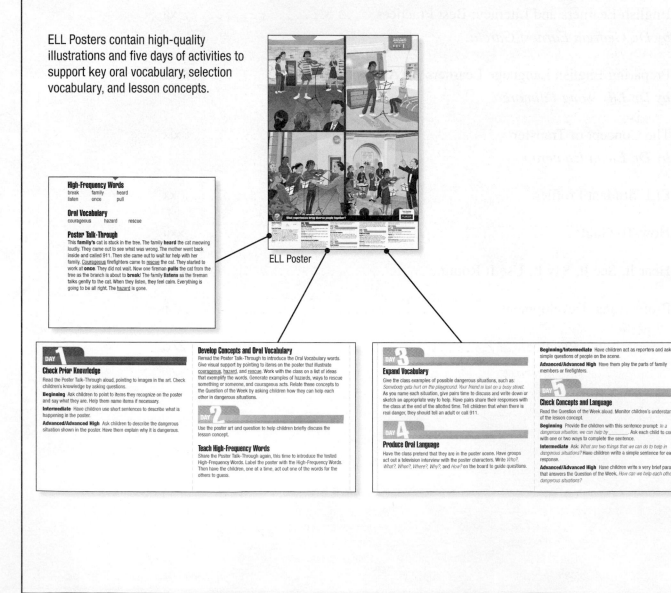

High-Frequency Words
break   family   heard
listen   once   pull

Oral Vocabulary
courageous   hazard   rescue

Poster Talk-Through
This **family's** cat is stuck in the tree. The family **heard** the cat meowing loudly. They came out to see what was wrong. The mother went back inside and called 911. Then she came out to wait for help with her family. Courageous firefighters came to rescue the cat. They started to work at **once**. They did not wait. Now one fireman **pulls** the cat from the tree as the branch is about to **break**! The family **listens** as the fireman talks gently to the cat. When they listen, they feel calm. Everything is going to be all right. The hazard is gone.

ELL Poster

DAY 1

Check Prior Knowledge
Read the Poster Talk-Through aloud, pointing to images in the art. Check children's knowledge by asking questions.

Beginning Ask children to point to items they recognize on the poster and say what they are. Help them name items if necessary.

Intermediate Have children use short sentences to describe what is happening in the poster.

Advanced/Advanced High Ask children to describe the dangerous situation shown in the poster. Have them explain why it is dangerous.

Develop Concepts and Oral Vocabulary
Reread the Poster Talk-Through to introduce the Oral Vocabulary words. Give visual support by pointing to items on the poster that illustrate courageous, hazard, and rescue. Work with the class on a list of ideas that exemplify the words. Generate examples of hazards, ways to rescue something or someone, and courageous acts. Relate these concepts to the Question of the Week by asking children how they can help each other in dangerous situations.

DAY 2

Use the poster art and question to help children briefly discuss the lesson concept.

Teach High-Frequency Words
Share the Poster Talk-Through again, this time to introduce the tested High-Frequency Words. Label the poster with the High-Frequency Words. Then have the children, one at a time, act out one of the words for the others to guess.

DAY 3

Expand Vocabulary
Give the class examples of possible dangerous situations, such as: Somebody gets hurt on the playground. Your friend is lost on a busy street. As you name each situation, give pairs time to discuss and write down or sketch an appropriate way to help. Have pairs share their responses with the class at the end of the allotted time. Tell children that when there is real danger, they should tell an adult or call 911.

DAY 4

Produce Oral Language
Have the class pretend that they are in the poster scene. Have groups act out a television interview with the poster characters. Write Who?, What?, When?, Where?, Why?, and How? on the board to guide questions.

Beginning/Intermediate Have children act as reporters and ask simple questions of people on the scene.

Advanced/Advanced High Have them play the parts of family members or firefighters.

DAY 5

Check Concepts and Language
Read the Question of the Week aloud. Monitor children's understanding of the lesson concept.

Beginning Provide the children with this sentence prompt: In a dangerous situation, we can help by _____. Ask each child to come up with one or two ways to complete the sentence.

Intermediate Ask: What are two things that we can do to help in dangerous situations? Have children write a simple sentence for each response.

Advanced/Advanced High Have children write a very brief paragraph that answers the Question of the Week, How can we help each other in dangerous situations?

The ELL Handbook includes phonics and grammar transition lessons, comprehension skill practice, selection vocabulary word cards, study guides for ELL Readers, and multilingual selection summaries and vocabulary charts. Weekly planners provide daily instructional plans.

ELL Handbook

Weekly Planner

Instructional-level fiction and nonfiction books are provided for readers at all proficiency levels. The ELL, ELD, and Concept Literacy Readers relate to weekly concepts and offer students opportunities to read texts and practice target skills and strategies.

ELD/ELL Reader Teaching Guide

ELD Reader

ELL Reader

Concept Literacy Reader

Technology

Concept Talk Video

Use the Concept Talk Video to activate an engaging discussion about the weekly concept. Use the Concept Talk Video Routine found in the ELL Handbook to guide students' understanding.

AudioText CD

Use the AudioText CD and the AudioText CD Routine in this ELL Handbook to help students build fluency and comprehension and prepare for reading the main selection.

I love my dog Thunder.

Grammar Jammer

Grammar Jammer provides additional practice with weekly grammar skills. For suggestions on how to use this learning tool, see the Grammar Jammer Routine in the ELL Handbook.

ELL Handbook

v

Language Development Student Outcomes

Language Learning Strategies	• Use prior knowledge and experiences to understand English. • Self-monitor oral or written language to recognize and correct errors or to seek help. • Use strategic learning techniques (such as concept mapping, drawing, memorizing, comparing, contrasting, or reviewing) to learn vocabulary. • Use learning strategies when speaking (request assistance, employ non-verbal cues, or use synonyms and descriptions in place of unknown English words). • Use and reuse newly acquired English words and expressions to improve proficiency and to build concepts. • Learn new essential language by using familiar or accessible language. • Distinguish between formal and informal English and use each language register in appropriate circumstances, in accord with grade-level expectations. • Develop and use language-learning strategies (such as looking for patterns in language or analyzing sayings and expressions), in accord with grade-level expectations.
Listening Skills	• Distinguish sounds and intonation patterns in English words and expressions with increasing clarity. • Distinguish phonetic sounds of English during word learning. • Learn English language structures, expressions, and vocabulary by listening to instruction and talking with peers and teachers. • Self-monitor for understanding of language during instruction and conversations, and seek clarification as needed. • Use visual resources, context, and familiar language to better understand unfamiliar spoken English. • Listen to a variety of media, paying attention to language meaning, to build concepts and acquire language. • Understand the meaning, main points, and important details of spoken language about familiar or unfamiliar topics. • Understand information and implied ideas in complex spoken language, in accord with grade-level expectations. • Demonstrate listening comprehension by following directions, responding to questions and requests, collaborating with peers, taking notes, or retelling and summarizing spoken messages.
Speaking Skills	• Produce phonetic sounds in newly acquired words and expressions in order to pronounce English words in an understandable manner. • Learn and use high-frequency English words to identify and describe people, places, animals, and objects. • Learn English vocabulary by retelling simple stories and information represented or supported by pictures. • Learn and use English words and expressions needed for classroom communication. • Speak using a variety of English grammatical structures, sentence lengths, sentence types, and connecting words with increasing accuracy and ease. • Speak using grade-appropriate content-area vocabulary in context to learn new English words and build academic language proficiency. • Share information interactively with peers and teachers. • Ask for and give information, using high-frequency, concrete words and expressions for basic communication and using abstract and content-based vocabulary during extended speaking assignments.

- Express opinions, ideas, and feelings, ranging from using words and short phrases to participating in discussions about various grade-appropriate topics.
- Explain, narrate, and describe with increasing specificity and detail as more English is acquired.
- Adapt spoken language appropriately for formal and informal purposes.
- Respond orally to information in print, electronic, audio, and visual media to build concepts and acquire language.

Reading Skills

- Learn relationships between sounds and letters in English, and decode words by recognizing sound-letter relationships and identifying cognates, affixes, roots, and base words.
- Recognize the directionality of written English: left to right and top to bottom.
- Develop basic English sight vocabulary.
- Derive meaning of environmental print.
- Comprehend English used routinely in grade-level texts.
- Use before-reading strategies such as previewing graphic organizers and illustrations or learning topic-related vocabulary to enhance comprehension of written text.
- Read adapted content-area material with a decreasing need for linguistic accommodations as more English is learned.
- Use visual resources and context to read grade-appropriate text with understanding and to acquire vocabulary including academic language.
- Use support from peers and teachers to read grade-appropriate text with understanding and to acquire vocabulary including academic language.
- Demonstrate comprehension of increasingly complex grade-appropriate texts in English by participating in shared reading, retelling, or summarizing; responding to questions; and taking notes.
- Read silently with increasing ease and comprehension for sustained periods.
- Demonstrate English comprehension by employing and expanding basic reading skills (such as summarizing, understanding supporting ideas and details in text and graphic sources, and distinguishing main ideas from details) in accord with grade-level needs.
- Demonstrate English comprehension by employing and expanding inferential skills (such as predicting, making connections between ideas, drawing conclusions from text and graphic sources, and finding supporting text evidence) in accord with grade-level needs.
- Demonstrate English comprehension by employing and expanding analytical skills (such as evaluating written information and critically examining texts) in accord with grade-level needs.

Writing Skills

- Represent the sounds of the English language with letters when writing words in English.
- Write using newly acquired basic English vocabulary and grade-level academic vocabulary.
- Spell common English words with increasing accuracy, and use spelling patterns correctly as more English is acquired.
- Edit writing for standard grammar and usage, including subject-verb agreement, pronoun agreement, and appropriate verb tenses, in accord with grade-level expectations as more English is acquired.
- Use grammatical structures (such as verbs in different tenses, pronouns, possessive nouns, contractions, and negatives) correctly in writing, in accord with grade-level expectations.
- Write using a variety of grade-appropriate sentence lengths, patterns, and connecting words to combine phrases, clauses, and sentences in increasingly accurate ways.
- Narrate, describe, and explain with increasing detail to fulfill grade-appropriate writing needs as more English is acquired.

Grade 4 Readers on Reading Street

Every week there are a variety of readers to choose from to target instruction and meet the language development needs and reading levels of all learners. Every reader supports weekly grade-level concept development and the Question of the Week.

Leveled Readers

Weekly fiction and nonfiction readers are provided for students at the On-Level, Strategic Intervention, and Advanced levels.

Build Concepts

The Concept Literacy Reader builds concepts and language.

| On-Level | Strategic Intervention | Advanced | Concept Literacy |

Build Language

Scaffolded versions build vocabulary and comprehension skills each week at different proficiency levels.

ELD Reader

ELL Reader

Beginning • Intermediate	Intermediate • Advanced • Advanced High
• Contains the same high-quality art as the ELL Reader.	• Contains the same high-quality art as the ELD Reader.
• Text adapted for Beginning and Intermediate proficiency levels.	• Text adapted for Intermediate to Advanced High proficiency levels.
• High-frequency and concept words are emphasized.	• Concept words that students need to know to understand the text are highlighted and defined.
• Graphic elements are simplified.	• Graphic elements such as captions, diagrams, maps, flow charts, and signs are included.
• Captions for photos are simple, then progress to either phrases or short sentences.	• Captions for photos are complete sentences.

Scott Foresman ELL Authors

Elena Izquierdo, Ph.D.
Associate Professor
University of Texas at El Paso

Jim Cummins, Ph.D.
Professor
Department of Curriculum,
Teaching and Learning
University of Toronto

Lily Wong Fillmore, Ph.D.
Professor Emerita
Graduate School of Education
University of California, Berkeley

Georgia Earnest García, Ph.D.
Professor
Language and Literacy Division
Department of Curriculum
and Instruction
University of Illinois at
Urbana-Champaign

George A. González, Ph.D.
Professor (Retired)
School of Education
University of Texas-Pan American,
Edinburg

The Three Pillars of English Language Learning

Dr. Jim Cummins, the University of Toronto

In order to understand how English learners develop second-language literacy and reading comprehension, we must distinguish between three different aspects of language proficiency:

Conversational fluency This dimension of proficiency represents the ability to carry on a conversation in face-to-face situations. Most native speakers of English have developed conversational fluency by age 5. This fluency involves use of high-frequency words and simple grammatical constructions. English learners generally develop fluency in conversational English within a year or two of intensive exposure to the language in school or in their neighborhood environments.

Discrete language skills These skills reflect specific phonological, literacy, and grammatical knowledge that students can acquire in two ways— through direct instruction and through immersion in a literacy-rich and language-rich environment in home or in school. The discrete language skills acquired early include:

- knowledge of the letters of the alphabet
- knowledge of the sounds represented by individual letters and combinations of letters
- the ability to decode written words

Children can learn these specific language skills concurrently with their development of basic English vocabulary and conversational fluency.

Academic language proficiency This dimension of proficiency includes knowledge of the less frequent vocabulary of English as well as the ability to interpret and produce increasingly complex written language. As students progress through the grades, they encounter:

- far more low-frequency words, primarily from Greek and Latin sources
- complex syntax (for example, sentences in passive voice)
- abstract expressions

Acquiring academic language is challenging. Schools spend at least 12 years trying to teach all students the complex language associated with academic success. It is hardly surprising that research has repeatedly shown that English language learners, on average, require *at least* 5 years of exposure to academic English to catch up to native-speaker norms.

Effective instruction for English language learners is built on three fundamental pillars.

English Language Learners

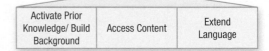

| Activate Prior Knowledge/ Build Background | Access Content | Extend Language |

Activate Prior Knowledge/ Build Background

No learner is a blank slate. Each person's prior experience provides the foundation for interpreting new information. In reading, we construct meaning by bringing our prior knowledge of language and of the world to the text. The more we already know about the topic in the text, the more of the text we can understand. Our prior knowledge enables us to make inferences about the meaning of words and expressions that we may not have come across before. Furthermore, the more of the text we understand, the more new knowledge we can acquire. This expands our knowledge base (what cognitive psychologists call *schemata*, or underlying patterns of concepts). Such comprehension, in turn, enables us to understand even more concepts and vocabulary.

It is important to *activate* students' prior knowledge because students may not realize what they know about a particular topic or issue. Their knowledge may not facilitate learning unless that knowledge is brought to consciousness.

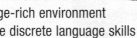

Teachers can use a variety of strategies to activate students' prior knowledge:	
Brainstorming/Discussion	Visual stimuli
Direct experience	Student writing
Dramatization	Drawing

When students don't already have knowledge about a topic, it is important to help them acquire that knowledge. For example, in order to comprehened texts such as *The Midnight Ride of Paul Revere,* students need to have background knowledge about the origin of the United States.

Access Content

How can teachers make complex academic English comprehensible for students who are still in the process of learning English?

We can *scaffold* students' learning by modifying the input itself. Here are a variety of ways of modifying the presentation of academic content to students so that they can more effectively gain access to the meaning.

Using Visuals Visuals enable students to "see" the basic concepts we are trying to teach much more effectively than if we rely only on words. Among the visuals we can use are:

- pictures/diagrams
- vocabulary cards
- real objects
- graphic organizers
- maps

Dramatization/Acting Out For beginning English learners, physical response, in which they follow commands such as "Turn around," can be highly effective. The meanings of words can be demonstrated through *gestures* and *pantomime.*

Language Clarification This category of teaching methods includes language-oriented activities that clarify the meaning of new words and concepts. *Use of dictionaries,* either bilingual or English-only, is still the most direct method of getting access to meaning.

Making Personal and Cultural Connections We should constantly search for ways to link academic content with what students already know or what is familiar to them from their family or cultural experiences. This not only validates children's sense of identity, but it also makes the learning more meaningful.

Extend Language

A systematic exploration of language is essential if students are to develop a curiosity about language and deepen their understanding of how words work. Students should become *language detectives* who investigate the mysteries of language and how it has been used throughout history to shape and change society.

Students also can explore the building blocks of language. A large percentage of the less frequently heard academic vocabulary of English derives from Latin and Greek roots. Word formation follows predictable patterns. These patterns are very similar in English and Spanish.

When students know rules or conventions of how words are formed, it gives them an edge in extending vocabulary. It helps them figure out the meanings of words and how to form different parts of speech from words. The exploration of language can focus on meaning, form, or use.

Focus on meaning Categories that can be explored within a focus on meaning include:

- home language equivalents or cognates
- synonyms, antonyms, and homonyms
- meanings of prefixes, roots, and suffixes

Focus on form Categories that can be explored within a focus on form include:

- word families
- grammatical patterns
- words with same prefixes, roots, or suffixes

Focus on use Categories that can be explored within a focus on use include:

- general uses
- idioms
- metaphorical use
- proverbs
- advertisements
- puns and jokes

The Three Pillars

- Activate Prior Knowledge/Build Background,
- Access Content,
- Extend Language,

establish a solid structure for the effective instruction of English language learners.

English Learners and Literacy: Best Practices

Dr. Georgia Earnest García, the University of Illinois at Urbana-Champaign

Like other children, English language learners come to school with much oral language knowledge and experience. Their knowledge and experience in languages other than English provide skills and world knowledge that teachers can build on.

Making literacy instruction comprehensible to English language learners is essential. Many of the teaching strategies developed for children who are proficient in English can be adapted for English learners, and many strategies from an English language learner curriculum are also useful in "mainstream" reading education.

Building on Children's Knowledge

It is vital to learn about each student's literacy development and proficiency in the home language. School personnel should ask parents:

- How many years of school instruction has the child received in the home language?
- Can the child read and write in that language?
- Can the child read in any other language?

Students can transfer aspects of home-language literacy to their English literacy development, such as phonological awareness and reading (or listening) comprehension strategies. If they already know key concepts and vocabulary in their home languages, then they can transfer that knowledge to English. For the vocabulary concepts they already know in their home languages, they only need to learn the English labels. Not all English learners automatically transfer what they have learned in the home language to their reading in English. Teachers can help facilitate relevant transfer by explicitly asking English learners to think about what they have learned about a topic in the home language.

A teacher need not speak each student's home language to encourage English language learners to work together and benefit from one another's knowledge. Students can communicate in their home languages and English, building the content knowledge, confidence, and English skills that they need to participate fully in learning. Devising activities in which students who share home languages can work together also allows a school to pool resources, such as bilingual dictionaries and other books, as well as home-language tutors or aides.

Sheltering Instruction in English

Often, beginning and intermediate English language learners may not understand what their classroom teachers say or read aloud in English. These students benefit when teachers shelter, or make comprehensible, their literacy instruction.

Sheltered techniques include using:

- consistent, simplified, clearly enunciated, and slower-paced oral language to explain literacy concepts or activities
- gestures, photos, illustrations, drawings, real objects, dramatization, and/or physical action to illustrate important concepts and vocabulary
- activities that integrate reading, writing, listening, and speaking, so students see, hear, read, and write new vocabulary, sentence structures, and content

When it is clear from students' actions and responses that they understand what is being said, teachers can vary their strategies. As students' comprehension expands, teachers can gradually curtail their use of adapted oral language and of gestures, illustrations, and dramatizations.

Adapting Literacy Activities

Teachers can use many instructional activities developed for native English speakers with English language learners. For example, teacher read-alouds, shared reading, and paired reading can allow an English learner to follow the text during a reading. Such techniques greatly improve students' learning skills and comprehension.

Similarly, interactive journal writing, in which the teacher and student take turns writing entries, allows students to explore topics and ask questions. It also allows teachers to engage in ongoing authentic assessment of student proficiency and to pinpoint areas of misunderstanding.

Small group instruction and discussion also are helpful. Beginning English language learners benefit from the repeated readings of predictable texts with illustrations, especially when the teacher has provided a brief preview of each text to introduce the topic of the story and preview new vocabulary.

Repeated reading aloud of such predictable, patterned, illustrated texts provides English language learners with multiple opportunities to match the text they read with the words they hear. When students participate in shared reading and echo the spoken text or read the words aloud chorally, anxiety about pronunciation or decoding errors is reduced. When teachers choose texts that are culturally familiar and ask English language learners personal questions related to the text, the result is a lower-risk learning environment and an increased opportunity for students to make accurate inferences.

Examples of Teaching Strategies

Before students read content material, provide them with hands-on or visual experience directly related to the content. Then have them use a graphic organizer to map what they have learned or seen about the topic. Let pairs or small groups of students brainstorm for words that are related to the concept. Then introduce other related words, including vocabulary from the reading. Illustrate new concepts or vocabulary with drawings,

photographs, or artifacts that represent the concepts. The hands-on experience and graphic organizer that precede the reading help introduce students to new concepts. Students will thus be familiar with the selection's subject before they begin to read.

Semantic Mapping Working with graphic organizers can help teach vocabulary and concepts in subject areas.

For example, before a reading on the subject of baby animals, have students help you to complete a semantic map showing pictures of animals and the names of baby animals. Ask them to volunteer the names for animal babies in their home language and transcribe their responses. Then show students examples of the different forms of writing. Ask students to meet in small groups to identify the examples. They may do this in English or their home language. If they use the home language, the teacher needs to write the English labels on the board for each form of writing. Then students need to enter the words for the different forms of writing, with drawings or home language equivalents, into a vocabulary notebook.

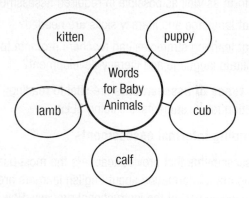

Summarizing After reading, students can dictate what they remember from their reading to the teacher. Students can then illustrate their summaries, and label the illustrations with vocabulary from the reading.

Preparing English Language Learners for Assessment

Dr. Lily Wong Fillmore, the University of California, Berkeley

Under federal and state law, all students—including English learners—must be assessed annually on their progress toward mastery of academic standards in reading, math, and science. Many questions arise when certain assessments are used with ELLs because their test scores are never easy to interpret when they are assessed in English. The most critical question is this: What do test scores mean when they are based on instruction and assessments given in a language students have not yet mastered? Although difficult to interpret, assessments are required of all students, so we must consider how to help ELLs perform as well as possible.

Addressed in this essay

- What can teachers do to fast-track their ELL students' mastery of the language and content needed to perform as well as possible in required assessments?
- What language and literacy skills are needed?
- What learning strategies can teachers promote to facilitate language and literacy development?

Three types of assessments are vital to reading instruction for all students, including ELLs.

1. Ongoing informal assessments

The assessments that provide teachers the most useful and important information about English learners are those used as part of the instructional process. How well do children understand the materials they are working with, and what needs adjustment or modification in instruction? These are built into these instructional materials and help teachers keep an ongoing record of student progress over time. Such assessments do not need to be elaborate. Asking children what they think is happening in a text can reveal how well they comprehend what they are reading. Asking children what they think words or phrases mean can show

whether they are trying to make sense of text. These types of questions are highly useful to teachers since they allow them to monitor participation levels and help them discover who understands the materials and who needs more attention and support.

2. Diagnostic assessments

A second type of assessment that some ELLs may require is diagnostic, and it is needed when individuals are not making the progress expected of them. The school must determine where student problems lie (e.g., skill development, or perception or awareness of English sounds, vocabulary, or grammar) before teachers can provide the corrective help needed.

3. Standardized assessments

The type of assessments that causes teachers of ELLs the greatest concern are the standards-based tests of English Language Arts and content area tests (especially in Math). These state tests are required of all students and are recognized as "high stakes" tests for students and for schools. They are often used to evaluate the effectiveness of a curriculum, the teacher, or the instructional approach used.

What's involved in reading?

Reading skills are built on several types of knowledge: linguistic, symbolic, experiential, and strategic. Each is crucial and is linked with the others. *Language is fundamental;* it is the medium through which meaning—information, story, knowledge, poetry, and thought—is communicated from writer to reader. Unlike speech, what is communicated by written language is indirect and *encoded in symbols* that must be deciphered before access to meaning is possible.

But reading goes beyond mere decoding. Texts call for readers to apply what they know about how language is used to convey thought and ideas to interpret what they are reading. Having *experienced reading as a sense-making activity*, readers will seek meaning as they learn to read. This calls for *special strategies:* They look for meaning if they assume it is to be found in texts. If they do not know

the language in which the texts are written, they will recognize that learning the code is the key to unlocking meaning. They will pay attention to the language and ask: *What is this saying? What does this mean? How does this relate to what I already know about the way the language works?*

English learners have an easier time learning to read in English if they have already learned to read in their first language. Without question, a language barrier makes learning to read a more difficult task. But if students have already learned to read in their primary language, they know what is involved, what to expect, and thus they are in a better position to deal with learning to read In the new language in order to access meaning.

Can children learn to read in a language before they are fully proficient in that language?

Can they in fact learn the language through reading? *Yes, but only with ample instructional assistance that supports the development of both.* Ideally, reading instruction in English comes after ELLs have gained some familiarity with the sounds and patterns of spoken English. Children need to hear the sounds of the new language before they can connect symbols to those sounds. For example, in order for children to gain confidence relating the many vowel sounds of English to the five vowel symbols used to "spell them," they need help hearing them and differentiating them in words.

Similarly, many ELLs need help dealing with the ways consonants pile up at the beginning and at the ends of syllables and words in English, which may be quite different than the way consonants are used in their primary language. Most crucially, ELLs need help in connecting the words they are learning to decode from the text to their referents. Using pictures, demonstrations, diagrams, gestures, and enactments, teachers can help ELLs see how the words, phrases, and sentences in the reading selections have meaning that can be accessed through the language they are learning.

Helping ELLs become successful readers

The most important way to help ELLs perform well in mandated reading assessments is by giving them the instructional support they need to become successful readers. This involves help in:

- Learning English
- Discovering the purpose of reading
- Becoming active learners
- Gaining access to academic language

Learning English

The more proficient children are in the language they are reading, the more readily they learn to read. For ELLs, support for learning English is support for learning to read. The most effective kind of help comes in content-focused language instruction, where learners are engaged in grade-level-appropriate instructional activities and their participation is scaffolded and supported as needed.

The most effective activities provide ELLs ample opportunity to hear English and to use it productively in meaningful communication. Teachers play a vital role in creating a supportive classroom environment. ELLs must be able to partIcIpate to the extent possible (again, with as much support as needed) in discussions with classmates who are more proficient in English. Peers can offer practice and support, but only teachers can ensure that ELLs get access to the kind of language needed for literacy development.

Purpose of reading

The greatest dangers ELLs face in learning to read in English before they are proficient in that language is that the effort involved in decoding takes precedence in their minds over all else. Connections between words and referents, between words and structures, and between text and meaning are overlooked when children focus on sounding out, figuring out symbols, and figuring out sounds. This is especially likely to happen when there is too little emphasis placed on reading as a sense-making activity in instructional programs. If meaning—no matter how difficult it is to come by—is not constantly emphasized in reading instruction, children end up believing that decoding is reading, and that there is nothing missing when they read without understanding.

Decoding becomes an end in itself, and the real purpose of reading is lost. Unfortunately, this is the outcome for many ELLs, who even after having learned English do not perform well in reading assessments.

Literacy in English begins as deciphering for ELLs; they must first figure out how the code in which the text is written works. It is not until the reader engages in an interpretive process in which the thoughts, information, concepts, situations, and relations encoded in the texts are manifested as meanings that there is real reading. This is true for both ELLs and for native English speakers. ELLs, however, will need a lot of guidance and instructional support from teachers to do that. Once children have gained enough familiarity with English to participate even at a rudimentary level in discussions about reading selections and content, they begin to learn that the materials they are reading have something to say to them and that hearing what they have to say is the real purpose of learning to read.

Active readers

Helping children become active learners of English and users of the literacy skills they are acquiring is a key to their becoming successful students and performing well in the assessments they have to take. This is accomplished by encouraging children to take an active role in instructional activities, asking questions, seeking answers, and trying to make sense of what they are studying in school.

Both teachers and students can have many preconceived ideas about the roles they play as teachers and learners. Children sometimes come to school believing that learning is something that will be done to them, rather than something they must take an active role in doing. In their view, the role of the teacher is active and the role they play as learners is passive. When teachers share that belief, there is little likelihood of active or independent learning. Instruction is most effective when teachers are knowledgeable about the subject matter they are teaching, and they create a classroom environment in which learners can take an active role in discovering how things work, what things mean, and how to get and make sense of information.

Academic English

Teachers are aware that the language used in written texts is sufficiently different from everyday spoken language to constitute a barrier to children who are not already familiar with it. Academic English is not just another name for "standard English." It is, instead, the special forms of standard English used in academic discourse and in written texts. It makes use of grammatical constructions, words, and rhetorical conventions that are not often used in everyday spoken language.

Paradoxically, academic language is both a prerequisite for full literacy and the outcome of it. Some children arrive at school with a running start in acquiring it. Children who come from homes where family members engage in frequent discussions of books and ideas are already familiar with it, and thus have an advantage learning to read.

It should be noted that the language used at home does not have to be English for children to benefit from such experiences. Teachers can provide their students, irrespective of background, experiences with academic language by reading to them and discussing readings, instructional activities, and experiences. By drawing children into instructional conversations focused on the language they encounter in their school texts and other materials, teachers get children to notice language itself and to figure out how it works.

Supporting language and literacy development for ELLs

Teachers support language development by engaging children as active participants in making sense of the texts they are working on. They do it by drawing the English learners into discussions relating to the texts. Even relative newcomers are able to participate in these discussions as long as ample scaffolding is provided:

It says here, "Her teacher picked up the paper and studied it carefully."

Hector, what does the text tell us Vashti's teacher did first?

Yes, she picked up the paper first.

Take a look at the picture. Marta, can you show us which part of the sentence tells us what the teacher is doing?

Can you tell us what she is doing?

Yes! She is studying the paper carefully.

Teachers draw attention to words, phrases, and sentences, by asking: "Let's see if we can figure out what that means!" By relating language to meaning, they help students gain access to meaning by demonstrating, referring to illustrations and diagrams, and paraphrasing in simpler language.

Instructional conversations about the texts they are reading are as essential for newcomers as they are for ELLs who have already gained some proficiency in English. It is vital to their literacy development to realize that what they are "reading" can be understood, even if its meaning is not immediately available to them as it would be to readers who are fully proficient in English. Without such help, ELLs sometimes come to believe that decoding without access to meaning is an empty exercise one does in school, and except for that, it has little relevance to their lives.

Teachers can help students discover how the language works and how to extract meaning from texts by considering how the language they encounter can convey information, ideas, stories, feelings, and images. This cannot wait until the learners are fully proficient in the language they are reading. It can enhance language development if done from the start, as soon as ELLs are introduced to English reading.

Strategies for supporting language and literacy development and preparing ELLs for assessment

The most effective support comes in the form of instructional conversations in which ELLs are drawn into discussions of reading selections and content. By hearing their teachers and other classmates discuss the materials they are reading, they gradually learn how the language works in texts and in conversation.

- Draw attention to the language used in reading selections and other text materials—words, phrases, and sentences—and relate them to meaning that is discussed and commented on, both locally and globally, to help ELLs learn how to get at meaning in texts.

- Provide students ample opportunity to use the language of texts in speaking (during discussions of the reading selections, for example) and in writing (in response to writing prompts).

- Teach English learners to be strategic readers by guiding them to assume that the text should make sense and that meaning can be accessed by figuring out what the words, phrases, and sentences mean.

- Teach students to ask questions about meaning as it unfolds in the text. Help them recognize that some parts of texts provide background knowledge while other parts reveal new information.

- Teach children how to relate new information presented in a text to what is already known. Train students to make inferences about meaning based on the words and phrases used in a text.

- Expect ELLs to make progress, and then ensure it by providing ample grade-level discussion of content. At the same time, recognize that it takes time to learn English, and that learners may differ in the amount and kind of help they need in order to make progress.

- Recognize that the most crucial kind of preparation for assessment is in helping children develop the *language and literacy skills* that are essential to successful performance in tests and for academic progress itself.

- Call children's attention to words, phrases, and constructions that often figure in text items. For example, words such as *both, not,* and *best* may not seem to be noteworthy, but their uses in test questions prove otherwise. ELLs need help in seeing how such words frame and constrain the ideas expressed in sentences in which they appear.

- Teach children the logic of test questions. Use released test items or models of test items (both of which are likely to be available online from your state department of education or district Web sites). Show children, for example, that the question, "Which of the following is NOT a sentence?" entails that all of the listed options except one *are* sentences.

- Teach children to read carefully. Children who are fully proficient in English may occasionally benefit from test-taking strategies such as reading the test question and answer options first and then skimming the test passage to find information that will aid in the selection of the correct answer to the question. This tactic does not serve English learners well. They need to read and understand the passage carefully, and then consider how to answer the questions asked.

- Teach children when the text calls for activation of prior knowledge. All children have such knowledge, but English learners need help in deciding where it is called for and how they should bring what they already know to interpret the texts they are reading.

- Expand children's horizons by reading them texts that may be too difficult to handle on their own. Help them make sense of such materials by commenting on meaning, drawing attention to how language is used

in them, and engaging children in discussions about aspects of the texts.

The texts that are read to children, and the ones they read themselves, provide reliable access to the academic language they need for literacy and for assessment, provided teachers call their attention to language and help children see how it works. Teachers do this by identifying interesting (not just new) phrases and commenting on them, inviting children to try using the phrases, and providing scaffolds as needed; they model the uses of language from texts in subsequent instructional activities; they encourage children to remember and keep records of words they learn from texts; they remind them when words and phrases encountered earlier show up again in different contexts.

The Concept of Transfer

Dr. Elena Izquierdo, the University of Texas at El Paso

Research continues to support the critical role of the child's first language (L1) in literacy development and its effect on literacy in (L2) English. Strong L1 literacy skills facilitate the transfer into English literacy, and students ultimately progress rapidly into learning in English. In reality, the concept of transfer refers to the child's facility in appropriating knowledge from one language to the other. Children do not know they know, but they know. They are constantly and indirectly, unconsciously and automatically, constructing the knowledge that is inherent in the contexts for which each of these languages can function. Reasearch by Jim Cummins has shown that the effective transfer of skills transpires as students develop their metalinguistic and metacognitive skills and as they engage in a contrastive analysis of the two languages.

Matters of transfer occur within essentials of language that are (1) common to L1 and L2; (2) similar, but not exact in both languages; and (3) specific to each language and not applicable to the other language. In essence, children develop a special awareness of language and its function;

learn that some sounds are the same in both languages; and also learn that there are certain boundaries for specific sounds depending on the language.

Children who have developed an awareness for phonemes, phonics, vocabulary building, and reading comprehension skills, can transfer these skills to English. They develop an enhanced awareness of the relationship between their L1 and English, which leads them to successfully appropriate strategies of transfer in similar types of word recognition processing; searching for cognates; making reference to prior knowledge, inferencing, questioning, and monitoring. Facilitating these cognitive skills in children will support their success in English literacy and their learning in English.

English Language Learner Profiles

English Language Learners—ELLs—are a quickly growing population in U.S. schools. While some are children of recent immigrants, many more were born in the United States but have spoken other languages in their homes. ELLs may come to classrooms with knowledge of other places as well as diverse cultures and customs. As you work with ELLs, you will want to consider how proficient your students are and how you can make the academic content accessible. You will be integrating language and content instruction, most likely within the context of a classroom of students with many abilities and proficiencies. As you consider how to best meet the needs of ELLs in your classroom, think about their characteristics, patterns of development, and literacy challenges.

General Characteristics of English Language Learners

- ELLs have a first language—also called a home language, primary language, or native language—other than English and are in the process of acquiring English.

- Some ELLs have newly arrived in the United States, while others were born in the United States but have lived for many years in households where family members do not speak English.

- Some ELLs have already acquired and developed literacy skills in their native languages, while others have not learned the academic vocabulary and background knowledge necessary for continued success in school.

- ELLs vary in that some have primary languages that resemble English in word order, sound system, and in the patterns of forming words. Spanish, French, and Portuguese, for example, are languages that share alphabets and left-to-right directionality with English. Some words in English and Spanish are cognates. Some languages, such as Swahili or Vietnamese, do not have as much in common with English. For children who speak these languages, initial learning of English is more difficult.

Types of English Language Learners

- **Newly Arrived English Language Learners** may come with adequate or limited schooling. Those with adequate schooling will make steady academic progress, although they may have difficulty on standardized tests in English. Those with limited formal schooling may lack a sense of school culture and routines. Their limited literacy development may lead to poor academic achievement until both their background knowledge and English proficiency grow.

- **Long Term English Language Learners** have been in the United States for some time, but they have had limited exposure to English in their communities and little reason to learn or know English. As they begin to acquire English, they may lose proficiency in their native languages and have difficulty grasping new content.

- **Older English Language Learners** may be more capable of quickly learning academic concepts even though they have not developed the language proficiency of other students their age. Curriculum challenges will help these students bridge their academic gaps while they gain English proficiency. Provide scaffolds for instruction and organize collaborative activities to help these students gain success.

Literacy Challenges for ELLs

1. **Phonemic Awareness** ELLs may find it difficult to differentiate between certain phonemes in English. Some children may find it difficult to separate groups of phonemes into words.

2. **Phonics** ELLs need to be able to match sounds to letters and letters to sounds in order to read and write English successfully. They need to develop both oral vocabularies of frequently used words and written vocabularies of sight words.

3. **Vocabulary Development** Some ELLs are able to repeat, pronounce, decode, and produce words in English without really knowing what these words mean. ELLs need opportunities to link vocabulary words to meaning through routines, concrete objects, pictures and gestures, physical movement, and experiences. These students need multiple exposures to words through explanation, discussion, and repeated readings.

4. **Fluency** Fluent reading involves reading quickly, accurately, and expressively. This can be challenging for ELLs, who need many opportunities to listen and speak English before they can feel comfortable and successful with fluent reading. In large groups, ELLs may be reluctant to read orally. They need opportunities to listen and follow along with read-alouds.

5. **Comprehension** Help ELLs gain comprehension in reading by choosing reading materials with familiar topics, settings, and concepts. Use nonfiction materials, such as photographs and science experiments. Use anticipation guides and graphic organizers to prepare ELLs for reading and allow them to comprehend more of what they read.

Best Practices

Scaffolding instruction for ELLs allows them to access content while gaining proficiency in English. Most strategies that help ELLs access content and language are appropriate for struggling readers in your classroom whose native language is English, so these strategies can be used with the whole class. Some best practices for teaching ELLs include:

- using questioning techniques to elicit experiences that relate to students' native cultures;

- using visual aids, including photographs, graphic organizers, and real objects;

- linking learning to a physical response, such as raising hands, doing a "thumbs up," nodding, and moving to a different part of the room;

- actively engaging students in the lesson by including less teacher talk and down time and keeping students involved;

- using scaffolding techniques, such as think-alouds, paraphrasing, partnering, and reciprocal teaching; and

- building background with such activities as cloze sentences, creating word walls, and working with students to make personal dictionaries.

English language learners are generally divided into proficiency levels. The chart below describes what you might expect from students at each level, and it compares different proficiency levels used across the United States. It also includes teaching strategies for your classroom. *Reading Street* provides systematic leveled support to meet the needs of all students.

	LEVELS OF PROFICIENCY		BEHAVIORS	TEACHING STRATEGIES
I	Beginning		• may be unfamiliar with sounds, rhythms, or patterns in English • respond by pointing, gesturing, or drawing • can use simple yes/no responses or one- to two-word answers • read simple language that they have already heard • write labels, patterned sentences, or short cloze sentences	• provide opportunities for active listening and visuals • model language with songs and chants • pair students with more proficient speakers • ask yes/no questions; require responses of one or two words • use manipulatives and pictures • provide writing frames
II	Early Intermediate	Intermediate	• may understand more details in spoken English • use longer phrases and sentences with better grammar • write for a variety of purposes using models • can read independently after oral previews	• allow students to make personal connections with the material • structure group discussion time • ask open-ended questions and then model, expand, restate, and enrich student language • allow students opportunities to create language for a variety of purposes and audiences
III	Intermediate		• participate in discussions about academic content • can use higher-order language to describe or persuade • write narratives and expository text • use vocabulary with more accuracy and correctness	• use graphic organizers to prepare students for reading and to discuss selections • promote academic concepts and vocabulary with nonfictional texts, magazines, newspapers, and so on • conference with students about writing to point out areas of progress and areas for improvement
IV	Early Advanced	Advanced	• have a deeper understanding of everyday language, including idioms • use more extensive vocabulary and produce language with fewer grammatical errors • use standard forms when writing • produce writing about varied topics	• structure discussion for the group • provide reference materials for students and guide them with the research • introduce more variety of literary forms • provide opportunities for more variation in writing assignments
V	Advanced	Advanced High	• use more complex and varied grammatical structures and vocabulary • read texts appropriate for grade level • write about a variety of topics on grade level • begin to self-monitor and correct as they read and write	• provide opportunities for students to publish their writing for others to read • increase students' production of language through drama and music • continue to make strong links between content-area materials and literacy activities

Essentials of ELL Instruction in *Reading Street*

Imagine students from diverse language backgrounds communicating in English on the playground. It's easy to think that they are fluent English speakers, but they may still be at the beginning stage of using English for learning purposes. Research proves that it takes at least five years of exposure to academic English to catch up with native-speaker proficiency in school.

How Do English Language Learners Differ from Other Learners?

ELLs face challenges because they have not acquired academic English. Student's reading and language skills may seem deficient because their language experiences have lacked academic instruction. ELLs need targeted instruction to participate fully in reading/language arts lessons with their peers. Helping ELLs achieve academically is critically important because they must meet the same state and federal grade-level standards as other students. Their academic success depends on learning to read well, and this depends on rich language knowledge.

> **Academic Language** is the language of the classroom. It's used for academic purposes, not social or personal ones.

Essentials of ELL Instruction

These five essential practices take into account language and academic needs of English language learners. They are incorporated into *Reading Street* as common-sense, everyday strategies that help you build an effective learning relationship between you and your ELL students.

Identify and Communicate Content Objectives and Language Objectives English language learners need instruction for the same grade-level skills and strategies as students whose first language is English. Deliver your instruction with clear, simple language. Provide extra support for academic vocabulary. Provide direct instruction for the academic language that students need to use to complete classroom tasks successfully.

Frontload the Lesson When new information arrives as a blur to ELL students, they are lost at the beginning of a lesson. Taking time to frontload, or preteach lesson elements, will bring them into mainstream instruction. Activating prior knowledge, building background, previewing, and setting a purpose for reading are frontloading methods that remove learning obstacles. Asking students to make personal connections helps them see relationships and gives you insight into their experiences and backgrounds.

Provide Comprehensible Input The instruction and content you present to ELL students may be unclear because of language barriers. Use visual supports, multimedia, examples of real items, and demonstrations to provide comprehensible instruction. Communicating with methods such as gestures, props, and dramatization can be an effective approach. Hands-on activities and multiple exposures to new concepts can lessen confusion.

Enable Language Production The listening, speaking, reading, and writing ELLs do for school is different from the language they use in everyday conversation. In school, ELLs need ample opportunities to demonstrate their use of English. Two critical methods for enabling student's English language production are direct instruction and modeling the use of a skill in a comprehensible way. Create scaffolds so that students can read and hear English language patterns and build on them to express their own thoughts. Paraphrasing, restatements, cloze sentences, writing prompts, and templated forms for note-taking are useful supports. Responding to student's strengths and needs by modifying instruction gives them opportunities to express themselves in an academic setting and gain proficiency in English.

Assess for Content and Language Understanding ELLs are required to achieve the same high standards as mainstream students. Keep in mind that children are at different stages for learning English language and literacy skills. Asking these questions frequently and using assessments will help you determine how to modify your instruction for different proficiency levels.

- Where are ELL students in their acquisition of English language proficiency?

- Where are they in their acquisition of literacy skills?

Just as for all students, you will rely on diagnostic, formative, and summative assessments for ELLs. Consistently integrate informal assessment into your lessons to target specific problem areas for learning, adapt your instruction, and intervene earlier rather than later.

You can modify both formal and informal assessments so that ELLs show their proficiency in literacy skills with a minimal amount of negative impact. These modifications include time extensions, use of bilingual dictionaries and glossaries, repeated readings of listening passages, use of dual-language assessments, and allowing written responses in the first language.

To meet ELLs at their own levels of English acquisition, teachers use instructional supports and tools. Through scaffolding and modifying instruction you can lead ELLs to achieve the same instructional goals that mainstream students do. The ELL strategies and supports in *Reading Street* have the five essential principles of ELL as their foundation. Use them throughout your instruction to modify or scaffold core instruction. With *Reading Street* ELL Leveled Support activities, you meet students where they are—from beginning to advanced levels of English proficiency.

Other English language learner resources include:

Student Edition The Student Edition builds every student's reading and language skills.

Teacher's Edition The Teacher's Edition has ELL instructional strategies built into the lesson plans. The ELL weekly lessons have pacing plans to help you carefully integrate instruction. The ELL Support lessons guide you in using sheltered techniques and routines for teaching concept development, academic vocabulary, listening comprehension, phonics, phonemic awareness, vocabulary, comprehension, and writing.

ELD/ELL Readers ELD/ELL Readers develop English learners' vocabulary and comprehension skills. Study guides support comprehension and provide writing and take-home activities.

ELL Posters ELL Posters contain high-quality illustrations and five days of activities supporting key oral vocabulary, selection vocabulary, and lesson concepts.

Essentials of ELL Instruction in *Reading Street*

- Identify and Communicate Content Objectives and Language Objectives
- Frontload the Lesson
- Provide Comprehensible Input
- Enable Language Production
- Assess for Content and Language Understanding

ELL Handbook The ELL Handbook supports teachers' professional development and the transition to advanced levels of English proficiency for all ELLs. The Handbook contains comprehension skill practice, selection vocabulary word cards, multilingual summaries of Student Edition literature, study guides for ELL Readers, and multilingual vocabulary charts. The English selection summaries and vocabulary charts are accompanied by translations in Spanish and in several other languages. The flexible bank of Phonics and Grammar Transition Lessons provides differentiated practice.

Ten Important Sentences The Ten Important Sentences reproducibles help students focus on comprehension while they expand their English proficiency.

English Language Proficiency—What, Why, and How
The next section, English Language Proficiency—What, Why, and How, provides ideas for how to use *Reading Street* across language proficiency levels and instructional strands. Using research from Dr. Jim Cummins, this section explains why and how *Reading Street* promotes literacy attainment for English language learners at all levels.

English Language Proficiency—What, Why, and How

Concept Development

 "No learner is a blank slate. The more we know about the topic in the text, the more of the text we can understand."—Dr. Jim Cummins

Why

Organizing concept development around big question themes is essential for ELLs. Through the use of themes, it is easier to connect the curriculum to students' lives and backgrounds. Themes help to make sense of the curriculum because students know what the topic is, even if the instruction is in English. By learning more about the topic through concept development, students will increase their social and academic vocabulary production and be more engaged when reading the text.

How

Reading Street promotes literacy attainment through Concept Development activities in the core and ELL Support lessons that encourage literacy engagement. These activities activate prior knowledge and build background, scaffold meaning, affirm identity, and extend language.

Activate Prior Knowledge/Build Background

Frontload the Lesson Build background and scaffold meaning to prepare for the core Anchored Talk lesson. In a small group, use Preteach Concepts from the Concept Development section of the ELL Support pages and the Poster Talk Through to frontload the lesson.

Access Content

Provide Comprehensible Input Use the linguistically accommodated questions in the Concept Development section of the ELL Support pages to reach all language proficiency levels and make personal and cultural connections that validate identity and link academic content with what students already know.

Scaffold Meaning Give visual support that students need to access academic content with the photographs in the Let's Talk About section in the Student Edition, the concept graphic organizer created during the week's discussion, the Concept Talk Video from the digital path, and the daily Poster Activities. The activities in the ELL Support pages for Concept Development and the ELL Support notes throughout the Teacher Edition give ideas to scaffold meaning for all language proficiency levels.

Extend Language

Enable Language Production Use the daily activities on the ELL Poster and the Anchored Talk questions in the core to build concept attainment and encourage oral language production. The Team-Talk Routine in the core instruction and the Poster Talk, Concept Talk activities from the *ELL Handbook* provide nonthreatening small group oral practice with social and academic vocabulary related to the concept. The Concept Literacy Reader builds both concepts and language.

	Student Behaviors	Teacher Behaviors	Examples
Beginning	• Actively listens • Responds nonverbally • Can follow one-step oral directions • Answers in one- or two-word phrases • May not seek clarification Student can: point, move, choose, match, mime, draw.	• Use gestures, repetition, slower speech, visuals, and simple language. *Point to the _____.* *Find the _____.* *Is this a _____?*	How does city life compare to life in the country? Use the *Let's Talk About It* photographs in the Student Edition to activate prior knowledge and build background. .... *Point to the city. Find the picture of the country.* *Are they the same or different?* *Is this a building?* *Is this a farm?* *Where is the cow?*
Intermediate	• Actively listens with greater understanding • Needs processing time • Uses short phrases • Identifies people and objects • Begins to seek clarification Student can: name, list, say, tell, restate.	• Model correct responses. • Don't call attention to grammar errors. • Ask general questions to encourage production. • Ask questions for two-word responses. *Is this a _____ or a _____?* *What is this?*	*Is this a building or a farm?* *Is this the city or the country?* *What do you see in the city?* *What do you see in the country?* *Are they the same or different?*
Advanced	• Actively listens to longer questions and directions • Uses language more freely • Sometimes needs more processing time and depends on visuals • Will seek clarification Student can: describe, restate, compare, contrast.	• Ask open-ended questions to encourage language production. • Check comprehension frequently. *Why?* *How?* *Tell me about _____.* *Describe _____.*	*Describe the city.* *Tell me about the country.* *How are they the same?* *How are they different?*
Advanced High	• Understands longer, elaborated discussions • Occasionally needs more processing time • Understands details and information comparable to a native speaker • Rarely seeks clarification • Produces a variety of sentence lengths Student can: explain, define, support, describe, summarize.	• Make lessons interactive and comprehensible. • Structure group discussions. *Describe/compare _____.* *How are these similar or different?* *What would happen if _____?* *What is your opinion of _____?*	*Compare the pictures of the city and country.* *How are they the same and different?* *Which place do you like better? Why?*

Listening Comprehension

"How can teachers make complex academic English comprehensible for children who are still in the process of learning English? We can scaffold students' learning by modifying the input itself."— Dr. Jim Cummins

Why

English language learners must be able to comprehend newly acquired language in all content areas. They must listen to a variety of speakers, including teachers and peers, as well as understand the language they hear in electronic media. In order for English language learners to meet grade-level learning expectations and have access to the core curriculum, all instruction delivered in English must be linguistically accommodated for all levels of English language proficiency.

How

Reading Street promotes literacy attainment with listening activities in the core lessons and ELL Support lessons that encourage literacy engagement. These activities activate prior knowledge and build background, scaffold meaning, affirm identity, and extend language.

Activate Prior Knowledge/Build Background

Frontload the Lesson Each adapted Read Aloud in the Listening Comprehension section of the ELL Support pages covers the same concept and information as the Read Aloud in the core curriculum. Use it with a small group to build background and scaffold meaning for Advanced and Advanced High levels before listening to the core Read Aloud. Each modified Read Aloud has frontloading activities that build background to improve comprehension before listening to the main selection. In the core Teacher's Edition, ELL notes offer suggestions for frontloading the regular Read Aloud at point of use.

Access Content

Provide Comprehensible Input For Beginning and Intermediate levels, use the grade-appropriate adapted Read Aloud in place of the regular Read Aloud until students no longer need the linguistic support and modification.

First Listening: Listen to Understand gives students a purpose for listening. The questions are designed to generate interest and help students understand the general meaning of the adapted Read Aloud, so all proficiency levels can achieve success without cognitive overload.

Language Clarification Second Listening: Listen to Check Understanding allows students to clarify what they have heard. Once students understand the main idea of the adapted Read Aloud, they can listen again on subsequent days to clarify understanding of important details of spoken language. The graphic organizers provide visual support for organizing information and taking notes.

Extend Language

Enable Language Production Discussing the adapted Read Aloud in a small group setting provides a nonthreatening environment, lowering the affective filter and facilitating increased language production.

The AudioText CD of the main reading selection and the digital products for each strand provide more opportunities for listening practice throughout each week in order to build, reinforce, and extend concept and language attainment.

	Student Behaviors	Teacher Behaviors	Examples
Beginning	• Needs accommodations to understand grade-appropriate stories • Responds non-verbally • Can follow one-step oral directions • Answers in one or two words • Can match oral statements to illustrations or objects Student can: point, move, choose, match, mime, draw, label.	• Use gestures, repetition, slower speech, visuals, and simple language. *Point to the _____.* *Find the _____.* *Is this a _____?*	In a small group, use the modified Read Aloud. Build background and scaffold comprehension by reviewing the concept or showing a visual. Read the text clearly. Stop at intervals to check for understanding and clarify language. Use gestures to scaffold meaning. Students may need to hear the text repeated multiple times.
Intermediate	• Needs accommodations to understand grade-appropriate stories • Actively listens with greater understanding • Uses short phrases • Understands simple directions • Identifies people and objects • Identifies key words and phrases • Begins to seek clarification Student can: name, list, say, tell, restate.	• Model correct responses. • Use visuals, gestures, and preteaching to preview topic-related vocabulary. • Don't call attention to errors. • Ask general questions to encourage production. • Ask questions that elicit two-word responses *Is this a _____ or a _____?* *What is this?*	In a small group, use the modified Read Aloud. Preview topic-related vocabulary and then read the text clearly. Stop at intervals to check for understanding and clarify language. Then use the Anchored Talk photographs to build vocabulary and concepts and to encourage discussion.
Advanced	• Actively listens to longer questions • Understands multistep directions • Understands main points and most important details • Will seek clarification • Uses language more freely Student can: describe, restate, compare, contrast.	• Ask open-ended questions to encourage language production. • Check comprehension frequently. • Give more time to process information and provide visual support as needed. *Why? How?* *Describe _____.*	In a small group, use the modified Read Aloud to prepare for listening to the oral reading in the core text. Then have partners restate some of the important points.
Advanced High	• Understands longer, elaborated discussions • Understands details and information comparable to a native speaker • Rarely seeks clarification • Produces a variety of sentence lengths Student can: explain, define, support, describe, summarize.	• Make lessons interactive and comprehensible. • Structure group discussions. • Give more processing time. *Describe/compare_____.* *How are these similar or different?* *What would happen if _____?* *What is your opinion of _____?*	In a small group, use the modified Read Aloud to prepare for listening to the oral reading in the core text. Then have students summarize the selection.

Phonics, Spelling, and Word Analysis

"A systematic exploration of language is essential if students are to develop a curiosity about language and deepen their understanding of how words work. Children should become language detectives who investigate the mysteries of language and how it has been used throughout history to shape and change society."— Dr. Jim Cummins

Why

Discrete language skills that English language learners need to develop second language literacy and comprehension include:

- knowledge of the letters of the alphabet
- knowledge of the sounds represented by individual letters and combinations of letters
- the ability to decode words
- knowledge of the rules and conventions of how words are formed

Students can learn these skills at the same time they are developing basic English vocabulary. While letter-sound correspondences in numerous languages are relatively simple, the relationships of letters to sounds in English can be complicated. The challenges of written English affect spelling, word recognition, comprehension of text, and confidence in language learning. *Reading Street* addresses these challenges in both the core curriculum and in the ELL Support pages.

How

Reading Street promotes literacy attainment through engaging phonics, spelling, and word analysis activities in the core lessons and ELL Support lessons. These activities activate prior knowledge and build background, scaffold meaning, affirm identity, and extend language.

Activate Prior Knowledge/Build Background

Frontload the Lesson Use the Phonics and Spelling and Word Analysis lessons in the ELL Support pages with a small group to preteach the skill before the core lesson. Then use the Reteach activities from the ELL Support pages to provide more practice and help students internalize language.

Affirm Identity Use the Transfer Skills Notes throughout the core Teacher Edition, on the ELL Support pages, and in the Phonics Transition Lessons in the *ELL Handbook* to activate prior knowledge about a phonics or word analysis skill before the core lesson or for reteaching the skill to a small group to scaffold meaning.

Access Content

Provide Comprehensible Input Use the Sound-Spelling Cards and the Envision it! Words to Know from the Student Edition to provide visual support and scaffold meaning for the phonics and spelling lessons at all proficiency levels. Choose appropriate Phonics Transition Lessons and reproducible practice pages from the bank of lessons in the *ELL Handbook* to provide instruction on consonant sounds and blends, varying English vowel sounds, and other phonics challenges for all proficiency levels. The *Words! Vocabulary Handbook* in the Student Edition provides visual support for explaining the Word Analysis skill. Use it to preteach or reteach the skill. Use the leveled ideas in the Word Analysis section of the ELL Support pages to differentiate instruction and reach all students. The Word Analysis lessons focus on word endings, contractions, prefixes, suffixes, compound words, cognates, and other vocabulary builders.

Extend Language

Enable Language Production Guide small groups of students in exploring the rules and conventions of how words are formed using the leveled Word Analysis lessons from the ELL Support pages. When students learn the patterns of English word formation, students will become more engaged in literacy activities, and oral and written production will increase.

Focus on Meaning and Form Use the Word Analysis lessons from the ELL Support pages to teach home language equivalents, synonyms, antonyms, and the meaning of prefixes, roots, and suffixes. This knowledge engages students in figuring out meanings of new words, increasing their comprehension and language production.

	Student Behaviors	Teacher Behaviors	Examples
Beginning	• Actively listens and responds non-verbally • Can follow one-step oral directions • Answers in one- to two-word phrases • Uses high-frequency words, concrete words, and phrases Student can: point, move, choose, match, mime, draw label.	• Use gestures, repetition, slower speech, visuals, and simple language. *Point to the _____.* *Find the _____.* *Is this a _____?*	prefixes *un-* and *in-* .... Give students a piece of cloth and model the difference between *cover* and *uncover.* Use Student Edition *Words! Vocabulary Handbook* to provide more visual support for meaning. Have students draw pictures to show *lock / unlock* and *happy / unhappy.* Use the *ELL Handbook* reproducible pages to provide more practice with prefixes.
Intermediate	• Actively listens with greater understanding • Needs more processing time • Uses short phrases • Identifies people and objects • Begins to seek clarification if he or she doesn't understand Student can: name, list, say, tell, restate.	• Model correct responses. • Don't call attention to grammar errors. • Ask general questions to encourage production. • Ask questions that elicit two-word responses. *Is this a _____ or a _____?* *What is this?*	Use the Student Edition *Words! Vocabulary Handbook* to provide visual support for meaning. Ask questions about the picture to clarify meaning. Provide more practice using *in-* with words *expensive* and *inexpensive.* Use the *ELL Handbook* reproducible pages to provide more practice with prefixes.
Advanced	• Actively listens to longer questions and directions • Uses language more freely • Sometimes needs more processing time and depends on visuals • Will seek clarification Student can: describe, restate, compare, contrast.	• Ask open-ended questions to encourage language production. • Check comprehension frequently. *Why? How?* *Tell me about _____.*	Use the Student Edition *Words! Vocabulary Handbook* to provide visual support for meaning. *Tell me about the first picture. Compare it to the second picture. Look at the chart. What does the prefix un- mean? Where do we find prefixes?* Repeat with prefix *in-.* Use the *ELL Handbook* reproducible pages to provide more practice with prefixes.
Advanced High	• Understands longer, elaborated discussions • Occasionally needs more processing time • Understands details and information comparable to a native speaker • Rarely seeks clarification Student can: explain, define, support, describe, summarize.	• Make lessons interactive and comprehensible. • Structure group discussions. *Describe/compare _____.* *How are these similar or different?* *What would happen if _____?* *What is your opinion of _____?*	Use the Student Edition *Words! Vocabulary Handbook* to provide visual support for meaning. *Compare the two pictures. Look at the chart. What do the prefixes un- and in- mean? Explain what else you know about prefixes.* Write the words *lock, happy, complete,* and *action* on the board. Have pairs add the appropriate prefix and then write sentences using the words. Use the *ELL Handbook* reproducible pages to provide more practice with prefixes.

Copyright © Pearson Education, Inc., or its affiliates. All Rights Reserved. 4

Vocabulary

"We should constantly search for ways to link academic content with what students already know or what is familiar to them from their family or cultural experiences. This not only validates children's sense of identity, but it also makes the learning more meaningful."— Dr. Jim Cummins

Why

Vocabulary development is critically important for English language learners, even more so than for their English-speaking peers. English learners need explicit instruction to acquire both social and academic language for literacy attainment. Research indicates that a broad knowledge of academic vocabulary is critical to student achievement and distinguishes students who experience academic success from those who struggle in school. Instruction in social and academic vocabulary should be explicit and systematic. Students need multiple exposures to new vocabulary through frequent listening, reading, writing, and oral language activities.

How

Reading Street promotes literacy attainment through interactive vocabulary activities in the core lessons and ELL Support pages that encourage literacy engagement. These activities activate prior knowledge and build background, scaffold meaning, affirm identity, and extend language.

Activate Prior Knowledge/Build Background

Frontload the Lesson The Concept Development activities from the ELL Support lessons, the Vocabulary Routines in the core and in the ELL Support pages, the ELL Poster, and the word cards from the *ELL Handbook* can be used to activate prior knowledge and build background for reading the selection. Use them in a small group to preteach, practice, and reinforce the grade-level lesson vocabulary. By using and reusing the words in meaningful interactions, students will internalize the words and be more engaged in reading the selection.

Access Content

Provide Comprehensible Input The Vocabulary Activities in the ELL Support lessons provide ideas for giving visual, contextual, and linguistic support so students can access grade-level lesson vocabulary. The activities are designed so students reuse the vocabulary using different modalities to confirm and enhance understanding. Give visual support that students need to access academic content vocabulary with the Anchored Talk photos and illustrations in the Student Edition, the Poster illustrations, Envision It! Words to Know in the Student Edition, and the digital vocabulary activities.

Affirm Identity Multilingual vocabulary lists in the *ELL Handbook* translate the selection vocabulary words from English into Spanish, Chinese, Vietnamese, Hmong, and Korean. Use the lists to preview the words or to check understanding.

Language Clarification Throughout the core and ELL Support pages, there are a variety of ideas for teachers to use to help students clarify meaning of language. Ideas range from activities using bilingual and English dictionaries to leveled questioning examples. In the core Teacher Edition, helpful ELL notes are located at point of use. These notes give language transfer support and a variety of ideas to clarify meaning for students.

Extend Language

Enable Language Production Use the Concept Talk and vocabulary activities on the ELL Support pages and the daily activities on the ELL Poster for ideas to give repeated exposure to social and academic vocabulary to build concept and language attainment.

The leveled vocabulary activities in the ELL Support lessons and the reproducible word cards in the *ELL Handbook* actively engage students in producing and reusing grade-level vocabulary in different contexts through spoken and written communication so that vocabulary becomes internalized.

	Student Behaviors	Teacher Behaviors	Examples
Beginning	• Actively listens • Answers in one- to two-word phrases • Uses and reads some high-frequency words, concrete words, and phrases represented by pictures Student can: point, move, choose, match, mime, draw, label, copy.	• Activate prior knowledge. • Use gestures, repetition, slower speech, and visuals. • Preteach topic-related vocabulary. *Point to the* _____. *Find the* _____. *Is this a* _____?	Use a word grid or word cards to preteach vocabulary. .... Students can write the new word in the circle in the middle and then draw or find a picture to illustrate the meaning of the word. Students can point to the squares while the other students describe the card to the class.
Intermediate	• Actively listens with greater understanding • Uses short phrases • Understands simple directions • Identifies people and objects • Begins to seek clarification if he or she doesn't understand Student can: name, list, say, tell, restate.	• Model correct responses. • Use visuals, gestures, and preteaching to preview topic-related vocabulary. • Ask general questions to encourage production. • Ask questions that elicit two-word responses. *Is this a* _____ *or a* _____? *What is this?*	Students can write a synonym or antonym for the word. They can assist beginners with creating a visual of the word. When sharing with the class, these students can list the synonyms and antonyms.
Advanced	• Understands longer, more elaborate directions and conversations • Understands main points and most important details • Sometimes needs more processing time; depends on more visuals • Will seek clarification Student can: describe, restate, compare, contrast.	• Ask open-ended questions to encourage language production. • Check comprehension frequently. • Give more time to process information. *Why?* *How?* *Tell me about* _____. *Describe* _____.	Students can write sentences with the word and identify cognates. They can describe their cards to the class when they are finished.
Advanced High	• May need more processing time • Understands details and information comparable to a native speaker • Rarely seeks clarification • Produces a variety of sentence lengths Student can: explain, define, support, describe, summarize.	• Make lessons interactive and comprehensible. • Structure group discussions. • Give extra processing time. *Describe/compare* _____. *How are these similar or different?* *What would happen if* _____? *What is your opinion of* _____?	Students can check the work of others and edit and revise the sentences so they are correct. They can describe the cards to the class when they are finished.

Reading Comprehension

"The more of the text we understand, the more new knowledge we can acquire. This expands our knowledge base, what cognitive psychologists call *schemata*, or underlying patterns of concepts. Such comprehension, in turn, enables us to understand even more concepts and vocabulary."— Dr. Jim Cummins

Why

English learners need guidance to become active readers who engage with texts on multiple levels before, during, and after reading. Comprehension instruction in *Reading Street* focuses on *metacognition*, a good reader's ability to independently reflect on the purpose of reading, select appropriate approaches to texts, ask questions as he or she reads, and actively resolve areas of confusion.

How

Core Comprehension Skill
Activate Prior Knowledge/Build Background
Frontload the Lesson Use the Preteach activities in the Guide Comprehension section of the ELL Support lessons with a small group to build background for the main Comprehension Skill. The Envision It! Visual Skills Handbook in the Student Edition and Envision It! Animations from the digital path provide visual support to fully engage students in the core skill instruction.

Access Content and Scaffold Meaning
Provide Comprehensible Input The leveled Reteach activities in the Guide Comprehension section of the ELL Support pages provide visual, contextual, and linguistic support for the grade-level Comprehension Skill. The interactive activities are designed so students reuse the academic vocabulary related to each Comprehension Skill using different modalities to enhance understanding. Topics range from basic reading skills, such as understanding supporting ideas and details in text, to expanded skills, such as making inferences.

Language Clarification The leveled support notes in the Reteach activities of the Guide Comprehension section of the ELL Support pages provide ideas for clarifying meaning for all proficiency levels.

Extend Language
Enable Language Production and Affirm Identity
The mini-lessons in the Guide Comprehension section of the ELL Support pages focus on the Comprehension Skill. Use them to encourage students to express ideas and participate in discussions using social and academic vocabulary.

Comprehension of Core Selection
Sheltered Reading
Activate Prior Knowledge/Build Background
Frontload the Lesson Use the Before Reading activities in the Sheltered Reading section in the ELL Support pages for ideas to preview the text and set a purpose for reading. The Multilingual Summaries in the *ELL Handbook* activate prior knowledge, affirm identity, and build background before reading the main selection.

Access Content and Scaffold Meaning
Provide Comprehensible Input Use the Sheltered Reading questions and the graphic organizer on the ELL Support pages to guide comprehension and clarify understanding of the selection.

Extend Language
Enable Language Production The Sheltered Reading section on the ELL Support pages has questions that encourage students to use oral language during reading to demonstrate understanding. The Fluency and the After Reading sections have ideas for shared reading, summarizing, and organizing information for each selection.

ELD and ELL Readers
There is an ELD and an ELL Reader for each week of instruction. Each Reader has a topic that supports grade-level concept development, tying into the Question of the Week. The ELD Readers are written for Beginning and Intermediate language proficiency levels, and the ELL Readers are designed for Intermediate to Advanced High levels. The rich language and information, sentence patterns, repetition, and visual support will unlock new words for students and give them models for using English words, phrases, and sentence structures.

Activate Prior Knowledge/Build Background
Frontload the Lesson Use the Before Reading section in the ELL Support pages for the ELL and ELD Readers for ideas to preview the text and set a purpose for reading.

Access Content and Scaffold Meaning
Provide Comprehensible Input Use the During Reading Routine along with the sheltered questions in the ELL/ELD Reader Support pages and visuals in the Readers to build background, model, and guide comprehension.

Extend Language
Enable Language Production and Affirm Identity Use the Anchored Talk and Let's Write About It activities on the inside back cover of each ELL Reader to have students apply the lesson's target comprehension skill. The reproducible Study Guide found in the ELL Handbook supports students' comprehension and provides writing and take-home activities.

	Student Behaviors	Teacher Behaviors	Examples
Beginning	• Uses vocabulary that includes environmental print, some high-frequency and concrete words represented by pictures • Depends on visuals and prior knowledge • Able to apply comprehension skills when reading texts at his or her level • May recognize a few letter-sound relationships • Reads word by word	• Use gestures, repetition, slower speech, visuals, and simple language. • Assess prior knowledge, build background, and frontload extensively before reading text. • Make sure text is linguistically accommodated for level or provide teacher/peer support for grade-level text.	Use gestures to explain first, next, and last. Hold up one finger as you say *first* and put on a shoe. Hold up two fingers as you say *next* and tie the shoe. Hold up three fingers as you say *last* and take a step forward. Then use the Envision It! Visual Skills Handbook picture in the Student Edition to identify sequence words *first, next,* and *last.* Use the Picture It! activity from the *ELL Handbook* to practice and assess sequence.
Intermediate	• Reads some everyday oral language, knows literal meanings of common words, and uses routine academic language • Reads slowly and in short phrases and may need to reread to clarify meaning • Can locate and classify information • Understands simple sentences but is dependent on visual cues, topic familiarity, prior knowledge, or pre-taught vocabulary • Can apply basic and higher-order thinking skills in texts that are linguistically accommodated	• Use gestures, repetition, slower speech, visuals, and simple language. • Assess prior knowledge, build background, and frontload extensively before reading text. • Make sure text is linguistically accommodated for level or provide support for grade-level text.	Use gestures to explain *first, next,* and *last.* As you tie your shoe, have students describe what you do first, next, and last. Then use the Envision It! Visual Skills Handbook in the Student Edition to have students identify sequence words *first, next,* and *last* and then describe the sequence in the pictures. Use the Picture It! activity from the *ELL Handbook* to practice and assess sequences.
Advanced	• Reads with greater ease • Uses a variety of comprehension strategies • Can understand words and phrases beyond their literal meanings • Able to apply basic and higher-order comprehension skills • Occasionally dependent on visuals and teacher/peer assistance with unfamiliar topics	• Frontload text and build background before reading. • Preteach unfamiliar concepts and related vocabulary. • Use visuals to clarify meanings of new topics. • Provide support for grade-level text.	Use the Envision It! Visual Skills Handbook in the Student Edition to preteach sequence. Students can describe what is happening in each picture and identify sequence words. After using the Routine to frontload the ELL Reader, guide students to find words that show sequence. Use the graphic organizer to fill in the sequence of events. Use the organizer to retell the sequence of events with a partner and then share with the class.
Advanced High	• Reads and understands vocabulary nearly comparable to native English-speaking peers • Can infer meaning, draw conclusions, and use context to infer meanings of new words • Can interpret information and find details that support main ideas	• Frontload text and build background before reading. • Preteach unfamiliar concepts and related vocabulary. • Use visuals to clarify meanings of new topics. • Provide support for grade-level text as needed.	Use the Envision It! Visual Skills Handbook in the Student Edition to preteach sequence. Students can describe what is happening in each picture and identify other sequence words they may know. After using the routine to frontload the ELL Reader, pairs can find words that show sequence. Use a graphic organizer to fill in the sequence of events and then retell the story. Use the organizer if needed.

Conventions and Writing

"Writing helps solve problems, affirms students' identities, and generates linguistic feedback from teachers that can increase language awareness and academic language proficiency." — Dr. Jim Cummins

Why

Research shows that students acquire language most readily when they are fully involved in all learning activities in the classroom. Activities should integrate listening, speaking, reading, and writing, since these language skills develop interdependently. Teachers can facilitate language learning and literacy development by ensuring that students hear language in natural ways, in real and practical contexts, and write it in structured formats.

Each English language learner comes from a unique background of language, literacy, and culture. Because students are at varying levels of English proficiency, it is important that each student has challenging work, appropriate for his or her level of English proficiency and literacy. The conventions and writing lessons in the ELL Support pages of *Reading Street* provide the systematic instruction that students need at each language proficiency level to scaffold use of increasingly complex grammatical structures in content area writing.

How

Reading Street promotes literacy attainment through engaging Conventions and Writing activities in the core Teacher Edition and ELL Support lessons. These activities activate prior knowledge and build background, scaffold meaning, affirm identity, and extend language.

Activate Prior Knowledge/Build Background

Frontload the Lesson Use the Preteach activities in the Conventions and Writing sections of the ELL Support pages with a small group of students before the lesson to introduce the concepts. Each Conventions lesson contains a helpful chart to convey grammatical forms and has ideas for addressing the functions of the grammatical structure to students. The Writing section contains a simple model to use when guiding instruction for beginning and intermediate levels.

Affirm Identity Use the Language Transfer notes in the core Teacher Edition, the Language Transfer Charts in the *ELL Handbook*, and the *ELL Handbook* Grammar Transition Lessons to lead students in transferring knowledge from their home languages to English.

Access Content and Scaffold Meaning

Provide Comprehensible Input Use the leveled Conventions practice activities in the ELL Support pages for contextual and linguistic support for each grade-level grammar skill. The interactive activities are designed so students reuse the language related to each core convention using different modalities to enhance understanding. For more practice on a core skill, or to meet the needs of beginners and intermediate students, use the Grammar Transition bank of flexible activities in the *ELL Handbook* or the Grammar Jammer from the digital path during small group time. Use the leveled writing ideas and the simplified writing models in the ELL Support pages to scaffold meaning for all students.

Language Clarification The leveled support notes throughout the Teacher Edition pages and the Grammar Transition Lessons in the *ELL Handbook* contain ideas for clarifying meaning for all proficiency levels.

Extend Language

Enable Language Production The Conventions and Writing sections of the ELL Support pages have practice activities for students to actively use grammar and writing skills. The sentence frames and leveled writing prompts guide and encourage oral and written language production for all levels of English proficiency. Use the ELL Notes throughout the core Teacher Edition Language Arts pages for ideas to support all levels of English language learners in prewriting, editing, revising, and publishing writing pieces.

References for English Language Proficiency— What, Why, and How

Gottlieb, Margo, M. Elizabeth Cranley, and Andrea R. Oliver. (2007). *The WIDA English Language Proficiency Standards and Resource Guide, Pre-Kindergarten through Grade 12.* Board of Regents of the University of Wisconsin on behalf of the WIDA Consortium.

Peregoy, Suzanne F., and Owen F. Boyle (2008). *Reading, Writing, and Learning in ESL: A Resource Book for Teaching K–12 English Learners.* New York: Pearson.

	Student Behaviors	Teacher Behaviors	Examples
Beginning	• Can label, list, copy, and use basic punctuation and capitalization • Uses some standard word order • Uses high-frequency words phrases and short sentences in present tense • May recognize a few letter-sound relationships • Responds to pictured events using words or phrases based on models	• Allow extra time for prewriting and build background before writing. • Use language experience stories. • Help students turn words and phrases into sentences. • Accept phonetic spelling, but show corrections. • Give a checklist for revising that has visual cues and help students use dictionaries or word walls.	Descriptive paragraph about a family member. . . . . Students can produce words or phrases about a family member using a drawing or photograph. Guide production of supporting details on a graphic organizer. Write out sentences and have students copy the sentences and read them to you or a partner.
Intermediate	• Communicates best when topics are familiar and concrete • Produces short phrases and simple sentences • May use simple future and past tenses inconsistently • Can compare and contrast • Can describe events, people, processes, and procedures with limited details	• Allow extra time for building background and prewriting. • Help students turn phrases into sentences. • Accept phonetic spelling, but show corrections. • Give a checklist for revising that has written cues and help students use dictionaries or word walls.	Students can write short sentences about a family member. Guide students to use a graphic organizer to add details. Have partners work together to write at least three interesting details describing the family member. Share their sentences with the class.
Advanced	• Can engage in grade-appropriate writing tasks with support • Can write phrases, sentences, and paragraphs with some errors • Can edit and revise using a checklist with a written description • Has a basic grasp of basic verb tenses, grammar features, sentence patterns, and cohesive devices • Provides increased detail and can summarize information from graphics and notes	• Allow extra time for prewriting. • Use brainstorming, concept mapping, peer conferencing, interviewing, and reading. • Help students with correct spelling, capitalization, and punctuation. • Clarify error correction by peers or teachers to make changes.	Use a graphic organizer to develop Ideas and details about a family member. Students can develop a paragraph based on the graphic organizer.
Advanced High	• Can express ideas in writing and engage meaningfully in grade-level writing assignments with minimal support • Writes comparable to native English speaker • Makes minor errors that rarely interfere with communication	• Use brainstorming, concept mapping, peer conferencing, interviewing, and reading. • Help students with correct spelling, capitalization, and punctuation if needed. • Clarify error correction by peers or teachers to make changes.	Use a graphic organizer to develop ideas about a family member. Students can develop a paragraph based on the graphic organizer. Share the details they find most interesting.

Hear It!   See It!   Say It!   Use It!

Use this flexible routine with all levels of English language learners to guide their language development as they learn new basic and academic vocabulary, increase conceptual knowledge, and improve their reading comprehension. The following instructional sequence will encourage production and guide language development.

Start with choral work (Whole Group), and then move to partners or small groups, followed by "on your own" activities. Because choral, partner, and small group practice activities are nonthreatening, the affective filter is lowered, increasing language production.

Academic Vocabulary Routine

Hear It!

Model the word so that students can hear the correct pronunciation. Provide a student-friendly definition and relate it to something that students know, affirming their identity.

See It!

Display the word, and use a picture or pantomime to visually clarify meaning. Ask questions, and have students respond to show their understanding of the word.

Say It!

Have students repeat the word chorally and then with a partner. Students will be able to use the word with more confidence and accuracy.

Use It!

Engage students in activities that encourage language production. Have them create their own definitions and use the word multiple times orally and in writing to internalize vocabulary and concept knowledge.

ELL Use the Academic Vocabulary Routine

This example shows how to use the Academic Vocabulary Routine to pre-teach the word *noun*.

How to Teach the Word *Noun*

Hear It!	Say the word **noun**. A **noun** is a naming word for people, places, animals, or things. Point to a desk. Say: *This is a desk. A desk is a thing, so the word* desk *is a **noun**.*
See It!	Write the word **noun** on the board and word wall. To clarify meaning, point to other items in the classroom. Ask: *What is this?* (a chair) *Is this a person?* (no) *Is this a place?* (no) *Is this a thing?* (yes) *So, the word* chair *must be a **noun**.*
Say It!	Have students repeat the word **noun**. In partners, have them say the word **noun** and the definition, *a **noun** is a naming word for people, places, animals, or things.*
Use It!	Have partners work together to identify more **nouns** for people and things they see in the classroom. Then have them write and illustrate their own definition of **noun**. Partners can then share their definitions orally with the class.

 Leveled Support

Beginning Pair students with more proficient speakers or students who speak the same language. Use more gestures and repetition. Allow students to answer by pointing, gesturing, or giving one-word responses.

Intermediate Continue to use visuals and gestures. Model correct responses. Ask questions that elicit two-word responses.

Advanced Continue to provide visual support. Give students more time to process information. Questions can be more open-ended, but be sure to check comprehension frequently.

Advanced High Provide visual support as needed. Have students work with beginners who speak the same language to clarify meaning.

Contents

Professional Development

Introduction: How to Use This Book

Across the United States, teachers are welcoming increasing numbers of English language learners (ELLs) into their classrooms. English language learners make up the fastest growing K–12 student population in the United States.

While English language learners share many characteristics with other students, they need support and scaffolding specific to their needs. They represent a highly diverse population. They come from many home language backgrounds and cultures, and they have a wide range of prior educational and literacy experiences acquiring in their home languages.

This Handbook is designed to help you identify and support the needs of ELLs in your classroom. The strategies and activities will allow you to scaffold and support instruction so that all students can learn in ways that are comprehensible and meaningful, and in ways that promote their academic success and achievement.

Carefully crafted **professional development articles** assist you in understanding and planning for the unique needs of English language learners in your classroom.

Weekly Planners outline all activities in a "week at a glance" format and include objectives for each instructional strand.

Each reading selection is supported by a set of reproducibles. **Word Cards** allow students to use key vocabulary for speaking, writing, and content acquisition. Each **Picture It!** focuses on a reading comprehension skill with leveled instruction targeted to English language learners. **Multilingual Selection Summaries,** in English, Spanish, Chinese, Vietnamese, Korean, and Hmong, allow students to access selection content and share their reading with their families. **Study Guides** for ELL Readers allow you to assess comprehension of content and the use of key reading strategies. All of these resources provide access to core content material, each unit and week of the year. Detailed instructions for using these resources are provided in the ELL Support pages of the Teacher's Edition.

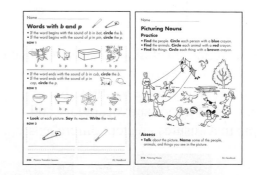

Phonics pages target instruction with consonants, vowels, and syllable patterns that may be challenging for English language learners. **Grammar** lessons supplement core instruction in speaking and writing. Use these lessons as students need additional support.

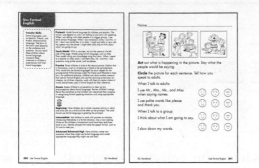

English Language Learner Workshops
provide direct and explicit instruction in such topics as using transactional language, retelling or summarizing in English, asking for assistance, giving and following directions, and using formal and informal English. A teacher-driven lesson as well as a student worksheet is provided for a model/teach/practice/assess progression as students gradually master these skills.

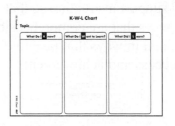

Teaching Routines for English language learners allow for a systematic approach to learning that yields results. Routines are tied to instruction, allowing students to master the skills needed to succeed.

Multilingual Vocabulary
charts translate the lesson words into Spanish, Korean, Hmong, Vietnamese, and Chinese to allow the frontloading of important vocabulary and concepts that ensures greater comprehension.

Graphic Organizers give students visual support to assist them in accessing the content. ELL teaching ideas are provided for each graphic organizer.

Poster Talk, Concept Talk
leveled activities encourage language production using the poster visuals and vocabulary related to the weekly concept.

Identifying Language Proficiency Levels

To differentiate both instruction and assessment for the English language learners in your classroom, it is important to identify their various levels of language proficiency across the four domains of listening, speaking, reading, and writing. Language proficiency is a collection of interdependent components. Fundamentally, language proficiency requires phonemic awareness and awareness of phonological relationships. It requires knowledge of vocabulary, grammar, syntax, and pronunciation. More subtle and sophisticated skills also apply. For instance, can a student switch his or her usage to match either a conversational or academic setting? The interplay of these abilities determines a student's linguistic competency.

Four or five levels of English proficiency are generally used to describe learners at various stages of language acquisition: **Beginning** (or pre-production), **Intermediate** (or early production), **Advanced** (or intermediate fluency), and **Advanced High** (or near proficient). The table below shows some responses you can expect from students at each level. The Comparative Oral Language Proficiency Chart on p. 6 provides more in-depth descriptions of what you might expect from students at each stage of oral language development, and it compares different proficiency levels used across the United States. Use the chart to plan instruction for your class.

	Listening	Speaking	Reading	Writing
Beginning	Can respond to simple commands or questions nonverbally.	Uses only single words or phrases and may be prone to echo others.	May match pictures to words or recognize a few letter-sound relationships.	May write single words and attempt to copy statements.
Intermediate	Understands short sentences and simple conversational language and can follow simple directions. Beginning to grasp concrete details and a few abstract concepts.	Learns common social phrases by heart and can communicate simple information. Begins to speak in complete sentences, and vocabulary increases.	Understands simple texts and can group words such as synonyms and antonyms. Comprehends texts on familiar topics and may be able to summarize a simple passage or identify its sequence of events.	Writing is error-prone, but can use correct word order in simple sentences. Begins to use basic rules of grammar and mechanics to write statements and questions.
Advanced	Grasps most conversational and some academic language.	Speaks in more complex sentences and uses a wider range of vocabulary.	Reads with greater ease and uses a variety of comprehension strategies, but may stumble over texts with unfamiliar concepts or vocabulary.	Can write multi-sentence paragraphs organized logically.
Advanced High	Follows multi-step directions and grasps speech with complex syntax and academic vocabulary.	Uses both conversational and academic language with ease and can speak on a range of topics, using idioms.	Reads grade-level appropriate texts, can infer meaning, draw conclusions, and use context to infer meanings of words.	Writes organized texts with few errors, sufficient detail, and specific vocabulary.

How can you differentiate instruction for the different proficiency levels?

You can use a variety of instructional techniques, activities, and assessment tools to support English language learners at different levels of proficiency—all within the same lesson. For example, to teach sequence of events, you might choose to adapt your instruction as follows:

Teach/Model

Read a short passage to the whole class, showing pictures of each event in the story as you do so. When you have finished reading, review the events in the story. Model using sequence words.

- Use gestures to explain "first," "next," and "last" to students at the **Beginning** level. For example, hold up one finger as you say "first" and put on a shoe. Hold up two fingers as you say "next" and lace up the shoe. Hold up three fingers as you say "last" and take a step.

- Have students at the **Intermediate** level echo you as you say "first," "next," and "last" and then add a detail to each to make a phrase or short sentence.

- Have students at the **Advanced** level answer questions about sequence of events as you read aloud.

- Have students at the **Advanced High** level answer questions about the sequence of inferred events as you read aloud. (For example, "What must have happened before Jack slipped in the paint?" "The paint can fell.")

Practice

- After you read, have students at the **Beginning** level arrange the pictures in the story in the correct order.

- Have students at the **Intermediate** level answer the questions, "What happened first?" "What happened next?" "What happened last?"

- Have students at the **Advanced** level verbally describe the events in the story using sequence words.

- Have students at the **Advanced High** level write the sequence of events in the story using complete sentences.

Assess

- Have students at the **Beginning** level arrange a new series of pictures in the correct order.

- Have students at the **Intermediate** level look at a new series of pictures and then answer the questions, "What happened first?" "What happened next?" "What happened last?"

- Have students at the **Advanced** level read a new passage and then verbally describe its events using sequence words.

- Have students at the **Advanced High** level read a new passage and answer questions about the sequence of inferred events.

Comparative Oral Language Proficiency Chart

Levels of Proficiency	Level I Entering — Beginning — **Beginning**	Level II Beginning — Early Intermediate — **Intermediate**	Level III Developing — Intermediate — **Intermediate**	Level IV Expanding — Early Advanced — **Advanced**	Level V Bridging — Advanced — **Advanced High**
Characteristics of the English Language Learner	• Minimal comprehension • May be very shy • No verbal production • Non-English speaker • Silent period (10 hours to 3 months) • Uses gestures and actions to communicate	• Limited comprehension • Gives one- or two-word responses • May use two- or three-word phrases • Stage may last 6 months to 2 years	• Comprehension increases • Errors still occur in speech • Simple sentences • Stage may last 2 to 4 years	• Good comprehension • Sentences become more complex • Engages in conversation • Errors in speech are more complex	• Few errors in speech • Orally proficient • Near-native vocabulary • Uses complex sentences
What They Can Do: Performance Indicators	• Listen • Point • Illustrate • Match • Choose	• Name • List and group • Categorize • Label • Demonstrate	• Compare and contrast • Recall and retell • Summarize • Explain	• Higher-order thinking skills • Analyze, debate, justify	• All performance indicators
Instructional Ideas for Teachers	• Visual cues • Tape passages • Pair students • Total Physical Response activities • Concrete objects • Graphic organizers	• Short homework assignments • Short-answer quizzes • Open-ended sentences	• Graphs • Tables • Group discussions • Student-created books • Cloze activities	• Group panels • Paraphrasing • Defending and debating	• Lessons on writing mechanics • Free reading of appropriate books • Cooperative learning groups

What Reading Teachers Should Know About Language

Why do reading teachers need to know about the structure of language?

English language learners are entering U.S. classrooms in steadily increasing numbers. The demands on teachers are also surging. To communicate effectively with these students, teachers need to know how to make their instructional talk more comprehensible. All teachers need to better understand their students' attempts at written and spoken language. To improve students' literacy skills in English, teachers must understand how language works *in education.* What should we know about English and other languages? What truths about language help teachers as communicators, as guides, and as evaluators?

Knowledge about the structure of languages—and particularly of English—is vital not only to linguists and ELL teachers. Reading and content-area teachers, too, can make practical, everyday use of the concepts that are posed and explored by the following questions.

What are the basic units of language?

Spoken language consists of units of different sizes:

Phonemes

Phonemes are the individual sounds in a word that affect meaning. The word *cat* consists of these three phonemes: /k/ /a/ /t/.

Different languages use different sets of phonemes. English language learners may not be familiar with some English phonemes and may need help recognizing and producing these sounds.

Phonemes signal different word meanings. For example, the different vowel sounds in the words *hit* and *heat* indicate that these are two different words.

Morphemes

Morphemes are the smallest units of meaning in a language. Some morphemes are **free** (or independent) units. Words such as *dog, jump,* and *happy* are free morphemes. Other morphemes are **bound** (or attached), such as inflected endings, prefixes, and suffixes:

- the noun ending *-s* in *dogs*
- the verb ending *-ed* in *jumped*
- the prefix *un-* in *unhappy*
- the adjective ending *-er* in *happier*
- the suffix *-ness* in *happiness*

These bound morphemes add meaning and, in fact, form new words.

Words

A word consists of one or more morphemes. A word also can be defined as a meaningful group of morphemes. Native English speakers may pronounce words in ways that make it difficult for English language learners to hear word boundaries. For example, in conversation, an English speaker may ask, "Did you eat?"—but pronounce it like "Jeet?"

Some languages use bound morphemes (for example, word endings) to convey the meanings of certain functional English words such as the prepositions *in, on,* and *between.* English language learners may need explicit instruction in order to use these functional words correctly. On the other hand, an English word such as *in* may seem familiar to a Spanish speaker who uses the similar preposition *en.*

Phrases

A phrase is a group of words that have meaning together but do not include a subject and a predicate. Since some languages allow the subject or verb to be understood, students may believe that certain phrases in English are equivalent to sentences.

Sentences

A sentence is a meaningful group of words that includes a subject and a predicate. English language learners may understand the concept of sentences, but they may apply word order conventions from their home languages. They also may struggle with the dense sentence structures of academic English.

Discourses

Discourses include speeches, essays, and many other kinds of communication made up of sentences. One kind of discourse frequently heard in U.S. classrooms involves the teacher asking questions and students responding aloud. Depending on their home cultures, some English language learners may find the question-and-answer form of discourse unfamiliar.

Why do English language learners need to learn about basic units of language?

It helps teachers to understand that units, such as bound and free morphemes, words, phrases, and sentences or clauses, operate differently in different languages. For example:

- In Chinese, the past tense is not expressed with verb endings, but by separate words that indicate the time of the action (similar to *yesterday* and *already*).

- In Spanish, verb endings indicate the person and number of sentence subjects, so the subject may not be stated in some sentences.

- In Arabic, related words share three-consonant roots. Speakers form related verbs, nouns, and adjectives by applying fixed patterns to these roots and sometimes adding prefixes and suffixes.

English language learners are working mentally to determine how units of English work—as they also try to understand texts and acquire content knowledge.

What is academic English?

Academic English might be described as the language of teachers, literature, textbooks, and content areas, such as science and social studies. Unlike conversational English, academic English is language of a cognitively demanding register, or range. Academic English does not depend as much upon the gestures and circumstances of speech as conversational English does.

Academic English includes content-area vocabulary embedded in complex grammatical structures. It features words about abstract ideas. Understanding this language requires knowledge of content, as well as experience with written materials and classroom discussions. Many English language learners can carry on conversations in English with their native-English-speaking classmates. But they still struggle with reading and writing English—and even understanding their teachers in class. They have acquired social English skills used in personal communication, but they have not yet mastered the academic English used at their grade level.

How do English language learners learn vocabulary?

English language learners must learn much more than the selected vocabulary words in a lesson. They also must make sense of the other unfamiliar words in the lesson—and thousands of other words they continually encounter in school.

Knowing a word involves much more than hearing it and learning its definition. Students must learn how each word relates to its other forms. They gradually learn how it relates to other words and concepts. Knowledge of a word grows during many encounters.

Students learn words in meaningful groups more effectively than in unrelated lists. Look for opportunities to group words in meaningful ways. For example, as students learn the word *invite*, they also can learn *invited, uninvited, invitation, inviting,* and other words in this family.

What is "regular" to English language learners?

Proficient English speakers often take for granted irregularities in English that can puzzle younger and less fluent learners.

For example, a student who learns the plural forms *dogs, cats,* and *turtles* may wonder why *mouses, mooses,* and *childs* meet with disapproval. A student who masters these past tense forms—*jumped, walked,* and *stopped*—may try to use *throwed, catched,* or *taked.* In both cases, the child demonstrates an awareness of English conventions, and a teacher should acknowledge this in a positive way. The teacher also should gradually help each student master the many exceptions to the rules. Teachers who are aware of the principles of word formation in English can help students acquire vocabulary. English has many helpful patterns for new speakers, readers, and writers to learn. Savvy teachers break up the instruction into manageable chunks so that students are not overwhelmed by the many English word patterns they encounter.

What characteristics of written words might challenge English language learners?

- Written English is an alphabetic language, and letters represent sounds in words. Languages such as Chinese and Japanese are not alphabetic; written symbols can represent larger parts of words than just individual sounds. For students whose home languages are not alphabetic, learning the alphabetic system is an early and continuing challenge.

- The home languages of many English language learners—including Spanish, Vietnamese, Hmong, Haitian Creole, and others—are alphabetic. Yet the letter-sound correspondences in these languages are different from those of English. Students can use literacy skills they may have in their home languages, but much new learning is needed to master English.

- While letter-sound correspondences in numerous languages are relatively simple, the relationships of letters to sounds in English can be complicated. In Spanish, for example, the vowel *a* has one sound. In English, *a* can represent many different sounds.

- Even in related English words, the same letters can stand for different sounds. Consider *c* in the words *electric, electricity,* and *electrician.* The spellings of these words may challenge English language learners.

- The challenges of written English affect not only spelling but also word recognition, comprehension of text, and confidence in language learning.

Welcoming Newcomers
to the Mainstream Classroom

The teacher's first concern when welcoming newcomers to the mainstream classroom must be to help each student learn the basic concepts and vocabulary needed to participate in school life.

Prepare

Learn as much as possible about your newcomer students in order to tailor instruction to their individual needs.

Find out from parents or other sources about educational practices in the student's home country or culture. For example, if the student is accustomed to memorizing and reciting material in a group, he or she may feel anxious about independent work or homework, particularly if the family is not able to help the child in English.

Newcomers who are acquiring English may experience identifiable stages of adjustment and adaptation.

- **A Silent Period** For a student quite new to an English-language environment, a "silent period" is normal. The student may be learning classroom routine and acquiring basic vocabulary by watching and listening.

- **Culture Shock** In this phase, newcomers may prefer to spend much of their time with family or friends from the home culture and to temporarily reject the new language and culture. Help children to cope with this phase by providing extra help and attention when possible. A bilingual friend or classroom aide can help to make the environment feel more navigable to the child and can help to alleviate any feeling of anxiety or sadness.

Getting Started in the Classroom

Before classes begin, you may wish to plan a small reception for newcomers. Invite the students' parents or other family members, and include someone who can translate.

- **Orient the newcomer to the classroom.** Have students help you to label the classroom and the objects in it with self-stick notes. Pronounce the name of each item as you do, and use the word in a short sentence. *"Desk. This is your desk."*

- **Show interest in and respect for each child's home culture.** Create opportunities for the class to learn more about the newcomer's home country and culture. Learn a few phrases in the student's home language. Correctly pronounce the student's name.

- **Demonstrate crucial skills.** Have students tour the school with older students who speak the same home language. Post seating charts and go through assigned textbooks with newcomers to help them understand what content is presented in each.

- **Try to provide a risk-free learning environment.** Create opportunities for students to practice speaking English in small groups or with a partner without worrying about errors they may make. Accept errors in speech without comment and model the correct phrasing.

- **Provide a "buddy."** A buddy system helps students feel more secure in their environment. Buddies need not speak the same home language, but pairing up buddies with the same home language can allow buddies to serve as tutors.

- **Include newcomers in classroom routines.** Assign newcomers their share of regular classroom chores. Such responsibilities can help them feel they are part of the group. Students can be shown how to successfully carry out routine tasks without using or needing extensive English.

Teaching Strategies

Educational strategies should assist students to learn in content areas at the same time that they acquire the new language. Remember that students' skills in the home language can be transferred to English learning. Encourage students to continue to speak and read in the home language.

- **Build on students' prior knowledge.** Newcomers often have knowledge bases that are much greater than their skill levels in English. Find ways to gauge students' familiarity with the topics of upcoming lessons. Regularly using visual aids, such as semantic maps, K-W-L charts, or time lines, can help you determine how much each student already knows or needs to learn about a topic.

- **Encourage students to use learning resources.** Teach students how to use a picture dictionary or a children's dictionary, and encourage them to use it frequently to find the words they need. Ask them to start their own word banks by listing frequently used vocabulary in a notebook. Provide bilingual dictionaries for extra support.

- **Use environmental print to teach.** Put up posters and other materials from periodicals and magazines. If possible, provide students with parallel texts about the same topic in English and in the home language.

- **Invite the families of newcomers to participate in school life.** Find ways to communicate information about homework and class projects in English and the home language. Make families aware that literacy skills in the home language can help students transfer those skills to English.

- **Build a support network.** Bilingual tutors or classroom aides can clarify assignments or lesson content for English language learners without disrupting the day's activities. Similarly, family members who volunteer to help in the classroom can greatly lessen students' anxiety levels.

- **Help students transfer their writing skills.** For English language learners who have developed any emergent writing skills in their home languages, build on these skills by occasionally having them write in both languages. Short sentences and picture labels written in a home language and English help students with writing and English acquisition.

- **Include culturally relevant assignments.** Try to find readings for students that refer to their home cultures. If writing skills are limited, encourage learners to show their understanding by talking about the stories and creating illustrations.

While it may take some time for English language learners to gain proficiency in academic English, newcomers need not feel like outsiders for very long.

Sheltering Instruction for English Language Learners

What is sheltered instruction?

Sheltered instruction is a combination of strategies for teaching academic content to English language learners at the same time that they are developing proficiency in the English language. This approach to instruction is called *sheltered* because it offers a haven, or refuge, for students who must comprehend subject matter presented in a language they are still learning. Sheltered instruction supports English language learners who do not have grade-level academic vocabulary or the familiarity with the American school system that their English speaking classmates have. It provides extended English language support that English language learners receive as they learn subject-area concepts.

How does sheltered instruction help students and teachers?

Sheltered instruction offers practical, easy-to-implement strategies that teachers can use in a mainstream classroom to extend and scaffold instruction about the English language. Sheltered instruction helps English language learners find the keys they need to make sense of instruction in English about the concepts and processes they need to perform grade-level work in all subjects.

Teachers can help students build mental bridges to new concepts and learning in English by encouraging them to connect their prior knowledge—the diverse skills, experiences, language, and cultural knowledge that they bring to the classroom—to their new learning activities. Finding ways for students to draw on their home language, cultural background, and prior experience can facilitate each English language learner's ability to grasp and retain abstract ideas and grade-level vocabulary. Finding connections between what they are learning and what they already know in their home language can motivate students to read, write, listen, and speak in English. As comprehension and vocabulary increase, students can transfer more and more concepts from their home languages into English.

This knowledge transfer can work for teachers, too. As teachers tap into students' prior knowledge, the teachers will discover when they need to supply background about American events, customs, and idioms that may be new to English language learners. At the same time, they will be expanding their knowledge about English language learners' backgrounds and traditions.

Some Basics

1. Use Appropriate Speech (Comprehensible Input)

   - ✓ **Enunciate.** Speak slowly and clearly, especially when introducing new content and vocabulary.
   - ✓ **Provide wait time.** English language learners often need extra time to process questions in English and to formulate responses.
   - ✓ **Explain and demonstrate the meanings of complex terms.** Use activities that help students practice speaking, hearing, writing, and reading key words and phrases.

Complex term	Activities to clarify meaning
weather	Write and say: weather Write and say: hot, cold Say: *The weather is hot today.* (Fan yourself to show you are hot.) Then say: *The weather is cold today.* (Hug yourself and shiver to show you are cold.) Have volunteers repeat each sentence with gestures. Then fan yourself and ask: *What is the weather like today?* (hot) Hug yourself and shiver and ask: *Is the weather hot or cold today?* (cold) Have partners take turns using gestures and asking and answering the questions. Start a wall chart of weather words with pictures.

✓ **Allow students to show comprehension at their levels of language proficiency.** Ask questions that can be answered with "yes" or "no," by choosing one of two words as the answer (*Is ice hot or cold?*), by pointing to a picture or object (*Point to the tree.*), or by following simple oral directions.

2. Develop Academic Concepts

✓ **Link concepts explicitly to students' prior knowledge and background.** For example, if you introduce a unit on weather, ask students to describe, illustrate, and share what they know about weather. Create and display a class chart that tells about weather in places where students have lived.

✓ **Use hands-on activities to build background for new information.** For example, introduce the idea of touch (The Five Senses) by having students touch objects with different textures and learn a word or words to describe how each object feels.

✓ **Use supplementary materials.** Picture books can clarify and support concept learning. Use picture books that show terms that are hard to explain, such as *covered wagons, rations,* or the *Pony Express.*

3. Emphasize and Develop Key Vocabulary

✓ **Repeat key words, phrases, and concepts, and have students practice using them.**

✓ **Provide feedback on students' language use.** Use gestures to indicate understanding, as well as supportive questions to prompt students to provide more details.

✓ **Make the development of proficiency in English an explicit goal in all of your teaching. To learn new academic vocabulary, students need to use it.** Provide situations that challenge students to push themselves to a higher level of proficiency.

4. Connect Written and Oral Language

✓ **Say and write new vocabulary.** When teaching new words or phrases, such as idioms, write the word or phrase where everyone can see it. Say it slowly as you point to it. Have students repeat the word or phrase. Use gestures, role play, or drawings to demonstrate what the word means. Have students practice saying, reading, and writing the word or phrase in sentences.

✓ **Use word and picture cards to explain vocabulary and content.**

✓ **Have students build personal word files.** Have them write a word on one side of a card and draw a picture to represent its meaning on the other side. The files can include target words for different content areas as well as words that students find interesting or important. Have students use the cards for sorting and categorizing activities (e.g., color words, animal names, weather words, math words, action words).

✓ **Provide letter and phoneme cards for phonics activities.** Pair English language learners with native English speakers to use cards in order to build and say words that contain target sounds and spelling patterns. Give English language learners extra time and support to hear, say, and practice sounds and to build words using those sounds.

5. Use Visuals, Dramatization, and Realia (Real Things)

✓ **Use picture walks to preview text, concepts, and vocabulary—and to build background knowledge.** Use pictures to introduce characters and the setting and to give a simple summary of a story. You can use this same strategy with nonfiction text, having students preview illustrations, captions, boldfaced words, and other text features.

✓ **Use realia and graphic organizers.** Whenever possible, show objects and pictures that will help students understand concepts and speak about them in English. Use graphic organizers, diagrams, drawings, charts, and maps to help students conceptualize abstract information.

✓ **Use Total Physical Response (TPR) for active learning, so that students can show comprehension through physical movement.** For example, have students hear and follow instructions: *Clap your hands for Carla. Go to the board and circle the noun in red.*

✓ **Use role play, drama, rhymes, songs, and movement.** All students need opportunities to be active learners. For English language learners, participating in a small group re-enactment of a story, for example, can allow them to show comprehension and personal responses beyond what their language abilities may allow them to express.

6. Ongoing Formal and Informal Assessment

✓ **Assess early to understand a student's language level and academic preparedness. Use your assessment to plan and guide instruction.**

✓ **Set personal goals for each student and monitor progress regularly.** A student who uses phrases might be pushed to say and write complete sentences. A student who uses simple sentences might be pushed to add clauses to the sentences.

✓ **Provide various ways to demonstrate knowledge, including acting, singing, retelling, demonstrating, and illustrating.**

✓ **Use a variety of formal assessments such as practice tests, real tests, and oral and written assessments.** Use multiple choice, cloze, and open-response formats to help students become familiar with various assessment formats.

Sheltered instruction provides English language learners with opportunities to understand and access content-area learning. Within this framework, teachers provide activities that integrate reading, writing, listening, and speaking. Teachers can address the range of cultural, linguistic, and literary experiences that English language learners bring to the classroom. Sheltered instruction provides English language learners with many opportunities to understand and access content-area learning. Within this kind of instruction, teachers support English language learners by providing activities that integrate reading, writing, listening, and speaking. Teachers use students' experiences and prior knowledge as the key to unlock doors to content and language learning.

Vocabulary Knowledge and Strategies

Knowing how to organize vocabulary instruction around a few key areas will go a long way toward ensuring that students achieve both language proficiency and overall academic success. The new vocabulary that you teach should be carefully selected. As you consider the vocabulary you will teach in your classroom, you'll need to be aware of both survival language and academic language.

Survival Language

Think of survival language as a useful toolkit for new English language learners—a practical store of words and phrases that can be used to navigate new environments and accomplish everyday tasks in the classroom and at home. Survival language not only involves teaching students labels for common objects, places, and people, but includes giving students instruction in how to understand and follow directions, ask for help, and function appropriately in social situations. While it is valuable to reinforce this type of vocabulary acquisition throughout the day, as spontaneous interactions with students arise, it is also important to offer structured and intentional instruction in survival language. Consider organizing related words and phrases under the heading of a topic such as "School," as in the following table.

People	Places	Objects	Phrases
principal	cafeteria	desk	May I have...?
teacher	classroom	chair	Please show
nurse	bathroom	chalkboard	me....
student	library	worksheet	I want to...
coach	gym	ruler	What is a ...?
			I need help
			with....

Teachers Support Vocabulary Learning

English language learners come to school with a wide range of home language literacy, English language proficiency, and previous educational experiences. All of these factors impact their learning in English.

Teachers can use various strategies to support vocabulary development. Students need multiple exposures to words. Understanding deepens over time through gradually increased and varied experiences with the words.

English language learners need opportunities to learn vocabulary through activities that integrate reading, writing, speaking, and listening skills in the context of meaningful literacy experiences. Language learning is an exploration. Students have a curiosity about learning, and effective teachers nurture this quality through engaging and meaningful activities. Teachers can use what students already know to help them extract meaning from text by teaching them ways to learn and think about words.

Strategies for Exploring Words

Use these strategies to build vocabulary.

Related Words

Provide opportunities for English language learners to learn new words by grouping words that are related to a specific theme, quality, or activity. Help students classify English words in meaningful categories.

Use word walls, graphic organizers, and concept maps to group related words and create visual references that can be used in future lessons. Teachers can help students group and relate words in different ways, depending on what they can notice and understand, as well as how students will use the vocabulary.

Color names are one example of related words that can be the focus of a lesson.

✓ Write the word *colors* at the top of a wall chart.

✓ With colored markers, make a column of squares under the heading: red, blue, yellow, green.

✓ Point to the word *colors* and tell students they are going to learn the names of colors.

✓ Point to the first square and say, *This color is red.* Write *red* and repeat it clearly as you underline it with your finger.

✓ Show a familiar red object, such as a block, and say: *This is a red block. The color of this block is red. What color is this block?* (red)

Repeat this process with the other colors, making sure that students hear, say, and read each color name, and connect it to the color itself.

Have students create other sections in their personal word card files such as "family names," "numbers," "days and months," "weather," and "time."

Whenever you introduce a new topic or concept, take time to teach English language learners words they will need to understand the lesson. Keep in mind that they may need to learn some words and phrases in the lesson—including idioms and background references—that may already be common knowledge to native speakers. Encourage native speakers to act as resources for English language learners when they encounter a word, phrase, or concept that puzzles them.

Charts such as the one here can help students learn how words change form, depending on their function.

Naming Word	Describing Word	Action Word
rain	rainy	rain, rains, rained, raining
dance, dancer	dancing	dance, dances, danced, dancing
sleep, sleeper	sleepy	sleep, sleeps, slept, sleeping

Cognates

When students hear or see a word that looks or sounds similar to a word they know in their home language, encourage them to explore the connection. For example, a Russian speaker hearing the word *music* may recognize its connection to the Russian word *musika*. Many words that sound similar in two or more languages are cognates—they have the same or similar meaning in both languages. Record cognates on a wall chart and add to it during the year.

Multiple-meaning Words

Many English words have multiple meanings. Illustrating and creating examples of the ways words are used can build English language learners' experiences and understanding of the multiple meanings that words may have. Teachers can help students expand their understanding of multiple meanings by sharing sentences, definitions, and pictures that demonstrate the different meanings. For example, contrasting *The pitcher is full of water* with *The pitcher threw the ball,* with illustrations, will help English language learners remember the two meanings of *pitcher.*

Academic Language

Research indicates that acquiring a strong grasp of academic vocabulary is perhaps the most vital factor that distinguishes successful students from those who struggle in school. Becoming fluent in academic language will enable English language learners to understand and analyze texts, write clearly about their ideas, and comprehend subject-area material. Academic vocabulary differs from conversational English. It is the language of classroom discourse, and it is used to accomplish academic, not social or personal, purposes. Academic vocabulary also includes words, phrases, and sentence structures not commonly found in oral language but used frequently in academic texts such as textbooks, reports, essays, articles, and test materials. Instruction in academic vocabulary should be explicit and systematic. Give students multiple exposures to academic terms through frequent reading, writing, and oral language activities. Because academic vocabulary involves the use of language that is not commonly encountered in conversational contexts, English language learners need structured opportunities to practice this vocabulary in formal settings where teachers and peers are modeling the use of effective academic language.

Below is a partial list of types of academic vocabulary to which students should be exposed:

- **Transition words**

  therefore; thus; however; similarly; alternatively

- **Content-specific words**

  cell (science); *era* (social studies); *graph* (math)

- **Difficult verb and tense forms**

  was written by (passive voice); *have voted* (present perfect); *had ended* (past perfect)

- **The language of written instructions**

  compare; define; analyze; calculate; summarize

<u>Home Language Activities</u>

Teachers can use home language activities to help students reinforce their learning of the concepts and meanings of vocabulary and literacy activities. English language learners can participate in a variety of activities such as discussion, telling or reading stories, listening to songs and music, hearing radio or television weather or sports reports, and interviewing family members, and then use those experiences as topics for discussion and sharing in the classroom. Students can transfer their understanding of a word or concept from their home language to English when they have experiences that illustrate meaning. Teachers can find ways to use the home environment as an educational resource by planning activities that involve reading, writing, listening, and speaking about students' family histories, cultures, and experiences.

<u>Technology</u>

Teachers can use various forms of technology (computer, Internet, audio, video recording) to meet the specific and varied needs of English language learners.

For example, you might choose target words and have students use computers to find images that illustrate their meanings.

Creating and Adapting Strategies

A great deal of reading in English, listening to selections read aloud, and conversing in English will help learners acquire thousands of words per year if they are engaged in learning. Continue using the instructional strategies that work, adapt (or discontinue) the ones that are not effective, and try new approaches as needed.

References

August, Diane (Principal Investigator), and T. Shanahan (Panel Chair) (2006). *Developing Literacy in Second-Language Learners: Report of the National Literacy Panel on Language-Minority Children and Youth.* Mahwah, New Jersey: Lawrence Erlbaum Associates.

Blachowicz, Camille L. Z., and Peter Fisher. *Teaching Vocabulary in All Classrooms.* Upper Saddle River, NJ: Prentice Hall, 2002.

Vocabulary Development for Reading Success. Scott Foresman Professional Development Series, Module 6. Glenview, IL: Scott Foresman, 2004.

Effective Comprehension Instruction for English Language Learners

Clear and explicit comprehension instruction is a key component of successful English language development. Traditionally, the main purpose of comprehension instruction has been limited to having students answer assigned questions related to a passage they have read. As a result, what can and should be a complex, analytical process has been diminished by a narrow focus on products. A greater benefit to English language learners, as for all students, is guidance in becoming active readers who are engaged in texts on multiple levels before, during, and after reading.

Jim Cummins identifies conditions that promote engaging with literacy for English language learners and, in fact, for all students. To attain literacy, students must be fully engaged in their reading and writing. Students need to read a variety of texts that reflect children's cultures and languages. Teachers must use strategies that promote a deep understanding of the text. Through engaging students by activating prior knowledge, frontloading to build background, affirming identity, scaffolding the language, and extending language through various experiences, students move from engagement in literacy to achievement in literacy.

Comprehension instruction that will achieve this more sophisticated goal focuses on *meta-cognition*, the name we give to a good reader's ability to independently reflect on the purpose of reading, select appropriate approaches to texts, ask questions as he or she reads, and actively resolve areas of confusion. Metacognitive strategies such as predicting, questioning, self-monitoring, summarizing, and making inferences should be transferable from one type of text to another. For this reason it is important to introduce these strategies to students using a variety of fiction and nonfiction texts. The following comprehension instruction techniques will help you encourage literacy engagement and the development of metacognition in your students.

What Is Frontloading?

Imagine that you are teaching someone how to bake a cake. If you knew that your pupil had no experience in the kitchen, you would not jump right into the recipe and instructions. Instead, you would start by naming and explaining the key ingredients in the cake—the flour, sugar, baking powder, eggs, and so on. You would demonstrate how to use measuring cups. You might explain how baking differs from frying or boiling. In other words, you would anticipate the knowledge that your budding baker requires in order to be successful at this new task and make sure to introduce that knowledge first. This is the essence of frontloading.

Frontloading for English language learners involves preteaching the vital vocabulary, background concepts, and sometimes the text structures that students need to know before they can understand an upcoming lesson. Prior to a lesson in which students will be reading a story from *Aesop's Fables*, for example, you might choose to frontload the following vocabulary using a graphic organizer.

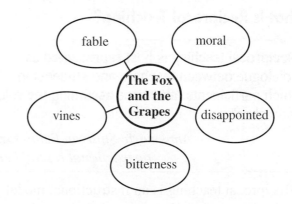

What Is Shared Reading?

Shared reading is reading that is rich with interactions between teacher and students. When using the shared reading model, the goal is to invite students to actively participate in the reading process. This is an excellent opportunity to encourage English language learners to use oral language in a relaxed and informal setting. Use an enlarged text as the central focus as you conduct a shared reading session, so that everyone in the group can clearly see the text. The basic elements of shared reading include:

✓ **Think Alouds:** Model making predictions, asking questions, and drawing conclusions about the text by thinking aloud as you read.

✓ **Guided Discussions:** Using open-ended questions, encourage students to respond to, analyze, and summarize the text.

✓ **Active Participation:** Students can contribute to the reading of the text by chorusing repetitive words or phrases or reading sight words that you point to.

✓ **Multiple Readings:** Return to the same text several times over a few days. Set a focus for each reading such as enjoyment, decoding, comprehension, or vocabulary.

What Is Reciprocal Teaching?

> "Reciprocal teaching is best represented as a dialogue between teachers and students in which participants take turns assuming the role of teacher."
>
> — *Annemarie Sullivan Palincsar,*
> *instructional researcher*

Reciprocal teaching is an instructional model that focuses on four key comprehension strategies: predicting, question generating, clarifying, and summarizing. First, you explain, discuss, and model the strategies. Then, while working in small groups, students gradually take responsibility for strategies while making their way through a text.

- **Predicting:** Make predictions about what an author will discuss next.
- **Question Generating:** Pose "teacher-like" questions about main ideas in the text.
- **Clarifying:** Notice potential areas of confusion and take steps to clarify them (e.g., reread, identify the definition of a word).
- **Summarizing:** Identify and recap the most important information.

Reciprocal teaching has proven to be of great help in developing the skills of English language learners. Although it can be used with a variety of text types, this technique is especially useful for deepening comprehension of expository text.

References

Cummins, Jim. *Reading Instruction and Reading Achievement Among EL Students* (Research Into Practice monograph). Glenview, IL: Pearson, 2009.

Drucker, M. J. "What Reading Teachers Should Know About ESL Learners." *The Reading Teacher,* 57(1) (2003), pp. 22–29.

Francis, D. J., et al. "Practical Guidelines for the Education of English Language Learners: Research-Based Recommendations for Instruction and Academic Interventions." Houston, TX: Center on Instruction, 2006.

Institute of Education Sciences, National Center for Educational Evaluation and Regional Assistance. "Effective Literacy and English Language Instruction for English Learners in the Elementary Grades." IES Practice Guide, 2007.

Effective Writing Instruction for English Language Learners

The Role of Writing in Language and Literacy Development

Research shows that students acquire language most readily when they are fully involved in all learning activities in the classroom. Classroom activities should integrate reading, writing, listening, and speaking, as these language skills develop interdependently. This approach supports English language development in the context of meaningful instructional content. That is, students will learn to write (in English) about real ideas and things.

Teachers can facilitate students' language learning and literacy development by ensuring that:

- students hear language in natural ways, in real and practical contexts—and write it in structured formats

- activities in which students participate regularly provide opportunities for listening and speaking so students can internalize the language

- opportunities for acquiring new vocabulary are always present in reading activities and environmental print, and are related to the content areas of the curriculum

- opportunities are always available for interesting conversations with English-speaking peers

- mistakes are accepted as part of learning

- students understand why they are being asked to complete various oral communication, reading, and writing tasks

English language learners who are already literate, or are emergent readers and writers in their home languages, no doubt have been influenced by their backgrounds and experiences with writing genres, writing styles, and cultural discourse. By learning more about the characteristics of English language learners' literacy experiences, teachers can recognize when students are transferring what they already know to their new, early literacy learning in English, and teachers can support these efforts. It is helpful to seek information about students in sensitive ways, appropriately respecting families' privacy and regarding home languages and cultures with respect.

Such efforts to find out students' strengths and needs are worthwhile. For example, teachers who compare spelling patterns between a home language and English will better understand the efforts students make to acquire and write English words. Teachers can point out the differences and similarities so that students can learn to compare the languages and develop metalinguistic understanding about how both languages work. This will help them sort out the ways they can use language in their writing.

ENGLISH	rose
SPANISH	rosa

Young English language learners also are emergent writers. For most children, the line between emergent writing and drawing (that is, art) is not a bold border. It helps learners to write in both words and pictures. Experts in English language learning advise, however, that English language learners who draw too often without writing any words are missing vital opportunities to practice writing in English. Encourage students to write about their pictures.

Scaffolding the Steps of the Writing Process

Writing, whether in a home language or especially in a new language, is the most difficult mode of language use to master (Collier and Ovando, 1998). Each English language learner has a unique background and set of experiences with language, literacy, and culture. Students access writing instruction at varying levels of English proficiency. It is important for teachers to provide each student with challenging work that is appropriate for his or her level of English proficiency and literacy.

By understanding the specific kinds of support English language learners need at each stage of the writing process, teachers can tailor their instruction to fit individual needs. The chart below provides suggestions to help you do this.

	Level I	Level II & III	Level IV & V
	Beginning (little experience in English)	**Intermediate** (conversational but not academic English)	**Advanced/ Advanced High** (gaining skills in academic English)
Prewrite	Allow extra time for prewriting. Use brainstorming. Have student draw or act out ideas. Map, or illustrate and label, words that the student needs.	Allow extra time for prewriting. Use brainstorming. Have student draw and label, or act out and describe, ideas. Help student learn and write the words he or she needs.	Allow extra time for prewriting. Use brainstorming, drawing, word mapping, and story mapping. Help student learn and write the words he or she needs.
Draft	Allow student to dictate, as appropriate. As skills emerge, student writes words and phrases. Accept phonetic invented spelling, but model correct spelling, capitalization, and punctuation.	Student writes words, phrases, and simple sentences. Help student turn phrases into sentences. Accept phonetic invented spelling, but show correct spelling, capitalization, and punctuation.	Student writes words, phrases, and simple sentences. Help student add details to sentences and create paragraphs. Accept phonetic invented spelling, but show correct spelling, capitalization, and punctuation.
Revise	With help, student revises work with the aid of a checklist that has visual clues about each task.	Student revises work with the aid of a checklist that has visual and written clues about each task. Help student incorporate written or oral commentary from teacher in revisions.	Student revises work with the aid of a checklist that has visual and written clues about each task—and asks for clarification. Help student incorporate written or oral comments from teacher in revisions.
Edit	Student sees teacher model how to correct errors and begins to correct errors.	Student corrects errors with help from the teacher.	Student corrects errors with help from the teacher and incorporates teacher's suggestions into writing.
Publish	Student creates final product of writing with teacher's guidance.	Student creates final product of writing with teacher's guidance.	Student creates final product of writing with teacher's guidance.

Structured Writing

Teachers can use **structured writing** to scaffold writing instruction. Structured writing aids include writing/sentence frames and graphic organizers, which help students record and organize their ideas.

Writing Assignments for English Language Learners

There are various kinds of assignments and activities that encourage English language learners to use their background knowledge and previous experiences to connect with the writing process. Establishing a daily or weekly **routine** for these assignments and activities helps cue students about what to expect and provides extra support for participating in classroom instruction.

Teachers can compile a **writing portfolio** to show progress and to facilitate home communication and teacher/student dialogue about writing.

Writing Products

While there are varieties of authentic writing assignments that encourage students to write about their interests and experiences, there are specific genres with which students must become familiar in order to build an understanding of text structures that reflect district and state standards/curriculum frameworks. The following examples suggest ways to approach each genre in relation to English language learners' needs.

Language Experience Approach
Students dictate stories to the teacher (or aide), who writes them down. Students then copy the words that the teacher wrote. In this way, reading and writing become processes directly related to children's experiences. They read and write to express themselves and communicate their experiences.

Dialogue Journals
Dialogue journals develop writing skills and provide authentic communication between a student and teacher. This writing is informal and may include pictures. It allows students to choose topics for writing. The teacher may suggest topics, but the choice is the writer's. The student writes as in conversation with the teacher. The teacher responds to the content of the writing, also in a conversational manner. Writing errors are not explicitly corrected, but the teacher's writing serves as a model (Collier and Ovando, 1998).

Home Literacy Activities
Home literacy activities encourage conversation between students and their families as they read together in their home language and/or in English. If parents are not literate, students can practice reading aloud and discussing stories with them. Teachers can plan activities such as interviewing family members in the home language and then sharing the responses with the class in English.

Students learning to write will benefit from writing in their home language as well as the new language, English. Bilingual parents, staff members, and students can help children write in home languages.

Rubrics to Evaluate Writing

Teachers can use school, district, state, or national standards for English language learners (which are aligned with English Language Arts standards) to create rubrics that adjust expectations for English language learners based on their individual English proficiency levels.

The sample rubric on the following page focuses on one of the traits of good writing: rules (or conventions) of English. It describes what English language learners at various levels (beginning, intermediate, advanced, and advanced high) would be expected to write. Teachers can develop similar evaluation forms that reflect the needs of the school, the grade, and the students involved. Other examples of traits of good writing may include Focus/Ideas, Order, Writer's Voice, Word Choice, and Sentences.

Traits of Good Writing: Rules (English Language Learners)

	Level	Capitalization	Punctuation	Sentence Structure and Grammar	Spelling
Beginning (little experience in English)	1	Uses capitalization when writing one's own name.	Adds a period to the end of a sentence and a question mark to the end of a question.	Begins to use some standard word order, with mostly inconsistent grammatical forms (for example, subject/verb agreement).	Produces some independent writing that includes inconsistent spelling.
Intermediate/ Advanced (conversational but not academic English)	2–4	Uses capitalization to begin sentences and proper nouns.	Produces independent writing that may include some inconsistent use of periods and question marks.	Uses standard word order but may use inconsistent grammatical forms.	Produces independent writing that includes some misspellings.
Advanced High (gaining skills in academic English)	5	Produces independent writing with consistent use of correct capitalization.	Produces independent writing with generally consistent use of correct punctuation.	Uses complete sentences and generally correct word order.	Produces independent writing with consistent use of correct spelling.

References

August, Diane (Principal Investigator), and T. Shanahan (Panel Chair) (2006). *Developing Literacy in Second-Language Learners: Report of the National Literacy Panel on Language-Minority Children and Youth.* Mahwah, New Jersey: Lawrence Erlbaum Associates.

Collier, V. P., and C. J. Ovando (1998). *Bilingual and ESL Classrooms: Teaching in Multicultural Contexts.* Boston, MA: McGraw Hill.

Echevarria, J.; M. Vogt; and D. Short (2004). *Making Content Comprehensible for English Learners: The SIOP Model.* Boston: Allyn & Bacon.

Fillmore, L. W., and C. E. Snow (2000). "*What Teachers Need to Know About Language.*" Washington, DC: ERIC Clearinghouse on Languages and Linguistics.

English Language Learners and Assessment

Assessment Needs of Diverse Learners

Because English language learners make up a dynamic group of learners who enter school with a wide range of linguistic, cultural, and learning experiences, it is important for teachers to learn about the unique background of each individual learner. Overall, assessment can provide important information about students' learning that can be used to plan appropriate and meaningful instruction. However, the kinds of assessment, the purposes for which they are used, and how the results are evaluated can directly impact how meaningful the assessments are (Cummins, 1981).

High-stakes Testing vs. Authentic Assessment

While so-called "high-stakes" testing has become increasingly influential, high-profile tests can be difficult for English language learners because they require proficiency in academic English, understanding of grade-level subject matter, and an understanding of cultural contexts. While high-stakes test results in the United States influence instructional decisions made in schools, these results often do not reflect what English language learners know. Consequently, the instructional decisions based on test results often do not reflect the specific learning needs of English language learners (Bielenberg and Fillmore, 2005).

It is important to find a variety of ways to assess English language learners that show what each learner is able to do. Focusing on what students already know—and what they are learning but have not mastered—helps teachers identify specific educational needs and enables educators to build their ongoing instruction upon all the resources, experiences, and abilities that English language learners bring to school. Authentic assessment, or ongoing classroom-based (often informal) assessment of students by teachers, allows students to show their strengths. Ongoing assessment also provides teachers with an accurate, dynamic picture of how to plan instruction and provide feedback in ways that meet the changing learning needs of each student (García, 1994).

Outcome-based/norm-referenced tests are different from ongoing authentic assessment because they evaluate, or make a judgment about, the performance of a student at a given time, while authentic assessment informs both teachers and students about day-to-day learning and provides feedback about how to proceed in order to meet the needs of individual learners.

English language learners must be taught test-taking strategies and must build background about the language and procedures of test taking. Use the suggestions below when preparing English language learners, who may not be experienced with the specialized language and implications of standardized tests. (Bielenberg and Fillmore, 2005):

- Point out text structures and conceptual references used in tests.
- Point out difficult language structures, and provide sufficient practice before the test.
- Preteach basic and content-area vocabulary.
- Build background and knowledge about test taking and procedural language.

Preteach Vocabulary and Question Types

- Make a T-chart to show examples of the question types students will find on tests. Explain what the structures mean and what they ask test-takers to do.
- Make a short list of test vocabulary, phrases, and instructions found on tests—such as *choose, write, fill in the circle, less than,* and *greater than.* Illustrate what these expressions ask students to do.

Example:

TEST DIRECTIONS	WHAT SHOULD I DO?
<u>Choose</u> the word that goes in the <u>blank</u>. <u>Mark</u> your answer. 1. Nancy rides her ____. ○ book ○ bike ○ store ○ gloves	• **Choose** = pick, decide on one • **Blank** = the line 1. Nancy rides her ____. • **Mark** = use pencil to fill in the circle

Example:

INSTRUCTIONS	WHAT SHOULD I DO?		
Find the **sum.**	Add numbers, + 10 + 1 = 11		
Compare the numbers using **>** , **<** , or **=**	<	less than	1 < 10
	>	greater than	9 > 2
	=	equals	3 = 3

Reading Fluency and Comprehension Assessment

Authentic assessment focuses on teachers making informed decisions based on authentic literacy tasks within the classroom context that reflect individual student's progress and learning (García, 1994). Finding ways to help English language learners develop reading fluency means finding out if students really comprehend what they read, rather than just decode words.

Student's English language proficiency levels, the kinds of literacy and learning experiences students have had, and how familiar they are with the topic of the reading passage will affect how much they struggle with understanding what they read. Literature also can be challenging for English language learners because of the use of figurative language, including metaphors, similes, and symbolism. Check students' reading comprehension and understanding of concepts such as *setting, characters, plot, beginning, middle,* and *end.*

When assessing fluency and comprehension, it is helpful for teachers to learn how students' home literacy and languages affect their learning in English. English language learners may draw on what they already know; for example, an English language learner whose home language is Spanish may use Spanish spelling patterns and/or phonetics when reading or writing words in English. Recognizing the influence of the home language, and the student's reliance upon the literacy skills and strategies he or she knows in the home language, will help teachers not only assess more accurately, but know how to point out similarities and differences between English and the home language as a way to develop awareness about how different languages are related. This helps develop metalinguistic awareness, or thinking about how language works.

Teachers must ultimately use all they know about each student's English proficiency and literacy skills in order to:

- monitor progress
- organize students in groups for effective learning
- differentiate instruction

Assessing English language learners and learning about their cultural, linguistic, and learning experiences can help teachers plan instruction that is comprehensible and challenging.

Scaffolding High-stakes Testing

While "high-stakes" testing presents various challenges for English language learners, there are various test-taking strategies that teachers can use to support students in preparing for eventual mastery of standardized testing. Showing students ways in which they can recognize test formats and decode the questions of a test will help them figure out what each question is asking them to do.

Assessment Accommodations for English Language Learners

While English language learners need time to acquire the academic language necessary to be able to practice and perform well on standardized tests in English, there are some accommodations that may support their attempts at extracting meaning from test language, questions, and passages. Accommodations for English language learners may include the following:

- Provide English language learners with extra time to complete the test.
- Allow the use of a bilingual dictionary or a picture dictionary to clarify words that may hinder comprehension.
- Read the question aloud in some cases.

References

August, D., and K. Hakuta. *Improving Schooling for Language Minority Children: A Research Agenda*. Washington, DC: National Academy Press, 1997.

Bielenberg, B., and L. W. Fillmore. "The English They Need for the Test." *Educational Leadership,* 62(4) (2004/2005), pp. 45–49.

Cummins, J. "The Role of Primary Language Development in Promoting Educational Success for Language Minority Students." *Schooling and Language Minority Students: A Theoretical Framework*. Sacramento, CA: California Department of Education, 1981.

García, G. E. "Assessing the Literacy Development of Second Language Students: A Focus on Authentic Assessment" in K. Spangenbergk-Urbschat and R. Pritchard, eds. *Kids Come in All Languages: Reading Instruction for ESL Students,* pp. 180–205. Newark, DE: International Reading Association, 1994.

Scott Foresman Reading Street
Overview of Weekly Support for English Language Learners

The ELL Handbook provides weekly lesson materials to support English language learners with scaffolded and leveled comprehension and vocabulary instruction for language development. It builds on the Student Edition and on literacy instruction in the Teacher's Edition. Each strand contains a wide variety of activities that promote literacy attainment for your English language learners.

Weekly Planners offer a quick reference to the ELL Support materials for each lesson of the year.

Weekly Resources Guide for English Language Learner Support

Unit 2 Week 1 *What Jo Did*

For this week's content and language objectives, see p. 59e.

This symbol indicates leveled instruction to address language proficiency levels.

Instructional Strand	Day 1	Day 2	Day 3	Day 4	Day 5
Concept Development/Academic Language	TEACHER'S EDITION • Academic Language, p. DI•16 • Concept Development, p. DI•16 • Anchored Talk, pp. 172j—172–173 • Preteach Academic Vocabulary, p. 175a • Concept Talk Video ELL HANDBOOK • Hear It, See It, Say It, Use It, pp. xxxvi–xxxvii • ELL Poster Talk, Concept Talk, p. 59c ELL POSTER 6 • Day 1 Activities	TEACHER'S EDITION • Academic Language, p. DI•16 • Concept Development, p. DI•16 • Anchored Talk, p. 176a • Concept Talk Video ELL HANDBOOK • ELL Poster Talk, Concept Talk, p. 59c • Concept Talk Video Routine, p. 477 ELL POSTER 6 • Day 2 Activities	TEACHER'S EDITION • Academic Language, p. DI•16 • Concept Development, p. DI•16 • Anchored Talk, p. 184a • Concept Talk Video ELL HANDBOOK • ELL Poster Talk, Concept Talk, p. 59c ELL POSTER 6 • Day 3 Activities	TEACHER'S EDITION • Academic Language, p. DI•16 • Concept Development, p. DI•16 • Anchored Talk, p. 192a • Concept Talk Video ELL HANDBOOK • ELL Poster Talk, Concept Talk, p. 59c ELL POSTER 6 • Day 4 Activities	TEACHER'S EDITION • Academic Language, p. DI•16 • Concept Development, p. DI•16 • Concept Talk Video ELL HANDBOOK • ELL Poster Talk, Concept Talk, p. 59c ELL POSTER 6 • Day 5 Activities
Phonics and Spelling	TEACHER'S EDITION • Phonics and Spelling, p. DI•20	TEACHER'S EDITION • Phonics and Spelling, p. DI•20	ELL HANDBOOK • Phonics Transition Lesson, pp. 268, 270	ELL HANDBOOK • Phonics Transition Lesson, pp. 268, 270	TEACHER'S EDITION • Phonics and Spelling, p. DI•20
Listening Comprehension	TEACHER'S EDITION • Modified Read Aloud, p. DI•19 • Read Aloud, p. 173b • Concept Talk Video ELL HANDBOOK • Concept Talk Video Routine, p. 477	TEACHER'S EDITION • Modified Read Aloud, p. DI•19 • AudioText of *What Jo Did* • Concept Talk Video ELL HANDBOOK • AudioText CD Routine, p. 477 • Story Map B, p. 484	TEACHER'S EDITION • AudioText of *What Jo Did* • Concept Talk Video ELL HANDBOOK • AudioText CD Routine, p. 477	TEACHER'S EDITION • Concept Talk Video	
Reading Comprehension	TEACHER'S EDITION • Preteach Cause and Effect, p. DI•21	TEACHER'S EDITION • Reteach Cause and Effect, p. DI•21 • Frontloading Reading, p. DI•22 ELL HANDBOOK • Picture It! Skill Instruction, pp. 60–60a • Multilingual Summaries, pp. 61–63	TEACHER'S EDITION • Sheltered Reading, p. DI•22 ELL HANDBOOK • Multilingual Summaries, pp. 61–63	TEACHER'S EDITION • ELL/ELD Reader Guided Reading, p. DI•23 ELL HANDBOOK • ELL Study Guide, p. 64	TEACHER'S EDITION • ELL/ELD Reader Guided Reading, p. DI•23 ELL HANDBOOK • ELL Study Guide, p. 64
Vocabulary **Basic and Lesson Vocabulary** **Word Analysis: Prefixes *un-* and *in-***	TEACHER'S EDITION • Basic Vocabulary, p. DI•17 • Preteach Lesson Vocabulary, p. DI•17 • Prefixes *un-* and *in-*, p. DI•20 ELL HANDBOOK • Word Cards, p. 59 • ELL Vocabulary Routine, p. 471 ELL POSTER 6 • Day 1 Activities	TEACHER'S EDITION • Basic Vocabulary, p. DI•17 • Reteach Lesson Vocabulary, p. DI•18 • Prefixes *un-* and *in-*, p. DI•20 ELL HANDBOOK • Word Cards, p. 59 • Multilingual Vocabulary List, p. 431 ELL POSTER 6 • Day 2 Activities	ELL HANDBOOK • High-Frequency Words Activity Bank, p. 446 ELL POSTER 6 • Day 3 Activities	ELL HANDBOOK • High-Frequency Words Activity Bank, p. 446	TEACHER'S EDITION • Prefixes *un-* and *in-*, p. 195i ELL HANDBOOK • High-Frequency Words Activity Bank, p. 446
Grammar and Conventions	TEACHER'S EDITION • Preteach Common and Proper Nouns, p. DI•24	TEACHER'S EDITION • Teach/Model Common and Proper Nouns, p. DI•24	TEACHER'S EDITION • Grammar Jammer ELL HANDBOOK • Grammar Transition Lesson, pp. 314, 318–319 • Grammar Jammer Routine, p. 478	TEACHER'S EDITION • Grammar Jammer ELL HANDBOOK • Grammar Transition Lesson, pp. 314, 318–319	TEACHER'S EDITION • Grammar Jammer ELL HANDBOOK • Grammar Transition Lesson, pp. 314, 318–319
Writing	TEACHER'S EDITION • Figurative Language, p. DI•25 • Introduce Poetry, pp. 175e–175f	TEACHER'S EDITION • Limerick, pp. 183d–183e	TEACHER'S EDITION • Let's Write It!, pp. 190–191 • Shape Poem, pp. 191a–191b	TEACHER'S EDITION • Shape Poem, pp. 195d–195e	TEACHER'S EDITION • Proofreading and Presenting, pp. 195p–195q

Weekly Planner

The daily Concept Development activities activate prior knowledge and build background, scaffold meaning, affirm identity, and develop and extend language.

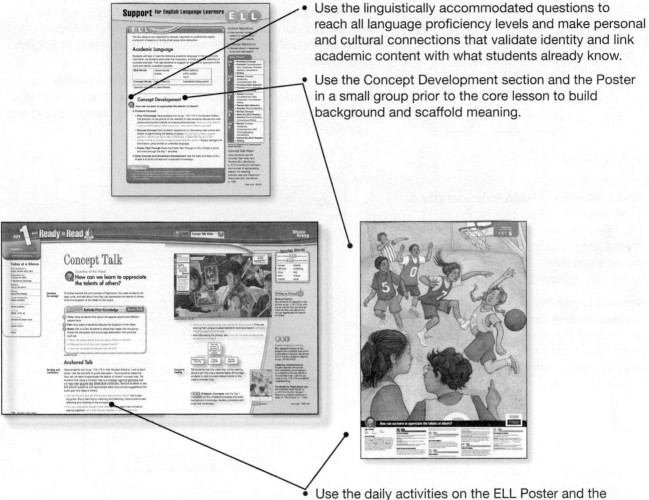

- Use the linguistically accommodated questions to reach all language proficiency levels and make personal and cultural connections that validate identity and link academic content with what students already know.

- Use the Concept Development section and the Poster in a small group prior to the core lesson to build background and scaffold meaning.

- Use the daily activities on the ELL Poster and the Anchored Talk questions in the core lesson to build concept attainment and encourage oral language development and production.

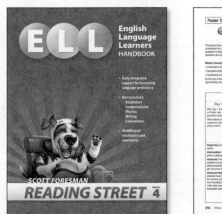

- Use the daily, leveled Poster Talk, Concept Talk in the ELL Handbook and the Team Talk activities in the core lesson to encourage oral language production.

Listening Comprehension

The adapted Read Aloud in the Listening Comprehension section of the ELL Support pages covers the same concept and information as the Read Aloud in the core curriculum.

In order for English language learners to meet grade-level learning expectations, have access to the core curriculum, and develop language, all instruction delivered in English must be linguistically accommodated for all levels of English language proficiency.

For Beginning and Intermediate levels, use the grade-appropriate adapted Read Aloud in place of the regular Read Aloud until students no longer need the linguistic support and modification.

- **First Listening: Listen to Understand** gives students a purpose for listening. The questions are designed to generate interest and help students get the gist of the adapted Read Aloud, so all proficiency levels can achieve success.

- **Second Listening: Listen to Check Understanding** Once students understand the main idea of the adapted Read Aloud, they can listen on subsequent days to clarify understanding of important details of spoken language.

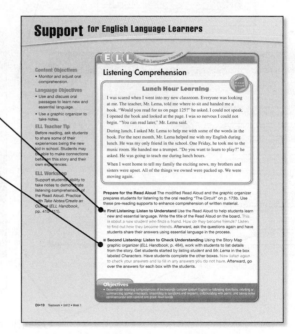

Additional Products

Concept Talk Video

Concept Talk Video Routine

AudioText CD

AudioText Routine

Discrete language skills that English language learners need include knowledge of the letters of the alphabet, familiarity with the sounds represented by letters, the ability to decode words, and the rules and conventions of how words are formed.

The Phonics support lessons work along with the Phonics Transition Lessons to help students learn phonics skills at the same time they are developing basic English vocabulary.

Language Transfer Notes activate prior knowledge about a phonics skill. Relating the skill being taught to a student's home language helps students build on what they already know and affirm their identities.

The flexible bank of Phonics Transition Lessons provides practice for developing and internalizing language at all proficiency levels. The Practice Pages provide visual support and context for the skills.

Additional Products

Modeled Pronunciation
Audio CD

The Modeled Pronunciation Audio CD and routine offers additional practice with sound-spelling correspondence.

Vocabulary

English learners need explicit and systematic instruction to acquire both social and academic language for literacy attainment. Students need multiple exposures to new vocabulary through frequent listening, reading, writing, and oral language activities.

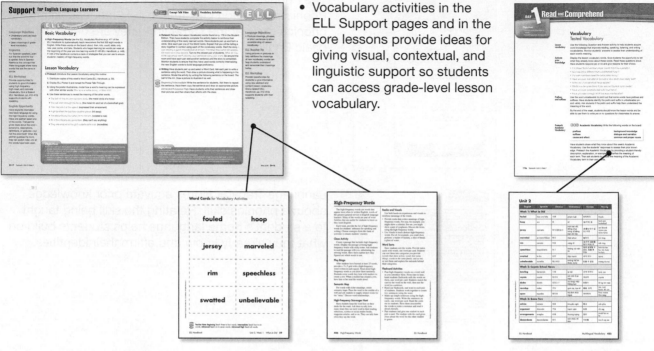

- Vocabulary activities in the ELL Support pages and in the core lessons provide ideas for giving visual, contextual, and linguistic support so students can access grade-level lesson vocabulary.

- Word Analysis lessons from the ELL Support and core lesson pages engage students in figuring out meanings of new words, thereby increasing their comprehension and language production.

Daily activities in the Poster increase oral and written production of newly acquired vocabulary.

- The Poster Talk, Concept Talk provides leveled support to meet the needs of all students.

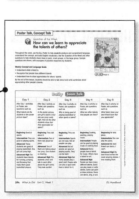

Engaging activities in the core lessons, the ELL Handbook, and the three Comprehension sections of the ELL Support lessons activate prior knowledge, build background, scaffold meaning, affirm identity, and develop and extend language.

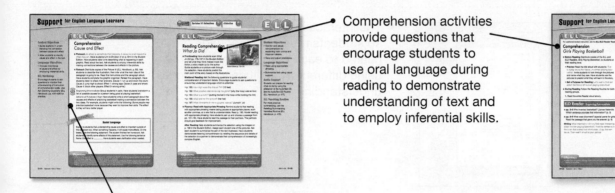

• Comprehension activities provide questions that encourage students to use oral language during reading to demonstrate understanding of text and to employ inferential skills.

• The leveled notes in the ELL Support and Picture It! instruction pages provide ideas for differentiating instruction at all proficiency levels.

• The ELD Readers are written for Beginning and Intermediate language proficiency levels, and the ELL Readers are designed for Advanced to Advanced High levels, allowing you to meet the needs of a diverse classroom.

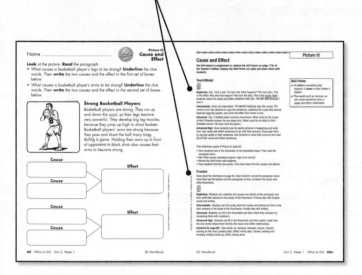

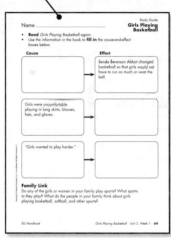

Additional Products

Multilingual Summaries

AudioText CD

AudioText CD Routine

ELL Handbook

Research into Practice **27f**

The Grammar and Conventions and Writing lessons provide the systematic instruction that students need at each language proficiency level to scaffold use of increasingly complex grammatical structures in content area reading and writing.

Grammar and Conventions

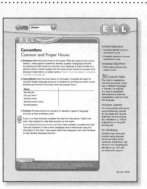

- The interactive activities are designed so students reuse the language related to each core convention, using different modalities to enhance understanding.

- The flexible bank of Grammar Transition Lessons leads students in transferring knowledge from their home languages to English and guides language development.

Writing

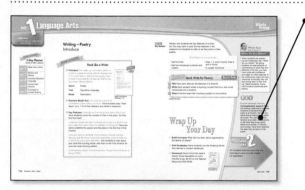

- ELL Notes throughout the core Language Arts pages provide ideas to support all levels of English language learners in prewriting, editing, revising, and publishing writing pieces.

- The writing model, sentence frames, and leveled writing prompts guide and encourage oral and written language production for all levels of English proficiency.

Concept Talk Video

- Use the Concept Talk Video to activate an engaging discussion about the weekly concept. Use the Concept Talk Video Routine found in the ELL Handbook to guide students' understanding.

AudioText CD

- Students can build fluency and comprehension and prepare for reading the main selection by using the AudioText CD and the AudioText CD Routine.

I love my dog Thunder.

Grammar Jammer

- Use the Grammar Jammer for additional practice with the target skill. For suggestions on how to use this learning tool, see the Grammar Jammer Routine in the ELL Handbook.

Concept Literacy Reader

- Use the Concept Literacy Reader for additional support to develop the weekly concept.

Contents

Unit 1

Unit 2

Unit 3

Unit 4

Unit 5

Unit 6

Weekly Resources Guide for English Language Learner Support

For this week's content and language objectives, see p. 29e.

Instructional Strand	Day 1	Day 2
Concept Development/Academic Language	**TEACHER'S EDITION** • Academic Language, p. DI•16 • Concept Development, p. DI•16 • Anchored Talk, pp. 20j—20–21 • Preteach Academic Vocabulary, p. 23a • Concept Talk Video **ELL HANDBOOK** • Hear It, See It, Say It, Use It, pp. xxxvi–xxxvii • ELL Poster Talk, Concept Talk, p. 29c **ELL POSTER 1** • Day 1 Activities	**TEACHER'S EDITION** • Academic Language, p. DI•16 • Concept Development, p. DI•16 • Anchored Talk, p. 24a • Concept Talk Video **ELL HANDBOOK** • ELL Poster Talk, Concept Talk, p. 29c • Concept Talk Video Routine, p. 477 **ELL POSTER 1** • Day 2 Activities
Phonics and Spelling	**TEACHER'S EDITION** • Phonics and Spelling, p. DI•20	**TEACHER'S EDITION** • Phonics and Spelling, p. DI•20
Listening Comprehension	**TEACHER'S EDITION** • Modified Read Aloud, p. DI•19 • Read Aloud, p. 21b • Concept Talk Video **ELL HANDBOOK** • Concept Talk Video Routine, p. 477	**TEACHER'S EDITION** • Modified Read Aloud, p. DI•19 • AudioText of *Because of Winn-Dixie* • Concept Talk Video **ELL HANDBOOK** • AudioText CD Routine, p. 477 • Story Map B, p. 484
Reading Comprehension	**TEACHER'S EDITION** • Preteach Sequence, p. DI•21	**TEACHER'S EDITION** • Reteach Sequence, p. DI•21 • Frontloading Reading, p. DI•22 **ELL HANDBOOK** • Picture It! Skill Instruction, pp. 30–30a • Multilingual Summaries, pp. 31–33
Vocabulary **Basic and Lesson Vocabulary** **Word Analysis: Word Ending -ed**	**TEACHER'S EDITION** • Basic Vocabulary, p. DI•17 • Preteach Lesson Vocabulary, p. DI•17 • Word Ending -ed, p. DI•20 **ELL HANDBOOK** • Word Cards, p. 29 • ELL Vocabulary Routine, p. 471 **ELL POSTER 1** • Day 1 Activities	**TEACHER'S EDITION** • Basic Vocabulary, p. DI•17 • Reteach Lesson Vocabulary, p. DI•18 • Word Ending -ed, p. DI•20 **ELL HANDBOOK** • Word Cards, p. 29 • Multilingual Vocabulary List, p. 431 **ELL POSTER 1** • Day 2 Activities
Grammar and Conventions	**TEACHER'S EDITION** • Preteach Declarative and Interrogative Sentences, p. DI•24	**TEACHER'S EDITION** • Reteach Declarative and Interrogative Sentences, p. DI•24
Writing	**TEACHER'S EDITION** • Vivid Words, p. DI•25 • Introduce Realistic Fiction, pp. 23e–23f	**TEACHER'S EDITION** • Writing Trait: Organization, pp. 31d–31e

This symbol indicates leveled instruction to address language proficiency levels.

Day 3	Day 4	Day 5
TEACHER'S EDITION • Academic Language, p. DI•16 • Concept Development, p. DI•16 • Anchored Talk, p. 32a • Concept Talk Video **ELL HANDBOOK** • ELL Poster Talk, Concept Talk, p. 29c **ELL POSTER 1** • Day 3 Activities	**TEACHER'S EDITION** • Academic Language, p. DI•16 • Concept Development, p. DI•16 • Anchored Talk, p. 42a • Concept Talk Video **ELL HANDBOOK** • ELL Poster Talk, Concept Talk, p. 29c **ELL POSTER 1** • Day 4 Activities	**TEACHER'S EDITION** • Academic Language, p. DI•16 • Concept Development, p. DI•16 • Concept Talk Video **ELL HANDBOOK** • ELL Poster Talk, Concept Talk, p. 29c **ELL POSTER 1** • Day 5 Activities
		TEACHER'S EDITION • Phonics and Spelling, p. DI•20
ELL HANDBOOK • Phonics Transition Lesson, pp. 246–252	**ELL HANDBOOK** • Phonics Transition Lesson, pp. 246–252	
TEACHER'S EDITION • AudioText of *Because of Winn-Dixie* • Concept Talk Video **ELL HANDBOOK** • AudioText CD Routine, p. 477	**TEACHER'S EDITION** • Concept Talk Video	**TEACHER'S EDITION** • Concept Talk Video
TEACHER'S EDITION • Sheltered Reading, p. DI•22 **ELL HANDBOOK** • Multilingual Summaries, pp. 31–33	**TEACHER'S EDITION** • ELL/ELD Reader Guided Reading, p. DI•23 **ELL HANDBOOK** • ELL Study Guide, p. 34	**TEACHER'S EDITION** • ELL/ELD Reader Guided Reading, p. DI•23 **ELL HANDBOOK** • ELL Study Guide, p. 34
		TEACHER'S EDITION • Word Ending -*ed*, p. 45i
ELL HANDBOOK • High-Frequency Words Activity Bank, p. 446 **ELL POSTER 1** • Day 3 Activities	**ELL HANDBOOK** • High-Frequency Words Activity Bank, p. 446	**ELL HANDBOOK** • High-Frequency Words Activity Bank, p. 446
TEACHER'S EDITION • Grammar Jammer **ELL HANDBOOK** • Grammar Transition Lesson, pp. 342, 352 • Grammar Jammer Routine, p. 478	**TEACHER'S EDITION** • Grammar Jammer **ELL HANDBOOK** • Grammar Transition Lesson, pp. 342, 352	**TEACHER'S EDITION** • Grammar Jammer **ELL HANDBOOK** • Grammar Transition Lesson, pp. 342, 352
TEACHER'S EDITION • Let's Write It!, p. 40–41 • Writer's Craft: Vivid Words, pp. 41a–41b	**TEACHER'S EDITION** • Revising Strategy, pp. 45d–45e	**TEACHER'S EDITION** • Declarative and Interrogative Sentences, pp. 45p–45q

Question of the Week
What experiences bring diverse people together?

E L L Poster 1

Throughout the week, use the ELL Poster to help students produce and comprehend language, understand the concept, and build English vocabulary. Use the Question of the Week and other questions to help students share ideas in pairs, small groups, or the large group. Sample questions are shown, with examples of possible responses by students.

Weekly Concept and Language Goals

• Understand diversity

• Recognize how people share music

• Describe an experience with people from other cultures

By the end of the lesson, students should be able to talk about and write sentences about experiences that bring different people together.

Daily Team Talk

Day 1	Day 2	Day 3	Day 4	Day 5
After Day 1 activities on Poster, ask questions such as *In the poster picture, how does the student share music with others?*	After Day 2 activity on Poster, ask questions such as *How does the poster picture show diversity?*	After Day 3 activity on Poster, ask questions such as *Why is music something diverse people can share?*	After Day 4 activity on Poster, ask questions such as *In the story* Because of Winn-Dixie, *are Miss Franny, Winn-Dixie, and Opal a group of diverse friends? Why or why not?*	After Day 5 activity on Poster, ask questions such as *What is something you did with a group of diverse people?*
Beginning She plays it. **Intermediate** She plays for other people. **Advanced** The student plays music for her friend, the teacher, and people at the concert. **Advanced High** The student shares music by playing for her friend, the conductor, and the audience at the concert. She also shares music with the other students in the orchestra.	**Beginning** People are different. **Intermediate** The people all look different. **Advanced** The students look like they come from many different cultures. **Advanced High** The student, her friend, and the members of the orchestra and audience come from many different cultures.	**Beginning** They like it. **Intermediate** They can listen to it together. **Advanced** People from many different cultures can listen to and play music. **Advanced High** Even though their cultures and languages may be different, people can enjoy listening to and playing all kinds of music.	**Beginning** Yes. Not the same. **Intermediate** Yes. They are different. **Advanced** Yes. One is a dog, one is a girl, and one is an older woman. **Advanced High** The characters are diverse friends because they are all different from one another. Miss Franny is an older woman, Winn-Dixie is a dog, and Opal is a little girl.	**Beginning** Went to camp. **Intermediate** Went to summer camp. **Advanced** At summer camp last year, I met people from different places and cultures. **Advanced High** When I went to camp last summer, I met people from different cultures. We taught each other our favorite games and songs.

This Week's Materials

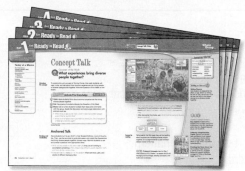

Teacher's Edition pages 20j–45q

See the support for English language learners throughout the lesson, including ELL strategies and scaffolded activities at points of use.

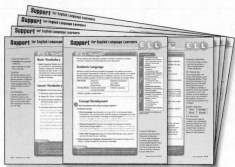

Teacher's Edition pages DI•16–DI•25

Differentiated Instruction for English language learners provides daily group activities that "frontload," or preteach, core instruction.

ELL Handbook pp. 29a–34

Find additional lesson materials that support the core lesson and the ELL instructional pages.

ELL Poster 1

ELL Reader 4.1.1

ELD Reader 4.1.1

Concept Literacy Reader

ELD, ELL Reader Teaching Guide

Concept Literacy Reader Teaching Guide

Technology

Online Teacher's Edition Use the digital version of the core Teacher's Edition for planning and instruction.

eReaders
This week's ELL and ELD Readers and Concept Literacy Reader are also available in digital format.

This Week's Content and Language Objectives by Strand

Concept Development/ Academic Language What experiences bring diverse people together?	**Content Objective** • Use concept vocabulary related to diversity. **Language Objectives** • Express ideas in response to discussion. • Express ideas in response to new academic vocabulary.
Phonics and Spelling Short Vowel VCCV	**Content Objectives** • Identify words with short vowel VCCV pattern. • Review mulitsyllabic words. **Language Objectives** • Write using phonics patterns with newly acquired vocabulary. • Use decoding skills with newly acquired vocabulary.
Listening Comprehension Modified Read Aloud: "A Perfect Match"	**Content Objective** • Monitor and adjust oral comprehension. **Language Objectives** • Discuss oral passages to learn new and essential language. • Use a graphic organizer for pre-reading support.
Reading Comprehension Sequence	**Content Objectives** • Order the sequence of events in a story. • Make and adjust comprehesion. **Language Objectives** • Retell sequence from a reading. • Discuss following directions in a text. • Write sequence from personal experience. • Read grade-level text with expression and intonation.
Vocabulary Basic and Lesson Vocabulary	**Language Objectives** • Understand and use basic and grade-level vocabulary. • Learn meanings of grade-level vocabulary. • Produce drawings, phrases, and short sentences to show understanding of Lesson Vocabulary.
Word Analysis Word Ending –ed	**Content Objective** • Identify and define words ending in –ed. **Language Objective** • Write and discuss the meaning and sounds of words ending in –ed.
Grammar and Conventions Declarative and Interrogative Sentences	**Content Objective** • Distinguish and use declarative and interrogative sentences. **Language Objective** • Speak using declarative and interrogative sentences. • Write declarative and interrogative sentences.
Writing Writing with vivid words	**Content Objective** • Identify vivid words in a text. **Language Objective** • Write a narrative paragraph using vivid words. • Edit for appropriate verb tense.

Word Cards for Vocabulary Activities

grand

memorial

peculiar

positive

prideful

recalls

selecting

Teacher Note: Beginning Teach three to four words. **Intermediate** Teach four to six words. **Advanced** Teach six to seven words. **Advanced High** Teach all words.

Name _____

Look at the pictures. **Read** the story.

- What happens first? **Write** that event in the *First circle.*
- What happens next? **Write** that event in the *Next circle.*
- What happens next? **Write** that event in the second *Next circle.*
- What happens last? **Write** that event in the *Last circle.*

Sharing Lunches

Ayako and Julie sit together every day in the lunch room. Today, they decided to share their lunches.

Ayako gave Julie a rice ball.

Julie gave Ayako her cheese sandwich.

"What a delicious rice ball!" said Julie. "I like this cheese sandwich!" said Ayako.

First   **Next**   **Next**   **Last**

Sequence

Use this lesson to supplement or replace the skill lesson on page 21c of the Teacher's Edition. Display the Skill Points (at right) and share them with students.

Teach/Model

Beginning Say: *I go to the library. I read some poems. I write my own poem! I show my poem to my mom.* Have students retell the events of the story in sequence, using the clue words *first, next, then,* and *last.*

Intermediate Say: *I went to the library this morning. At noon, I stopped at the store. By three o'clock I was home again.* Ask students to tell the story's sequence of events. Have them identify time phrases that helped them identify the sequence.

Advanced Write and read aloud: *I walk to the library. I return a book. I walk home. I check out another book.* Explain that the sentences are out of sequence. Have students write them in the correct sequence, adding the clue words *first, next, then,* and *last.*

Advanced High Have each student write a story in three or four sentences. Remind students to use clue words such as *first, next, then,* and *last* to show the sequence of events. Have students read their stories to a partner.

Then distribute copies of Picture It! page 30.

- Have students look at the pictures and tell what is happening.
- Read the story aloud. Ask: *What happens first in this story?* (Ayako and Julie decide to share their lunches.)
- Review the Skill Points with students.
- Have students tell what happens next and last in the story.

Practice

Read aloud the directions on page 30. Have volunteers take turns rereading the story aloud. Tell students to look at the pictures and the story as they fill in the circles in the sequence flowchart.

Beginning Students can point to and use the pictures as they say what they want to write before writing in the circles. Provide help with English words, including sequence words, and writing.

Intermediate Students can first orally answer and then write words and phrases in the circles. Provide help with English words and writing.

Advanced Students can write their answers in the circles to complete the sequence flowchart and check their answers by rereading the story and making any changes they think are needed.

Advanced High Students can write their answers in the circles to complete the graphic organizer and then orally retell the story events using sequence words.

Answers for page 30: *First:* Ayako and Julie decide to share lunches. *Next:* Ayako gives Julie a rice ball. *Next:* Julie gives Ayako a cheese sandwich. *Last:* The girls praise each other's lunches.

Skill Points

✔ Events in a story happen in an order, or **sequence**.
✔ Understanding the sequence helps you understand the story.
✔ Sometimes events in a story are told out of sequence. Something that happens earlier may be told after something that happens later.

Multilingual Summaries

Because of Winn-Dixie

Opal moves to a new town. She is lonely for friends. Her only friend is a dog named Winn-Dixie. Opal goes to the library. Dogs are not allowed. Opal tells the dog to wait outside.

The librarian, Miss Franny, sees Winn-Dixie through the window. She thinks it is a bear. She screams. Opal tells her Winn-Dixie is only a dog. Miss Franny lets Winn-Dixie come into the library.

Miss Franny tells Opal a story. In the story, a real bear came into the library. Miss Franny threw a large book to scare away the bear. The bear ran away with the book. After she tells the story, Miss Franny becomes friends with Opal and Winn-Dixie.

Spanish

Gracias a Winn-Dixie

Opal se muda a otra ciudad. Se siente sola y sin amigos. Su único amigo, es el perro Winn-Dixie. Opal va a la biblioteca. No se permiten perros. Opal deja al perro afuera.

La señora Franny, la bibliotecaria, ve a Winn-Dixie desde su ventana. Cree que es un oso, y grita. Opal le dice que es un perro. La señora deja que Winn-Dixie entre a la biblioteca.

La señora Franny le cuenta a Opal una historia. En la historia, un oso real entró a la biblioteca. La señora le lanzó un libro. El oso se fue con el libro. Después de que le cuenta la historia, la señora se hace amiga de Opal y su perro.

Multilingual Summaries

全因为韦戴茜

澳宝搬到另一个镇，她没有朋友，很寂寞，她的唯一朋友是一只狗叫韦戴茜。澳宝去图书馆，但图书馆不准狗进入，她只好要韦戴茜在外面等她。

图书馆员弗兰尼小姐看见韦戴茜在窗口外面。她以为韦戴茜是一只熊，所以她尖叫，澳宝告诉她韦戴茜是一只狗，弗兰尼小姐就让它进入图书馆。

弗兰尼小姐给澳宝讲一个很久以前的故事。这个故事说一只熊走进图书馆，弗兰尼小姐就把图书馆里的一本大书扔去那只熊，希望把它吓走，那只熊果然受惊跑掉。

弗兰尼小姐讲完了这个故事以后，她和澳宝、韦戴茜成了朋友。

Nhờ Có Winn-Dixie

Opal dọn nhà đến một thị trấn mới. Cô ta cô đơn không có bạn bè. Cho đến nay, bạn duy nhất của cô là một con chó tên là Winn-Dixie. Opal đến thư viện. Chó không được phép vào thư viện. Opal bảo Winn-Dixie đợi bên ngoài.

Cô Franny, người quản thủ thư viện, nhìn thấy Winn-Dixie qua cửa sổ. Cô ta tưởng Winn-Dixie là con gấu. Cô ta thét lên. Opal nói với cô ta Winn-Dixie chỉ là con chó. Co Franny để cho Winn-Dixie vào trong thư viện.

Cô Franny kể cho Opal một câu chuyện từ lâu rồi. Trong câu chuyện, một con gấu thật đã đến thư viện. Cô Frannie đã liệng một cuốn sách lớn để xua đuổi con gấu. Con gấu chạy đi, mang theo cuốn sách.

Sau khi kể xong câu chuyện, Cô Franny trở thành bạn của Opal và Winn-Dixie.

Multilingual Summaries

Korean

윈-딕시 때문에

오팔은 새 읍으로 이사를 왔습니다. 그녀는 친구들이 그립습니다. 여지껏 그녀의 유일한 친구라고는 윈-딕시라는 이름의 개입니다. 오팔은 도서관에 갔습니다. 개는 도서관에 들어갈 수 없습니다. 오팔은 윈-딕시에게 밖에서 기다리라고 말합니다.

도서관 프레니 선생님은 창문을 통해 윈-딕시를 보았습니다. 선생님은 윈-딕시가 곰이라고 생각했어요. 그리고 비명을 질렀지요. 오팔은 윈-딕시가 단지 개라고 얘기했습니다. 프레니 선생님은 윈-딕시가 도서관에 들어오도록 허락했습니다.

선생님은 아주 오랜 옛날 이야기를 해주셨습니다. 그 이야기에서는 진짜 곰이 도서관에 들어왔어요. 선생님이 곰을 위협해서 내보내려고 큰 책을 집어던졌습니다. 곰은 책을 가지고 달아났습니다.

이야기를 마친 후에, 페니 선생님은 오팔과 윈-딕시와 친구가 되었답니다.

Hmong

Vim Yog Winn-Dixie

Opal nyaib mus rau lub zos tshiab. Nwg khua siab tsi muaj phoojywg. Nwg tus phoojywg tamsim no yog ib tus aub hu ua Winn-Dixie. Opal mus tim lub tsev saib ntawv. Pub tsi tau aub nkag rau hauv lub tsev saib ntawv. Opal kom Winn-Dixie tog nrau zoov.

Tus poj saib ntawv, Miss Franny, xauj qhovrais pom Winn-Dixie. Nwg xav tias Winn-Dixie yog ib tus dais. Nwg qw nrov nrov. Opal qhia nwg tias Winn-Dixie yog ib tus aub xwb. Miss Franny cia Winn-Dixie nkag los rau hauv lub tsev saib ntawv.

Miss Franny qhia Opal txog ib zaj dabneeg txheej thau u los. Hauv zaj dabneeg no, ib tus dais tiag tiag nkag tuaj rau hauv lub tsev saib ntawv. Miss Franny muab ib phau ntawv loj loj pov rau kom tus dais ntshai es khiav tsiv. Tus dais coj phau ntawv tsiv tibsi.

Tom qab nwg qhia zaj dabneeg tag lawm, Miss Franny ua phoojywg nrog rau Opal thiab Winn-Dixie.

- **Read** *World Concert* again.
- Use the information in the story to **answer** the questions.

pages 2–3

1. Why do you think that the children are nervous?

_____

2. Name two children and where they are from.

_____

page 4

3. Why does Pedro say he has butterflies in his stomach?

_____

_____

pages 5–6

4. Why do the children practice for a long time?

_____

pages 7–8

5. How do you know that the children did a good job?

_____

_____

Family Link

Has anyone in your family been to a concert? Ask family members to describe a concert they have seen.

Weekly Resources Guide for English Language Learner Support

For this week's content and language objectives, see p. 35e.

Instructional Strand	Day 1	Day 2
Concept Development/Academic Language	**TEACHER'S EDITION** • Academic Language, p. DI•41 • Concept Development, p. DI•41 • Anchored Talk, pp. 46j—46–47 • Preteach Academic Vocabulary, p. 49a • Concept Talk Video **ELL HANDBOOK** • Hear It, See It, Say It, Use It, pp. xxxvi–xxxvii • ELL Poster Talk, Concept Talk, p. 35c **ELL POSTER 2** • Day 1 Activities	**TEACHER'S EDITION** • Academic Language, p. DI•41 • Concept Development, p. DI•41 • Anchored Talk, p. 50a • Concept Talk Video **ELL HANDBOOK** • ELL Poster Talk, Concept Talk, p. 35c • Concept Talk Video Routine, p. 477 **ELL POSTER 2** • Day 2 Activities
Phonics and Spelling	**TEACHER'S EDITION** • Phonics and Spelling, p. DI•45	**TEACHER'S EDITION** • Phonics and Spelling, p. DI•45
Listening Comprehension	**TEACHER'S EDITION** • Modified Read Aloud, p. DI•44 • Read Aloud, p. 47b • Concept Talk Video **ELL HANDBOOK** • Concept Talk Video Routine, p. 477	**TEACHER'S EDITION** • Modified Read Aloud, p. DI•44 • AudioText of *Lewis and Clark and Me* • Concept Talk Video **ELL HANDBOOK** • AudioText CD Routine, p. 477 • Story Map A, p. 483
Reading Comprehension	**TEACHER'S EDITION** • Preteach Author's Purpose, p. DI•46	**TEACHER'S EDITION** • Reteach Author's Purpose, p. DI•46 • Frontloading Reading, p. DI•47 **ELL HANDBOOK** • Picture It! Skill Instruction, pp. 36–36a • Multilingual Summaries, pp. 37–39
Vocabulary **Basic and Lesson Vocabulary** **Word Analysis: Suffixes *-or, -er***	**TEACHER'S EDITION** • Basic Vocabulary, p. DI•42 • Preteach Lesson Vocabulary, p. DI•42 • Suffixes *-or, -er,* p. DI•45 **ELL HANDBOOK** • Word Cards, p. 35 • ELL Vocabulary Routine, p. 471 **ELL POSTER 2** • Day 1 Activities	**TEACHER'S EDITION** • Basic Vocabulary, p. DI•42 • Reteach Lesson Vocabulary, p. DI•43 • Suffixes *-or, -er,* p. DI•45 **ELL HANDBOOK** • Word Cards, p. 35 • Multilingual Vocabulary List, p. 431 **ELL POSTER 2** • Day 2 Activities
Grammar and Conventions	**TEACHER'S EDITION** • Preteach Imperative and Exclamatory Sentences, p. DI•49	**TEACHER'S EDITION** • Reteach Imperative and Exclamatory Sentences, p. DI•49
Writing	**TEACHER'S EDITION** • Organize Ideas Around a Main Idea, p. DI•50 • Introduce Expository Composition, pp. 49e–49f	**TEACHER'S EDITION** • Writing Trait: Organization, pp. 61d–61e

This symbol indicates leveled instruction to address language proficiency levels.

Day 3	Day 4	Day 5
TEACHER'S EDITION • Academic Language, p. DI•41 • Concept Development, p. DI•41 • Anchored Talk, p. 62a • Concept Talk Video **ELL HANDBOOK** • ELL Poster Talk, Concept Talk, p. 35c **ELL POSTER 2** • Day 3 Activities	**TEACHER'S EDITION** • Academic Language, p. DI•41 • Concept Development, p. DI•41 • Anchored Talk, p. 72a • Concept Talk Video **ELL HANDBOOK** • ELL Poster Talk, Concept Talk, p. 35c **ELL POSTER 2** • Day 4 Activities	**TEACHER'S EDITION** • Academic Language, p. DI•41 • Concept Development, p. DI•41 • Concept Talk Video **ELL HANDBOOK** • ELL Poster Talk, Concept Talk, p. 35c **ELL POSTER 2** • Day 5 Activities
		TEACHER'S EDITION • Phonics and Spelling, p. DI•45
ELL HANDBOOK • Phonics Transition Lesson, pp. 253–255, 257	**ELL HANDBOOK** • Phonics Transition Lesson, pp. 253–255, 257	
TEACHER'S EDITION • AudioText of *Lewis and Clark and Me* • Concept Talk Video **ELL HANDBOOK** • AudioText CD Routine, p. 477	**TEACHER'S EDITION** • Concept Talk Video	**TEACHER'S EDITION** • Concept Talk Video
TEACHER'S EDITION • Sheltered Reading, p. DI•47 **ELL HANDBOOK** • Multilingual Summaries, pp. 37–39	**TEACHER'S EDITION** • ELL/ELD Reader Guided Reading, p. DI•48 **ELL HANDBOOK** • ELL Study Guide, p. 40	**TEACHER'S EDITION** • ELL/ELD Reader Guided Reading, p. DI•48 **ELL HANDBOOK** • ELL Study Guide, p. 40
		TEACHER'S EDITION • Suffixes *-or, -er*, p. 77i
ELL HANDBOOK • High-Frequency Words Activity Bank, p. 446 **ELL POSTER 2** • Day 3 Activities	**ELL HANDBOOK** • High-Frequency Words Activity Bank, p. 446	**ELL HANDBOOK** • High-Frequency Words Activity Bank, p. 446
TEACHER'S EDITION • Grammar Jammer **ELL HANDBOOK** • Grammar Transition Lesson, pp. 343, 353–354 • Grammar Jammer Routine, p. 478	**TEACHER'S EDITION** • Grammar Jammer **ELL HANDBOOK** • Grammar Transition Lesson, pp. 343, 353–354	**TEACHER'S EDITION** • Grammar Jammer **ELL HANDBOOK** • Grammar Transition Lesson, pp. 343, 353–354
TEACHER'S EDITION • Let's Write It!, p. 70–71 • Writer's Craft: Chronological Order, pp. 71a–71b	**TEACHER'S EDITION** • Revising Strategy, pp. 77d–77e	**TEACHER'S EDITION** • Imperative and Exclamatory Sentences, pp. 77p–77q

Question of the Week
What opportunities can be found in new places?

ELL Poster 2

Throughout the week, use the ELL Poster to help students produce and comprehend language, understand the concept, and build English vocabulary. Use the Question of the Week and other questions to help students share ideas in pairs, small groups, or the large group. Sample questions are shown, with examples of possible responses by students.

Weekly Concept and Language Goals

- Explain different types of opportunities
- Understand why opportunities are important
- Describe opportunities from the past and opportunities today

By the end of the lesson, students should be able to talk about and write sentences about opportunities in new places.

Daily Team Talk

Day 1	Day 2	Day 3	Day 4	Day 5
After Day 1 activities on Poster, ask questions such as	After Day 2 activity on Poster, ask questions such as	After Day 3 activity on Poster, ask questions such as	After Day 4 activity on Poster, ask questions such as	After Day 5 activity on Poster, ask questions such as
In the poster picture, what new opportunity does the girl in the pink outfit have?	*Why is taking pictures a new opportunity for the girl on the boat?*	*Why is it good to have new opportunities?*	*In the story* Lewis and Clark and Me, *what is one opportunity people had?*	*What is one opportunity people have today that they did not have in the past?*
Beginning She wants to fish.	**Beginning** It's a new place.	**Beginning** They are fun.	**Beginning** To see new places.	**Beginning** They can fly places.
Intermediate The girl will learn how to fish.	**Intermediate** She never saw the water.	**Intermediate** It is good to try new things.	**Intermediate** People went to find out about new places.	**Intermediate** People can fly in planes to get places.
Advanced The man is going to teach the girl how to fish.	**Advanced** She may not have seen the sea before. It is new to her.	**Advanced** You can learn a lot when you try new things.	**Advanced** People in the past traveled to new places to find out about them.	**Advanced** People can get places faster by flying in a plane.
Advanced High The girl is taking the opportunity to learn how to fish. The fisherman will teach her.	**Advanced High** This may be the girl's first trip to the sea. She may never have seen seagulls or big boats before.	**Advanced High** New opportunities give us chances to try new things.	**Advanced High** In the past, people explored new land. They traveled across the land and learned about the new things they saw.	**Advanced High** People today can travel by flying in an airplane. This helps them go farther and faster than they could in the past.

This Week's Materials

Teacher's Edition pages 46j–77q

See the support for English language learners throughout the lesson, including ELL strategies and scaffolded activities at points of use.

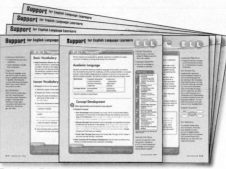

Teacher's Edition pages DI•41–DI•50

Differentiated Instruction for English language learners provides daily group activities that "frontload," or preteach, core instruction.

ELL Handbook pp. 35a–40

Find additional lesson materials that support the core lesson and the ELL instructional pages.

ELL Poster 2

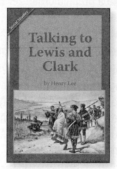

ELL Reader 4.1.2

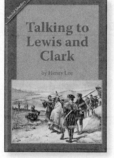

ELD Reader 4.1.2

The Dog That Discovered the West

By Jennifer Blizin Gillis

Concept Literacy Reader

ELD, ELL Reader Teaching Guide

Concept Literacy Reader Teaching Guide

Technology

Online Teacher's Edition Use the digital version of the core Teacher's Edition for planning and instruction.

eReaders
This week's ELL and ELD Readers and Concept Literacy Reader are also available in digital format.

This Week's Content and Language Objectives by Strand

Concept Development/ Academic Language What opportunities can be found in new places?	**Content Objective** • Use concept vocabulary related to finding opportunities in new places. **Language Objectives** • Express ideas in response to art and discussion. • Use prior knowledge to understand meanings.
Phonics and Spelling Long *a* and Long *i*	**Content Objective** • Identify various spelling relationships with the long *a* and *i* sounds. **Language Objectives** • Apply phonics skills to vocabulary. • Apply decoding skills to vocabulary.
Listening Comprehension Modified Read Aloud: "Planting Apple Trees"	**Content Objective** • Monitor and adjust oral comprehension. **Language Objectives** • Discuss oral passages to confirm understanding. • Use a graphic organizer to take notes and summarize spoken messages.
Reading Comprehension Author's Purpose	**Content Objectives** • Identify the author's purpose to aid understanding. • Monitor and adjust comprehension. **Language Objectives** • Determine how to identify an author's purpose. • Read with appropriate phrasing and punctuation cues. • Summarize text using visual and contextual support for general understanding.
Vocabulary Basic and Lesson Vocabulary	**Language Objectives** • Understand and use basic and grade-level vocabulary. • Learn meanings of grade-level vocabulary. • Produce drawings, phrases, and short sentences to show understanding of Lesson Vocabulary.
Word Analysis Suffixes *-or, -er*	**Content Objective** • Identify and define words with the suffix *–or* and *–er*. **Language Objective** • Learn meanings of words with the *–or* and *–er* suffixes.
Grammar and Conventions Imperative and Exclamatory Sentences	**Content Objective** • Decode and identify imperative and exclamatory sentences. **Language Objectives** • Read imperative and exclamatory sentences. • Write imperative and exclamatory sentences.
Writing Organize Ideas Around a Main Idea	**Content Objective** • Identify the ideas organized around the main idea. **Language Objectives** • Write organizing ideas around a main idea. • Share feedback for editing and revising.

Word Cards for Vocabulary Activities

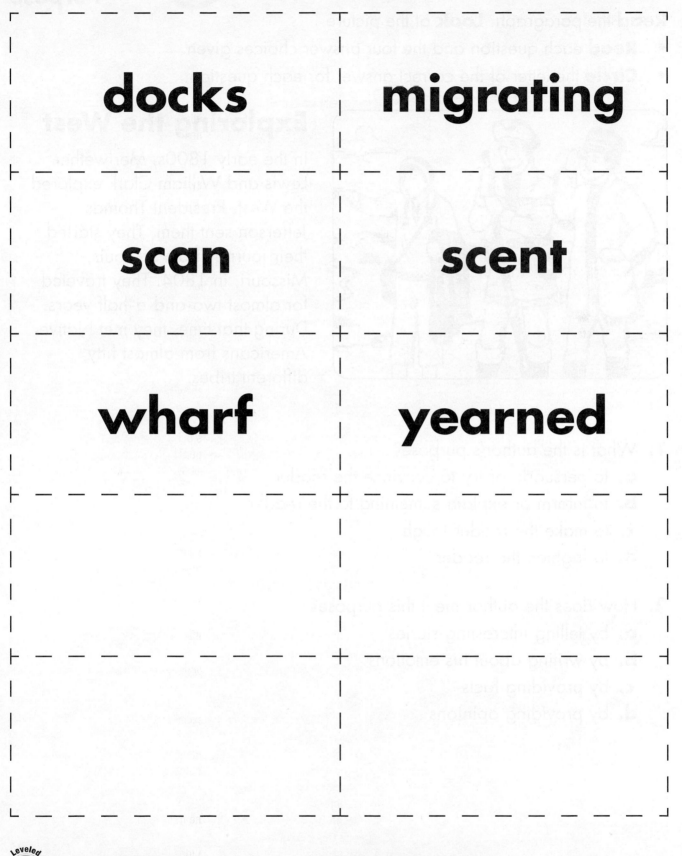

docks	migrating
scan	scent
wharf	yearned

Teacher Note: Beginning Teach two to three words. **Intermediate** Teach three to four words. **Advanced** Teach four to five words. **Advanced High** Teach all words.

Name _____

Read the paragraph. **Look** at the picture.
- **Read** each question and the four answer choices given.
- **Circle** the letter of the correct answer for each question.

Exploring the West

In the early 1800s, Meriwether Lewis and William Clark explored the West. President Thomas Jefferson sent them. They started their journey from St. Louis, Missouri, in 1804. They traveled for almost two-and-a-half years. During that time, they met Native Americans from almost fifty different tribes.

1. What is the author's purpose?
   a. to persuade or try to convince the reader
   b. to inform or explain something to the reader
   c. to make the reader laugh
   d. to frighten the reader

2. How does the author meet this purpose?
   a. by telling interesting stories
   b. by writing about his emotions
   c. by providing facts
   d. by providing opinions

Author's Purpose

Use this lesson to supplement or replace the skill lesson on page 47c of the Teacher's Edition. Display the Skill Points (at right) and share them with students.

Teach/Model

Beginning Write and read aloud: *I think Missouri is beautiful.* Ask: W*hat is the author's purpose?* (to express an opinion) Guide students in finding clue words that show the author's purpose. (think, beautiful)

Intermediate Say: *I love Texas! Texas is a large state. You should visit Texas.* Ask: *Which sentence was written to inform?* (the second sentence) Have students identify the author's purpose for the other sentences. (to share feelings; to persuade)

Advanced Say: *While I am on a trip, I will write in a journal. My journal will help me record how I feel about what I see and do. What is my purpose for writing in the journal?* (to express feelings) Repeat this process with other forms of writing and have students identify the author's purpose for each form.

Advanced High Assign each student a purpose for writing (to inform, to entertain, to persuade, to express feelings). Have students write a three-sentence paragraph about the West that uses their assigned purpose.

Then distribute copies of Picture It! page 36.

- Have students look at the picture and the title and predict what the paragraph will be about.
- Read the paragraph aloud. Ask: *What is the author's purpose, or reason, for writing this paragraph?* (to inform the reader)
- Review the Skill Points with students.
- Have students discuss the author's purpose and how the author achieves it.

Practice

Read aloud the directions on page 36. Have students reread the paragraph with partners. Have them look at the picture and the paragraph as they answer the questions.

Beginning Students can say the answers to the questions before circling the letters. Provide help with circling the correct choices.

Intermediate Students can first orally answer and then point to the answers and circle the letters. Provide help if necessary.

Advanced Students can circle the letters of their answers and then check them by comparing their answers with a partner's.

Advanced High Students can circle the letters of their answers and then orally explain how they chose their answers.

Answers for page 36: 1. b; 2. c

Skill Points

✔ The **author's purpose** is the reason or reasons why an author writes something.

✔ Common author's purposes are to persuade or convince the reader of something; to inform, or explain something; to entertain, or make the reader laugh or feel good; or to share or express ideas or feelings.

Multilingual Summaries

Lewis and Clark and Me: A Dog's Tale

Lewis and Clark are explorers. They are planning their journey west in 1803. Lewis is looking for a dog to take on the trip. Seaman is a big dog and a good swimmer. Lewis knows right away he is the best dog for the trip. Lewis buys him. Seaman and Lewis like each other right away.

On the trip, Seaman helps the explorers hunt. They discover a new kind of animal. Seaman helps them catch it. Later, they meet some Indians. The Indians think Seaman looks like a bear. They try to buy Seaman, but Lewis refuses. Lewis and Seaman become even closer friends.

Spanish

Lewis, Clark y yo: Historia de un perro

Lewis y Clark son exploradores. Están planeando un viaje hacia el Oeste en 1803. Lewis busca un perro que puedan llevar al viaje. Seaman es un perro grande y nada muy bien. Lewis sabe que es un buen perro para el viaje. Lewis lo compra. Seaman y Lewis se entienden de inmediato.

En el viaje, Seaman los ayuda a cazar. Descubren un nuevo tipo de animal. Seaman los ayuda a atraparlo. Luego ven unos indígenas. Los indígenas piensan que Seaman parece un oso y quieren comprarlo. Lewis se niega. Lewis y Seaman se vuelven buenos amigos.

Multilingual Summaries

Chinese

刘易斯、克拉克和我：一个有关狗的故事

　　刘易斯和克拉克是探险者。一八零三年他们计划一起去西部探险，刘易斯去寻找一只狗和他们同行。希曼是一只大狗，也善于游泳，刘易斯一看见它，就知道它很适合，所以把它买下。希曼和刘易斯很快已经很喜欢对方。

　　旅途上，希曼帮助两个探险者捕猎。他们发现了一种不为人知的动物，希曼帮助他们抓获这种动物。他们也遇见一些印第安人，印第安人以为希曼是一只熊，所以很想把它买下，可是刘易斯拒绝了；刘易斯和希曼的感情越来越深厚。

Vietnamese

Lewis, Clark Và Tôi. Chuyện Một Con Chó

　　Lewis và Clark là những nhà thám hiểm. Họ dự định du hành về miền Tây trong năm 1803. Lewis đang tìm một con chó để đem theo chuyến đi. Seaman là một con chó lớn và bơi lội giỏi. Lewis biết ngay nó là con chó thích hợp nhất cho chuyến đi. Lewis mua nó. Seaman và Lewis ưa thích nhau ngay.

　　Trong chuyến đi, Seaman giúp các nhà du hành săn bắn. Họ phát hiện một loài thú mới. Seaman giúp họ bắt con thú. Các nhà thám hiểm gặp vài người Da đỏ. Các người Da đỏ thấy Seaman giống con gấu. Họ cố mua nó nhưng Lewis từ chối. Lewis và Seaman trở thành bạn thân hơn nữa.

Multilingual Summaries

Korean

루이스와 클락과 나: 개 이야기

루이스와 클락은 탐험가입니다. 그들은 1803년에 여행을 계획했습니다. 루이스는 여행에 데리고 갈 개를 찾았습니다. 씨만은 큰 개이며 수영을 잘 했습니다. 루이스는 곧바로 씨만이 여행에 가장 적합한 개라는 것을 알았습니다. 루이스는 씨만을 샀습니다. 씨만과 루이스는 곧바로 서로 좋아하게 되었습니다.

여행에서 씨만은 탐험가들이 사냥하는 것을 도왔습니다. 그들은 새로운 종류의 동물을 발견했습니다. 씨만은 그 동물을 잡는 것을 도왔습니다. 탐험가들은 인디언들을 만났습니다. 인디언들은 씨만이 곰처럼 생겼다고 생각했습니다. 그들은 씨만을 사려고 했으나 루이스는 거절했습니다. 루이스와 씨만은 심지어 더 가까운 친구가 되었습니다.

Hmong

Lewis thiab Clark thiab Kuv: Aub Zaj Dabneeg

Lewis thiab Clark yog tibneeg nrhiav xyuas tebchaws. Nkawv tab tom npaaj yuav mus ncig rau sab nub poob thaus 1803. Lewis nrhiav ib tus aub coj nrog pais. Seaman yog ib tus aub loj loj thiab txawj luam dej. Lewis paub tamsiv tias nwg yog tus aub uas yuav zoo coj nrog pais. Lewis them nyiaj yuav nwg. Seaman thiab Lewis nkawv sis nyiam tam sim ntawd.

Thaus lawv mus lawm, Seaman pab nkawv tua noj. Lawv nrhiav tau ib tug tsiaj tshiab. Seaman pab nkawv nteg tus tsiaj. Nkawv ntsib ib cov khab. Cov khab xav tias Seaman zoo li ib tus dais. Lawv sim yuav Seaman, tiamsis Lewis tsi kam. Lewis thiab Seaman haj yam ua phoojywg zoo ntxiv.

Name _____

- **Read** *Talking to Lewis and Clark* again.
- Use the information in the book to **answer** the questions below.

Pages	Question	Answer
2	**1.** Which country sold the Louisiana Territory to the United States?	
3	**2.** What languages did Meriwether Lewis and William Clark speak?	
4	**3.** How did the Native American tribes living in the Great Plains communicate with one another?	
5	**4.** How did Lewis and Clark communicate with the tribes that lived in the Great Plains?	
6–7	**5.** Who was Sacajawea?	

Family Link

Does anyone in your family know a sign language? Ask family members to share what they know.

Weekly Resources Guide for English Language Learner Support

For this week's content and language objectives, see p. 41e.

Instructional Strand	Day 1	Day 2
Concept Development/Academic Language	TEACHER'S EDITION • Academic Language, p. DI•66 • Concept Development, p. DI•66 • Anchored Talk, pp. 78j—78–79 • Preteach Academic Vocabulary, p. 81a • Concept Talk Video ELL HANDBOOK • Hear It, See It, Say It, Use It, pp. xxxvi–xxxvii • ELL Poster Talk, Concept Talk, p. 41c ELL POSTER 3 • Day 1 Activities	TEACHER'S EDITION • Academic Language, p. DI•66 • Concept Development, p. DI•66 • Anchored Talk, p. 82a • Concept Talk Video ELL HANDBOOK • ELL Poster Talk, Concept Talk, p. 41c • Concept Talk Video Routine, p. 477 ELL POSTER 3 • Day 2 Activities
Phonics and Spelling	TEACHER'S EDITION • Phonics and Spelling, p. DI•70	TEACHER'S EDITION • Phonics and Spelling, p. DI•70
Listening Comprehension	TEACHER'S EDITION • Modified Read Aloud, p. DI•69 • Read Aloud, p. 79b • Concept Talk Video ELL HANDBOOK • Concept Talk Video Routine, p. 477	TEACHER'S EDITION • Modified Read Aloud, p. DI•69 • AudioText of *On the Banks of Plum Creek* • Concept Talk Video ELL HANDBOOK • AudioText CD Routine, p. 477 • T-Chart, p. 493
Reading Comprehension	TEACHER'S EDITION • Preteach Literary Elements: Character, Setting, Plot, p. DI•71	TEACHER'S EDITION • Reteach Literary Elements: Character, Setting, Plot, p. DI•71 • Frontloading Reading, p. DI•72 ELL HANDBOOK • Picture It! Skill Instruction, pp. 42–42a • Multilingual Summaries, pp. 43–45
Vocabulary **Basic and Lesson Vocabulary** **Word Analysis: Words Ending in -*ing***	TEACHER'S EDITION • Basic Vocabulary, p. DI•67 • Preteach Lesson Vocabulary, p. DI•67 • Words Ending in -*ing*, p. DI•70 ELL HANDBOOK • Word Cards, p. 41 • ELL Vocabulary Routine, p. 471 ELL POSTER 3 • Day 1 Activities	TEACHER'S EDITION • Basic Vocabulary, p. DI•67 • Reteach Lesson Vocabulary, p. DI•68 • Words Ending in -*ing*, p. DI•70 ELL HANDBOOK • Word Cards, p. 41 • Multilingual Vocabulary List, p. 431 ELL POSTER 3 • Day 2 Activities
Grammar and Conventions	TEACHER'S EDITION • Teach/Model Complete Subjects and Predicates, p. DI•74	TEACHER'S EDITION • Teach/Model Complete Subjects and Predicates, p. DI•74
Writing	TEACHER'S EDITION • Language Matches Purpose, p. DI•75 • Introduce Parody, pp. 81e–81f	TEACHER'S EDITION • Writing Trait: Organization, pp. 93d–93e

Unit 1 Week 3 On the Banks of Plum Creek

This symbol indicates leveled instruction to address language proficiency levels.

Day 3	Day 4	Day 5
TEACHER'S EDITION • Academic Language, p. DI•66 • Concept Development, p. DI•66 • Anchored Talk, p. 94a • Concept Talk Video **ELL HANDBOOK** • ELL Poster Talk, Concept Talk, p. 41c **ELL POSTER 3** • Day 3 Activities	**TEACHER'S EDITION** • Academic Language, p. DI•66 • Concept Development, p. DI•66 • Anchored Talk, p. 104a • Concept Talk Video **ELL HANDBOOK** • ELL Poster Talk, Concept Talk, p. 41c **ELL POSTER 3** • Day 4 Activities	**TEACHER'S EDITION** • Academic Language, p. DI•66 • Concept Development, p. DI•66 • Concept Talk Video **ELL HANDBOOK** • ELL Poster Talk, Concept Talk, p. 41c **ELL POSTER 3** • Day 5 Activities
		TEACHER'S EDITION • Phonics and Spelling, p. DI•70
ELL HANDBOOK • Phonics Transition Lesson, pp. 254, 256, 258	**ELL HANDBOOK** • Phonics Transition Lesson, pp. 254, 256, 258	
TEACHER'S EDITION • AudioText of *On the Banks of Plum Creek* • Concept Talk Video **ELL HANDBOOK** • AudioText CD Routine, p. 477	**TEACHER'S EDITION** • Concept Talk Video	**TEACHER'S EDITION** • Concept Talk Video
TEACHER'S EDITION • Sheltered Reading, p. DI•72 **ELL HANDBOOK** • Multilingual Summaries, pp. 43–45	**TEACHER'S EDITION** • ELL/ELD Reader Guided Reading, p. DI•73 **ELL HANDBOOK** • ELL Study Guide, p. 46	**TEACHER'S EDITION** • ELL/ELD Reader Guided Reading, p. DI•73 **ELL HANDBOOK** • ELL Study Guide, p. 46
		TEACHER'S EDITION • Word Ending -*ing*, p. 109i
ELL HANDBOOK • High-Frequency Words Activity Bank, p. 446 **ELL POSTER 3** • Day 3 Activities	**ELL HANDBOOK** • High-Frequency Words Activity Bank, p. 446	**ELL HANDBOOK** • High-Frequency Words Activity Bank, p. 446
TEACHER'S EDITION • Grammar Jammer **ELL HANDBOOK** • Grammar Transition Lesson, pp. 340, 348 • Grammar Jammer Routine, p. 478	**TEACHER'S EDITION** • Grammar Jammer **ELL HANDBOOK** • Grammar Transition Lesson, pp. 340, 348	**TEACHER'S EDITION** • Grammar Jammer **ELL HANDBOOK** • Grammar Transition Lesson, pp. 340, 348
TEACHER'S EDITION • Let's Write It!, p. 102–103 • Writer's Craft: Voice, pp. 103a–103b	**TEACHER'S EDITION** • Revising Strategy, pp. 109d–109e	**TEACHER'S EDITION** • Complete Subjects and Predicates, pp. 109p–109q

Question of the Week
Why do we want to explore new places?

Throughout the week, use the ELL Poster to help students produce and comprehend language, understand the concept, and build English vocabulary. Use the Question of the Week and other questions to help students share ideas in pairs, small groups, or the large group. Sample questions are shown, with examples of possible responses by students.

ELL Poster 3

Weekly Concept and Language Goals

• Name things people see when they explore nature

• Recognize that we can learn things when we explore new places

• Tell how tools can help us explore new places

By the end of the lesson, students should be able to talk about and write sentences about exploring new places.

Daily Team Talk

Day 1	Day 2	Day 3	Day 4	Day 5
After Day 1 activities on Poster, ask questions such as	After Day 2 activity on Poster, ask questions such as	After Day 3 activity on Poster, ask questions such as	After Day 4 activity on Poster, ask questions such as	After Day 5 activity on Poster, ask questions such as
What things in nature do you see in the park in the poster picture?	*What do you think the people climbing the mountain will learn?*	*What do you think the bike riders will learn about as they explore the woods?*	*What tools are people in the poster picture using to help them explore the park?*	*Where has your family gone exploring?*
Beginning Trees and a river. **Intermediate** There are rocks, trees, grass, and a river. **Advanced** The park has a mountain and a river with reeds, rocks, and trees. **Advanced High** I see many trees, a mountain with a cliff, and a river. I also see a badger, a frog, and a bird.	**Beginning** What's on top. **Intermediate** They will learn what grows on top. **Advanced** They will learn what kinds of plants grow on top of a mountain. **Advanced High** The climbers will learn how hard it is to climb a cliff. They will also learn about the plants and animals on top of a mountain.	**Beginning** Trees. **Intermediate** They will learn about trees. **Advanced** They will learn about different trees and animals in the woods. **Advanced High** The bike riders will learn about the different kinds of trees that grow in the woods. They will also learn about the animals that live in the woods.	**Beginning** They use maps. **Intermediate** Some people are looking at a map. **Advanced** Some people are looking at maps, and others might use the visitor center. **Advanced High** The people in the poster picture are using maps, binoculars, and signs to help them explore the park.	**Beginning** To a lake. **Intermediate** We went on a lake. **Advanced** My family used a boat to explore a lake. **Advanced High** My family explored a lake. First, we went across the lake in a boat. Then we hiked around the lake.

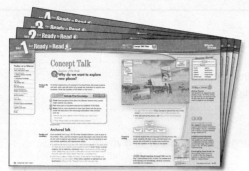

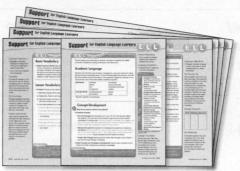

Teacher's Edition pages 78j–109q

Teacher's Edition pages DI•66–DI•75

ELL Handbook pp. 41a–46

See the support for English language learners throughout the lesson, including ELL strategies and scaffolded activities at points of use.

Differentiated Instruction for English language learners provides daily group activities that "frontload," or preteach, core instruction.

Find additional lesson materials that support the core lesson and the ELL instructional pages.

 Poster 3

ELL Reader 4.1.3

ELD Reader 4.1.3

Concept Literacy Reader

ELD, ELL Reader
Teaching Guide

Concept Literacy Reader
Teaching Guide

Technology

Online Teacher's Edition Use the digital version of the core Teacher's Edition for planning and instruction.

eReaders
This week's ELL and ELD Readers and Concept Literacy Reader are also available in digital format.

This Week's Content and Language Objectives by Strand

Concept Development/ Academic Language Why do we want to explore new places?	**Content Objective** • Use concept vocabulary related to exploring new places. **Language Objectives** • Express ideas in response to art and discussion. • Learn and use academic vocabulary.
Phonics and Spelling Long *e* and *o*	**Content Objective** • Identify spelling and intonation patterns of long vowel sounds. **Language Objectives** • Apply phonics skills to vocabulary. • Apply decoding skills to vocabulary.
Listening Comprehension Modified Read Aloud: "Travel Across the Country"	**Content Objective** • Use contextual support to enhance and confirm understanding of spoken language. **Language Objectives** • Discuss oral passages to confirm understanding. • Use a graphic organizer to take notes.
Reading Comprehension Literary Elements: Character, Setting, Plot	**Content Objectives** • Identify the literary elements of a story. • Use literary elements to aid comprehension. **Language Objectives** • Demonstrate knowledge of when to use informal language. • Read grade-level text with appropriate rate and accuracy. • Summarize text using visual support.
Vocabulary Basic and Lesson Vocabulary	**Language Objectives** • Internalize new basic language by using and revising it in meaning speaking activities. • Learn meanings of grade-level vocabulary. • Produce drawings, phrases, and short sentences to show understanding of Lesson Vocabulary.
Word Analysis Words Ending in *–ing*	**Content Objective** • Identify the suffix *–ing*. **Language Objective** • Identify the use of words ending in *–ing*.
Grammar and Conventions Complete Subjects and Predicates	**Content Objective** • Identify complete subjects and predicates. **Language Objectives** • Speak using complete subjects and predicates. • Write sentences with complete subjects and predicates.
Writing Language Matches Purpose	**Content Objective** • Identify the purpose of a piece of writing. **Language Objectives** • Adapt spoken language appropriately for informal purposes. • Write with a specific purpose in mind.

Word Cards for Vocabulary Activities

badger

bank

bristled

jointed

patched

ruffled

rushes

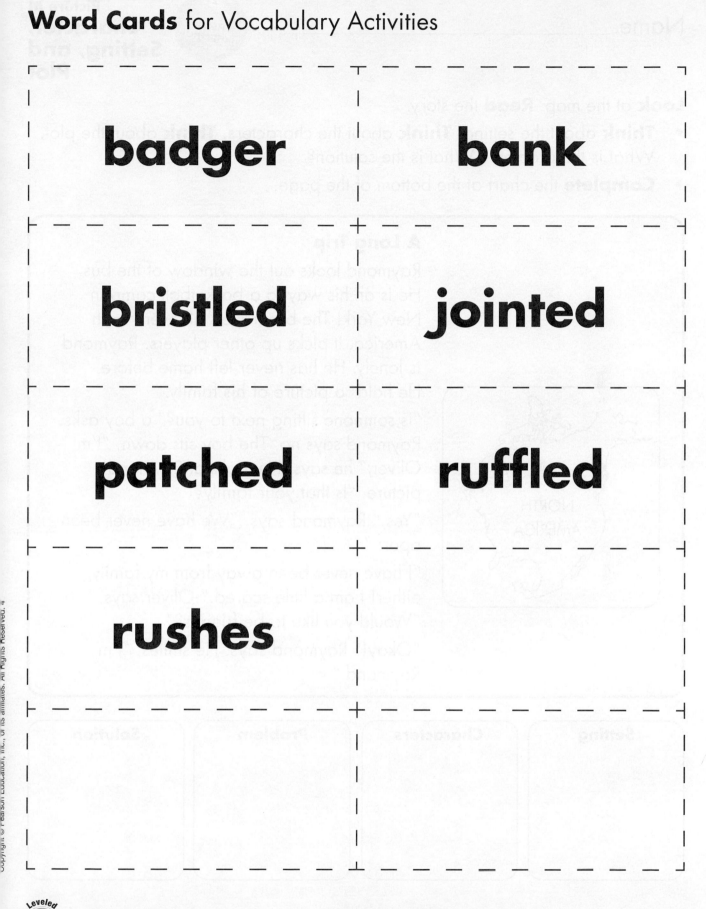

Teacher Note: Beginning Teach three to four words. **Intermediate** Teach four to six words. **Advanced** Teach six to seven words. **Advanced High** Teach all words.

Look at the map. **Read** the story.

- **Think** about the setting. **Think** about the characters. **Think** about the plot. What is the problem? What is the solution?

- **Complete** the chart at the bottom of the page.

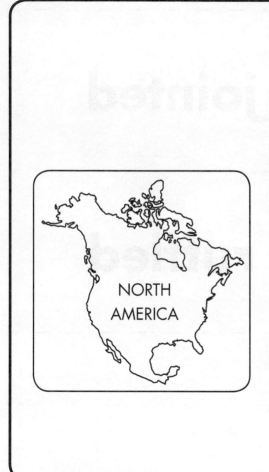

NORTH AMERICA

A Long Trip

Raymond looks out the window of the bus. He is on his way to a basketball camp in New York! The bus travels all over North America. It picks up other players. Raymond is lonely. He has never left home before. He holds a picture of his family.

"Is someone sitting next to you?" a boy asks. Raymond says no. The boy sits down. "I'm Oliver," he says. He looks at Raymond's picture. "Is that your family?"

"Yes," Raymond says. "We have never been apart."

"I have never been away from my family, either! I am a little scared." Oliver says. "Would you like to be friends?"

"Okay!" Raymond says. He smiles. "I'm Raymond."

Setting	Characters	Problem	Solution

Character, Setting, and Plot

Use this lesson to supplement or replace the skill lesson on page 79c of the Teacher's Edition. Display the Skill Points (at right) and share them with students.

Teach/Model

Beginning Say: *Sam and Lin hiked in the woods. Sam hurt his foot. Lin helped him walk. They got home safely.* Ask: *Who are the characters in this story?* (Sam and Lin) *What is the problem in the story?* (Sam hurt his foot.) *How do the characters solve the problem?* (Lin helps Sam walk.)

Intermediate Say: *Carlos went to camp. At first, he was lonely. Then he went to swimming class. He met Tina there. They had fun swimming.* Have pairs of students work together to write three sentences to describe the characters, setting, and plot of the story.

Advanced Say: *I am writing a story about Jim and his mom. The setting of the story is a train. What will happen in the story?* Have students brainstorm ideas for a plot that includes a problem and a solution. Use their ideas to write a group story.

Advanced High Have students write and illustrate short stories with two characters, one setting, and at least four plot events. Remind them that plots often include a problem that is solved by the characters. Have students read aloud their stories to the group.

Then distribute copies of Picture It! page 42.

- Have students look at the picture and the title.
- Read the paragraph aloud. Ask: *Who is in the story?* (Raymond and Oliver) *Where are Raymond and Oliver?* (on a bus) *How does Raymond feel?* (lonely)
- Review the Skill Points with students.
- Have students discuss the characters, setting, and plot of the story.

Practice

Read aloud the directions on page 42. Have students look at the picture and the story as they fill in the boxes.

Beginning Students can say what they want to write about the setting, characters, problem, and solution before they fill in the boxes. Provide help with English words and writing.

Intermediate Students can first orally answer and then write words and phrases to fill in the boxes. Provide help with English words and writing.

Advanced Students can write their answers in the boxes and then check their answers by comparing them to a partner's.

Advanced High Students can write their answers in the boxes and then orally explain how they decided what the story's problem and solution are.

Answers for page 42: *Setting:* on a bus in North America; *Characters:* Raymond and Oliver; *Problem:* Raymond is lonely. *Solution:* He makes friends with Oliver.

> ## Skill Points
> ✔ A **character** is a person or animal in a story. What characters say or do helps us know what they are like.
> ✔ The **setting** is the time and place of a story.
> ✔ The **plot** is the sequence of events in a story.
> ✔ A plot is often based on a problem that someone in the story has.
> ✔ The plot usually ends with the resolution, or solution, of the problem.

Multilingual Summaries

On the Banks of Plum Creek

Every morning, Laura and her sister go to the creek to play. There is a pool of water along the creek. They are not allowed to go near the pool because it is too deep. It would be dangerous if the girls fell in.

One day, Laura goes for a walk by herself. She starts to go to the pool. A badger scares her away. She feels sorry for disobeying her parents. Laura tells her father she went to the pool. To punish Laura, her father tells her she must stay at home for a day. The next day, Laura helps her mother do chores. The next morning, Laura and her mother go to look for the badger. They cannot find it.

A orillas del arroyo Plum

Todas las mañanas, Laura y su hermana van al arroyo a jugar. Hay un estanque a lo largo del arroyo. No tienen permiso de ir porque es muy hondo. Sería muy peligroso si se cayeran en el estanque.

Un día, Laura sale sola a caminar. Va al estanque. Un tejón la asusta y ella se aleja. Laura se siente mal por desobedecer. Le dice a su padre que fue al estanque. Para castigar a Laura, su padre le dice que debe permanecer en casa por un día. Al día siguiente, Laura ayuda a su mamá con los quehaceres. La mañana siguiente, Laura y su madre van a buscar al tejón. No lo encuentran.

Multilingual Summaries

Chinese

梅子溪的两岸

劳拉和妹妹每天早上都去小溪里玩，溪的旁边有一潭水，因为水太深，父母不准她们走近，恐怕她们会掉进水里，发生危险。

一天，劳拉一个人去散步；她走去水潭，一只獾把她吓走。她为自己不听父母的话感到难过，所以就告诉爸爸她去了水潭。为了惩罚劳拉，爸爸整天不让她出去。第二天，劳拉在家里帮妈妈做家务，第三天早上，劳拉和妈妈去寻找那只獾，可是她们什么也找不到。

Vietnamese

Trên Bờ Con Lạch Plum

Mỗi buổi sáng, Laura và chị thường ra con lạch chơi. Dọc theo con lạch có một vũng nước. Họ không được phép đến gần vũng nước vì nó rất sâu. Nếu hai cô gái té xuống đó thì rất nguy hiểm.

Một hôm, Laura đi dạo chơi một mình. Cô bắt đầu đi đến vũng nước. một con chồn lửng khiến cô kinh hãi chạy đi. Cô cảm thấy buồn vì đã không vâng lời cha mẹ. Laura nói với cha là cô đã đến vũng nước. Cha phạt cô phải ở nhà một ngày. Ngày hôm sau, cô giúp mẹ làm công việc lặt vặt trong nhà. Sáng hôm sau, Laura và mẹ đi tìm con chồn lửng. Nhưng họ không thể tìm thấy nó.

Multilingual Summaries

Korean

플럼 시내둑 위에서

매일 아침, 로라와 언니는 시냇가에 가서 놉니다. 시냇가를 따라 물이 한가득 고여있습니다. 그 물은 너무 깊기 때문에, 로라와 언니는 물 가까이 가지 못하게 되어있습니다. 만약 물에 빠진다면 너무 위험하겠지죠.

어느 날 로라는 혼자서 산책을 갔습니다. 그리고시냇물 쪽으로 걷기 시작했습니다. 오소리가 로라를 놀래키었지요. 로라는 부모님 말씀을 듣지 않은 것을 후회했습니다. 로라는 아버지께 시냇가에 갔다고 말씀드렸어요. 아버지는 로라에게 하루동안 집에만 있으라고 벌을 내리셨어요. 다음 날 로라는 엄마를 도와 집안 일을 했습니다. 그 다음 날 로라와 엄마는 오소리를 찾으로 갔습니다. 그러나 찾지 못했습니다.

Hmong

Nyob Ntawm Plum Creek sab Ntus Dej

Naj tagkig sawv ntxov, Laura thiab nwg tus vivncaus nkawv mus uasi tom tus kwg dej. Nwg muaj ib lub pag dej me lawv tus kwg dej. Nkawv txwv tsi pub mus ze lub pag dej me rau qhov nwg tub tub. Yuav muaj teebmeem loj yog hais tias ob vivncaus poob rau hauv.

Muaj ib nub, Laura mus taugkev ib leeg. Nwg mus ncaj rau ntawm lub pag dej me. Tug hmab ntxhi rau nwg ntshai thiab kiav tsiv. Nwg tu siab uas nwg tsi noog nwg niam thiab txiv hais. Laura qhia nwg txiv tias nwg mus rau tim lub pag dej me. Thaus rau txim Laura, nwg txiv hais tias nwg yuav tsum nyob tsev ib nub. Nub tom qab, Laura pab nwg niam tu vaj tu tsev. Tagkig sawv ntxov tom qab ntawd, Laura thiab nwg niam mus nrhiav tug hmab. Tiamsis, nkawv nrhiav tsi tau.

Name _____

- **Read** *Our Trip Out East* again.
- Use information in the book to **fill in** the sequence organizer.
  Describe all of the events that happened in each place, in the order in which they happened.

Chicago, Illinois

Flemington, New Jersey

Chicago, Illinois

Family Link

Has anyone in your family taken a long trip in the United States? Where did they go? What did they see? Ask family members to describe a trip they took.

For this week's content and language objectives, see p. 47e.

Instructional Strand	Day 1	Day 2
Concept Development/Academic Language	**TEACHER'S EDITION** • Academic Language, p. DI•91 • Concept Development, p. DI•91 • Anchored Talk, pp. 110j—110–111 • Preteach Academic Vocabulary, p. 113a • Concept Talk Video **ELL HANDBOOK** • Hear It, See It, Say It, Use It, pp. xxxvi–xxxvii • ELL Poster Talk, Concept Talk, p. 47c **ELL POSTER 4** • Day 1 Activities	**TEACHER'S EDITION** • Academic Language, p. DI•91 • Concept Development, p. DI•91 • Anchored Talk, p. 114a • Concept Talk Video **ELL HANDBOOK** • ELL Poster Talk, Concept Talk, p. 47c • Concept Talk Video Routine, p. 477 **ELL POSTER 4** • Day 2 Activities
Phonics and Spelling	**TEACHER'S EDITION** • Phonics and Spelling, p. DI•95	**TEACHER'S EDITION** • Phonics and Spelling, p. DI•95
Listening Comprehension	**TEACHER'S EDITION** • Modified Read Aloud, p. DI•94 • Read Aloud, p. 111b • Concept Talk Video **ELL HANDBOOK** • Concept Talk Video Routine, p. 477	**TEACHER'S EDITION** • Modified Read Aloud, p. DI•94 • AudioText of *The Horned Toad Prince* • Concept Talk Video **ELL HANDBOOK** • AudioText CD Routine, p. 477 • T-Chart, p. 493
Reading Comprehension	**TEACHER'S EDITION** • Preteach Literary Elements: Author's Purpose, p. DI•96	**TEACHER'S EDITION** • Reteach Literary Elements: Author's Purpose, p. DI•96 • Frontloading Reading, p. DI•97 **ELL HANDBOOK** • Picture It! Skill Instruction, pp. 48–48a • Multilingual Summaries, pp. 49–51
Vocabulary **Basic and Lesson Vocabulary** **Word Analysis: Compound Words**	**TEACHER'S EDITION** • Basic Vocabulary, p. DI•92 • Preteach Lesson Vocabulary, p. DI•92 • Compound Words, p. DI•95 **ELL HANDBOOK** • Word Cards, p. 47 • ELL Vocabulary Routine, p. 471 **ELL POSTER 4** • Day 1 Activities	**TEACHER'S EDITION** • Basic Vocabulary, p. DI•92 • Reteach Lesson Vocabulary, p. DI•93 • Compound Words, p. DI•95 **ELL HANDBOOK** • Word Cards, p. 47 • Multilingual Vocabulary List, p. 431 **ELL POSTER 4** • Day 2 Activities
Grammar and Conventions	**TEACHER'S EDITION** • Teach/Model Compound Sentences, p. DI•99	**TEACHER'S EDITION** • Reteach Compound Sentences, p. DI•99
Writing	**TEACHER'S EDITION** • Correct Use of Commas, p. DI•100 • Introduce Friendly Letter, pp. 113e–113f	**TEACHER'S EDITION** • Writing Trait: Organization, pp. 123d–123e

This symbol indicates leveled instruction to address language proficiency levels.

Day 3	Day 4	Day 5
TEACHER'S EDITION • Academic Language, p. DI•91 • Concept Development, p. DI•91 • Anchored Talk, p. 124a • Concept Talk Video **ELL HANDBOOK** • ELL Poster Talk, Concept Talk, p. 47c **ELL POSTER 4** • Day 3 Activities	**TEACHER'S EDITION** • Academic Language, p. DI•91 • Concept Development, p. DI•91 • Anchored Talk, p. 134a • Concept Talk Video **ELL HANDBOOK** • ELL Poster Talk, Concept Talk, p. 47c **ELL POSTER 4** • Day 4 Activities	**TEACHER'S EDITION** • Academic Language, p. DI•91 • Concept Development, p. DI•91 • Concept Talk Video **ELL HANDBOOK** • ELL Poster Talk, Concept Talk, p. 47c **ELL POSTER 4** • Day 5 Activities
		TEACHER'S EDITION • Phonics and Spelling, p. DI•95
ELL HANDBOOK • Phonics Transition Lesson, pp. 254, 256	**ELL HANDBOOK** • Phonics Transition Lesson, pp. 254, 256	
TEACHER'S EDITION • AudioText of *The Horned Toad Prince* • Concept Talk Video **ELL HANDBOOK** • AudioText CD Routine, p. 477	**TEACHER'S EDITION** • Concept Talk Video	**TEACHER'S EDITION** • Concept Talk Video
TEACHER'S EDITION • Sheltered Reading, p. DI•97 **ELL HANDBOOK** • Multilingual Summaries, pp. 49–51	**TEACHER'S EDITION** • ELL/ELD Reader Guided Reading, p. DI•98 **ELL HANDBOOK** • ELL Study Guide, p. 52	**TEACHER'S EDITION** • ELL/ELD Reader Guided Reading, p. DI•98 **ELL HANDBOOK** • ELL Study Guide, p. 52
		TEACHER'S EDITION • Compound Words, p. 137i
ELL HANDBOOK • High-Frequency Words Activity Bank, p. 446 **ELL POSTER 4** • Day 3 Activities	**ELL HANDBOOK** • High-Frequency Words Activity Bank, p. 446	**ELL HANDBOOK** • High-Frequency Words Activity Bank, p. 446
TEACHER'S EDITION • Grammar Jammer **ELL HANDBOOK** • Grammar Transition Lesson, pp. 344, 355 • Grammar Jammer Routine, p. 478	**TEACHER'S EDITION** • Grammar Jammer **ELL HANDBOOK** • Grammar Transition Lesson, pp. 344, 355	**TEACHER'S EDITION** • Grammar Jammer **ELL HANDBOOK** • Grammar Transition Lesson, pp. 344, 355
TEACHER'S EDITION • Let's Write It!, p. 132–133 • Writing Trait: Conventions, p. 133a–133b	**TEACHER'S EDITION** • Revising Strategy, pp. 137d–137e	**TEACHER'S EDITION** • Compound Sentences, pp. 137p–137q

Question of the Week

What can we discover in the landscape of the Southwest?

Throughout the week, use the ELL Poster to help students produce and comprehend language, understand the concept, and build English vocabulary. Use the Question of the Week and other questions to help students share ideas in pairs, small groups, or the large group. Sample questions are shown, with examples of possible responses by students.

ELL Poster 4

Weekly Concept and Language Goals

• Describe the unique animal and plant life in America's Southwest deserts

• Understand how the harsh climate affects wildlife

• Identify an animal that lives in the desert

By the end of the lesson, students should be able to talk about and write sentences about plants and animals of the Southwest.

Daily Team Talk

Day 1	Day 2	Day 3	Day 4	Day 5
After Day 1 activities on Poster, ask questions such as *In the poster picture, what plants do you see that live in the Southwest deserts?*	After Day 2 activity on Poster, ask questions such as *In the poster picture, what animals do you see that live in the Southwest deserts?*	After Day 3 activity on Poster, ask questions such as *How do you think the dry weather affects the plants and animals that live in the desert?*	After Day 4 activity on Poster, ask questions such as *What desert plants and animals are in the story* The Horned Toad Prince *but are not in the poster picture?*	After Day 5 activity on Poster, ask questions such as *What is one way that life in our area is different from life in the Southwest deserts?*
Beginning Cactuses. **Intermediate** There are cactuses and some grass. **Advanced** I see different kinds of cactuses and small bunches of grass. **Advanced High** Not many plants live in the Southwest deserts. The poster picture shows bushes, grasses, tumbleweeds, and two kinds of cactuses.	**Beginning** A toad. **Intermediate** There is a toad and a bird. **Advanced** I see a horned toad on a rock and a large hawk in the sky. **Advanced High** The horned toad and the red-tailed hawk live in the Southwest deserts.	**Beginning** No water. **Intermediate** They don't have much water. **Advanced** The plants and animals can survive without much water. **Advanced High** The plants and animals that live in the desert have adapted to the climate. They can survive with very little water.	**Beginning** A vulture. **Intermediate** She sees a vulture and there is a sagebrush. **Advanced** In the story, the girl sees a vulture. The story also talks about sagebrush. **Advanced High** The story tells about the sagebrush. It also says rattlesnakes and vultures live in the desert.	**Beginning** We have trees. **Intermediate** Our area has trees and grass. **Advanced** In our area, the ground is covered with grass, trees, and other plants. **Advanced High** In our area, trees, grass, and bushes cover the ground. In the desert, the ground is covered with sand or dry dirt and a few plants.

This Week's Materials

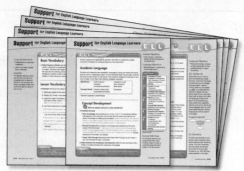

Teacher's Edition pages 110j–137q

See the support for English language learners throughout the lesson, including ELL strategies and scaffolded activities at points of use.

Teacher's Edition pages DI•91–DI•100

Differentiated Instruction for English language learners provides daily group activities that "frontload," or preteach, core instruction.

ELL Handbook pp. 47a–52

Find additional lesson materials that support the core lesson and the ELL instructional pages.

ELL Poster 4

ELL Reader 4.1.4

ELD Reader 4.1.4

Concept Literacy Reader

ELD, ELL Reader
Teaching Guide

Concept Literacy Reader
Teaching Guide

Technology

Online Teacher's Edition Use the digital version of the core Teacher's Edition for planning and instruction.

eReaders
This week's ELL and ELD Readers and Concept Literacy Reader are also available in digital format.

This Week's Content and Language Objectives by Strand

Concept Development/ Academic Language What can we discover in the landscape of the Southwest?	**Content Objective** • Use concept vocabulary related to the landscape of the Southwest. **Language Objectives** • Express ideas in response to art and discussion. • Learn and use academic vocabulary.
Phonics and Spelling Long *e*	**Content Objective** • Identify different spellings of long *e*. **Language Objectives** • Apply phonics skills to vocabulary. • Apply decoding skills to vocabulary.
Listening Comprehension Modified Read Aloud: "Children in the Old West"	**Content Objective** • Monitor and adjust oral comprehension. **Language Objectives** • Discuss oral passages. • Use accessible language to help learn essential language.
Reading Comprehension Author's Purpose	**Content Objectives** • Identify the author's purpose for writing. • Use the author's purpose to aid comprehension. **Language Objectives** • Use text and illustrations to identify an author's purpose. • Read grade-level text with appropriate phrasing. • Summarize text using visual support.
Vocabulary Basic and Lesson Vocabulary	**Language Objectives** • Understand and use basic vocabulary. • Learn meanings of grade-level vocabulary. • Produce drawings, phrases, and short sentences to show understanding of Lesson Vocabulary.
Word Analysis Compound Words	**Content Objective** • Identify and define words in compound words. **Language Objective** • Discuss meanings of compound words.
Grammar and Conventions Compound Sentences	**Content Objective** • Identify compound sentences. **Language Objectives** • Combine simple sentences to create a compound sentence. • Write simple and compound sentences.
Writing Correct Use of Commas	**Content Objective** • Identify and use grade-appropriate connecting words to combine phrases, clauses, and sentences. **Language Objectives** • Write using informal language, commas, and connecting words. • Share feedback for editing and revising.

Word Cards for Vocabulary Activities

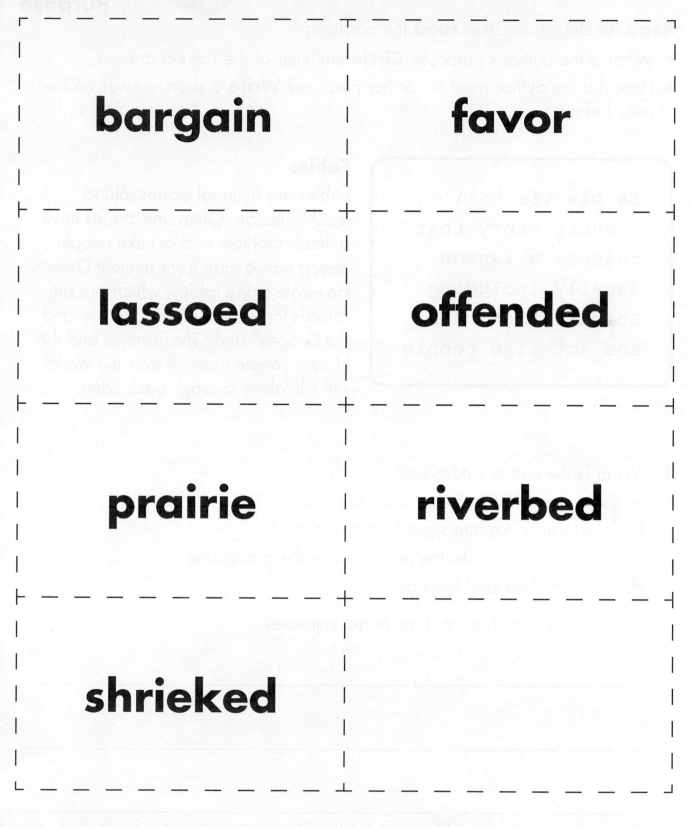

bargain

favor

lassoed

offended

prairie

riverbed

shrieked

Teacher Note: Beginning Teach three to four words. **Intermediate** Teach four to six words. **Advanced** Teach six to seven words. **Advanced High** Teach all words.

Name _____

Read the definition. Then **read** the paragraph.

- What is the author's purpose? **Circle** the letter of the correct answer.
- How did the author meet his or her purpose? **Write** a short answer on the lines below.

fa·ble \fā′bəl\ *n.* :
a short story that
teaches a lesson,
usually including
animals that talk
and act like people

Fables

Fables are fictional stories told to teach a lesson. Often, the stories have animals that talk and act like people. Aesop was a man from ancient Greece. He wrote many fables, which are still famous today. He wrote "The Fox and the Grapes" and "The Tortoise and the Hare." People from all over the world still tell fables to teach each other.

1. What is the author's purpose?
   a. to persuade or try to convince the reader
   b. to inform or explain something to the reader
   c. to entertain or make the reader enjoy the paragraph
   d. to write ideas and feelings

2. How does the author meet his or her purpose?

_____

_____

_____

_____

Author's Purpose

Use this lesson to supplement or replace the skill lesson on page 111c of the Teacher's Edition. Display the Skill Points (at right) and share them with students.

Teach/Model

Beginning Play a children's song. Ask: *What is the author's purpose for writing this song?* (to entertain) Display a dictionary entry. Ask: *What is the author's purpose for writing this dictionary entry?* (to inform)

Intermediate Read aloud a paragraph about animals from a science textbook. Ask: *What is the author's purpose?* (to inform) *How do you know?* (The paragraph gives information about animals.) *I want to write a poem about this information. What is my purpose?* (to entertain; to express feelings)

Advanced Provide each student with an advertisement. Ask: *How can you tell the author's purpose is to persuade?* (clue words such as *should, best*) Encourage students to support their responses with specific details from their ad.

Advanced High Tell students they will write three sentences about a country of their own choice. Assign each student an author's purpose: to *explain* something about the country; to *persuade* readers to visit the country; to *entertain* with a story from the country; or to *express* their feelings about the country. Have students share their writing.

Then distribute copies of Picture It! page 48.

- Have students read the dictionary definition. Then read the paragraph aloud.
- Ask: *What is the author's purpose?* (to inform or explain something to the reader)
- Review the Skill Points with students.
- Have students discuss the ways the author shows the purpose.

Practice

Read aloud the directions on page 48. Have a volunteer reread the paragraph aloud. Have students look at the definition and the paragraph as they answer the questions.

Beginning Students can point to the correct answer and tell what they want to write before circling and writing their answers. Provide help with circling the correct choice and writing.

Intermediate Students can first orally answer the questions and then circle and write their answers. Provide help with English words and writing.

Advanced Students can circle and write their answers and then check them by rereading the text and making any changes they think are needed.

Advanced High Students can circle and write their answers and then orally explain the reasons for their answers to a partner.

Answers for page 48: 1. b; 2. To inform readers about fables, the author gives a definition of the word *fable* and information about fables.

Skill Points

✔ The **author's purpose** is the reason or reasons an author writes something.

✔ Common author's purposes are to persuade or convince the reader of something; to inform, or explain something; to entertain, or make the reader laugh or feel good; or to share or express ideas or feelings.

Multilingual Summaries

English

The Horned Toad Prince

Reba Jo played guitar. She roped things with her lasso. One day, she rode her horse to an old, dry riverbed. Suddenly, the wind blew her hat off. The hat blew into an old well.

A horned toad said he would find her hat. He asked for three things in return. He wanted some chili. He wanted to hear Reba Jo play her guitar. He wanted to take a nap in her hat. Reba Jo agreed. The toad found Reba Jo's hat. She rode away without thanking the toad.

The toad followed her home. Reba Jo gave him his wishes. The toad ate some chili and heard a song. Instead of his last wish, the toad asked for a kiss. Reba Jo agreed so the toad would leave. When she kissed him, the toad turned into a prince. Then he went away.

Spanish

El príncipe sapo

Reba Jo tocaba guitarra. Enlazaba cosas con su lazo. Un día, llegó en su caballo hasta el lecho de un río seco. De repente, el viento le voló el sombrero. El sombrero cayó dentro de un viejo pozo.

Un sapo le dijo que él podía encontrar el sombrero. Le pidió tres cosas a cambio. Quería comer un poco de chile. Quería escuchar a Reba Jo tocar la guitarra. Quería dormir una siesta en su sombrero. Reba Jo estuvo de acuerdo. El sapo le encontró el sombrero y ella se fue sin darle las gracias.

El sapo la siguió hasta la casa. Reba Jo le cumplió los tres deseos que había prometido. Le dio un poco de chile, le cantó una canción. En lugar de pedir su último deseo, el sapo le pidió un beso. Reba Jo estuvo de acuerdo porque así el sapo se podía ir. Cuando lo besó, el sapo se convirtió en un príncipe. Después, se fue.

Multilingual Summaries

Chinese

蟾蜍王子

麗巴不僅能彈吉它，還會使用套索。有一天，她騎馬去乾涸的老河床。突然帽子讓一陣風吹走，掉進井裏面。

蟾蜍保證為她找回帽子，但先要答應三件事。它想要一些辣椒，聽麗巴彈吉它，還想在帽子裏打個盹。麗巴全都同意了。可找回帽子後，麗巴沒說謝謝就騎馬走了。

蟾蜍一直跟到家裏，麗巴只好滿足它的願望。讓它吃了辣椒，為它彈了歌曲。蟾蜍說不想打盹，最好能吻一下。為了讓它趕快走，麗巴勉強同意了。輕輕一吻，蟾蜍竟然變成了英俊的王子！可是王子轉身離開了麗巴的家。

Vietnamese

Hoàng Tử Cóc Sừng

Reba Jo chơi đàn ghi-ta. Cô buộc đồ vật bằng sợi dây thòng lọng của mình. Ngày nọ, cô cỡi ngựa đến một lòng sông xưa cũ đã khô. Thình lình, gió thổi bay nón của cô. Nón bay xuống một cái giếng cũ.

Một con cóc sừng nói là nó sẽ tìm được cái nón của cô. Để bù lại cóc yêu cầu ba điều. Cóc muốn được một ít súp đậu. Cóc muốn được nghe Reba Jo chơi đàn ghi-ta. Cóc muốn ngủ trưa trong cái nón của cô. Reba Jo đồng ý. Cóc tìm ra chiếc nón của Reba Jo. Cô cỡi ngựa đi mà không cám ơn chàng cóc.

Chàng cóc theo cô về tận nhà. Reba Jo cho cóc được những điều ước. Cóc ăn một ít súp đậu và nghe một bài hát. Thay vào điều ước cuối cùng của mình, cóc xin được một nụ hôn. Reba Jo đồng ý làm để cho cóc đi chỗ khác. Khi cô hôn cóc, cóc trở thành một chàng hoàng tử. Rồi chàng bỏ đi.

Multilingual Summaries

뿔 달린 두꺼비 왕자

레바 조는 기타를 연주한다. 그녀는 올가미로 물건을 낚아채기도 한다. 어느 날 그녀는 말을 타고 오래되어 말라버린 강바닥에 갔다가 갑자기 바람이 불어 그녀의 모자가 날아가서 오래된 우물 속에 빠져버린다.

그러자 뿔 달린 두꺼비 한 마리가 나타나 모자를 찾아주겠다고 말한다. 두꺼비는 그 대신 그녀에게 세 가지를 요구하는데 그것은 칠리 고추 몇 개, 레바 조의 기타 연주 듣기, 그리고 그녀의 모자 안에서 낮잠을 자는 것이었다. 레바 조가 그러겠다고 하자 두꺼비는 모자를 찾아 주지만 레바 조는 두꺼비에게 고맙다는 말도 없이 말을 타고 떠나 버린다.

두꺼비가 그녀의 집까지 따라오자 레바 조는 두꺼비의 소원을 들어준다. 두꺼비는 칠리 고추 몇 개를 먹고 음악을 듣고는 마지막 소원 대신 키스를 해달라고 한다. 레바 조는 두꺼비를 내보내기 위해 그러겠다고 하고 두꺼비에게 키스하자 두꺼비는 왕자로 변한다. 하지만 왕자는 떠나가버린다.

Tub Qav Kaws Vaj Ntxwv Tuaj Kub

Reba Jo ntaus kij taj. Nws muab nws txoj hlua pov khi ntau yam. Muaj ib hnub, nws tau caij nees mus txog ib tug dej qub thiab qhuav lawm. Tos nco xwb, cua cia li tshuab nws lub kaus mom ya lawm. Lub kaus mom raug tshuab mus poob rau ib lub qhov dej.

Ib tug qav kaws tuaj kub hais tias nws mam li nrhiav lub kaus mom. Nws tau nug peb yam khoom rov qab. Nws xav tau ib cov kua txob ntxuag taum thiab nqaij nyuj (chili) los noj. Nws xav hnov Reba Jo ntaus kij taj. Thiab, nws xav pw ib tsig hauv lub kaus mom. Reba Jo pom zoo li. Tus qav nrhiav tau Reba Jo lub kaus mom. Reba Jo caij nees mus tsis nco ua tus qav kaws tsaug.

Tus qav kaws raws nws los tsev. Reba Jo thiaj li muaj tej yam uas tus qav kaws xav tau. Tus qav noj kua txob ntxuag taum thiab mloog ib zaj nkauj. Tabsis tus qav kaws tsis yuav yam kawg nws thov lawm, tus qav kaws txawm thov nwj ib pas xwb. Reba Jo pom zoo li, kom tus qav kaws thiaj li khiav mus. Thaum nws nwj tus qav kaws, tus qav kaws cia li txias los ua ib tug tub vaj ntxwv. Ces nws thiaj li khiav mus lawm.

Name _____

- **Read** *Painting the Southwest* again.
- Use the information in the book to **answer** the questions below.

---

pages 2–4

1. How do artists "talk" to people?

_____

_____

2. What stories does Williams tell through his paintings?

_____

_____

---

pages 5–9

3. What types of people does Williams paint?

_____

_____

4. Which people have lived in the Southwest?

_____

_____

---

pages 10–12

5. What were the author's purposes in writing this book?

_____

_____

Family Link

Does anyone in your family paint or draw? If they were to paint people or places, what would they paint?

For this week's content and language objectives, see p. 53e.

Instructional Strand	Day 1	Day 2
Concept Development/Academic Language	TEACHER'S EDITION • Academic Language, p. DI•116 • Concept Development, p. DI•116 • Anchored Talk, pp. 138j—138–139 • Preteach Academic Vocabulary, p. 141a • Concept Talk Video ELL HANDBOOK • Hear It, See It, Say It, Use It, pp. xxxvi–xxxvii • ELL Poster Talk, Concept Talk, p. 53c ELL POSTER 5 • Day 1 Activities	TEACHER'S EDITION • Academic Language, p. DI•116 • Concept Development, p. DI•116 • Anchored Talk, p. 142a • Concept Talk Video ELL HANDBOOK • ELL Poster Talk, Concept Talk, p. 53c • Concept Talk Video Routine, p. 477 ELL POSTER 5 • Day 2 Activities
Phonics and Spelling	TEACHER'S EDITION • Phonics and Spelling, p. DI•120	TEACHER'S EDITION • Phonics and Spelling, p. DI•120
Listening Comprehension	TEACHER'S EDITION • Modified Read Aloud, p. DI•119 • Read Aloud, p. 139b • Concept Talk Video ELL HANDBOOK • Concept Talk Video Routine, p. 477	TEACHER'S EDITION • Modified Read Aloud, p. DI•119 • AudioText of *Letters Home from Yosemite* • Concept Talk Video ELL HANDBOOK • AudioText CD Routine, p. 477 • K-W-L Chart, p. 480
Reading Comprehension	TEACHER'S EDITION • Preteach Literary Elements: Main Idea and Details, p. DI•121	TEACHER'S EDITION • Reteach Literary Elements: Main Idea and Details, p. DI•121 • Frontloading Reading, p. DI•122 ELL HANDBOOK • Picture It! Skill Instruction, pp. 54–54a • Multilingual Summaries, pp. 55–57
Vocabulary **Basic and Lesson Vocabulary** **Word Analysis: Related Words**	TEACHER'S EDITION • Basic Vocabulary, p. DI•117 • Preteach Lesson Vocabulary, p. DI•117 • Related Words, p. DI•120 ELL HANDBOOK • Word Cards, p. 53 • ELL Vocabulary Routine, p. 471 ELL POSTER 5 • Day 1 Activities	TEACHER'S EDITION • Basic Vocabulary, p. DI•117 • Reteach Lesson Vocabulary, p. DI•118 • Related Words, p. DI•120 ELL HANDBOOK • Word Cards, p. 53 • Multilingual Vocabulary List, p. 431 ELL POSTER 5 • Day 2 Activities
Grammar and Conventions	TEACHER'S EDITION • Preteach Clauses and Complex Sentences, p. DI•124	TEACHER'S EDITION • Teach/Model Clauses and Complex Sentences, p. DI•124
Writing	TEACHER'S EDITION • Personal Narrative, p. DI•125 • Writing for Tests: Personal Narrative, pp. 141e–141f	TEACHER'S EDITION • Writing for Tests: Personal Narrative, pp. 151d–151e

Unit 1 Week 5 · Letters Home from Yosemite

This symbol indicates leveled instruction to address language proficiency levels.

Day 3	Day 4	Day 5
TEACHER'S EDITION • Academic Language, p. DI•116 • Concept Development, p. DI•116 • Anchored Talk, p. 152a • Concept Talk Video **ELL HANDBOOK** • ELL Poster Talk, Concept Talk, p. 53c **ELL POSTER 5** • Day 3 Activities	**TEACHER'S EDITION** • Academic Language, p. DI•116 • Concept Development, p. DI•116 • Anchored Talk, p. 160a • Concept Talk Video **ELL HANDBOOK** • ELL Poster Talk, Concept Talk, p. 53c **ELL POSTER 5** • Day 4 Activities	**TEACHER'S EDITION** • Academic Language, p. DI•116 • Concept Development, p. DI•116 • Concept Talk Video **ELL HANDBOOK** • ELL Poster Talk, Concept Talk, p. 53c **ELL POSTER 5** • Day 5 Activities
		TEACHER'S EDITION • Phonics and Spelling, p. DI•120
ELL HANDBOOK • Phonics Transition Lesson, pp. 254, 259	**ELL HANDBOOK** • Phonics Transition Lesson, pp. 254, 259	
TEACHER'S EDITION • AudioText of *Letters Home from Yosemite* • Concept Talk Video **ELL HANDBOOK** • AudioText CD Routine, p. 477	**TEACHER'S EDITION** • Concept Talk Video	**TEACHER'S EDITION** • Concept Talk Video
TEACHER'S EDITION • Sheltered Reading, p. DI•122 **ELL HANDBOOK** • Multilingual Summaries, pp. 55–57	**TEACHER'S EDITION** • ELL/ELD Reader Guided Reading, p. DI•123 **ELL HANDBOOK** • ELL Study Guide, p. 58	**TEACHER'S EDITION** • ELL/ELD Reader Guided Reading, p. DI•123 **ELL HANDBOOK** • ELL Study Guide, p. 58
		TEACHER'S EDITION • Related Words, p. 165i
ELL HANDBOOK • High-Frequency Words Activity Bank, p. 446 **ELL POSTER 5** • Day 3 Activities	**ELL HANDBOOK** • High-Frequency Words Activity Bank, p. 446	**ELL HANDBOOK** • High-Frequency Words Activity Bank, p. 446
TEACHER'S EDITION • Grammar Jammer **ELL HANDBOOK** • Grammar Transition Lesson, pp. 345, 357–358 • Grammar Jammer Routine, p. 478	**TEACHER'S EDITION** • Grammar Jammer **ELL HANDBOOK** • Grammar Transition Lesson, pp. 345, 357–358	**TEACHER'S EDITION** • Grammar Jammer **ELL HANDBOOK** • Grammar Transition Lesson, pp. 345, 357–358
TEACHER'S EDITION • Let's Write It!, p. 158–159 • Writing for Tests: Evaluation, pp. 159a–159b	**TEACHER'S EDITION** • Writing for Tests, pp. 165d–165e	**TEACHER'S EDITION** • Writing for Tests: Conventions, pp. 165p–165q

This Week's Content and Language Objectives by Strand

Concept Development/ Academic Language How does Yosemite reflect the unique qualities of the West?	**Content Objective** • Use concept vocabulary related to Yosemite. **Language Objectives** • Express ideas in response to art and discussion. • Use prereading supports, such as illustrations, to enhance comprehension.
Phonics and Spelling Long *u*	**Content Objective** • Identify different spellings of long *u*. **Language Objectives** • Apply phonics skills to vocabulary. • Apply decoding skills to vocabulary.
Listening Comprehension Modified Read Aloud: "The Volcano Explodes"	**Content Objective** • Monitor and adjust oral comprehension. **Language Objectives** • Discuss oral passages. • Use a graphic organizer to take notes.
Reading Comprehension Main Idea and Details	**Content Objectives** • Identify the main idea and details. • Use the main idea and details to aid comprehension. **Language Objectives** • Identify details that support the main idea. • Write a main idea and its details. • Summarize text using visual support.
Vocabulary Basic and Lesson Vocabulary	**Language Objectives** • Understand and use basic vocabulary. • Learn meanings of grade-level vocabulary. • Produce drawings, phrases, and short sentences to show understanding of Lesson Vocabulary.
Word Analysis Related Words	**Content Objective** • Identify related words. **Language Objective** • Discuss how words can be related.
Grammar and Conventions Clauses and Complex Sentences	**Content Objective** • Identify complex sentences. **Language Objectives** • Speak using complex sentences. • Write complex sentences.
Writing Writing a Personal Narrative	**Content Objective** • Identify the features of a personal narrative. **Language Objectives** • Write a personal narrative using sequence and descriptive details. • Share feedback for editing and revising.

Word Cards for Vocabulary Activities

glacier

impressive

naturalist

preserve

slopes

species

wilderness

Teacher Note: Beginning Teach three to four words. **Intermediate** Teach four to six words. **Advanced** Teach six to seven words. **Advanced High** Teach all words.

Name _____

Look at the map. **Read** the paragraph.
- Which sentence tells the main idea? **Write** it in the *Main Idea* box.
- Which sentences give details? **Write** those sentences in the *Detail* boxes.

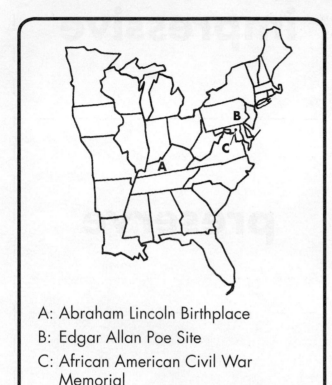

A: Abraham Lincoln Birthplace
B: Edgar Allan Poe Site
C: African American Civil War Memorial

National Parks in the United States

Some national parks in the United States are historic places. These parks teach visitors about America's past. At the Abraham Lincoln Birthplace National Historic Site, visitors can see a cabin similar to the boyhood home of the 16th President. At the Edgar Allan Poe National Historic Site, visitors can see where a famous writer lived. Visitors to the African American Civil War Memorial can learn about African Americans' contributions during the Civil War.

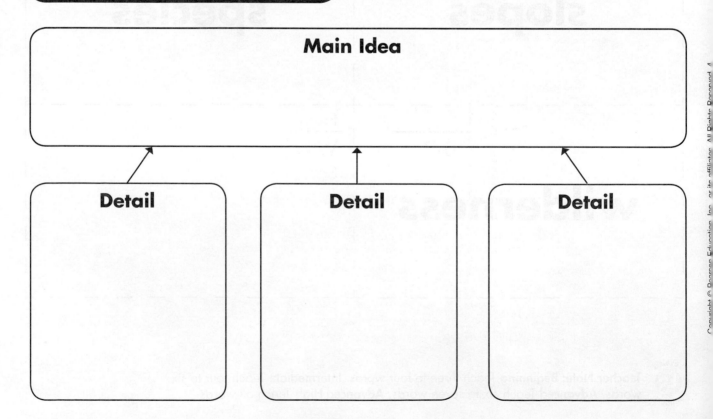

Main Idea

Detail

Detail

Detail

Main Idea and Details

Use this lesson to supplement or replace the skill lesson on page 139c of the Teacher's Edition. Display the Skill Points (at right) and share them with students.

Teach/Model

Beginning Display photographs showing three famous places in Washington, D.C. Say: *These photos show details about Washington, D.C.* Guide students in stating a main idea sentence that is supported by these details. (Possible answer: Washington, D.C., has many interesting places to visit.)

Intermediate Write and read aloud: *Yellowstone National Park is a special place. It is known for its geysers and hot springs. Grizzly bears, bison, and wolves live there.* Ask students to identify the main idea and to explain how the details support it.

Advanced Say: *Boston is an old city. You can visit many historic sites there. These places are part of the early history of our country.* Ask students to write a main idea sentence for the paragraph. (Possible answer: Boston is important to American history.)

Advanced High Ask students to write a brief paragraph with a main idea and supporting details. Pair students. Have partners read each other's paragraphs and identify the main idea and supporting details.

Then distribute copies of Picture It! page 54.

- Have students look at the map and read the title. Then read the paragraph aloud.
- Ask: *What is this paragraph about?* (national parks)
- Review the Skill Points with students.
- Have students find the sentence that tells the main idea. Then have them find the sentences that give details.

Practice

Read aloud the directions on page 54. Have students reread the paragraph silently. Have them look at the map and the paragraph as they fill in the graphic organizer.

Beginning Students can orally identify the main idea and three details before writing their answers in the boxes. Provide help with English words and writing.

Intermediate Students can first orally answer and then write their answers to fill in the graphic organizer. Provide help with English words and writing.

Advanced Students can write their answers to fill in the graphic organizer and then check them by comparing them to a partner's answers.

Advanced High Students can write their answers to fill in the graphic organizer and then orally explain the process of identifying the main idea and supporting details.

Answers for page 54: *Main Idea:* Some national parks in the United States are historic places. *Details:* Details should be the three historical sites and what they teach visitors.

Skill Points

✔ The most important idea in a paragraph is the **main idea.**

✔ To find the main idea, ask: *What is this paragraph mostly about?* See if there is a sentence that gives the main idea.

✔ Other sentences in the paragraph tell about the main idea. They give details about the main idea.

Multilingual Summaries

Letters Home from Yosemite

Yosemite became a national park in 1890. It is in the mountains of the Sierra Nevada. The park is named for a Native American word for grizzly bear. More than 3.5 million people visit Yosemite every year.

Bridal Veil Falls is one of the highest waterfalls in America. More than half of the highest waterfalls in America are in Yosemite. Giant old sequoia trees grow in Yosemite. Wild animals such as black bears and bighorn sheep live in the park.

Glacier Point is a little more than one-half mile above the floor of Yosemite Valley. El Capitan is the biggest block of granite in the country. Yosemite Falls is three waterfalls in one. A glacier is on Mt. Lyell, the park's highest peak. Tioga Pass runs through the park. It is the highest highway in the Sierra Nevada.

Spanish

Cartas desde Yosemite

Yosemite se convirtió en un parque nacional en 1890. Está situado en las montañas de la Sierra Nevada. El parque recibió este nombre por el nombre que le daban al oso pardo los indígenas norteamericanos. Más de 3.5 millones de personas visitan Yosemite cada año.

La catarata de Bridal Veil es una de las cataratas más altas en América del Norte. Más de la mitad de las cataratas más altas de América del Norte están en Yosemite. Enormes y viejos árboles de secuoya crecen en Yosemite. Animales salvajes como osos negros y carneros de cuernos grandes viven en el parque.

Glacier Point está a un poco más de la mitad de una milla encima del valle Yosemite. El Capitán es el bloque más grande de granito del país. Las cataratas de Yosemite son tres cataratas en una. Un glaciar está en el monte Lyell, la cima más alta del parque. El paso de Tioga corre a través del parque. Es la carretera más alta en las montañas de la Sierra Nevada.

Multilingual Summaries

Chinese

優勝美地公園

優勝美地於1890年成為國家公園，它位於內華達山區，在印地安語中是"大灰熊"的意思。每年有超過350萬人來這裏觀光。

新娘面紗瀑布是美國最高的瀑布之一，全國最高的瀑布有一半以上在優勝美地。這裏還有古老的美洲巨杉，生活著黑熊、大角羊等野生動物。

冰川點距離優勝美地谷底800多米。酋長石是美國最大的花崗岩巨石。優勝美地瀑布分三段俯衝直下。公園最高的萊爾峰上也有冰川。迪歐戈公路穿過公園，是內華達山區海拔最高的公路。

Vietnamese

Thư Gởi Về Nhà từ Yosemite

Yosemite trở thành khu vườn quốc gia vào năm 1890. Nó nằm trong Dãy Núi Sierra Nevada. Khu vườn được đặt tên theo chữ gấu lớn màu nâu (grizzly bear) của tiếng Thổ Dân Mỹ. Có hơn 3.5 triệu người đến tham quan Yosemite mỗi năm.

Thác nước Bridal Veil (Mạng Che Mặt Cô Dâu) là một trong những thác nước cao nhất ở Hoa Kỳ. Yosemite có trên phân nửa số thác nước cao nhất ở Hoa Kỳ. Những cây tùng đồ sộ lâu đời mọc lên ở Yosemite. Thú rừng như gấu đen và cừu to sừng sinh sống trong khu vườn này.

Điểm Glacier ở bên trên nền thung lũng Yosemite hơn nửa dặm. El Capitan là một trong những tảng hoa cương lớn nhất của cả nước. Thác nước Yosemite là ba thác nước nhập một. Một dãy băng trên ngọn Mt. Lyell, đỉnh cao nhất của khu vườn. Đường đèo Tioga Pass đi xuyên qua khu vườn. Đó là xa lộ cao nhất trong Dãy Núi Sierra Nevada.

Multilingual Summaries

Korean

요세미티에서 온 편지

시에라 네바다 산맥 속에 있는 요세미티는 1890년에 국립공원으로 지정되었다. 요세미티란 이름은 아메리카 원주민어의 회색 곰이라는 말에서 따왔으며 매년 350만 명 이상이 이 공원을 찾는다.

브라이들 베일(면사포) 폭포는 미국에서 가장 높은 폭포 중 하나로 이런 폭포의 반 이상이 요세미티 안에 자리잡고 있다. 거대하고 오래된 세쿼이아 나무들이 요세미티에서 자라고 있으며 흑곰이나 큰뿔양 같은 야생동물도 이곳에 살고 있다.

글래시어 포인트는 요세미티 계곡 바닥에서 위쪽으로 반 마일보다 약간 더 높은 곳에 있다. 엘 캐피턴은 미국에서 가장 큰 화강암 바위이다. 요세미티 폭포는 폭포 세 개가 하나로 합쳐진 것이다. 공원에서 가장 높은 봉우리인 라이엘 산에는 빙하가 하나 있다. 티오가 패스는 공원을 관통해 이어져있는데 이것은 시에라 네바다 산맥에서 가장 높은 고속도로이다.

Hmong

Sau Tsab Ntawv Mus Tsev los ntawm Yosemite

Xyoo 1890, Yosemite raug tsa ua ib lub thaj chaw national park. Nws nyob rau hauv roob toj siab Sierra Nevada. Thaj chaw park ntawd raug tis npe los ntawm ib lo lus Qhab Miskas rau ib tug dais. Niaj xyoo, ntau tshaj li 3.5 lab neeg tuaj xyuas Yosemite.

Bridal Veil Falls yog ib tug dej tsaws tsag ntawm cov loj tshaj hauv teb chaws Miskas. Cov dej tsaws tsag loj tshaj plaws feem coob nyob Miskas teb nyob rau hauv Yosemite. Tsob ntoo sequoia loj tuaj hauv Yosemite. Tsiaj txhu qus xws li cov dais dub thiab cov yaj tuaj kub loj nyob rau hauv thaj chaw park no.

Lub Roob Glacier Point siab siab tshaj ib nrab las (mile) los ntawm Tiaj Yosemite. El Capitan yog lub roob ua pob zeb granite loj tshaj plaws hauv teb chaws Miskas. Yosemite Falls yog peb dej tsaws tsag los ua ib lub. Muaj ib thooj dej khov nyob rau saum lub roob Mt. Lyell, thaj chaw park ntawd lub ncov roob siab tshaj. Txoj kev Tioga Pass nyob rau hauv thaj chaw park ntawd thiab yog txoj kev siab tshaj nyob rau hauv cov roob Sierra Nevada.

Name _____

- **Read** *For Purple Mountain Majesties* again.
- Use the information in the book. **Write** the supporting details for the main idea shown below.

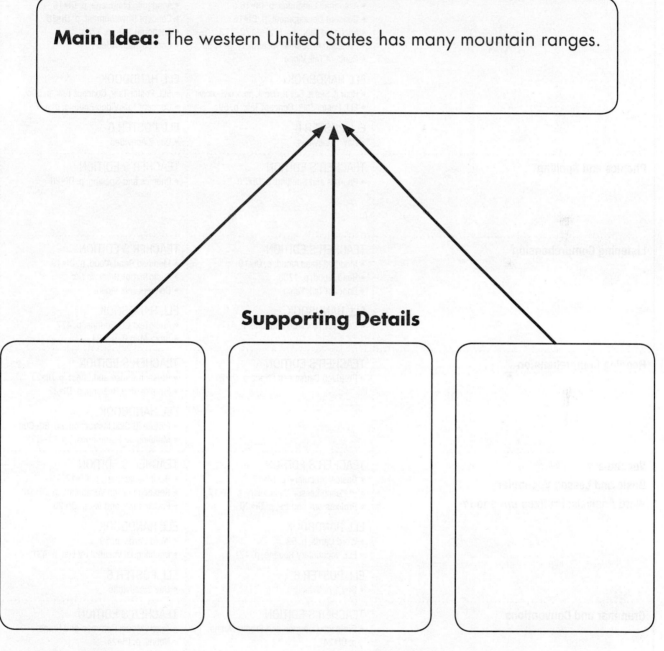

Main Idea: The western United States has many mountain ranges.

Supporting Details

Family Link

Has anyone in your family ever been to the mountain ranges described in this book? Ask family members to share what they know about mountain ranges they have seen.

For this week's content and language objectives, see p. 59e.

Instructional Strand	Day 1	Day 2
Concept Development/Academic Language	**TEACHER'S EDITION** • Academic Language, p. DI•16 • Concept Development, p. DI•16 • Anchored Talk, pp. 172j—172–173 • Preteach Academic Vocabulary, p. 175a • Concept Talk Video **ELL HANDBOOK** • Hear It, See It, Say It, Use It, pp. xxxvi–xxxvii • ELL Poster Talk, Concept Talk, p. 59c **ELL POSTER 6** • Day 1 Activities	**TEACHER'S EDITION** • Academic Language, p. DI•16 • Concept Development, p. DI•16 • Anchored Talk, p. 176a • Concept Talk Video **ELL HANDBOOK** • ELL Poster Talk, Concept Talk, p. 59c • Concept Talk Video Routine, p. 477 **ELL POSTER 6** • Day 2 Activities
Phonics and Spelling	**TEACHER'S EDITION** • Phonics and Spelling, p. DI•20	**TEACHER'S EDITION** • Phonics and Spelling, p. DI•20
Listening Comprehension	**TEACHER'S EDITION** • Modified Read Aloud, p. DI•19 • Read Aloud, p. 173b • Concept Talk Video **ELL HANDBOOK** • Concept Talk Video Routine, p. 477	**TEACHER'S EDITION** • Modified Read Aloud, p. DI•19 • AudioText of *What Jo Did* • Concept Talk Video **ELL HANDBOOK** • AudioText CD Routine, p. 477 • Story Map B, p. 484
Reading Comprehension	**TEACHER'S EDITION** • Preteach Cause and Effect, p. DI•21	**TEACHER'S EDITION** • Reteach Cause and Effect, p. DI•21 • Frontloading Reading, p. DI•22 **ELL HANDBOOK** • Picture It! Skill Instruction, pp. 60–60a • Multilingual Summaries, pp. 61–63
Vocabulary **Basic and Lesson Vocabulary** **Word Analysis: Prefixes *un-* and *in-***	**TEACHER'S EDITION** • Basic Vocabulary, p. DI•17 • Preteach Lesson Vocabulary, p. DI•17 • Prefixes *un-* and *in-*, p. DI•20 **ELL HANDBOOK** • Word Cards, p. 59 • ELL Vocabulary Routine, p. 471 **ELL POSTER 6** • Day 1 Activities	**TEACHER'S EDITION** • Basic Vocabulary, p. DI•17 • Reteach Lesson Vocabulary, p. DI•18 • Prefixes *un-* and *in-*, p. DI•20 **ELL HANDBOOK** • Word Cards, p. 59 • Multilingual Vocabulary List, p. 431 **ELL POSTER 6** • Day 2 Activities
Grammar and Conventions	**TEACHER'S EDITION** • Preteach Common and Proper Nouns, p. DI•24	**TEACHER'S EDITION** • Teach/Model Common and Proper Nouns, p. DI•24
Writing	**TEACHER'S EDITION** • Figurative Language, p. DI•25 • Introduce Poetry, pp. 175e–175f	**TEACHER'S EDITION** • Limerick, pp. 183d–183e

This symbol indicates leveled instruction to address language proficiency levels.

Day 3	Day 4	Day 5
TEACHER'S EDITION • Academic Language, p. DI•16 • Concept Development, p. DI•16 • Anchored Talk, p. 184a • Concept Talk Video **ELL HANDBOOK** • ELL Poster Talk, Concept Talk, p. 59c **ELL POSTER 6** • Day 3 Activities	**TEACHER'S EDITION** • Academic Language, p. DI•16 • Concept Development, p. DI•16 • Anchored Talk, p. 192a • Concept Talk Video **ELL HANDBOOK** • ELL Poster Talk, Concept Talk, p. 59c **ELL POSTER 6** • Day 4 Activities	**TEACHER'S EDITION** • Academic Language, p. DI•16 • Concept Development, p. DI•16 • Concept Talk Video **ELL HANDBOOK** • ELL Poster Talk, Concept Talk, p. 59c **ELL POSTER 6** • Day 5 Activities
		TEACHER'S EDITION • Phonics and Spelling, p. DI•20
ELL HANDBOOK • Phonics Transition Lesson, pp. 268, 270	**ELL HANDBOOK** • Phonics Transition Lesson, pp. 268, 270	
TEACHER'S EDITION • AudioText of *What Jo Did* • Concept Talk Video **ELL HANDBOOK** • AudioText CD Routine, p. 477	**TEACHER'S EDITION** • Concept Talk Video	**TEACHER'S EDITION** • Concept Talk Video
TEACHER'S EDITION • Sheltered Reading, p. DI•22 **ELL HANDBOOK** • Multilingual Summaries, pp. 61–63	**TEACHER'S EDITION** • ELL/ELD Reader Guided Reading, p. DI•23 **ELL HANDBOOK** • ELL Study Guide, p. 64	**TEACHER'S EDITION** • ELL/ELD Reader Guided Reading, p. DI•23 **ELL HANDBOOK** • ELL Study Guide, p. 64
		TEACHER'S EDITION • Prefixes *un-* and *in-*, p. 195i
ELL HANDBOOK • High-Frequency Words Activity Bank, p. 446 **ELL POSTER 6** • Day 3 Activities	**ELL HANDBOOK** • High-Frequency Words Activity Bank, p. 446	**ELL HANDBOOK** • High-Frequency Words Activity Bank, p. 446
TEACHER'S EDITION • Grammar Jammer **ELL HANDBOOK** • Grammar Transition Lesson, pp. 314, 318–319 • Grammar Jammer Routine, p. 478	**TEACHER'S EDITION** • Grammar Jammer **ELL HANDBOOK** • Grammar Transition Lesson, pp. 314, 318–319	**TEACHER'S EDITION** • Grammar Jammer **ELL HANDBOOK** • Grammar Transition Lesson, pp. 314, 318–319
TEACHER'S EDITION • Let's Write It!, p. 190–191 • Shape Poem, pp. 191a–191b	**TEACHER'S EDITION** • Shape Poem, pp. 195d–195e	**TEACHER'S EDITION** • Proofreading and Presenting, pp. 195p–195q

Question of the Week

How can we learn to appreciate the talents of others?

Throughout the week, use the ELL Poster to help students produce and comprehend language, understand the concept, and build English vocabulary. Use the Question of the Week and other questions to help students share ideas in pairs, small groups, or the large group. Sample questions are shown, with examples of possible responses by students.

Weekly Concept and Language Goals

• Explain what a talent is

• Recognize that people have different talents

• Tell how to show appreciation for others' talents

By the end of the lesson, students should be able to talk about and write sentences about appreciating other people's talents.

ELL Poster 6

Daily Team Talk

Day 1	Day 2	Day 3	Day 4	Day 5
After Day 1 activities on Poster, ask questions such as	After Day 2 activity on Poster, ask questions such as	After Day 3 activity on Poster, ask questions such as	After Day 4 activity on Poster, ask questions such as	After Day 5 activity on Poster, ask questions such as
What talents do the students in the poster picture have?	*In the poster picture, one girl's talent is that she can jump really high. How do the other students show that they appreciate her talent?*	*Why is being good at playing basketball or other sports a talent?*	*What are other talents that people can have?*	*What talent does your best friend have that you appreciate?*
Beginning Good at sports.	**Beginning** They talk about it.	**Beginning** They are hard.	**Beginning** Cooking, painting, playing music.	**Beginning** He plays piano.
Intermediate They are good at playing sports.	**Intermediate** Two of them talk about her jump.	**Intermediate** Sports are not easy.	**Intermediate** People can be good at playing music or cooking food.	**Intermediate** She can tell funny jokes.
Advanced These students are good at playing basketball. One girl can jump high.	**Advanced** Two of them are talking about her jump. One student is cheering.	**Advanced** Not all people are good at playing sports.	**Advanced** Some people have a talent for music. Others have a talent for art.	**Advanced** My best friend can dance. I can't.
Advanced High The students have talents for running, jumping, and throwing that make them good basketball players.	**Advanced High** The students cheer and talk to each other about the girl's jump. They look excited.	**Advanced High** Not many people play a sport well. People who can play a sport well have a talent for it.	**Advanced High** People can have many different talents. Some can play music or write stories. Some can paint or draw pictures.	**Advanced High** My best friend writes the most amazing stories. I love reading them.

This Week's Materials

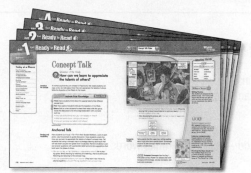

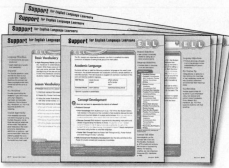

Teacher's Edition pages 172j–195q

Teacher's Edition pages DI•16–DI•25

ELL Handbook pp. 59a–64

See the support for English language learners throughout the lesson, including ELL strategies and scaffolded activities at points of use.

Differentiated Instruction for English language learners provides daily group activities that "frontload," or preteach, core instruction.

Find additional lesson materials that support the core lesson and the ELL instructional pages.

ELL Poster 6

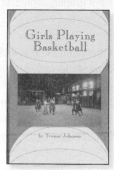

ELL Reader 4.2.1

ELD Reader 4.2.1

Concept Literacy Reader

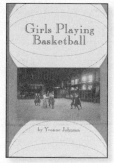

ELD, ELL Reader
Teaching Guide

Concept Literacy Reader
Teaching Guide

Technology

Online Teacher's Edition Use the digital version of the core Teacher's Edition for planning and instruction.

eReaders
This week's ELL and ELD Readers and Concept Literacy Reader are also available in digital format.

This Week's Content and Language Objectives by Strand

Concept Development/ Academic Language How can we learn to appreciate the talents of others?	**Content Objective** • Use concept vocabulary related to people's talents. **Language Objectives** • Express ideas in response to art and discussion. • Learn and use new academic vocabulary.
Phonics and Spelling Add –s or -es	**Content Objective** • Use spelling rules to add –s or –es to make words plural. **Language Objectives** • Apply decoding skills to vocabulary. • Write plural words correctly.
Listening Comprehension Modified Read Aloud: "Lunch Hour Learning"	**Content Objective** • Monitor and adjust oral comprehension. **Language Objectives** • Discuss oral passages to learn new and essential language. • Use a graphic organizer to take notes for pre-reading support.
Reading Comprehension Cause and Effect	**Content Objectives** • Understand the connection between cause and effect. • Allow students to identify cause and effect in a text. **Language Objectives** • Discuss the importance of cause and effect. • Use inferential skills to determine cause and effect. • Summarize text using visual support.
Vocabulary Basic and Lesson Vocabulary	**Language Objectives** • Understand and use basic vocabulary. • Learn meanings of grade-level vocabulary. • Produce drawings, phrases, and short sentences to show understanding of Lesson Vocabulary.
Word Analysis Prefixes un- and in-	**Content Objective** • Identify prefixes un- and in-. **Language Objective** • Use prefixes un- and in- correctly.
Grammar and Conventions Common and Proper Nouns	**Content Objective** • Correctly identify common and proper nouns. **Language Objectives** • Speak using common and proper nouns. • Write using common and proper nouns.
Writing Figurative Language	**Content Objective** • Understand the importance of using figurative language in your writing. **Language Objective** • Write narrative sentences that includes specific examples of figurative language.

Word Cards for Vocabulary Activities

fouled

hoop

jersey

marveled

rim

speechless

swatted

unbelievable

Teacher Note: Beginning Teach three to four words. **Intermediate** Teach four to six words. **Advanced** Teach six to seven words. **Advanced High** Teach all words.

Name _____

Look at the picture. **Read** the paragraph.

- What causes a basketball player's legs to be strong? **Underline** the clue words. Then **write** the two causes and the effect in the first set of boxes below.

- What causes a basketball player's arms to be strong? **Underline** the clue words. Then **write** the two causes and the effect in the second set of boxes below.

Strong Basketball Players

Basketball players are strong. They run up and down the court, so their legs become very powerful. They develop big leg muscles, because they jump up high to shoot baskets. Basketball players' arms are strong because they pass and shoot the ball many times during a game. Holding their arms up in front of opponents to block shots also causes their arms to become strong.

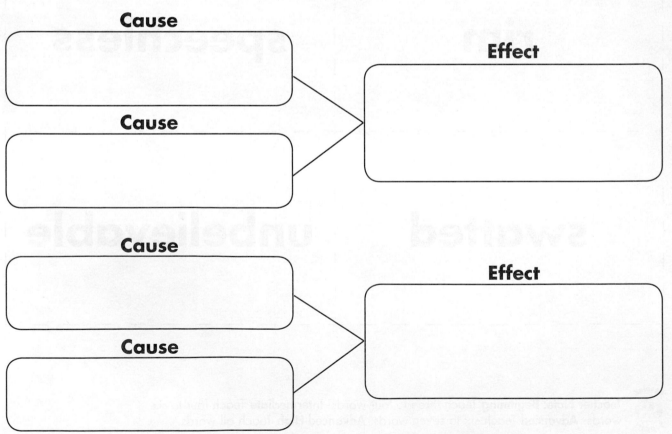

Cause

Cause

Effect

Cause

Cause

Effect

Cause and Effect

Use this lesson to supplement or replace the skill lesson on page 173c of the Teacher's Edition. Display the Skill Points (at right) and share them with students.

Teach/Model

Beginning Say: *I kick a ball. The ball rolls. What happens?* (The ball rolls.) *This is the effect. Why does this happen?* (You kick the ball.) *This is the cause.* Have students repeat the cause-and-effect sentence after you: *The ball rolls because I kick it.*

Intermediate Write and read aloud: *The second baseman tags the runner. The runner is out.* Ask students to copy the sentences, underline the cause (the second baseman tags the runner), and circle the effect (the runner is out).

Advanced Say: *A football player scores a touchdown. What could be the cause of this?* (Possible answer: No one stops him.) *What could be an effect of this?* (Possible answer: His team wins the game.)

Advanced High Have students look for sports pictures in magazines and write their own cause-and-effect sentences to go with their pictures. Encourage them to use clue words in their sentences. Ask students to show their pictures and read aloud their cause-and-effect sentences.

Then distribute copies of Picture It! page 60.

- Have students look at the illustration of the basketball player. Then read the paragraph aloud.
- Ask: *What causes basketball players' legs to be strong?*
- Review the Skill Points with students.
- Have students find the clue words. Then have them find the causes and effects.

Practice

Read aloud the directions on page 60. Have students reread the paragraph aloud. Have them use the picture and the paragraph as they complete the cause-and-effect flowcharts.

Beginning Students can underline the causes and effects in the paragraph and then write their answers in the boxes of the flowcharts. Provide help with English words and writing.

Intermediate Students can first orally state the causes and effects and then write their answers in the boxes of the flowcharts. Provide help with writing.

Advanced Students can fill in the flowcharts and then check their answers by comparing them with a partner's.

Advanced High Students can fill in the flowcharts and then explain orally how the clue words helped them identify the cause-and-effect relationships.

Answers for page 60: *Clue words:* so, because, because, causes; *Causes:* running on the court, jumping high; *Effect:* strong legs; *Causes:* passing and shooting, holding hands up; *Effect:* strong arms

Skill Points

- ✔ An **effect** is something that happens. A **cause** is what makes it happen.
- ✔ Clue words such as *because, so,* and *cause* sometimes show a cause-and-effect relationship.

Multilingual Summaries

What Jo Did

Joanna plays basketball at home. Her basket is sixteen feet high. Her parents do not know that regulation baskets are only ten feet high. Joanna learns to jump very high.

One day, Joanna's mother sends her to the store. On her way home, she sees boys playing basketball. They ask her to play with them. She is wearing a hat that covers her hair. They think that she is a boy. She tells them that her name is Jo.

Everyone sees that Jo is good at basketball. They ask her to dunk the ball. She does! Her hat falls off and they see that she is a girl. They are surprised. They ask her to play with them again.

Spanish

Lo que hizo Jo

Joanna juega baloncesto en casa. Su canasta está a dieciséis pies de altura. Sus padres no saben que las regulaciones para las canastas son sólo de diez pies hasta el aro. Joanna aprende a saltar muy alto.

Un día, la mamá de Joanna la manda a la tienda. En el camino de regreso, ella ve a unos niños jugando baloncesto. Ellos la invitan a jugar. Joanna tiene puesto un sombrero que le cubre su cabello. Los niños piensan que es un niño. Ella les dice que se llama Jo.

Todos ven que Jo es buena jugadora de baloncesto. Ellos la invitan a clavar la pelota. ¡Ella lo hace! Su sombrero se cae y ellos ven que es una niña. Están sorprendidos, pero la invitan a volver a jugar con ellos.

Multilingual Summaries

Read

Use the

boxes

Cause

Chinese

School + Home

喬的故事

喬安娜常在家裏打籃球。父母親不知道標準是10英尺，將她的籃筐提高到16英尺，因此喬安娜學會跳得很高。

有一次媽媽叫喬安娜去買東西，她回來時看見男孩們在打籃球。喬安娜戴著帽子，遮住了頭髮，大家以為她是男孩，叫她一塊打籃球。她說自己名字叫喬。

每人都說喬是好球員。請她做扣籃，她輕鬆地完成！可是帽子掉了，大家發現喬原來是女孩，不過還是請她一起玩。

Vietnamese

School + Home

Điều Jo Đã Làm

Joanna chơi bóng rổ ở nhà. Khung rổ của cô cao đến mười sáu bộ. Ba mẹ của cô không biết là theo quy định thì những khung rổ chỉ được cao mười bộ. Joanna học nhảy lên rất cao.

Ngày kia, mẹ của Joanna nhờ cô đi đến một cửa tiệm. Trên đường về nhà, cô thấy các cậu con trai đang chơi bóng rổ. Họ rủ cô chơi với họ. Cô đang đội một cái nón che hết tóc của mình. Họ tưởng cô là một cậu con trai. Cô nói cho họ biết tên mình là Jo.

Mọi người thấy là Jo chơi bóng rổ giỏi. Họ kêu cô đánh bóng vào rổ. Cô làm được! Nón rơi xuống và họ nhận ra cô là một cô gái. Họ ngạc nhiên. Họ rủ cô chơi với họ nữa.

Korean

조안
부모님은
높이 점크

어느
남자아이
제안한다
남자아이

모두
덩크슛을
모자가
놀라워한

Hmong

Joar
rau feet
tawb pa
Mua
ib tog k
nws nro
Lawv xa
lub npe
Sav
pov lub
kaus ma
Lawv ce

Poster Talk, Concept Talk

ELL Poster 7

? Question of the Week

How can we work together to achieve a goal?

Throughout the week, use the ELL Poster to help students produce and comprehend language, understand the concept, and build English vocabulary. Use the Question of the Week and other questions to help students share ideas in pairs, small groups, or the large group. Sample questions are shown, with examples of possible responses by students.

Weekly Concept and Language Goals

- Discuss goals people might have
- Understand how people everywhere work together to achieve common goals
- Recognize a variety of team goals

By the end of the lesson, students should be able to talk about and write sentences about working together to achieve goals.

Daily Team Talk

Day 1	Day 2	Day 3	Day 4	Day 5
After Day 1 activities on Poster, ask questions such as *In the poster picture, what goal are the cowgirls and cowboys working together to achieve?*	After Day 2 activity on Poster, ask questions such as *In the poster picture, what is the man with the rope doing to help round up cattle?*	After Day 3 activity on Poster, ask questions such as *In the poster picture, how will the woman at the gate help round up the cattle?*	After Day 4 activity on Poster, ask questions such as *In the story* Coyote School News, *what goals does Monchi help achieve by working together with others?*	After Day 5 activity on Poster, ask questions such as *What is one goal you have achieved by working together with others?*
Beginning Get the cows in. **Intermediate** They want to get the cows inside. **Advanced** They want to bring all the cows inside the fence where they will be safe. **Advanced High** The cowboys and cowgirls are working together to round up the cows and bring them into the corral.	**Beginning** He gets a cow. **Intermediate** A cow is running away. He is getting it. **Advanced** He is using his rope to catch a cow that is trying to run away. **Advanced High** The man with the rope is helping the roundup by bringing in stray cows. One cow is running away, so he is using his rope to catch it.	**Beginning** She closes it. **Intermediate** She will close the gate. **Advanced** She will shut the gate when the last cow is inside the fence. **Advanced High** The woman at the gate will help by shutting the gate after all the cows are in the corral so they cannot get back out.	**Beginning** He writes stories. **Intermediate** He writes stories for the school. **Advanced** He helps write stories for the school news. He helps bring in cattle. **Advanced High** Monchi works with other students to write stories for the school news. He works with his family to bring in cattle.	**Beginning** A science report. **Intermediate** I helped my group do a science project. **Advanced** I worked with a group to make a project for science class. **Advanced High** My group's goal was to create a science project about clouds. We all worked on it, and we finished on time.

Teacher's Edition pages 196j–227q

See the support for English language learners throughout the lesson, including ELL strategies and scaffolded activities at points of use.

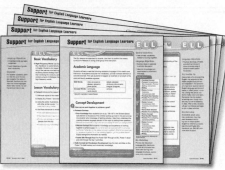

Teacher's Edition pages DI•41–DI•50

Differentiated Instruction for English language learners provides daily group activities that "frontload," or preteach, core instruction.

ELL Handbook pp. 65a–70

Find additional lesson materials that support the core lesson and the ELL instructional pages.

ELL Poster 7

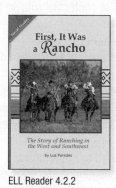

ELL Reader 4.2.2

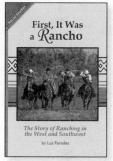

ELD Reader 4.2.2

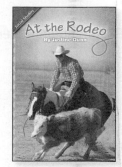

Concept Literacy Reader

ELD, ELL Reader Teaching Guide

Concept Literacy Reader Teaching Guide

Technology

Online Teacher's Edition Use the digital version of the core Teacher's Edition for planning and instruction.

eReaders
This week's ELL and ELD Readers and Concept Literacy Reader are also available in digital format.

This Week's Content and Language Objectives by Strand

Concept Development/ Academic Language How can we work together to achieve a goal?	**Content Objective** • Use concept vocabulary related to working together. **Language Objectives** • Express ideas in response to art and discussion. • Use prior knowledge and experiences to understand meanings.
Phonics and Spelling Irregular Plural Nouns	**Content Objective** • Identify irregular plural nouns. **Language Objectives** • Spell familiar English words with increasing accuracy. • Discuss the meaning of irregular plural nouns.
Listening Comprehension Modified Read Aloud: "Luz's Dream Garden"	**Content Objective** • Monitor and adjust oral comprehension. **Language Objectives** • Discuss oral passages. • Use contextual support to confirm understanding of spoken language.
Reading Comprehension Draw Conclusions	**Content Objective** • Draw conclusions to aid comprehension. **Language Objectives** • Discuss supporting facts for drawing conclusions. • Retell supporting facts and draw conclusions from a reading. • Summarize text using visual support.
Vocabulary Basic and Lesson Vocabulary	**Language Objectives** • Understand and use basic vocabulary. • Learn meanings of grade-level vocabulary. • Produce drawings, phrases, and short sentences to show understanding of Lesson Vocabulary.
Grammar and Conventions Regular Plural Nouns	**Content Objective** • Decode and use regular plural nouns. **Language Objectives** • Speak using the pattern of regular plural nouns. • Write phrases and sentences using regular plural nouns.
Writing Know Your Purpose for Writing	**Content Objective** • Identify purpose in a text. **Language Objectives** • Write a paragraph with a clear purpose. • Use specific details in writing to express purpose.

Word Cards for Vocabulary Activities

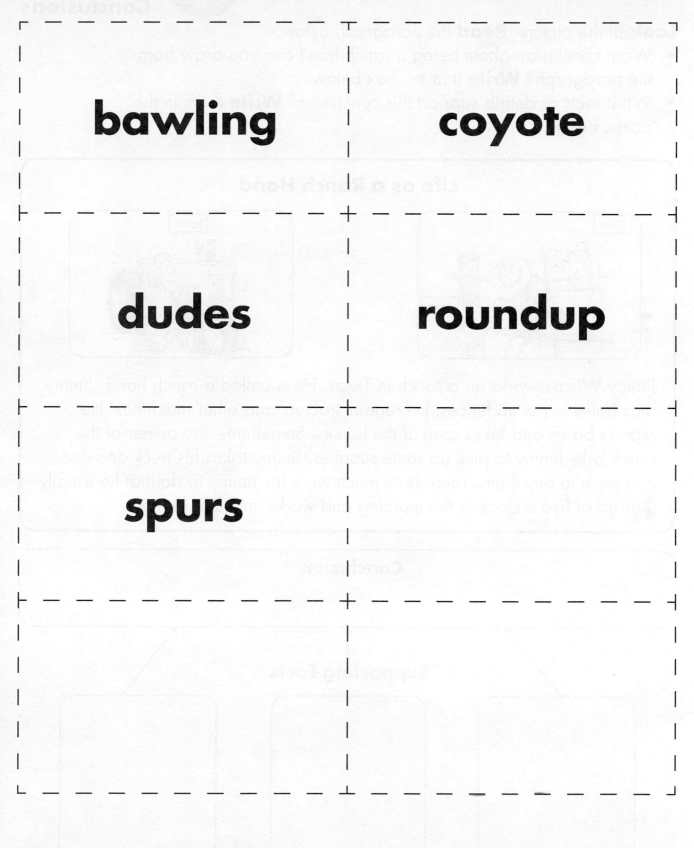

bawling

coyote

dudes

roundup

spurs

Teacher Note: Beginning Teach two to three words. **Intermediate** Teach three to four words. **Advanced** Teach four to five words. **Advanced High** Teach all words.

Name _____

Look at the picture. **Read** the paragraph below.

• What conclusion about being a ranch hand can you draw from the paragraph? **Write** it in the box below.

• What facts or details support this conclusion? **Write** them in the boxes below.

Life as a Ranch Hand

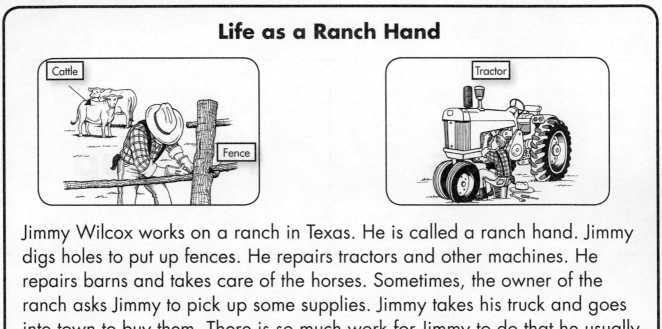

Jimmy Wilcox works on a ranch in Texas. He is called a ranch hand. Jimmy digs holes to put up fences. He repairs tractors and other machines. He repairs barns and takes care of the horses. Sometimes, the owner of the ranch asks Jimmy to pick up some supplies. Jimmy takes his truck and goes into town to buy them. There is so much work for Jimmy to do that he usually gets up at five o'clock in the morning and works until late at night.

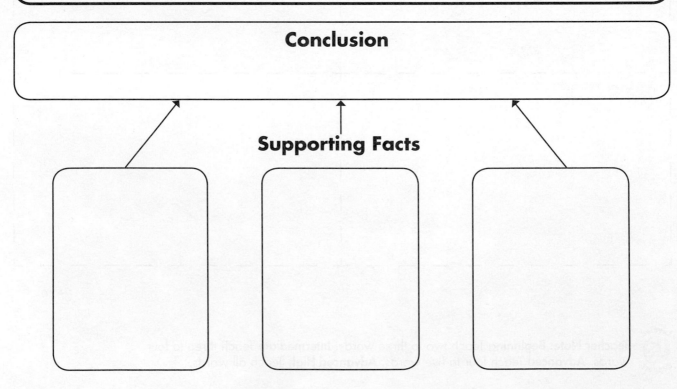

Conclusion

Supporting Facts

Draw Conclusions

Use this lesson to supplement or replace the skill lesson on page 197c of the Teacher's Edition. Display the Skill Points (at right) and share them with students.

Teach/Model

Beginning Display a picture of a construction worker wearing a hard hat. Say: *This construction worker is wearing a hard hat. What conclusion can you make about why she does that?* (It keeps her head safe while she is working.)

Intermediate Say: *Firefighters have to take a test. They wear 50 pounds of clothing and carry a 50-pound hose at least 75 feet. They carry equipment up stairs and put up a big ladder. What conclusion can you draw about being a firefighter?* (A firefighter has to be strong and in great physical shape.)

Advanced Ask students to draw conclusions about the skills a teacher needs or the characteristics that make a good teacher. Have them explain how they used what they already know to draw their conclusions.

Advanced High Display pictures of different workers such as a police officer, librarian, judge, and doctor. Briefly describe each job. Ask students to use what they see in the picture and what they already know to draw conclusions about each job.

Then distribute copies of Picture It! page 66.

- Have students describe what they see in the illustrations.
- Read the paragraph aloud. Ask: *What are some of the things a ranch hand does?* (puts up fences, repairs machines, repairs barns, takes care of horses, goes into town to buy supplies)
- Review the Skill Points with students.
- Have students identify a conclusion they can draw from the paragraph about life as a ranch hand.

Practice

Read aloud the directions on page 66. Have students reread the paragraph with a partner. Then have them use the illustrations and the paragraph as they fill in the boxes.

Beginning Students can orally state their conclusion and supporting facts before writing their answers in the boxes. Provide help with English words and writing.

Intermediate Students can first orally answer and then write their answers in the boxes on the page.

Advanced Students can write their answers to fill in the graphic organizer and then check their answers by comparing them to a partner's.

Advanced High Students can write their answers to fill in the graphic organizer and then orally explain how they used information in the paragraph to draw their conclusion.

Answers for page 66: *Conclusion:* Being a ranch hand is hard work. *Supporting Facts:* digs holes for fences, repairs machines and barns, takes care of horses

Skill Points

✔ When you read, you use what you already know and the facts and details in the text to form an idea, or **draw a conclusion.**

✔ You can check your conclusions or an author's conclusions by asking: *Does this conclusion make sense? Is it supported by the facts and details?*

Multilingual Summaries

English

Coyote School News

Monchi lives on a ranch in Arizona. He goes to Coyote School. The teacher, Miss Byers, helps the students to start a newspaper called *Coyote News*. All the students write stories for it. Miss Byers offers a prize for perfect attendance—a silver dollar.

Monchi and his family pick chiles after school. Monchi is hurt when a bag of chiles falls on him. He breaks his wrist.

Monchi's family has a big Christmas Eve party. They make a piñata and eat and dance. This year Monchi's present is a silver belt buckle with a hole for a silver dollar.

Monchi and his older brother help with the roundup on the ranch. They stay home from school. Monchi is sad he will not get a perfect attendance award.

At the end of the school year, Monchi wins a silver dollar for helping with the newspaper. He puts the dollar in his buckle.

Spanish

Noticias de la escuela Coyote

Monchi vive en un rancho de Arizona. Él va a la escuela Coyote. La maestra, la señorita Byers, ayuda a los estudiantes a hacer un periódico que se llama *Noticias Coyote*. Todos los estudiantes escriben historias para el periódico. La señorita Byers promete dar un dólar de plata como premio por la asistencia perfecta.

Monchi y su familia recolectan chiles después de la escuela. Monchi se hace daño con una bolsa de chiles que se le cae encima. Se rompe la muñeca.

La familia de Monchi hace una gran fiesta de Nochebuena. Hacen una piñata y comen y bailan. Este año el regalo de Monchi es una hebilla de cinturón con un hueco para un dólar de plata.

Monchi y su hermano ayudan en el rodeo del rancho. Ellos no van a la escuela. Monchi está triste porque no tendrá el premio de asistencia perfecta.

Al final del año escolar, Monchi gana un dólar de plata por su ayuda en el periódico. Él coloca el dólar en su hebilla.

Multilingual Summaries

Chinese

凱奧特學校新聞報

蒙奇住在亞利桑那州的農場，他的學校名叫凱奧特。同學們跟著白老師辦報紙，起名叫凱奧特新聞報，每個人都給報紙投稿。白老師說哪位同學不缺課，就給予獎勵一銀元。

放學後，蒙奇幫家裏摘辣椒。一不小心，大包辣椒掉下來，扭傷了他的手腕。

聖誕前夕，蒙奇家舉行盛大的宴會。他們製做彼那塔陶罐、吃許多東西和一起跳舞。今年蒙奇收到的禮物是銀帶扣，上面有個小洞要放一個銀元。

可是蒙奇與哥哥要幫農場趕牛群，不能按時去學校。拿不到老師的獎勵，蒙奇心裏很傷心。

學期結束時，由於蒙奇辦報紙出色，還是獲得銀元獎，他高興地把它放在帶扣上。

Vietnamese

Tin Của Trường Coyote

Monchi sống trong một trang trại ở Arizona. Cậu đi học ở Trường Coyote. Cô giáo, Cô Byers, giúp học sinh khởi sự làm một tờ báo gọi là Tin Của Coyote. Tất cả học sinh đều phải viết bài cho báo. Cô Byers đưa ra một giải thưởng cho ai đi học đều đặn—một đồng đô-la bằng bạc.

Monchi và gia đình cậu hái ớt sau giờ học. Monchi bị thương khi một túi ớt ngả lên mình. Cậu bị gẫy cổ tay.

Gia đình của Monchi có một bữa tiệc lớn trước ngày lễ Giáng Sinh. Họ làm một con thú nhồi kẹo và ăn uống và nhảy múa. Năm nay món quà cho Monchi là một cái khóa thắt lưng bằng bạc với một cái lỗ trống để nhét đồng đô-la bạc.

Monchi và người anh giúp lùa súc vật ở trang trại. Họ phải nghỉ học. Monchi buồn vì cậu sẽ không được phần thưởng đi học đều.

Vào cuối niên học, Monchi đạt được đồng đô-la bạc vì đã giúp đỡ tờ báo. Cậu để đồng đô-la vào cái khóa thắt lưng của mình.

Multilingual Summaries

코요테 학교 뉴스

애리조나의 대농장에서 살고 있는 몬치는 코요테 학교에 다닌다. 바이어스 선생님은 학생들이 코요테 뉴스라는 신문을 만들 수 있도록 도왔고 학생들은 모두 신문에 실을 이야기를 쓴다. 바이어스 선생님은 1년 개근한 학생에게 상으로 은화 1달러를 주겠다고 제안한다.

몬치는 방과 후 가족과 칠레 고추를 따다가 고추가 든 가방이 떨어지는 바람에 손목이 부러진다.

몬치의 가족은 크리스마스 이브 파티를 성대하게 열어 피나타를 만들어 먹고 춤을 춘다. 올해 몬치가 받은 선물은 은화 달러를 달 수 있는 구멍이 나있는 은 벨트 버클이다.

몬치와 형은 농장의 가축을 모는 일을 돕느라 학교에 가지 못한다. 몬치는 개근상을 받지 못한다고 슬퍼한다.

학기말이 되었을 때 몬치는 신문 발행을 도운 공로로 은화 달러를 받고 그 은화를 벨트 버클에 끼워 넣는다.

Tsev Kawm Ntawv Coyote Xov Xwm

Monchi nyob rau ib lub tsev yaj sab yug tsiaj nyob rau Arizona. Nws mus lub tsev kawm ntawv Coyote. Tus xib fwb, Miss Byers, pab nws cov tub ntxhais kawm ntawv tsim ib daim xov xwm hu ua Xov Xwm Coyote. Tag nrho cov tub ntxhais kawm ntawv sau dab neeg rau hauv. Miss Byers muaj khoom plig rau tus ua tuaj kawm ntawv txhua hnub - ib lub nyiaj duas-las.

Monchi thiab nws tsev neeg khaws kua txob tom qab tsev kawm ntawv lawb. Monchi tau raug mob thaum ib hnab kua txob poob ntaus nws. Nws qis tes thiaj li dam.

Monchi tsev neeg muaj ib lub koom txoos hmo ua ntej Christmas. Lawv ua Pinata thiab noj mov thiab seev ceev. Xyoo no, Monchi's qhov khoom plig yog ib txoj siv muaj lub pov siv nyiaj nrog ib lub qhov rau lub nyiaj duas-las.

Monchi thiab nws tus tij laug pab sau cov tsiaj mus khaws cia nyob rau tom tsev. Nkawv nyob tsev tsis mus kawm ntawv. Monchi tu siab tias nws yuav tsis tau qhov khoom plig ua tuaj txhua hnub tom tsev kawm ntawv.

Thaum xyoo yuav kawg, Monchi yeej ib lub nyiaj duas-las vim nws pab lawv ua daim xov xwm. Nws muab lub nyiaj duas-las rau nws lub pob siv.

- **Read** *First, It Was a Rancho* again.
- Use the information in the book to **draw** a picture and **write** a description of a ranch.

_____

_____

_____

_____

Family Link

How would your family like to live on a cattle ranch? Ask them what they think life would be like there. Ask them what they think would be the best part and the worst part of living on a ranch.

Weekly Resources Guide for English Language Learner Support

For this week's content and language objectives, see p. 71e.

Instructional Strand	Day 1	Day 2
Concept Development/Academic Language	**TEACHER'S EDITION** • Academic Language, p. DI•66 • Concept Development, p. DI•66 • Anchored Talk, pp. 228j—228–229 • Preteach Academic Vocabulary, p. 231a • Concept Talk Video **ELL HANDBOOK** • Hear It, See It, Say It, Use It, pp. xxxvi–xxxvii • ELL Poster Talk, Concept Talk, p. 71c **ELL POSTER 8** • Day 1 Activities	**TEACHER'S EDITION** • Academic Language, p. DI•66 • Concept Development, p. DI•66 • Anchored Talk, p. 232a • Concept Talk Video **ELL HANDBOOK** • ELL Poster Talk, Concept Talk, p. 71c • Concept Talk Video Routine, p. 477 **ELL POSTER 8** • Day 2 Activities
Phonics and Spelling	**TEACHER'S EDITION** • Phonics and Spelling, p. DI•70	**TEACHER'S EDITION** • Phonics and Spelling, p. DI•70
Listening Comprehension	**TEACHER'S EDITION** • Modified Read Aloud, p. DI•69 • Read Aloud, p. 229b • Concept Talk Video **ELL HANDBOOK** • Concept Talk Video Routine, p. 477	**TEACHER'S EDITION** • Modified Read Aloud, p. DI•69 • AudioText of *Scene Two* • Concept Talk Video **ELL HANDBOOK** • AudioText CD Routine, p. 477 • K-W-L Chart, p. 480
Reading Comprehension	**TEACHER'S EDITION** • Preteach Draw Conclusions, p. DI•71	**TEACHER'S EDITION** • Reteach Draw Conclusions, p. DI•71 • Frontloading Reading, p. DI•72 **ELL HANDBOOK** • Picture It! Skill Instruction, pp. 72–72a • Multilingual Summaries, pp. 73–75
Vocabulary **Basic and Lesson Vocabulary** **Word Analysis: Latin Prefixes *dis-, re-, non-***	**TEACHER'S EDITION** • Basic Vocabulary, p. DI•67 • Preteach Lesson Vocabulary, p. DI•67 • Latin Prefixes *dis-, re-, non-*, p. DI•70 **ELL HANDBOOK** • Word Cards, p. 71 • ELL Vocabulary Routine, p. 471 **ELL POSTER 8** • Day 1 Activities	**TEACHER'S EDITION** • Basic Vocabulary, p. DI•67 • Reteach Lesson Vocabulary, p. DI•68 • Latin Prefixes *dis-, re-, non-*, p. DI•70 **ELL HANDBOOK** • Word Cards, p. 71 • Multilingual Vocabulary List, p. 431 **ELL POSTER 8** • Day 2 Activities
Grammar and Conventions	**TEACHER'S EDITION** • Teach/Model Irregular Plural Nouns, p. DI•74	**TEACHER'S EDITION** • Reteach Irregular Plural Nouns, p. DI•74
Writing	**TEACHER'S EDITION** • Figurative Language, p. DI•75 • Introduce Poetry, pp. 231e–231f	**TEACHER'S EDITION** • Cinquain, pp. 241d–241e

This symbol indicates leveled instruction to address language proficiency levels.

Day 3	Day 4	Day 5
TEACHER'S EDITION • Academic Language, p. DI•66 • Concept Development, p. DI•66 • Anchored Talk, p. 242a • Concept Talk Video **ELL HANDBOOK** • ELL Poster Talk, Concept Talk, p. 71c **ELL POSTER 8** • Day 3 Activities	**TEACHER'S EDITION** • Academic Language, p. DI•66 • Concept Development, p. DI•66 • Anchored Talk, p. 252a • Concept Talk Video **ELL HANDBOOK** • ELL Poster Talk, Concept Talk, p. 71c **ELL POSTER 8** • Day 4 Activities	**TEACHER'S EDITION** • Academic Language, p. DI•66 • Concept Development, p. DI•66 • Concept Talk Video **ELL HANDBOOK** • ELL Poster Talk, Concept Talk, p. 71c **ELL POSTER 8** • Day 5 Activities
		TEACHER'S EDITION • Phonics and Spelling, p. DI•70
ELL HANDBOOK • Phonics Transition Lesson, pp. 262–265	**ELL HANDBOOK** • Phonics Transition Lesson, pp. 262–265	
TEACHER'S EDITION • AudioText of *Scene Two* • Concept Talk Video **ELL HANDBOOK** • AudioText CD Routine, p. 477	**TEACHER'S EDITION** • Concept Talk Video	**TEACHER'S EDITION** • Concept Talk Video
TEACHER'S EDITION • Sheltered Reading, p. DI•72 **ELL HANDBOOK** • Multilingual Summaries, pp. 73–75	**TEACHER'S EDITION** • ELL/ELD Reader Guided Reading, p. DI•73 **ELL HANDBOOK** • ELL Study Guide, p. 76	**TEACHER'S EDITION** • ELL/ELD Reader Guided Reading, p. DI•73 **ELL HANDBOOK** • ELL Study Guide, p. 76
		TEACHER'S EDITION • Latin Prefixes *dis-, re-, non-*, p. 255i
ELL HANDBOOK • High-Frequency Words Activity Bank, p. 446 **ELL POSTER 8** • Day 3 Activities	**ELL HANDBOOK** • High-Frequency Words Activity Bank, p. 446	**ELL HANDBOOK** • High-Frequency Words Activity Bank, p. 446
TEACHER'S EDITION • Grammar Jammer **ELL HANDBOOK** • Grammar Transition Lesson, pp. 316, 322 • Grammar Jammer Routine, p. 478	**TEACHER'S EDITION** • Grammar Jammer **ELL HANDBOOK** • Grammar Transition Lesson, pp. 316, 322	**TEACHER'S EDITION** • Grammar Jammer **ELL HANDBOOK** • Grammar Transition Lesson, pp. 316, 322
TEACHER'S EDITION • Let's Write It!, p. 250–251 • Free Verse, pp. 251a–251b	**TEACHER'S EDITION** • Free Verse, pp. 255d–255e	**TEACHER'S EDITION** • Editing and Presenting, pp. 255p–255q

Question of the Week
What can teams accomplish?

Throughout the week, use the ELL Poster to help students produce and comprehend language, understand the concept, and build English vocabulary. Use the Question of the Week and other questions to help students share ideas in pairs, small groups, or the large group. Sample questions are shown, with examples of possible responses by students.

E L L Poster 8

Weekly Concept and Language Goals

- Identify what obstacles are
- Recognize obstacles that can stand in the way of teamwork
- Tell ways in which some obstacles, such as disagreements, can be overcome

By the end of the lesson, students should be able to talk about and write sentences about team accomplishments.

Daily Team Talk

Day 1	Day 2	Day 3	Day 4	Day 5
After Day 1 activities on Poster, ask questions such as	After Day 2 activity on Poster, ask questions such as	After Day 3 activity on Poster, ask questions such as	After Day 4 activity on Poster, ask questions such as	After Day 5 activity on Poster, ask questions such as
What obstacles do the students in the poster picture face as they get ready to put on a play?	*Why can arguments between students make putting on the play together difficult?*	*In the poster picture, the girl wants the boy to repaint the scenery, but he does not want to. How can they overcome this obstacle?*	*In the poster picture, the girl talking to her teacher is nervous about being in the play. How are they working together to overcome this obstacle?*	*Imagine you and your classmates are putting on a play. You cannot remember your lines. How can teamwork help you overcome this obstacle?*
Beginning They fight. **Intermediate** They are fighting. They are scared. **Advanced** Some students are fighting. Some are still learning their lines for the play. **Advanced High** Two of the students are arguing about something. Two other students are still learning their lines. One student looks unhappy and scared.	**Beginning** They can't work. **Intermediate** They cannot get their work done when they fight. **Advanced** If the students are fighting, they cannot finish their work for the play. **Advanced High** The students who are fighting are not working together so they will not be able to finish their work and put on the play.	**Beginning** She can help. **Intermediate** She can help him paint it. **Advanced** He might repaint the scenery if she will help him do it. **Advanced High** The boy and girl can work together to repaint the scenery. The work will be done much faster if they work together.	**Beginning** Her teacher helps. **Intermediate** Her teacher talks to her about it. **Advanced** Her teacher is talking to her about how to feel less nervous. **Advanced High** Her teacher is giving the girl advice on how to overcome being nervous.	**Beginning** Friends can help. **Intermediate** They can help me learn the lines. **Advanced** My classmates can help me learn my lines for the play. **Advanced High** My classmates can help me by practicing my lines with me until I have learned them.

This Week's Materials

 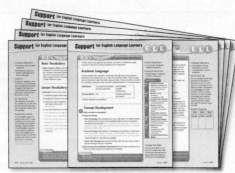 

Teacher's Edition pages 228j–255q

Teacher's Edition pages DI•66–DI•75

ELL Handbook pp. 71a–76

See the support for English language learners throughout the lesson, including ELL strategies and scaffolded activities at points of use.

Differentiated Instruction for English language learners provides daily group activities that "frontload," or preteach, core instruction.

Find additional lesson materials that support the core lesson and the ELL instructional pages.

Poster 8

ELL Reader 4.2.3

ELD Reader 4.2.3

Concept Literacy Reader

ELD, ELL Reader
Teaching Guide

Concept Literacy Reader
Teaching Guide

Technology

Online Teacher's Edition Use the digital version of the core Teacher's Edition for planning and instruction.

eReaders
This week's ELL and ELD Readers and Concept Literacy Reader are also available in digital format.

This Week's Content and Language Objectives by Strand

Concept Development/ Academic Language What can teams accomplish?	**Content Objective** • Use concept vocabulary related to teamwork. **Language Objectives** • Express ideas in response to art and discussion. • Learn and use new academic vocabulary.
Phonics and Spelling Words with *ar, or*	**Content Objective** • Identify words with *r*-controlled vowels. **Language Objectives** • Apply phonics and decoding skills to vocabulary. • Speak using *r*-controlled vowels.
Listening Comprehension Modified Read Aloud: "Teamwork with Taste"	**Content Objective** • Monitor and adjust oral comprehension. **Language Objectives** • Discuss oral passages to learn new and essential language. • Use a graphic organizer to take notes.
Reading Comprehension Draw Conclusions	**Content Objectives** • Draw conclusions from text. • Monitor and adjust comprehension. **Language Objectives** • Use visual support to discuss facts and details for drawing conclusions. • Use visual support to write conclusions based on text.
Vocabulary Basic and Lesson Vocabulary	**Language Objectives** • Understand and use basic vocabulary. • Use linguistic support to confirm understanding of spoken language. • Use strategic learning techniques to acquire understanding of Lesson Vocabulary.
Word Analysis Latin Prefixes *dis-, re-, non-*	**Content Objective** • Identify and define prefixes in words. **Language Objective** • Discuss meanings of words with prefixes.
Grammar and Conventions Irregular Plural Nouns	**Content Objective** • Identify and use irregular plural nouns. **Language Objectives** • Work with a partner to give feedback. • Write phrases and sentences with irregular plural nouns.
Writing Figurative Language	**Content Objective** • Identify elements of figurative language in text. **Language Objectives** • Write using figurative language. • Write with increasing specificity and detail.

Word Cards for Vocabulary Activities

advice

argument

arrangements

descendants

dishonest

script

snag

Teacher Note: Beginning Teach three to four words. **Intermediate** Teach four to six words. **Advanced** Teach six to seven words. **Advanced High** Teach all words.

Name _____

Look at the pictures. **Read** the scenes.

- How do Denya, Jamal, and Alisha work together? Draw a conclusion. **Write** it in the *Conclusion* box below.

- What facts and details help you make that conclusion? **Write** facts and details in the *Facts* and *Details* boxes below.

The Time Machine

Denya: Jamal and Alisha. Come here! Do you want to travel back in time?

Jamal and Alisha: Okay!

Denya: Oh, no! I think that the machine doesn't work.

Alisha: I think that I can help.

Alisha: You have to press this button.

Denya: That doesn't seem to work either.

Jamal: You need to plug in the machine!

Denya and Alisha: Thanks, Jamal! Let's go to your first birthday party.

Jamal: Is that me? I look so little!

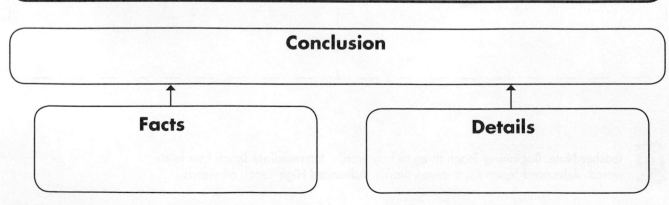

Conclusion

Facts

Details

Draw Conclusions

Use this lesson to supplement or replace the skill lesson on page 229c of the Teacher's Edition. Display the Skill Points (at right) and share them with students.

Teach/Model

Beginning Say and pantomime: *I am in a theater. People are clapping. The actors on the stage are bowing. What conclusions can you draw?* (You saw a play. The play just ended. The audience liked the play.) *What words are clues that helped you draw your conclusions?* (theater, clapping, actors, stage, bowing)

Intermediate Say: *Actors get flowers at the end of the first performance of a play. Elly gets flowers after her play on Friday night. What conclusion can you draw?* (The play's first performance was on Friday night.) *How do the details support your conclusion?*

Advanced Say: *Randy is the lead in the play. Tonight is his first performance. He looks out and sees the audience. He gulps and his hands start to shake. What conclusion can you draw?* (Randy is nervous and scared.) Have students explain how they used what they already know to draw that conclusion.

Advanced High Discuss with students what a director does for a play. Ask: *What conclusions can you draw about the kinds of skills a director needs?* (Possible answers: A director needs to be a leader. A director has to know about plays.) Ask students to explain how they drew that conclusion.

Then distribute copies of Picture It! page 72.

- Have students look at the pictures and tell what is happening.
- Read the scenes aloud. Ask: *How do the children visit the past?* (by watching videos of themselves when they were younger)
- Review the Skill Points with students.
- Have students find the details that support their conclusion.

Practice

Read aloud the directions on page 72. Have three volunteers read the parts of the play. Explain to students what a VCR is and how it works. Have students use the pictures and the story as they fill in the boxes.

Beginning Students can say what their conclusion, facts, and details are before they write their answers in the boxes. Provide help with English words and writing.

Intermediate Students can first orally answer and then write their answers in the boxes of the graphic organizer.

Advanced Students can write their answers to complete the graphic organizer and then check them by discussing them with a partner.

Advanced High Students can write their answers to complete the graphic organizer and then orally explain how they used what they know and what they read to draw their conclusion.

Answers for page 72: *Conclusion:* They work together to make the VCR work. *Facts:* Jamal suggests plugging in the VCR. *Details:* Alisha suggests pressing a button on the VCR.

Skill Points

✔ When you **draw a conclusion,** you form an idea based on what you already know and on the facts and details in a text.

✔ Details should support any conclusion you or the author draws.

Multilingual Summaries

Scene Two

Mitch, Jasmine, Hap, Angie, Kerry, and Delores are writing a script for the Founder's Day talent show. Their script is about their town's history. They have finished Scene One. Mitch, Jasmine, and Hap all write a separate Scene Two.

Jasmine reads her scene. Her scene is historically accurate and is about the town's founding fathers. Mitch reads his scene. It is not based completely on history, but it is entertaining. Mitch and Jasmine argue.

Angie tells them they have to listen to each other. Jasmine wants to bring history alive. Mitch wants people to be entertained. They decide to use both scenes and explain to the audience that Mitch's story is probably untrue.

Spanish

Escena dos

Mitch, Jasmine, Hap, Angie, Kerry y Delores están escribiendo el guión para el espectáculo de talentos del Día de los Fundadores. El guión es sobre la historia de su propio pueblo. Ellos ya terminaron la Escena uno. Mitch, Jasmine, y Hap están escribiendo la Escena dos, por separado.

Jasmine lee su escena. La escena debe ser históricamente exacta y trata sobre los fundadores de su pueblo. Mitch lee su escena. No está basada completamente en la historia verdadera, pero es entretenida. Mitch y Jasmine discuten.

Angie les sugiere que se escuchen el uno al otro. Jasmine quiere revivir la historia. Mitch quiere que las personas se diviertan. Ellos deciden usar ambas escenas y le explican al público que las escenas de Mitch tal vez no sea cierta.

Multilingual Summaries

Chinese

第二幕劇本

米契、潔思明、哈普、安琪、凱立和迪羅斯正在為鎮慶才藝表演寫劇本。 他們的劇本講的是這個鎮的歷史。 他們已經寫好了第一幕。米契、潔思明和哈普三個人將各自寫一份第二幕劇本。

潔思明讀著自己寫的第二幕劇本。 她的第二幕劇本完全符合史實，描寫了創鎮者的故事。 米契讀著自己寫的第二幕劇本。 他的第二幕劇本並非完全符合史實，但是很有娛樂效果。 米契和潔思明彼此爭論起來。

安琪告訴他們兩個，他們必須聽聽彼此的看法。 潔思明希望讓歷史重現， 而米契則希望能讓觀眾得到娛樂。 他們最後決定兩個第二幕的劇本都用，並向觀眾說明米契的故事很可能並不真實。

Vietnamese

Màn Hai

Mitch, Jasmine, Hap, Angie, Kerry, và Delores đang viết kịch bản cho ngày Trình Diễn Tài Năng của Người Sáng Lập. Kịch bản nói về lịch sử thành phố của họ ở. Họ đã viết xong màn một. Mitch, Jasmine, và Hap viết riêng Màn Hai.

Jasmine đọc màn kịch của cô. Màn kịch này có lịch sử chính xác và nói về các vị cha sáng lập thành phố. Mitch đọc màn kịch của nó. Nó không dựa hoàn toàn vào lịch sử, nhưng màn kịch đó hay. Mitch và Jasmine tranh luận nhau.

Angie cho biết hai người cần lắng nghe lẫn nhau. Jasmine thì muốn cho lịch sử sống động. Còn Mitch thì muốn mọi người được giải trí vui. Họ quyết định dùng cả hai màn kịch và giải thích cho khán giả rằng chuyện của Mitch có thể không là thật.

Multilingual Summaries

장면 2

미치, 쟈스민, 햅, 앤지, 케리와 델로어는 창립자의 날 탤런트쇼를 위한 대본을 쓰고 있다. 대본은 마을 역사에 관한 것이다. 그들은 장면 1을 끝냈다. 미치와 쟈스민과 햅은 모두 서로 다른 장면 2를 쓴다.

쟈스민이 자신의 장면을 읽는다. 그녀가 쓴 장면은 역사적으로 정확하며 마을의 창립자에 관한 것이다. 미치가 자신의 장면을 읽는다. 그것은 역사에 바탕을 둔 것이 아니지만 재미있다. 미치와 쟈스민이 논쟁한다.

앤지가 그들에게 서로 귀 기울여야 한다고 말한다. 쟈스민은 역사를 생생하게 쓰고 싶다. 미치는 사람들을 즐겁게 하고 싶다. 그들은 두 장면을 모두 사용한 후 관중에게 미치의 이야기는 사실이 아닐 수 있다고 설명해주기로 한다.

Kas Xabdia Zaum 2

Mitch, Jasmine, Hap, Angie, Kerry, thiab Delores tab tom sau cov lus xabdia rau zaj dab neeg Founder's Day. Lawv zaj dab neeg no yog hais txog lub zos no li dab neeg. Lawv twb sau task as xabdia Zaum 1 tas lawm. Mitch, Jasmine, thiab Hap txhua tus sau qhov sib txawv rau Kas Xabdia Zaum 2 no.

Jasmine nyeem qhov nws yuav ua. Qhov nws yuav ua no yog qhov tseeb thiab nws ua txog cov neeg tsim tsa lub zos no tiag. Mitch ho nyeem nws qhov. Nws kuj yuav yog tas nro txog lub zos li dab neeg, tabsis nws yeej yog kev lom zem. Mitch thiab Jasmine sib cav li ntawd.

Angie hais kom lawv mloog saib leej twg zaj yog. Jasmine xav ua kom zaj dab neeg ciaj sia los. Mitch xav kom cov neeg tuaj saib los tau kev lom zem nrog. Lawv txiav txim siab yuav ob leeg zaj tib si thiab qhia rau cov neeg tuaj saib hais tias qhov Mitch ua kuj yuav tsis yog tseeb tas tib si.

- **Read** *Teamwork* again.
- Use the information in the story to **answer** the questions below.

---

pages 2–3

1. Why do you think that John Buck is listening to his coach?

_____

2. Is Coach Phillips a good coach? Why do you think so?

_____

_____

---

pages 4–5

3. Why are the Cougar fans excited?

_____

---

pages 6–8

4. How do you know that John Buck is the best player on the team?

_____

5. Why do you think that John Buck is happy?

_____

_____

Family Link

Ask family members if they enjoy watching soccer. Have them describe a soccer game they have seen. Did their favorite team win or lose?

Weekly Resources Guide for English Language Learner Support

For this week's content and language objectives, see p. 77e.

Instructional Strand	Day 1	Day 2
Concept Development/Academic Language	**TEACHER'S EDITION** • Academic Language, p. DI•91 • Concept Development, p. DI•91 • Anchored Talk, pp. 256j—256–257 • Preteach Academic Vocabulary, p. 259a • Concept Talk Video **ELL HANDBOOK** • Hear It, See It, Say It, Use It, pp. xxxvi–xxxvii • ELL Poster Talk, Concept Talk, p. 77c **ELL POSTER 9** • Day 1 Activities	**TEACHER'S EDITION** • Academic Language, p. DI•91 • Concept Development, p. DI•91 • Anchored Talk, p. 260a • Concept Talk Video **ELL HANDBOOK** • ELL Poster Talk, Concept Talk, p. 77c • Concept Talk Video Routine, p. 477 **ELL POSTER 9** • Day 2 Activities
Phonics and Spelling	**TEACHER'S EDITION** • Phonics and Spelling, p. DI•95	**TEACHER'S EDITION** • Phonics and Spelling, p. DI•95
Listening Comprehension	**TEACHER'S EDITION** • Modified Read Aloud, p. DI•94 • Read Aloud, p. 257b • Concept Talk Video **ELL HANDBOOK** • Concept Talk Video Routine, p. 477	**TEACHER'S EDITION** • Modified Read Aloud, p. DI•94 • AudioText of *Horse Heroes* • Concept Talk Video **ELL HANDBOOK** • AudioText CD Routine, p. 477 • K-W-L Chart, p. 480
Reading Comprehension	**TEACHER'S EDITION** • Preteach Fact and Opinion, p. DI•96	**TEACHER'S EDITION** • Reteach Fact and Opinion, p. DI•96 • Frontloading Reading, p. DI•97 **ELL HANDBOOK** • Picture It! Skill Instruction, pp. 78–78a • Multilingual Summaries, pp. 79–81
Vocabulary **Basic and Lesson Vocabulary** **Word Analysis: Compound Words**	**TEACHER'S EDITION** • Basic Vocabulary, p. DI•92 • Preteach Lesson Vocabulary, p. DI•92 • Compound Words, p. DI•95 **ELL HANDBOOK** • Word Cards, p. 77 • ELL Vocabulary Routine, p. 471 **ELL POSTER 9** • Day 1 Activities	**TEACHER'S EDITION** • Basic Vocabulary, p. DI•92 • Reteach Lesson Vocabulary, p. DI•93 • Compound Words, p. DI•95 **ELL HANDBOOK** • Word Cards, p. 77 • Multilingual Vocabulary List, p. 431 **ELL POSTER 9** • Day 2 Activities
Grammar and Conventions	**TEACHER'S EDITION** • Preteach Singular Possessive Nouns, p. DI•99	**TEACHER'S EDITION** • Reteach Singular Possessive Nouns, p. DI•99
Writing	**TEACHER'S EDITION** • Topic Sentences, p. DI•100 • Introduce Expository Composition, pp. 259e–259f	**TEACHER'S EDITION** • Writing Trait: Organization, pp. 267d–267e

This symbol indicates leveled instruction to address language proficiency levels.

Day 3	Day 4	Day 5
TEACHER'S EDITION • Academic Language, p. DI•91 • Concept Development, p. DI•91 • Anchored Talk, p. 268a • Concept Talk Video ELL HANDBOOK • ELL Poster Talk, Concept Talk, p. 77c ELL POSTER 9 • Day 3 Activities	TEACHER'S EDITION • Academic Language, p. DI•91 • Concept Development, p. DI•91 • Anchored Talk, p. 278a • Concept Talk Video ELL HANDBOOK • ELL Poster Talk, Concept Talk, p. 77c ELL POSTER 9 • Day 4 Activities	TEACHER'S EDITION • Academic Language, p. DI•91 • Concept Development, p. DI•91 • Concept Talk Video ELL HANDBOOK • ELL Poster Talk, Concept Talk, p. 77c ELL POSTER 9 • Day 5 Activities
		TEACHER'S EDITION • Phonics and Spelling, p. DI•95
ELL HANDBOOK • Phonics Transition Lesson, pp. 240–243	ELL HANDBOOK • Phonics Transition Lesson, pp. 240–243	
TEACHER'S EDITION • AudioText of *Horse Heroes* • Concept Talk Video ELL HANDBOOK • AudioText CD Routine, p. 477	TEACHER'S EDITION • Concept Talk Video	TEACHER'S EDITION • Concept Talk Video
TEACHER'S EDITION • Sheltered Reading, p. DI•97 ELL HANDBOOK • Multilingual Summaries, pp. 79–81	TEACHER'S EDITION • ELL/ELD Reader Guided Reading, p. DI•98 ELL HANDBOOK • ELL Study Guide, p. 82	TEACHER'S EDITION • ELL/ELD Reader Guided Reading, p. DI•98 ELL HANDBOOK • ELL Study Guide, p. 82
		TEACHER'S EDITION • Compound Words, p. 283i
ELL HANDBOOK • High-Frequency Words Activity Bank, p. 446 ELL POSTER 9 • Day 3 Activities	ELL HANDBOOK • High-Frequency Words Activity Bank, p. 446	ELL HANDBOOK • High-Frequency Words Activity Bank, p. 446
TEACHER'S EDITION • Grammar Jammer ELL HANDBOOK • Grammar Transition Lesson, pp. 317, 323 • Grammar Jammer Routine, p. 478	TEACHER'S EDITION • Grammar Jammer ELL HANDBOOK • Grammar Transition Lesson, pp. 317, 323	TEACHER'S EDITION • Grammar Jammer ELL HANDBOOK • Grammar Transition Lesson, pp. 317, 323
TEACHER'S EDITION • Let's Write It!, p. 276–277 • Writer's Craft: Topic Sentences, pp. 277a–277b	TEACHER'S EDITION • Revising Strategy, pp. 283d–283e	TEACHER'S EDITION • Possessive Nouns, pp. 283p–283q

Question of the Week
How can people and animals work as a team?

Throughout the week, use the ELL Poster to help students produce and comprehend language, understand the concept, and build English vocabulary. Use the Question of the Week and other questions to help students share ideas in pairs, small groups, or the large group. Sample questions are shown, with examples of possible responses by students.

ELL Poster 9

Weekly Concept and Language Goals

- Tell how trained animals can help people live and work
- Explain how animals can help people overcome obstacles
- Recognize that animals can help people on the job

By the end of the lesson, students should be able to talk about and write sentences about service animals.

Daily Team Talk

Day 1	Day 2	Day 3	Day 4	Day 5
After Day 1 activities on Poster, ask questions such as *In the poster picture, which animals are helping people, and which are not?*	After Day 2 activity on Poster, ask questions such as *What obstacle do you think the dog can help the pioneers overcome?*	After Day 3 activity on Poster, ask questions such as *The farmer wants to plant crops, but the ground is hard and rocky. How do the oxen help him overcome this obstacle?*	After Day 4 activity on Poster, ask questions such as *In the story* Horse Heroes, *how did horses and people work together to accomplish something in the past?*	After Day 5 activity on Poster, ask questions such as *What is a job people have today that animals help them with?*
Beginning The horses help. **Intermediate** The horses and oxen help. The bird does not. **Advanced** The horses and the oxen are helping people, but the birds are not. **Advanced High** The horses and the oxen are helping people by pulling the wagon and the plow. The birds and the buffalo are not helping people in this picture.	**Beginning** Protect them. **Intermediate** It can bark when wild animals get too close. **Advanced** The dog can keep wild animals away from the pioneers. **Advanced High** The dog can protect the pioneers and the horses from wild animals.	**Beginning** They pull it. **Intermediate** They pull the plow. **Advanced** The oxen pull the plow through the ground to get the soil ready. **Advanced High** The oxen help the farmer by pulling the plow through the hard ground. This breaks the soil and gets it ready for planting.	**Beginning** They got mail. **Intermediate** They took mail across the country. **Advanced** Horses and people rode across the country together to deliver mail. **Advanced High** Horses and people worked together to travel quickly across the country and deliver mail.	**Beginning** Police use dogs. **Intermediate** The police use dogs to help them. **Advanced** Police officers have dogs that help them find things. **Advanced High** Dogs are good at tracking smells. The police use dogs when they need help finding things.

This Week's Materials

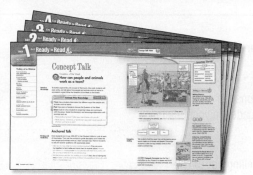

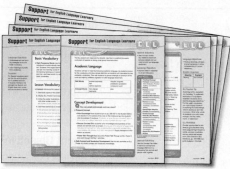

Teacher's Edition pages 256j–283q

Teacher's Edition pages DI•91–DI•100

ELL Handbook pp. 77a–82

See the support for English language learners throughout the lesson, including ELL strategies and scaffolded activities at points of use.

Differentiated Instruction for English language learners provides daily group activities that "frontload," or preteach, core instruction.

Find additional lesson materials that support the core lesson and the ELL instructional pages.

Poster 9

ELL Reader 4.2.4

ELD Reader 4.2.4

Concept Literacy Reader

ELD, ELL Reader
Teaching Guide

Concept Literacy Reader
Teaching Guide

Technology

Online Teacher's Edition Use the digital version of the core Teacher's Edition for planning and instruction.

eReaders
This week's ELL and ELD Readers and Concept Literacy Reader are also available in digital format.

This Week's Content and Language Objectives by Strand

Concept Development/ Academic Language How can people and animals work as a team?	**Content Objective** • Use concept vocabulary related to teamwork between people and animals. **Language Objectives** • Express ideas in response to art and discussion. • Learn and use new academic vocabulary.
Phonics and Spelling Words Consonant Patterns *ng, nk, wh*	**Content Objective** • Review consonant spelling patterns. **Language Objectives** • Apply phonics and decoding skills to vocabulary. • Write using spelling patterns *ng, nk, wh.*
Listening Comprehension Modified Read Aloud: "To the Rescue"	**Content Objective** • Monitor and adjust oral comprehension. **Language Objectives** • Discuss oral passages to learn new and essential language. • Use a graphic organizer to take notes.
Reading Comprehension Fact and Opinion	**Content Objectives** • Distinguish between facts and opinions. • Monitor and adjust comprehension. **Language Objectives** • Discuss evidence for facts and opinions. • Retell facts and opinions from a reading. • Write facts and opinions from personal experience.
Vocabulary Basic and Lesson Vocabulary	**Language Objectives** • Understand and use learning strategies to acquire basic vocabulary. • Learn meanings of grade-level vocabulary. • Produce drawings, phrases, or short sentences to show understanding of Lesson Vocabulary.
Word Analysis Compound Words	**Content Objective** • Identify and define words in compound words. **Language Objective** • Discuss meanings of compound words.
Grammar and Conventions Singular Possessive Nouns	**Content Objective** • Decode and use singular possessive nouns. **Language Objectives** • Speak using the pattern of singular possessive nouns. • Write phrases and sentences with singular possessive nouns.
Writing Writing Topic Sentences	**Content Objective** • Identify the topic sentence and details in a text. **Language Objectives** • Write descriptive paragraphs using a topic sentence and details. • Share feedback for editing and revising.

Word Cards for Vocabulary Activities

ambition

infested

landslide

quicksand

resistance

rickety

roamed

vast

Teacher Note: Beginning Teach three to four words. **Intermediate** Teach four to six words. **Advanced** Teach six to seven words. **Advanced High** Teach all words.

Name _____

Read Together

Look at the picture. **Read** the paragraph.

• **Read** each sentence below the paragraph. **Put a check** to show whether it is a fact or an opinion.

Special Dogs

There are special dogs that help people. I think that they are more than pets. Some dogs can help people who can't walk. Other dogs help people who can't talk. There are even dogs that let people know when there is a fire. Some dog owners take their dogs to hospitals and nursing homes. These dogs make someone who is sick feel better. In my opinion, these dogs are the most helpful animals in the world!

1. There are special dogs that help people.

Fact _____ Opinion _____

2. I think that they are more than pets.

Fact _____ Opinion _____

3. There are even dogs that let people know when there is a fire.

Fact _____ Opinion _____

4. Some dog owners take their dogs to hospitals and nursing homes.

Fact _____ Opinion _____

5. In my opinion, these dogs are the most helpful animals in the world!

Fact _____ Opinion _____

Fact and Opinion

Use this lesson to supplement or replace the skill lesson on page 257c of the Teacher's Edition. Display the Skill Points (at right) and share them with students.

Teach/Model

Beginning Display a photo of a giraffe. Write and read aloud: *Giraffes are interesting animals. Is this a fact or an opinion?* (an opinion) *How do you know?* (It tells what someone thinks. *Interesting* is a clue word.) Have students use the picture to tell you a fact to write about giraffes. (Possible answer: Giraffes have long necks.)

Intermediate Say: *I have a pet goldfish. A goldfish is a great pet because it is easy to take care of. Which sentence is a fact? Which sentence is an opinion?* Ask students to explain how they decided which is fact and which is opinion.

Advanced Pair students. Have one partner tell a fact and an opinion about any animal. The other partner identifies the fact and the opinion and explains how he or she decided. Then the partners trade roles.

Advanced High Ask each student to choose an animal and use reference materials or background knowledge to write two facts about the animal. Have students write a three-sentence report that uses the facts and includes their opinion.

Then distribute copies of Picture It! page 78.

- Have students read the title and look at the picture. Then read the paragraph aloud.
- Ask: *What words are clues that the author is expressing an opinion?* (I think, in my opinion, most helpful)
- Review the Skill Points with students.
- Have students first identify all the facts in the paragraph and then identify all the opinions.

Practice

Read aloud the directions on page 78. Have students reread the paragraph silently. Then have them use the picture and the paragraph as they mark their answers.

Beginning Students can say whether they think each sentence is a fact or an opinion before they put checks by their answers. Provide help with making and placing checks correctly.

Intermediate Students can first orally answer whether each sentence is a fact or an opinion and then put checks by their answers on the page.

Advanced Students can put checks by their answers and then discuss their answers with a partner and see if they want to make any changes.

Advanced High Students can put checks by their answers and then orally explain their answers by pointing out clue words or other details that helped them choose.

Answers for page 78: 1. fact; 2. opinion; 3. fact; 4. fact; 5. opinion

---

Skill Points

✔ A **fact** tells something that can be proven true or false. To prove a fact, you can look in a book, check the Internet, or ask an expert.

✔ An **opinion** tells what someone thinks or believes. Clue words that indicate an opinion include *best, should, beautiful, fun,* and *like.*

Multilingual Summaries

Horse Heroes

In 1860, the Pony Express began delivering the mail. It was a horse relay for the mail. It was a dangerous job. There were attacks and bad weather. The riders insisted that the mail must get through.

In 1925, Tschiffely, with his two horses Gato and Mancha, became the first man ever to ride from Buenos Aires, Argentina, to Washington, D.C. Both horses helped save Tschiffely's life during the journey. He set the horses free after their journey.

In 1938, a horse named Golden Cloud made his movie debut. He became the horse used in the Roy Rogers western movies. He was renamed Trigger. He loved the camera and knew many tricks. Trigger died in 1965.

Spanish

Caballos héroes

En 1860, el Pony Express comenzó a entregar el correo. Era un carrera de relevos a caballo para llevar la correspondencia. Esta labor era peligrosa. Había bandidos y el clima era malo. Pero los jinetes insistían en que el correo debía llegar.

En 1925, Tschiffely, con sus dos caballos Gato y Mancha, se convirtió en el primer hombre en cabalgar desde Buenos Aires, Argentina hasta Washington, D.C. Ambos caballos ayudaron a salvar la vida de Tschiffely durante la jornada. Después de esta hazaña, él liberó a los caballos.

En 1938, un caballo llamado Golden Cloud hizo su debut en el cine. Este se convirtió en el caballo utilizado en las películas del viejo oeste de Roy Rogers. Luego cambiaron su nombre a Trigger, él adoraba las cámaras y sabía hacer varios trucos. Trigger murió en 1965.

Multilingual Summaries

Chinese

騎馬的英雄

1860 年時，快馬郵遞就開始提供郵件遞送服務。 那時候是以騎馬接力的方式遞送郵件。 這是一份危險的差事， 騎士可能會遭到攻擊或遇上惡劣的天氣。 不過，騎士卻堅持要把郵件送達。

1925 年時，史福利帶著他的兩匹馬（加圖和曼恰）成為第一個從阿根廷的布宜諾斯艾利斯一路騎馬抵達華盛頓特區的人。這兩匹馬在路上幫助救了史福利的命。 完成任務後，他放走了這兩匹馬。

1938 年，一匹名為「黃金雲朵」的馬拍攝了牠的第一部電影。 後來在 Roy Rogers 西部片中也使用了這匹馬。 牠被改名為「扳機」。牠喜歡面對鏡頭，而且還知道許多表演技巧。 「扳機」在 1965 年過世。

Vietnamese

Những Con Ngựa Anh Hùng

Trong năm 1860 hãng Pony Express bắt đầu công việc đưa thơ. Đây là một công việc gởi thơ dựa vào con ngựa. Một việc làm nguy hiểm. Có lúc bị tấn công và đôi khi gặp thời tiết xấu. Người đem thơ cố gắng trao thơ đến tận nơi.

Trong năm 1925, Tschiffely, cùng với hai con ngựa Gato và Mancha, trở thành người đầu tiên cởi ngựa từ Buenos Aires, Á Can Đình (Argentina) đến Hoa Thịnh Đốn (Washington), D.C. Cả hai con ngựa đã cứu Tschiffely trong cuộc hành trình. Ông thả chúng tự do sau đó.

Trong năm 1938 một con ngựa tên Golden Cloud bắt đầu cuộc đời trong một cuốn phim. Nó trở thành con ngựa được đóng trong các phim cao bồi của Roy Rogers. Nó được đổi tên là Trigger. Nó thích quay phim và biết làm nhiều trò. Trigger chết năm 1965.

Multilingual Summaries

Korean

말 영웅들

1860년에 조랑말 속달우편이 우편물을 배달하기 시작했다. 이것은 우편물 배달을 위한 말들의 릴레이였는데, 위험한 일이었다. 습격을 받기도 했고 날씨가 나빠지기도 했다.

1925년에 치펠리는 가토와 만차라는 말 두 마리와 함께 아르헨티나의 부에노스 아이레스에서 워싱턴 디시로 가는 최초의 사람이 되었다. 두 마리의 말은 여행 도중 치펠리의 생명을 구했다. 여행이 끝난 후 그는 말 두 마리를 놓아주었다.

1938년에 골든 클라우드라는 이름의 말이 영화에 데뷔했다. 그 말은 로이 로저스의 서부영화에 나오게 되었다. 말에게 트리거라는 새 이름이 생겼다. 그 말은 카메라를 사랑했으며 수많은 요령을 알았다. 트리거는 1965년에 사망했다.

Hmong

Nee Phaib Ej

Nyob rau xyoo 1860 qhov hu ua Pony Express pib xa ntawv. Nws yogib tug nee siv los xa ntawv. Nws yog txoj hauj lwm kas das kawg. Muaj neeg tos kev tua thiab huav cua phem. Tus neeg caij nee mas phaj hais tias xa kom tau ntawv xwb xwb.

Nyob rau xyoo 1925, Tschiffely, nrog rau nws ob tug nee phaib ej hu ua Gato thiab Mancha, yog thawj tus neeg uas caij nee nram Buenos Aires, Argentina mus txog Washington, D.C. Ob tug nee pas cawm tau yawg Tschiffely txoj sia nyob rau zaum ntawd. Nws tso nws ob tug nee mus dawb mus do thaum lawv mus txog chaw lawm.

Nyob rau xyoo 1938 muaj ib tug nee hu ua Golden Cloud tau ua xis nes mas zaj deb neeg no. Nws yog tus nee uas raug siv los nrog Roy Rogers ua cov xis nes mas sab hnub poob no. Nws raug tis lub npe tshiab hu uaTrigger. Nws nyiam koob thaij duab thiab nws paub ua ntau yam. Tus neeg Trigger tuag xyoo 1965.

Name _____

- **Read** *Dogs With Jobs* again.
- Use the information in the book. **Write** facts and opinions in the chart. The first row has been done.
- In the fact column, **write** three more facts from the book. In the opinion column, **write** three opinions of your own based on the information in the book.

Fact	Opinion
Today most dogs are pets.	I think that dogs make great pets.
1.	
2.	
3.	

Family Link
Does anyone in your family have a pet dog? Ask family members to talk about any jobs their dog may have.

Weekly Resources Guide for English Language Learner Support

For this week's content and language objectives, see p. 83e.

Instructional Strand	Day 1	Day 2
Concept Development/Academic Language	**TEACHER'S EDITION** • Academic Language, p. DI•116 • Concept Development, p. DI•116 • Anchored Talk, pp. 284j—284–285 • Preteach Academic Vocabulary, p. 287a • Concept Talk Video **ELL HANDBOOK** • Hear It, See It, Say It, Use It, pp. xxxvi–xxxvii • ELL Poster Talk, Concept Talk, p. 83c **ELL POSTER 10** • Day 1 Activities	**TEACHER'S EDITION** • Academic Language, p. DI•116 • Concept Development, p. DI•116 • Anchored Talk, p. 288a • Concept Talk Video **ELL HANDBOOK** • ELL Poster Talk, Concept Talk, p. 83c • Concept Talk Video Routine, p. 477 **ELL POSTER 10** • Day 2 Activities
Phonics and Spelling	**TEACHER'S EDITION** • Phonics and Spelling, p. DI•120	**TEACHER'S EDITION** • Phonics and Spelling, p. DI•120
Listening Comprehension	**TEACHER'S EDITION** • Modified Read Aloud, p. DI•119 • Read Aloud, p. 285b • Concept Talk Video **ELL HANDBOOK** • Concept Talk Video Routine, p. 477	**TEACHER'S EDITION** • Modified Read Aloud, p. DI•119 • AudioText of *So You Want to Be President?* • Concept Talk Video **ELL HANDBOOK** • AudioText CD Routine, p. 477 • K-W-L Chart, p. 480
Reading Comprehension	**TEACHER'S EDITION** • Preteach Main Idea and Details, p. DI•121	**TEACHER'S EDITION** • Reteach Main Idea and Details, p. DI•121 • Frontloading Reading, p. DI•122 **ELL HANDBOOK** • Picture It! Skill Instruction, pp. 84–84a • Multilingual Summaries, pp. 85–87
Vocabulary **Basic and Lesson Vocabulary** **Word Analysis: Suffix -ly**	**TEACHER'S EDITION** • Basic Vocabulary, p. DI•117 • Preteach Lesson Vocabulary, p. DI•117 • Suffix -ly, p. DI•120 **ELL HANDBOOK** • Word Cards, p. 83 • ELL Vocabulary Routine, p. 471 **ELL POSTER 10** • Day 1 Activities	**TEACHER'S EDITION** • Basic Vocabulary, p. DI•117 • Reteach Lesson Vocabulary, p. DI•118 • Suffix -ly, p. DI•120 **ELL HANDBOOK** • Word Cards, p. 83 • Multilingual Vocabulary List, p. 431 **ELL POSTER 10** • Day 2 Activities
Grammar and Conventions	**TEACHER'S EDITION** • Preteach Plural Possessive Nouns, p. DI•124	**TEACHER'S EDITION** • Reteach Plural Possessive Nouns, p. DI•124
Writing	**TEACHER'S EDITION** • Transitions, p. DI•125 • Writing for Tests: Persuasive Essay, pp. 287e–287f	**TEACHER'S EDITION** • Writing for Tests: Persuasive Essay, pp. 297d–297e

Unit 2 Week 5   *So You Want to Be President?*

Day 3	Day 4	Day 5
TEACHER'S EDITION • Academic Language, p. DI•116 • Concept Development, p. DI•116 • Anchored Talk, p. 298a • Concept Talk Video **ELL HANDBOOK** • ELL Poster Talk, Concept Talk, p. 83c **ELL POSTER 10** • Day 3 Activities	**TEACHER'S EDITION** • Academic Language, p. DI•116 • Concept Development, p. DI•116 • Anchored Talk, p. 306a • Concept Talk Video **ELL HANDBOOK** • ELL Poster Talk, Concept Talk, p. 83c **ELL POSTER 10** • Day 4 Activities	**TEACHER'S EDITION** • Academic Language, p. DI•116 • Concept Development, p. DI•116 • Concept Talk Video **ELL HANDBOOK** • ELL Poster Talk, Concept Talk, p. 83c **ELL POSTER 10** • Day 5 Activities
		TEACHER'S EDITION • Phonics and Spelling, p. DI•120
ELL HANDBOOK • Phonics Transition Lesson, pp. 263, 265	**ELL HANDBOOK** • Phonics Transition Lesson, pp. 263, 265	
TEACHER'S EDITION • AudioText of *So You Want to Be President?* • Concept Talk Video **ELL HANDBOOK** • AudioText CD Routine, p. 477	**TEACHER'S EDITION** • Concept Talk Video	**TEACHER'S EDITION** • Concept Talk Video
TEACHER'S EDITION • Sheltered Reading, p. DI•122 **ELL HANDBOOK** • Multilingual Summaries, pp. 85–87	**TEACHER'S EDITION** • ELL/ELD Reader Guided Reading, p. DI•123 **ELL HANDBOOK** • ELL Study Guide, p. 88	**TEACHER'S EDITION** • ELL/ELD Reader Guided Reading, p. DI•123 **ELL HANDBOOK** • ELL Study Guide, p. 88
		TEACHER'S EDITION • Suffix -*ly*, p. 309i
ELL HANDBOOK • High-Frequency Words Activity Bank, p. 446 **ELL POSTER 10** • Day 3 Activities	**ELL HANDBOOK** • High-Frequency Words Activity Bank, p. 446	**ELL HANDBOOK** • High-Frequency Words Activity Bank, p. 446
TEACHER'S EDITION • Grammar Jammer **ELL HANDBOOK** • Grammar Transition Lesson, pp. 317, 323 • Grammar Jammer Routine, p. 478	**TEACHER'S EDITION** • Grammar Jammer **ELL HANDBOOK** • Grammar Transition Lesson, pp. 317, 323	**TEACHER'S EDITION** • Grammar Jammer **ELL HANDBOOK** • Grammar Transition Lesson, pp. 317, 323
TEACHER'S EDITION • Let's Write It!, p. 304–305 • Writing for Tests: Evaluation, pp. 305a–305b	**TEACHER'S EDITION** • Writing for Tests: Persuasive Essay, pp. 309d–309e	**TEACHER'S EDITION** • Writing for Tests: Conventions, pp. 309p–309q

Question of the Week
What is the job of the President of the United States?

Throughout the week, use the ELL Poster to help students produce and comprehend language, understand the concept, and build English vocabulary. Use the Question of the Week and other questions to help students share ideas in pairs, small groups, or the large group. Sample questions are shown, with examples of possible responses by students.

Weekly Concept and Language Goals

• Tell about the U.S. President's job

• Explain why the President has to work with other leaders in the United States and in other countries

• Understand that American citizens elect their leaders

By the end of the lesson, students should be able to talk about and write sentences about what the President of the United States does.

Daily Team Talk

Day 1	Day 2	Day 3	Day 4	Day 5
After Day 1 activities on Poster, ask questions such as	After Day 2 activity on Poster, ask questions such as	After Day 3 activity on Poster, ask questions such as	After Day 4 activity on Poster, ask questions such as	After Day 5 activity on Poster, ask questions such as
In the poster picture, what is the President of the United States doing?	*Why does the President of the United States give a State of the Union address every year?*	*Besides giving a State of the Union address, what else does the President of the United States do?*	*How did the man in the poster picture become the President of the United States?*	*Why do you think the President of the United States works with the leaders in other countries?*
Beginning Talking to people. **Intermediate** He is making a speech. **Advanced** The President is explaining what he has done for the country in the last year. **Advanced High** The President is giving his State of the Union address. In this speech, he explains some of the decisions he made in the last year.	**Beginning** It is his job. **Intermediate** It is part of the President's job to do it. **Advanced** The Constitution says it is part of the President's job to give the address. **Advanced High** The United States Constitution says that one of the President's responsibilities is to give a State of the Union address every year.	**Beginning** Leads the army. **Intermediate** He leads the army and picks judges. **Advanced** He leads the army, picks new judges, and works with Congress. **Advanced High** The President leads the armed forces, chooses judges for the Supreme Court, and works with Congress.	**Beginning** People elected him. **Intermediate** People elected him to be President. **Advanced** He is President because Americans voted for him. **Advanced High** He was elected to be President. American citizens voted for the person they wanted to be the President, and this man received the most votes.	**Beginning** To be friends. **Intermediate** He works with the leaders so they will be our friends. **Advanced** He works with the leaders in other countries to try to keep peace in the world. **Advanced High** The President works with the leaders in other countries to solve problems among all the countries of the world.

This Week's Materials

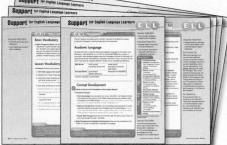

Teacher's Edition pages 284j–313a

See the support for English language learners throughout the lesson, including ELL strategies and scaffolded activities at points of use.

Teacher's Edition pages DI•116–DI•125

Differentiated Instruction for English language learners provides daily group activities that "frontload," or preteach, core instruction.

ELL Handbook pp. 83a–88

Find additional lesson materials that support the core lesson and the ELL instructional pages.

 Poster 10

ELL Reader 4.2.5

ELD Reader 4.2.5

Concept Literacy Reader

ELD, ELL Reader
Teaching Guide

Concept Literacy Reader
Teaching Guide

Technology

Online Teacher's Edition Use the digital version of the core Teacher's Edition for planning and instruction.

eReaders
This week's ELL and ELD Readers and Concept Literacy Reader are also available in digital format.

This Week's Content and Language Objectives by Strand

Concept Development/ Academic Language What is the job of the President of the United States?	**Content Objective** • Use concept vocabulary related to the President. **Language Objectives** • Express ideas in response to art and discussion. • Use students prior knowledge and experience to understand meanings.
Phonics and Spelling Words with *ear, ir, ur*	**Content Objective** • Identify *r*-controlled vowels. **Language Objective** • Apply phonics and decoding skills to vocabulary.
Listening Comprehension Modified Read Aloud: "A Built-to-Order Capital"	**Content Objective** • Monitor and adjust oral comprehension. **Language Objectives** • Discuss oral passages. • Use a graphic organizer to take notes.
Reading Comprehension Main Idea and Details	**Content Objectives** • Distinguish between main idea and details. • Identify main idea and details to aid comprehension. **Language Objectives** • Discuss the difference between main idea and details. • Write the main idea and details based on a text.
Vocabulary Basic and Lesson Vocabulary	**Language Objectives** • Understand and use learning strategies to acquire basic vocabulary. • Learn meanings of grade-level vocabulary. • Produce drawings, phrases, or short sentences to show understanding of Lesson Vocabulary.
Word Analysis Suffix *–ly*	**Content Objective** • Identify and define words with the suffix *–ly*. **Language Objective** • Discuss and spell words with the suffix *–ly*.
Grammar and Conventions Plural Possessive Nouns	**Content Objective** • Decode and use plural possessive nouns. **Language Objectives** • Speak using the pattern of plural possessive nouns. • Write phrases and sentences with plural possessive nouns.
Writing Writing Transitions	**Content Objective** • Identify transitions in a text. **Language Objectives** • Write paragraphs using transitions by combining phrases, clauses, or connecting words. • Speak using transitions by combining phrases, clauses, or connecting words.

Word Cards for Vocabulary Activities

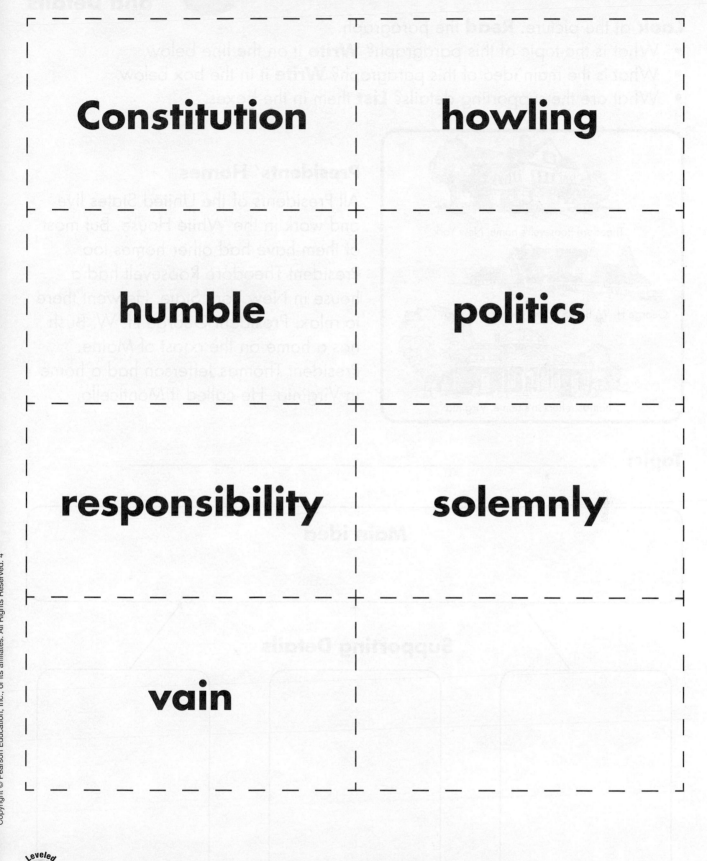

Constitution

howling

humble

politics

responsibility

solemnly

vain

Teacher Note: Beginning Teach three to four words. **Intermediate** Teach four to six words. **Advanced** Teach six to seven words. **Advanced High** Teach all words.

Name _____

Look at the picture. **Read** the paragraph.
- What is the topic of this paragraph? **Write** it on the line below.
- What is the main idea of this paragraph? **Write** it in the box below.
- What are the supporting details? **List** them in the boxes.

Theodore Roosevelt's home, New York

George H. W. Bush's home, Maine

Thomas Jefferson's home, Virginia

Presidents' Homes

All Presidents of the United States live and work in the White House. But most of them have had other homes too. President Theodore Roosevelt had a house in New York State. He went there to relax. President George H. W. Bush has a home on the coast of Maine. President Thomas Jefferson had a home in Virginia. He called it Monticello.

Topic: _____

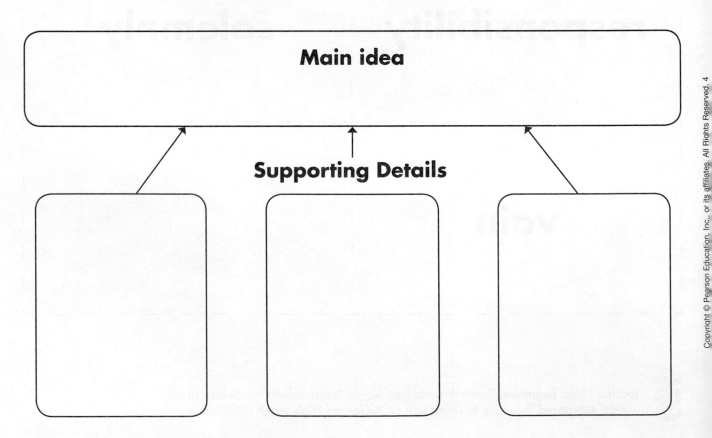

Main idea

Supporting Details

Main Idea and Details

Use this lesson to supplement or replace the skill lesson on page 285c of the Teacher's Edition. Display the Skill Points (at right) and share them with students.

Teach/Model

Beginning Say: *My friend Joe would be a great class president. He is organized, responsible, and nice.* Help students identify which sentence is the main idea and which sentence tells details that supports the main idea.

Intermediate Display pictures of and identify several countries' flags. Say: *These pictures show details that support this main idea: Every country's flag is unique.* Have students write a sentence that tells about one of the details and supports the main idea.

Advanced Read aloud part of the entry about the White House in a children's encyclopedia. Say: *The topic is the White House. Here is a main idea: The White House is important to the American people. What details support this main idea?* (Students can tell how long the White House has existed or how many Presidents have lived in it.)

Advanced High Read aloud information about Abraham Lincoln from an encyclopedia. Have students use the information to write a main idea about Lincoln, such as *Abraham Lincoln did many things when he was President.* Then have them write two details that support their main idea.

Then distribute copies of Picture It! page 84.

- Have students look at the pictures and read the captions. Then read the paragraph aloud.
- Ask: *What is the paragraph all about?* (Presidents' homes)
- Review the Skill Points with students.
- Have students identify the main idea of the paragraph and find the supporting details for the main idea.

Practice

Read aloud the directions on page 84. Reread the paragraph aloud. Have students use the pictures and the paragraph as they fill in the boxes.

Beginning Students can underline or circle their answers in the paragraph before they write their answers. Suggest that they use the text to help them as they write.

Intermediate Students can first orally answer and then write their answers. Encourage them to use the paragraph to check their spelling.

Advanced Students can write their answers on the line and in the boxes and then check their answers by silently rereading the paragraph and comparing their answers to the text.

Advanced High Students can write their answers on the line and in the boxes and then orally explain how the topic and the main idea are different and how the details support the main idea.

Answers for page 84: *Topic:* Presidents' homes; *Main Idea:* Most Presidents have their own houses. *Supporting Details:* President Roosevelt had a house in New York State. President George H. W. Bush has a home on the coast of Maine. President Thomas Jefferson had a house in Virginia.

Skill Points

✔ The **topic** is what a paragraph is all about.

✔ The **main idea** is the most important thing an author has to say about the topic.

✔ **Supporting details** are pieces of information that tell about the main idea.

Multilingual Summaries

So You Want to Be President?

The President of the United States can have fun. The White House has a swimming pool, a movie theater, and a bowling alley. Presidents can eat anything that they want to.

However, the President must dress up every day. The President must always be polite. The President has homework every day.

Presidents have been tall, short, thin, and fat. Some were outgoing. Some were shy. To be President, you must be at least 35 years old.

Some Presidents have had a father or cousin who also served as President. Presidents have had all kinds of pets.

Nine Presidents never went to college. Other Presidents have worked as engineers, farmers, lawyers, surveyors, shopkeepers, soldiers, or sailors before they were elected.

Being President is a big responsibility. The President must serve the country and the people.

Spanish

Entonces, ¿quieres ser presidente?

El presidente de Estados Unidos puede divertirse. La Casa Blanca tiene una piscina, un cine y una pista para jugar a los bolos. Los presidentes pueden comer lo que quieran.

Sin embargo, el presidente se tiene que vestir con ropa elegante todos los días. También, tiene que comportarse siempre con cortesía. El presidente tiene trabajo todos los días.

Los presidentes han sido altos, bajos, delgados y gordos. Algunos eran extrovertidos. Algunos eran tímidos. Para ser presidente tienes que tener por lo menos 35 años.

Algunos presidentes han tenido un padre o un primo que también fue presidente. Los presidentes han tenido todo tipo de mascotas.

Nueve presidentes nunca fueron a la universidad. Otros presidentes han trabajado como ingenieros, granjeros, abogados, topógrafos, comerciantes, soldados o marinos antes de haber sido elegidos.

Ser presidente es una gran responsabilidad. El presidente tiene que servir al país y a la gente.

Multilingual Summaries

你想成為總統嗎？

做美國總統有許多樂趣。白宮裏有游泳池、電影院和保齡球道。總統想吃什麼，就能馬上吃到。

但是，總統必須天天穿得整整齊齊，要很有禮貌，每天還要做很多工作。

總統有高的矮的，有胖的瘦的；有些性格外向，而有些卻很內向。不過，所有總統都必須年滿35歲。

有些總統的父親或堂兄也當過總統。總統的寵物也各不相同。有位總統讓兒子在白宮的電梯裏養了匹小馬。

有九位總統從來沒上過大學。其他總統原先是工程師、農民、律師、測量師、商人、士兵或海員。

總統要擔負很大的責任，必須為國家與人民服務。

Vậy Bạn Muốn Làm Tổng Thống Chăng?

Làm Tổng Thống của Hoa Kỳ có thể vui. Tòa Bạch Ốc có hồ bơi, rạp chiếu phim, và nhà chơi bóng gỗ lăn. Tổng Thống có thể được ăn bất cứ món gì họ muốn.

Tuy nhiên, Tổng Thống phải ăn mặc đẹp mỗi ngày. Tổng Thống lúc nào cũng phải lịch sự. Tổng Thống có bài tập làm ở nhà mỗi ngày.

Các Tổng Thống cao, thấp, gầy, và béo. Vài vị bặt thiệp. Vài vị rụt rè. Để làm Tổng Thống, bạn phải ít nhất là 35 tuổi.

Vài vị Tổng Thống đã có cha hoặc anh em họ cũng từng là Tổng Thống. Các vị Tổng Thống có đủ loại thú nuôi trong nhà. Có con trai của một vị Tổng Thống đã đem một con lừa vào trong thang máy của Tòa Bạch Ốc!

Có chín vị Tổng Thống không bao giờ học đại học. Các Tổng Thống khác đã từng làm kỹ sư, nhà nông, luật sư, thanh tra trắc đạc, chủ tiệm, binh sĩ, hoặc thủy thủ trước khi đắc cử.

Làm Tổng Thống là một trách nhiệm to lớn. Tổng Thống phải phục vụ tổ quốc và dân chúng.

Multilingual Summaries

대통령이 되고 싶다고?

미국 대통령이 되면 즐거운 일이 가득하다. 백악관에는 수영장과 영화관 그리고 볼링장도 있다. 대통령은 먹고 싶은 것은 무엇이든 먹을 수 있다.

하지만 대통령은 매일 정장을 갖춰 입어야 하고 항상 정중해야 하며 매일 숙제가 있다.

대통령들은 키가 크기도, 작기도, 마르기도, 뚱뚱하기도 하다. 어떤 대통령들은 외향적이었고 어떤 대통령들은 부끄럼을 타기도 했다. 대통령이 되려면 최소한 35살은 되어야 한다.

어떤 대통령들은 아버지나 사촌이 대통령직을 수행하기도 했다. 대통령들은 온갖 종류의 애완동물을 키우는데 어느 대통령의 아들은 백악관 엘리베이터 안에 조랑말을 데려다 놓기도 했다.

대통령들 중 열에 아홉은 전혀 대학을 다닌 적이 없다. 다른 대통령들은 대통령으로 뽑히기 전에 기술자나 농부, 변호사, 측량 기사, 소매 상인, 군인, 선원이었다.

대통령이 되는 일에는 큰 책임감이 따르며 대통령은 국가와 국민들을 위해 봉사해야 한다.

Koj Xav Ua Thawj Tswj hwm lub Teb chaws Mis kas, Lov?

Tus thawj tswj hwm nyob rau mis kas muaj kev lom zem. Lub tsev dawb muaj ib lub pas dej, ib lub tsev saib yeeb yaj kiab, thiab ib qhov chaw kiv npas tshum cov koob ntoo (bowling). Tus thawj tswj hwm xav noj dab tsi los tau.

Tab sis, tus thawj tswj hwm yuav tsum hnav khaub ncaws zoo txhua hnub. Tus thawj tswj hwm yuav tsum paub cai txhua lub sij hawm. Tus thawj tswj hwm muaj hauj lwm ua txhua hnub.

Cov thawj tswj hwm dhau los, muaj cov siab, qis taub, yuag, thiab rog. Ib co kuj nquag thiab nyiam ua ntau yam. Ib co kuj txaj muag. Los ua tus thawj tswj hwm, koj yuav tsuam muaj hnub nyoog li 35 xyoos.

Ib cov thawj tswj hwm kuj muaj txiv los sis kwv tij tau ua tus thawj tswj hwm dhau los lawm. Cov Thawj tswj hwm nyiam yug ntau yam tsiaj. Ib tug thawj tswj hwm tus tub muab ib tug me nyuam nees rau hauv lub tsev dawb lub cav nqa tib neeg (elevator).

Cuaj tus thawj tswj hwm yeej tsis tau mus kawm ntawv qib siab ib zaug li! Lwm tus thawj tswj hwm twb ua hauj lwm ua cov kws txuj, cov qoob loo ua teb, cov kws li choj, cov kws soj ntsuam thaj av, cov neeg muag khoom tom taj laj, cov tub rog, los sis cov kws tsav nkoj dej ua ntej lawv raug tsa ua tus thawj tswj hwm.

Ua tus thawj tswj hwm yog ib txoj hauj lwm loj heev li. Tus thawj tswj hwm yuav tsum ua hauj lwm rau nws lub teb chaws thiab pej xeem sawv daws.

Name _____

- **Read** *The Fourth Grade Election* again.
- Use the information in the book. **Write** supporting details for the main idea shown below.

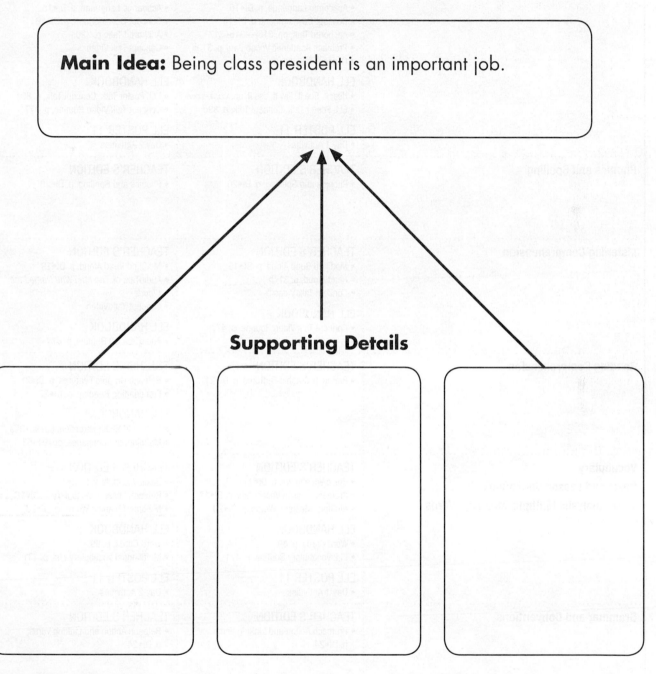

Main Idea: Being class president is an important job.

Supporting Details

Family Link

Has anyone in your family voted in an election? Ask family members to share their experiences voting. Ask them if they used a voting machine like the one shown in the book.

Weekly Resources Guide for English Language Learner Support

For this week's content and language objectives, see p. 89e.

Instructional Strand	Day 1	Day 2
Concept Development/Academic Language	**TEACHER'S EDITION** • Academic Language, p. DI•16 • Concept Development, p. DI•16 • Anchored Talk, pp. 316j—316–317 • Preteach Academic Vocabulary, p. 319a • Concept Talk Video **ELL HANDBOOK** • Hear It, See It, Say It, Use It, pp. xxxvi–xxxvii • ELL Poster Talk, Concept Talk, p. 89c **ELL POSTER 11** • Day 1 Activities	**TEACHER'S EDITION** • Academic Language, p. DI•16 • Concept Development, p. DI•16 • Anchored Talk, p. 320a • Concept Talk Video **ELL HANDBOOK** • ELL Poster Talk, Concept Talk, p. 89c • Concept Talk Video Routine, p. 477 **ELL POSTER 11** • Day 2 Activities
Phonics and Spelling	**TEACHER'S EDITION** • Phonics and Spelling, p. DI•20	**TEACHER'S EDITION** • Phonics and Spelling, p. DI•20
Listening Comprehension	**TEACHER'S EDITION** • Modified Read Aloud, p. DI•19 • Read Aloud, p. 317b • Concept Talk Video **ELL HANDBOOK** • Concept Talk Video Routine, p. 477	**TEACHER'S EDITION** • Modified Read Aloud, p. DI•19 • AudioText of *The Man Who Named the Clouds* • Concept Talk Video **ELL HANDBOOK** • AudioText CD Routine, p. 477
Reading Comprehension	**TEACHER'S EDITION** • Preteach Graphic Features, p. DI•21	**TEACHER'S EDITION** • Reteach Graphic Features, p. DI•21 • Frontloading Reading, p. DI•22 **ELL HANDBOOK** • Picture It! Skill Instruction, pp. 90–90a • Multilingual Summaries, pp. 91–93
Vocabulary **Basic and Lesson Vocabulary** **Word Analysis: Multiple-Meaning Words**	**TEACHER'S EDITION** • Basic Vocabulary, p. DI•17 • Preteach Lesson Vocabulary, p. DI•17 • Multiple-Meaning Words, p. DI•20 **ELL HANDBOOK** • Word Cards, p. 89 • ELL Vocabulary Routine, p. 471 **ELL POSTER 11** • Day 1 Activities	**TEACHER'S EDITION** • Basic Vocabulary, p. DI•17 • Reteach Lesson Vocabulary, p. DI•18 • Multiple-Meaning Words, p. DI•20 **ELL HANDBOOK** • Word Cards, p. 89 • Multilingual Vocabulary List, p. 431 **ELL POSTER 11** • Day 2 Activities
Grammar and Conventions	**TEACHER'S EDITION** • Preteach Action and Linking Verbs, p. DI•24	**TEACHER'S EDITION** • Reteach Action and Linking Verbs, p. DI•24
Writing	**TEACHER'S EDITION** • Poetic Structure, p. DI•25 • Introduce Narrative Poem, pp. 319e–319f	**TEACHER'S EDITION** • Writing Trait: Organization, pp. 329d–329e

Unit 3 Week 1 The Man Who Named the Clouds

This symbol indicates leveled instruction to address language proficiency levels.

Day 3	Day 4	Day 5
TEACHER'S EDITION • Academic Language, p. DI•16 • Concept Development, p. DI•16 • Anchored Talk, p. 330a • Concept Talk Video **ELL HANDBOOK** • ELL Poster Talk, Concept Talk, p. 89c **ELL POSTER 11** • Day 3 Activities	**TEACHER'S EDITION** • Academic Language, p. DI•16 • Concept Development, p. DI•16 • Anchored Talk, p. 340a • Concept Talk Video **ELL HANDBOOK** • ELL Poster Talk, Concept Talk, p. 89c **ELL POSTER 11** • Day 4 Activities	**TEACHER'S EDITION** • Academic Language, p. DI•16 • Concept Development, p. DI•16 • Concept Talk Video **ELL HANDBOOK** • ELL Poster Talk, Concept Talk, p. 89c **ELL POSTER 11** • Day 5 Activities
ELL HANDBOOK • Phonics Transition Lesson, pp. 269, 271	**ELL HANDBOOK** • Phonics Transition Lesson, pp. 269, 271	**TEACHER'S EDITION** • Phonics and Spelling, p. DI•20
TEACHER'S EDITION • AudioText of *The Man Who Named the Clouds* • Concept Talk Video **ELL HANDBOOK** • AudioText CD Routine, p. 477	**TEACHER'S EDITION** • Concept Talk Video	**TEACHER'S EDITION** • Concept Talk Video
TEACHER'S EDITION • Sheltered Reading, p. DI•22 **ELL HANDBOOK** • Multilingual Summaries, pp. 91–93	**TEACHER'S EDITION** • ELL/ELD Reader Guided Reading, p. DI•23 **ELL HANDBOOK** • ELL Study Guide, p. 94	**TEACHER'S EDITION** • ELL/ELD Reader Guided Reading, p. DI•23 **ELL HANDBOOK** • ELL Study Guide, p. 94
ELL HANDBOOK • High-Frequency Words Activity Bank, p. 446 **ELL POSTER 11** • Day 3 Activities	**ELL HANDBOOK** • High-Frequency Words Activity Bank, p. 446	**TEACHER'S EDITION** • Multiple-Meaning Words, p. 343h **ELL HANDBOOK** • High-Frequency Words Activity Bank, p. 446
TEACHER'S EDITION • Grammar Jammer **ELL HANDBOOK** • Grammar Transition Lesson, pp. 327, 336 • Grammar Jammer Routine, p. 478	**TEACHER'S EDITION** • Grammar Jammer **ELL HANDBOOK** • Grammar Transition Lesson, pp. 327, 336	**TEACHER'S EDITION** • Grammar Jammer **ELL HANDBOOK** • Grammar Transition Lesson, pp. 327, 336
TEACHER'S EDITION • Let's Write It!, p. 338–339 • Writing Trait: Organization, pp. 339a–339c	**TEACHER'S EDITION** • Revising Strategy, pp. 343d–343e	**TEACHER'S EDITION** • Action and Linking Verbs, pp. 343p–343q

Question of the Week
What is the value of looking at patterns in nature?

ELL Poster 11

Throughout the week, use the ELL Poster to help students produce and comprehend language, understand the concept, and build English vocabulary. Use the Question of the Week and other questions to help students share ideas in pairs, small groups, or the large group. Sample questions are shown, with examples of possible responses by students.

Weekly Concept and Language Goals

• Understand that the seasons bring changes in nature

• Identify patterns in nature

• Discuss why it is important to look at patterns in nature

By the end of the lesson, students should be able to talk about and write sentences about patterns in nature.

Daily Team Talk

Day 1	Day 2	Day 3	Day 4	Day 5
After Day 1 activities on Poster, ask questions such as	After Day 2 activity on Poster, ask questions such as	After Day 3 activity on Poster, ask questions such as	After Day 4 activity on Poster, ask questions such as	After Day 5 activity on Poster, ask questions such as
Look at the poster behind the globe in the poster picture. What happens as the seasons change?	*What patterns in nature are the students in the poster picture studying?*	*Why is it important to understand changes in air pressure?*	*Why is it important to understand chemicals that affect the atmosphere?*	*Besides the patterns in the poster picture, what other things in nature have patterns?*
Beginning It gets cold. **Intermediate** It gets cold in winter and warm in summer. **Advanced** The weather changes with the seasons. Trees lose their leaves in fall. **Advanced High** As the seasons change, so does the weather. Trees also grow leaves in spring and lose them in fall.	**Beginning** They study weather. **Intermediate** They are studying weather. **Advanced** They are studying weather. They learn about the sun and the air. **Advanced High** The students are studying weather. They study air pressure, the sun, and chemicals that affect the atmosphere.	**Beginning** It means a storm. **Intermediate** The air pressure tells about the weather. **Advanced** A change in air pressure means there will be a change in weather. **Advanced High** When the air pressure changes, people know the weather is changing. Knowing about changes in air pressure can help people predict the weather.	**Beginning** They make the air dirty. **Intermediate** Some chemicals make the air dirty. **Advanced** Some chemicals can pollute the atmosphere. **Advanced High** Some chemicals pollute and hurt our atmosphere. If we know which chemicals are harmful, we can try to not use them.	**Beginning** Plants and animals. **Intermediate** How plants and animals grow have patterns. **Advanced** The lives of plants and animals have patterns. The way rain is formed is also a pattern. **Advanced High** Other patterns in nature are plant and animal life cycles and the water cycle.

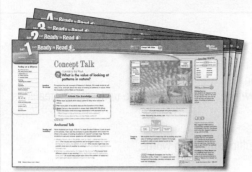

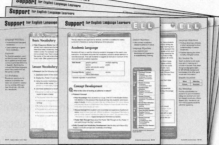

Teacher's Edition pages 316j–343q

Teacher's Edition pages DI•16–DI•25

ELL Handbook pp. 89a–94

See the support for English language learners throughout the lesson, including ELL strategies and scaffolded activities at points of use.

Differentiated Instruction for English language learners provides daily group activities that "frontload," or preteach, core instruction.

Find additional lesson materials that support the core lesson and the ELL instructional pages.

ELL Poster 11

ELL Reader 4.3.1

ELD Reader 4.3.1

Concept Literacy Reader

ELD, ELL Reader
Teaching Guide

Concept Literacy Reader
Teaching Guide

Technology

Online Teacher's Edition Use the digital version of the core Teacher's Edition for planning and instruction.

eReaders
This week's ELL and ELD Readers and Concept Literacy Reader are also available in digital format.

This Week's Content and Language Objectives by Strand

Concept Development/ Academic Language What is the value of looking at patterns in nature?	**Content Objective** • Use concept vocabulary related to patterns in nature. **Language Objectives** • Express ideas in response to art and discussion. • Use students prior knowledge and experience to understand meanings.
Phonics and Spelling Multiple-Meaning Words	**Content Objective** • Identify and decode multiple-meaning words. **Language Objective** • Discuss meanings of multiple-meaning words.
Listening Comprehension Modified Read Aloud: "Why We Have Seasons"	**Content Objective** • Monitor and adjust oral comprehension. **Language Objectives** • Discuss oral passages. • Take notes about story structure.
Reading Comprehension Graphic Sources	**Content Objectives** • Identify graphic sources in a text. • Use graphic sources to aid comprehension. **Language Objectives** • Discuss uses for graphic sources • Read and interpret graphic sources in a text.
Vocabulary Basic and Lesson Vocabulary	**Language Objectives** • Understand and use basic vocabulary. • Learn meanings of grade-level vocabulary. • Produce drawings, phrases, or short sentences to show understanding of Lesson Vocabulary.
Word Analysis Multiple-Meaning Words	**Content Objective** • Identify and decode multiple-meaning words. **Language Objective** • Discuss meanings of multiple-meaning words.
Grammar and Conventions Action and Linking Verbs	**Content Objective** • Decode and use action and linking verbs. **Language Objectives** • Speak using action and linking verbs. • Write phrases and sentences with action and linking verbs.
Writing Poetic Structure	**Content Objective** • Identify poetic structure in a text. **Language Objectives** • Write poems using poetic structure. • Distinguish between formal and informal language.

Word Cards for Vocabulary Activities

apprentice

atmosphere

chemical

club

essay

manufacturing

pressure

scales

Name_____

Read Together

Look at the picture. **Read** the story.

Trees

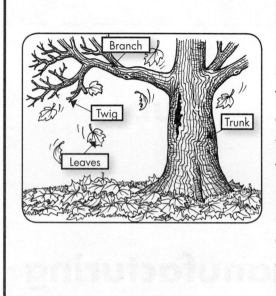

Trees are a beautiful part of nature. Many people think about the leaves and the branches, but an important part of a tree is underground. Deep in the earth, **roots** stretch out to hold the tree in the ground. Did you know that the roots can grow as long as the tree is high? The roots are connected to the trunk. The **trunk** is covered in bark which is like a protective skin. The **branches** reach out from the trunk. The branches have smaller **twigs** attached to them. Leaves grow on the twigs. The leaves are the powerhouse of the tree making energy for it to grow. The **leaves** of many trees drop off in the fall.

Answer the questions.

1. What does the diagram illustrate?

_____

2. Are all of the boldfaced words illustrated? Why do you think this is so?

_____

_____

3. How could the diagram be changed to show all of the boldfaced words?

Graphic Sources

Use this lesson to supplement or replace the skill lesson on page 317c of the Teacher's Edition. Display the Skill Points (at right) and share them with students.

Teach/Model

Beginning Ask: *Where do we see maps?* (in books, on the wall, on the Internet) *What do maps tell us?* (where things are located) Have students discuss maps they have seen. Repeat this process for other graphic sources such as photos, diagrams, charts, and graphs.

Intermediate Display a chart, diagram, or graph from a science textbook. Have students identify the kind of graphic source. Discuss with them how the graphic source can help them understand the information in the text.

Advanced Write and read aloud: *A plant's roots take in food and water. A plant has a stem to support it. Leaves grow on the stem and take in sunlight.* Ask: *What kind of graphic source can best help us understand this information?* (diagram) *Why?* (It can show the parts.) Have students draw a diagram to show the information.

Advanced High Ask students to find a paragraph in their science textbook that describes a machine. Have them create an appropriate graphic source to help show the information in the paragraph.

Then distribute copies of Picture It! page 90.

- Have students look at the diagram and read the labels. Then read the paragraph aloud.
- Ask: *What do the labels in the diagram identify?* (the parts—a branch, a twig, leaves, and the trunk—of a tree)
- Review the Skill Points with students.
- Have students compare information in the illustration with information in the paragraph.

Practice

Read aloud the directions on page 90. Have volunteers read the paragraph aloud. Have students look at the diagram and the paragraph as they answer the questions.

Beginning Students can say or explain their answers to the questions before they write or draw them on the page. Provide help with English words and writing.

Intermediate Students can first orally answer the questions and then write or draw their answers on the page. Provide help with writing.

Advanced Students can write or draw their answers and then check them by silently rereading the paragraph and comparing their writing to the text.

Advanced High Students can write or draw their answers and then orally explain why some words are boldfaced in the text.

Answers for page 90: 1. the parts of a tree; 2. Roots are not illustrated. They are underground, so they are not shown in the diagram. 3. Students should draw the roots of a tree and label them.

> ### Skill Points
> ✔ A **graphic source** shows or explains the information in the text. Charts, maps, pictures, time lines, and diagrams are examples of graphic sources.
> ✔ As you read, use graphic sources to help you understand information. Compare the information in the text with the information in the graphic sources.

Multilingual Summaries

The Man Who Named the Clouds

Luke Howard was born in London, England, in 1772. At that time, people did not know what clouds were. They did not know very much about what caused weather. They looked for signs in nature to predict the weather.

Luke was very interested in the weather. He thought if there were names for types of clouds, it would be easier to study them. He wrote a paper about different types of clouds. He gave each type of cloud a name. His cloud names became popular. Now, scientists still use some of his names for types of clouds.

Spanish

El hombre que nombró las nubes

Luke Howard nació en Londres, Inglaterra, en 1772. En esa época, las personas no sabían qué eran las nubes. Tampoco sabían mucho acerca de las causas del clima. Ellos buscaban señales de la naturaleza para predecir el clima.

Luke estaba muy interesado en el clima. Él pensó que si hubiera nombres para los tipos de nubes, sería más fácil estudiarlas. Escribió un artículo sobre los diferentes tipos de nubes. Le puso un nombre a cada tipo de nube. Sus nombres se volvieron populares. Hoy en día, los científicos todavía usan algunos de estos nombres.

Multilingual Summaries

为云改名的人

卢克·霍华德生于一七七二年的英国伦敦，那时候，人们不知道天上的云是什么东西，也不大清楚什么导致天气的转变；他们只凭借大自然的迹象来预测天气。

卢克对天气很感兴趣；他想如果每一种云都有一个名字，研究起来就方便一点，所以他写了一篇有关不同种类的云的文章，并给每一种一个名字。他用的名字开始流行起来，科学家现在仍然沿用一些他为云改的名字。

Người Đặt Tên Cho Mây

Luke Howard sinh tại Luân đôn, Anh quốc, năm 1772. Lúc bấy giờ, người ta không biết mây là cái gì. Người ta không biết nhiều về nguyên nhân của thời tiết. Họ nhìn vào dấu hiệu của thiên nhiên để dự đoán thời tiết.

Luke rất quan tâm đến thời tiết. Ông nghĩ rằng nếu các loại mây có tên thì sẽ dễ nghiên cứu mây hơn. Ông viết một luận văn về các loại mây. Ông đặt cho mỗi loại mây một cái tên. Tên mây của ông trở thành phổ cập. Ngày nay các nhà khoa học vẫn còn dùng một vài tên ông đã đặt để gọi các loại mây.

Multilingual Summaries

구름 이름을 지은 사람

루크 하워드는 1772년 영국 런던에서 태어났다. 그 당시에는 사람들은 구름이 무엇인지 몰랐다. 사람들은 날씨의 원인원인이 무엇인지 잘 몰랐다. 사람들은 날씨를 예측하기 위해서 자연의 신호를 찾곤 했다.

루크는 날씨에 관심이 많았다. 그는 구름에 이름이 있다면 연구하기가 쉬울 것이라고 생각했다. 그는 다른 종류의 구름에 관한 논문을 썼다. 그는 각기 다른 구름에 이름을 붙였다. 루크가 지은 구름 이름은 유명해졌다. 오늘날 과학자들은 루크가 지은 구름 이름의 일부를 여전히 사용한다.

Tus Txivneej Uas Tis Npe Rau Cov Huab

Luke Howard yug hauv London, England rau 1772. Lub sijhawm ntawd, tibneeg tsi paub tias huab yog dabtsi. Lawv tsi tshuam paub txog tias dab tsi ua rau askaj hloov. Lawv tsuas yog saib kablig saib askaj yuav hloov li cas xwb.

Luke nyiam sojntsuam txog askaj heev. Nwg xav tias yog cov huab muaj npe no yuav kawm txog yoojyim dua. Nwg sau ib daim ntawv txog ntau ntau hom huab. Nwg tis npe rau txhua hom huab. Nwg cov npe huab pib nto npe. Nim no, cov tub txawg tub ntse tseem niaj nub siv cov npe nwg tis rua cov huab.

Name _____

- **Read** *Leaves* again.
- Use the information in the book to **answer** the questions below.

---

pages 2–3

1. During the fall, what color are leaves like the one shown on page 3?

_____

_____

---

pages 4–5

2. During which time of the year does photosynthesis take place?

_____

_____

3. Why does photosynthesis stop in the fall?

_____

_____

---

pages 6–7

4. What happens to the leaves in the fall?

_____

_____

5. What do buds do in the spring?

_____

_____

Family Link

Talk to your family about the different seasons of the year.
Which season do they like best? What color are the trees at
that time of year?

Weekly Resources Guide for English Language Learner Support

For this week's content and language objectives, see p. 95e.

Instructional Strand	Day 1	Day 2
Concept Development/Academic Language	**TEACHER'S EDITION** • Academic Language, p. DI•41 • Concept Development, p. DI•41 • Anchored Talk, pp. 344j—344–345 • Preteach Academic Vocabulary, p. 347a • Concept Talk Video **ELL HANDBOOK** • Hear It, See It, Say It, Use It, pp. xxxvi–xxxvii • ELL Poster Talk, Concept Talk, p. 95c **ELL POSTER 12** • Day 1 Activities	**TEACHER'S EDITION** • Academic Language, p. DI•41 • Concept Development, p. DI•41 • Anchored Talk, p. 348a • Concept Talk Video **ELL HANDBOOK** • ELL Poster Talk, Concept Talk, p. 95c • Concept Talk Video Routine, p. 477 **ELL POSTER 12** • Day 2 Activities
Phonics and Spelling	**TEACHER'S EDITION** • Phonics and Spelling, p. DI•45	**TEACHER'S EDITION** • Phonics and Spelling, p. DI•45
Listening Comprehension	**TEACHER'S EDITION** • Modified Read Aloud, p. DI•44 • Read Aloud, p. 345b • Concept Talk Video **ELL HANDBOOK** • Concept Talk Video Routine, p. 477	**TEACHER'S EDITION** • Modified Read Aloud, p. DI•44 • AudioText of *Adelina's Whales* • Concept Talk Video **ELL HANDBOOK** • AudioText CD Routine, p. 477
Reading Comprehension	**TEACHER'S EDITION** • Preteach Fact and Opinion, p. DI•46	**TEACHER'S EDITION** • Reteach Fact and Opinion, p. DI•46 • Frontloading Reading, p. DI•47 **ELL HANDBOOK** • Picture It! Skill Instruction, pp. 96–96a • Multilingual Summaries, pp. 97–99
Vocabulary **Basic and Lesson Vocabulary** **Word Analysis: Greek Roots *bio, phon, graph***	**TEACHER'S EDITION** • Basic Vocabulary, p. DI•42 • Preteach Lesson Vocabulary, p. DI•42 • Greek Roots *bio, phon, graph*, p. DI•45 **ELL HANDBOOK** • Word Cards, p. 95 • ELL Vocabulary Routine, p. 471 **ELL POSTER 12** • Day 1 Activities	**TEACHER'S EDITION** • Basic Vocabulary, p. DI•42 • Reteach Lesson Vocabulary, p. DI•43 • Greek Roots *bio, phon, graph*, p. DI•45 **ELL HANDBOOK** • Word Cards, p. 95 • Multilingual Vocabulary List, p. 431 **ELL POSTER 12** • Day 2 Activities
Grammar and Conventions	**TEACHER'S EDITION** • Preteach Main and Helping Verbs, p. DI•49	**TEACHER'S EDITION** • Reteach Main and Helping Verbs, p. DI•49
Writing	**TEACHER'S EDITION** • Writer's Personality, p. DI•50 • Introduce Invitation, pp. 347e–347f	**TEACHER'S EDITION** • Writing Trait: Voice, pp. 357d–357e

This symbol indicates leveled instruction to address language proficiency levels.

Day 3	Day 4	Day 5
TEACHER'S EDITION • Academic Language, p. DI•41 • Concept Development, p. DI•41 • Anchored Talk, p. 358a • Concept Talk Video **ELL HANDBOOK** • ELL Poster Talk, Concept Talk, p. 95c **ELL POSTER 12** • Day 3 Activities	**TEACHER'S EDITION** • Academic Language, p. DI•41 • Concept Development, p. DI•41 • Anchored Talk, p. 366a • Concept Talk Video **ELL HANDBOOK** • ELL Poster Talk, Concept Talk, p. 95c **ELL POSTER 12** • Day 4 Activities	**TEACHER'S EDITION** • Academic Language, p. DI•41 • Concept Development, p. DI•41 • Concept Talk Video **ELL HANDBOOK** • ELL Poster Talk, Concept Talk, p. 95c **ELL POSTER 12** • Day 5 Activities
		TEACHER'S EDITION • Phonics and Spelling, p. DI•45
ELL HANDBOOK • Phonics Transition Lesson, pp. 279, 282	**ELL HANDBOOK** • Phonics Transition Lesson, pp. 279, 282	
TEACHER'S EDITION • AudioText of *Adelina's Whales* • Concept Talk Video **ELL HANDBOOK** • AudioText CD Routine, p. 477	**TEACHER'S EDITION** • Concept Talk Video	**TEACHER'S EDITION** • Concept Talk Video
TEACHER'S EDITION • Sheltered Reading, p. DI•47 **ELL HANDBOOK** • Multilingual Summaries, pp. 97–99	**TEACHER'S EDITION** • ELL/ELD Reader Guided Reading, p. DI•48 **ELL HANDBOOK** • ELL Study Guide, p. 100	**TEACHER'S EDITION** • ELL/ELD Reader Guided Reading, p. DI•48 **ELL HANDBOOK** • ELL Study Guide, p. 100
		TEACHER'S EDITION • Greek Roots, p. 371i
ELL HANDBOOK • High-Frequency Words Activity Bank, p. 446 **ELL POSTER 12** • Day 3 Activities	**ELL HANDBOOK** • High-Frequency Words Activity Bank, p. 446	**ELL HANDBOOK** • High-Frequency Words Activity Bank, p. 446
TEACHER'S EDITION • Grammar Jammer **ELL HANDBOOK** • Grammar Transition Lesson, pp. 327, 335 • Grammar Jammer Routine, p. 478	**TEACHER'S EDITION** • Grammar Jammer **ELL HANDBOOK** • Grammar Transition Lesson, pp. 327, 335	**TEACHER'S EDITION** • Grammar Jammer **ELL HANDBOOK** • Grammar Transition Lesson, pp. 327, 335
TEACHER'S EDITION • Let's Write It!, p. 364–365 • Writing Trait: Voice, pp. 365a–365b	**TEACHER'S EDITION** • Revising Strategy, pp. 371d–371e	**TEACHER'S EDITION** • Verb Phrases, pp. 371p–371q

Question of the Week
What patterns in nature guide the lives of animals?

Throughout the week, use the ELL Poster to help students produce and comprehend language, understand the concept, and build English vocabulary. Use the Question of the Week and other questions to help students share ideas in pairs, small groups, or the large group. Sample questions are shown, with examples of possible responses by students.

ELL Poster 12

Weekly Concept and Language Goals

• Tell how patterns in nature guide the lives of animals

• Name an animal behavior that is guided by nature

• Describe the things that animals do when they are guided by patterns in nature

By the end of the lesson, students should be able to talk about and write sentences about patterns in nature and animal behavior.

Daily Team Talk

Day 1	Day 2	Day 3	Day 4	Day 5
After Day 1 activities on Poster, ask questions such as *In the poster picture, why do the flamingos come to the tropical lagoon?*	After Day 2 activity on Poster, ask questions such as *Why are the biologists observing the flamingos?*	After Day 3 activity on Poster, ask questions such as *What do you think the flamingos will do when winter is over?*	After Day 4 activity on Poster, ask questions such as *In the story* Adelina's Whales, *why does Adelina walk to the beach every afternoon in January?*	After Day 5 activity on Poster, ask questions such as *Besides flamingos and whales, what is another animal that is guided by patterns in nature? What do these animals do?*
Beginning It's warm. **Intermediate** It is winter, so they come to a warm place. **Advanced** Flamingos migrate to someplace warm in the winter. **Advanced High** Flamingos come to the tropical lagoon because they migrate to warm locations in the winter to have their young.	**Beginning** To learn about them. **Intermediate** They want to learn what flamingos eat. **Advanced** The scientists watch the flamingos to learn what they eat and how they eat. **Advanced High** The biologists are observing the flamingos to learn about their behavior. They want to know what the flamingos eat and how they feed their young.	**Beginning** Go away. **Intermediate** The flamingos will leave. **Advanced** The flamingos will leave the lagoon and go home. **Advanced High** When winter is over, the flamingos will migrate again. They will leave the tropical lagoon and go to the place where they spend the summer.	**Beginning** To see whales. **Intermediate** To see if the whales have come yet. **Advanced** She knows the whales come in winter. She wants to see if they have come yet. **Advanced High** Each winter, whales come to the beach near Adelina's town. So every afternoon in January, Adelina checks the beach to see if the whales have arrived.	**Beginning** Bears sleep in winter. **Intermediate** Bears go to sleep when it is winter. They get up when it is spring. **Advanced** Bears hibernate in winter. They do not wake up until spring. **Advanced High** The behavior of bears is guided by the seasons. They hibernate through the winter. They are active in spring, summer, and fall.

This Week's Materials

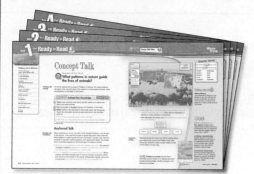

Teacher's Edition pages 344j–371q

See the support for English language learners throughout the lesson, including ELL strategies and scaffolded activities at points of use.

Teacher's Edition pages DI•41–DI•50

Differentiated Instruction for English language learners provides daily group activities that "frontload," or preteach, core instruction.

ELL Handbook pp. 95a–100

Find additional lesson materials that support the core lesson and the ELL instructional pages.

ELL Poster 12

ELL Reader 4.3.2

ELD Reader 4.3.2

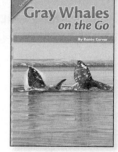

Concept Literacy Reader

ELD, ELL Reader Teaching Guide

Concept Literacy Reader Teaching Guide

Technology

Online Teacher's Edition Use the digital version of the core Teacher's Edition for planning and instruction.

eReaders
This week's ELL and ELD Readers and Concept Literacy Reader are also available in digital format.

This Week's Content and Language Objectives by Strand

Concept Development/ Academic Language What patterns in nature guide the lives of animals?	**Content Objective** • Use concept vocabulary related to how patterns in nature guide the lives of animals. **Language Objectives** • Express ideas in response to art and discussion. • Use students prior knowledge and experience to understand meanings.
Phonics and Spelling Homophones	**Content Objective** • Identify homophones. **Language Objective** • Apply phonics and decoding skills to vocabulary.
Listening Comprehension Modified Read Aloud: "The Swans Fly South"	**Content Objective** • Monitor and adjust oral comprehension. **Language Objectives** • Use contextual support to enhance understanding of spoken language. • Discuss oral passages.
Reading Comprehension Fact and Opinion	**Content Objectives** • Distinguish between facts and opinions. • Use learning strategies to identify facts and opinions. **Language Objectives** • Develop a repertoire of learning strategies to discuss facts and opinions. • Retell facts and opinions in a reading. • Write facts and opinions from personal experience.
Vocabulary Basic and Lesson Vocabulary	**Language Objectives** • Understand and use basic vocabulary. • Learn meanings of grade-level vocabulary. • Produce drawings, phrases, or short sentences to show understanding of Lesson Vocabulary.
Word Analysis Greek Roots *bio, phon, graph*	**Content Objective** • Identify words with the Greek roots *bio, phon,* and *graph.* **Language Objective** • Learn new language structures by reading and writing words with Greek roots *bio, phon,* and *graph.*
Grammar and Conventions Main and Helping Verbs	**Content Objective** • Decode and use main and helping verbs. **Language Objectives** • Speak using main and helping verbs. • Write grammatically correct sentences with main and helping verbs.
Writing Writer's Personality	**Content Objective** • Identify the writer's personality in a text. **Language Objectives** • Write paragraphs with strong verbs. • Write paragraphs with a variety of words and descriptive details.

Word Cards for Vocabulary Activities

biologist	**bluff**
lagoon	**massive**
rumbling	**tropical**

Teacher Note: Beginning Teach two to three words. **Intermediate** Teach three to four words. **Advanced** Teach four to five words. **Advanced High** Teach all words.

Name _____

Look at the pictures. **Read** the paragraph.

- **Read** the sentences below the paragraph. Which ones are facts? **Write** an *F* next to sentences that tell facts.
- Which sentences are opinions? **Write** an *O* next to sentences that tell opinions.

Two Kinds of Whales

To prevent whales from becoming extinct, the countries of the world signed an agreement. They agreed not to allow whales to be killed. In my opinion, this agreement was very good. It protected the most beautiful sea animal in the world. Unfortunately, some countries still kill whales. Iceland and Japan say that they allow whale hunting for scientific reasons. Norway allows whale hunting because it says the whales eat too many fish. These are terrible reasons for hunting whales. All whale hunting should be stopped.

1. Whales are the most beautiful sea animals in the world. _____

2. Whales should be protected. _____

3. Iceland, Japan, and Norway allow whale hunting. _____

4. The countries of the world signed an agreement making it illegal to kill whales. _____

5. Whale hunting should be stopped. _____

Fact and Opinion

Use this lesson to supplement or replace the skill lesson on page 345c of the Teacher's Edition. Display the Skill Points (at right) and share them with students.

Teach/Model

Beginning Say: *Whales live in all oceans. Is this a fact or an opinion?* (a fact) *How can you tell?* (I can do research to check this fact. I can look in a book or on the Internet.) Have students state their opinion about whales.

Intermediate Write and read aloud: *Seals, the cutest creatures in the sea, are mammals.* Say: *This sentence tells both a fact and an opinion. What is the fact?* (Seals are mammals.) *What is the opinion?* (They are the cutest creatures in the sea.)

Advanced Say: *An opinion cannot be proven true or false, but it can be supported with facts.* Write and read aloud: *It is important to protect whales.* Ask students to write a fact that supports this opinion.

Advanced High Have each student write one fact and one opinion about sea mammals. Pair students and have them share their sentences with partners. Have the partners take turns identifying facts and opinions.

Then distribute copies of Picture It! page 96.

- Have students describe what they see in the picture. Then read the paragraph aloud.
- Ask: *What clue words tell you when an opinion is being stated?* (in my opinion, very good, most beautiful, unfortunately, terrible, should)
- Review the Skill Points with students.
- Have students identify facts and opinions in the paragraph.

Practice

Read aloud the directions on page 96. Have students reread the paragraph aloud. Have them look at the picture and the paragraph as they write their answers.

Beginning Students can say whether each sentence is a fact or an opinion before they write their answers on the page. Provide help with marking the answers correctly.

Intermediate Students can first orally answer and then write their answers on the page. Remind them that they are writing only the letter *F* or *O*.

Advanced Students can write their answers and then check them by comparing their answers with a partner's.

Advanced High Students can write their answers and then orally explain how they used clue words to identify the opinions in the paragraph.

Answers for page 96: 1. O; 2. O; 3. F; 4. F; 5. O

Skill Points

- ✔ **A fact** can be proven true or false. You can prove a fact by doing research.
- ✔ An **opinion** cannot be proven true or false, but it should be supported. A valid opinion is well supported. A faulty opinion is not.
- ✔ Look for clue words that indicate an opinion. Examples include *best, should, good, beautiful, fun,* and *like.*

Multilingual Summaries

Adelina's Whales

Adelina lives on the shore of Laguna San Ignacio in Baja California, Mexico. Gray whales come to the lagoon in January to have their babies. They stay for three months. The whales are friendly there. They let people touch them.

Adelina's grandfather was the first person to tell about a visit from a whale. One day he was fishing with his partner. A whale came alongside their boat, and they were afraid. But the whale was friendly.

Adelina loves the time of year when the whales visit La Laguna. She likes to learn about the whales and watch them. Some day she may have a job working with or studying whales.

Spanish

Las ballenas de Adelina

Adelina vive a orillas de la Laguna de San Ignacio, en Baja California, México. Las ballenas grises llegan en enero para tener a sus bebés en la laguna y se quedan allí durante tres meses. Las ballenas son amistosas. Dejan que la gente las toque.

El abuelo de Adelina fue la primera persona que habló de la visita de una ballena. Un día, estaba pescando con un amigo. Una ballena se acercó al bote y ellos sintieron miedo. Pero la ballena se mostró amistosa.

Adelina adora la epoca del año en que las ballenas visitan La Laguna. Le gusta aprender de las ballenas y observarlas. Algún día, tal vez ella trabajará con las ballenas o estudiará algo relacionado con ellas.

Multilingual Summaries

阿德莉娜的鯨魚

阿德莉娜住在墨西哥下加州省的拉古拿聖伊格納西奧湖旁邊。每年一月，灰鯨都會來這個礁湖生小鯨魚，並待上三個月。那地方的鯨魚非常友善，會讓人摸牠們的身體。

阿德莉娜的祖父是第一個把看見鯨魚的事講出來的人。有一天，正當祖父和他的夥伴一起捕魚的時候，有一隻鯨魚突然游到他們的小船旁邊，他們害怕極了，不過幸好那鯨魚表現得很友善。

一年裡面阿德莉娜最喜歡的時候，就是鯨魚來拉拉古拿的季節。她喜歡研究鯨魚，也喜歡盯著他們看。她以後很可能跟鯨魚一起工作，或者是變成專門研究鯨魚的專家。

Những Con Cá Voi của Adelina

Adelina sống ở bờ biển Laguna San Ignacio ở Baja California, Mexico. Vào tháng Giêng, các cá voi sám đến vùng hồ nước biển này để đẻ con. Chúng ở đó ba tháng. Các con cá voi rất thân thiện. Chúng cho người ta sờ vào mình.

Ông nội của Adelina là người đầu tiên kể chuyện cá voi đến thăm. Một ngày kia ông đang đi đánh cá với người bạn của mình. Một con cá voi bơi dọc theo chiếc thuyền của họ, và họ lo sợ. Nhưng chú cá voi rất thân thiện.

Adelina thích khoản thời gian có các cá voi đến thăm vùng La Laguna. Cô bé thích học hỏi về cá voi và quan sát chúng. Một ngày nào đó cô bé có thể sẽ có công việc làm với cá voi hoặc nghiên cứu chúng.

Multilingual Summaries

아델리나의 고래

아델리나는 멕시코의 바자 켈리포니아에 있는 라구나 산 이그나시오 해변에 산다. 1월에 회색 고래가 새끼를 갖기 위해 환초로 둘러싸인 얕은 바다로 와서 3개월 동안 머문다. 회색 고래들은 우호적이어서 사람들이 만져도 가만히 있는다.

아델리나의 할아버지는 고래의 방문에 대해 얘기해 준 첫 번째 사람이다. 어느 날 할아버지가 동료와 낚시를 즐기고 있는데 고래 한 마리가 배 근처로 다가온다. 그들은 무서웠지만 고래는 친근하게 군다.

아델리나는 고래들이 라 라구나에 오는 시기를 좋아하며 고래에 대해 배우고 고래를 관찰하는 것을 좋아한다. 나중에 그녀는 고래와 일하는 직업을 갖거나 고래를 연구할 지도 모른다.

Adelina tus Ntses Loj

Adelina nyob ze tus ciam dej Laguna San Ignacio hauv Baja California, Mexico. Cov ntses loj los hauv lub me nyuam pas dej los yug cov lawv me nyuam. Lawv nyob hauv lub pas dej peb lub lim tiam. Cov ntses loj yeej tsis qus. Lawv cia tib neeg los kov lawv.

Adelina yawm txiv yog thawj tus neeg ua tau qhia txog ib lub sij hawm thaum ib tug ntses loj los xyuas nws. Muaj ib hnub thaum nws mus nus ntses nrog nws ib tug phooj ywg. Ib tug ntses loj tau los ntawm lub nkoj ib sab, thiab nkawv ntshai heev. Tiam sis tus ntses loj no tsis qus.

Adelina nyiam heev thaum muaj ib lub sij hawm thaum cov ntses loj los xyuas La Laguna. Nws nyiam kawm txog cov ntses loj thiab saib lawv. Ib hnub tej zaum nws yuav tau ib txoj hauj lwm nrog cov ntses loj thiab kawm cov ntses loj.

Name _____

- **Read** *Friendly Giants: California Gray Whales* again.
- Use the information in the book. **Write** facts and opinions in the chart. The first fact has been done.
- In the fact column, **write** three more facts from the book. In the opinion column, **write** four opinions of your own based on the information in the book.

Fact	Opinion
1. There are about 26,000 California gray whales.	**1.** _____
2.	**2.** _____
3.	**3.** _____
4.	**4.** _____

Family Link

Has anyone in your family ever seen or touched a whale? Ask family members to share what they know about whales and what they would like to know.

Weekly Resources Guide for English Language Learner Support

For this week's content and language objectives, see p. 101e.

Instructional Strand	Day 1	Day 2
Concept Development/Academic Language	**TEACHER'S EDITION** • Academic Language, p. DI•66 • Concept Development, p. DI•66 • Anchored Talk, pp. 372j—372–373 • Preteach Academic Vocabulary, p. 375a • Concept Talk Video **ELL HANDBOOK** • Hear It, See It, Say It, Use It, pp. xxxvi–xxxvii • ELL Poster Talk, Concept Talk, p. 101c **ELL POSTER 13** • Day 1 Activities	**TEACHER'S EDITION** • Academic Language, p. DI•66 • Concept Development, p. DI•66 • Anchored Talk, p. 376a • Concept Talk Video **ELL HANDBOOK** • ELL Poster Talk, Concept Talk, p. 101c • Concept Talk Video Routine, p. 477 **ELL POSTER 13** • Day 2 Activities
Phonics and Spelling	**TEACHER'S EDITION** • Phonics and Spelling, p. DI•70	**TEACHER'S EDITION** • Phonics and Spelling, p. DI•70
Listening Comprehension	**TEACHER'S EDITION** • Modified Read Aloud, p. DI•69 • Read Aloud, p. 373b • Concept Talk Video **ELL HANDBOOK** • Concept Talk Video Routine, p. 477	**TEACHER'S EDITION** • Modified Read Aloud, p. DI•69 • AudioText of *How Night Came from the Sea* • Concept Talk Video **ELL HANDBOOK** • AudioText CD Routine, p. 477
Reading Comprehension	**TEACHER'S EDITION** • Preteach Generalize, p. DI•71	**TEACHER'S EDITION** • Reteach Generalize, p. DI•71 • Frontloading Reading, p. DI•72 **ELL HANDBOOK** • Picture It! Skill Instruction, pp. 102–102a • Multilingual Summaries, pp. 103–105
Vocabulary **Basic and Lesson Vocabulary** **Word Analysis: Related Words**	**TEACHER'S EDITION** • Basic Vocabulary, p. DI•67 • Preteach Lesson Vocabulary, p. DI•67 • Related Words, p. DI•70 **ELL HANDBOOK** • Word Cards, p. 101 • ELL Vocabulary Routine, p. 471 **ELL POSTER 13** • Day 1 Activities	**TEACHER'S EDITION** • Basic Vocabulary, p. DI•67 • Reteach Lesson Vocabulary, p. DI•68 • Related Words, p. DI•70 **ELL HANDBOOK** • Word Cards, p. 101 • Multilingual Vocabulary List, p. 431 **ELL POSTER 13** • Day 2 Activities
Grammar and Conventions	**TEACHER'S EDITION** • Preteach Subject-Verb Agreement, p. DI•74	**TEACHER'S EDITION** • Reteach Subject-Verb Agreement, p. DI•74
Writing	**TEACHER'S EDITION** • Sentence Variety, p. DI•75 • Introduce Myth, pp. 375e–375f	**TEACHER'S EDITION** • Writing Trait: Sentences, pp. 387d–387e

Unit 3 Week 3   How Night Came from the Sea

This symbol indicates leveled instruction to address language proficiency levels.

Day 3	Day 4	Day 5
TEACHER'S EDITION • Academic Language, p. DI•66 • Concept Development, p. DI•66 • Anchored Talk, p. 388a • Concept Talk Video **ELL HANDBOOK** • ELL Poster Talk, Concept Talk, p. 101c **ELL POSTER 13** • Day 3 Activities	**TEACHER'S EDITION** • Academic Language, p. DI•66 • Concept Development, p. DI•66 • Anchored Talk, p. 396a • Concept Talk Video **ELL HANDBOOK** • ELL Poster Talk, Concept Talk, p. 101c **ELL POSTER 13** • Day 4 Activities	**TEACHER'S EDITION** • Academic Language, p. DI•66 • Concept Development, p. DI•66 • Concept Talk Video **ELL HANDBOOK** • ELL Poster Talk, Concept Talk, p. 101c **ELL POSTER 13** • Day 5 Activities
		TEACHER'S EDITION • Phonics and Spelling, p. DI•70
ELL HANDBOOK • Phonics Transition Lesson, pp. 260–261	**ELL HANDBOOK** • Phonics Transition Lesson, pp. 260–261	
TEACHER'S EDITION • AudioText of *How Night Came from the Sea* • Concept Talk Video **ELL HANDBOOK** • AudioText CD Routine, p. 477	**TEACHER'S EDITION** • Concept Talk Video	**TEACHER'S EDITION** • Concept Talk Video
TEACHER'S EDITION • Sheltered Reading, p. DI•72 **ELL HANDBOOK** • Multilingual Summaries, pp. 103–105	**TEACHER'S EDITION** • ELL/ELD Reader Guided Reading, p. DI•73 **ELL HANDBOOK** • ELL Study Guide, p. 106	**TEACHER'S EDITION** • ELL/ELD Reader Guided Reading, p. DI•73 **ELL HANDBOOK** • ELL Study Guide, p. 106
		TEACHER'S EDITION • Related Words, p. 401i
ELL HANDBOOK • High-Frequency Words Activity Bank, p. 446 **ELL POSTER 13** • Day 3 Activities	**ELL HANDBOOK** • High-Frequency Words Activity Bank, p. 446	**ELL HANDBOOK** • High-Frequency Words Activity Bank, p. 446
TEACHER'S EDITION • Grammar Jammer **ELL HANDBOOK** • Grammar Transition Lesson, pp. 340, 349 • Grammar Jammer Routine, p. 478	**TEACHER'S EDITION** • Grammar Jammer **ELL HANDBOOK** • Grammar Transition Lesson, pp. 340, 349	**TEACHER'S EDITION** • Grammar Jammer **ELL HANDBOOK** • Grammar Transition Lesson, pp. 340, 349
TEACHER'S EDITION • Let's Write It!, p. 394–395 • Writing Trait: Sentence Variety, pp. 395a–395b	**TEACHER'S EDITION** • Revising Strategy, pp. 401d–401e	**TEACHER'S EDITION** • Subject-Verb Agreement, pp. 401p–401q

Question of the Week
How have people explained the pattern of day and night?

Throughout the week, use the ELL Poster to help students produce and comprehend language, understand the concept, and build English vocabulary. Use the Question of the Week and other questions to help students share ideas in pairs, small groups, or the large group. Sample questions are shown, with examples of possible responses by students.

ELL Poster 13

Weekly Concept and Language Goals

• Understand how people have explained patterns in nature such as day and night

• Tell why patterns in nature happen

• Describe different patterns in nature

By the end of the lesson, students should be able to talk about and write sentences about the pattern of day and night.

Daily Team Talk

Day 1	Day 2	Day 3	Day 4	Day 5
After Day 1 activities on Poster, ask questions such as	After Day 2 activity on Poster, ask questions such as	After Day 3 activity on Poster, ask questions such as	After Day 4 activity on Poster, ask questions such as	After Day 5 activity on Poster, ask questions such as
In the poster picture, how does the father explain the pattern of day and night?	*What tools does the father use to help him explain the pattern of day and night to his son?*	*Is the father telling a story or using science to explain the pattern of day and night? How do you know?*	*How does the story How Night Came from the Sea explain the pattern of day and night?*	*Besides the pattern of day and night, what is another pattern in nature you can try to explain through stories or science?*
Beginning The Sun makes day and night. **Intermediate** One part of Earth has day, and one part of Earth has night. **Advanced** When our part faces the Sun, it is day, and when our part does not face the Sun, it is night. **Advanced High** As Earth turns, one part of Earth faces the Sun, so it is day in that part. One part of Earth does not face the Sun, so it is night in that part.	**Beginning** A light. **Intermediate** He uses a flashlight and a globe. **Advanced** The father shines a flashlight on a globe. **Advanced High** The father uses a flashlight and a globe. He shines the flashlight on the globe to show that the Sun can only light half of Earth at a time.	**Beginning** Using science. **Intermediate** He is using science. He uses tools. **Advanced** The father explains day and night using science. He uses tools as he explains. **Advanced High** I know the father is using science because he uses a flashlight and a globe to represent the Sun and Earth as he explains the pattern of day and night.	**Beginning** The girl misses it. **Intermediate** The girl misses the dark sea. **Advanced** Sunlight hurts the girl's eyes. She misses the dark of the sea. **Advanced High** When a girl from the sea marries a man, she has to live in the daylight. The light begins to hurt her eyes, so her mother sends the girl night from the sea.	**Beginning** Fall trees. **Intermediate** I can explain what happens to trees in the fall. **Advanced** I can try to explain why leaves fall off the trees in the autumn. **Advanced High** I can use stories or science to explain why trees lose their leaves in the fall.

Teacher's Edition pages 372j–401q

See the support for English language learners throughout the lesson, including ELL strategies and scaffolded activities at points of use.

Teacher's Edition pages DI•66–DI•75

Differentiated Instruction for English language learners provides daily group activities that "frontload," or preteach, core instruction.

ELL Handbook pp. 101a–106

Find additional lesson materials that support the core lesson and the ELL instructional pages.

ELL Poster 13

ELL Reader 4.3.3

ELD Reader 4.3.3

Concept Literacy Reader

ELD, ELL Reader
Teaching Guide

Concept Literacy Reader
Teaching Guide

Technology

Online Teacher's Edition Use the digital version of the core Teacher's Edition for planning and instruction.

eReaders
This week's ELL and ELD Readers and Concept Literacy Reader are also available in digital format.

This Week's Content and Language Objectives by Strand

Concept Development/ Academic Language How have people explained the pattern of day and night?	**Content Objective** • Use concept vocabulary related to explanations of night and day. **Language Objectives** • Express ideas in response to art and discussion. • Use students' prior knowledge and experience to understand meanings.
Phonics and Spelling Vowel Sound in *shout*	**Content Objective** • Understand and spell words with the vowel sound pattern in *shout*. **Language Objective** • Apply phonics and decoding skills to newly acquired vocabulary.
Listening Comprehension Modified Read Aloud: "The Story of the Stars and the Moon"	**Content Objective** • Monitor and adjust oral comprehension. **Language Objectives** • Discuss oral passages and monitor understanding of spoken language. • Use graphic organizer to take notes.
Reading Comprehension Generalize	**Content Objectives** • Interpret generalizations. • Identify clue words that indicate generalizations. **Language Objectives** • Use grade-level content vocabulary to discuss generalizations in a story. • Cite content from generalizations. • Summarize text using visual support.
Vocabulary Basic and Lesson Vocabulary	**Language Objectives** • Understand and use basic vocabulary. • Learn meanings of grade-level vocabulary. • Produce drawings, phrases, or short sentences to show understanding of Lesson Vocabulary.
Word Analysis Related Words	**Content Objective** • Understand related words. **Language Objective** • Write lists of related words using basic vocabulary.
Grammar and Conventions Subject-Verb Agreement	**Content Objective** • Use subject-verb agreement correctly. **Language Objectives** • Speak with subject-verb agreement. • Write sentences using subject-verb agreement.
Writing Sentence Variety	**Content Objective** • Use sentence variety in writing. **Language Objectives** • Listen to example of good sentence variety. • Share feedback for editing and revising.

Word Cards for Vocabulary Activities

brilliant

chorus

coward

gleamed

shimmering

Teacher Note: Beginning Teach two to three words. **Intermediate** Teach three to four words. **Advanced** Teach four to five words. **Advanced High** Teach all words.

Name _____

Look at the pictures. **Read** the paragraph.

- What generalization clue words can you find? **Write** them in the chart below.
- What generalizations do the clue words show? **Write** them in the boxes next to their clue words.

Short and Long Days

Children generally like the summer because the weather is warm and the days are longer. In many places in the United States, daylight lasts until after eight o'clock at night. In countries farther north, it stays light until eleven o'clock at night! In the winter, the days are much shorter. Most children do not like the short days of the winter. They do not like having to go to school in the dark.

Clue Word	Generalization

Generalize

Use this lesson to supplement or replace the skill lesson on page 373c of the Teacher's Edition. Display the Skill Points (at right) and share them with students.

Teach/Model

Beginning Write and read aloud: *Summer days are long. Most people stay outside longer.* Ask: *Which sentence is a generalization?* (the second one) Guide students in recognizing *many* as a clue word for a generalization.

Intermediate Write and read aloud: *Many birds fly south in the winter.* Ask: *What word tells you this is a generalization?* (Many) Have students use another clue word, such as *most, generally, all, always,* or *usually,* to write their own generalization about birds.

Advanced Say: *In winter, people generally spend more time inside.* Ask students to identify the clue word that shows this is a generalization. (generally) Then have them write a sentence that supports the generalization. (Possible answer: Some outdoor activities are not possible in cold weather.)

Advanced High Ask students to write a generalization about summer. Then pair students and have them exchange generalizations. Have each partner tell a fact that supports the other generalization.

Then distribute copies of Picture It! page 102.

- Have students describe what they see in the pictures. Then read the paragraph aloud.
- Ask: *What generalization does the author make about how children feel about winter?* (Most children do not like the short days of winter.)
- Review the Skill Points with students.
- Have students find the clue words. Then have them find the generalizations that go with the clue words.

Practice

Read aloud the directions on page 102. Have students reread the paragraph with partners. Have them look at the pictures and the paragraph as they fill in the chart.

Beginning Students can say and point to the clue words and generalizations in the paragraph before writing their answers in the chart. Provide help with English words and writing.

Intermediate Students can first orally identify clue words and generalizations and then write their answers in the chart. Provide help with English words and writing.

Advanced Students can write words and sentences to fill in the chart and then check their answers by underlining the generalizations and circling the clue words in the paragraph.

Advanced High Students can write words and sentences to fill in the chart and then orally explain why their generalizations are generalizations.

Answers for page 102: *Clue Word:* generally, most; *Generalization:* Children generally like the summer because the weather is warm and the days are longer. Most children do not like the short days of the winter.

Skill Points

✔ A **generalization** is a sentence or rule that explains many examples.

✔ Clue words such as *all, many, most, always, usually,* and *generally* show that an author is making a generalization.

✔ Generalizations should be supported by facts or details.

Multilingual Summaries

How Night Came from the Sea

At the beginning of time, the only darkness was under the sea, in the kingdom ruled by Iemanjá (yay-mahn-JAH). Iemanjá's daughter married a man from the land. She loved the land. But the light was too bright for her. She wanted darkness to rest her eyes.

Her husband sent three men to Iemanjá to ask for some night. Iemanjá gave them a bag of night. She warned that only her daughter could open it. But when the men returned to land, one of them opened the bag. The night creatures escaped, and the moon and stars jumped out. Luckily Iemanjá's daughter was there. She calmed the creatures. Then she went to sleep. When she woke up, she gave three gifts: the morning star, the rooster to announce the morning, and the birds singing beautiful morning songs.

Spanish

Cómo la noche fue creada del mar

Al principio, la única oscuridad estaba debajo del mar, en el reino gobernado por Yemayá. La hija de Yemayá se casó con un hombre de la tierra. Amaba la tierra, pero la luz era demasiado brillante para ella. Quería también oscuridad para descansar sus ojos.

Su esposo mandó tres hombres a ver a Yemayá y a pedirle un poco de noche. Yemayá les dio un saco lleno de noche y les dijo que sólo su hija podía abrirlo. Sin embargo, cuando llegaron a la tierra, uno de los hombres abrió el saco. Las criaturas de la noche se escaparon y la luna y las estrellas saltaron fuera del saco. Afortunadamente, la hija de Yemayá estaba allí. Calmó a las criaturas y después se fue a dormir. Cuando se levantó, regaló tres cosas: la estrella de la mañana, el gallo para anunciar el amanecer y los pájaros cantando bellas canciones matutinas.

Multilingual Summaries

Chinese

夜晚的由來

在時間巨輪剛剛開始運轉的時候，這世界上唯一的黑暗就在海底下，那是一個由海洋女神所統治的王國。海洋女神的女兒嫁給一個陸地上的男人，她愛陸地上的一切，可是唯一不適應的地方是那裡的光線太亮了，她實在受不了，真希望有點黑暗讓眼睛好好休息一下。

她的丈夫派了三個人去海洋女神那兒要點黑暗，海洋女神給了他們一袋黑暗，不過卻警告他們，只有她女兒才能打開袋子。這三個男人回到陸地之後，其中有一個人實在忍不住好奇心，偷偷打開了袋子。一瞬間，有好多夜晚的動物從袋子裡逃了出來，月亮和星星也蹦蹦跳跳地跑了出來。還好有海洋女神的女兒在，她讓動物們安靜下來，然後她自己也趁著這難得的黑夜上床睡個好覺。隔天早上醒來，她給了大家三份禮物：晨星、宣佈早晨來臨的公雞，還有在早上唱出美妙樂曲的鳥兒。

Vietnamese

Vì Sao Đêm Tối Đến Từ Biển

Từ thuở xa xưa, bóng tối duy nhất là ở dưới biển, trong vương quốc do nữ vương Iemanjá (đọc là dê-man-giá) cai trị. Con gái của Iemanjá có chồng là người trên đất liền. Cô yêu đất liền. Nhưng ánh sáng quá chói chang cho cô. Cô muốn có được bóng tối để đôi mắt của cô được nghỉ.

Chồng của cô sai ba người đi đến Iemanjá xin một ít đêm tối. Iemanjá cho họ một túi đêm tối. Bà ấy dặn là chỉ có con gái của bà mới có thể mở túi này. Nhưng khi ba người trở về đất liền, một người trong bọn mở túi đó. Những con vật của đêm tối thoát ra, rồi trăng và sao nhảy ra. May là con gái của Iemanjá có mặt ở đó. Cô trấn an những con vật. Rồi cô đi ngủ. Khi cô thức dậy, cô tặng ba món quà: sao mai, gà trống để báo bình minh, và các con chim líu lo hót những bài ca bình minh tươi đẹp.

Multilingual Summaries

밤이 바다에서 온 방법

태초에 야만야가 통치하는 왕국의 바다 아래에는 오직 어둠만이 있었다. 야만야의 딸은 육지에서 온 남자와 결혼한다. 그녀는 육지를 좋아한다. 하지만 빛이 너무 밝아서 눈을 쉬게 해주는 어둠을 원했다.

그녀의 남편은 세 명의 남자를 야만야에게 보내 어두운 밤을 달라고 요청한다. 야만야는 그들에게 어두운 밤 한 자루를 주었는데 오직 자신의 딸만 자루를 열어볼 수 있다고 주의를 준다. 하지만 육지로 돌아올 때 그들 중 한 명이 자루를 열고 만다. 그러자 밤이 도망가고 달과 별이 자루에서 뛰어나온다. 다행히 야만야의 딸이 그곳에 있다. 그녀는 그 생물들을 진정시키고 나서 잠을 청한다. 그녀가 깨어났을 때 그녀는 자루에 담긴 생물 대신 세 가지 선물을 주는데 그것은 샛별, 아침을 알리는 수탉 그리고 아름다운 아침 노래를 부르는 새들이다.

Ua Li Cas Yav Tsaus Ntuj Los Hauv Dej Hiav Txwv Los

Txij thaum ntuj tsim teb raug los, qhov uas tsuas tsaus ntuj yog hauv dej hiav txwv, hauv ib lub nceeg vaj uas raug kav los ntawm ib tug hu ua lemanjá (yay-mahn-JAH). lemanjá tus ntxhais tau yuav ib tug txiv neej nyob hauv qhuab nruab. Nws nyiam nyob saum qhuab nruab. Tiam sis lub hnub ci ci heev rau nws. Nws xav kom muaj yav tsaus ntuj kom nws qi tau muag.

Nws tus txiv txib peb tug txiv neej mus thov kom lemanjá muab yav tsaus ntuj. lemanjá tau muab ib lub hnab ntim yav tsaus ntuj rau hauv. Nws ceeb toom tias tsaus yog nws tus ntxhais thiaj li qhib tau lub hnab. Cov tsiaj txu tau dim, thiab lub hli thiab cov hnub qub tau khiav tawm hauv lub hnab. Muaj hmoo kawg lemanjá tus ntxhais tau nyob ntawd thaum lub hnab tau qhib. Nws ua kom cov tsiaj txu nyob twj ywm. Ces nws mus pw tsaug zog. Thaum nws tau sawv, nws pub peb qho khoom plig: cov hnub qub thaum yav sawv ntxov, tus qaij kom nws qua yav sawv ntxov, thiab cov noog uas hu nkauj yav sawv ntxov.

- **Read** *Day and Night* again.
- In the box, **draw** a sunrise or sunset.
- **Write** four things you learned about day and night from the book.

1. _____

2. _____

3. _____

4. _____

Family Link

Look at a map or globe with a family member. Ask for help in finding a country that has night when it is day in your hometown. Share the country you found with your class.

Weekly Resources Guide for English Language Learner Support

For this week's content and language objectives, see p. 107e.

Instructional Strand	Day 1	Day 2
Concept Development/Academic Language	TEACHER'S EDITION • Academic Language, p. DI•91 • Concept Development, p. DI•91 • Anchored Talk, pp. 402j—402–403 • Preteach Academic Vocabulary, p. 405a • Concept Talk Video ELL HANDBOOK • Hear It, See It, Say It, Use It, pp. xxxvi–xxxvii • ELL Poster Talk, Concept Talk, p. 107c ELL POSTER 14 • Day 1 Activities	TEACHER'S EDITION • Academic Language, p. DI•91 • Concept Development, p. DI•91 • Anchored Talk, p. 406a • Concept Talk Video ELL HANDBOOK • ELL Poster Talk, Concept Talk, p. 107c • Concept Talk Video Routine, p. 477 ELL POSTER 14 • Day 2 Activities
Phonics and Spelling	TEACHER'S EDITION • Phonics and Spelling, p. DI•95	TEACHER'S EDITION • Phonics and Spelling, p. DI•95
Listening Comprehension	TEACHER'S EDITION • Modified Read Aloud, p. DI•94 • Read Aloud, p. 403b • Concept Talk Video ELL HANDBOOK • Concept Talk Video Routine, p. 477	TEACHER'S EDITION • Modified Read Aloud, p. DI•94 • AudioText of *Eye of the Storm* • Concept Talk Video ELL HANDBOOK • AudioText CD Routine, p. 477 • Web, p. 486
Reading Comprehension	TEACHER'S EDITION • Preteach Cause and Effect, p. DI•96	TEACHER'S EDITION • Reteach Cause and Effect, p. DI•96 • Frontloading Reading, p. DI•97 ELL HANDBOOK • Picture It! Skill Instruction, pp. 108–108a • Multilingual Summaries, pp. 109–111
Vocabulary **Basic and Lesson Vocabulary** **Word Analysis: Latin Roots *struct, scrib, script***	TEACHER'S EDITION • Basic Vocabulary, p. DI•92 • Preteach Lesson Vocabulary, p. DI•92 • Latin Roots *struct, scrib, script*, p. DI•95 ELL HANDBOOK • Word Cards, p. 107 • ELL Vocabulary Routine, p. 471 ELL POSTER 14 • Day 1 Activities	TEACHER'S EDITION • Basic Vocabulary, p. DI•92 • Reteach Lesson Vocabulary, p. DI•93 • Latin Roots *struct, scrib, script*, p. DI•95 ELL HANDBOOK • Word Cards, p. 107 • Multilingual Vocabulary List, p. 431 ELL POSTER 14 • Day 2 Activities
Grammar and Conventions	TEACHER'S EDITION • Preteach Past, Present, and Future Tenses, p. DI•99	TEACHER'S EDITION • Teach Past, Present, and Future Tenses, p. DI•99
Writing	TEACHER'S EDITION • Salutation, Body, and Closing, p. DI•100 • Introduce Formal Letter, pp. 405e–405f	TEACHER'S EDITION • Writing Trait: Organization, pp. 415d–415e

This symbol indicates leveled instruction to address language proficiency levels.

Day 3	Day 4	Day 5
TEACHER'S EDITION • Academic Language, p. DI•91 • Concept Development, p. DI•91 • Anchored Talk, p. 416a • Concept Talk Video **ELL HANDBOOK** • ELL Poster Talk, Concept Talk, p. 107c **ELL POSTER 14** • Day 3 Activities	**TEACHER'S EDITION** • Academic Language, p. DI•91 • Concept Development, p. DI•91 • Anchored Talk, p. 424a • Concept Talk Video **ELL HANDBOOK** • ELL Poster Talk, Concept Talk, p. 107c **ELL POSTER 14** • Day 4 Activities	**TEACHER'S EDITION** • Academic Language, p. DI•91 • Concept Development, p. DI•91 • Concept Talk Video **ELL HANDBOOK** • ELL Poster Talk, Concept Talk, p. 107c **ELL POSTER 14** • Day 5 Activities
		TEACHER'S EDITION • Phonics and Spelling, p. DI•95
ELL HANDBOOK • Phonics Transition Lesson, pp. 278, 281	**ELL HANDBOOK** • Phonics Transition Lesson, pp. 278, 281	
TEACHER'S EDITION • AudioText of *Eye of the Storm* • Concept Talk Video **ELL HANDBOOK** • AudioText CD Routine, p. 477	**TEACHER'S EDITION** • Concept Talk Video	**TEACHER'S EDITION** • Concept Talk Video
TEACHER'S EDITION • Sheltered Reading, p. DI•97 **ELL HANDBOOK** • Multilingual Summaries, pp. 109–111	**TEACHER'S EDITION** • ELL/ELD Reader Guided Reading, p. DI•98 **ELL HANDBOOK** • ELL Study Guide, p. 112	**TEACHER'S EDITION** • ELL/ELD Reader Guided Reading, p. DI•98 **ELL HANDBOOK** • ELL Study Guide, p. 112
		TEACHER'S EDITION • Latin Roots *struct, scrib, script*, p. 429i
ELL HANDBOOK • High-Frequency Words Activity Bank, p. 446 **ELL POSTER 14** • Day 3 Activities	**ELL HANDBOOK** • High-Frequency Words Activity Bank, p. 446	**ELL HANDBOOK** • High-Frequency Words Activity Bank, p. 446
TEACHER'S EDITION • Grammar Jammer **ELL HANDBOOK** • Grammar Transition Lesson, pp. 324–325, 330–332 • Grammar Jammer Routine, p. 478	**TEACHER'S EDITION** • Grammar Jammer **ELL HANDBOOK** • Grammar Transition Lesson, pp. 324–325, 330–332	**TEACHER'S EDITION** • Grammar Jammer **ELL HANDBOOK** • Grammar Transition Lesson, pp. 324–325, 330–332
TEACHER'S EDITION • Let's Write It!, p. 422–423 • Writing Trait: Organization, p. 423a • Writer's Craft: Parts of a Letter, p. 423b	**TEACHER'S EDITION** • Revising Strategy, pp. 429d–429e	**TEACHER'S EDITION** • Verb Tenses, pp. 429p–429q

Question of the Week

How do weather patterns affect our lives?

Throughout the week, use the ELL Poster to help students produce and comprehend language, understand the concept, and build English vocabulary. Use the Question of the Week and other questions to help students share ideas in pairs, small groups, or the large group. Sample questions are shown, with examples of possible responses by students.

ELL Poster 14

Weekly Concept and Language Goals

• Understand the concept of weather patterns

• Tell how weather patterns affect our lives

• Name different weather patterns and their effects

By the end of the lesson, students should be able to talk about and write sentences about weather patterns and their effects.

Daily Team Talk

Day 1	Day 2	Day 3	Day 4	Day 5
After Day 1 activities on Poster, ask questions such as *What are some weather patterns you can see in the poster picture?*	After Day 2 activity on Poster, ask questions such as *Look for the snow symbol in the poster picture. How does the snow affect the people who live in that place?*	After Day 3 activity on Poster, ask questions such as *Look for the sun symbol in the poster picture. How does the sunshine affect the people who live in that place?*	After Day 4 activity on Poster, ask questions such as *How can people in the poster picture learn about weather patterns?*	After Day 5 activity on Poster, ask questions such as *What is the weather pattern today? How does it affect you?*
Beginning Snow and rain. **Intermediate** There is snow, rain, and sunshine in places. **Advanced** In different places, snow fell, the sun is shining, and there is a storm. **Advanced High** Different places are having different kinds of weather. One place has snow, and another has clouds. It is sunny in one place and stormy in another.	**Beginning** They wear coats. **Intermediate** They have to shovel the snow. **Advanced** The people have to shovel the sidewalk. **Advanced High** The people have to shovel the snow off the sidewalk. They look cold.	**Beginning** It is warm. **Intermediate** The sun makes it warm. **Advanced** That place is sunny and warm. People are outside enjoying the sun. **Advanced High** People are riding bikes outside. They are enjoying the sunshine and the warm air.	**Beginning** From the man. **Intermediate** The man tells about the weather. **Advanced** The weatherman shows people the weather each day. **Advanced High** The weather forecaster reports about the weather each day. People can watch him to find out about weather patterns.	**Beginning** It's raining. **Intermediate** It is raining outside. I got wet. **Advanced** It is rainy and cold. I had to use an umbrella. **Advanced High** The weather pattern today is cold and rainy. I had to wear a jacket and use an umbrella on my way to school.

Teacher's Edition pages 402j–429q

See the support for English language learners throughout the lesson, including ELL strategies and scaffolded activities at points of use.

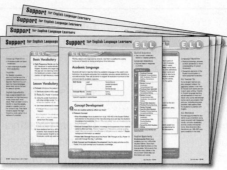

Teacher's Edition pages DI•91–DI•100

Differentiated Instruction for English language learners provides daily group activities that "frontload," or preteach, core instruction.

ELL Handbook pp. 107a–112

Find additional lesson materials that support the core lesson and the ELL instructional pages.

ELL Poster 14

ELL Reader 4.3.4

ELD Reader 4.3.4

Concept Literacy Reader

ELD, ELL Reader
Teaching Guide

Concept Literacy Reader
Teaching Guide

Technology

Online Teacher's Edition Use the digital version of the core Teacher's Edition for planning and instruction.

eReaders
This week's ELL and ELD Readers and Concept Literacy Reader are also available in digital format.

This Week's Content and Language Objectives by Strand

Concept Development/ Academic Language How do weather patterns affect our lives?	**Content Objective** • Use concept vocabulary related to weather patterns. **Language Objectives** • Express ideas in response to art and discussion. • Use students prior knowledge and experience to understand meanings.
Phonics and Spelling Compound Words	**Content Objective** • Understand compound words. **Language Objective** • Apply phonics and decoding skills to vocabulary.
Listening Comprehension Modified Read Aloud: "Amazing Tornados"	**Content Objective** • Monitor and adjust oral comprehension. **Language Objectives** • Discuss oral passages. • Use graphic organizer to take notes.
Reading Comprehension Cause and Effect	**Content Objectives** • Interpret causes and effects. • Identify clue words that indicate causes and effects. **Language Objectives** • Discuss cause-and-effect relationships in a story. • Cite causes and effects in an example. • Summarize text using visual support.
Vocabulary Basic and Lesson Vocabulary	**Language Objectives** • Understand and use basic vocabulary. • Learn meanings of grade-level vocabulary. • Produce drawings, phrases, or short sentences to show understanding of Lesson Vocabulary.
Word Analysis Latin Roots *struct, scrib, script*	**Content Objective** • Understand words with the Latin roots *struct, scrib,* and *script*. **Language Objective** • Learn new language structures heard during instruction.
Grammar and Conventions Past, Present, and Future Tenses	**Content Objective** • Use past, present, and future tenses correctly. **Language Objectives** • Speak using sentences that contain past, present, and future tenses. • Write sentences using verb tenses correctly.
Writing Salutation, Body, and Closing	**Content Objective** • Recognize the parts of a letter. **Language Objectives** • Listen to example of well-written letters. • Share feedback for editing and revising.

destruction

expected

forecasts

inland

shatter

surge

Teacher Note: Beginning Teach two to three words. **Intermediate** Teach three to four words. **Advanced** Teach four to five words. **Advanced High** Teach all words.

Look at the pictures. **Read** the paragraphs.

• In the boxes below, **write** the effects for each cause shown.

Snow Dangers

You can have fun in the snow, but snow can also be dangerous. **Blizzards** are huge, powerful snowstorms. They usually cover a large area of land with many inches of snow. When this much snow falls, many schools and businesses are closed. The snow may knock down power lines.

In mountains, snow can cause another problem. **Avalanches** happen when snow slides down a mountain or slope. As the snow slides, it picks up speed and power and gathers more snow. As a result, it can cover anything in its path with piles of deep snow including people and houses.

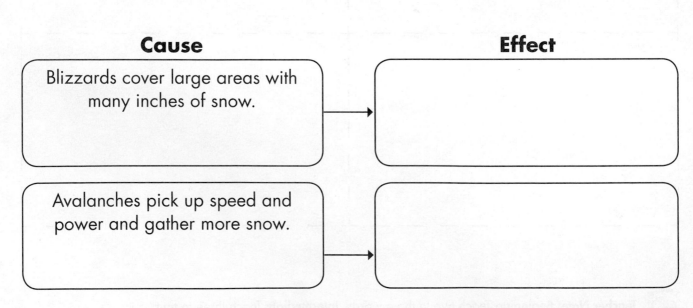

Cause	**Effect**
Blizzards cover large areas with many inches of snow.	
Avalanches pick up speed and power and gather more snow.	

Cause and Effect

Use this lesson to supplement or replace the skill lesson on page 403c of the Teacher's Edition. Display the Skill Points (at right) and share them with students.

Teach/Model

Beginning Say: *The road is full of snow. Cars can't get through.* Have students identify the cause (the road is full of snow) and the effect (cars can't get through). Show students how to combine the sentences using the clue word *because*.

Intermediate Write and read aloud: *Leaves blow everywhere. It is windy today.* Have students copy the sentences and label the cause (It is windy today) and the effect (Leaves blow everywhere). Then have them combine the sentences using a clue word.

Advanced Say: *I am opening an umbrella. Opening an umbrella is an effect. Why would I open an umbrella?* (It is raining.) *The rain is the cause.* Have students write a sentence using that cause and effect and think of other effects that could result from that cause.

Advanced High Pair students. One partner writes a cause-and-effect sentence using a clue word such as *because, so,* or *cause.* The other partner reads the sentence and labels the cause, the effect, and the clue word. Then partners trade roles.

Then distribute copies of Picture It! page 108.

- Have students look at the pictures. Then read the paragraph aloud.
- Ask: *What could cause power lines to be knocked down?* (heavy snow from a blizzard)
- Review the Skill Points with students.
- Have students write an effect for each cause shown.

Practice

Read aloud the directions on page 108. Have students reread the paragraph silently. Have them look at the pictures and the paragraph as they fill in the cause-and-effect boxes.

Beginning Students can say what effects they want to write and point to the evidence in the paragraph that supports their answers before writing in the boxes. Provide help with English words and writing.

Intermediate Students can underline the effects in the paragraph and then write their answers in the boxes. Provide help with writing.

Advanced Students can write effect sentences in the boxes and then check their answers by finding the causes and effects in the paragraph.

Advanced High Students can write effect sentences in the boxes and then orally identify other effects of blizzards or avalanches.

Answers for page 108: *Effect:* Many schools and businesses are closed. The snow may knock down power lines. *Effect:* It can cover anything in its path with piles of deep snow.

Skill Points

✔ An **effect** is something that happens. A **cause** is why it happens.

✔ Sometimes clue words such as *because, so,* and *cause* show causes and effects. Sometimes causes and effects do not have clue words.

Multilingual Summaries

Eye of the Storm

Warren Faidley is a storm chaser. He travels around the United States to photograph tornadoes, thunderstorms, and hurricanes. Warren pays close attention to weather forecasts. When the forecast says a hurricane is coming, Warren flies to the place where it will be. He went to Florida in 1992 to see Hurricane Andrew.

Warren and two other storm chasers stayed in a parking garage. They listened to weather reports. The storm came at 2:30 in the morning. The wind was loud and strong. Around 5:15, the storm reached its peak and the parking garage started to shake. They heard car alarms and windows breaking.

Around 6:00, it began to get light outside. Warren carefully went out. Broken boats were on the beach and in the streets. Trees were bent by the wind. Buildings were damaged. Warren took lots of pictures.

Spanish

El ojo de la tormenta

Warren Faidley es un cazador de tormentas. Viaja por todo el territorio de Estados Unidos para sacar fotografías de tornados, tormentas y huracanes. Warren siempre está muy atento a lo que dicen los pronósticos del tiempo. Cuando un pronóstico dice que se acerca un huracán, Warren vuela al sitio donde la tormenta llegará. Él fue a la Florida en 1992 para ver el huracán Andrew.

Warren y otros dos cazadores de tormentas estaban en un estacionamiento. Escuchaban los reportes del tiempo. La tormenta llegó a las 2:30 de la madrugada. El viento era fuerte y hacía mucho ruido. Alrededor de las 5:15, la tormenta alcanzó su máximo y el estacionamiento comenzó a temblar. Escucharon el sonido de muchas alarmas de autos y de vidrios de las ventanas rompiéndose.

Alrededor de las 6:00, comenzó a amanecer. Con mucho cuidado, Warren salió del lugar donde se encontraba. Había botes destrozados tanto en la playa como en las calles. Los árboles se habían doblado por la fuerza del viento. Muchos edificios estaban destruidos. Warren tomó muchísimas fotos.

Multilingual Summaries

風暴的眼睛

　　華倫˙費德萊是一名風暴追逐者，他跑遍整個美國，為的是要拍下龍捲風、大雷雨和颶風的照片。華倫非常注意天氣預報，只要預報說有颶風要來，華倫一定馬上搭飛機飛到將會出現颶風的地方。1992 年的時候他曾經到佛羅里達州親身經歷安德魯颶風的威力。

　　華倫和其他兩名風暴追逐者待在車庫裡，他們留心聽著天氣預報，預報說風暴會在凌晨兩點三十分的時候來。外面的風好強，風呼呼吹的聲音好大。大概在五點十五分的時候，風暴開始發揮它最強的威力，連車庫都開始震動，還可以聽到汽車警報和窗子破裂的聲音。

　　大約六點時，外面風雨開始變小，天也漸漸亮了。華倫小心翼翼地走出去一探究竟。被風吹壞的小船散佈在海灘和街道上，樹被吹歪，大樓也被風吹起來的東西砸得亂七八糟。華倫等的就是這個，他興奮地拍了好多照片。

Mắt Bão

　　Warren Faidley là một người săn đuổi bão. Ông ấy du lịch vòng quanh Hoa Kỳ để chụp ảnh những cơn lốc xoáy, mưa bão sấm sét, và bão lớn. Warren rất chú ý đến các dự báo thời tiết. Khi dự báo nói rằng có cơn bão lớn sắp đến. Warren bay đến nơi sẽ có bão. Ông đã đi đến Florida vào năm 1992 để xem cơn Bão Andrew.

　　Warren và hai người săn đuổi bão khác ở trong một khu nhà đậu xe. Họ nghe báo cáo thời tiết. Cơn bão đến vào lúc 2:30 giờ sáng. Gió ầm ĩ và mạnh. Vào khoảng 5:15 giờ, cơn bão lên đến mức mạnh nhất và khu nhà đậu xe bắt đầu rung chuyển. Họ nghe những máy báo động chống trộm trong các chiếc xe kêu vang và cửa sổ xe rạn vỡ.

　　Vào khoảng 6:00 giờ, bên ngoài trời bắt đầu sáng lại. Warren thận trọng bước ra ngoài. Tàu thuyền gẫy vỡ nằm trên bãi biển và trên đường. Cây cối bị gió uốn cong. Nhà cửa bị hư hại. Warren chụp được nhiều ảnh.

Multilingual Summaries

Korean

폭풍의 눈

워렌 페이들리는 폭풍을 추적하는 사람으로 미국 전역을 여행하며 토네이도, 뇌우, 허리케인 등을 사진에 담는다. 워렌은 일기예보에 특히 귀를 기울이는데 허리케인이 예보되면 비행기를 타고 예보된 장소로 날아간다. 그는 1992년 허리케인 앤드류를 보기 위해 플로리다로 갔다.

워렌과 두 명의 다른 폭풍 추적자들이 차고에서 일기예보를 듣고 있었다. 폭풍은 새벽 2시 30분에 닥쳤다. 바람은 요란했다. 5시15분쯤 폭풍은 최고조에 달했고 차고가 흔들거리기 시작했다. 그들은 차의 경보음과 창문이 깨지는 소리를 들었다.

6시경에는 밖이 환해지기 시작했다. 워렌은 조심스럽게 밖으로 나갔다. 부서진 배들이 해변과 길가에 즐비했고 나무들은 바람에 휘어졌으며 건물들도 손상을 입었다. 워렌은 많은 사진을 찍었다.

Hmong

Hauv Nruab Nrab Ntawm Kob Nag Loj

Warren Faidley yog ib tug uas caum nag xob nag cua. Nws mus ncig lub United States mus thaij duab txog tej cua kauj zig, tej nag xob nag cua, thiab tej cua daj cua dub. Warrens saib ntsoov tej huab cua. Thaum lawv qhuaj hais tias yuav muaj ib kob cua daj cua dub, Warren ya dav hlau mus rau qhov chaw ntawd. Nws tau mus hauv Florida thaum lub 1992 mus saib Kob Cua Daj Cua Dub Andrew.

Warren thiab ob tug uas caum nag xob nag cua tau nyob hauv ib qhov chaw nres tshej. Lawv mloog xov xwm huab cua. Tau muaj kob nag xob thaum 2:30 yas sawv ntxov. Cov cua nrov thiab muaj zog heev. Thaum li 5:15, kob nag xob tau muaj zog heev thiab qhov chaw nres tshej tau pib co. Lawv hnov tej tshej pib quaj thiab tej tshej tej qhov rais pib txawg.

Thaum li 6:00, nws pib kab nraum zoov. Warren maj mam mus nraum zoov. Tej nkoj tau piam tau nyob ntawm ntug dej hiav txwv thiab ntawv tej kev. Cov cua tau ua tej ntoo lov. Tej tsev tau piam. Warren tau thaij ntau daim duab.

Name_____

- **Read** *Watch Out for Hurricanes!* again.
- **Look** at the time line. These are important dates from the story.
- **Write** what happened in each of these years.

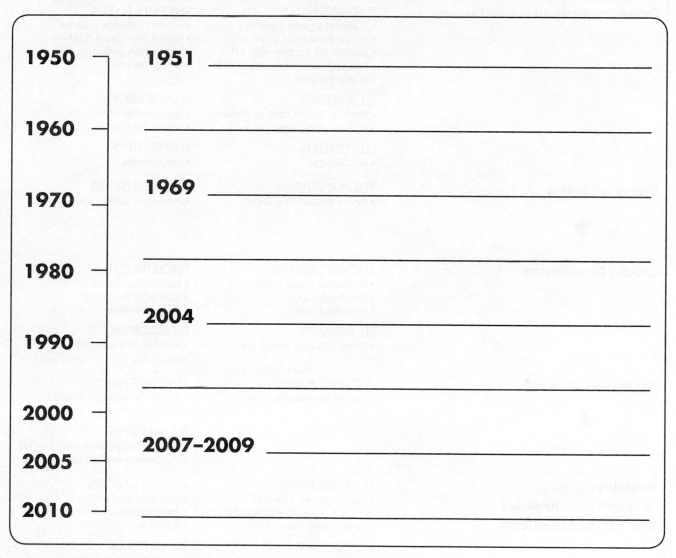

Family Link

Has anyone in your family ever been in a bad storm or a hurricane?
Ask family members to share their experiences with very bad rainstorms
and windstorms.

Weekly Resources Guide for English Language Learner Support

For this week's content and language objectives, see p. 113e.

Instructional Strand	Day 1	Day 2
Concept Development/Academic Language	**TEACHER'S EDITION** • Academic Language, p. DI•116 • Concept Development, p. DI•116 • Anchored Talk, pp. 430j—430–431 • Preteach Academic Vocabulary, p. 433a • Concept Talk Video **ELL HANDBOOK** • Hear It, See It, Say It, Use It, pp. xxxvi–xxxvii • ELL Poster Talk, Concept Talk, p. 113c **ELL POSTER 15** • Day 1 Activities	**TEACHER'S EDITION** • Academic Language, p. DI•116 • Concept Development, p. DI•116 • Anchored Talk, p. 434a • Concept Talk Video **ELL HANDBOOK** • ELL Poster Talk, Concept Talk, p. 113c • Concept Talk Video Routine, p. 477 **ELL POSTER 15** • Day 2 Activities
Phonics and Spelling	**TEACHER'S EDITION** • Phonics and Spelling, p. DI•120	**TEACHER'S EDITION** • Phonics and Spelling, p. DI•120
Listening Comprehension	**TEACHER'S EDITION** • Modified Read Aloud, p. DI•119 • Read Aloud, p. 431b • Concept Talk Video **ELL HANDBOOK** • Concept Talk Video Routine, p. 477	**TEACHER'S EDITION** • Modified Read Aloud, p. DI•119 • AudioText of *Paul Bunyan* • Concept Talk Video **ELL HANDBOOK** • AudioText CD Routine, p. 477 • Web, p. 486
Reading Comprehension	**TEACHER'S EDITION** • Preteach Generalization, p. DI•121	**TEACHER'S EDITION** • Reteach Generalization, p. DI•121 • Frontloading Reading, p. DI•122 **ELL HANDBOOK** • Picture It! Skill Instruction, pp. 114–114a • Multilingual Summaries, pp. 115–117
Vocabulary **Basic and Lesson Vocabulary** **Word Analysis: Related Words**	**TEACHER'S EDITION** • Basic Vocabulary, p. DI•117 • Preteach Lesson Vocabulary, p. DI•117 • Related Words, p. DI•120 **ELL HANDBOOK** • Word Cards, p. 113 • ELL Vocabulary Routine, p. 471 **ELL POSTER 15** • Day 1 Activities	**TEACHER'S EDITION** • Basic Vocabulary, p. DI•117 • Reteach Lesson Vocabulary, p. DI•118 • Related Words, p. DI•120 **ELL HANDBOOK** • Word Cards, p. 113 • Multilingual Vocabulary List, p. 431 **ELL POSTER 15** • Day 2 Activities
Grammar and Conventions	**TEACHER'S EDITION** • Preteach Irregular Verbs, p. DI•124	**TEACHER'S EDITION** • Reteach Irregular Verbs, p. DI•124
Writing	**TEACHER'S EDITION** • Eliminate Wordy or Run-on Sentences, p. DI•125 • Writing for Tests: Summary, pp. 433e–433f	**TEACHER'S EDITION** • Writing for Tests: Summary, pp. 443d–443e

This symbol indicates leveled instruction to address language proficiency levels.

Day 3	Day 4	Day 5
TEACHER'S EDITION • Academic Language, p. DI•116 • Concept Development, p. DI•116 • Anchored Talk, p. 444a • Concept Talk Video **ELL HANDBOOK** • ELL Poster Talk, Concept Talk, p. 113c **ELL POSTER 15** • Day 3 Activities	**TEACHER'S EDITION** • Academic Language, p. DI•116 • Concept Development, p. DI•116 • Anchored Talk, p. 454a • Concept Talk Video **ELL HANDBOOK** • ELL Poster Talk, Concept Talk, p. 113c **ELL POSTER 15** • Day 4 Activities	**TEACHER'S EDITION** • Academic Language, p. DI•116 • Concept Development, p. DI•116 • Concept Talk Video **ELL HANDBOOK** • ELL Poster Talk, Concept Talk, p. 113c **ELL POSTER 15** • Day 5 Activities
		TEACHER'S EDITION • Phonics and Spelling, p. DI•120
ELL HANDBOOK • Phonics Transition Lesson, pp. 268, 270	**ELL HANDBOOK** • Phonics Transition Lesson, pp. 268, 270	
TEACHER'S EDITION • AudioText of *Paul Bunyan* • Concept Talk Video **ELL HANDBOOK** • AudioText CD Routine, p. 477	**TEACHER'S EDITION** • Concept Talk Video	**TEACHER'S EDITION** • Concept Talk Video
TEACHER'S EDITION • Sheltered Reading, p. DI•122 **ELL HANDBOOK** • Multilingual Summaries, pp. 115–117	**TEACHER'S EDITION** • ELL/ELD Reader Guided Reading, p. DI•123 **ELL HANDBOOK** • ELL Study Guide, p. 118	**TEACHER'S EDITION** • ELL/ELD Reader Guided Reading, p. DI•123 **ELL HANDBOOK** • ELL Study Guide, p. 118
		TEACHER'S EDITION • Related Words, p. 459i
ELL HANDBOOK • High-Frequency Words Activity Bank, p. 446 **ELL POSTER 15** • Day 3 Activities	**ELL HANDBOOK** • High-Frequency Words Activity Bank, p. 446	**ELL HANDBOOK** • High-Frequency Words Activity Bank, p. 446
TEACHER'S EDITION • Grammar Jammer **ELL HANDBOOK** • Grammar Transition Lesson, pp. 325–326, 334 • Grammar Jammer Routine, p. 478	**TEACHER'S EDITION** • Grammar Jammer **ELL HANDBOOK** • Grammar Transition Lesson, pp. 325–326, 334	**TEACHER'S EDITION** • Grammar Jammer **ELL HANDBOOK** • Grammar Transition Lesson, pp. 325–326, 334
TEACHER'S EDITION • Let's Write It!, p. 452–453 • Writing for Tests: Evaluation, pp. 453a–453b	**TEACHER'S EDITION** • Writing for Tests: Summary, pp. 459d–459e	**TEACHER'S EDITION** • Writing for Tests: Conventions, pp. 459p–459q

Question of the Week
What causes changes in nature?

ELL Poster 15

Throughout the week, use the ELL Poster to help students produce and comprehend language, understand the concept, and build English vocabulary. Use the Question of the Week and other questions to help students share ideas in pairs, small groups, or the large group. Sample questions are shown, with examples of possible responses by students.

Weekly Concept and Language Goals

• Explain how people cause changes in nature
• Name various natural features and landscapes
• Describe how events in nature cause changes to the Earth

By the end of the lesson, students should be able to talk about and write sentences about changes in nature.

Daily Team Talk

Day 1	Day 2	Day 3	Day 4	Day 5
After Day 1 activities on Poster, ask questions such as *In the poster picture, what natural features do you see?*	After Day 2 activity on Poster, ask questions such as *What is happening in the poster picture that will change nature?*	After Day 3 activity on Poster, ask questions such as *People are cutting down trees. Is this change in nature caused by natural events? Why or why not?*	After Day 4 activity on Poster, ask questions such as *In the poster picture, what is one change in nature that is caused by natural events?*	After Day 5 activity on Poster, ask questions such as *Besides snow melting, what is another natural event that can change nature?*
Beginning Trees and snow. **Intermediate** There are trees and snow on the ground. **Advanced** I see woods, a mountain, and snow on the ground. **Advanced High** The natural features I see are a forest with many tall pine trees, a high mountain with snow on the top, and snow covering the ground.	**Beginning** Making a house. **Intermediate** They are making a house with wood. **Advanced** The men are building a house using logs. **Advanced High** The lumberjacks are cutting down trees to make logs for a house.	**Beginning** No. People do it. **Intermediate** No. People are changing it. **Advanced** It is not natural because it is caused by people. **Advanced High** The change is not caused by natural events because people are changing nature.	**Beginning** Snow going away. **Intermediate** The snow is melting. **Advanced** The snow is melting off the trees and on the ground. **Advanced High** The snow melting is a change in nature that is caused by natural events. Warm weather and spring are natural causes that cause snow to melt.	**Beginning** Wind blowing. **Intermediate** The wind can blow things over. **Advanced** The wind can cause change by breaking things and blowing things away. **Advanced High** The wind blowing is a natural event that can change nature. Strong winds can tear branches off trees or even knock trees down.

Teacher's Edition pages 430j–463a

See the support for English language learners throughout the lesson, including ELL strategies and scaffolded activities at points of use.

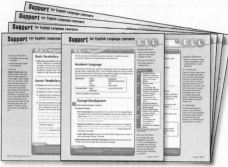

Teacher's Edition pages DI•116–DI•125

Differentiated Instruction for English language learners provides daily group activities that "frontload," or preteach, core instruction.

ELL Handbook pp. 113a–118

Find additional lesson materials that support the core lesson and the ELL instructional pages.

 Poster 15

ELL Reader 4.3.5

ELD Reader 4.3.5

Concept Literacy Reader

ELD, ELL Reader Teaching Guide

Concept Literacy Reader Teaching Guide

Technology

Online Teacher's Edition Use the digital version of the core Teacher's Edition for planning and instruction.

eReaders
This week's ELL and ELD Readers and Concept Literacy Reader are also available in digital format.

This Week's Content and Language Objectives by Strand

Concept Development/ Academic Language What causes changes in nature?	**Content Objective** • Use concept vocabulary related to what causes changes in nature. **Language Objectives** • Use verbal support to express ideas. • Use academic language.
Phonics and Spelling Possessives	**Content Objective** • Understand possessives. **Language Objective** • Apply phonics and decoding skills to vocabulary.
Listening Comprehension Modified Read Aloud: "Water—The Stuff of Life"	**Content Objective** • Monitor and adjust oral comprehension. **Language Objectives** • Discuss oral passages. • Use graphic organizer to take notes. • Use accessible language and learn essential language in process.
Reading Comprehension Generalization	**Content Objectives** • Interpret generalizations. • Identify clue words that indicate generalizations. **Language Objectives** • Discuss the generalization in a story. • Cite content from generalizations. • Internalize new academic language through writing.
Vocabulary Basic and Lesson Vocabulary	**Language Objectives** • Understand and use basic vocabulary. • Learn meanings of grade-level vocabulary. • Produce drawings, phrases, or short sentences to show understanding of Lesson Vocabulary.
Word Analysis Related Words	**Content Objective** • Understand related words. **Language Objective** • Correctly use related words.
Grammar and Conventions Irregular Verbs	**Content Objective** • Use irregular verbs correctly. **Language Objectives** • Speak using sentences that contain irregular verbs. • Write sentences using irregular verbs correctly.
Writing Eliminate Wordy or Run-on Sentences	**Content Objective** • Recognize wordy or run-on sentences. **Language Objectives** • Write using a variety of sentence lengths. • Write and edit to eliminate wordy or run-on sentences.

Word Cards for Vocabulary Activities

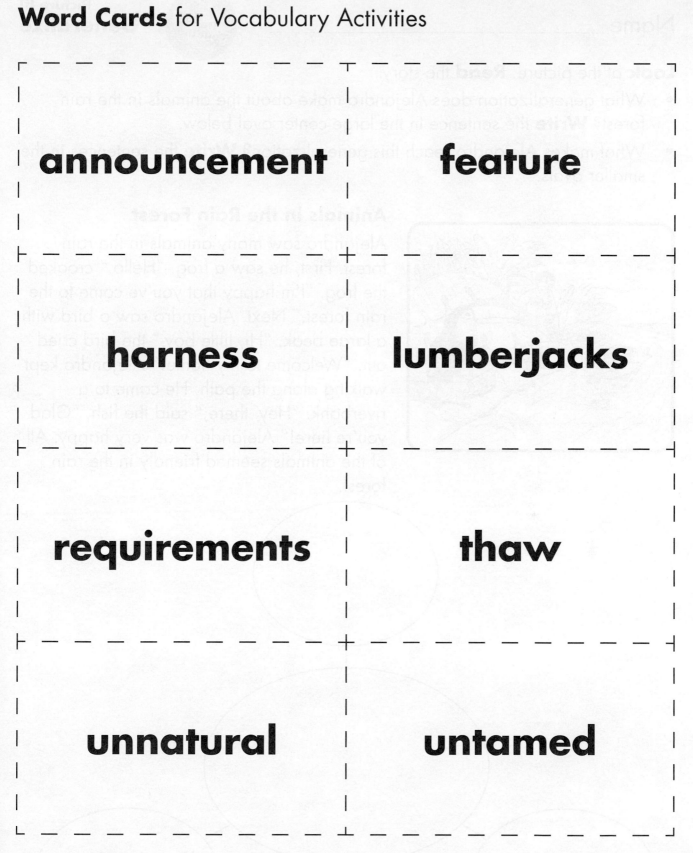

announcement

feature

harness

lumberjacks

requirements

thaw

unnatural

untamed

Teacher Note: Beginning Teach three to four words. **Intermediate** Teach four to six words. **Advanced** Teach six to seven words. **Advanced High** Teach all words.

Look at the picture. **Read** the story.

• What generalization does Alejandro make about the animals in the rain forest? **Write** the sentence in the large center oval below.

• What makes Alejandro reach this generalization? **Write** the sentences in the smaller ovals.

Animals in the Rain Forest

Alejandro saw many animals in the rain forest. First, he saw a frog. "Hello," croaked the frog. "I'm happy that you've come to the rain forest." Next, Alejandro saw a bird with a large beak. "Hi, little boy," the bird cried out. "Welcome to my home!" Alejandro kept walking along the path. He came to a riverbank. "Hey, there," said the fish. "Glad you're here!" Alejandro was very happy. All of the animals seemed friendly in the rain forest.

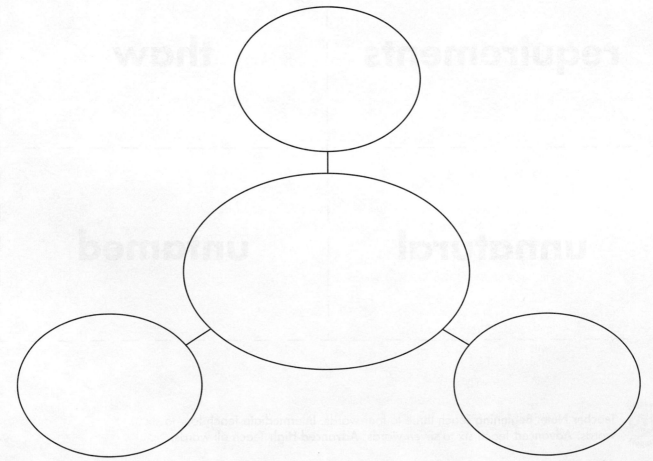

Generalize

Use this lesson to supplement or replace the skill lesson on page 431c of the Teacher's Edition. Display the Skill Points (at right) and share them with students.

Teach/Model

Beginning Write and read aloud: *Many insects are unusual. One insect looks like a stick. Another insect can glow.* Ask: *Which sentence is a generalization?* (Many insects are unusual.) Guide students in recognizing that the other sentences are examples that support the generalization.

Intermediate Write and read aloud: *Many kinds of plants grow only in the rain forest.* Ask: *What word tells you this is a generalization?* (Many) Ask students where they could find support for this generalization. (in reference books; on the Internet)

Advanced Write and read aloud: *Forests are always full of life.* Ask students how they know the sentence is a generalization. (It tells how forests are all alike. It contains the clue word *always*.) Have them write a sentence that supports the generalization. (Possible answers: Many animals live in forests. Many plants grow in forests.)

Advanced High Ask students to write a generalization about trees. Have them exchange generalizations with a partner. Each partner writes a sentence that supports the other partner's generalization.

Then distribute copies of Picture It! page 114.

- Have students look at the picture and name things they recognize.
- Read the paragraph aloud. Ask: *What does Alejandro think about the animals in the rain forest?* (He thinks they seem friendly.)
- Review the Skill Points with students.
- Have students identify the generalization in the story and find details that support it.

Practice

Read aloud the directions on page 114. Have volunteers reread the story aloud. Have students look at the picture and the story as they fill in the web.

Beginning Students can say the generalization and examples they want to write, pointing to the sentences that support their ideas, and then fill in the web. Provide help with filling in the web and with English words and writing.

Intermediate Students can first orally answer the questions at the top of the page and then write their answers in the web. Provide help with filling in the web if necessary.

Advanced Students can write sentences to fill in the web and then check their answers by comparing them to a partner's answers.

Advanced High Students can write sentences to fill in the web and then orally explain how they identified Alejandro's generalization and make their own generalizations about rain forests, using prior knowledge.

Answers for page 114: *Generalization:* The animals in the rain forest are generally friendly. *Details:* Students should write about the three animals and their friendly actions.

ELL Handbook

Skill Points

✔ A **generalization** is a sentence or rule that explains many examples.

✔ A good generalization is supported by many examples.

Unit 3, Week 5 *Paul Bunyan* **114a**

Multilingual Summaries

Paul Bunyan: American Tall Tales

A 100-pound baby was born in Maine. When he started to crawl, he caused an earthquake. The neighbors complained. His parents left him in a cave with an ax and other tools.

The baby caught a fish and used his tools to make dinner. After that, Paul Bunyan took care of himself in the woods and lived alone for twenty years. He rescued a big blue baby ox and called him Babe.

Paul Bunyan decided to invent logging. He and Babe traveled all over America. There are many stories about their travels. After traveling, he decided to start a logging camp. He and Babe moved on to the Arctic Circle. Loggers still tell stories of Paul Bunyan and Babe today.

Spanish

Paul Bunyan: Grandes cuentos americanos

En Maine nació un bebé que pesó 100 libras. Cuando él comenzó a gatear, causó un terremoto. Los vecinos se quejaron y us padres lo abandonaron en una cueva con un hacha y otras herramientas.

El bebé atrapó un pez y utilizó sus herramientas para preparar la comida. Tiempo después, Paul Bunyan aprendió a cuidarse solo en el bosque y vivió por su cuenta durante veinte años. Él rescató a un enorme y azul buey bebé y lo llamó Babe.

Paul Bunyan fue el primer leñador. Él y Babe viajaron por toda América. Existen muchas historias acerca de sus travesías. Después de viajar, él decidió abrir un campamento de leñadores. Luego, decidió irse con Babe a vivir al Ártico. Hoy en día, los leñadores todavía cuentan historias sobre Paul Bunyan y Babe.

Multilingual Summaries

Chinese

美國奇聞 (Paul Bunyan)

緬因州有一個新生兒重達 100 磅。 在他開始學會爬時，造成了地震。 鄰居頻頻抱怨。 於是，他的父母把他放到了一個洞穴裡，還在他身邊留下了一把斧頭和其他工具。

這名嬰兒抓到了一條魚，並利用工具做晚餐。 之後，保羅 班揚就在森林裡過活，自己獨自生活了二十年。 他救了一頭體型很大的藍色小牛，並叫他「寶貝」。

保羅 班揚決定開始伐木。 他和寶貝遊遍了美國各地。 流傳著許許多多他們旅程中的故事。 旅行結束後，他決定創立一個伐木營地。他和寶貝搬到了北極圈去住。 直到現在，伐木工人仍然在傳頌著保羅 班揚和寶貝的故事。

Vietnamese

Chuyện Dân Gian Mỹ (Paul Bunyan)

Có một em bé nặng100 cân được sanh ra tại Maine. Khi bắt đầu biết bò, nó gây động đất. Hàng xóm phàn nàn về nó. Cha mẹ nó mới bỏ nó vào hang núi và cho thêm cái búa và các dụng cụ khác.

Em bé bắt cá và dùng dụng cụ để làm bữa ăn. Sau đó, Paul Bunyan sống một mình trong rừng và cô đơn trong hai mươi năm. Ông ta cứu được một con bò con lớn màu xanh và gọi nó là Babe.

Paul Bunyan bắt đầu khai khẩn rừng núi. Ông ta và Babe du hành toàn khắp nước Mỹ. Có rất nhiều câu chuyện về cuộc hành trình của họ. Sau cuộc hành trình, họ làm một cái trại bằng gỗ. Ông ta và Babe dời lên vùng cực Arctic Circle ở. Hiện nay những người bán gỗ vẫn còn kể nhiều chuyện về Paul Bunyan và Babe.

Multilingual Summaries

믿기 어려운 미국의 전설
(Paul Bunyan)

메인 주에서 무게가 백 파운드나 되는 아기가 태어난다. 아기가 기기 시작하자 지진이 일어났으며, 이웃들이 불평했다. 부모는 아기를 도끼와 다른 도구들과 함께 동굴에 버려두었다.

아기는 도구를 이용하여 물고기를 잡아서 저녁식사를 만들었다. 그 이후에 폴 버냔은 스스로를 돌보며 숲속에서 이십 년 동안 혼자 살았다. 그는 커다란 파란 송아지를 구해준 후 베이브라는 이름을 붙였다.

폴 버냔은 벌목을 하기로 결심했다. 그와 베이비는 미국 전역을 여행했다. 그들의 여행에 관한 이야기는 아주 많다. 여행 후에 그는 벌목 캠프를 시작했다. 그 후에 그와 베이브는 북극권으로 옮겨갔다. 벌목꾼들은 오늘날에도 여전히 폴 버냔과 베이브의 이야기를 한다.

Dab Neeg Asmesliskas
(Paul Bunyan)

Muaj ib tug me nyuam 100-pound yug nyob luv lav Maine. Thaum nws pib txawj nkag, nws ua rau av qeeg. Tej neeg nyob ze ib koog ntawd tsis txaus siab. Nws niam thiab nws txiv tso nws nyob tim qhov tsua nrog ib ib rab taus thiab lwm khoom siv.

Tus me nyuam ntawd ntes tau ib tug ntses thiab siv nws cov khoom coj los npaj ua hmo. Lawv qab ntawd, Paul Bunyan zov nws nyob tom hav zoov thiab nws nyob ib leeg tau 20 lub xyoo. Nws kuj pab cawm tau ib me nyuam nyuj qus xiav xiav thiab muab hu ua Babe.

Paul Bunyan txiav txim siab los txiav ntoo. Nws thiab Babe mus ncig thoov lub Asmeslikas teb no. Nws muaj ntau zaj dab neeg txog nkawd qhov kev ncig no. Lawv qab ntawm nkawd ncig, nws txiav txim siab ua lub chaw so rau txiav ntoo. Nws thiab Babe thiaj tsiv mus nyob rau Arctic Circle. Niaj hnub no neeg txiv ntoo tseem piav txog Paul Bunyan thiab Babe zaj dab neeg.

Name _____

- **Read** *Changes in Nature* again.
- In the box, **draw** a way an animal or a plant changes when the seasons change.
- **Write** four facts about the change you drew.

1. _____

2. _____

3. _____

4. _____

Family Link

Show your drawing to family members. Explain what you learned about changes in nature. Ask if they can think of another example of a change in nature.

Weekly Resources Guide for English Language Learner Support

For this week's content and language objectives, see p. 119e.

Instructional Strand	Day 1	Day 2
Concept Development/Academic Language	**TEACHER'S EDITION** • Academic Language, p. DI•16 • Concept Development, p. DI•16 • Anchored Talk, pp. 20j—20–21 • Preteach Academic Vocabulary, p. 23a • Concept Talk Video **ELL HANDBOOK** • Hear It, See It, Say It, Use It, pp. xxxvi–xxxvii • ELL Poster Talk, Concept Talk, p. 119c **ELL POSTER 16** • Day 1 Activities	**TEACHER'S EDITION** • Academic Language, p. DI•16 • Concept Development, p. DI•16 • Anchored Talk, p. 24a • Concept Talk Video **ELL HANDBOOK** • ELL Poster Talk, Concept Talk, p. 119c • Concept Talk Video Routine, p. 477 **ELL POSTER 16** • Day 2 Activities
Phonics and Spelling	**TEACHER'S EDITION** • Phonics and Spelling, p. DI•20	**TEACHER'S EDITION** • Phonics and Spelling, p. DI•20
Listening Comprehension	**TEACHER'S EDITION** • Modified Read Aloud, p. DI•19 • Read Aloud, p. 21b • Concept Talk Video **ELL HANDBOOK** • Concept Talk Video Routine, p. 477	**TEACHER'S EDITION** • Modified Read Aloud, p. DI•19 • AudioText of *The Case of the Gasping Garbage* • Concept Talk Video **ELL HANDBOOK** • AudioText CD Routine, p. 477 • Story Map A, p. 483
Reading Comprehension	**TEACHER'S EDITION** • Preteach Compare and Contrast, p. DI•21	**TEACHER'S EDITION** • Reteach Compare and Contrast, p. DI•21 • Frontloading Reading, p. DI•22 **ELL HANDBOOK** • Picture It! Skill Instruction, pp. 120–120a • Multilingual Summaries, pp. 121–123
Vocabulary **Basic and Lesson Vocabulary** **Word Analysis: Related Words**	**TEACHER'S EDITION** • Basic Vocabulary, p. DI•17 • Preteach Lesson Vocabulary, p. DI•17 • Related Words, p. DI•20 **ELL HANDBOOK** • Word Cards, p. 119 • ELL Vocabulary Routine, p. 471 **ELL POSTER 16** • Day 1 Activities	**TEACHER'S EDITION** • Basic Vocabulary, p. DI•17 • Reteach Lesson Vocabulary, p. DI•18 • Related Words, p. DI•20 **ELL HANDBOOK** • Word Cards, p. 119 • Multilingual Vocabulary List, p. 431 **ELL POSTER 16** • Day 2 Activities
Grammar and Conventions	**TEACHER'S EDITION** • Preteach Singular and Plural Pronouns, p. DI•24	**TEACHER'S EDITION** • Reteach Singular and Plural Pronouns, p. DI•24
Writing	**TEACHER'S EDITION** • Create Rhythm and Style, p. DI•25 • Introduce Mystery, pp. 23e–23f	**TEACHER'S EDITION** • Strategy: Story Sequence Chart, pp. 35d–35e

The Case of the Gasping Garbage

This symbol indicates leveled instruction to address language proficiency levels.

Day 3	Day 4	Day 5
TEACHER'S EDITION • Academic Language, p. DI•16 • Concept Development, p. DI•16 • Anchored Talk, p. 36a • Concept Talk Video **ELL HANDBOOK** • ELL Poster Talk, Concept Talk, p. 119c **ELL POSTER 16** • Day 3 Activities	**TEACHER'S EDITION** • Academic Language, p. DI•16 • Concept Development, p. DI•16 • Anchored Talk, p. 46a • Concept Talk Video **ELL HANDBOOK** • ELL Poster Talk, Concept Talk, p. 119c **ELL POSTER 16** • Day 4 Activities	**TEACHER'S EDITION** • Academic Language, p. DI•16 • Concept Development, p. DI•16 • Concept Talk Video **ELL HANDBOOK** • ELL Poster Talk, Concept Talk, p. 119c **ELL POSTER 16** • Day 5 Activities
		TEACHER'S EDITION • Phonics and Spelling, p. DI•20
ELL HANDBOOK • Phonics Transition Lesson, pp. 280, 283	**ELL HANDBOOK** • Phonics Transition Lesson, pp. 280, 283	
TEACHER'S EDITION • AudioText of *The Case of the Gasping Garbage* • Concept Talk Video **ELL HANDBOOK** • AudioText CD Routine, p. 477	**TEACHER'S EDITION** • Concept Talk Video	**TEACHER'S EDITION** • Concept Talk Video
TEACHER'S EDITION • Sheltered Reading, p. DI•22 **ELL HANDBOOK** • Multilingual Summaries, pp. 121–123	**TEACHER'S EDITION** • ELL/ELD Reader Guided Reading, p. DI•23 **ELL HANDBOOK** • ELL Study Guide, p. 124	**TEACHER'S EDITION** • ELL/ELD Reader Guided Reading, p. DI•23 **ELL HANDBOOK** • ELL Study Guide, p. 124
		TEACHER'S EDITION • Suffixes *-ian, ist, ism,* p. 51i **ELL HANDBOOK** • High-Frequency Words Activity Bank, p. 446
ELL HANDBOOK • High-Frequency Words Activity Bank, p. 446 **ELL POSTER 16** • Day 3 Activities	**ELL HANDBOOK** • High-Frequency Words Activity Bank, p. 446	
TEACHER'S EDITION • Grammar Jammer **ELL HANDBOOK** • Grammar Transition Lesson, pp. 362–369 • Grammar Jammer Routine, p. 478	**TEACHER'S EDITION** • Grammar Jammer **ELL HANDBOOK** • Grammar Transition Lesson, pp. 362–369	**TEACHER'S EDITION** • Grammar Jammer **ELL HANDBOOK** • Grammar Transition Lesson, pp. 362–369
TEACHER'S EDITION • Let's Write It!, p. 44–45 • Writing Trait: Word Choice, pp. 45a–45b	**TEACHER'S EDITION** • Revising Strategy, pp. 51d–51e	**TEACHER'S EDITION** • Singular and Plural Pronouns, pp. 51p–51q

Poster Talk, Concept Talk

Question of the Week
Why can't you always believe what you think you see?

Throughout the week, use the ELL Poster to help students produce and comprehend language, understand the concept, and build English vocabulary. Use the Question of the Week and other questions to help students share ideas in pairs, small groups, or the large group. Sample questions are shown, with examples of possible responses by students.

ELL Poster 16

Weekly Concept and Language Goals

• Understand perception

• Identify how perception can change

• Tell how scientists test a hypothesis

By the end of the lesson, students should be able to talk about and write sentences about perception.

Daily Team Talk

Day 1	Day 2	Day 3	Day 4	Day 5
After Day 1 activities on Poster, ask questions such as *Before the students in the poster picture study the water, what do they think about the water? What is their perception?*	After Day 2 activity on Poster, ask questions such as *What do the students think about the water after they study it? How does their perception change?*	After Day 3 activity on Poster, ask questions such as *How do the students in the poster picture study the water?*	After Day 4 activity on Poster, ask questions such as *In the story* The Case of the Gasping Garbage, *what is Gabby's perception of the garbage can?*	After Day 5 activity on Poster, ask questions such as *How do Doyle and Fossey test their hypothesis in the story* The Case of the Gasping Garbage?
Beginning It's clear. **Intermediate** They think there is nothing in it. **Advanced** The students think the water has nothing in it. **Advanced High** Before they study the water, the students believe that there is nothing in it.	**Beginning** It has things in it. **Intermediate** The water has things in it. **Advanced** The pond water has living things in it. **Advanced High** When you look at pond water through a microscope, you will see living things in the water.	**Beginning** With a microscope. **Intermediate** They put water on slides and look at it. **Advanced** They put pond water on a slide and look at it through the microscope. **Advanced High** The students put a precise amount of pond water on a slide and examine the slide through a microscope.	**Beginning** It has a monster. **Intermediate** She thinks it has a monster in it. **Advanced** Gabby thinks there is a monster in the garbage can. **Advanced High** Gabby's perception of the garbage can is that it contains a gasping monster, but it is only growing yeast.	**Beginning** They do tests. **Intermediate** They do experiments on the garbage can. **Advanced** They make their lab hot, just like Gabby's garage, so they can test the can. **Advanced High** Doyle and Fossey recreate the conditions in Gabby's garage to see what makes the garbage gasp.

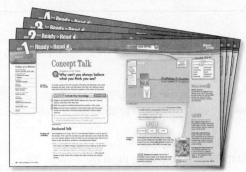

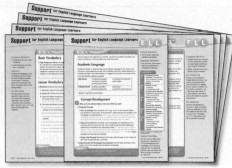

Teacher's Edition pages 20j–51q

Teacher's Edition pages DI•16–DI•25

ELL Handbook pp. 119a–124

See the support for English language learners throughout the lesson, including ELL strategies and scaffolded activities at points of use.

Differentiated Instruction for English language learners provides daily group activities that "frontload," or preteach, core instruction.

Find additional lesson materials that support the core lesson and the ELL instructional pages.

ELL Poster 16

ELL Reader 4.4.1

ELD Reader 4.4.1

Concept Literacy Reader

ELD, ELL Reader Teaching Guide

Concept Literacy Reader Teaching Guide

Technology

Online Teacher's Edition Use the digital version of the core Teacher's Edition for planning and instruction.

eReaders
This week's ELL and ELD Readers and Concept Literacy Reader are also available in digital format.

This Week's Content and Language Objectives by Strand

Concept Development/ Academic Language Why can't you always believe what you think you see?	**Content Objective** • Use concept vocabulary related to not always believing what you think you see. **Language Objectives** • Express ideas in response to art and discussion. • Use students' prior knowledge and experience to understand meanings.
Phonics and Spelling Contractions	**Content Objective** • Identify contractions and the words that make them up. **Language Objective** • Apply phonics and decoding skills to vocabulary.
Listening Comprehension Modified Read Aloud: "New Clothes for the Emperor"	**Content Objective** • Monitor and adjust oral comprehension. **Language Objectives** • Discuss oral passages. • Use a graphic organizer to take notes.
Reading Comprehension Compare and Contrast	**Content Objectives** • Monitor and adjust comprehension. • Make and adjust predictions. **Language Objectives** • Read grade-level text with expression. • Use learned vocabulary to summarize text using visual support.
Vocabulary Basic and Lesson Vocabulary	**Language Objectives** • Understand and use basic vocabulary. • Learn meanings of grade-level vocabulary. • Produce drawings, phrases, and short sentences to show and internalize understanding of Lesson Vocabulary. • Speak using learning strategies by using synonyms.
Word Analysis Related Words	**Content Objective** • Identify words with suffixes *–ian, -ist,* and *-ism.* **Language Objective** • Read and write words with suffixes *–ian, -ist,* and *-ism.*
Grammar and Conventions Singular and Plural Pronouns	**Content Objectives** • Decode and use singular and plural pronouns. • Correctly form singular and plural pronouns. **Language Objectives** • Speak using singular and plural pronouns. • Write and edit phrases and sentences for pronoun agreement.
Writing Create Rhythm and Style	**Content Objective** • Recognize the use of rhythm and style in a text. **Language Objectives** • Write paragraphs with rhythm and style. • Share feedback for editing and revising using appropriate sentence lengths.

Word Cards for Vocabulary Activities

analysis	**beakers**
hollow	**identify**
lecture	**microscope**
precise	**relentless**

Teacher Note: Beginning Teach three to four words. **Intermediate** Teach four to six words. **Advanced** Teach six to seven words. **Advanced High** Teach all words.

Name _____

Look at the picture. **Read** the paragraph.

- How are Harry Houdini and David Copperfield similar? **Write** your ideas in the middle section of the Venn diagram.
- How are they different? **Describe** Houdini in the left-hand side of the diagram. **Describe** Copperfield in the right-hand side of the diagram.

Famous Magicians of the Past and Present

Harry Houdini was born in Hungary in 1874. He came to the United States when he was four years old. When he was fifteen, he decided to be an escape artist. He became the most famous magician of his time. He starred in many movies. He died in 1926.

David Copperfield was born in New Jersey in 1956. He is an illusionist: he knows how to make things seem to disappear. He has starred in many television shows and is the most famous magician of his time. Like Houdini, he became interested in magic as a young boy.

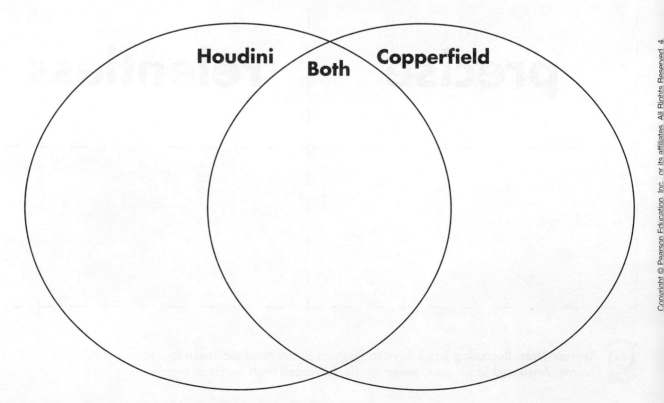

Houdini   **Both**   **Copperfield**

ELL Handbook

Compare and Contrast

Use this lesson to supplement or replace the skill lesson on page 21c of the Teacher's Edition. Display the Skill Points (at right) and share them with students.

Teach/Model

Beginning Ask students to think about football and baseball. Ask: *How are these two sports similar? How are they different?* Draw a Venn diagram on the board and complete it with students' ideas. Remind students they are using information they already know about the two sports.

Intermediate Say: *Travis and Jane like to go to the circus. Travis loves the clowns. Jane admires the trapeze artists. They both want to become circus performers.* Guide students in completing a Venn diagram that compares and contrasts Travis and Jane. Repeat the story if necessary.

Advanced Tell students to find something in the classroom that can be described with an adjective such as *red* or *small*. When everyone has an object, choose two volunteers and discuss how their objects are alike and different. Repeat this process with other volunteers or a different adjective.

Advanced High Pair students. Ask partners to share information about their favorite hobbies. Have them work together to complete a Venn diagram that compares and contrasts their hobbies.

Then distribute copies of Picture It! page 120.

- Have students look at the picture. Then read the paragraph aloud.
- Ask: *How was Harry Houdini different from other magicians?* (He performed real acts of escape.)
- Review the Skill Points with students.
- Have students describe how Houdini and David Copperfield are similar and different.

Practice

Read aloud the directions on page 120. Have two volunteers reread the information about each magician. Have students use the paragraphs as they fill in the Venn diagram.

Beginning Students can say what they want to write in each section of the diagram before writing their answers on the page. Provide help with filling in a Venn diagram and with writing.

Intermediate Students can first orally tell how the two magicians are similar and different and then write their answers in the Venn diagram.

Advanced Students can write their answers in the Venn diagram and then check them by comparing their Venn diagram with a partner's.

Advanced High Students can write their answers in the Venn diagram and then check them by reviewing the paragraphs.

Answers for page 120: *Houdini:* born in Hungary in 1874, escape artist, starred in movies, died in 1926; *Both:* most famous magicians of their times; became interested in magic very young; *Copperfield:* born in New Jersey in 1956, illusionist, starred in TV shows, still alive

Multilingual Summaries

The Case of the Gasping Garbage

Drake and Nell are science detectives. They work in a laboratory in Drake's home. Gabby calls Drake. She says there is a gasping monster in her garbage can. Is there a monster? They go to find out.

Drake and Nell gather information. The garbage can sounds hollow. It is next to a warm furnace. The can smells like fresh-baked bread. Gabby's father is a baker.

Nell and Gabby study the problem. They decide there is yeast in the garbage can. Bakers use yeast to make bread. Yeast grows when it is warm. When it grows, it makes a gas. The gas made noises in the can.

Spanish

El caso de la basura jadeante

Drake y Nell son detectives científicos. Trabajan en un laboratorio en la casa de Drake. Gabby llama a Drake. Dice que hay un monstruo jadeante en su bote de basura. ¿Hay un monstruo? Van a investigarlo.

Drake y Nell reúnen información. El bote de basura suena hueco. Está junto a una caldera caliente. El bote huele a pan recién horneado. El papá de Gabby es panadero.

Nell y Gabby estudian el caso. Deciden que hay levadura en el bote. Los panaderos usan levadura para hacer pan. La levadura crece cuando está caliente. Cuando crece, despide un gas. El gas hacía el ruido.

Multilingual Summaries

喘气的垃圾

德雷克·多伊尔和尼尔·佛西是科学侦探，他们在德雷克的家的实验室做调查工作。加比·塔伯格给德雷克打了一个电话，说她的垃圾桶里面有一个喘气的怪物。到底是不是一个怪物呢？德雷克和尼尔去加比的家调查一下。

德雷克和尼尔收集证据：从垃圾桶里发出的声音有一点空洞；垃圾桶放在炉子的旁边；垃圾里发出烘面包的鲜味；加比的爸爸是一个面包师傅。

尼尔和加比研究了一会，发现原因在于垃圾桶里面的酵母：面包师傅用酵母来烘面包；在暖和的环境下，酵母菌会繁殖，当繁殖的时候，酵母菌会呼吸，而呼吸就在垃圾桶里放出喘气的声音。

Vụ Thùng Rác thở hổn hển

Drake Doyle và Nell Fossey là những thám tử khoa học. Họ làm việc trong một phòng thí nghiệm tại mha` Drake. Gabby Talberg gọi Drake. Cô ta nói có một con quỷ thở hổn hển trong thùng rác của cô. Có con quỷ thật không? Drake và Nell đến nhà Gabby để tìm.

Drake và Nell thu thập thông tin. Thùng rác nghe như trống rỗng. Nó nằm kế một cái lò ấm. Thùng rác có mùi như bánh mì mới nướng. Cha của Gabby là thợ làm bánh mì.

Nell và Gabby nghiên cứu vấn đề . Họ quyết định có men trong thùng rác. Thợ làm bánh mì dùng men để làm bánh. Khi có hơi ấm thì men nở ra. Khi nó nở, khí thoát ra. Khí gây ra tiếng động trong thùng.

Multilingual Summaries

Korean

숨을 헐떡거리는 쓰레기의 비밀

드레이크 도일과 넬 포시는 과학 탐정들입니다. 그들은 드레이크의 집에 있는 실험실에서 일하지요. 게비 톨버그가 드레이크한테 전화를 하네요. 그녀는 자신의 쓰레기통에 숨을 헐떡거리는 괴물이 있다고 얘기합니다. 드레이크와 넬은 무슨 일인지 알아보려고 게비의 집으로 갑니다.

드레이크와 넬은 정보를 수집합니다. 쓰레기통은 속이 텅 빈 것처럼 들립니다. 그것은 따뜻한 난로 옆에 놓여있지요. 쓰레기통은 갓 구워낸 빵 냄새가 납니다. 게비의 아버지는 빵 굽는 사람이지요.

넬과 게비는 문제점이 무엇인지 연구합니다. 그들은 쓰레기통 안에 누룩이 있다고 결론냅니다. 빵 굽는 사람은 빵을 만들기 위해 누룩을 사용하지요. 누룩은 따듯할 때 자랍니다. 그것이 자라면 기체를 만듭니다. 그 기체가 통 속에서 소리를 낸 것입니다.

Hmong

Rooj Plaub txog lub Nab Kibnyuab Huas Pa

Drake thiab Nell yog tibneeg soj ntsuam xaij. Nkawv ua haujlwm hauv ib lub chaw soj ntsuam xaij nyob hauv Drake lub tsev. Gabby hu Drake. Nwg hais tias muaj ib niag dab huas pa nyob hauv nwg lub thoob kibnyuab. Puas muaj ib tus dab tiag ma? Drake thiab Nell mus tom Gabby tsev mus xauj saib zoo li cas.

Drake thiab Nell khaws ntaub ntawv txog. Lub nab kibnyuab nrov khoob khoob. Nwg nyob ib sab ntawm lub cua sov. Lub thoob kibnyuab tsw li qhaubcij uas nyiav ci siav. Gabby txiv yog ib tus tub ci qhaubcij.

Nell thiab Gabby sojntsuam qhov teeb meem. Nkawv txiav txim tias nwg muaj poovxab nyob hauv lub thoob kibnyuab. Cov tub ci qhaubcij siv poovxab los ua qhaubcij. Poovxab sawv tuaj thaus nwg sov. Thaus sawv tuaj lawm, nwg ua ib cov pa. Cov pa ntawd ua suab nrov nrov hauv lub thoob.

Name _____

- **Read** *Two Master Magicians* again.
- Use the information in the book. In the chart below, **write** four similarities and four differences between Robert-Houdin and Houdini. The first has been done for you.

Similarities	Differences
Robert-Houdin and Houdini both used science.	Robert-Houdin made magic look easy. But Houdini made it look hard.
1. _____	1. _____
2. _____	2. _____
3. _____	3. _____
4. _____	4. _____

Family Link

Does anyone in your family know magic tricks? Ask family members to share what they know about magicians and magic tricks.

Weekly Resources Guide for English Language Learner Support

For this week's content and language objectives, see p. 125e.

Instructional Strand	Day 1	Day 2
Concept Development/Academic Language	TEACHER'S EDITION • Academic Language, p. DI•41 • Concept Development, p. DI•41 • Anchored Talk, pp. 52j—52–53 • Preteach Academic Vocabulary, p. 55a • Concept Talk Video ELL HANDBOOK • Hear It, See It, Say It, Use It, pp. xxxvi–xxxvii • ELL Poster Talk, Concept Talk, p. 125c ELL POSTER 17 • Day 1 Activities	TEACHER'S EDITION • Academic Language, p. DI•41 • Concept Development, p. DI•41 • Anchored Talk, p. 56a • Concept Talk Video ELL HANDBOOK • ELL Poster Talk, Concept Talk, p. 125c • Concept Talk Video Routine, p. 477 ELL POSTER 17 • Day 2 Activities
Phonics and Spelling	TEACHER'S EDITION • Phonics and Spelling, p. DI•45	TEACHER'S EDITION • Phonics and Spelling, p. DI•45
Listening Comprehension	TEACHER'S EDITION • Modified Read Aloud, p. DI•44 • Read Aloud, p. 53b • Concept Talk Video ELL HANDBOOK • Concept Talk Video Routine, p. 477	TEACHER'S EDITION • Modified Read Aloud, p. DI•44 • AudioText of *Encantado* • Concept Talk Video ELL HANDBOOK • AudioText CD Routine, p. 477 • Story Map B, p. 484
Reading Comprehension	TEACHER'S EDITION • Preteach Compare and Contrast, p. DI•46	TEACHER'S EDITION • Reteach Compare and Contrast, p. DI•46 • Frontloading Reading, p. DI•47 ELL HANDBOOK • Picture It! Skill Instruction, pp. 126–126a • Multilingual Summaries, pp. 127–129
Vocabulary **Basic and Lesson Vocabulary** **Word Analysis: Latin Roots**	TEACHER'S EDITION • Basic Vocabulary, p. DI•42 • Preteach Lesson Vocabulary, p. DI•42 • Latin Roots, p. DI•45 ELL HANDBOOK • Word Cards, p. 125 • ELL Vocabulary Routine, p. 471 ELL POSTER 17 • Day 1 Activities	TEACHER'S EDITION • Basic Vocabulary, p. DI•42 • Reteach Lesson Vocabulary, p. DI•43 • Latin Roots, p. DI•45 ELL HANDBOOK • Word Cards, p. 125 • Multilingual Vocabulary List, p. 431 ELL POSTER 17 • Day 2 Activities
Grammar and Conventions	TEACHER'S EDITION • Preteach Pronouns, p. DI•49	TEACHER'S EDITION • Reteach Pronouns, p. DI•49
Writing	TEACHER'S EDITION • Poetic Structure, p. DI•50 • Introduce Song, pp. 55e–55f	TEACHER'S EDITION • Strategy: Brainstorming, pp. 67d–67e

This symbol indicates leveled instruction to address language proficiency levels.

Day 3	Day 4	Day 5
TEACHER'S EDITION • Academic Language, p. DI•41 • Concept Development, p. DI•41 • Anchored Talk, p. 68a • Concept Talk Video ELL HANDBOOK • ELL Poster Talk, Concept Talk, p. 125c ELL POSTER 17 • Day 3 Activities	TEACHER'S EDITION • Academic Language, p. DI•41 • Concept Development, p. DI•41 • Anchored Talk, p. 76a • Concept Talk Video ELL HANDBOOK • ELL Poster Talk, Concept Talk, p. 125c ELL POSTER 17 • Day 4 Activities	TEACHER'S EDITION • Academic Language, p. DI•41 • Concept Development, p. DI•41 • Concept Talk Video ELL HANDBOOK • ELL Poster Talk, Concept Talk, p. 125c ELL POSTER 17 • Day 5 Activities
		TEACHER'S EDITION • Phonics and Spelling, p. DI•45
ELL HANDBOOK • Phonics Transition Lesson, pp. 232–234, 236–238	ELL HANDBOOK • Phonics Transition Lesson, pp. 232–234, 236–238	
TEACHER'S EDITION • AudioText of *Encantado* • Concept Talk Video ELL HANDBOOK • AudioText CD Routine, p. 477	TEACHER'S EDITION • Concept Talk Video	TEACHER'S EDITION • Concept Talk Video
TEACHER'S EDITION • Sheltered Reading, p. DI•47 ELL HANDBOOK • Multilingual Summaries, pp. 127–129	TEACHER'S EDITION • ELL/ELD Reader Guided Reading, p. DI•48 ELL HANDBOOK • ELL Study Guide, p. 130	TEACHER'S EDITION • ELL/ELD Reader Guided Reading, p. DI•48 ELL HANDBOOK • ELL Study Guide, p. 130
		TEACHER'S EDITION • Latin Roots *aqua, dict*, p. 81i
ELL HANDBOOK • High-Frequency Words Activity Bank, p. 446 ELL POSTER 17 • Day 3 Activities	ELL HANDBOOK • High-Frequency Words Activity Bank, p. 446	ELL HANDBOOK • High-Frequency Words Activity Bank, p. 446
TEACHER'S EDITION • Grammar Jammer ELL HANDBOOK • Grammar Transition Lesson, pp. 362–369 • Grammar Jammer Routine, p. 478	TEACHER'S EDITION • Grammar Jammer ELL HANDBOOK • Grammar Transition Lesson, pp. 362–369	TEACHER'S EDITION • Grammar Jammer ELL HANDBOOK • Grammar Transition Lesson, pp. 362–369
TEACHER'S EDITION • Let's Write It!, p. 74–75 • Writing Trait: Word Choice, pp. 75a–75b	TEACHER'S EDITION • Revising Strategy, p. 81d	TEACHER'S EDITION • Pronouns, pp. 81p–81q

Question of the Week
Why do animals behave the way they do?

Throughout the week, use the ELL Poster to help students produce and comprehend language, understand the concept, and build English vocabulary. Use the Question of the Week and other questions to help students share ideas in pairs, small groups, or the large group. Sample questions are shown, with examples of possible responses by students.

Weekly Concept and Language Goals

• Understand animal behavior

• Explain how different animals behave

• Describe how different animals communicate

By the end of the lesson, students should be able to talk about and write sentences about how animals behave.

ELL Poster 17

Daily Team Talk

Day 1	Day 2	Day 3	Day 4	Day 5
After Day 1 activities on Poster, ask questions such as *What is the underwater dolphin doing in the poster picture?*	After Day 2 activity on Poster, ask questions such as *What are the other two dolphins doing in the poster picture?*	After Day 3 activity on Poster, ask questions such as *How are the trainers communicating with the dolphins in the poster picture?*	After Day 4 activity on Poster, ask questions such as *Why do the dolphins in the poster picture do what their trainers ask them to do?*	After Day 5 activity on Poster, ask questions such as *How do you communicate with an animal?*
Beginning Swimming. **Intermediate** Swimming to a trainer. **Advanced** It is swimming toward a trainer. **Advanced High** The underwater dolphin is swimming toward the trainer with a whistle.	**Beginning** Jumping up. **Intermediate** They are jumping up. **Advanced** The dolphins are jumping out of the water together. **Advanced High** The two dolphins are jumping up toward the trainer with a fish.	**Beginning** Use a whistle. **Intermediate** They are blowing a whistle and holding a fish. **Advanced** The trainers are blowing a whistle and holding a fish above the water. **Advanced High** One trainer is blowing a whistle. The other trainer is encouraging the dolphins to jump toward a fish treat she is holding.	**Beginning** For food. **Intermediate** They want the fish. **Advanced** The trainers give the dolphins fish. **Advanced High** If the dolphins do what their trainers ask them to do, the dolphins are rewarded with fish and other treats.	**Beginning** I talk to my dog. **Intermediate** I call my dog and she comes to me. **Advanced** When I want my dog to come, I call her name. Then I give her a treat. **Advanced High** I have taught my dog several commands, such as *sit*, *shake*, and *lie down*. When she does what I say, I give her a treat.

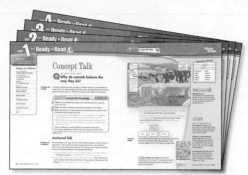

Teacher's Edition pages 52j–81q

See the support for English language learners throughout the lesson, including ELL strategies and scaffolded activities at points of use.

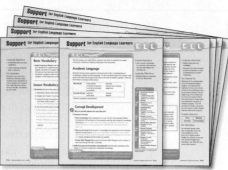

Teacher's Edition pages DI•41–DI•50

Differentiated Instruction for English language learners provides daily group activities that "frontload," or preteach, core instruction.

ELL Handbook pp. 125a–130

Find additional lesson materials that support the core lesson and the ELL instructional pages.

ELL Poster 17

ELL Reader 4.4.2

ELD Reader 4.4.2

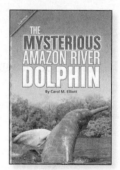

Concept Literacy Reader

ELD, ELL Reader Teaching Guide

Concept Literacy Reader Teaching Guide

Technology

Online Teacher's Edition Use the digital version of the core Teacher's Edition for planning and instruction.

eReaders
This week's ELL and ELD Readers and Concept Literacy Reader are also available in digital format.

This Week's Content and Language Objectives by Strand

Concept Development/ Academic Language Why do animals behave the way they do?	**Content Objective** • Use concept vocabulary to understand the reasons why animals behave the way they do. **Language Objectives** • Express ideas in response to art and discussion. • Express ideas in response to new academic vocabulary
Phonics and Spelling Final Syllable Patterns	**Content Objectives** • Identify final syllable patterns. • Correctly spell words in which the final syllable begins with a consonant or a vowel. **Language Objective** • Apply phonics and decoding skills to vocabulary.
Listening Comprehension Modified Read Aloud: "The Amazing Cat, Sugar"	**Content Objective** • Monitor and adjust oral comprehension. **Language Objectives** • Monitor students' understanding of spoken language by discussing oral passages. • Use a graphic organizer to take notes.
Reading Comprehension Compare and Contrast	**Content Objectives** • Compare and contrast components of a text. • Compare and contrast to aid comprehension. • Make and adjust predictions. **Language Objectives** • Discuss characteristics that can be compared and contrasted. • Compare and contrast personal experiences in writing. • Summarize text using visual support.
Vocabulary Basic and Lesson Vocabulary	**Language Objectives** • Understand and use basic vocabulary. • Learn meanings of grade-level vocabulary. • Speak using learning strategies. • Produce drawings, phrases, or short sentences to show understanding of Lesson Vocabulary.
Word Analysis Latin Roots	**Content Objective** • Identify Latin roots *aqua* and *dict*. **Language Objective** • Discuss Latin roots *aqua* and *dict*.
Grammar and Conventions Pronouns	**Content Objective** • Decode and use pronouns. **Language Objectives** • Speak using pronouns. • Write phrases or sentences that use pronouns.
Writing Poetic Structure	**Content Objective** • Identify vivid nouns and adjectives. **Language Objective** • Share feedback for editing and revising.

Word Cards for Vocabulary Activities

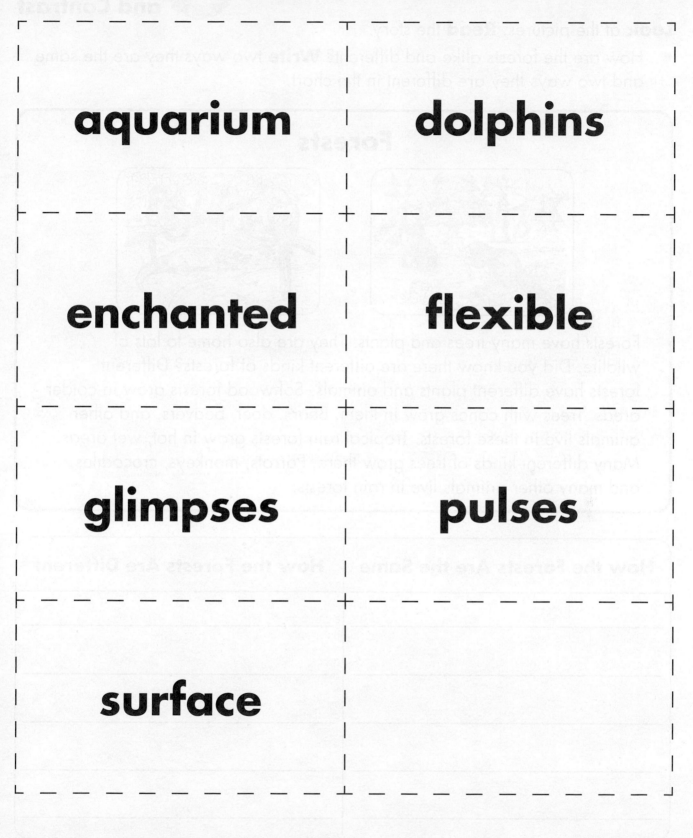

aquarium

dolphins

enchanted

flexible

glimpses

pulses

surface

Teacher Note: Beginning Teach three to four words. **Intermediate** Teach four to six words. **Advanced** Teach six to seven words. **Advanced High** Teach all words.

Name _____

Look at the pictures. **Read** the story.

- How are the forests alike and different? **Write** two ways they are the same and two ways they are different in the chart.

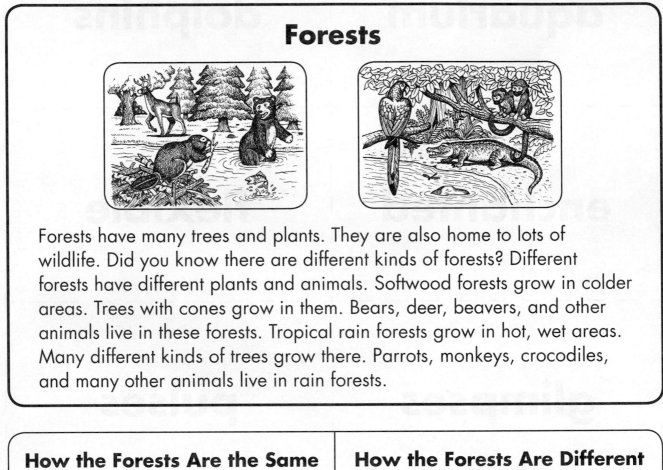

Forests

Forests have many trees and plants. They are also home to lots of wildlife. Did you know there are different kinds of forests? Different forests have different plants and animals. Softwood forests grow in colder areas. Trees with cones grow in them. Bears, deer, beavers, and other animals live in these forests. Tropical rain forests grow in hot, wet areas. Many different kinds of trees grow there. Parrots, monkeys, crocodiles, and many other animals live in rain forests.

How the Forests Are the Same	How the Forests Are Different

Compare and Contrast

Use this lesson to supplement or replace the skill lesson on page 53c of the Teacher's Edition. Display the Skill Points (at right) and share them with students.

Teach/Model

Beginning Display pictures of a farm and a city that show details. Ask: *How are the farm and the city alike and different?* Write students' responses in two lists labeled *Alike* and *Different*.

Intermediate Display pictures of different kinds of trees, such as a palm tree, maple tree, and pine tree. Ask students to use their observations as you listen and fill in a chart with two columns labeled *How the Trees Are the Same* and *How the Trees Are Different.*

Advanced Write and read aloud: *Ben and Anne go to the zoo. Ben likes the monkeys, but Anne likes the giraffes. Unlike Ben, Anne will look at the snakes. They both visit the elephants.* Have students tell how Ben and Anne are alike and different and identify the clue words that helped them.

Advanced High Ask each student to write about his or her favorite animal, including what it looks like, where it lives, and what it eats. Have pairs of students compare and contrast their favorite animals and write sentences using clue words to tell how the animals are alike and different.

Then distribute copies of Picture It! page 126.

- Have students look at the pictures and describe what they see.
- Read the paragraph aloud. Ask: *How are tropical rain forests and softwood forests different?*
- Review the Skill Points with students.
- Have students write how the two types of forests are alike and different.

Skill Points

✔ To **compare** is to tell how two or more things are alike. To **contrast** is to tell how two or more things are different.

✔ Clue words such as *both, like*, and *as* show a comparison. Clue words such as *but, instead,* and *unlike* show a contrast.

Practice

Read aloud the directions on page 126. Have students reread the paragraph with a partner. Then have them use the pictures and the paragraph as they fill in the chart.

Beginning Students can say what they want to write in each column before writing their answers in the chart on the page. Provide help with English words and writing.

Intermediate Students can first orally answer the question at the top of the page and then write their answers in the chart. Provide help with writing.

Advanced Students can write sentences in the chart and then check their answers by silently rereading the paragraph or comparing their answers with a partner's.

Advanced High Students can write sentences in the chart and then change the chart into a Venn diagram, explaining what information goes in each section as they write it.

Answers for page 126: *How the Forests Are the Same:* They have many trees, plants, and animals. *How the Forests Are Different:* Softwood forests grow in colder areas. Trees with cones grow in them. Bears, deer, and beavers live there. Tropical rain forests grow in hot, wet areas. Parrots, monkeys, and crocodiles live there.

Multilingual Summaries

Encantado: Pink Dolphin of the Amazon

In the wet season, you might see pink dolphins, which live in the rivers of the Amazon. They are called encantados. Pink dolphins are different from ocean dolphins. They swim slowly and do not have a fin on their backs. Their bodies bend so they can swim around the plants in the rivers.

A guide takes you through the rain forest in a canoe. You are going to a lake to see pink dolphins. Along the way, you see huge spiders and stinging ants. There are trees with sharp spines and trees with sap that burns the skin.

At the lake, you can hear the dolphins. They are hard to see. The water is very dark. You can only see a head or a tail. The guide says encantados are mysterious.

Spanish

Encantado: El delfín rosado del Amazonas

En la estación de las lluvias puedes ver delfines rosados que viven en los ríos del Amazonas. Los llaman encantados. Los delfines rosados son diferentes a los delfines del océano. Nadan lentamente y no tienen una aleta en el dorso. Sus cuerpos se arquean para poder nadar entre las plantas de los ríos.

Un guía te lleva a través de la selva en una canoa. Vas al lago a ver los delfines rosados. A lo largo del trayecto ves enormes arañas y hormigas que pican. Allí hay árboles con espinas puntiagudas y árboles con savia que quema la piel.

En el lago puedes escuchar a los delfines. Es difícil verlos porque el agua es muy oscura. Puedes ver solamente una cabeza o una cola. El guía dice que los delfines encantados son misteriosos.

Multilingual Summaries

Chinese

恩肯塔多：亞馬遜河的粉紅海豚

在潮濕的季節裡，你或許可以在亞馬遜河看到粉紅海豚，大家都叫牠們「恩肯塔多」。粉紅海豚和生活在海洋裡的海豚不同，牠們游得很慢而且背上也沒有鰭，身體會彎曲，這樣游泳的時候就可以繞著河裡面的植物游過去。

導遊會帶你坐獨木舟穿過雨林，你們的目的地是一個湖，在那裡可以看到粉紅海豚。沿路上，你會看到巨型蜘蛛和會咬人的螞蟻，有些樹長有尖刺，有些樹的汁液還會灼傷人的皮膚。

在這個湖上，你可以聽到粉紅海豚的聲音，但是很難看得到牠們，因為湖水的顏色很深，故只能看見頭或者尾鰭的部分。導遊說恩肯塔多像謎一樣的非常神秘。

Vietnamese

Encantado: Cá Heo Màu Hồng của Vùng Amazon

Vào mùa mưa, bạn có thể thấy những con cá heo màu hồng, sống trong những con sông ở Amazon. Chúng được gọi là "encantados". Cá heo màu hồng khác với cá heo đại dương. Cá heo màu hồng bơi chậm hơn và không có vây ở trên lưng. Thân hình có thể uốn cong để chúng có thể bơi quanh các thực vật dưới sông.

Một người hướng dẫn đưa bạn xuyên qua khu rừng rậm trong một chiếc ca-nô. Bạn sẽ đi đến một cái hồ để xem cá heo màu hồng. Trên đường đi bạn thấy những con nhện khổng lồ và các con kiến chích. Có cây có gai và cây có nhựa làm phỏng da.

Tại hồ, bạn có thể nghe được tiếng cá heo. Khó mà thấy được chúng. Nước có màu rất sậm. Bạn chỉ có thể thấy cái đầu hoặc cái đuôi. Người hướng dẫn nói rằng những con cá heo màu hồng là rất bí ẩn.

Multilingual Summaries

엔칸타도: 아마존의 핑크색 돌고래

습기가 많은 계절에는 아마존 강에 살고 있는 핑크색 돌고래를 볼 수 있을 지도 모른다. 핑크색 돌고래는 엔칸타도라고 불린다. 핑크색 돌고래는 바다에 사는 돌고래와는 달리, 천천히 수영하며 등에 지느러미가 없고 몸을 굽혀 강에 서식하는 식물 주위를 수영할 수도 있다.

한 여행 안내자가 카누를 타고 열대 우림으로 안내한다. 호수에 가면 핑크색 돌고래를 볼 수 있다. 가는 도중엔 큰 거미와 독개미도 만난다. 날카로운 가시가 있는 나무와 살도 태워버리는 수액을 가진 나무도 있다.

호수에 가면 돌고래 소리를 들을 수 있지만 돌고래는 잘 보이지 않는다. 물은 매우 탁해서 단지 돌고래의 머리와 꼬리만 볼 수 있을 뿐이다. 여행 안내자는 엔칸타도가 신비롭다고 말한다.

Encantado: Cov Dolphin Xim Liab Dawb Muag Hauv Amazon

Thaum lub ciaj los nag, tej zaum koj pom tau tej dolphine xim liab dawb muag, uas nyob hauv cov dej ntawm Amazon. Lawv hu ua encantados. Cov dolphine xim liab dawb muag yeej txawv cov dolphine hauv dej hiav txwv. Lawv ua luam dej qeeb zog thiab tsis muaj tus nqa txaj qaum saum lawv dab qaum. Lawv lub cev txawj lov kom lawv thiaj ua luam dej ib ncig tau ntawm tej hmab ntoov nyob hauv cov dej.

Ib tug coj kev coj koj mus hauv lub hav zoov nuj txeeg siv ib lub nkoj me me. Koj tam tom mus hauv lub pas dej mus saib cov dolphin xim liab dawb muag. Hauv koj txoj kev koj pom cov kab laug sab loj loj thiab cov ntsaum uas txawj plev. Muaj cov ntoo uas muaj muaj pos thiab cov ntoo uas muaj tej kua ua kom nqaij tawv khaus khuas.

Hauv lub pas dej, koj yeej hnov tau cov dolphin. Kom pom lawv mas yeej nyuaj. Cov dej tsaus tsaus heev. Koj tsuas pom tau lub taub hau los sis tusk o tw xwb. Tus coj kev hais tias neeg yeej tsis paub dab tsi txog cov encantados li.

Name _____

- **Read** *Life in the Amazon Rain Forest* again.
- Use the information in the book. **Look** at the question below.
  Write the answers in each of the boxes.

Who lives here?

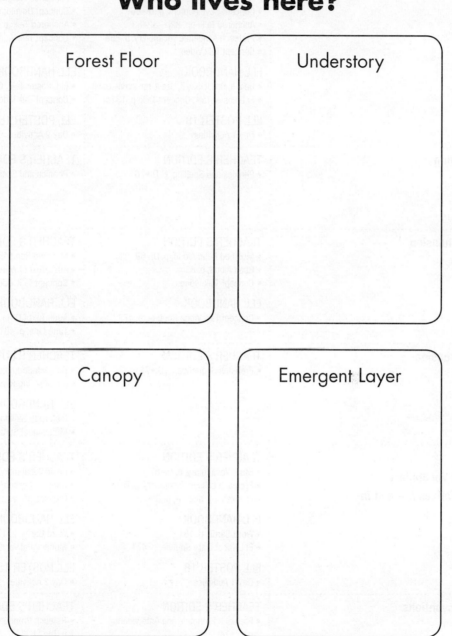

| Forest Floor | Understory |
| Canopy | Emergent Layer |

Family Link

Has anyone in your family ever been to a rain forest? Ask family
members to share what they know about rain forests.

Weekly Resources Guide for English Language Learner Support

For this week's content and language objectives, see p. 131e.

Instructional Strand	Day 1	Day 2
Concept Development/Academic Language	**TEACHER'S EDITION** • Academic Language, p. DI•66 • Concept Development, p. DI•66 • Anchored Talk, pp. 82j—82–83 • Preteach Academic Vocabulary, p. 85a • Concept Talk Video **ELL HANDBOOK** • Hear It, See It, Say It, Use It, pp. xxxvi–xxxvii • ELL Poster Talk, Concept Talk, p. 131c **ELL POSTER 18** • Day 1 Activities	**TEACHER'S EDITION** • Academic Language, p. DI•66 • Concept Development, p. DI•66 • Anchored Talk, p. 86a • Concept Talk Video **ELL HANDBOOK** • ELL Poster Talk, Concept Talk, p. 131c • Concept Talk Video Routine, p. 477 **ELL POSTER 18** • Day 2 Activities
Phonics and Spelling	**TEACHER'S EDITION** • Phonics and Spelling, p. DI•70	**TEACHER'S EDITION** • Phonics and Spelling, p. DI•70
Listening Comprehension	**TEACHER'S EDITION** • Modified Read Aloud, p. DI•69 • Read Aloud, p. 83b • Concept Talk Video **ELL HANDBOOK** • Concept Talk Video Routine, p. 477	**TEACHER'S EDITION** • Modified Read Aloud, p. DI•69 • AudioText of *Navajo Code Talkers* • Concept Talk Video **ELL HANDBOOK** • AudioText CD Routine, p. 477 • Time Line, p. 491
Reading Comprehension	**TEACHER'S EDITION** • Preteach Sequence, p. DI•71	**TEACHER'S EDITION** • Reteach Sequence, p. DI•71 • Frontloading Reading, p. DI•72 **ELL HANDBOOK** • Picture It! Skill Instruction, pp. 132–132a • Multilingual Summaries, pp. 133–135
Vocabulary **Basic and Lesson Vocabulary** **Word Analysis: Prefixes *im-* and *in-***	**TEACHER'S EDITION** • Basic Vocabulary, p. DI•67 • Preteach Lesson Vocabulary, p. DI•67 • Prefixes *im-* and *in-*, p. DI•70 **ELL HANDBOOK** • Word Cards, p. 131 • ELL Vocabulary Routine, p. 471 **ELL POSTER 18** • Day 1 Activities	**TEACHER'S EDITION** • Basic Vocabulary, p. DI•67 • Reteach Lesson Vocabulary, p. DI•68 • Prefixes *im-* and *in-*, p. DI•70 **ELL HANDBOOK** • Word Cards, p. 131 • Multilingual Vocabulary List, p. 431 **ELL POSTER 18** • Day 2 Activities
Grammar and Conventions	**TEACHER'S EDITION** • Preteach Pronouns and Antecedents, p. DI•74	**TEACHER'S EDITION** • Reteach Pronouns and Antecedents, p. DI•74
Writing	**TEACHER'S EDITION** • Use Logical Order, p. DI•75 • Introduce Instructions, pp. 85e–85f	**TEACHER'S EDITION** • Writing Trait: Organization, pp. 95d–95e

This symbol indicates leveled instruction to address language proficiency levels.

Day 3	Day 4	Day 5
TEACHER'S EDITION • Academic Language, p. DI•66 • Concept Development, p. DI•66 • Anchored Talk, p. 96a • Concept Talk Video **ELL HANDBOOK** • ELL Poster Talk, Concept Talk, p. 131c **ELL POSTER 18** • Day 3 Activities	**TEACHER'S EDITION** • Academic Language, p. DI•66 • Concept Development, p. DI•66 • Anchored Talk, p. 108a • Concept Talk Video **ELL HANDBOOK** • ELL Poster Talk, Concept Talk, p. 131c **ELL POSTER 18** • Day 4 Activities	**TEACHER'S EDITION** • Academic Language, p. DI•66 • Concept Development, p. DI•66 • Concept Talk Video **ELL HANDBOOK** • ELL Poster Talk, Concept Talk, p. 131c **ELL POSTER 18** • Day 5 Activities
		TEACHER'S EDITION • Phonics and Spelling, p. DI•70
ELL HANDBOOK • Phonics Transition Lesson, pp. 224, 227	**ELL HANDBOOK** • Phonics Transition Lesson, pp. 224, 227	
TEACHER'S EDITION • AudioText of *Navajo Code Talkers* • Concept Talk Video **ELL HANDBOOK** • AudioText CD Routine, p. 477	**TEACHER'S EDITION** • Concept Talk Video	**TEACHER'S EDITION** • Concept Talk Video
TEACHER'S EDITION • Sheltered Reading, p. DI•72 **ELL HANDBOOK** • Multilingual Summaries, pp. 133–135	**TEACHER'S EDITION** • ELL/ELD Reader Guided Reading, p. DI•73 **ELL HANDBOOK** • ELL Study Guide, p. 136	**TEACHER'S EDITION** • ELL/ELD Reader Guided Reading, p. DI•73 **ELL HANDBOOK** • ELL Study Guide, p. 136
		TEACHER'S EDITION • Prefixes *im-* and *in-*, p. 111i
ELL HANDBOOK • High-Frequency Words Activity Bank, p. 446 **ELL POSTER 18** • Day 3 Activities	**ELL HANDBOOK** • High-Frequency Words Activity Bank, p. 446	**ELL HANDBOOK** • High-Frequency Words Activity Bank, p. 446
TEACHER'S EDITION • Grammar Jammer **ELL HANDBOOK** • Grammar Transition Lesson, pp. 363, 368 • Grammar Jammer Routine, p. 478	**TEACHER'S EDITION** • Grammar Jammer **ELL HANDBOOK** • Grammar Transition Lesson, pp. 363, 368	**TEACHER'S EDITION** • Grammar Jammer **ELL HANDBOOK** • Grammar Transition Lesson, pp. 363, 368
TEACHER'S EDITION • Let's Write It!, p. 106–107 • Writer's Craft: Using Logical Order, pp. 107a–107b	**TEACHER'S EDITION** • Revising Strategy, pp. 111d–111e	**TEACHER'S EDITION** • Instructions, pp. 111p–111q

Question of the Week
Why are secret codes necessary?

Throughout the week, use the ELL Poster to help students produce and comprehend language, understand the concept, and build English vocabulary. Use the Question of the Week and other questions to help students share ideas in pairs, small groups, or the large group. Sample questions are shown, with examples of possible responses by students.

ELL Poster 18

Weekly Concept and Language Goals

• Understand secret codes

• Describe how secret codes help people communicate

• Tell how messages can be passed using secret codes

By the end of the lesson, students should be able to talk about and write sentences about secret codes.

Daily Team Talk

Day 1	Day 2	Day 3	Day 4	Day 5
After Day 1 activities on Poster, ask questions such as	After Day 2 activity on Poster, ask questions such as	After Day 3 activity on Poster, ask questions such as	After Day 4 activity on Poster, ask questions such as	After Day 5 activity on Poster, ask questions such as
Why are the soldiers in the poster picture using a secret code?	*What message do you think the soldier with the radio is sending to headquarters?*	*How does the soldier who is taking notes know what the message says?*	*According to the selection* Navajo Code Talkers, *why was the Navajo code so successful?*	*When would you use a secret code?*
Beginning To be safe. **Intermediate** They need to send messages. **Advanced** They need to tell headquarters what is happening. **Advanced High** The soldiers need to send messages to headquarters about what is happening in battle. They use a secret code so the enemy will not be able to read the messages.	**Beginning** Send help. **Intermediate** Please send us help. **Advanced** We are under attack, so please send more soldiers. **Advanced High** I think the message says that the soldiers are under attack and they need to know what to do next.	**Beginning** Uses the code. **Intermediate** He uses the code. **Advanced** He uses the secret code to see what it says. **Advanced High** The soldier uses the secret code to figure out what the message says.	**Beginning** It was secret. **Intermediate** Navajo is hard. **Advanced** The Navajo language is hard to understand. **Advanced High** The Navajo language is hard for non-Navajo to understand. That makes it the perfect language to use for a secret code.	**Beginning** With my friend. **Intermediate** To send a message to my friend. **Advanced** I would put a message in code and send it to a friend. **Advanced High** I would use a secret code to send a message to my best friend if I didn't want my sister to read it.

Teacher's Edition pages 82j–111q

See the support for English language learners throughout the lesson, including ELL strategies and scaffolded activities at points of use.

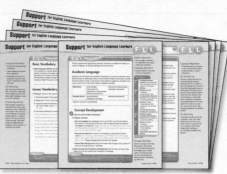

Teacher's Edition pages DI•66–DI•75

Differentiated Instruction for English language learners provides daily group activities that "frontload," or preteach, core instruction.

ELL Handbook pp. 131a–136

Find additional lesson materials that support the core lesson and the ELL instructional pages.

ELL Poster 18

ELL Reader 4.4.3

ELD Reader 4.4.3

Concept Literacy Reader

ELD, ELL Reader
Teaching Guide

Concept Literacy Reader
Teaching Guide

Technology

Online Teacher's Edition Use the digital version of the core Teacher's Edition for planning and instruction.

eReaders
This week's ELL and ELD Readers and Concept Literacy Reader are also available in digital format.

This Week's Content and Language Objectives by Strand

Concept Development/ Academic Language Why are secret codes necessary?	**Content Objective** • Use concept vocabulary to understand why secret codes are necessary. **Language Objectives** • Express ideas in response to art and discussion. • Express ideas in response to new academic vocabulary.
Phonics and Spelling Consonant Digraph /sh/	**Content Objective** • Identify the consonant digraph /sh/. **Language Objective** • Apply phonics and decoding skills to vocabulary.
Listening Comprehension Modified Read Aloud: "Using Codes"	**Content Objective** • Monitor and adjust oral comprehension. **Language Objectives** • Discuss oral passages. • Use a graphic organizer to take notes.
Reading Comprehension Sequence	**Content Objectives** • Sequence of events of a text. • Make and adjust predictions. • Sequence events to aid comprehension. **Language Objectives** • Discuss events that can be sequenced. • Write sequenced events from personal experience. • Read grade-level text with expression. • Summarize text using visual support.
Vocabulary Basic and Lesson Vocabulary	**Language Objectives** • Understand and use basic vocabulary • Learn meanings of grade-level vocabulary • Internalize new basic language by using and reusing it in meaningful writing activities.
Word Analysis Prefixes *im-* and *in-*	**Content Objective** • Identify prefixes *im-* and *in-*. **Language Objective** • Discuss prefixes *im-* and *in-*.
Grammar and Conventions Pronouns and Antecedents	**Content Objective** • Decode and use pronouns and antecedents. **Language Objectives** • Speak using pronouns and antecedents. • Write phrases or sentences that use pronouns and antecedents.
Writing Use Logical Order	**Content Objectives** • Identify the logical order of events. • Use newly acquired vocabulary. **Language Objectives** • Write a paragraph using a logical order of events. • Distinguish between formal and informal language.

Word Cards for Vocabulary Activities

advance	developed
exhausting	**headquarters**
impossible	**intense**
messages	**reveal**

Teacher Note: Beginning Teach three to four words. **Intermediate** Teach four to six words. **Advanced** Teach six to seven words. **Advanced High** Teach all words.

Name _____

Look at the picture. **Read** the story.

• **Write** the events of the story in correct sequence.

How a Peasant Helped a Princess

Once there was a foolish king who had a smart daughter. He didn't want her to learn to read or write. Every month, a peasant brought them something new. The king paid the peasant well. One month he brought books. The king laughed, but his daughter learned to read. One month the peasant brought a pen and paper. The king fell asleep, but his daughter learned how to write. The princess later became a wise queen. She never forgot the peasant who helped her to read and write in secret. The peasant became a rich man. But the king remained foolish.

First, _____

_____

Then, _____

_____

Next, _____

_____

Next, _____

_____

Last, _____

_____

Sequence

Use this lesson to supplement or replace the skill lesson on page 83c of the Teacher's Edition. Display the Skill Points (at right) and share them with students.

Teach/Model

Beginning Write and read aloud: *I eat my lunch. I go to the grocery store after work. My alarm clock wakes me up in the morning. I watch TV before I go to bed.* Say: *These story events are out of order.* Tell students to use clues in the sentences to tell you how to write the story events in the correct sequence.

Intermediate Say: *Listen to this story: Jack uses the library computer to search for a book. He writes down the book's number. He finds the book on the shelf. The librarian scans Jack's library card and the book.* Ask students to retell the story using the sequence words *first, then, next,* and *last.*

Advanced Write this story starter: *When Joshua woke up today, the first thing he thought about was his math test.* Ask students to add sentences to continue the story. Encourage them to use sequence words such as *next, then,* and *last.*

Advanced High Ask students to think about a good day they have had. Have them write four sentences that tell the sequence of events on that day. Remind them to use sequence words. Then have them tell their story to a partner.

Then distribute copies of Picture It! page 132.

- Have students look at the picture and read the title.
- Read the paragraph aloud. Ask: *What is the first thing the peasant brings to the king?* (books)
- Review the Skill Points with students.
- Have students tell what the peasant brings next.

Practice

Read aloud the directions on page 132. Have volunteers reread the story aloud. Have students use the picture and the story to write the events in sequence.

Beginning Students can act out the story events in the correct sequence before writing their answers on the page. Provide help with English words and writing.

Intermediate Students can first orally retell the story events in the correct sequence and then write the events on the lines. Provide help with English words and writing.

Advanced Students can write their answers on the lines and then check them by rereading them aloud or comparing them with a partner's answers.

Advanced High Students can write their answers on the lines and then check them by retelling the story in their own words but using the sequence words *first, then, next,* and *last.*

Answers for page 132: *First,* a peasant brought the king and princess some books. *Then* the king laughed, but his daughter learned to read. *Next,* the peasant brought the king and princess a pen and paper. *Next,* the king fell asleep, but the daughter learned to write. *Last,* the princess later became a wise queen. The peasant became a rich man.

Skill Points

✔ The **sequence** is the order of the events in a story or paragraph.

✔ Time order is one way of organizing the events in a story or paragraph.

Multilingual Summaries

English

Navajo Code Talkers

In the 1930s, Navajo children were not allowed to speak the Navajo language in school. That changed when the United States declared war on Japan. The military needed a code to use with the new wireless radios. Philip Johnston suggested they use the Navajo language.

The military recruited marines from the Navajo reservation. They were told to create an unbreakable code. The code included Navajo words for letters and for military terms.

The code talkers were sent to the front lines. The code was never broken.

The code talkers returned home. They could not talk about their role in the war. In 2001, the code talkers and their families were finally awarded Congressional medals.

Spanish

Los códigos navajo

Durante los años treintas, a los niños navajos no les permitían hablar su lenguaje en la escuela. Eso cambió cuando Estados Unidos le declaró la guerra a Japón. Los militares necesitaban un código para usarlo con las nuevas radios inalámbricas. Philip Johnston sugirió que se usara el lenguaje navajo.

Los militares reclutaron soldados de la reservación navajo. Se les pidió que crearan un código indescifrable para el enemigo. Este código incluía palabras del lenguaje navajo para las letras y los términos militares. Los lectores del código fueron enviados al frente de batalla. Y el código jamás fue descifrado por los japoneses.

Los lectores del código regresaron a casa. No se les permitió hablar sobre su trabajo en la guerra.

Finalmente, en el año 2001 a los lectores y a sus familias se les reconoció otorgándoles las medallas del Congreso.

Multilingual Summaries

Chinese

講納瓦伙語的密碼兵

1930 年代時，學校不准納瓦伙族的小朋友在學校里講納瓦伙語。這種情況在美國對日本宣戰後有了改變。 軍方需要一種可在新的無線電台系統中使用的密碼。 菲立普 強斯頓建議軍方使用納瓦伙族語。

於是，軍方從納瓦伙族保留區招募了一些海軍。 軍方要求這些新兵建立一種無法破解的密碼。 該密碼採用納瓦伙族語來代表字母和軍事術語。

密碼兵被派往前線。 密碼從未被破解過。

密碼兵退役返家後， 他們不能對外透露自己在戰爭中的角色。2001 年時，這些密碼兵及他們的家人獲頒國會勳章。

Vietnamese

Người Nói Ám Hiệu Navajo

Trong năm 1930, trẻ em Navajo bị cấm không được nói tiếng mẹ đẻ của mình trong trường học. Sự việc này thay đổi khi Hoa Kỳ tuyên bố chiến tranh với Nhật Bản. Quân đội cần có một ám hiệu để dùng với máy truyền thanh không dây mới. Ông Philip Johnston mới đề nghị dùng tiếng Navajo.

Quân đội tuyển mộ lính thủy quân lục chiến từ các lãnh thổ Da Đỏ Navajo. Họ được cho biết là phải tạo ra một ám hiệu không thể giải được. Ám hiệu gồm có chữ Navajo dùng cho các mẫu tự và các chữ riêng trong quân đội. Người lính nói ám hiệu được gởi đến trận tuyến. Ám hiệu này chưa bao giờ bị giải.

Những người lính nói ám hiệu trở về quê nhà. Họ không thể nói ra nhiệm vụ của mình trong cuộc chiến. Trong năm 2001, những người lính nói ám hiệu và gia đình họ được tuyên dương huy chương Quốc Hội.

Multilingual Summaries

Korean

나바호 암호병

1930년대에 나바호 어린이들이 학교에서 나바호어를 쓰는 것은 허용되지 않았다. 그것은 미국이 일본에 전쟁을 선포하면서 바뀌었다. 군대에서 새로운 무선 통신에 사용할 암호가 필요했기 때문이다. 필립 존스톤이 나바호어를 이용하자고 제안했다.

군대는 나바호 보호 거주지에서 해병대원을 징집했다. 그들은 해독되지 않는 암호를 만들라는 명령을 받았다. 글자와 군사 용어에 해당하는 나바호 단어들이 암호에 포함되었다. 암호병들이 최전선으로 보내졌다. 암호는 적들에게 절대로 해독되지 않았다.

암호병들은 집으로 돌아갔다. 그들은 전쟁에서의 역할에 대해 말해선 안 되었다. 2001년에 암호병들과 그들의 가족들은 의회 명예 훈장을 받았다.

Hmong

Cov Kab Navajo Tham Lus

Nyob rau thaum xyoo 1930s, Cov me nyuam kab Navajo raug txwv tsis pub hais lawv cov lus Navajo nyob tom tsev kawm ntawv. Qhov li hais no hloov thaum lub teb chaw United States tau paj kaj ua rog nrog lub teb chaw Japan. Cov tub rog toob kas ib yam lus los siv rau lawv cov xov tooj sib tham. Philip Johnston hais kom lawv siv yam lus Navajo.

Cov tub rog thiaj tau mus nriav peeb zej hauv cov chaw nyob ntawm cov neeg Navajo. Lawv tau lav lus hais tias kom lawv tsim ib yam lus tsis muaj leeg twg paub li. Cov lus tshiab no muaj lus Navajo nrog tsiaj ntaw rau cov tub rog siv.

Cov neeg ua tham tau cov lus no raug xa mus nyob pem hauv ntej. Cov lus li hai no yeej tsis muaj neeg paub tiag.

Cov neeg tham yom lus no rov qab los txog tsev. Lawv yeej muaj cai tham txog lawv tes hauj lwm nyob hauv npluav rog no. Nyob rau xyoo 2001, cov neeg tham cov lus no thiab lawv tsev neeg thiaj tau txais lub liam Congressional medals.

Name _____ **Computer Secrets**

- **Read** *Computer Secrets* again.
- Use the information in the book. **Write** five facts about secret codes in the order in which they are presented in the book.

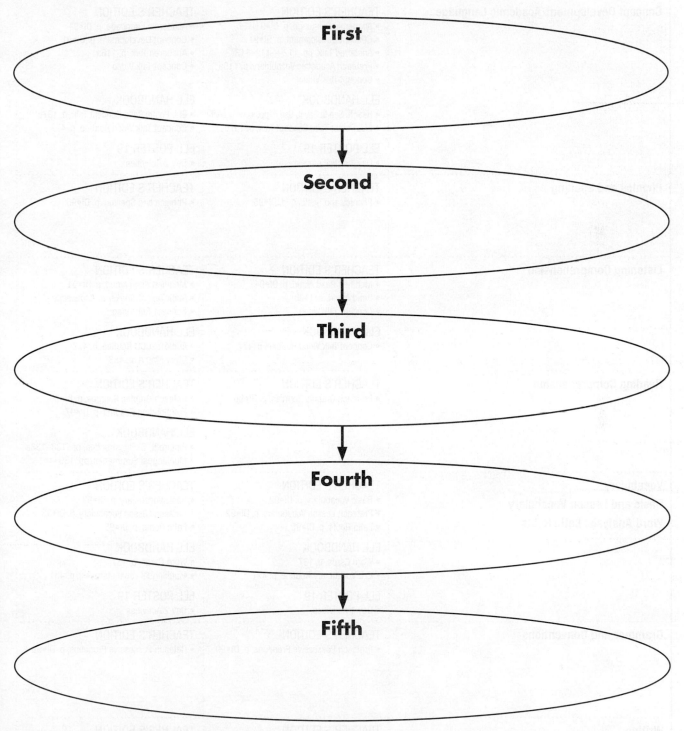

First

Second

Third

Fourth

Fifth

Family Link

Does anyone in your family use secret codes? Ask family members to share what they know about secret codes.

Weekly Resources Guide for English Language Learner Support

For this week's content and language objectives, see p. 137e.

Instructional Strand	Day 1	Day 2
Concept Development/Academic Language	**TEACHER'S EDITION** • Academic Language, p. DI•91 • Concept Development, p. DI•91 • Anchored Talk, pp. 112j—112–113 • Preteach Academic Vocabulary, p. 115a • Concept Talk Video **ELL HANDBOOK** • Hear It, See It, Say It, Use It, pp. xxxvi–xxxvii • ELL Poster Talk, Concept Talk, p. 137c **ELL POSTER 19** • Day 1 Activities	**TEACHER'S EDITION** • Academic Language, p. DI•91 • Concept Development, p. DI•91 • Anchored Talk, p. 116a • Concept Talk Video **ELL HANDBOOK** • ELL Poster Talk, Concept Talk, p. 137c • Concept Talk Video Routine, p. 477 **ELL POSTER 19** • Day 2 Activities
Phonics and Spelling	**TEACHER'S EDITION** • Phonics and Spelling, p. DI•95	**TEACHER'S EDITION** • Phonics and Spelling, p. DI•95
Listening Comprehension	**TEACHER'S EDITION** • Modified Read Aloud, p. DI•94 • Read Aloud, p. 113b • Concept Talk Video **ELL HANDBOOK** • Concept Talk Video Routine, p. 477	**TEACHER'S EDITION** • Modified Read Aloud, p. DI•94 • AudioText of *Seeker of Knowledge* • Concept Talk Video **ELL HANDBOOK** • AudioText CD Routine, p. 477 • Story Map A, p. 483
Reading Comprehension	**TEACHER'S EDITION** • Preteach Graphic Sources, p. DI•96	**TEACHER'S EDITION** • Reteach Graphic Sources, p. DI•96 • Frontloading Reading, p. DI•97 **ELL HANDBOOK** • Picture It! Skill Instruction, pp. 138–138a • Multilingual Summaries, pp. 139–141
Vocabulary **Basic and Lesson Vocabulary** **Word Analysis: Latin Roots**	**TEACHER'S EDITION** • Basic Vocabulary, p. DI•92 • Preteach Lesson Vocabulary, p. DI•92 • Latin Roots, p. DI•95 **ELL HANDBOOK** • Word Cards, p. 137 • ELL Vocabulary Routine, p. 471 **ELL POSTER 19** • Day 1 Activities	**TEACHER'S EDITION** • Basic Vocabulary, p. DI•92 • Reteach Lesson Vocabulary, p. DI•93 • Latin Roots, p. DI•95 **ELL HANDBOOK** • Word Cards, p. 137 • Multilingual Vocabulary List, p. 431 **ELL POSTER 19** • Day 2 Activities
Grammar and Conventions	**TEACHER'S EDITION** • Preteach Possessive Pronouns, p. DI•99	**TEACHER'S EDITION** • Reteach Possessive Pronouns, p. DI•99
Writing	**TEACHER'S EDITION** • Include Essential Information, p. DI•100 • Introduce Problem-Solution Essay, pp. 115e–115f	**TEACHER'S EDITION** • Writing Trait: Focus/Ideas, pp. 125d–125e

137a *Seeker of Knowledge* Unit 4, Week 4

ELL Handbook

This symbol indicates leveled instruction to address language proficiency levels.

Day 3	Day 4	Day 5
TEACHER'S EDITION • Academic Language, p. DI•91 • Concept Development, p. DI•91 • Anchored Talk, p. 126a • Concept Talk Video **ELL HANDBOOK** • ELL Poster Talk, Concept Talk, p. 137c **ELL POSTER 19** • Day 3 Activities	**TEACHER'S EDITION** • Academic Language, p. DI•91 • Concept Development, p. DI•91 • Anchored Talk, p. 134a • Concept Talk Video **ELL HANDBOOK** • ELL Poster Talk, Concept Talk, p. 137c **ELL POSTER 19** • Day 4 Activities	**TEACHER'S EDITION** • Academic Language, p. DI•91 • Concept Development, p. DI•91 • Concept Talk Video **ELL HANDBOOK** • ELL Poster Talk, Concept Talk, p. 137c **ELL POSTER 19** • Day 5 Activities
		TEACHER'S EDITION • Phonics and Spelling, p. DI•95
ELL HANDBOOK • Phonics Transition Lesson, pp. 272, 275	**ELL HANDBOOK** • Phonics Transition Lesson, pp. 272, 275	
TEACHER'S EDITION • AudioText of *Seeker of Knowledge* • Concept Talk Video **ELL HANDBOOK** • AudioText CD Routine, p. 477	**TEACHER'S EDITION** • Concept Talk Video	**TEACHER'S EDITION** • Concept Talk Video
TEACHER'S EDITION • Sheltered Reading, p. DI•97 **ELL HANDBOOK** • Multilingual Summaries, pp. 139–141	**TEACHER'S EDITION** • ELL/ELD Reader Guided Reading, p. DI•98 **ELL HANDBOOK** • ELL Study Guide, p. 142	**TEACHER'S EDITION** • ELL/ELD Reader Guided Reading, p. DI•98 **ELL HANDBOOK** • ELL Study Guide, p. 142
		TEACHER'S EDITION • Greek and Latin Prefixes *trans-, tele-*, p. 139i **ELL HANDBOOK** • High-Frequency Words Activity Bank, p. 446
ELL HANDBOOK • High-Frequency Words Activity Bank, p. 446 **ELL POSTER 19** • Day 3 Activities	**ELL HANDBOOK** • High-Frequency Words Activity Bank, p. 446	
TEACHER'S EDITION • Grammar Jammer **ELL HANDBOOK** • Grammar Transition Lesson, pp. 363, 367 • Grammar Jammer Routine, p. 478	**TEACHER'S EDITION** • Grammar Jammer **ELL HANDBOOK** • Grammar Transition Lesson, pp. 363, 367	**TEACHER'S EDITION** • Grammar Jammer **ELL HANDBOOK** • Grammar Transition Lesson, pp. 363, 367
TEACHER'S EDITION • Let's Write It!, p. 132–133 • Writer's Craft: Topic Sentences, pp. 133a–133b	**TEACHER'S EDITION** • Revising Strategy, pp. 139d–139e	**TEACHER'S EDITION** • Possessive Pronouns, pp. 139p–139q

Question of the Week
How can knowing another language create understanding?

Throughout the week, use the ELL Poster to help students produce and comprehend language, understand the concept, and build English vocabulary. Use the Question of the Week and other questions to help students share ideas in pairs, small groups, or the large group. Sample questions are shown, with examples of possible responses by students.

Weekly Concept and Language Goals

• Share ideas about why communication is important

• Describe ways that cultures communicate

• Explain how people communicate

By the end of the lesson, students should be able to talk about and write sentences about communication.

ELL Poster 19

Daily Team Talk

Day 1	Day 2	Day 3	Day 4	Day 5
After Day 1 activities on Poster, ask questions such as *How are the students in the poster picture communicating information about ancient Greece to the audience?*	After Day 2 activity on Poster, ask questions such as *How is the girl on the side of the stage helping people in the audience understand the play?*	After Day 3 activity on Poster, ask questions such as *According to the students' play, how did people in ancient Greece communicate?*	After Day 4 activity on Poster, ask questions such as *Why do we need to be able to communicate with others?*	After Day 5 activity on Poster, ask questions such as *Other than through language, how do people communicate in your native culture?*
Beginning In a play. **Intermediate** They are putting on an old play. **Advanced** They are performing a Greek play for the audience. **Advanced High** The students are communicating information about ancient Greece by performing an ancient Greek play.	**Beginning** With sign language. **Intermediate** She is telling the play in sign language. **Advanced** The girl is translating the play into American Sign Language. **Advanced High** The girl is helping people in the audience who are hearing impaired understand the play by translating it into American Sign Language.	**Beginning** By talking. **Intermediate** They talked and they wrote. **Advanced** They talked and they wrote on paper. **Advanced High** People in ancient Greece communicated by talking and by writing on scrolls.	**Beginning** To talk to each other. **Intermediate** To understand each other. **Advanced** If we couldn't talk to each other, we would be lonely. **Advanced High** We need to communicate with others to give and get information.	**Beginning** We dance. **Intermediate** With dancing and music. **Advanced** We communicate through our dancing and music. **Advanced High** People in my native culture communicate through our music and our dancing.

Teacher's Edition pages 112j–139q

See the support for English language learners throughout the lesson, including ELL strategies and scaffolded activities at points of use.

Teacher's Edition pages DI•91–DI•100

Differentiated Instruction for English language learners provides daily group activities that "frontload," or preteach, core instruction.

ELL Handbook pp. 137a–142

Find additional lesson materials that support the core lesson and the ELL instructional pages.

ELL Poster 19

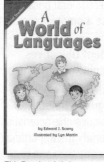

ELL Reader 4.4.4

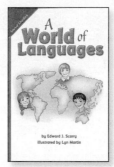

ELD Reader 4.4.4

Concept Literacy Reader

ELD, ELL Reader Teaching Guide

Concept Literacy Reader Teaching Guide

Technology

Online Teacher's Edition Use the digital version of the core Teacher's Edition for planning and instruction.

eReaders
This week's ELL and ELD Readers and Concept Literacy Reader are also available in digital format.

This Week's Content and Language Objectives by Strand

Concept Development/ Academic Language How long can knowing another language create understanding?	**Content Objective** • Use concept vocabulary to understand how knowing another language can create understanding. **Language Objectives** • Use prior knowledge and experience to understand meaning. • Express ideas in response to new academic vocabulary
Phonics and Spelling Consonant Sounds /j/, /ks/, /kw/	**Content Objective** • Identify consonant sounds /j/, /ks/, /kw/. **Language Objectives** • Apply phonics and decoding skills to vocabulary. • Learn relationships between sounds and letters to represent sounds when writing.
Listening Comprehension Modified Read Aloud: "The Scholar"	**Content Objective** • Monitor and adjust oral comprehension. **Language Objectives** • Discuss oral passages. • Use a graphic organizer to take notes.
Reading Comprehension Graphic Sources	**Content Objectives** • Identify graphic sources of a text. • Use graphic sources to aid comprehension. **Language Objectives** • Discuss characteristics of graphic sources. • Identify the importance of graphic sources through personal experiences and writing.
Vocabulary Basic and Lesson Vocabulary	**Language Objectives** • Understand and use basic and grade-level vocabulary. • Learn meanings of grade-level vocabulary • Produce drawings, phrases, and short sentences to show understanding of Lesson Vocabulary.
Word Analysis Latin Roots	**Content Objective** • Identify Greek and Latin prefixes *trans-* and *tele-*. **Language Objective** • Discuss Greek and Latin prefixes *trans-* and *tele-*.
Grammar and Conventions Possessive Pronouns	**Content Objective** • Decode and use possessive pronouns. **Language Objectives** • Speak using possessive pronouns. • Write and edit phrases or sentences that use possessive pronouns.
Writing Include Essential Information	**Content Objective** • Identify essential information. **Language Objective** • Write a paragraph including essential information.

Word Cards for Vocabulary Activities

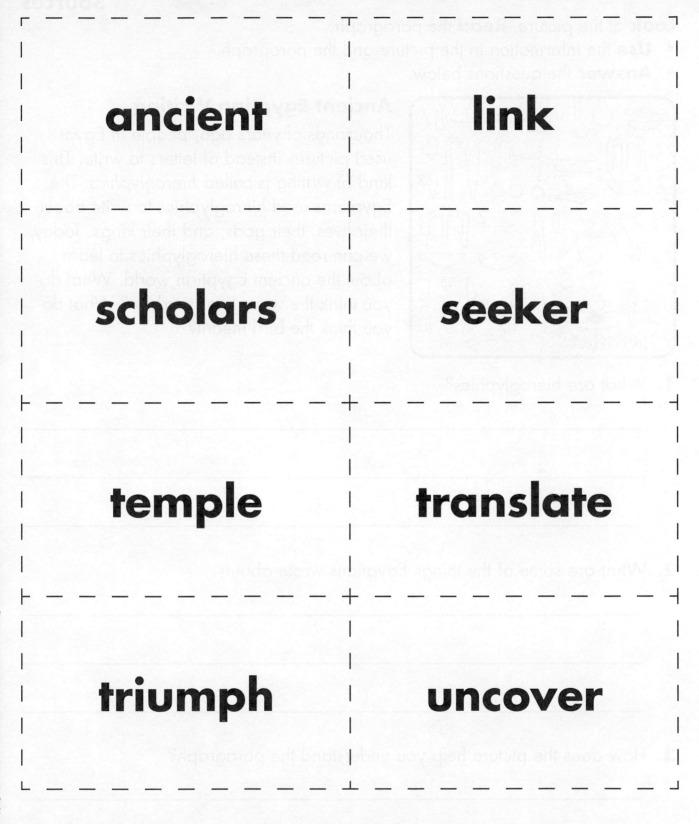

ancient

link

scholars

seeker

temple

translate

triumph

uncover

Teacher Note: Beginning Teach three to four words. **Intermediate** Teach four to six words. **Advanced** Teach six to seven words. **Advanced High** Teach all words.

Name _____

Look at the picture. **Read** the paragraph.
- **Use** the information in the picture and the paragraph.
- **Answer** the questions below.

Ancient Egyptian Writing

Thousands of years ago, people in Egypt used pictures instead of letters to write. This kind of writing is called *hieroglyphics.* The Egyptians used hieroglyphics to write about their lives, their gods, and their kings. Today, we can read these hieroglyphics to learn about the ancient Egyptian world. What do you think the wavy line stood for? What do you think the bird meant?

1. What are hieroglyphics?

_____

_____

_____

2. What are some of the things Egyptians wrote about?

_____

_____

_____

3. How does the picture help you understand the paragraph?

_____

_____

_____

Graphic Sources

Use this lesson to supplement or replace the skill lesson on page 113c of the Teacher's Edition. Display the Skill Points (at right) and share them with students.

Teach/Model

Beginning Display a map of the school. Ask: *What information does this graphic source tell us?* (where places are in our school) Display a world map. Ask: *What information does this graphic source tell us?* (where countries, bodies of water, cities, etc., are located) Say: *These are both maps, but they tell us different kinds of information.*

Intermediate Display a photograph of a platypus and read a description of it from a children's encyclopedia. Ask: *How does the photo help you understand the text?* (The photo shows what the platypus looks like. It makes the text clearer.)

Advanced Discuss the parts of a bicycle, what they look like, and where they are located. Ask: *What is a good way to show this information?* Have students draw a diagram of a bike and label its parts. Ask them why the graphic source helps them understand the information better.

Advanced High Ask students to name their favorite sport. Record their responses in a chart. Ask: *How does this chart help you understand the results of my survey?* (I can see how many chose each sport.) Have students help you make a bar graph showing the same information. Discuss how the graph makes the results even clearer.

Then distribute copies of Picture It! page 138.

- Have students look at and discuss the hieroglyphics. Then read the paragraph aloud.
- Ask: *What are hieroglyphics?* (pictures used to write)
- Review the Skill Points with students.
- Have students discuss how the graphic source—the picture—helps them understand what hieroglyphics are.

Practice

Read aloud the directions on page 138. Reread the paragraph aloud. Then have students use the picture and the paragraph as they answer the questions.

Beginning Students can say the answers to the questions before writing phrases or sentences on the lines. Provide help with English words and writing.

Intermediate Students can first orally answer the questions and then write phrases or simple sentences on the lines. Provide help with writing.

Advanced Students can write their answers on the lines and then check them by comparing them to a partner's.

Advanced High Students can write their answers on the lines and then check them by reviewing the information in the paragraph.

Answers for page 138: 1. They are a kind of writing in which pictures are used instead of letters. 2. They wrote about their lives, their gods, and their kings. 3. The paragraph tells about hieroglyphics. The picture shows what some hieroglyphics look like.

Skill Points

✔ **Graphic sources** include photos, illustrations, maps, charts, time lines, graphs, and diagrams.

✔ Many graphic sources organize information in a way that makes it easier to read and understand.

✔ You can use graphic sources to help you understand what you read.

Multilingual Summaries

Seeker of Knowledge

In the 1790s in Grenoble, France, a boy named Jean-François Champollion went with his brother to visit a scientist's home. The home was filled with things from ancient Egypt. The scientist told him that no one could read the writings of the ancient Egyptians, called hieroglyphics. Jean-François read many books about Egypt and the hieroglyphics. He claimed he would read them someday.

When he finished school, he went to Paris to study hieroglyphics with historians. They turned him away. Jean-François returned to Grenoble and began to teach. He often spoke about ancient Egypt. Even Napoleon came to listen to Jean-François speak.

Years later, Jean-François returned to Paris. He was determined to translate the hieroglyphics. After years of study, Jean-François became the first modern person to translate ancient Egyptian writing. He finally got to go to Egypt.

Spanish

El buscador de conocimiento

En la década de 1790, en Grenoble, Francia, un niño llamado Jean-François Champollion fue con su hermano a visitar la casa de un científico. La casa estaba llena de cosas del antiguo Egipto. El científico le dijo que nadie podía leer los escritos de los antiguos egipcios, llamados jeroglíficos. Jean-François leyó muchos libros sobre Egipto y los jeroglíficos. Dijo que él los leería algún día.

Cuando terminó la escuela, fue a París a estudiar jeroglíficos con los historiadores. Ellos no le hicieron caso. Jean-François volvió a Grenoble y comenzó a enseñar. A menudo hablaba del antiguo Egipto. Hasta Napoleón fue a escuchar las charlas sobre Egipto de Jean-François.

Años después, Jean-François regresó a París. Estaba decidido a traducir los jeroglíficos. Después de años de estudio, Jean-François se convirtió en la primera persona de este tiempo que tradujo la escritura egipcia antigua. Finalmente, pudo viajar a Egipto.

Multilingual Summaries

追求知識的人

　　1790 年代在法國格勒諾伯這個地方，有個男孩名字叫做向波倫。有一天，向波倫和他的兄弟一起去拜訪一位科學家，那科學家的家裡到處都是古埃及的東西。科學家告訴他，世界上沒有人看得懂古埃及人寫的文字，那種文字叫做象形文字。向波倫看了很多跟埃及和象形文字有關的書，他說有一天他一定會看得懂埃及象形文字。

　　在學校畢業以後，向波倫出發往巴黎，想跟史學家學習象形文字，可是被拒絕了，所以他就回格勒諾伯，然後開始教書。向波倫經常談到古埃及，後來連拿破崙都跑來聽向波倫講有關古埃及的事。

　　幾年後，向波倫又回到巴黎，這次他決定要翻譯埃及象形文字。經過好幾年的研究之後，向波倫終於成為現代第一個翻譯古埃及文字的人，最後他還去了埃及。

Người Tìm Kiến Thức

Trong những thập niên 1790 ở Grenoble, nước Pháp, một cậu bé tên Jean-François Champollion đi với anh mình đến thăm nhà của một khoa học gia. Ngôi nhà đầy các vật từ thời Ai Cập cổ xưa. Nhà khoa học nói với cậu bé rằng không ai có thể đọc những chữ viết của những người Ai Cập cổ xưa, được gọi là chữ viết tượng hình (hieroglyphics). Jean-François Champollion đã đọc nhiều sách về Ai Cập và kiểu chữ viết tượng hình. Cậu tuyên bố rằng một ngày nào đó cậu sẽ đọc được những chữ này.

Khi học xong, cậu đi đến Paris để học chữ viết tượng hình với các sử gia. Họ từ chối không nhận cậu. Jean-François Champollion trở về Grenoble và bắt đầu dạy học. Cậu thường nói về Ai Cập cổ xưa. Ngay cả Napoleon cũng đến nghe Jean-François giảng thuyết.

Nhiều năm trôi qua, Jean-François trở lại Paris. Ông cương quyết dịch ra những chữ viết tượng hình. Sau nhiều năm nghiên cứu, Jean-François trở thành người đầu tiên của thời hiện đại có thể dịch chữ viết của người Ai Cập cổ xưa. Cuối cùng ông được đi sang Ai Cập.

Multilingual Summaries

지식 탐구자

1790년대 프랑스의 그르노블에서 장 프랑수아 샹폴리옹이라는 한 남자 아이가 동생과 함께 한 과학자의 집으로 갔다. 그 집은 고대 이집트 물건들로 가득했는데 그 과학자는 아이에게 상형문자라고 하는 고대 이집트 사람들의 글자를 읽을 수 있는 사람은 아무도 없다고 말했다. 장 프랑수아는 이집트와 상형문자에 관한 많은 책을 읽었고, 언젠가 그는 상형문자를 읽을 수 있게 될 것이라고 주장했다.

그는 학교를 마치고 파리로 가서 역사학자들과 함께 상형문자를 공부하려 했지만 역사학자들은 그를 돌려보냈다. 장 프랑수아는 그르노블로 돌아와 선생님이 되었다. 그는 종종 고대 이집트에 대한 이야기를 했고 심지어 나폴레옹도 장 프랑수아의 연설을 들으러 왔다.

몇 년 후 장 프랑수아는 파리로 돌아왔고 상형문자를 해석하기로 결심한다. 몇 년 간의 연구 후 장 프랑수아는 고대 이집트 문자를 해석한 최초의 현대인이 되었고 그는 결국 이집트로 갔다.

Tus Neeg Nrhiav Kev Txawj Kev Ntse

Thaum xyoo 1790 hauv lub zos Grenoble, France, ib tug me nyuam tub uas muaj lub npe hu ua Jean-Francois Champollion tau mus nrog nws tus tij laug mus xyuas ib tug neeg txawj ntse lub tsev. Lub tsev muaj ntau yam khoom qub qub uas tau hauv nyob I-yiv. Tus neeg txawj ntse hais tias tsis muaj leej twg uas nyeem tau I-yiv cov ntawv txheej puag thaum ub uas hu ua cov ntawv hieroglyphics. Jean-Francois tau nyeem ntau phau ntawv txog I-yiv thiab cov ntawv hieroglyphics. Nws hais tias yuav muaj ib hnub nws yuav nyeem tau cov ntawv no.

Thaum nws kawm ntawv tas, nws tau mus hauv Paris mus kawm cov ntawv hieroglyphics nrog cov neeg paub keeb kwm. Lawv tsis kam nws nrog lawv. Jean-Francois rov qab mus rau Grenoble thiab pib qhia ntawv. Ntau zaus nws yeej hais txog I-yiv txheej puag thuam ub. Napoleon los kuj tau tuaj mloog Jean-Francois hais lus thiab.

Ntau xyoo dhau mus, Jean-Francois tau rov qab mus hauv Paris. Nws muaj siab xav txhais cov ntawv hieroglyphics. Tom qab ntau xyoo uas nws kawm cov ntawv no, Jean-Francois tau los yog thawj tug neeg niaj hnub nim no uas txhais tau I-yiv cov ntawv txheej puag thaum ub. Ces thaum kawg nws tau mus hauv I-yiv.

Name _____

- **Read** *A World of Languages* again.
- Use the information from the art in the book to **answer** the questions.

1. From the map on page 2, where do each of the three children live?

_____

2. Look at the art on page 3. Who can say "Hello" in three different languages?

_____

3. Look at the chart on page 4. In which countries is Mandarin spoken?

_____

4. On the map on page 5, name the four countries that border Switzerland.

_____

5. On the map on page 6, what country is next to the United States?

_____

Family Link

Does anyone in your family know more than one language? What are these languages?

Weekly Resources Guide for English Language Learner Support

For this week's content and language objectives, see p. 143e.

Instructional Strand	Day 1	Day 2
Concept Development/Academic Language	TEACHER'S EDITION • Academic Language, p. DI•116 • Concept Development, p. DI•116 • Anchored Talk, pp. 140j—140–141 • Preteach Academic Vocabulary, p. 143a • Concept Talk Video ELL HANDBOOK • Hear It, See It, Say It, Use It, pp. xxxvi–xxxvii • ELL Poster Talk, Concept Talk, p. 143c ELL POSTER 20 • Day 1 Activities	TEACHER'S EDITION • Academic Language, p. DI•116 • Concept Development, p. DI•116 • Anchored Talk, p. 144a • Concept Talk Video ELL HANDBOOK • ELL Poster Talk, Concept Talk, p. 143c • Concept Talk Video Routine, p. 477 ELL POSTER 20 • Day 2 Activities
Phonics and Spelling	TEACHER'S EDITION • Phonics and Spelling, p. DI•120	TEACHER'S EDITION • Phonics and Spelling, p. DI•120
Listening Comprehension	TEACHER'S EDITION • Modified Read Aloud, p. DI•119 • Read Aloud, p. 141b • Concept Talk Video ELL HANDBOOK • Concept Talk Video Routine, p. 477	TEACHER'S EDITION • Modified Read Aloud, p. DI•119 • AudioText of *Encyclopedia Brown* • Concept Talk Video ELL HANDBOOK • AudioText CD Routine, p. 477 • Story Map A, p. 483
Reading Comprehension	TEACHER'S EDITION • Preteach Character and Plot, p. DI•121	TEACHER'S EDITION • Reteach Character and Plot, p. DI•121 • Frontloading Reading, p. DI•122 ELL HANDBOOK • Picture It! Skill Instruction, pp. 144–144a • Multilingual Summaries, pp. 145–147
Vocabulary **Basic and Lesson Vocabulary** **Word Analysis: Greek Prefixes *amphi-, anti-***	TEACHER'S EDITION • Basic Vocabulary, p. DI•117 • Preteach Lesson Vocabulary, p. DI•117 • Greek Prefixes *amphi-, anti-*, p. DI•120 ELL HANDBOOK • Word Cards, p. 143 • ELL Vocabulary Routine, p. 471 ELL POSTER 20 • Day 1 Activities	TEACHER'S EDITION • Basic Vocabulary, p. DI•117 • Reteach Lesson Vocabulary, p. DI•118 • Greek Prefixes *amphi-, anti-*, p. DI•120 ELL HANDBOOK • Word Cards, p. 143 • Multilingual Vocabulary List, p. 431 ELL POSTER 20 • Day 2 Activities
Grammar and Conventions	TEACHER'S EDITION • Teach/Model Contractions and Negatives, p. DI•124	TEACHER'S EDITION • Reteach Contractions and Negatives, p. DI•124
Writing	TEACHER'S EDITION • Strong Action Verbs, p. DI•125 • Writing for Tests: Adventure Story, pp. 143e–143f	TEACHER'S EDITION • Writing for Tests: Adventure Story, pp. 151d–151e

Unit 4 Week 5 Encyclopedia Brown

This symbol indicates leveled instruction to address language proficiency levels.

Day 3	Day 4	Day 5
TEACHER'S EDITION • Academic Language, p. DI•116 • Concept Development, p. DI•116 • Anchored Talk, p. 152a • Concept Talk Video **ELL HANDBOOK** • ELL Poster Talk, Concept Talk, p. 143c **ELL POSTER 20** • Day 3 Activities	**TEACHER'S EDITION** • Academic Language, p. DI•116 • Concept Development, p. DI•116 • Anchored Talk, p. 160a • Concept Talk Video **ELL HANDBOOK** • ELL Poster Talk, Concept Talk, p. 143c **ELL POSTER 20** • Day 4 Activities	**TEACHER'S EDITION** • Academic Language, p. DI•116 • Concept Development, p. DI•116 • Concept Talk Video **ELL HANDBOOK** • ELL Poster Talk, Concept Talk, p. 143c **ELL POSTER 20** • Day 5 Activities
		TEACHER'S EDITION • Phonics and Spelling, p. DI•120
ELL HANDBOOK • Phonics Transition Lesson, pp. 284–285, 291–292	**ELL HANDBOOK** • Phonics Transition Lesson, pp. 284–285, 291–292	
TEACHER'S EDITION • AudioText of *Encyclopedia Brown* • Concept Talk Video **ELL HANDBOOK** • AudioText CD Routine, p. 477	**TEACHER'S EDITION** • Concept Talk Video	**TEACHER'S EDITION** • Concept Talk Video
TEACHER'S EDITION • Sheltered Reading, p. DI•122 **ELL HANDBOOK** • Multilingual Summaries, pp. 145–147	**TEACHER'S EDITION** • ELL/ELD Reader Guided Reading, p. DI•123 **ELL HANDBOOK** • ELL Study Guide, p. 148	**TEACHER'S EDITION** • ELL/ELD Reader Guided Reading, p. DI•123 **ELL HANDBOOK** • ELL Study Guide, p. 148
		TEACHER'S EDITION • Greek Prefixes *amphi-* and *anti-*, p. 165i **ELL HANDBOOK** • High-Frequency Words Activity Bank, p. 446
ELL HANDBOOK • High-Frequency Words Activity Bank, p. 446 **ELL POSTER 20** • Day 3 Activities	**ELL HANDBOOK** • High-Frequency Words Activity Bank, p. 446	
TEACHER'S EDITION • Grammar Jammer **ELL HANDBOOK** • Grammar Transition Lesson, pp. 328, 337 • Grammar Jammer Routine, p. 478	**TEACHER'S EDITION** • Grammar Jammer **ELL HANDBOOK** • Grammar Transition Lesson, pp. 328, 337	**TEACHER'S EDITION** • Grammar Jammer **ELL HANDBOOK** • Grammar Transition Lesson, pp. 328, 337
TEACHER'S EDITION • Let's Write It!, p. 158–159 • Writing for Tests: Evaluation, pp. 159a–159b	**TEACHER'S EDITION** • Writing for Tests: Adventure Story, pp. 165d–165e	**TEACHER'S EDITION** • Writing for Tests: Adventure Story, pp. 165p–165q

ELL Handbook

Question of the Week

How can attention to detail help solve a problem?

Throughout the week, use the ELL Poster to help students produce and comprehend language, understand the concept, and build English vocabulary. Use the Question of the Week and other questions to help students share ideas in pairs, small groups, or the large group. Sample questions are shown, with examples of possible responses by students.

ELL Poster 20

Weekly Concept and Language Goals

• Understand how details are related to solving problems

• Describe how asking questions can help find details

• Explain how paying attention to details can help solve problems

By the end of the lesson, students should be able to talk about and write sentences about attention to detail and problem solving.

Daily Team Talk

Day 1	Day 2	Day 3	Day 4	Day 5
After Day 1 activities on Poster, ask questions such as	After Day 2 activity on Poster, ask questions such as	After Day 3 activity on Poster, ask questions such as	After Day 4 activity on Poster, ask questions such as	After Day 5 activity on Poster, ask questions such as
What problem does the pet store owner need to solve?	*What do you think is the first question the police officer asks?*	*What detail about the empty cage helps solve part of the mystery?*	*What important details does the girl notice that help solve the rest of the mystery?*	*Why should you pay attention to details when you are solving a problem?*
Beginning No lizards. **Intermediate** His lizards are gone. **Advanced** He does not know where his lizards are. **Advanced High** One terrarium is empty, and two lizards are missing. The pet store owner needs to find them.	**Beginning** Where are they? **Intermediate** Did someone steal them? **Advanced** How could the lizards get out? **Advanced High** When did you last see the lizards?	**Beginning** A hole. **Intermediate** There is a hole. **Advanced** The lid of the cage has a hole in it. **Advanced High** The lizards chewed a hole in the lid of their cage and escaped through the hole.	**Beginning** The lizards. **Intermediate** She sees the lizards. **Advanced** The girl sees where the lizards are. **Advanced High** The girl sees one lizard hiding under the table and the other lizard hiding on the side of the bookcase.	**Beginning** It helps you. **Intermediate** Details can help you with the problem. **Advanced** You need to look at all the details to solve the problem. **Advanced High** Paying attention to details can help you solve the problem. The solution to the problem is probably in the details.

This Week's Materials

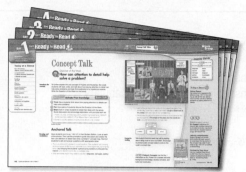

Teacher's Edition pages 140j–169a

See the support for English language learners throughout the lesson, including ELL strategies and scaffolded activities at points of use.

Teacher's Edition pages DI•116–DI•125

Differentiated Instruction for English language learners provides daily group activities that "frontload," or preteach, core instruction.

ELL Handbook pp. 143a–148

Find additional lesson materials that support the core lesson and the ELL instructional pages.

ELL Poster 20

ELL Reader 4.4.5

ELD Reader 4.4.5

Concept Literacy Reader

ELD, ELL Reader Teaching Guide

Concept Literacy Reader Teaching Guide

Technology

Online Teacher's Edition Use the digital version of the core Teacher's Edition for planning and instruction.

eReaders
This week's ELL and ELD Readers and Concept Literacy Reader are also available in digital format.

This Week's Content and Language Objectives by Strand

Concept Development/ Academic Language How can attention to detail help solve a problem?	**Content Objective** • Use concept vocabulary related to the idea of being attentive to details. **Language Objectives** • Express ideas in response to art and discussion. • Express ideas in response to new academic vocabulary.
Phonics and Spelling Prefixes *un-*, *dis-*, and *in-*	**Content Objective** • Identify prefixes *un-*, *dis-*, and *in-*. **Language Objective** • Apply phonics and decoding skills to vocabulary.
Listening Comprehension Modified Read Aloud: "Smell of Fish"	**Content Objective** • Monitor and adjust oral comprehension. **Language Objectives** • Discuss oral passages. • Use a graphic organizer to take notes.
Reading Comprehension Character and Plot	**Content Objectives** • Identify the characters of a story. • Monitor and adjust comprehension. **Language Objectives** • Discuss the characters and plot from the story. • Give examples to identify the characters and plot. • Monitor understanding of spoken language. • Read grade-level text with expression.
Vocabulary Basic and Lesson Vocabulary	**Language Objectives** • Use visual support to understand and use basic vocabulary. • Learn meanings of grade-level vocabulary. • Produce drawings, phrases, and short sentences to show understanding of Lesson Vocabulary.
Word Analysis Greek Prefixes *amphi-*, *anti-*	**Content Objective** • Identify Greek prefixes *amphi-* and *anti-*. **Language Objective** • Correctly use words that contain the Greek prefixes *amphi-* and *anti-*.
Grammar and Conventions Contractions and Negatives	**Content Objective** • Use contractions and negatives correctly. **Language Objectives** • Speak using contractions and negatives. • Write sentences using contractions and negatives correctly.
Writing Strong Action Verbs	**Content Objective** • Identify and use strong verbs. **Language Objective** • Write paragraphs using strong verbs.

Word Cards for Vocabulary Activities

amphibians

crime

exhibit

lizards

reference

reptiles

salamanders

stumped

Teacher Note: Beginning Teach three to four words. **Intermediate** Teach four to six words. **Advanced** Teach six to seven words. **Advanced High** Teach all words.

Name _____

Look at the picture. **Read** the story.

• **Answer** the questions below.

Leo the Lost Lizard

Katie looked everywhere for her pet lizard, Leo. She could not find him anywhere. She had tears in her eyes as she looked around the cage and under her bed. Where could Leo be? Katie hoped he was okay. Finally, Katie asked her brother to help her find her lizard. Her brother looked in Leo's cage for clues. Then he laughed out loud. "Katie," he said, "Leo isn't lost! He's sleeping under his log!" Katie smiled. She hugged her brother and thanked him.

---

1. What is Katie's problem?

_____

2. How does Katie feel at the beginning of the story?

_____

3. How is the problem solved?

_____

_____

4. How does Katie feel at the end of the story?

_____

Character and Plot

Use this lesson to supplement or replace the skill lesson on page 141c of the Teacher's Edition. Display the Skill Points (at right) and share them with students.

Teach/Model

Beginning Say: *Listen to this very short story: Sarah is driving to work. Her car gets a flat tire. She changes the tire.* Ask students to identify the character and plot of the story. Then have them identify the problem and solution in the plot.

Intermediate Say: *It is cold today. David's mom tells him to wear his coat, a hat, and gloves. He finds his coat and hat in the closet. But where are his gloves? His hands will freeze without them!* Ask students to identify the character, the plot so far, and the problem. Then have them suggest a solution to finish the plot and the story.

Advanced Say: *Once again Jana is late starting her homework. As she hurries to finish before bedtime, her pencil breaks. She starts to cry.* Ask: *Who is the character in this story? What do her actions tell about her?* (She puts things off and gets upset easily.) Ask students to suggest a solution to Jana's broken-pencil problem.

Advanced High As a group, decide on a problem for a story, such as *The bathroom sink is overflowing.* Then discuss characters, events leading up to the problem, and possible solutions. Finally, have individual students write the story in their own words.

Then distribute copies of Picture It! page 144.

- Have students look at the picture and describe what they see.
- Read the story aloud. Ask: *What is Katie's problem?* (She can't find Leo, her pet lizard.)
- Review the Skill Points with students.
- Have students discuss the characters and plot of the story.

Practice

Read aloud the directions on page 144. Have volunteers reread the story aloud. Then have students use the picture and the story as they answer the questions.

Beginning Students can say their answers to the questions before writing them on the lines. Provide help with English words and writing.

Intermediate Students can first orally answer the questions and then write their answers on the lines. Provide help with writing.

Advanced Students can write their answers to the questions on the lines and then check them by rereading them silently to make sure they make sense.

Advanced High Students can write their answers to the questions on the lines and then check them by reviewing the story and making any necessary changes.

Answers for page 144: 1. Katie can't find her pet lizard, Leo. 2. Katie is upset and worried. 3. Katie's brother finds Leo sleeping under his log inside the cage. 4. Katie is happy and grateful to her brother.

Skill Points

✔ A **character** is a person or animal in a story or play. You use what characters say and do to learn about them.

✔ The **plot** is the sequence of events in a story.

✔ A plot is often based on a problem that someone in the story has.

✔ The plot usually ends with the resolution, or solution, of the problem.

Multilingual Summaries

Encyclopedia Brown and the Case of the Slippery Salamander

No one got away with breaking the law in the town of Idaville. The police chief's son was called Encyclopedia Brown because he knew so many things. He was a great detective and helped his father solve crimes.

One night the police chief was upset. That day a salamander had been stolen from the town's aquarium. Encyclopedia Brown asked his father many questions about that. They talked about the suspects, Doctor Donnell, Mrs. King, and Sam Maine. Sam Maine, the new caretaker, had told Chief Brown that he had worked with salamanders and other lizards for many years. Encyclopedia said Sam was lying, because salamanders are not lizards. Lizards are reptiles, and salamanders are amphibians. Sam admitted to stealing the salamander, gave the salamander back, and was fired from his job.

Enciclopedia Brown y el caso de la escurridiza salamandra

En el pueblo de Idaville nadie se escapaba si traspasa la ley. Al hijo del jefe de la policía le decían Enciclopedia Brown porque sabía muchas cosas. Era un gran detective y le ayudaba a su padre a resolver muchos crímenes.

Una noche, el jefe de la policía estaba preocupado. Ese día se habían robado una salamandra del acuario del pueblo. Enciclopedia Brown le hizo a su padre muchas preguntas relacionadas con el robo. Hablaron de los sospechosos, como el Doctor Donnell, la Sra. King y Sam Maine. Sam Maine, el nuevo conserje, le había dicho al Jefe Brown que él había trabajado con salamandras y otros lagartos durante muchos años. Enciclopedia dijo que Sam estaba mintiendo porque las salamandras no son lagartos. Los lagartos son reptiles, y las salamandras son anfibios. Sam admitió que se había robado la salamandra, devolvió la salamandra y fue despedido de su trabajo.

Multilingual Summaries

Chinese

「萬事通」布朗與狡猾的火蜥蝪賊

在印達維爾鎮，所有違法的人都不可能逍遙法外，因為警長的兒子—「萬事通」布朗知道很多事，是一個非常厲害的偵探，他還會幫助他父親打擊犯罪。

有一天晚上，警長很不高興，因為那天有人偷了水族館裡的火蜥蝪。「萬事通」布朗問了父親很多有關的問題。兩人討論到最後，覺得嫌疑犯有三個人：唐奈醫生、金太太，和薩姆‧緬因。薩姆‧緬因是水族館裡新來的動物管理員，他告訴布朗警長，他照顧火蜥蝪和其他蜥蝪已經有好多年了。「萬事通」布朗說薩姆說謊，因為火蜥蝪不是蜥蝪，而是兩棲類動物。薩姆最後終於承認偷了火蜥蝪，他把火蜥蝪還給水族館，不過也被辭退了。

Vietnamese

Cậu Bé Brown Bách Khoa Thư và Vụ Kỳ Nhông Nan Giải

Không ai có thể chạy tội khi phạm luật ở thành phố Idaville. Con trai của viên cảnh sát trưởng được gọi là Brown Bách Khoa Thư vì cậu bé biết rất nhiều điều. Cậu là một thám tử giỏi và đã giúp ba giải quyết nhiều vụ tội phạm.

Một tối nọ viên cảnh sát trưởng buồn bực. Hôm đó một con kỳ nhông đã bị ăn cắp từ tòa nhà có bể nuôi cá của thành phố. Brown Bách Khoa Thư hỏi ba nhiều câu hỏi về việc này. Hai cha con nói về những kẻ bị tình nghi, Bác sĩ Donnell, Bà King, và Sam Maine. Sam Maine, người mới nhận việc chăm sóc kỳ nhông, đã nói với Cảnh Sát Trưởng Brown là ông ta đã làm việc nhiều năm với các kỳ nhông và thằn lằn. Bách Khoa Thư bảo là Sam nói dối, vì kỳ nhông không thuộc giống thằn lằn, mà thuộc loại động vật lưỡng cư. Sam thừa nhận đã ăn cắp con kỳ nhông, giao trả con kỳ nhông lại, và bị đuổi việc.

Multilingual Summaries

Korean

브라운 백과사전과 미끌미끌 도롱뇽 사건

아이다빌이라는 마을에서는 법을 어기면 누구나 처벌을 받는다. 경찰서장의 아들은 지식이 해박하여 브라운 백과사전이라고 불린다. 그는 훌륭한 탐정이고 아버지가 범죄를 해결하도록 도와준다.

어느 날 밤 경찰서장이 매우 화가 났다. 그날 도롱뇽 한 마리가 마을의 수족관에서 도난 당한 것이다. 브라운 백과사전은 아버지에게 그 사건에 대해 이것 저것을 물어보고 용의자인 도넬 의사, 킹 아줌마, 그리고 샘 메인에 대해 얘기한다. 새로운 관리자인 샘 메인은 브라운 서장에게 자신은 수년 동안 도롱뇽뿐만 아니라 다른 도마뱀과 함께 일해왔다고 말한다. 브라운 백과사전은 도롱뇽은 도마뱀이 아니고 양서류이기 때문에 샘이 거짓말을 한다고 말한다. 샘은 도롱뇽을 훔친 것을 인정하고 도롱뇽을 돌려주지만 직장에서 해고된다.

Hmong

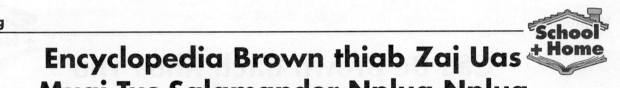

Encyclopedia Brown thiab Zaj Uas Muaj Tus Salamander Nplua Nplua

Tsis muaj leej twg uas mus dawb thaum lawv tau ua txhaum txoj cai hauv lub zos Idaville. Tus thawj tub ceev xwm tus tub uas muaj lub npe hu ua Encyclopedia Brown vim nws paub txhua yam txhua tsav. Nws yog ib tug tub ceev xwm siv tswv yim zoo heev thiab nws pab nws txiv nrhiav tau cov neeg phem.

Muaj ib hmo tus thawj tub ceev xwm tau chim. Hnub ntawd tau muaj leej twg uas nyiag ib tug salamander hauv qhov chaw rau cov salamander. Encyclopedia Brown nug nws txiv ntau yam txog qhov ntawd. Nkawd sib tham ntau txog cov neeg uas tej zaum tau nyiag tus salamander, xws li Doctor Donnel, Mrs. King, thiab Sam Maine. Sam Maine, tus neeg tshiab saib xyuas qhov chaw yug salamander, tau qhia Chief Brown tias nws tau ua hauj lwm nrog cov salamander thiab lwm cov nab qa tau ntau xyoo los lawm. Encyclopedia tau hais tias Sam dag xwb, vim cov salamander tsis nab qa, tiam sis yog amphibians. Sam tau lees hais tias nws tau nyiag tus salamander, rov muab tus salamander los, thiab tau raug ntiab tawv hauj lwm.

Name _____

- **Read** *The Case of the Disappearing Sugar* again.
- Use the information in the book to **answer** the questions below.

pages 2–3

1. Why didn't people like the lemonade Marco brought to the last soccer game?

_____

_____

pages 4–5

2. How did Marco's father help him?

_____

_____

pages 6–7

3. Why didn't Marco add the sugar to the lemonade at home?

_____

_____

pages 8–9

4. Why was Inéz unhappy with her brother?

_____

_____

pages 10–12

5. What happened when Inéz added the sugar to the water and lemon juice?

_____

_____

Family Link

Does anyone in your family make fruit drinks or desserts out of fruit?
Ask your family to share their recipes with you.

Weekly Resources Guide for English Language Learner Support

For this week's content and language objectives, see p. 149e.

Instructional Strand	Day 1	Day 2
Concept Development/Academic Language	**TEACHER'S EDITION** • Academic Language, p. DI•16 • Concept Development, p. DI•16 • Anchored Talk, pp. 172j—172–173 • Preteach Academic Vocabulary, p. 175a • Concept Talk Video **ELL HANDBOOK** • Hear It, See It, Say It, Use It, pp. xxxvi–xxxvii • ELL Poster Talk, Concept Talk, p. 149c **ELL POSTER 21** • Day 1 Activities	**TEACHER'S EDITION** • Academic Language, p. DI•16 • Concept Development, p. DI•16 • Anchored Talk, p. 176a • Concept Talk Video **ELL HANDBOOK** • ELL Poster Talk, Concept Talk, p. 149c • Concept Talk Video Routine, p. 477 **ELL POSTER 21** • Day 2 Activities
Phonics and Spelling	**TEACHER'S EDITION** • Phonics and Spelling, p. DI•20	**TEACHER'S EDITION** • Phonics and Spelling, p. DI•20
Listening Comprehension	**TEACHER'S EDITION** • Modified Read Aloud, p. DI•19 • Read Aloud, p. 173b • Concept Talk Video **ELL HANDBOOK** • Concept Talk Video Routine, p. 477	**TEACHER'S EDITION** • Modified Read Aloud, p. DI•19 • AudioText of *Smokejumpers* • Concept Talk Video **ELL HANDBOOK** • AudioText CD Routine, p. 477 • T-Chart, p. 493
Reading Comprehension	**TEACHER'S EDITION** • Preteach Author's Purpose, p. DI•21	**TEACHER'S EDITION** • Reteach Author's Purpose, p. DI•21 • Frontloading Reading, p. DI•22 **ELL HANDBOOK** • Picture It! Skill Instruction, pp. 150–150a • Multilingual Summaries, pp. 151–153
Vocabulary **Basic and Lesson Vocabulary**	**TEACHER'S EDITION** • Basic Vocabulary, p. DI•17 • Preteach Lesson Vocabulary, p. DI•17 **ELL HANDBOOK** • Word Cards, p. 149 • ELL Vocabulary Routine, p. 471 **ELL POSTER 21** • Day 1 Activities	**TEACHER'S EDITION** • Basic Vocabulary, p. DI•17 • Reteach Lesson Vocabulary, p. DI•18 **ELL HANDBOOK** • Word Cards, p. 149 • Multilingual Vocabulary List, p. 431 **ELL POSTER 21** • Day 2 Activities
Grammar and Conventions	**TEACHER'S EDITION** • Teach/Model Adjectives and Articles, p. DI•24	**TEACHER'S EDITION** • Reteach Adjectives and Articles, p. DI•24
Writing	**TEACHER'S EDITION** • Complete Sentences, p. DI•25 • Introduce Fantasy, pp. 175e–175f	**TEACHER'S EDITION** • Writer's Craft: Story Sequence, pp. 185d–185e

This symbol indicates leveled instruction to address language proficiency levels.

Day 3	Day 4	Day 5
TEACHER'S EDITION • Academic Language, p. DI•16 • Concept Development, p. DI•16 • Anchored Talk, p. 186a • Concept Talk Video **ELL HANDBOOK** • ELL Poster Talk, Concept Talk, p. 149c **ELL POSTER 21** • Day 3 Activities	**TEACHER'S EDITION** • Academic Language, p. DI•16 • Concept Development, p. DI•16 • Anchored Talk, p. 196a • Concept Talk Video **ELL HANDBOOK** • ELL Poster Talk, Concept Talk, p. 149c **ELL POSTER 21** • Day 4 Activities	**TEACHER'S EDITION** • Academic Language, p. DI•16 • Concept Development, p. DI•16 • Concept Talk Video **ELL HANDBOOK** • ELL Poster Talk, Concept Talk, p. 149c **ELL POSTER 21** • Day 5 Activities
		TEACHER'S EDITION • Phonics and Spelling, p. DI•20
ELL HANDBOOK • Phonics Transition Lesson, pp. 302, 307	**ELL HANDBOOK** • Phonics Transition Lesson, pp. 302, 307	
TEACHER'S EDITION • AudioText of *Smokejumpers* • Concept Talk Video **ELL HANDBOOK** • AudioText CD Routine, p. 477	**TEACHER'S EDITION** • Concept Talk Video	**TEACHER'S EDITION** • Concept Talk Video
TEACHER'S EDITION • Sheltered Reading, p. DI•22 **ELL HANDBOOK** • Multilingual Summaries, pp. 151–153	**TEACHER'S EDITION** • ELL/ELD Reader Guided Reading, p. DI•23 **ELL HANDBOOK** • ELL Study Guide, p. 154	**TEACHER'S EDITION** • ELL/ELD Reader Guided Reading, p. DI•23 **ELL HANDBOOK** • ELL Study Guide, p. 154
		TEACHER'S EDITION • French Word Origins, p. 199i
ELL HANDBOOK • High-Frequency Words Activity Bank, p. 446 **ELL POSTER 21** • Day 3 Activities	**ELL HANDBOOK** • High-Frequency Words Activity Bank, p. 446	**ELL HANDBOOK** • High-Frequency Words Activity Bank, p. 446
TEACHER'S EDITION • Grammar Jammer **ELL HANDBOOK** • Grammar Transition Lesson, pp. 370, 373–374 • Grammar Jammer Routine, p. 478	**TEACHER'S EDITION** • Grammar Jammer **ELL HANDBOOK** • Grammar Transition Lesson, pp. 370, 373–374	**TEACHER'S EDITION** • Grammar Jammer **ELL HANDBOOK** • Grammar Transition Lesson, pp. 370, 373–374
TEACHER'S EDITION • Let's Write It!, p. 194–195 • Writer's Craft: Complete Sentences, pp. 195a–195b	**TEACHER'S EDITION** • Revising Strategy, pp. 199d–199e	**TEACHER'S EDITION** • Adjectives and Articles, pp. 199p–199q

Question of the Week
How can we prepare for emergencies?

Throughout the week, use the ELL Poster to help students produce and comprehend language, understand the concept, and build English vocabulary. Use the Question of the Week and other questions to help students share ideas in pairs, small groups, or the large group. Sample questions are shown, with examples of possible responses by students.

Weekly Concept and Language Goals

• Participate in a discussion about emergencies

• Tell how to stay safe in emergencies

• Describe how to prepare for emergencies

By the end of the lesson, students should be able to talk about and write sentences about preparing for emergencies.

ELL Poster 21

Daily Team Talk

Day 1	Day 2	Day 3	Day 4	Day 5
After Day 1 activities on Poster, ask questions such as	After Day 2 activity on Poster, ask questions such as	After Day 3 activity on Poster, ask questions such as	After Day 4 activity on Poster, ask questions such as	After Day 5 activity on Poster, ask questions such as
What emergency is happening in the poster picture?	*How are the people in the poster picture trying to stay safe during the emergency?*	*How do you think the rescuers in the poster picture prepared for this emergency?*	*In the selection Smokejumpers, what things help the smokejumpers stay safe while they are putting out fires?*	*How have you stayed safe during an emergency?*
Beginning A flood. **Intermediate** There is a flood. **Advanced** A lot of rain fell during a storm and flooded this neighborhood. **Advanced High** This neighborhood has flooded during a huge rainstorm. Now the people and animals are stranded.	**Beginning** On top of their houses. **Intermediate** They are up on the roofs of their houses. **Advanced** The people are on the roofs of their houses waiting for help. **Advanced High** The people are trying to stay safe by getting above the water. They have climbed onto the roofs of their houses.	**Beginning** They practiced. **Intermediate** They practiced using the harness and the parachute. **Advanced** The rescuers had practice emergencies so they would be ready for real ones. **Advanced High** The rescuers had many practice drills and equipment checks so they are prepared for emergencies.	**Beginning** Gloves and helmets. **Intermediate** They wear gloves, helmets, and jumpsuits. **Advanced** The smokejumpers wear jumpsuits that are fireproof, gloves, and helmets. **Advanced High** The smokejumpers wear fireproof jumpsuits, gloves, and helmets with face masks. They use parachutes.	**Beginning** Go downstairs. **Intermediate** I went to the basement during a storm. **Advanced** When there was a tornado in our area, we went to the basement. **Advanced High** A tornado was spotted nearby, so our town's siren went off. My family took our bag of emergency supplies and went to the basement.

This Week's Materials

Teacher's Edition pages 172j–199q

See the support for English language learners throughout the lesson, including ELL strategies and scaffolded activities at points of use.

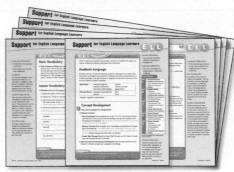

Teacher's Edition pages DI•16–DI•25

Differentiated Instruction for English language learners provides daily group activities that "frontload," or preteach, core instruction.

ELL Handbook pp. 149a–154

Find additional lesson materials that support the core lesson and the ELL instructional pages.

Poster 21

ELL Reader 4.5.1

ELD Reader 4.5.1

Concept Literacy Reader

ELD, ELL Reader
Teaching Guide

Concept Literacy Reader
Teaching Guide

Technology

Online Teacher's Edition Use the digital version of the core Teacher's Edition for planning and instruction.

eReaders
This week's ELL and ELD Readers and Concept Literacy Reader are also available in digital format.

This Week's Content and Language Objectives by Strand

Concept Development/ Academic Language How can we prepare for emergencies?	**Content Objective** • Use concept vocabulary related to preparing for emergencies. **Language Objectives** • Use prior knowledge and experiences to understand meanings. • Express ideas in response to new academic vocabulary.
Phonics and Spelling Multisyllabic Words	**Content Objectives** • Identify syllables of multisyllabic words. • Divide multisyllabic words between syllables. **Language Objectives** • Apply phonics and decoding skills to vocabulary. • Explain details of the meanings of homographs.
Listening Comprehension Modified Read Aloud: "My Job"	**Content Objective** • Monitor and adjust oral comprehension. **Language Objectives** • Discuss oral passages. • Use linguistic support to enhance and confirm understanding.
Reading Comprehension Author's Purpose	**Content Objectives** • Identify formal and informal language. • Identify the author's purpose and informal language. **Language Objectives** • Discuss author's purpose and genre. • Discuss usage of formal and informal language. • Improve rate and accuracy with grade-level text. • Reinforce comprehension with visual and contextual support.
Vocabulary Basic and Lesson Vocabulary	**Language Objectives** • Understand and use basic and grade-level vocabulary. • Learn meanings of grade-level vocabulary. • Produce drawings, phrases, and short sentences to show understanding of Lesson Vocabulary.
Grammar and Conventions Adjectives and Articles	**Content Objectives** • Identify adjectives and articles. • Correctly use adjectives and articles. **Language Objective** • Write sentences with adjectives and articles.
Writing Writing Complete Sentences	**Content Objectives** • Identify complete sentences in a text. • Identify that formal English is written and spoken in complete sentences. **Language Objectives** • Write complete sentences using appropriate sentences lengths and patterns. • Share feedback for editing and revising.

Word Cards for Vocabulary Activities

concentrating

dedication

essential

method

parachute

steer

underbrush

wind

Teacher Note: Beginning Teach three to four words. **Intermediate** Teach four to six words. **Advanced** Teach six to seven words. **Advanced High** Teach all words.

Name _____

Look at the pictures. Read the passage.
• **Answer** the questions below.

How to Dial 9-1-1

Be familiar with the steps below.

• Know your full name and address.

• Always call from a safe place.

• Give the operator your name and address. Tell them the problem.

• Be calm when you talk.

• Wait until the 9-1-1 operator tells you it's okay to hang up.

• Always talk to an adult family member after the emergency.

---

1. What are three ideas about calling 9-1-1 the author wants the reader to know?

_____

_____

_____

2. What was the author's purpose in writing this passage?

_____

_____

_____

Author's Purpose

Use this lesson to supplement or replace the skill lesson on page 173c of the Teacher's Edition. Display the Skill Points (at right) and share them with students.

Teach/Model

Beginning Write and read aloud these sentences: *Call 9-1-1 to reach the fire department. I think fighting fires is the hardest job.* Ask students which sentence was written to express the author's feelings (the second) and which sentence was written to inform readers (the first).

Intermediate Read aloud part of the entry for firefighters in a children's encyclopedia. Ask: *What is the author's purpose?* (to give information about firefighters) Have students tell details that helped them identify the author's purpose.

Advanced Say: *An author wrote a letter asking people to donate money to an animal shelter. What is the author's purpose?* (to persuade) *Why do you think that?* Repeat this process with other writing forms written for different purposes.

Advanced High Ask students to select a fiction or nonfiction book about rescue animals from the library. Have them look for words and phrases that suggest the author's purpose. Ask students to identify the author's purpose and to explain their reasoning to a partner.

Then distribute copies of Picture It! page 150.

- Have students look at the picture and tell what is happening.
- Read the passage aloud. Ask: *Why do you think the author wrote this passage?* (to teach children how to call 9-1-1)
- Review the Skill Points with students.
- Have students discuss the author's purpose and explain what the author did to achieve it.

Practice

Read aloud the directions on page 150. Have volunteers take turns rereading parts of the passage aloud. Have students look at the picture and the passage as they answer the questions.

Beginning Students can say their answers to the questions before writing words or phrases on the lines. Provide help with writing. Point out cognates such as *operator/operador* and *emergency/emergencia* to Spanish speakers.

Intermediate Students can first orally answer the questions and then write their answers on the lines. Provide help with writing and spelling English words.

Advanced Students can write their answers to the questions and then check them by rereading the passage and making any necessary corrections.

Advanced High Students can write their answers to the questions and then orally explain how they decided what the author's purpose is.

Answers for page 150: 1. Sample answers: Know your full name and address. Call from a safe place. Do not hang up until the operator tells you. 2. The author's purpose is to explain how to use 9-1-1 in an emergency.

Skill Points

✔ Authors have different **purposes,** or reasons, for writing. Four common reasons are to persuade, to inform, to express ideas or feelings, and to entertain.

✔ An author may have more than one reason for writing.

Multilingual Summaries

Smokejumpers: Life Fighting Fires

Forest fires are dangerous. Firefighters fight fires on the ground near roads. Smokejumpers are dropped from planes into remote areas of the forest. They create a firebreak.

Smokejumpers wear jumpsuits made of fire-retardant material and other gear. A parachute is attached to their backs. The smokejumpers, pilots, and jumpmasters study the ground. They look for landing zones, rocky land, clearings, and the wildfire. The smokejumpers jump. The plane drops more parachutes that hold packages. These packages have tools, food, and other equipment. When they land, they gather their supplies. They work to smother the fire.

When the fire is smothered, they radio for a pickup. They have to walk to a clearing so a helicopter can land.

Spanish

Saltadores de humo: Una vida combatiendo los incendios

Los incendios forestales son peligrosos. Los bomberos apagan fuegos en tierra cerca de los caminos. Los Saltadores de Humo son lanzados desde aviones hasta áreas remotas del bosque. Ellos bloquean el avance de los incendios.

Los Saltadores de Humo usan overoles o monos hechos con un material que resiste el fuego y otros implementos. Un paracaídas es atado a sus espaldas. Los Saltadores de Humo, los pilotos y paracaidistas expertos estudian el terreno. Tratan de encontrar buenos sitios donde poder saltar. Ellos buscan sitios de aterrizaje, terrenos rocosos y los incendios que están fuera de control. Los Saltadores de Humo saltan. Desde el avión les lanzan más paracaídas con el resto del equipo. Estos paquetes contienen herramientas, alimento y demás equipo necesario. Después de aterrizar, ellos recogen los paquetes. Ellos trabajan tratando de aplacar los incendios.

Después de que el incendio está controlado, llaman por radio al avión para que los recojan, entonces caminan hacia un claro para que el helicóptero pueda aterrizar.

Multilingual Summaries

空降森林消防員： 用生命對抗火災

森林火災是非常危險的。 地面消防隊員在靠近道路的地上滅火。而空降消防隊員則從飛機上跳到森林裡的偏遠地帶。 他們會開闢一條防火道。

空降消防隊員穿著防火材質做成的跳傘衣，並配備其它裝置。 他們的背上還附有降落傘。 空降消防隊員、飛行員及跳傘指導員共同研判地面情況， 並尋找降落區、岩石地面、空地及野火所在的地方。空降消防隊員先跳下去， 然後飛機會投下更多帶有包裹的降落傘。這些包裹裡面有工具、食物和其它裝備。 空降消防隊員著陸後就開始收集他們的用品。 之後就努力去滅火。

火被熄滅之後，他們會用無線電通知飛機來接他們。 他們必須走到空地上，這樣直昇機才能降落。

Lính Nhảy Dù Chữa Lửa: Cuộc Đời Chữa Lửa

Cháy rừng rất nguy hiểm. Những lính cứu hoả được dùng để chữa lửa trên mặt đất gần đường xá. Người lính nhảy dù chữa lửa được phi cơ thả xuống các vùng xa trong rừng. Họ dập tắt một khoảng để lửa không lan đi xa.

Lính chữa lửa mặc bộ áo liền quần làm bằng vật liệu cháy chậm và những thiết bị khác. Một cây dù được gắn trên lưng của họ. Người lính nhảy dù, phi công và người giám thị nghiên cứu mặt đất. Họ tìm nơi để nhảy dù, vùng có đá, chỗ trống, và nơi đang bị cháy. Sau đó người chữa lửa nhảy xuống. Còn phi cơ thì thả thêm dù có các kiện hàng xuống. Những kiện hàng này chứa dụng cụ, thực phẩm, và các thiết bị khác. Khi xuống đến đất họ gom các đồ tiếp tế lại. Và bắt đầu công việc dật tắt lửa.

Sau khi lửa tắt, họ gọi truyền thanh để máy bay đến rước. Họ phải đi đến một nơi trống trải để trực thăng có thể hạ xuống được.

Multilingual Summaries

삼림 소방대원: 불에 맞서는 삶

산불은 위험하다. 길 근처에서는 소방관들이 불에 맞선다. 삼림 소방대원들은 비행기에서 멀리 떨어진 숲으로 내려가 산불저지선을 만든다.

삼림 소방대원들은 방화 물질과 여러 장비로 이루어진 낙하복을 입는다. 등에는 낙하산이 달려있다. 삼림 소방대원, 비행기 조종사와 낙하산 강하 지휘관이 지면을 살핀 후 낙하 지점, 바위투성이의 땅, 착륙 장소, 연소물 등을 파악한다. 삼림 소방대원이 뛰어내리고, 비행기가 꾸러미를 실은 낙하산들도 떨어뜨린다. 이 꾸러미에는 연장과 음식과 다른 장비들이 들어있다. 소방대원들이 착륙하면 보급품을 모아서 불을 끄기 시작한다.

불이 꺼지면 돌아가기 위해 무전으로 연락한다. 그들은 헬리콥터가 착륙할 수 있는 착륙 장소까지 걸어가야 한다.

Neeg Dhia Pa Taw: Lub Neej Tua Hluav Taw

Hav zoo kub nyiab txaus ntshai heev. Kev tua hluav taw kub kub nyob ze tej ntug kev. Neeg dhia pa taw raug dav hlaus coj mus pov rau tim tej hav zoov. Lawv txoj hauj lwm yog ua kom hluav taw txhob kub tuaj lawm.

Neeg dhia pa taw hnav tej ris tsho uas hluav taw kub tsis tau thiab muaj lwm yam khoom nrog. Muaj ib lub kaus txuas nraum lawv nraub qaum. Tus neeg dhia pa taw, tus nais dav hlaus, thiab tus neeg nyob hauv av qhia lawv. Lawv nriav chaw dhia mus rau, toj zeb roob tsuas, luaj nroj tsuag, thiab hlawv toj tos. Tus neeg dhia pa taw. Lub dav hlaus pov ib co kaus uas muaj khoom. Nyob hauv cov khoom yog khoom siv, khoom noj, thiab lwm yam cuab yeej. Thaum lawv poob los txog lawm lawv mus nriav lawv tej khoom. Lawv ua cov hawj lwm kom hluav tawv tuag.

Thaum tuag me ntsis lawm, lawv hu xov tooj kom tuaj muab lawv. Lawv yuav tau mus rau qhov chaw do kom dav hlaus tsaw tau.

Name _____ **When a Storm Comes**

- **Read** *When a Storm Comes* again.
- Use the information from the book to **answer** the questions.

pages 2–3
1. What tells you the strength of a hurricane?

_____

pages 4–5
2. What is in Luis and his family's emergency kit?

_____

pages 6–7
3. How is a tornado different from a hurricane?

_____

pages 7–8
4. Where is the safest place in a building?

_____

5. How are Luis and Anita ready for big storms?

_____

_____

Family Link

Has anyone in your family been in a hurricane or snowstorm? Ask them to tell you how they prepared for this storm.

For this week's content and language objectives, see p. 155e.

Instructional Strand	Day 1	Day 2
Concept Development/Academic Language	**TEACHER'S EDITION** • Academic Language, p. DI•41 • Concept Development, p. DI•41 • Anchored Talk, pp. 200j—200–201 • Preteach Academic Vocabulary, p. 203a • Concept Talk Video **ELL HANDBOOK** • Hear It, See It, Say It, Use It, pp. xxxvi–xxxvii • ELL Poster Talk, Concept Talk, p. 155c **ELL POSTER 22** • Day 1 Activities	**TEACHER'S EDITION** • Academic Language, p. DI•41 • Concept Development, p. DI•41 • Anchored Talk, p. 204a • Concept Talk Video **ELL HANDBOOK** • ELL Poster Talk, Concept Talk, p. 155c • Concept Talk Video Routine, p. 477 **ELL POSTER 22** • Day 2 Activities
Phonics and Spelling	**TEACHER'S EDITION** • Phonics and Spelling, p. DI•45	**TEACHER'S EDITION** • Phonics and Spelling, p. DI•45
Listening Comprehension	**TEACHER'S EDITION** • Modified Read Aloud, p. DI•44 • Read Aloud, p. 201b • Concept Talk Video **ELL HANDBOOK** • Concept Talk Video Routine, p. 477	**TEACHER'S EDITION** • Modified Read Aloud, p. DI•44 • AudioText of *Lost City* • Concept Talk Video **ELL HANDBOOK** • AudioText CD Routine, p. 477 • Main Idea, p. 487
Reading Comprehension	**TEACHER'S EDITION** • Preteach Compare and Contrast, p. DI•46	**TEACHER'S EDITION** • Reteach Compare and Contrast, p. DI•46 • Frontloading Reading, p. DI•47 **ELL HANDBOOK** • Picture It! Skill Instruction, pp. 156–156a • Multilingual Summaries, pp. 157–159
Vocabulary **Basic and Lesson Vocabulary** **Word Analysis: Suffixes *-ous, -able, -ible***	**TEACHER'S EDITION** • Basic Vocabulary, p. DI•42 • Preteach Lesson Vocabulary, p. DI•42 • Suffixes *-ous, -able, -ible*, p. DI•45 **ELL HANDBOOK** • Word Cards, p. 155 • ELL Vocabulary Routine, p. 471 **ELL POSTER 22** • Day 1 Activities	**TEACHER'S EDITION** • Basic Vocabulary, p. DI•42 • Reteach Lesson Vocabulary, p. DI•43 • Suffixes *-ous, -able, -ible*, p. DI•45 **ELL HANDBOOK** • Word Cards, p. 155 • Multilingual Vocabulary List, p. 431 **ELL POSTER 22** • Day 2 Activities
Grammar and Conventions	**TEACHER'S EDITION** • Teach/Model Adverbs, p. DI•49	**TEACHER'S EDITION** • Reteach Adverbs, p. DI•49
Writing	**TEACHER'S EDITION** • Strong Verbs, p. DI•50 • Introduce A Legend, pp. 203e–203f	**TEACHER'S EDITION** • Writer's Craft: Story Sequence, pp. 213d–213e

This symbol indicates leveled instruction to address language proficiency levels.

Day 3	Day 4	Day 5
TEACHER'S EDITION • Academic Language, p. DI•41 • Concept Development, p. DI•41 • Anchored Talk, p. 214a • Concept Talk Video **ELL HANDBOOK** • ELL Poster Talk, Concept Talk, p. 155c **ELL POSTER 22** • Day 3 Activities	**TEACHER'S EDITION** • Academic Language, p. DI•41 • Concept Development, p. DI•41 • Anchored Talk, p. 222a • Concept Talk Video **ELL HANDBOOK** • ELL Poster Talk, Concept Talk, p. 155c **ELL POSTER 22** • Day 4 Activities	**TEACHER'S EDITION** • Academic Language, p. DI•41 • Concept Development, p. DI•41 • Concept Talk Video **ELL HANDBOOK** • ELL Poster Talk, Concept Talk, p. 155c **ELL POSTER 22** • Day 5 Activities
		TEACHER'S EDITION • Phonics and Spelling, p. DI•45
TEACHER'S EDITION • AudioText of *Lost City* • Concept Talk Video **ELL HANDBOOK** • AudioText CD Routine, p. 477	**TEACHER'S EDITION** • Concept Talk Video	**TEACHER'S EDITION** • Concept Talk Video
TEACHER'S EDITION • Sheltered Reading, p. DI•47 **ELL HANDBOOK** • Multilingual Summaries, pp. 157–159	**TEACHER'S EDITION** • ELL/ELD Reader Guided Reading, p. DI•48 **ELL HANDBOOK** • ELL Study Guide, p. 160	**TEACHER'S EDITION** • ELL/ELD Reader Guided Reading, p. DI•48 **ELL HANDBOOK** • ELL Study Guide, p. 160
ELL HANDBOOK • High-Frequency Words Activity Bank, p. 446 **ELL POSTER 22** • Day 3 Activities	**ELL HANDBOOK** • High-Frequency Words Activity Bank, p. 446	**TEACHER'S EDITION** • Suffixes *-ous, -able, -ible*, p. 227i **ELL HANDBOOK** • High-Frequency Words Activity Bank, p. 446
TEACHER'S EDITION • Grammar Jammer **ELL HANDBOOK** • Grammar Transition Lesson, pp. 372, 377–378 • Grammar Jammer Routine, p. 478	**TEACHER'S EDITION** • Grammar Jammer **ELL HANDBOOK** • Grammar Transition Lesson, pp. 372, 377–378	**TEACHER'S EDITION** • Grammar Jammer **ELL HANDBOOK** • Grammar Transition Lesson, pp. 372, 377–378
TEACHER'S EDITION • Let's Write It!, p. 220–221 • Writer's Craft: Sentences, pp. 221a–221b	**TEACHER'S EDITION** • Revising Strategy, pp. 227d–227e	**TEACHER'S EDITION** • Adverbs, pp. 227p–227q

Poster Talk, Concept Talk

Question of the Week

What surprises can happen on an expedition?

Throughout the week, use the ELL Poster to help students produce and comprehend language, understand the concept, and build English vocabulary. Use the Question of the Week and other questions to help students share ideas in pairs, small groups, or the large group. Sample questions are shown, with examples of possible responses by students.

ELL Poster 22

Weekly Concept and Language Goals

• Identify an ancient civilization

• Describe an expedition

• Tell about problems on an expedition

By the end of the lesson, students should be able to talk about and write sentences about expeditions and ancient civilizations.

Daily Team Talk

Day 1	Day 2	Day 3	Day 4	Day 5
After Day 1 activities on Poster, ask questions such as *Which ancient civilization built the pyramid shown in the poster picture?*	After Day 2 activity on Poster, ask questions such as *What do the people in the poster picture see on their expedition?*	After Day 3 activity on Poster, ask questions such as *What problems could the people in the poster picture have on their expedition?*	After Day 4 activity on Poster, ask questions such as *What tools do the people in the poster picture use to help them on their expedition?*	After Day 5 activity on Poster, ask questions such as *If you were going on an expedition, where would you go and why?*
Beginning Mayan people. **Intermediate** Mayan people made it. **Advanced** Mayan people who lived a long time ago built the pyramid. **Advanced High** The ancient Mayan civilization, or group of people who lived long ago, built the pyramid.	**Beginning** A building. **Intermediate** They see a building, a waterfall, and jungle. **Advanced** The people see Mayan ruins, a Mayan pyramid, a waterfall, and birds. **Advanced High** On their expedition, the people see Mayan ruins, terraced gardens, a waterfall, and colorful birds.	**Beginning** Get lost. **Intermediate** The girl can fall off the rock. **Advanced** The girl could fall in the water. **Advanced High** The people could get lost in the jungle, or the girl could drop the binoculars into the stream.	**Beginning** Binoculars. **Intermediate** Binoculars and a camera. **Advanced** They use binoculars, a camera, and backpacks. **Advanced High** The people use binoculars, a camera, backpacks, hats, and gym shoes to help them on their expedition.	**Beginning** To the ocean. I like it. **Intermediate** I would go to the ocean to see the animals. **Advanced** I would go deep in the ocean to see the animals that live there. **Advanced High** I would go on an expedition in the ocean. I would travel in a small submarine to learn about the animals that live there.

This Week's Materials

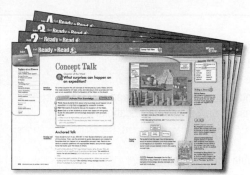

Teacher's Edition pages 200j–227q

See the support for English language learners throughout the lesson, including ELL strategies and scaffolded activities at points of use.

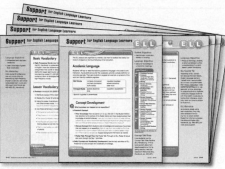

Teacher's Edition pages DI•41–DI•50

Differentiated Instruction for English language learners provides daily group activities that "frontload," or preteach, core instruction.

ELL Handbook pp. 155a–160

Find additional lesson materials that support the core lesson and the ELL instructional pages.

ELL Poster 22

ELL Reader 4.5.2

ELD Reader 4.5.2

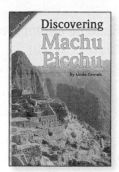

Concept Literacy Reader

ELD, ELL Reader Teaching Guide

Concept Literacy Reader Teaching Guide

Technology

Online Teacher's Edition Use the digital version of the core Teacher's Edition for planning and instruction.

eReaders
This week's ELL and ELD Readers and Concept Literacy Reader are also available in digital format.

This Week's Content and Language Objectives by Strand

Concept Development/ Academic Language What surprises can happen on an expedition?	**Content Objective** • Use concept vocabulary related to traveling to far-away and unfamiliar places. **Language Objectives** • Use prior knowledge and experience to understand meanings. • Express ideas in response to new academic vocabulary.
Phonics and Spelling Words with Double Consonants	**Content Objective** • Review words with double consonants. **Language Objective** • Apply phonics and decoding skills to vocabulary.
Listening Comprehension Modified Read Aloud: "Inca Farmers"	**Content Objective** • Monitor and adjust oral comprehension. **Language Objectives** • Discuss oral passages. • Use a graphic organizer to take notes.
Reading Comprehension Character and Plot	**Content Objectives** • Compare and contrast information in a text. • Monitor and adjust comprehension. **Language Objectives** • Compare two or more things in a text. • Contrast two or more things in a text. • Summarize text using visual support.
Vocabulary Basic and Lesson Vocabulary	**Language Objectives** • Understand and use basic and vocabulary. • Learn meanings of grade-level vocabulary. • Produce drawings, phrases, and short sentences to show understanding of Lesson Vocabulary.
Word Analysis Suffixes *–ous, -able, -ible*	**Content Objective** • Identify and use the suffixes *–ous, -able,* and *-ible*. **Language Objective** • Discuss the meaning of suffixes *–ous, -able,* and *-ible*.
Grammar and Conventions Adverbs	**Content Objectives** • Identify adverbs. • Correctly use adverbs. **Language Objective** • Write sentences with adverbs.
Writing Strong Verbs	**Content Objectives** • Analyze the structure of sentences. • Recognize short, choppy sentence patterns. **Language Objectives** • Combine short, choppy sentences. • Share feedback for editing and revising.

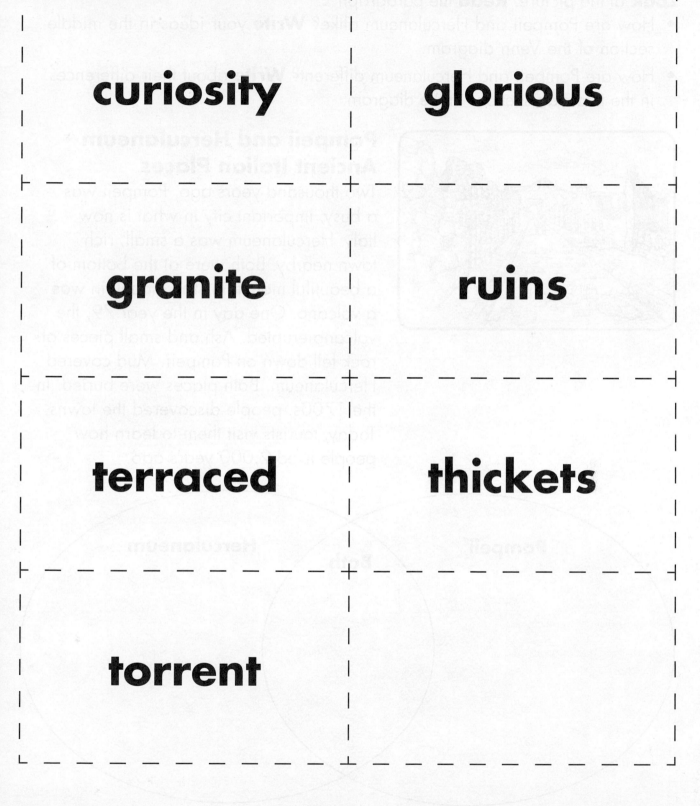

curiosity

glorious

granite

ruins

terraced

thickets

torrent

Teacher Note: Beginning Teach three to four words. **Intermediate** Teach four to six words. **Advanced** Teach six to seven words. **Advanced High** Teach all words.

Name _____

Look at the picture. **Read** the paragraph.

• How are Pompeii and Herculaneum alike? **Write** your ideas in the middle section of the Venn diagram.

• How are Pompeii and Herculaneum different? **Write** about their differences in the two side sections of the diagram.

Pompeii and Herculaneum— Ancient Italian Places

Two thousand years ago, Pompeii was a busy, important city in what is now Italy. Herculaneum was a small, rich town nearby. Both were at the bottom of a beautiful mountain. The mountain was a volcano. One day in the year 79, the volcano erupted. Ash and small pieces of rock fell down on Pompeii. Mud covered Herculaneum. Both places were buried. In the 1700s, people discovered the towns. Today, tourists visit them to learn how people lived 2,000 years ago.

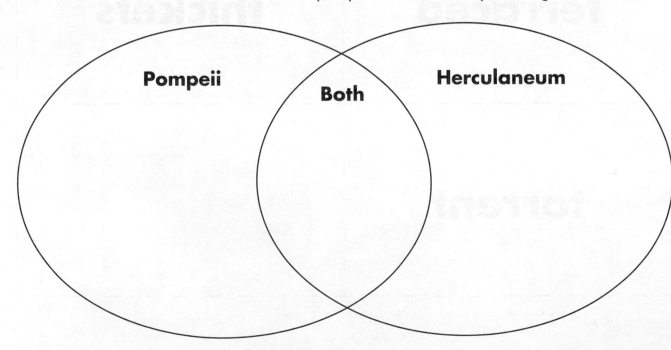

Pompeii   Both   Herculaneum

Compare and Contrast

Use this lesson to supplement or replace the skill lesson on page 201c of the Teacher's Edition. Display the Skill Points (at right) and share them with students.

Teach/Model

Beginning Draw a Venn diagram with the circles labeled *Big City* and *Small Town* and the intersection labeled *Both*. Display pictures of a big city and a small town. Ask: *How are these alike?* Write students' responses under *Both*. Ask: *How are these different?* Write their responses under either *Big City* or *Small Town*.

Intermediate Say: *Chicago is a big city. San Francisco is a big city. Chicago is on a lake. San Francisco is on the ocean.* Ask students to write a sentence that compares the cities and a sentence that contrasts the cities. (Both Chicago and San Francisco are big cities. Chicago is on a lake, but San Francisco is on the ocean.)

Advanced Display pictures of an ancient city and a modern city. Have students draw and fill in a Venn diagram telling how ancient and modern cities are alike and different.

Advanced High Write these sentence frames: ___ *and* ___ *are alike because* ___. *They are different because* ___. Ask students to choose a city or town to compare and contrast to their home city or town. Have them complete the sentence frames to tell how the two cities or towns are alike and different.

Then distribute copies of Picture It! page 156.

- Have students describe what they see in the illustration. Then read the paragraph aloud.
- Ask: *How was Pompeii different from Herculaneum?*
- Review the Skill Points with students.
- Have students discuss how Pompeii and Herculaneum were different and alike.

Skill Points

✔ To **compare** means to tell how two or more things are the same. To **contrast** means to tell how two or more things are different.

✔ Authors may use clue words such as *both, like,* and *same* to show comparisons. They may use clue words such as *but, unlike,* and *different* to show contrasts.

Practice

Read aloud the directions on page 156. Reread the paragraph aloud, explaining the words *volcano* and *erupted*. Have students look at the picture and the paragraph as they fill in the Venn diagram.

Beginning Students can say the similarities and differences between the two places and point out where they will write these ideas in the Venn diagram before writing their answers on the page. Provide help with English words and writing.

Intermediate Students can first state orally what they will write in each section of the Venn diagram and then write their answers on the page. Provide help with writing.

Advanced Students can write their answers in the Venn diagram and then check them by comparing them to a partner's.

Advanced High Students can write their answers in the Venn diagram and then use the information to orally compare and contrast the two places in complete sentences.

Answers for page 156: *Pompeii:* busy, important city; buried by ash and rock; *Both:* ancient cities in what is now Italy; located at the bottom of a mountain; buried by eruption of volcano; dug up in the 1700s; tourists visit today; *Herculaneum:* small, rich town; buried by mud

Multilingual Summaries

Lost City:
The Discovery of Machu Picchu

In 1911, Professor Hiram Bingham went to Peru. He hoped to find the lost city of Vilcapampa. He started in Cusco. There, he saw old stone walls and a stone temple. He knew the lost city would have stones like those.

Bingham went to the village of Ollantaytambo. No one knew about the lost city or about any ruins. Bingham was discouraged. Then he met a farmer who knew of ruins on top of a mountain. He took Bingham to the ruins.

After a long climb through the jungle, Bingham and the farmer met a young boy. The boy took them to an old city covered with vines. It was not Vilcapampa. Bingham had found the lost city of Machu Picchu.

Spanish

La ciudad perdida:
El descubrimiento de Machu Picchu

En 1911, el profesor Hiram Bingham viajó a Perú. Esperaba encontrar la ciudad perdida de Vilcapampa. Comenzó su viaje en Cuzco. Allí vio unas paredes de piedra antiguas y un templo de piedra. Él sabía que la ciudad perdida tendría piedras como ésas.

Bingham fue al pueblo de Ollantaytambo. Nadie sabía nada sobre la ciudad perdida o sobre ningunas ruinas. Bingham estaba desanimado. Luego conoció a un campesino que le dio información sobre unas ruinas en la cima de una montaña. Él llevó a Bingham a las ruinas.

Después de subir a través de la selva, Bingham y el campesino se encontraron con un muchacho. El muchacho los llevó a una antigua ciudad cubierta de enredaderas. No era Vilcapampa. ¡Bingham había encontrado la ciudad perdida de Machu Picchu!

Multilingual Summaries

失落之城

1911年，希蘭姆·賓漢教授前往秘魯，希望找到失落之城韋可帕母帕。他在庫斯科發現了古代的石墙和石廟，他知道韋可帕母帕也有一樣的石塊。

賓漢教授來到歐陽戴丹坡村。可是沒有人知道失落之城，也沒見過殘留的廢墟。賓漢教授非常失望。這時有一個農夫說，他知道山頂上有廢墟，可以帶賓漢教授去考察。

他們穿越叢林爬上了山頂，遇到一個小男孩，領他們去看野藤覆蓋的古代城市。原來它不是韋可帕母帕，而是另一個失落之城馬丘比丘。

Thành Phố Diệt Vong

Vào năm 1911, Giáo Sư Hiram Bingham đi đến nước Peru. Ông ấy hy vọng tìm ra một thành phố đã diệt vong tên Vilcapampa. Ông bắt đầu ở Cusco. Ở đó, ông thấy những bức tường đá cổ và một đền thờ bằng đá. Ông biết là thành phố bị diệt vong cũng có những viên đá giống như vậy.

Bingham đi đến ngôi làng Ollantaytambo. Không ai biết về thành phố bị diệt vong, hoặc về những tàn tích của thành phố này. Bingham bị nản lòng. Rồi ông gặp một ông nông phu, ông này biết về những tàn tích trên một ngọn núi. Ông dẫn Bingham đến tàn tích này.

Sau một cuộc leo trèo xa xôi xuyên qua rừng, Bingham và bác nhà nông gặp một cậu thiếu niên. Cậu này đưa họ đến thành phố cổ phủ đầy dây leo. Không phải Vilcapampa. Bingham đã tìm ra thành phố diệt vong tên Machu Picchu.

Multilingual Summaries

잃어버린 도시

1911년 하이램 빙엄 교수는 페루에 갔다. 그는 그곳에서 빌까밤바의 잃어버린 도시를 발견하길 바랬다. 그는 쿠스코에서부터 발굴을 시작했고 거기서 오래된 돌 벽과 돌로 된 신전을 발견했다. 그는 잃어버린 도시에 그와 비슷한 돌들이 있을 것이라고 생각했다.

빙엄은 올란타이탐보의 마을로 갔지만 아무도 잃어버린 도시나 유적에 관해서 알지 못했다. 실망한 빙엄은 그리고 나서 산꼭대기에 있는 유적지에 대해 알고 있던 한 농부를 만났다. 농부는 빙엄을 그 유적지로 데리고 갔다.

정글을 지나 한참을 오른 후 빙엄과 그 농부는 한 어린 소년을 만났다. 그 소년은 덩굴로 뒤덮인 어느 고대 도시로 그들을 데리고 갔다. 하지만 그것은 빌까밤바가 아니었다. 빙엄은 잃어버린 도시인 마추피추를 발견한 것이었다.

Lub Zos Uas Xiam Lawm

Nyob rau xyoo ib txhiab cuaj pua kaum ib, tus xibhwb hu ua Hiram Bingham mus rau Peru. Nws cia siab yuav mus nrhiav kom tau lub zos uas xiam lawm uas hu ua Vilcapampa. Nws xub pib nyob rau Cusco. Ntawd, nws pom ib cov phab ntsa pobzeb qub qub thiab ib lub tuam tsev pobzeb. Nws paub tias lus zos uas xiam lawm yuav muaj pobzeb zoo li ntawd thiab.

Bingham mus rau lus zos me me hu ua Ollantaytambo. Tsis muaj leej twg paub txog lub zos ua xiam ntawd lawm, lossis paub txog tej qub zog ntawd li. Bingham tsis muaj siab tag. Ces nws cia li ntsib ib tug neeg ua liaj ua teb uas paub txog ib lub qub zog nyob puag saum ib lub roob. Nws coj Bingham mus rau lub qub zog ntawd.

Tom qab nkawd nce mus siab siab rau puag hauv hav zoov lawm, Bingham thiab tus neeg ua liaj ua teb ntawd ntsib ib tug menyuam tub. Tus menyuam tub ntawd coj nkawd mus rau ib lub qub zog uas hmab ntoo tej muab vov tag lawm. Kuj tsis yog Vilcapampa thiab. Bingham nrhiav tau lub zos xiam lawm uas hu ua Machu Picchu.

Study Guide

Sylvia Earle: Doctor of the Deep

- **Read** *Sylvia Earle: Doctor of the Deep* again.
- Use the information in the book to **answer** the questions.

---

pages 2–4

1. How did Sylvia first become interested in the ocean?

_____

2. Compare and contrast snorkeling and scuba diving.

---

pages 5–6

3. How is coral reef like a rock? How is it different?

_____

_____

4. What did Sylvia do on Aquarius? Why?

_____

_____

_____

---

pages 7–8

5. What made Sylvia's submarine different from other submarines?

_____

6. What things can harm the ocean?

_____

Family Link

Ask family members what they like best about the ocean. Tell them some facts about the ocean that you learned from the reading.

Weekly Resources Guide for English Language Learner Support

For this week's content and language objectives, see p. 161e.

Instructional Strand	Day 1	Day 2
Concept Development/Academic Language	**TEACHER'S EDITION** • Academic Language, p. DI•66 • Concept Development, p. DI•66 • Anchored Talk, pp. 228j—228–229 • Preteach Academic Vocabulary, p. 231a • Concept Talk Video **ELL HANDBOOK** • Hear It, See It, Say It, Use It, pp. xxxvi–xxxvii • ELL Poster Talk, Concept Talk, p. 161c **ELL POSTER 23** • Day 1 Activities	**TEACHER'S EDITION** • Academic Language, p. DI•66 • Concept Development, p. DI•66 • Anchored Talk, p. 232a • Concept Talk Video **ELL HANDBOOK** • ELL Poster Talk, Concept Talk, p. 161c • Concept Talk Video Routine, p. 477 **ELL POSTER 23** • Day 2 Activities
Phonics and Spelling	**TEACHER'S EDITION** • Phonics and Spelling, p. DI•70	**TEACHER'S EDITION** • Phonics and Spelling, p. DI•70
Listening Comprehension	**TEACHER'S EDITION** • Modified Read Aloud, p. DI•69 • Read Aloud, p. 229b • Concept Talk Video **ELL HANDBOOK** • Concept Talk Video Routine, p. 477	**TEACHER'S EDITION** • Modified Read Aloud, p. DI•69 • AudioText of *Cliff Hanger* • Concept Talk Video **ELL HANDBOOK** • AudioText CD Routine, p. 477 • Three-Column Chart, p. 494
Reading Comprehension	**TEACHER'S EDITION** • Preteach Literary Elements: Character, Plot, Theme, p. DI•71	**TEACHER'S EDITION** • Reteach Literary Elements: Character, Plot, Theme, p. DI•71 • Frontloading Reading, p. DI•72 **ELL HANDBOOK** • Picture It! Skill Instruction, pp. 162–162a • Multilingual Summaries, pp. 163–165
Vocabulary **Basic and Lesson Vocabulary** **Word Analysis: Related Words**	**TEACHER'S EDITION** • Basic Vocabulary, p. DI•67 • Preteach Lesson Vocabulary, p. DI•67 • Related Words, p. DI•70 **ELL HANDBOOK** • Word Cards, p. 161 • ELL Vocabulary Routine, p. 471 **ELL POSTER 23** • Day 1 Activities	**TEACHER'S EDITION** • Basic Vocabulary, p. DI•67 • Reteach Lesson Vocabulary, p. DI•68 • Related Words, p. DI•70 **ELL HANDBOOK** • Word Cards, p. 161 • Multilingual Vocabulary List, p. 431 **ELL POSTER 23** • Day 2 Activities
Grammar and Conventions	**TEACHER'S EDITION** • Preteach Comparative and Superlative Adjectives, p. DI•74	**TEACHER'S EDITION** • Reteach Comparative and Superlative Adjectives, p. DI•74
Writing	**TEACHER'S EDITION** • Using Exact Words, p. DI•75 • Introduce Thank-You Note, pp. 231e–231f	**TEACHER'S EDITION** • Writing Trait: Word Choice, pp. 241d–241e

This symbol indicates leveled instruction to address language proficiency levels.

Day 3	Day 4	Day 5
TEACHER'S EDITION • Academic Language, p. DI•66 • Concept Development, p. DI•66 • Anchored Talk, p. 242a • Concept Talk Video **ELL HANDBOOK** • ELL Poster Talk, Concept Talk, p. 161c **ELL POSTER 23** • Day 3 Activities	**TEACHER'S EDITION** • Academic Language, p. DI•66 • Concept Development, p. DI•66 • Anchored Talk, p. 250a • Concept Talk Video **ELL HANDBOOK** • ELL Poster Talk, Concept Talk, p. 161c **ELL POSTER 23** • Day 4 Activities	**TEACHER'S EDITION** • Academic Language, p. DI•66 • Concept Development, p. DI•66 • Concept Talk Video **ELL HANDBOOK** • ELL Poster Talk, Concept Talk, p. 161c **ELL POSTER 23** • Day 5 Activities
ELL HANDBOOK • Phonics Transition Lesson, pp. 299, 304	**ELL HANDBOOK** • Phonics Transition Lesson, pp. 299, 304	**TEACHER'S EDITION** • Phonics and Spelling, p. DI•70
TEACHER'S EDITION • AudioText of *Cliff Hanger* • Concept Talk Video **ELL HANDBOOK** • AudioText CD Routine, p. 477	**TEACHER'S EDITION** • Concept Talk Video	**TEACHER'S EDITION** • Concept Talk Video
TEACHER'S EDITION • Sheltered Reading, p. DI•72 **ELL HANDBOOK** • Multilingual Summaries, pp. 163–165	**TEACHER'S EDITION** • ELL/ELD Reader Guided Reading, p. DI•73 **ELL HANDBOOK** • ELL Study Guide, p. 166	**TEACHER'S EDITION** • ELL/ELD Reader Guided Reading, p. DI•73 **ELL HANDBOOK** • ELL Study Guide, p. 166
ELL HANDBOOK • High-Frequency Words Activity Bank, p. 446 **ELL POSTER 23** • Day 3 Activities	**ELL HANDBOOK** • High-Frequency Words Activity Bank, p. 446	**TEACHER'S EDITION** • Related Words, p. 255i **ELL HANDBOOK** • High-Frequency Words Activity Bank, p. 446
TEACHER'S EDITION • Grammar Jammer **ELL HANDBOOK** • Grammar Transition Lesson, pp. 371, 375 • Grammar Jammer Routine, p. 478	**TEACHER'S EDITION** • Grammar Jammer **ELL HANDBOOK** • Grammar Transition Lesson, pp. 371, 375	**TEACHER'S EDITION** • Grammar Jammer **ELL HANDBOOK** • Grammar Transition Lesson, pp. 371, 375
TEACHER'S EDITION • Let's Write It!, p. 248–249 • Writer's Craft: Word Choice, pp. 249a–249b	**TEACHER'S EDITION** • Revising Strategy, pp. 255d–255e	**TEACHER'S EDITION** • Comparative and Superlative Adjectives and Adverbs, pp. 255p–255q

Poster Talk, Concept Talk

Question of the Week
What does it take to be a hero?

ELL Poster 23

Throughout the week, use the ELL Poster to help students produce and comprehend language, understand the concept, and build English vocabulary. Use the Question of the Week and other questions to help students share ideas in pairs, small groups, or the large group. Sample questions are shown, with examples of possible responses by students.

Weekly Concept and Language Goals

• Identify heroes and what they do

• Describe characteristics of heroes

• Tell about heroic acts

By the end of the lesson, students should be able to talk about and write sentences about heroes.

Daily Team Talk

Day 1	Day 2	Day 3	Day 4	Day 5
After Day 1 activities on Poster, ask questions such as *Why are the people in the poster picture wearing harnesses and helmets and using ropes?*	After Day 2 activity on Poster, ask questions such as *Who is being heroic in the poster picture? What is that person doing?*	After Day 3 activity on Poster, ask questions such as *Why is the climbing instructor a hero?*	After Day 4 activity on Poster, ask questions such as *Who is the hero in the story* Cliff Hanger? *Why is that person a hero?*	After Day 5 activity on Poster, ask questions such as *What are some characteristics that heroes have?*
Beginning To climb. **Intermediate** To keep them safe. **Advanced** They need the harnesses, helmets, and ropes to climb safely. **Advanced High** The people wear harnesses and helmets and use ropes for safety.	**Beginning** The woman helping the dog. **Intermediate** The woman is rescuing the dog. **Advanced** The instructor is being heroic by rescuing the dog. **Advanced High** The climbing instructor is being heroic by going down the mountain to rescue the trapped dog.	**Beginning** It's good. **Intermediate** It is a brave thing to do. **Advanced** She could fall or hurt herself. She does not have to do it. **Advanced High** The instructor is rescuing the dog even though it is difficult and dangerous to do.	**Beginning** The boy. **Intermediate** The boy is the hero. **Advanced** Axel is the hero because he saves his dog. **Advanced High** Axel is a hero because he climbs up the mountain to save Grits.	**Beginning** They are brave. **Intermediate** They are brave and not scared. **Advanced** Heroes are brave and know what to do. **Advanced High** Heroes are brave and confident. They are willing to risk their own lives to help others.

This Week's Materials

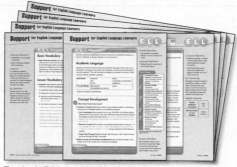

Teacher's Edition pages 228j–255q

Teacher's Edition pages DI•66–DI•75

ELL Handbook pp. 161a–166

See the support for English language learners throughout the lesson, including ELL strategies and scaffolded activities at points of use.

Differentiated Instruction for English language learners provides daily group activities that "frontload," or preteach, core instruction.

Find additional lesson materials that support the core lesson and the ELL instructional pages.

Poster 23

ELLReader 4.5.3

ELD Reader 4.5.3

Concept Literacy Reader

ELD, ELL Reader Teaching Guide

Concept Literacy Reader Teaching Guide

Technology

Online Teacher's Edition Use the digital version of the core Teacher's Edition for planning and instruction.

eReaders
This week's ELL and ELD Readers and Concept Literacy Reader are also available in digital format.

This Week's Content and Language Objectives by Strand

Concept Development/ Academic Language What does it take to be a hero?	**Content Objective** • Use content vocabulary related to what it takes to be a hero. **Language Objectives** • Express ideas in response to art and discussion. • Express ideas in response to new academic vocabulary.
Phonics and Spelling Greek Word Parts	**Content Objective** • Identify and define Greek parts of words. **Language Objective** • Speak using grade-level content and vocabulary.
Listening Comprehension Modified Read Aloud: "Heroes and Heroines"	**Content Objective** • Monitor and adjust oral comprehension. **Language Objectives** • Discuss oral passages. • Use a graphic organizer to take notes. • Learn new and essential language.
Reading Comprehension Literary Elements: Character, Plot, Theme	**Content Objectives** • To identify literary elements of character, plot, and theme. • Make and adjust predictions. **Language Objectives** • Retell plot of a picture story. • Write sentences about plot and theme of story. • Distinguish intonation patterns in English. • Read grade-level text with expression.
Vocabulary Basic and Lesson Vocabulary	**Language Objectives** • Understand and use basic and grade-level vocabulary. • Learn meanings of grade-level vocabulary. • Produce drawings, phrases, and short sentences to show understanding of Lesson Vocabulary.
Word Analysis Related Words	**Content Objective** • Review related words with Greek parts. **Language Objective** • Discuss meaning of words with Greek parts.
Grammar and Conventions Comparative and Superlative Adjectives	**Content Objective** • Decode, use, and form comparative and superlative adjectives. **Language Objective** • Speak and write sentences with comparative and superlative adjectives.
Writing Using Exact Words	**Content Objective** • Choose the most exact word. **Language Objectives** • Write an e-mail using exact words and details to explain. • Write using content-based vocabulary.

Word Cards for Vocabulary Activities

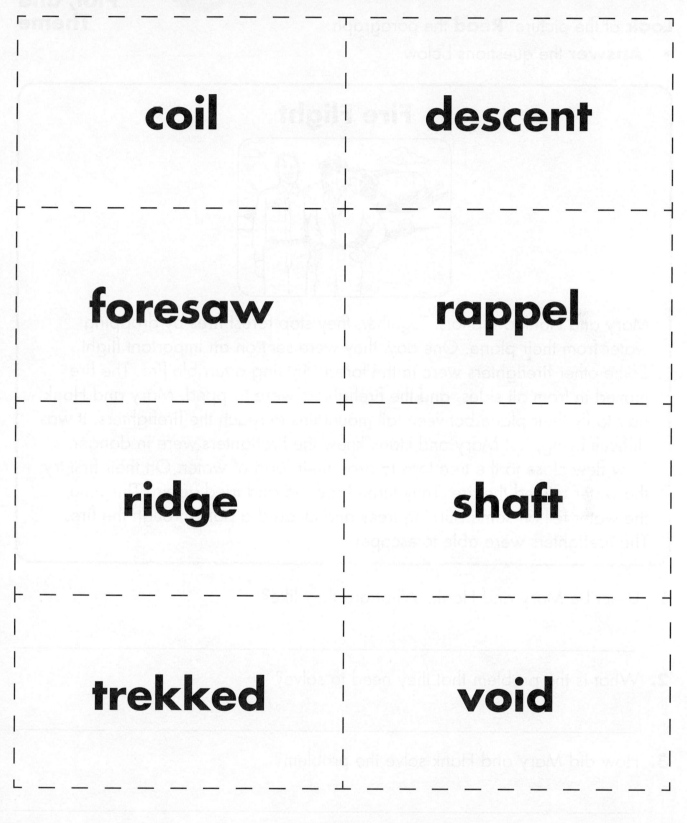

coil	**descent**
foresaw	**rappel**
ridge	**shaft**
trekked	**void**

Teacher Note: Beginning Teach three to four words. **Intermediate** Teach four to six words. **Advanced** Teach six to seven words. **Advanced High** Teach all words.

Name _____

Look at the picture. **Read** the paragraph.

• **Answer** the questions below.

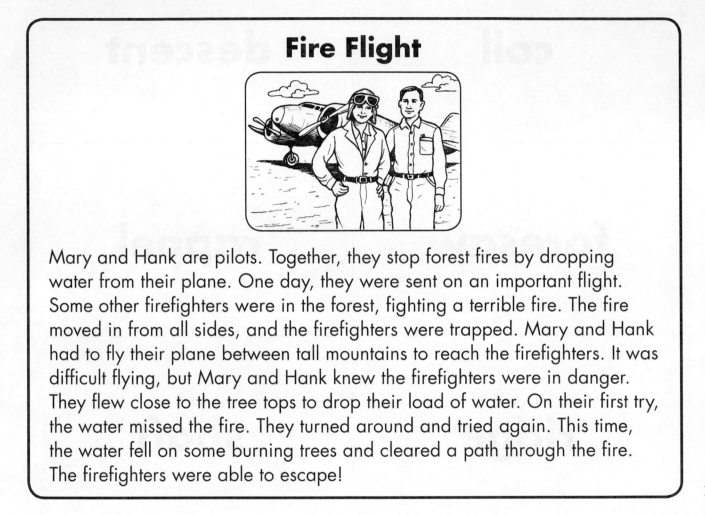

Fire Flight

Mary and Hank are pilots. Together, they stop forest fires by dropping water from their plane. One day, they were sent on an important flight. Some other firefighters were in the forest, fighting a terrible fire. The fire moved in from all sides, and the firefighters were trapped. Mary and Hank had to fly their plane between tall mountains to reach the firefighters. It was difficult flying, but Mary and Hank knew the firefighters were in danger. They flew close to the tree tops to drop their load of water. On their first try, the water missed the fire. They turned around and tried again. This time, the water fell on some burning trees and cleared a path through the fire. The firefighters were able to escape!

1. Describe Mary and Hank. What are they like?

_____

2. What is the problem that they need to solve?

_____

3. How did Mary and Hank solve the problem?

_____

4. What is the theme of the story?

_____

Character, Plot, and Theme

Use this lesson to supplement or replace the skill lesson on page 229c of the Teacher's Edition. Display the Skill Points (at right) and share them with students.

Teach/Model

Review a familiar story or fable such as "The Fox and the Crow."

Beginning Ask students to draw two pictures that show the problem and the solution in "The Fox and the Crow." Have them label the characters. Together decide what the meaning, or theme, of the story is.

Intermediate Ask: *Who are the characters?* (the fox and crow) *What is the fox's problem, and how does he solve it?* (He wants the crow's cheese. He tricks the crow to get it.) *These are part of the plot of the story. What is the theme of the story?* (Watch out for those who flatter.)

Advanced Have students discuss the characters and the plot of "The Fox and the Crow." Ask: *What is the theme of the story?* (Possible answer: Beware of those who flatter.) *Why is this an important lesson to learn?*

Advanced High Write and read aloud: *Two wrongs don't make a right.* Say: *We are going to write a story with this theme.* Together make up a story based on the big idea. Have students discuss the characters, their problem, and how they solve it.

Then distribute copies of Picture It! page 162.

- Have students look at the picture and describe what they see.
- Read the story aloud. Ask: *What is Mary and Hank's problem?* (They need to save firefighters who are trapped.)
- Review the Skill Points with students.
- Have students discuss the characters, plot, and theme of the story.

Practice

Read aloud the directions on page 162. Have students reread the story silently. Have them look at the picture and the story as they answer the questions.

Beginning Students can say their answers to the questions before writing their answers on the lines. Provide help with unfamiliar concepts and vocabulary.

Intermediate Students can first orally answer and then write their answers on the lines. Provide help with spelling English words.

Advanced Students can write their answers to the questions and then check them by rereading the story and making any necessary changes.

Advanced High Students can write their answers to the questions and then orally explain how they determined the theme of the story.

Answers for page 162: 1. They are brave pilots who do important work. 2. They need to save firefighters who are trapped by a fire. 3. They drop water from their plane to clear a path through the fire so that firefighters can escape. 4. Possible answer: Brave people will face danger to help others.

Skill Points

- ✔ A **character** is a person or animal in a story or play. You use what characters say and do to learn about them.
- ✔ The **plot** is the sequence of events in a story.
- ✔ A plot is often based on a problem that someone in the story has.
- ✔ The plot usually ends with the resolution, or solution, of the problem.
- ✔ The **theme** is the meaning of the story. Sometimes the author says what the theme is. Sometimes readers have to think about the story to find the theme.

Multilingual Summaries

Cliff Hanger

A storm is coming to Death Canyon. Two climbers tell Axel that his dog is at the top of Cathedral Wall. Dag decides that they have enough time to get Grits. Axel and Dag begin to climb.

Grits is on Monkey Ledge. Dag thinks that they can't make the climb because of the storm. Axel begins to climb anyway. Axel climbs on to the rim of Monkey Ledge and picks up his dog. The storm arrives and then moves away.

Axel lowers Grits down to Dag. He does not have enough rope to make it down. He has to free climb. He jumps down to his father. He did it.

Spanish

Escaladores de montañas

Una tormenta va a llegar a Death Canyon. Dos escaladores le dicen a Axel que su perro se encuentra en la cima de Catedral Wall. Dag decide que tienen tiempo para rescatar a Grits. Axel y Dag comienzan a escalar.

Grits se encuentra en Monkey Ledge. Dag opina que no podrán escalar debido a la tormenta. Pero Axel comienza a escalar de todos modos. Axel escala hasta la orilla de Monkey Ledge y rescata al perro. La tormenta llega y luego se retira.

Axel hace descender a Grits hasta Dag. No tienen suficiente cuerda para hacerlo bajar. Tendrá que escalar sin cuerdas. Él desciende hasta llegar donde está su padre. Lo logró.

Multilingual Summaries

Chinese

攀崖人

　　暴風雨即將侵襲「死亡峽谷」。　兩名攀岩者告訴艾克索，他的狗還在「教堂岩壁」的頂部。　戴格認為他們有充份的時間去救葛瑞特。於是，艾克索便開始往上攀登。

　　葛瑞特在「猴子岩峰」上。　戴格認為暴風雨使他們沒辦法往上爬。　但艾克索還是開始往上爬。　艾克索爬上了「猴子岩峰」的邊緣，並抓住他的狗。　暴風雨來了又走了。

　　艾克索把葛瑞特往下放，交給下面的戴格。　他沒有足夠的繩索往下降。　他必須徒手攀爬。　他向下跳到他爸爸所在的地方。　他辦到了。

Vietnamese

Người Treo Trên Vực

　　Cơn bão đang di chuyển đến Death Canyon (Thung Lũng Tử Thần). Có hai người leo núi nói với Axel rằng con chó của anh ta đang ở trên đỉnh của Cathedral Wall. Dag nghĩ là họ có đủ thời giờ để đem Grits xuống. Axel và Dag bắt đầu leo núi.

　　Grits đang ở tại Monkey Ledge. Dag nghĩ rằng họ không thể leo được nữa vì bão đến. Axel không nghe và vẫn leo như thường. Axel leo đến rìa của Monkey Ledge và cứu con chó xuống. Cơn bão đến và bay đi.

　　Axel hạ Grits xuống cho Dag xong. Anh không có đủ dây để xuống. Anh phải tự nhảy xuống. Anh nhảy trúng chỗ của cha anh. Anh đã xuống được.

Multilingual Summaries

Korean

클리프행어

'죽음의 협곡'에 폭풍이 몰려온다. 두 명의 등산가가 악셀에게 그의 개가 '성당의 벽' 꼭대기에 있다고 말한다. 댁은 그리츠를 데려올 시간이 충분하다고 판단한다. 알렉스와 댁이 암벽 등반을 시작한다.

그리츠가 '원숭이 암붕'에 있다. 댁은 폭풍 때문에 등반을 계속할 수 없다고 생각한다. 그렇지만 악셀은 올라가기 시작한다. 악셀이 원숭이 암붕 가장자리로 올라가서 개를 들어올린다. 폭풍이 왔다가 간다.

악셀이 댁에게 그리츠를 내려주는데, 그럴 만큼 밧줄이 충분하지 않다. 그래서 그는 자유 등반을 해야 한다. 그가 아버지에게로 뛰어내린다. 그가 해냈다.

Hmong

Neeg Nce Tsua

Kob nag xob nag cua los rau Death Canyon. Ob tug neeg nce tsua qhia rau Axel hais tias nws tus aub nyob puag saum tus Cathedral Wall. Dag txiav txim siab hais tias nkawv yuav tsum muaj sij hawm txaum mus muab Grits. Axel thiab Dag thiaj lis pib.

Grits yog nyob rau Monkey Ledge. Dag xav hais tias nkawv yuav nce mus tsis tau vim los nag xob nag cua lawm. Axel yeej nce mus lawm lis. Axel nce raw ib sab mus rau Monkey Ledge thiab mus muab nws tus aub. Nag xob nag cua los thiab tu mus lawm.

Axel txo lub Grits mus hauv Dag. Nws tsis hlua txaus cev mus txog rau hauv. Nws yuav cawm kom tau tus neeg nce ntawd. Nws dhia mus rau hauv nws txiv. Nws ua tau lawm.

165 *Cliff Hanger* Unit 5, Week 3

ELL Handbook

Copyright © Pearson Education, Inc., or its affiliates. All Rights Reserved. 4

Name _____

- **Read** *Women Who Dared to Fly* again.
- Use the information in the book to **complete** the chart below about three women aviators.

Who?: Katherine Cheung

Where?: _____

_____

When?: 1904, 1932

Who?: _____

Where?: space

When?: 1999, 1990s

Who?: Kalpana Chawla

Where?: _____

_____

When?: _____

Family Link

Would anyone in your family like to fly? Would they like to be astronauts? Ask people in your family if they think it would be exciting to be an aviator.

Weekly Resources Guide for English Language Learner Support

For this week's content and language objectives, see p. 167e.

Instructional Strand	Day 1	Day 2
Concept Development/Academic Language	**TEACHER'S EDITION** • Academic Language, p. DI•91 • Concept Development, p. DI•91 • Anchored Talk, pp. 256j—256–257 • Preteach Academic Vocabulary, p. 259a • Concept Talk Video **ELL HANDBOOK** • Hear It, See It, Say It, Use It, pp. xxxvi–xxxvii • ELL Poster Talk, Concept Talk, p. 167c **ELL POSTER 24** • Day 1 Activities	**TEACHER'S EDITION** • Academic Language, p. DI•91 • Concept Development, p. DI•91 • Anchored Talk, p. 260a • Concept Talk Video **ELL HANDBOOK** • ELL Poster Talk, Concept Talk, p. 167c • Concept Talk Video Routine, p. 477 **ELL POSTER 24** • Day 2 Activities
Phonics and Spelling	**TEACHER'S EDITION** • Phonics and Spelling, p. DI•95	**TEACHER'S EDITION** • Phonics and Spelling, p. DI•95
Listening Comprehension	**TEACHER'S EDITION** • Modified Read Aloud, p. DI•94 • Read Aloud, p. 257b • Concept Talk Video **ELL HANDBOOK** • Concept Talk Video Routine, p. 477	**TEACHER'S EDITION** • Modified Read Aloud, p. DI•94 • AudioText of *Antarctic Journal* • Concept Talk Video **ELL HANDBOOK** • AudioText CD Routine, p. 477 • Three-Column Chart, p. 494
Reading Comprehension	**TEACHER'S EDITION** • Preteach Main Idea and Details, p. DI•96	**TEACHER'S EDITION** • Reteach Main Idea and Details, p. DI•96 • Frontloading Reading, p. DI•97 **ELL HANDBOOK** • Picture It! Skill Instruction, pp. 168–168a • Multilingual Summaries, pp. 169–171
Vocabulary **Basic and Lesson Vocabulary** **Word Analysis: Suffix *-ion***	**TEACHER'S EDITION** • Basic Vocabulary, p. DI•92 • Preteach Lesson Vocabulary, p. DI•92 • Suffix *-ion*, p. DI•95 **ELL HANDBOOK** • Word Cards, p. 167 • ELL Vocabulary Routine, p. 471 **ELL POSTER 24** • Day 1 Activities	**TEACHER'S EDITION** • Basic Vocabulary, p. DI•92 • Reteach Lesson Vocabulary, p. DI•93 • Suffix *-ion*, p. DI•95 **ELL HANDBOOK** • Word Cards, p. 167 • Multilingual Vocabulary List, p. 431 **ELL POSTER 24** • Day 2 Activities
Grammar and Conventions	**TEACHER'S EDITION** • Preteach Time Order Words, p. DI•99	**TEACHER'S EDITION** • Practice Time Order Words, p. DI•99
Writing	**TEACHER'S EDITION** • Clear Purpose for Writing, p. DI•100 • Introduce Persuasive Ad, pp. 259e–259f	**TEACHER'S EDITION** • Writing Trait: Focus/Ideas, pp. 269d–269e

This symbol indicates leveled instruction to address language proficiency levels.

Day 3	Day 4	Day 5
TEACHER'S EDITION • Academic Language, p. DI•91 • Concept Development, p. DI•91 • Anchored Talk, p. 270a • Concept Talk Video **ELL HANDBOOK** • ELL Poster Talk, Concept Talk, p. 167c **ELL POSTER 24** • Day 3 Activities	**TEACHER'S EDITION** • Academic Language, p. DI•91 • Concept Development, p. DI•91 • Anchored Talk, p. 282a • Concept Talk Video **ELL HANDBOOK** • ELL Poster Talk, Concept Talk, p. 167c **ELL POSTER 24** • Day 4 Activities	**TEACHER'S EDITION** • Academic Language, p. DI•91 • Concept Development, p. DI•91 • Concept Talk Video **ELL HANDBOOK** • ELL Poster Talk, Concept Talk, p. 167c **ELL POSTER 24** • Day 5 Activities
		TEACHER'S EDITION • Phonics and Spelling, p. DI•95
ELL HANDBOOK • Phonics Transition Lesson, pp. 284, 291, 300, 305	**ELL HANDBOOK** • Phonics Transition Lesson, pp. 284, 291, 300, 305	
TEACHER'S EDITION • AudioText of *Antarctic Journal* • Concept Talk Video **ELL HANDBOOK** • AudioText CD Routine, p. 477	**TEACHER'S EDITION** • Concept Talk Video	**TEACHER'S EDITION** • Concept Talk Video
TEACHER'S EDITION • Sheltered Reading, p. DI•97 **ELL HANDBOOK** • Multilingual Summaries, pp. 169–171	**TEACHER'S EDITION** • ELL/ELD Reader Guided Reading, p. DI•98 **ELL HANDBOOK** • ELL Study Guide, p. 172	**TEACHER'S EDITION** • ELL/ELD Reader Guided Reading, p. DI•98 **ELL HANDBOOK** • ELL Study Guide, p. 172
		TEACHER'S EDITION • Suffix -*ion*, p. 287i
ELL HANDBOOK • High-Frequency Words Activity Bank, p. 446 **ELL POSTER 24** • Day 3 Activities	**ELL HANDBOOK** • High-Frequency Words Activity Bank, p. 446	**ELL HANDBOOK** • High-Frequency Words Activity Bank, p. 446
TEACHER'S EDITION • Grammar Jammer **ELL HANDBOOK** • Grammar Transition Lesson, pp. 372, 377 • Grammar Jammer Routine, p. 478	**TEACHER'S EDITION** • Grammar Jammer **ELL HANDBOOK** • Grammar Transition Lesson, pp. 372, 377	**TEACHER'S EDITION** • Grammar Jammer **ELL HANDBOOK** • Grammar Transition Lesson, pp. 372, 377
TEACHER'S EDITION • Let's Write It!, p. 280–281 • Writer's Craft: Clear Purpose for Writing, pp. 281a–281b	**TEACHER'S EDITION** • Revising Strategy, pp. 287d–287e	**TEACHER'S EDITION** • A Persuasive Ad, pp. 287p–287q

Question of the Week
What does a person sacrifice to explore the unknown?

Throughout the week, use the ELL Poster to help students produce and comprehend language, understand the concept, and build English vocabulary. Use the Question of the Week and other questions to help students share ideas in pairs, small groups, or the large group. Sample questions are shown, with examples of possible responses by students.

E L L Poster 24

Weekly Concept and Language Goals

• Explain why the Arctic climate is called harsh

• Tell about different harsh climates

• Describe sacrifices explorers make

By the end of the lesson, students should be able to talk about and write sentences about exploring and harsh climates.

Daily Team Talk

Day 1	Day 2	Day 3	Day 4	Day 5
After Day 1 activities on Poster, ask questions such as	After Day 2 activity on Poster, ask questions such as	After Day 3 activity on Poster, ask questions such as	After Day 4 activity on Poster, ask questions such as	After Day 5 activity on Poster, ask questions such as
In the poster picture, these explorers are crossing the Arctic. What and where is the Arctic?	*Why do people think the climate in the Arctic is a harsh climate?*	*These explorers made sacrifices to travel in the Arctic. What do you think Robert Peary misses most?*	*Other than their families, what else do you think the explorers miss as they travel in the Arctic?*	*What is another harsh climate you have learned about? Why is that climate harsh?*
Beginning It is ice. **Intermediate** It is thick ice. **Advanced** The Arctic is an area of frozen ocean in the North. **Advanced High** The Arctic is the area around the North Pole. It is frozen ocean.	**Beginning** It is cold. **Intermediate** It is very cold there. **Advanced** It is very cold in the Arctic. There is only ice and snow. **Advanced High** The Arctic is a very cold place. It is mostly ice and snow. No plants grow there.	**Beginning** His family. **Intermediate** He misses his family. **Advanced** I think he misses his family. He keeps a picture with him. **Advanced High** Robert Peary brought a picture of a woman with him. He is looking at the picture. Maybe she is his wife. I think he misses his family most.	**Beginning** Their homes. **Intermediate** They probably miss their beds. **Advanced** They might miss being able to eat fresh food. **Advanced High** I think the explorers miss sleeping inside a warm house instead of outside in the cold.	**Beginning** The desert. **Intermediate** The desert is very dry. **Advanced** The climate in a desert is harsh. It is very dry. **Advanced High** A desert has a harsh climate. It gets very little rain, so it is very dry. This makes it difficult for people to travel or live there.

Teacher's Edition pages 256j–287q

See the support for English language learners throughout the lesson, including ELL strategies and scaffolded activities at points of use.

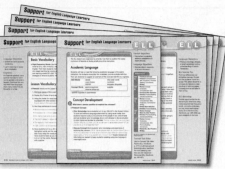

Teacher's Edition pages DI•91–DI•100

Differentiated Instruction for English language learners provides daily group activities that "frontload," or preteach, core instruction.

ELL Handbook pp. 167a–172

Find additional lesson materials that support the core lesson and the ELL instructional pages.

ELL Poster 24

ELL Reader 4.5.4

ELD Reader 4.5.4

Concept Literacy Reader

ELD, ELL Reader
Teaching Guide

Concept Literacy Reader
Teaching Guide

Technology

Online Teacher's Edition Use the digital version of the core Teacher's Edition for planning and instruction.

eReaders
This week's ELL and ELD Readers and Concept Literacy Reader are also available in digital format.

This Week's Content and Language Objectives by Strand

Concept Development/ Academic Language What does a person sacrifice to explore the unknown?	**Content Objective** • Use concept vocabulary related to adaptations to harsh climates. **Language Objectives** • Express ideas in response to art and discussion. • Express ideas in response to new academic vocabulary.
Phonics and Spelling Prefixes and Suffixes	**Content Objective** • Distinguish between main idea and details. **Language Objectives** • Discuss evidence for main idea and details. • Retell the main idea and details from a reading.
Listening Comprehension Modified Read Aloud: "The Eskimo Woman and the Polar Bear"	**Content Objective** • Monitor and adjust oral comprehension. **Language Objectives** • Discuss oral passages. • Use a graphic organizer to take notes.
Reading Comprehension Main Idea and Details	**Content Objectives** • Distinguish between main idea and details. • Monitor and adjust comprehension. **Language Objectives** • Discuss author's purpose and genre. • Discuss usage of formal and informal language in writing. • Read grade-level text with correct intonation.
Vocabulary Basic and Lesson Vocabulary	**Language Objectives** • Understand and use basic and grade-level vocabulary. • Learn meanings of grade-level vocabulary. • Produce drawings, phrases, and short sentences to show understanding of Lesson Vocabulary.
Word Analysis Suffix *-ion*	**Content Objective** • Identify main idea and details to aid comprehension. **Language Objective** • Write a main idea and details from personal experience.
Grammar and Conventions Time Order Words	**Content Objective** • Decode and use time order words appropriately. **Language Objectives** • Speak using time order words appropriately. • Write sentences that follow directions and use time order words.
Writing Clear Purpose for Writing	**Content Objective** • Identify purposes for writing a text. **Language Objectives** • Write a text with a clear purpose. • Explain with increasing specificity and detail.

Word Cards for Vocabulary Activities

anticipation | **continent**

convergence | **depart**

forbidding | **heaves**

icebergs

Teacher Note: Beginning Teach three to four words. **Intermediate** Teach four to six words. **Advanced** Teach six to seven words. **Advanced High** Teach all words.

Name _____

Look at the picture. **Read** the paragraph.

- What is the main idea of this paragraph? **Write** the main idea in the box below.

- What details support the main idea? **Write** the details in the boxes below.

An Age of Ice

Twenty thousand years ago, ice sheets, called glaciers, covered the northern parts of the Earth. The Earth was so cold that it was hard for plants and animals to survive. Only short grasses and trees could grow. Only strong people and animals could survive. Early humans, wolves, bears, and long-toothed tigers lived during this time. They had thick fur coats to help them survive in the icy world.

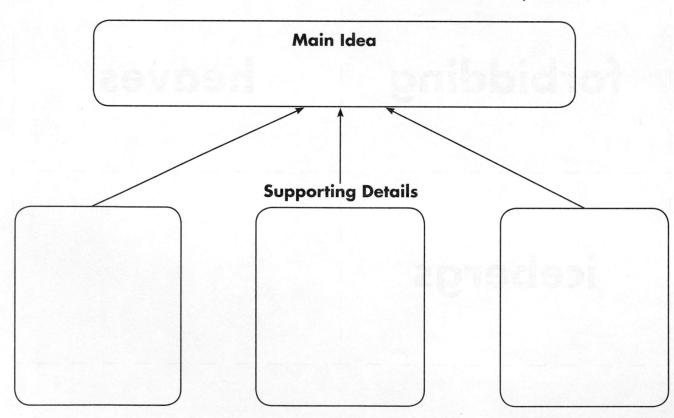

Main Idea

Supporting Details

Main Idea and Details

Use this lesson to supplement or replace the skill lesson on page 257c of the Teacher's Edition. Display the Skill Points (at right) and share them with students.

Teach/Model

Beginning Display a map of glacier coverage on Earth during the last Ice Age. Ask: *What is this map about? What is its main idea?* (Possible answer: Long ago, Earth was an icy place.) *What details in the map tell about the main idea?* (Possible answer: Ice sheets covered most of North America, Europe, and Asia.)

Intermediate Say: *The Arctic hare's fur changes from brown to white in winter. So does the fur of the snow fox. In winter, the Arctic wolf grows extra fur.* Work with students to decide what main idea these details tell about. (Possible answer: Some Arctic animals go through changes for winter.)

Advanced Say: *Arctic hares have adaptations that help them survive the Arctic winter. Their thick, white fur keeps them warm and blends in with the snow. Their short ears lose less heat than the longer ears of other hares.* Ask: *Which sentence tells the main idea?* (the first sentence) *Which sentences tell details?* (the second and third sentences)

Advanced High Have students identify the main idea of a section in their science textbook. Ask them to find details in the section that support the main idea. Have them explain how these details support the main idea.

Then distribute copies of Picture It! page 168.

- Have students look at and describe the picture. Then read the paragraph aloud.
- Ask: *What is the main idea of this paragraph?* (It was hard to survive on Earth twenty thousand years ago because it was very cold then.)
- Review the Skill Points with students.
- Have students identify details that support the main idea.

Practice

Read aloud the directions on page 168. Have volunteers take turns reading the paragraph aloud. Have students look at the picture and the paragraph as they fill in the graphic organizer.

Beginning Students can say what main idea and supporting details they want to write before writing words and phrases in the boxes. Provide help with English words and writing.

Intermediate Students can first answer orally and then write their answers in the boxes. Provide help with writing.

Advanced Students can write their answers in the boxes and then check their answers by rereading the paragraph and comparing what they wrote to the information in the paragraph.

Advanced High Students can write their answers in the boxes and then orally explain how they determined the main idea of the paragraph.

Answers for page 168: *Main Idea:* It was hard to survive on Earth twenty thousand years ago because it was very cold then. *Supporting Details:* Possible answers: The Earth was so cold that it was hard for plants and animals to survive. Only short grasses and trees could grow. Only strong people and animals could survive.

Skill Points

✔ The topic is what a text is about.
✔ The **main idea** is the most important idea about the topic.
✔ **Supporting details** give small pieces of information about the main idea.

Multilingual Summaries

Antarctic Journal

Jennifer Owings Dewey kept a journal during her trip to Antarctica. She flew in a plane to Chile. Then she took a boat to Palmer Station. During the trip, the boat stopped to let whales pass by.

The camp was cold. The weather was often dangerous. Everyone followed safety rules.

Dewey spent time exploring. She visited islands and old base camps. At one of the old camps, she watched a colony of penguins. She saw orca whales hunting for food.

The sun never sets in Antarctica during part of the year. The sun keeps many people awake. When she could not sleep, she wrote letters. She ate krill, a kind of plankton, with the other people in her camp.

Early one morning, she climbed a glacier. The summer sun had made cracks in the glacier. She almost fell through. But she made it back to camp. Jennifer Owings Dewey had many wonderful adventures to remember.

Spanish

El diario de la Antártida

Jennifer Owings Dewey escribió un diario del viaje que hizo a la Antártida. Primero voló en un avión a Chile y después tomó un bote para llegar a la estación Palmer. Durante el viaje, el bote se detuvo para dejar pasar a las ballenas.

El campamento era frío. Con frecuencia, el tiempo era peligroso. Todos seguían las reglas de seguridad.

Dewey dedicó tiempo a explorar. Visitó las islas y los viejos campamentos. En uno de los viejos campamentos vio una colonia de pingüinos. Vio ballenas orca cazando para comer.

En la Antártida el sol nunca se pone durante parte del año. El sol mantiene a mucha gente despierta. Cuando no podía dormir, Jennifer escribía cartas. Comió kril, un tipo de plancton, con la otra gente del campamento.

Una mañana, temprano, la autora escalaba un glaciar. El sol del verano había hecho grietas al glaciar y ella casi se cae, pero pudo regresar al campamento sin problemas. La autora tenía muchas aventuras maravillosas para recordar.

Multilingual Summaries

Chinese

南極日誌
四個月的極地生活

作家杜薇去南極旅行時，把每天的活動都記在日誌上。她先是乘飛機到智利，然後坐船去帕默研究站。途中，船還停下來讓大鯨魚先通過。

研究站的天氣非常寒冷，經常會有各種危險，因此每個人都要嚴格遵守安全規定。

杜薇經常尋訪南極各地，看過許多島嶼與以前留下的舊營地。還曾在那裏觀察一群企鵝，看見逆戟鯨獵食。

南極的太陽永遠不下山，令許多人睡不著。難以入睡時，杜薇經常寫寫書信。她和研究站裏的人一樣也吃磷蝦，這是一種浮游生物。

有一天清晨，她去爬冰川。夏季的陽光融化出許多冰縫，杜薇差點掉進去，但她還是努力克服困難返回營地。南極的經歷真是非常奇妙令人難忘！

Vietnamese

Nhật Ký ở Nam Cực
Bốn Tháng ở Tận Cùng Thế Giới

Jennifer Owings Dewey viết nhật ký trong suốt chuyến đi của cô đến Nam Cực. Cô bay đến Chilê. Rồi cô đi bằng thuyền đến Trạm Palmer. Trong chuyến đi này, chiếc thuyền ngừng để cho các cá voi đi qua.

Trại lạnh. Thời tiết thường nguy hiểm. Mọi người đều tuân theo các quy định an toàn.

Dewey dành thì giờ để thám hiểm. Cô tham quan các đảo và các trại căn cứ cũ. Tại một trong những trại cũ, cô quan sát bầy chim cánh cụt. Cô thấy những con cá voi orca đi săn mồi.

Mặt trời không bao giờ lặn ở Nam Cực. Mặt trời làm cho nhiều người không ngủ được. Khi cô không ngủ được, cô viết những lá thư. Cô ăn những con tôm nhỏ tí, một loại sinh vật phù du, với những người khác ở trại.

Một buổi sáng sớm, cổ trèo lên một khối băng. Trời mùa hè làm khối băng nứt nhiều chỗ. Cô suýt bị lọt vào trong khối băng. Nhưng cô ấy trở về trại được. Jennifer Owings Deweỷ có nhiều cuộc phiêu lưu tuyệt vời để ghi nhớ.

Multilingual Summaries

Korean

남극 일기 지구 최남단에서의 4개월

제니퍼 오잉스 듀이는 남극 여행 동안 일기를 적었다. 그녀는 비행기를 타고 칠레에 갔고 거기서 또 배를 타고 팔머 스테이션으로 갔다. 항해 중 고래들이 지나가도록 배가 멈추기도 했다.

캠프는 추웠다. 날씨는 가끔 위험스러울 정도였고 모든 이들이 안전 수칙을 따랐다.

듀이는 탐험을 하며 시간을 보냈고 주변 섬들과 오래된 베이스 캠프을 방문했다. 오래된 캠프 중 한 곳에서 그녀는 펭귄들의 서식지와 먹이를 사냥하는 범고래를 보았다.

남극에서의 태양은 결코 지지 않으며 많은 사람들을 깨어있게 한다. 잠을 이룰 수 없을 때 그녀는 작가가 되어 편지를 썼다. 그녀는 캠프에서 다른 사람들과 함께 플랑크톤의 일종인 크릴새우를 먹었다.

어느 날 아침 일찍 작가는 빙하를 올라갔다. 여름의 태양이 빙하에 균열을 내 놓았다. 그녀는 갈라진 틈 사이로 떨어질 뻔했지만 가까스로 캠프로 다시 돌아왔다. 작가는 잊지 못할 멋진 경험들을 많이 갖게 됐다.

Hmong

Phaum Ntawv Sau Txog Antartic Plaub Hlis Nyob Rau Sab Hauv Qab Ntiaj Teb No

Jennifer Owings Dewey khaws ib phau ntawd uas nws sau thaum nws mus rau Antartica. Nws ya nyoj hoom mus rau Chile. Ces nws caij ib lub nkoj mus rau Palmer Station. Thaum mus rau qhov ntawd, lub nkoj tau nres thiaj li cia tau cov ntses hiav txwv loj (whales) hla dhau lawm.

Lub chaws sob no kawg. Feem ntau mas, huab cua kuj txaus ntshai kawg. Txhua leej txhua tus ua zoo ua raws li kevcai ceeb faj.

Dewey tau siv sij hawm mus taug kev ncig xyuas ub no thiab. Nws tau mus xyuas tej koog pov txwv thiab tej chaws sob qub. Nyob rau ntawm ib qhov chaws sob qub, nws ntsia ib pab noog ntses uas tsuas nyob pem saum nabkuab thiab hauv hiavtxwv txias txias xwb (penguin). Nws pom ib cov ntses hiavtxwv loj hu ua orca no nrhiav mov noj.

Nyob Antartica mas lub hnub yeej tsis poob li. Lub hnub ua rau sawvdaws tsis paub pw. Thaum nws pw tsis tau, tus sau ntawd sau ntawv. Nws noj krill, ua yog ib yam nroj nyob hauv hiavtxwv, nrog cov neeg uas nrog nws sob ntawm lub chaws sob ntawd thiab.

Muaj ib tag kis txov txov, tus sau ntawv nce mus rau saum ib lub roob nab kuab. Lub hnub ntawm lub caij ntuj sov ntawd tau rau lub roob nab kuab ntawd thawg pleb. Nws yuav luag poob hauv. Tiam sis, nws rov mus tau txog rau pem qhov chaws sob lawm. Tus sau ntawd muaj ntau zaj nco txog.

Name _____

- **Read** *Antarctica: The Science Continent* again.
- Use the information in the book to **answer** the questions.

---

pages 2–5

1. Why did some of the first explorers die in Antarctica?

_____

_____

2. How did other explorers learn to survive in Antarctica?

_____

_____

_____

---

pages 6–8

3. What are some of the things scientists are interested in studying in Antarctica?

_____

_____

---

pages 9–12

4. About how many people come to Antarctica every year?

_____

5. Why did many countries come together to write the Antarctica Treaty?

_____

_____

Family Link

Ask family members what they think it would be like to spend six months in Antarctica. What would be the most interesting part of living there? What would they miss most?

Weekly Resources Guide for English Language Learner Support

For this week's content and language objectives, see p. 173e.

Instructional Strand	Day 1	Day 2
Concept Development/Academic Language	**TEACHER'S EDITION** • Academic Language, p. DI•116 • Concept Development, p. DI•116 • Anchored Talk, pp. 288j—288–289 • Preteach Academic Vocabulary, p. 291a • Concept Talk Video **ELL HANDBOOK** • Hear It, See It, Say It, Use It, pp. xxxvi–xxxvii • ELL Poster Talk, Concept Talk, p. 173c **ELL POSTER 25** • Day 1 Activities	**TEACHER'S EDITION** • Academic Language, p. DI•116 • Concept Development, p. DI•116 • Anchored Talk, p. 292a • Concept Talk Video **ELL HANDBOOK** • ELL Poster Talk, Concept Talk, p. 173c • Concept Talk Video Routine, p. 477 **ELL POSTER 25** • Day 2 Activities
Phonics and Spelling	**TEACHER'S EDITION** • Phonics and Spelling, p. DI•120	**TEACHER'S EDITION** • Phonics and Spelling, p. DI•120
Listening Comprehension	**TEACHER'S EDITION** • Modified Read Aloud, p. DI•119 • Read Aloud, p. 289b • Concept Talk Video **ELL HANDBOOK** • Concept Talk Video Routine, p. 477	**TEACHER'S EDITION** • Modified Read Aloud, p. DI•119 • AudioText of *Moonwalk* • Concept Talk Video **ELL HANDBOOK** • AudioText CD Routine, p. 477 • K-W-L Chart, p. 480
Reading Comprehension	**TEACHER'S EDITION** • Preteach Draw Conclusions, p. DI•121	**TEACHER'S EDITION** • Reteach Draw Conclusions, p. DI•121 • Frontloading Reading, p. DI•122 **ELL HANDBOOK** • Picture It! Skill Instruction, pp. 174–174a • Multilingual Summaries, pp. 175–177
Vocabulary **Basic and Lesson Vocabulary**	**TEACHER'S EDITION** • Basic Vocabulary, p. DI•117 • Preteach Lesson Vocabulary, p. DI•117 **ELL HANDBOOK** • Word Cards, p. 173 • ELL Vocabulary Routine, p. 471 **ELL POSTER 25** • Day 1 Activities	**TEACHER'S EDITION** • Basic Vocabulary, p. DI•117 • Reteach Lesson Vocabulary, p. DI•118 **ELL HANDBOOK** • Word Cards, p. 173 • Multilingual Vocabulary List, p. 431 **ELL POSTER 25** • Day 2 Activities
Grammar and Conventions	**TEACHER'S EDITION** • Preteach Prepositions and Prepositional Phrases, p. DI•124	**TEACHER'S EDITION** • Teach/Model Prepositions and Prepositional Phrases, p. DI•124
Writing	**TEACHER'S EDITION** • Sentences, p. DI•125 • Writing for Tests: Personal Narrative, pp. 291e–291f	**TEACHER'S EDITION** • Writing for Tests: Personal Narrative, pp. 301d–301e

This symbol indicates leveled instruction to address language proficiency levels.

Day 3	Day 4	Day 5
TEACHER'S EDITION • Academic Language, p. DI•116 • Concept Development, p. DI•116 • Anchored Talk, p. 302a • Concept Talk Video **ELL HANDBOOK** • ELL Poster Talk, Concept Talk, p. 173c **ELL POSTER 25** • Day 3 Activities	**TEACHER'S EDITION** • Academic Language, p. DI•116 • Concept Development, p. DI•116 • Anchored Talk, p. 310a • Concept Talk Video **ELL HANDBOOK** • ELL Poster Talk, Concept Talk, p. 173c **ELL POSTER 25** • Day 4 Activities	**TEACHER'S EDITION** • Academic Language, p. DI•116 • Concept Development, p. DI•116 • Concept Talk Video **ELL HANDBOOK** • ELL Poster Talk, Concept Talk, p. 173c **ELL POSTER 25** • Day 5 Activities
		TEACHER'S EDITION • Phonics and Spelling, p. DI•120
ELL HANDBOOK • Phonics Transition Lesson, pp. 301, 306	**ELL HANDBOOK** • Phonics Transition Lesson, pp. 301, 306	
TEACHER'S EDITION • AudioText of *Moonwalk* • Concept Talk Video **ELL HANDBOOK** • AudioText CD Routine, p. 477	**TEACHER'S EDITION** • Concept Talk Video	**TEACHER'S EDITION** • Concept Talk Video
TEACHER'S EDITION • Sheltered Reading, p. DI•122 **ELL HANDBOOK** • Multilingual Summaries, pp. 175–177	**TEACHER'S EDITION** • ELL/ELD Reader Guided Reading, p. DI•123 **ELL HANDBOOK** • ELL Study Guide, p. 178	**TEACHER'S EDITION** • ELL/ELD Reader Guided Reading, p. DI•123 **ELL HANDBOOK** • ELL Study Guide, p. 178
		TEACHER'S EDITION • Word Origins: German, p. 315i
ELL HANDBOOK • High-Frequency Words Activity Bank, p. 446 **ELL POSTER 25** • Day 3 Activities	**ELL HANDBOOK** • High-Frequency Words Activity Bank, p. 446	**ELL HANDBOOK** • High-Frequency Words Activity Bank, p. 446
TEACHER'S EDITION • Grammar Jammer **ELL HANDBOOK** • Grammar Transition Lesson, pp. 379–380 • Grammar Jammer Routine, p. 478	**TEACHER'S EDITION** • Grammar Jammer **ELL HANDBOOK** • Grammar Transition Lesson, pp. 379–380	**TEACHER'S EDITION** • Grammar Jammer **ELL HANDBOOK** • Grammar Transition Lesson, pp. 379–380
TEACHER'S EDITION • Let's Write It!, p. 308–309 • Writing for Tests: Evaluation, pp. 309a–309b	**TEACHER'S EDITION** • Writing for Tests: Personal Narrative, pp. 315d–315e	**TEACHER'S EDITION** • Writing for Tests: Personal Narrative, pp. 315p–315q

ELL Poster 25

Question of the Week

What are the risks when walking on the moon?

Throughout the week, use the ELL Poster to help students produce and comprehend language, understand the concept, and build English vocabulary. Use the Question of the Week and other questions to help students share ideas in pairs, small groups, or the large group. Sample questions are shown, with examples of possible responses by students.

Weekly Concept and Language Goals

• Discuss moon exploration

• Describe risks of walking on the moon

• Tell about the first walk on the moon

By the end of the lesson, students should be able to talk about and write sentences about the risks of walking on the moon.

Daily Team Talk

Day 1	Day 2	Day 3	Day 4	Day 5
After Day 1 activities on Poster, ask questions such as *What did the people in the poster picture do for the first time?*	After Day 2 activity on Poster, ask questions such as *What do you think would make walking on the moon difficult for the astronauts?*	After Day 3 activity on Poster, ask questions such as *Why do you think the astronauts want to be careful as they walk on the moon?*	After Day 4 activity on Poster, ask questions such as *Why do you think the astronauts put up a United States flag on the moon?*	After Day 5 activity on Poster, ask questions such as *Imagine you are one of the astronauts walking on the moon for the first time. How do you feel and why do you feel that way?*
Beginning Walk on the moon. **Intermediate** They walked on the moon. **Advanced** They were the first people to walk on the moon. **Advanced High** Neil Armstrong and Buzz Aldrin were the first men to walk on the moon.	**Beginning** The rocks. **Intermediate** There are lots of rocks and bumps. **Advanced** The moon has rocks and ditches. They might trip. **Advanced High** The surface of the moon has trenches and rocks of many sizes. The astronauts might trip and fall as they are walking.	**Beginning** So they do not fall. **Intermediate** They do not want to fall and hurt themselves. **Advanced** If they fall, they might get hurt. There is no doctor to help them. **Advanced High** The astronauts are careful not to trip because they do not want to fall. They could get hurt or they could rip their spacesuits.	**Beginning** They are first. **Intermediate** They are from the United States. **Advanced** They are proud of what their country has done. **Advanced High** The astronauts are proud of their country's achievement. Also, they want to show which country got to the moon first.	**Beginning** Scared. **Intermediate** I am scared but excited. **Advanced** I feel nervous and excited because I am on the moon! **Advanced High** I feel excited because I am one of the first people to ever walk on the moon. I also feel nervous because I am a long way from home.

This Week's Materials

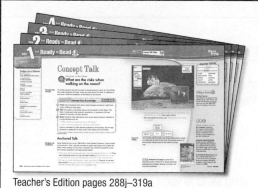

Teacher's Edition pages 288j–319a

See the support for English language learners throughout the lesson, including ELL strategies and scaffolded activities at points of use.

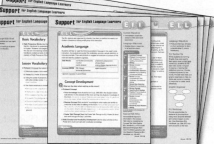

Teacher's Edition pages DI•116–DI•125

Differentiated Instruction for English language learners provides daily group activities that "frontload," or preteach, core instruction.

ELL Handbook pp. 173a–178

Find additional lesson materials that support the core lesson and the ELL instructional pages.

Poster 25

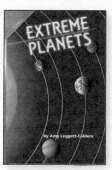

ELL Reader 4.5.5

ELD Reader 4.5.5

Concept Literacy Reader

ELD, ELL Reader Teaching Guide

Concept Literacy Reader Teaching Guide

Technology

Online Teacher's Edition Use the digital version of the core Teacher's Edition for planning and instruction.

eReaders
This week's ELL and ELD Readers and Concept Literacy Reader are also available in digital format.

This Week's Content and Language Objectives by Strand

Concept Development/ Academic Language What are the risks when walking on the moon?	**Content Objective** • Use concept vocabulary related to risks and moon exploration. **Language Objectives** • Express ideas in response to art and discussion. • Express ideas in response to new academic vocabulary.
Phonics and Spelling Related Words	**Content Objective** • Review related words. **Language Objectives** • Apply phonics and decoding skills to vocabulary. • Discuss meanings of compound words.
Listening Comprehension Modified Read Aloud: "Life on the Moon"	**Content Objective** • Monitor and adjust oral comprehension. **Language Objectives** • Discuss oral passages. • Use a graphic organizer to take notes.
Reading Comprehension Draw Conclusions	**Content Objectives** • Draw conclusions to aid comprehension. • Make and adjust predictions. **Language Objectives** • Discuss facts and details that can be used to draw a conclusion. • Write a conclusion based on personal experience. • Improve reading rate and accuracy with grade-level text.
Vocabulary Basic and Lesson Vocabulary	**Language Objectives** • Understand and use basic and grade-level vocabulary. • Learn meanings of grade-level vocabulary. • Produce drawings, phrases, and short sentences to show understanding of Lesson Vocabulary.
Grammar and Conventions Prepositions and Prepositional Phrases	**Content Objectives** • Decode and use prepositional phrases. • Correctly form prepositional phrases. **Language Objectives** • Use prepositional phrases in speech. • Write phrases and sentences with prepositional phrases.
Writing Sentences	**Content Objective** • Identify features of sentences that flow smoothly. **Language Objectives** • Write paragraphs with sentences that flow smoothly by using connecting words. • Speak using a variety of connecting words.

Word Cards for Vocabulary Activities

loomed

rille

runt

staggered

summoning

taunted

trench

trudged

Teacher Note: Beginning Teach three to four words. **Intermediate** Teach four to six words. **Advanced** Teach six to seven words. **Advanced High** Teach all words.

Name _____

Look at the picture. **Read** the story. **Answer** the questions.

A New Day on Mars

Jena and Jed were drinking breakfast in their Mars home. "I cleaned your spacesuits," Mom said. "I also put two extra batteries in them. I know you want to have a lot of energy today!" Four new kids were starting school today. Jena and Jed were excited to show them the school. It was their job to show the new kids how to use the flying machines. They also were excited for the kids to meet the robots at school. "Beep!" The space mobile was waiting. Jena and Jed put on their helmets. They ran outside. They hoped the new kids liked Mars School X-241!

1. Why do Jena and Jed want extra energy?
    a. They are tired.
    b. The new kids are coming.
    c. They were late for school.
    d. They did not have a good breakfast.

2. What can you conclude about Jenna and Jed?
    a. They have dirty spacesuits.
    b. They are aliens.
    c. They are starting a new school.
    d. They are brother and sister.

3. What can you conclude about when the story takes place?
    a. It is in the past.
    b. It happens today.
    c. It is in the future.

ELL Handbook

Draw Conclusions

Use this lesson to supplement or replace the skill lesson on page 289c of the Teacher's Edition. Display the Skill Points (at right) and share them with students.

Teach/Model

Beginning Say: *My favorite books are* Mars Mission, Adventures on Venus, *and* Journey to Mercury. *What conclusion can you make?* (You like books about other planets.) *How did you make that conclusion?* (The book titles mention other planets.)

Intermediate Say: *It is a dark night. I bring my telescope outside.* Ask students to draw a conclusion from the details. (You are going to look at the stars.) Ask them to identify clue words that helped them draw that conclusion. (dark, night, telescope, outside)

Advanced Say: *I read that we can see meteors tonight. I go out when it gets dark. I see something flash across the sky! What conclusion can you draw?* (You saw a meteor.) Have students explain how they drew that conclusion.

Advanced High Write and read aloud: *We need oxygen and water to live. Mars has little oxygen. Mars may have ice but no water.* Ask students to think about these facts. Have them write and share a conclusion. (Possible answer: We cannot live on Mars unless we bring oxygen and water with us.)

Then distribute copies of Picture It! page 174.

- Have students look at and describe the picture. Then read the paragraph aloud.
- Ask: *Is life on Mars similar to or different from life on Earth?* (different from)
- Review the Skill Points with students.
- Have students find details that support their conclusion about life on Mars.

Practice

Read aloud the directions on page 174. Have students reread the story silently. Have them look at the picture and the story as they answer the questions.

Beginning Students can first orally answer the questions and then mark their answers. Provide help with circling the correct choices.

Intermediate Students can read the questions, look for the answers in the story, and then mark their answers on the page.

Advanced Students can mark their answers and then check them by silently rereading the story and making any necessary corrections.

Advanced High Students can mark their answers and then orally explain how what they read in the story and what they already knew helped them draw the conclusions.

Answers for page 174: 1. b; 2. d; 3. c

Skill Points

- ✔ Facts are statements that can be proven true or false.
- ✔ Details are small pieces of information in a text.
- ✔ When you put facts and details together, you can form an idea or **draw a conclusion** about the text.

Multilingual Summaries

Moonwalk

Gerry and Vern Kandel visit the moon with their father. Vern always calls Gerry "Runt." Their father goes to work, and tells the boys to stay inside the shelter. But Vern wants to go for a moonwalk.

Vern dares Gerry to jump over rilles. Gerry jumps over a very big one, but Vern does not. Vern falls into the rille and hurts his leg. His moonsuit loses power. Gerry helps Vern to climb out of the rille and walk back to the shelter. They must get back before sunrise. Without power, Vern's moonsuit will get too hot, and he may run out of air.

Gerry takes Vern all the way back. Vern thanks him for saving his life. Vern promises never to call Gerry "Runt" again.

Spanish

Paseo lunar

Gerry y Vern Kandel visitan la Luna con su papá. Vern siempre llama a Gerry "Pequeño". Su papá se va a trabajar y le dice a los niños que se queden dentro del refugio. Pero Vern quiere dar un paseo lunar.

Vern desafía a Gerry a saltar sobre los *rilles* (valles lunares). Gerry salta uno muy grande, pero Vern no lo hace. Vern se cae dentro de un *rille* y se hace daño en la pierna. Su traje espacial pierde poder. Gerry ayuda a Vern a salir del *rille* y a regresar al refugio. Ellos tienen que llegar antes del amanecer. Sin poder, el traje lunar de Vern se calentará demasiado y puede quedarse sin aire.

Gerry lleva a Vern todo el camino de vuelta. Vern le da las gracias por salvarle la vida. Vern le promete que nunca más lo volverá a llamar "Pequeño".

Multilingual Summaries

月球漫步

　　格裏、弗恩和他們的爸爸一起來到月球。弗恩常把格裏叫做"矮子"。爸爸去上班時，囑咐他們不要走出生活站，可是弗恩非常想出去做月球漫步。

　　弗恩慫恿格裏跳月球溝。格裏一下跳過很寬的溝，但弗恩沒跳過。他掉進溝裏，摔傷了腳，而且月球服也弄壞了，失去了電力。格裏把弗恩拉出深溝，扶著他往回走。他們必須在太陽升起前趕回生活站，不然弄壞了的月球服會很燙，而且弗恩的氧氣也會用完。

　　一路上全靠格裏的幫助，他們安全返回。弗恩非常感謝格裏救了他，發誓以後再也不叫他"矮子"。

Đi Trên Mặt Trăng

Gerry và Vern Kandel đến mặt trăng với ba của họ. Vern lúc nào cũng gọi Gerry là "Runt" (thằng nhóc tì). Ba của họ đi làm, và dặn các cậu con trai ở trong khu trú ẩn. Nhưng Vern muốn được đi trên mặt trăng.

Vern thách thức Gerry nhảy qua các rãnh trên mặt trăng. Gerry nhảy qua một rãnh rất lớn, nhưng Vern không nhảy qua được. Vern bị rơi vào rãnh này và bị thương ở chân. Bộ đồ để mặc trên mặt trăng của nó bị mất năng lượng. Gerry giúp Vern leo ra khỏi cái rãnh và đi trở về khu trú ẩn. Họ phải trở về trước bình minh. Không có năng lượng bộ đồ mặt trăng của Vern sẽ trở nên rất nóng, và nó có thể bị hết khí để thở.

Gerry đưa Vern trở về. Vern cám ơn cậu bé đã cứu sống nó. Vern hứa không bao giờ gọi Gerry là "Runt" nữa.

Multilingual Summaries

Korean

달 산책

　게리와 번 캔들은 아버지와 함께 달을 방문한다. 번은 게리를 항상 "꼬마"라고 부른다. 아버지는 일을 하러 나가며 두 아들에게 숙소 안에 남아 있으라고 하지만 번은 달을 산책하고 싶어한다.

　번이 게리보고 골짜기를 뛰어 넘어 보라고 하자 게리는 굉장히 큰 골짜기를 뛰어 넘는다. 하지만 번은 하지 않는다. 번은 골짜기로 떨어져서 다리를 다치게 된다. 그러자 그의 우주복이 동력을 잃어버리고 게리는 번이 골짜기 밖으로 나오도록 도운 후 숙소로 걸어 돌아간다. 그들은 해가 지기 전까지 돌아가야만 하지만 동력이 떨어진 번의 우주복은 너무 뜨거워져서 산소가 바닥 날지도 모른다.

　게리는 번을 데리고 숙소까지 내내 간다. 번은 게리에게 자신의 생명을 구해준 데 대해 고마워하고 게리를 다시는 "꼬마"라고 부르지 않겠다며 약속한다.

Hmong

Nchim Lub Hli

Gerry thiab Vern Kandel nkawd mus xyuas lub hli nrog nkawd txiv. Vern yeej muab Gerry hu ua "Runt" tas mus li. Nkawd txiv mus ua hauj lwm, thiab hais rau ob tug tub tias kom nkawd nyob twj ywm hauv tsev. Tiam si Vern xav mus ncig lub hli.

Vern npav seb Gerry dhia puas dhau tej hav sauv. Gerry dhia dhau ib lub hav loj kawg, tiam sis Vern dhia tsis tau dhau. Vern poob rau hauv ib lub hav thiab ua raug nws txais ceg mob. Lub cev khaub ncaws hli poob hwj chim tag lawm. Gerry pab Vern nce tawm ntawm lub hav thiab rov qab mus tsev. Nkawd yuav tsum rov mus txog tsev ua ntej hnub tuaj. Vim Vern ces khaub ncaws tsis muaj xuj cim lawm nws yuav sov heev tuaj, thiab nws yuav tsis tau pab lawm los kuj muaj thiab.

Gerry coj Vern rov qab mus txog duab tsev. Vern ua nws tsaug uas nws tau cawm nws txog siab. Vern cog lus tias nws yuav tsis muab Gerry hu ua "Runt" tsiv lawm.

Name _____

- **Read** *Extreme Planets* again.
- Use the information in the book to **answer** the questions.

pages 2–5

1. Name three things humans need that are found on Earth.

_____

2. Why are people not able to live on either Venus or Mercury?

_____

pages 6–8

3. How are Mars and Earth alike?

_____

4. Make a conclusion about why people cannot live on Jupiter.

_____

pages 9–11

5. What makes Saturn different from any other planets?

_____

6. Draw a conclusion about why Uranus and Neptune are so cold.

_____

Family Link

Tell your family what you learned about the planets in our solar system. Explain why humans cannot live on many other planets.

For this week's content and language objectives, see p. 179e.

Instructional Strand	Day 1	Day 2
Concept Development/Academic Language	**TEACHER'S EDITION** • Academic Language, p. DI•16 • Concept Development, p. DI•16 • Anchored Talk, pp. 322j—322–323 • Preteach Academic Vocabulary, p. 325a • Concept Talk Video **ELL HANDBOOK** • Hear It, See It, Say It, Use It, pp. xxxvi–xxxvii • ELL Poster Talk, Concept Talk, p. 179c **ELL POSTER 26** • Day 1 Activities	**TEACHER'S EDITION** • Academic Language, p. DI•16 • Concept Development, p. DI•16 • Anchored Talk, p. 326a • Concept Talk Video **ELL HANDBOOK** • ELL Poster Talk, Concept Talk, p. 179c • Concept Talk Video Routine, p. 477 **ELL POSTER 26** • Day 2 Activities
Phonics and Spelling	**TEACHER'S EDITION** • Phonics and Spelling, p. DI•20	**TEACHER'S EDITION** • Phonics and Spelling, p. DI•20
Listening Comprehension	**TEACHER'S EDITION** • Modified Read Aloud, p. DI•19 • Read Aloud, p. 323b • Concept Talk Video **ELL HANDBOOK** • Concept Talk Video Routine, p. 477	**TEACHER'S EDITION** • Modified Read Aloud, p. DI•19 • AudioText of *My Brother Martin* • Concept Talk Video **ELL HANDBOOK** • AudioText CD Routine, p. 477 • Three-Column Chart, p. 494
Reading Comprehension	**TEACHER'S EDITION** • Preteach Cause and Effect, p. DI•21	**TEACHER'S EDITION** • Reteach Cause and Effect, p. DI•21 • Frontloading Reading, p. DI•22 **ELL HANDBOOK** • Picture It! Skill Instruction, pp. 180–180a • Multilingual Summaries, pp. 181–183
Vocabulary **Basic and Lesson Vocabulary** **Word Analysis: Latin Roots *gener* and *port***	**TEACHER'S EDITION** • Basic Vocabulary, p. DI•17 • Preteach Lesson Vocabulary, p. DI•17 • Latin Roots *gener* and *port*, p. DI•20 **ELL HANDBOOK** • Word Cards, p. 179 • ELL Vocabulary Routine, p. 471 **ELL POSTER 26** • Day 1 Activities	**TEACHER'S EDITION** • Basic Vocabulary, p. DI•17 • Reteach Lesson Vocabulary, p. DI•18 • Latin Roots *gener* and *port*, p. DI•20 **ELL HANDBOOK** • Word Cards, p. 179 • Multilingual Vocabulary List, p. 431 **ELL POSTER 26** • Day 2 Activities
Grammar and Conventions	**TEACHER'S EDITION** • Preteach Conjunctions, p. DI•24	**TEACHER'S EDITION** • Reteach Conjunctions, p. DI•24
Writing	**TEACHER'S EDITION** • Defining New Terms, p. DI•25 • Introduce Cause-and-Effect Essay, pp. 325e–325f	**TEACHER'S EDITION** • Writing Trait: Focus/Ideas, pp. 335d–335e

This symbol indicates leveled instruction to address language proficiency levels.

Day 3	Day 4	Day 5
TEACHER'S EDITION • Academic Language, p. DI•16 • Concept Development, p. DI•16 • Anchored Talk, p. 336a • Concept Talk Video **ELL HANDBOOK** • ELL Poster Talk, Concept Talk, p. 179c **ELL POSTER 26** • Day 3 Activities	**TEACHER'S EDITION** • Academic Language, p. DI•16 • Concept Development, p. DI•16 • Anchored Talk, p. 346a • Concept Talk Video **ELL HANDBOOK** • ELL Poster Talk, Concept Talk, p. 179c **ELL POSTER 26** • Day 4 Activities	**TEACHER'S EDITION** • Academic Language, p. DI•16 • Concept Development, p. DI•16 • Concept Talk Video **ELL HANDBOOK** • ELL Poster Talk, Concept Talk, p. 179c **ELL POSTER 26** • Day 5 Activities
ELL HANDBOOK • Phonics Transition Lesson, pp. 266–267	**ELL HANDBOOK** • Phonics Transition Lesson, pp. 266–267	**TEACHER'S EDITION** • Phonics and Spelling, p. DI•20
TEACHER'S EDITION • AudioText of *My Brother Martin* • Concept Talk Video **ELL HANDBOOK** • AudioText CD Routine, p. 477	**TEACHER'S EDITION** • Concept Talk Video	**TEACHER'S EDITION** • Concept Talk Video
TEACHER'S EDITION • Sheltered Reading, p. DI•22 **ELL HANDBOOK** • Multilingual Summaries, pp. 181–183	**TEACHER'S EDITION** • ELL/ELD Reader Guided Reading, p. DI•23 **ELL HANDBOOK** • ELL Study Guide, p. 184	**TEACHER'S EDITION** • ELL/ELD Reader Guided Reading, p. DI•23 **ELL HANDBOOK** • ELL Study Guide, p. 184
ELL HANDBOOK • High-Frequency Words Activity Bank, p. 446 **ELL POSTER 26** • Day 3 Activities	**ELL HANDBOOK** • High-Frequency Words Activity Bank, p. 446	**TEACHER'S EDITION** • Latin Roots *gener* and *port*, p. 349i **ELL HANDBOOK** • High-Frequency Words Activity Bank, p. 446
TEACHER'S EDITION • Grammar Jammer **ELL HANDBOOK** • Grammar Transition Lesson, pp. 379, 381 • Grammar Jammer Routine, p. 478	**TEACHER'S EDITION** • Grammar Jammer **ELL HANDBOOK** • Grammar Transition Lesson, pp. 379, 381	**TEACHER'S EDITION** • Grammar Jammer **ELL HANDBOOK** • Grammar Transition Lesson, pp. 379, 381
TEACHER'S EDITION • Let's Write It!, p. 344–345 • Writer's Craft: Topic Sentence, pp. 345a–345b	**TEACHER'S EDITION** • Revising Strategy, pp. 349d–349e	**TEACHER'S EDITION** • Cause-and-Effect Essay, pp. 349p–349q

Question of the Week
How can words change people's lives?

ⒺⓁⓁ Poster 26

Throughout the week, use the ELL Poster to help students produce and comprehend language, understand the concept, and build English vocabulary. Use the Question of the Week and other questions to help students share ideas in pairs, small groups, or the large group. Sample questions are shown, with examples of possible responses by students.

Weekly Concept and Language Goals

• Understand that art can contain words as well as pictures

• Identify people who use words to change lives

• Tell how people's words can change lives

By the end of the lesson, students should be able to talk about and write sentences about the effect words can have on people's lives.

Daily Team Talk

Day 1	Day 2	Day 3	Day 4	Day 5
After Day 1 activities on Poster, ask questions such as	After Day 2 activity on Poster, ask questions such as	After Day 3 activity on Poster, ask questions such as	After Day 4 activity on Poster, ask questions such as	After Day 5 activity on Poster, ask questions such as
Which work of art in the poster picture do you think might have words on it? Why?	*Who stands up in front of a large group of people and makes a speech to them?*	*When the President speaks to people, how can his words change people's lives?*	*In the story* My Brother Martin, *why did M. L. want to use his words to turn the world upside down?*	*When did a person's words change something in your life?*
Beginning The statue. **Intermediate** The statue because it is holding a paper. **Advanced** The statue might have words on it. The woman is holding a piece of paper. **Advanced High** The statue of a woman might have words on it. The woman is holding a scroll, which could have writing on it.	**Beginning** A teacher. **Intermediate** A teacher or a principal. **Advanced** Leaders make speeches to people all the time. **Advanced High** Leaders such as the mayor, the governor, and the President make speeches to large groups of people.	**Beginning** He can help them. **Intermediate** He can use words to help people. **Advanced** His words can get people to help one another. **Advanced High** The President's words can inspire people to help one another and make their communities better places to live.	**Beginning** They were mean. **Intermediate** He was sad that people were so mean. **Advanced** M. L. wanted to change the world so people were not so mean to one another. **Advanced High** M. L. did not know why people were so mean to one another. He wanted everyone to be treated equally and with kindness.	**Beginning** My mom's. **Intermediate** My mom told me to try soccer. **Advanced** My mom told me to try playing soccer. Now I love it. **Advanced High** My mom encouraged me to try something new. I tried soccer and now I love it.

Teacher's Edition pages 322j–349q

See the support for English language learners throughout the lesson, including ELL strategies and scaffolded activities at points of use.

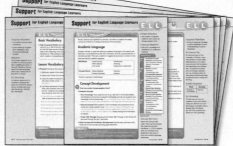

Teacher's Edition pages DI•16–DI•25

Differentiated Instruction for English language learners provides daily group activities that "frontload," or preteach, core instruction.

ELL Handbook pp. 179a–184

Find additional lesson materials that support the core lesson and the ELL instructional pages.

ELL Poster 26

ELL Reader 4.6.1

ELD Reader 4.6.1

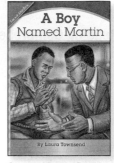

Concept Literacy Reader

ELD, ELL Reader
Teaching Guide

Concept Literacy Reader
Teaching Guide

Technology

Online Teacher's Edition Use the digital version of the core Teacher's Edition for planning and instruction.

eReaders
This week's ELL and ELD Readers and Concept Literacy Reader are also available in digital format.

This Week's Content and Language Objectives by Strand

Concept Development/ Academic Language How can words change people's lives?	**Content Objective** • Use concept vocabulary related to how words can change people's lives. **Language Objectives** • Use prior knowledge and experience, to understand meaning. • Express ideas in response to new academic vocabulary.
Phonics and Spelling Schwa	**Content Objectives** • Identify the schwa sound. • Say the schwa sound. **Language Objective** • Apply phonics and decoding skills to vocabulary.
Listening Comprehension Modified Read Aloud: "A Lonely Class"	**Content Objective** • Monitor and adjust oral comprehension. **Language Objectives** • Discuss oral passages. • Use a graphic organizer to take notes.
Reading Comprehension Cause and Effect	**Content Objectives** • Distinguish between cause and effect. • Make and adjust predictions. **Language Objectives** • Discuss evidence for cause and effect. • Write causes and effects from personal experience. • Read grade-level text with appropriate phrasing.
Vocabulary Basic and Lesson Vocabulary	**Language Objectives** • Understand and use basic vocabulary. • Learn meanings of grade-level vocabulary using visual and contextual support. • Produce drawings, phrases, and short sentences to show understanding of Lesson Vocabulary.
Word Analysis Latin Roots *gener* and *port*	**Content Objective** • Identify words with Latin roots *gener* and *port*. **Language Objective** • Discuss meaning of Latin roots *gener* and *port*.
Grammar and Conventions Conjunctions	**Content Objective** • Identify and use conjunctions correctly. **Language Objectives** • Speak using conjunctions correctly. • Write conjunctions correctly.
Writing Defining New Terms	**Content Objective** • Understand how new terms can be defined within a sentence. **Language Objective** • Share feedback for editing and revising.

Word Cards for Vocabulary Activities

ancestors

avoided

generations

minister

numerous

pulpit

shielding

Teacher Note: Beginning Teach three to four words. **Intermediate** Teach four to six words. **Advanced** Teach six to seven words. **Advanced High** Teach all words.

Name _____

Look at the picture. **Read** the paragraph.
• **Underline** the cause-and-effect clue words in the paragraph.
• **Write** the cause for the effect shown.
• **Write** the effect for the cause shown.

Fighting for Equal Schools

Linda Brown grew up in Topeka, Kansas, during the 1950s. At that time, white children and African American children could not go to the same school in many states. The school closest to Linda's home was for white children only, so she could not go to it. Because of the law, she had to walk a mile to get to school every morning. Linda's father thought the law separating children by skin color was unfair. He went to court to force the white school to accept his daughter. He won his case. Because of what he did, separate schools for people of different skin colors are not legal in the United States.

Cause

Effect

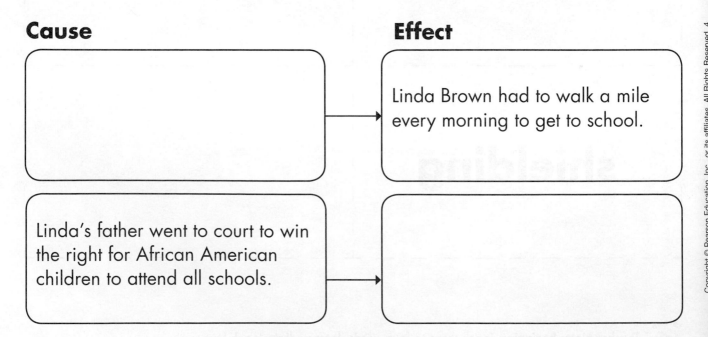

Linda Brown had to walk a mile every morning to get to school.

| Linda's father went to court to win the right for African American children to attend all schools. | |

Cause and Effect

Use this lesson to supplement or replace the skill lesson on page 323c of the Teacher's Edition. Display the Skill Points (at right) and share them with students.

Teach/Model

Beginning Write and read aloud: *It was raining, so we had recess inside.* Ask students to copy the sentence. Tell them to underline the cause once (it was raining), underline the effect twice (we had recess inside), and circle the cause-and-effect clue word (so).

Intermediate Say: *Jen studied last night. She got a good grade on her test today. What happened today?* (Jen got a good grade on her test.) *This is the effect. Why did this happen?* (Jen studied last night.) *This is the cause.* Combine the sentences using the word *because,* say the new sentence, and ask students to identify the clue word.

Advanced Provide an effect: *I missed the school bus.* Ask students to think of possible causes. (I woke up late. I was at the wrong place. I went back for my lunch.) Ask students to choose one cause and write a cause-and-effect sentence using a clue word.

Advanced High Pair students. Each partner writes a cause-and-effect sentence with a clue word. Partners exchange papers and identify the cause and the effect in each other's sentences.

Then distribute copies of Picture It! page 180.

- Have students tell you what they see in the picture. Then read the paragraph aloud.
- Ask: *What caused African American and white children to go to separate schools in many states in the 1950s?* (laws that said they could not go to the same school)
- Review the Skill Points with students.

Practice

Read aloud the directions on page 180. Reread the paragraph aloud, explaining any unfamiliar concepts or vocabulary. Have students use the picture and the paragraph as they fill in the cause-and-effect boxes.

Beginning Students can say what they want to write for the cause and the effect before writing their ideas in the boxes. Provide help with English words and writing.

Intermediate Students can first orally respond and then write their answers in the boxes. Provide help with writing English words.

Advanced Students can write their answers in the boxes and then check them by comparing them with a partner's.

Advanced High Students can write their answers in the boxes and then orally state each cause-and-effect relationship using an appropriate clue word.

Answers for page 180: *Clue words:* so, because; *Cause:* The law wouldn't allow Linda Brown to go to the school that was closest to her home. *Effect:* Separate schools for people of different skin colors are not legal in the United States.

Skill Points

- ✔ The **effect** is what happens. The **cause** is what makes it happen.
- ✔ Clue words such as *so, therefore, because,* and *as a result* can show causes and effects.

Multilingual Summaries

My Brother Martin

Christine was the sister of Martin Luther King Jr. and their brother Alfred Daniel. The family called the boys M. L. and A. D.

They lived in a town with unfair laws. The laws kept black people separate from white people.

M. L. and A. D. played with the white boys across the street. One day, the boys across the street said that they could not play together anymore because M. L. and A. D. were black. The children did not understand. Their mother explained that many white people did not understand that everyone is the same. M. L. wanted to change this.

His father showed him how to stand up for what is right. Later, M. L. gave speeches and organized marches. The speeches and marches helped end the unfair laws. He dreamed a dream that changed the world.

Spanish

Mi hermano Martin

Martin Luther King Jr. y Alfred Daniel eran los hermanos de Christine. La familia los llamaba M. L. y A. D.

Vivían en un pueblo que tenía leyes muy injustas. La ley mantenía separadas a las personas de raza negra y de raza blanca.

M. L. y A. D. jugaban con los niños blancos que vivían en la calle del frente. Un día los niños dijeron que no podrían jugar más con M. L. y A. D. porque ellos eran negros. Los niños no comprendían por qué las cosas eran así. Su madre les explicó que muchas de las personas blancas no entendían que todas las personas son iguales. M. L. quería que esto cambiara.

Su padre le enseñó cómo luchar por lo que es correcto. Más tarde, M. L. dio discursos y organizó marchas. Los discursos y las marchas ayudaron a terminar con las leyes injustas. Él tenía un sueño que cambió al mundo.

Multilingual Summaries

Chinese

我 的 兄 弟 — 馬 丁

　　克麗斯汀是小馬丁・路德・金恩的姐妹，他們還有一個兄弟叫做艾弗雷德・丹尼爾。家裡的人都叫他們 M.L. 和 A.D.。

　　他們住的小鎮法律很不公平，因為法律規定黑人不能接近白人。

　　馬丁和艾弗雷德時常和對街的白人男孩一起玩。有一天，那些對街男孩說他們不可以一起玩，因為馬丁和艾弗雷德是黑人。兄弟倆不明白為什麼黑人不能跟白人玩，他們的母親說，那是因為有很多白人不懂得其實每一個人都是平等的。馬丁不喜歡這樣，他想要改變這種不平等的情況。

　　馬丁的父親教他怎樣為正確的事挺身而出，據理力爭。長大以後，馬丁經常演講，而且還號召大家上街遊行，抗議不公平的法律。馬丁的演講和遊行終於讓不公平的法律廢除了，他追求公平的夢想改變了這個世界。

Vietnamese

Anh Martin của Tôi

　　Christine là em của Martin Luther King Jr. và người anh khác là Alfred Daniel. Gia đình gọi hai người con trai là M.L. và A.D.

　　Họ sống trong một thành phố có những luật lệ bất công. Các luật lệ này tách rời người da đen với người da trắng.

　　M.L. và A.D. từng chơi chung với những đứa con trai da trắng ở bên kia đường. Một ngày kia, những đứa con trai bên kia đường nói là họ không thể chơi chung với nhau được nữa vì M.L. và A.D. là người da đen. Hai cậu bé không hiểu. Mẹ của họ giải thích rằng nhiều người da trắng không hiểu là mọi người đều như nhau. M.L. muốn thay đổi điều này.

　　Ba của ông chỉ cho ông cách tranh đấu cho những điều đúng. Sau này, M.L. đi diễn thuyết và tổ chức những cuộc tuần hành. Các bài diễn văn và những cuộc tuần hành giúp chấm dứt các luật lệ bất công. Ông đã mơ một giấc mơ làm thay đổi thế giới.

Multilingual Summaries

Korean

우리 형 마틴

크리스틴과 마틴 루터 킹 주니어 그리고 알프레드 다니엘은 남매이며, 그들 가족은 두 형제를 M.L과 A.D로 불렀다.

그들이 사는 마을의 법은 공평하지 않았고 백인과 흑인을 차별했다.

M.L과 A.D는 길 건너편의 백인 아이들과 놀고 있었는데 어느 날 길 건너편의 아이들이 M.L과 A.D가 흑인이라서 더 이상 같이 놀 수 없다고 말했다. 아이들은 이것을 이해하지 못했고 그들의 어머니는 아이들에게 많은 백인들은 모두가 평등하다는 것을 이해하지 못한다고 설명해주었다. M.L은 이것을 바꾸고 싶었다.

M.L의 아버지는 그에게 옳은 것을 옹호하는 방법을 보여주었다. 훗날 M.L은 연설을 하고 행진을 주도했다. 연설과 행진은 불평등한 법을 폐지하는 데 도움이 되었다. 그는 세상을 바꾸는 꿈을 꾸었던 것이다.

Hmong

Kuv Nus Martin

Christine tau yog Martin Luther King Jr. tus muam thiab lawv tus nus Alfred Daniel tus muam. Tsev neeg hu nkawd hu ua M.L. thiab A.D.

Lawv nyob hauv ib lub zos uas tsis muaj txoj cai ncaaj ncees. Txoj cai hais kom cov neeg dub tsis txhob poo nrog cov neeg dawb.

M.L. thiab A.D. ua siv nrog cov me nyuam dawb nyob ze lawv. Muaj ib hnub, cov me nyuam dawb nyob ze lawv hais tias lawv ua siv tsis tau nrog lawv lawm vim M.L. thiab A.D. yog neeg dub. Cov me nyuam tsis to taub. Nkawd niam piav hais tias muaj ntau cov neeg dawb tsis to taub hais tias sawv daws yeej zoo ib yam. M.L. xav muaj qhov no pauv.

Nws txiv tau qhia nws kom sawv khov kho rau tej yam yog. Tom qab ntawd, M.L. tau hais ntau zaj lus thiab tau coj ntau txoj kev sawv mus kev. Tej lus thiab tej kev mus kev pab kom muab tej cai tsis ncaj ncees tso pov tseg. Nws ua ib zaj npau suav uas tau hloov lub ntiaj teb.

Name _____

- **Read** *Ralph Bunche: Quiet Hero* again.
- Use the information in the book to fill in the time line below.
  Write one important event from Ralph Bunche's life for each year shown.
- **Answer** the questions below.

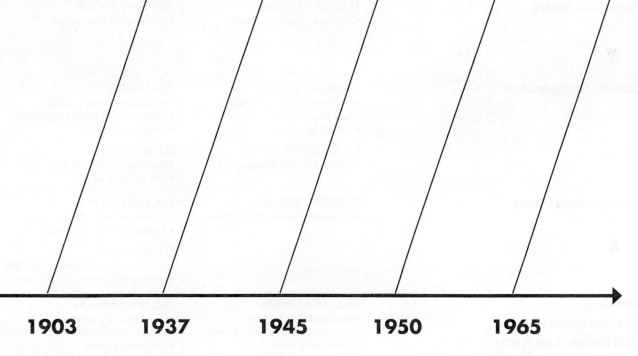

1903   **1937**   **1945**   **1950**   **1965**

Which of these events is the cause of another? Which is the effect?

_____

_____

Family Link

Has anyone in your family ever worked to help people? Ask family members to share what they know about working to help people.

Weekly Resources Guide for English Language Learner Support

For this week's content and language objectives, see p. 185e.

Instructional Strand	Day 1	Day 2
Concept Development/Academic Language	**TEACHER'S EDITION** • Academic Language, p. DI•41 • Concept Development, p. DI•41 • Anchored Talk, pp. 350j—350–351 • Preteach Academic Vocabulary, p. 353a • Concept Talk Video **ELL HANDBOOK** • Hear It, See It, Say It, Use It, pp. xxxvi–xxxvii • ELL Poster Talk, Concept Talk, p. 185c **ELL POSTER 27** • Day 1 Activities	**TEACHER'S EDITION** • Academic Language, p. DI•41 • Concept Development, p. DI•41 • Anchored Talk, p. 354a • Concept Talk Video **ELL HANDBOOK** • ELL Poster Talk, Concept Talk, p. 185c • Concept Talk Video Routine, p. 477 **ELL POSTER 27** • Day 2 Activities
Phonics and Spelling	**TEACHER'S EDITION** • Phonics and Spelling, p. DI•45	**TEACHER'S EDITION** • Phonics and Spelling, p. DI•45
Listening Comprehension	**TEACHER'S EDITION** • Modified Read Aloud, p. DI•44 • Read Aloud, p. 351b • Concept Talk Video **ELL HANDBOOK** • Concept Talk Video Routine, p. 477	**TEACHER'S EDITION** • Modified Read Aloud, p. DI•44 • AudioText of *Jim Thorpe's Bright Path* • Concept Talk Video **ELL HANDBOOK** • AudioText CD Routine, p. 477 • K-W-L Chart, p. 480
Reading Comprehension	**TEACHER'S EDITION** • Preteach Fact and Opinion, p. DI•46	**TEACHER'S EDITION** • Reteach Fact and Opinion, p. DI•46 • Frontloading Reading, p. DI•47 **ELL HANDBOOK** • Picture It! Skill Instruction, pp. 186–186a • Multilingual Summaries, pp. 187–189
Vocabulary **Basic and Lesson Vocabulary** **Word Analysis: Latin Roots**	**TEACHER'S EDITION** • Basic Vocabulary, p. DI•42 • Preteach Lesson Vocabulary, p. DI•42 • Latin Roots, p. DI•45 **ELL HANDBOOK** • Word Cards, p. 185 • ELL Vocabulary Routine, p. 471 **ELL POSTER 27** • Day 1 Activities	**TEACHER'S EDITION** • Basic Vocabulary, p. DI•42 • Reteach Lesson Vocabulary, p. DI•43 • Latin Roots, p. DI•45 **ELL HANDBOOK** • Word Cards, p. 185 • Multilingual Vocabulary List, p. 431 **ELL POSTER 27** • Day 2 Activities
Grammar and Conventions	**TEACHER'S EDITION** • Preteach Capitalization and Abbreviations, p. DI•49	**TEACHER'S EDITION** • Reteach Capitalization and Abbreviations, p. DI•49
Writing	**TEACHER'S EDITION** • Varying Sentence Beginnings, p. DI•50 • Introduce Review, pp. 353e–353f	**TEACHER'S EDITION** • Writing Trait: Organization, pp. 363d–363e

Day 3	Day 4	Day 5
TEACHER'S EDITION • Academic Language, p. DI•41 • Concept Development, p. DI•41 • Anchored Talk, p. 364a • Concept Talk Video **ELL HANDBOOK** • ELL Poster Talk, Concept Talk, p. 185c **ELL POSTER 27** • Day 3 Activities	**TEACHER'S EDITION** • Academic Language, p. DI•41 • Concept Development, p. DI•41 • Anchored Talk, p. 376a • Concept Talk Video **ELL HANDBOOK** • ELL Poster Talk, Concept Talk, p. 185c **ELL POSTER 27** • Day 4 Activities	**TEACHER'S EDITION** • Academic Language, p. DI•41 • Concept Development, p. DI•41 • Concept Talk Video **ELL HANDBOOK** • ELL Poster Talk, Concept Talk, p. 185c **ELL POSTER 27** • Day 5 Activities
		TEACHER'S EDITION • Phonics and Spelling, p. DI•45
ELL HANDBOOK • Phonics Transition Lesson, pp. 284–285, 291–292	**ELL HANDBOOK** • Phonics Transition Lesson, pp. 284–285, 291–292	
TEACHER'S EDITION • AudioText of *Jim Thorpe's Bright Path* • Concept Talk Video **ELL HANDBOOK** • AudioText CD Routine, p. 477	**TEACHER'S EDITION** • Concept Talk Video	**TEACHER'S EDITION** • Concept Talk Video
TEACHER'S EDITION • Sheltered Reading, p. DI•47 **ELL HANDBOOK** • Multilingual Summaries, pp. 187–189	**TEACHER'S EDITION** • ELL/ELD Reader Guided Reading, p. DI•48 **ELL HANDBOOK** • ELL Study Guide, p. 190	**TEACHER'S EDITION** • ELL/ELD Reader Guided Reading, p. DI•48 **ELL HANDBOOK** • ELL Study Guide, p. 190
		TEACHER'S EDITION • Latin Roots *dur, ject*, p. 381i
ELL HANDBOOK • High-Frequency Words Activity Bank, p. 446 **ELL POSTER 27** • Day 3 Activities	**ELL HANDBOOK** • High-Frequency Words Activity Bank, p. 446	**ELL HANDBOOK** • High-Frequency Words Activity Bank, p. 446
TEACHER'S EDITION • Grammar Jammer **ELL HANDBOOK** • Grammar Transition Lesson, pp. 315, 320–321 • Grammar Jammer Routine, p. 478	**TEACHER'S EDITION** • Grammar Jammer **ELL HANDBOOK** • Grammar Transition Lesson, pp. 315, 320–321	**TEACHER'S EDITION** • Grammar Jammer **ELL HANDBOOK** • Grammar Transition Lesson, pp. 315, 320–321
TEACHER'S EDITION • Let's Write It!, p. 374–375 • Writer's Craft: Vary Sentence Beginnings, pp. 375a–375b	**TEACHER'S EDITION** • Revising Strategy, pp. 381d–381e	**TEACHER'S EDITION** • Capitalization and Abbreviations, pp. 381p–381q

Question of the Week
How can our abilities influence our dreams and goals?

Throughout the week, use the ELL Poster to help students produce and comprehend language, understand the concept, and build English vocabulary. Use the Question of the Week and other questions to help students share ideas in pairs, small groups, or the large group. Sample questions are shown, with examples of possible responses by students.

ELL Poster 27

Weekly Concept and Language Goals

• Identify challenges people may face

• Understand how abilities affect goals

• Discuss people who have faced and overcome challenges

By the end of the lesson, students should be able to talk about and write sentences about abilities, challenges, and goals.

Daily Team Talk

Day 1	Day 2	Day 3	Day 4	Day 5
After Day 1 activities on Poster, ask questions such as	After Day 2 activity on Poster, ask questions such as	After Day 3 activity on Poster, ask questions such as	After Day 4 activity on Poster, ask questions such as	After Day 5 activity on Poster, ask questions such as
In the poster picture, what ability does the runner at the front have?	*In the poster picture, how does the girl's ability to run affect her goals?*	*What challenges do you think the girl will face in reaching her goal of becoming an Olympic runner?*	*In the story* Jim Thorpe's Bright Path, *Jim Thorpe wants to be a football player. What challenge does he face, and how does he overcome it?*	*What ability do you have? How does this ability affect your goals?*
Beginning She runs.	**Beginning** She wants to run.	**Beginning** Much practice.	**Beginning** He is small.	**Beginning** I play the guitar.
Intermediate She can run fast.	**Intermediate** She wants to be a good runner.	**Intermediate** She will have to run and practice a lot.	**Intermediate** He is too small. He shows he is fast.	**Intermediate** I tell great jokes. I like to make people laugh.
Advanced The girl can run fast. She beats the other girls.	**Advanced** The girl wants to keep practicing and be a great runner.	**Advanced** The girl will have to practice a lot. Practicing will take a lot of time.	**Advanced** Jim is too little to play football, but he shows he is fast and strong.	**Advanced** I am good at science, so maybe I will become a scientist.
Advanced High The girl at the front can run longer and faster than the other girls.	**Advanced High** The girl dreams of being a runner in the Olympics. She might not dream about going to the Olympics if she did not have the ability to run fast.	**Advanced High** The girl will have to practice every day if she wants to be an Olympic runner. She will also have to be faster than many other runners.	**Advanced High** The coach thinks Jim Thorpe is too little to play football. Jim shows how fast and tough he is, and the coach lets him play on the team.	**Advanced High** One ability I have is I play baseball well. This could help me be a professional baseball player someday.

Teacher's Edition pages 350j–381q

See the support for English language learners throughout the lesson, including ELL strategies and scaffolded activities at points of use.

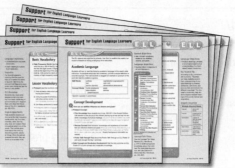

Teacher's Edition pages DI•41–DI•50

Differentiated Instruction for English language learners provides daily group activities that "frontload," or preteach, core instruction.

ELL Handbook pp. 185a–190

Find additional lesson materials that support the core lesson and the ELL instructional pages.

Poster 27

ELL Reader 4.6.2

ELD Reader 4.6.2

Concept Literacy Reader

ELD, ELL Reader Teaching Guide

Concept Literacy Reader Teaching Guide

Technology

Online Teacher's Edition Use the digital version of the core Teacher's Edition for planning and instruction.

eReaders
This week's ELL and ELD Readers and Concept Literacy Reader are also available in digital format.

This Week's Content and Language Objectives by Strand

Concept Development/ Academic Language How can our abilities influence our dreams and goals?	**Content Objective** • Use concept vocabulary related to our abilities, dreams, and goals. **Language Objectives** • Express ideas in response to art and discussion. • Express ideas in response to new academic vocabulary.
Phonics and Spelling Prefixes *mis-, non-, re-*	**Content Objective** • Identify prefixes in words. **Language Objective** • Apply phonics and decoding skills to vocabulary.
Listening Comprehension Modified Read Aloud: "A Big Hurdle!"	**Content Objective** • Monitor and adjust oral comprehension. **Language Objectives** • Discuss oral passages. • Use accessible language and learn new language.
Reading Comprehension Fact and Opinion	**Content Objectives** • Use grade-level learning strategies to distinguish between facts and opinions. • Make and adjust predictions. **Language Objectives** • Retell facts and opinions from a reading. • Discuss evidence for facts and opinions. • Write facts and opinions from personal experience. • Read grade-level text with expression.
Vocabulary Basic and Lesson Vocabulary	**Language Objectives** • Understand and use basic vocabulary. • Learn meanings of grade-level vocabulary. • Produce drawings, phrases, and short sentences to show understanding of Lesson Vocabulary.
Word Analysis Latin Roots	**Content Objective** • Identify and define Latin roots in words. **Language Objective** • Discuss meanings of Latin roots.
Grammar and Conventions Capitalization and Abbreviations	**Content Objective** • Identify and use correct capitalization and abbreviations. **Language Objectives** • Recognize which months have abbreviations. • Write sentences using correct capitalization and abbreviations for days and months.
Writing Varying Sentence Beginnings	**Content Objective** • Identify and use a variety of sentence beginnings. **Language Objective** • Write a paragraph, varying sentence beginnings.

Word Cards for Vocabulary Activities

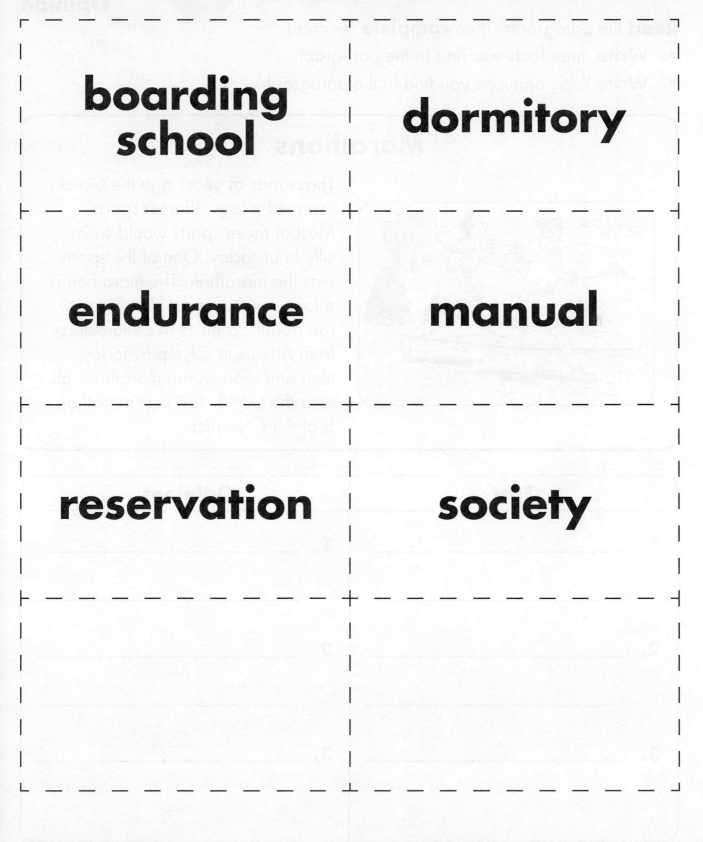

boarding school

dormitory

endurance

manual

reservation

society

Teacher Note: Beginning Teach two to three words. **Intermediate** Teach three to four words. **Advanced** Teach four to five words. **Advanced High** Teach all words.

Name _____

Read the paragraph. Then **complete** the chart.

- **Write** three facts you find in the paragraph.
- **Write** three opinions you find in the paragraph.

Marathons

Thousands of years ago the Greeks invented many different sports. Most of those sports would seem silly to us today. One of the sports was the marathon. The marathon is a long, exciting race. Greek men ran about 26 miles (42 kilometers) from Athens to Olympia. Today, men and women run marathons all over the world. The best marathon is at the Olympics.

Facts	Opinions
1. _____ _____	1. _____ _____
2. _____ _____	2. _____ _____
3. _____	3. _____

Fact and Opinion

Use this lesson to supplement or replace the skill lesson on page 351c
of the Teacher's Edition. Display the Skill Points (at right) and share them
with students.

Teach/Model

Beginning Say: *Running is the best way to exercise. I run three miles every day.*
Ask students to identify the fact (the second sentence) and the opinion (the first
sentence). Ask: *How do you know the second sentence is a fact?* (It can be
proven true.)

Intermediate Write and read aloud: *A marathon is 26 miles long. I think that is
too far to run.* Have volunteers label the fact (the first sentence) and the opinion
(the second sentence), circle the clue words in the opinion (I think, too far), and
explain how they can prove the fact.

Advanced Say: *One mile is 5,280 feet. Is this a fact?* (yes) *How can we prove it?*
(Look in a reference book or on the Internet; ask an expert.) *What is your opinion
about running a mile?* Have each student share his or her opinion and one reason
to support it.

Advanced High Explain a relay race and have four volunteers demonstrate.
Ask students to tell a fact and an opinion about a relay race. Encourage them to
use what they know and what they saw in the demonstration.

Then distribute copies of Picture It! page 186.

- Have students look at the picture and describe what is happening. Then read the
  paragraph aloud.
- Ask: *Which sentences in the paragraph tell opinions?*
- Review the Skill Points with students.
- Have students find support for an opinion in the paragraph.

Practice

Read aloud the directions on page 186. Have volunteers reread the paragraph
aloud. Then have students use the picture and the paragraph as they fill in
the chart.

Beginning Students can say facts and opinions from the paragraph before
writing them in the chart. Provide help with writing and spelling English words.

Intermediate Students can first orally answer and then write their answers on
the lines in the chart. Provide help with writing.

Advanced Students can write their answers on the lines and then check their
answers by comparing them with a partner's.

Advanced High Students can write their answers on the lines and then orally
explain how they decided which sentences were facts and which were opinions.

Answers for page 186: *Facts:* 1. Greeks invented many different sports.
2. Greek men ran 26 miles from Athens to Olympia. 3. Today, men and women run
marathons all over the world. *Opinions:* 1. Most of these sports would seem silly
to us today. 2. The marathon is a long, exciting race. 3. The best marathon is at
the Olympics.

Skill Points

- ✔ A **fact** can be proven true or false.
  You can prove a fact by doing
  research.
- ✔ An **opinion** cannot be proven true
  or false, but it should be supported.
  A valid opinion is well supported. A
  faulty opinion is not.
- ✔ Look for clue words that indicate an
  opinion. Examples include adjectives
  such as *best, beautiful,* and *silly* and
  verbs such as *should* and *like.*

Multilingual Summaries

Jim Thorpe's Bright Path

Jim Thorpe and his twin brother, Charlie, were born on an Indian reservation in 1887. Jim and Charlie played outdoors. Jim was always a faster runner than Charlie.

When the twins were six years old, their father sent them to boarding school. Jim hated being inside all day. Charlie encouraged Jim to keep studying. In their third year at school, Charlie got sick and died.

Jim did not want to go back to school. His father said he had to. Jim ran away. His father sent him to another school. At his new school, Jim was on the track team. He learned to play football. Later, he went to an Indian college. He was the best athlete on the track team, and he played football. Charlie had been right. Continuing his education helped Jim Thorpe find his path in life.

Spanish

El futuro brillante de Jim Thorpe

Jim Thorpe y su hermano gemelo Charlie nacieron en una reserva indígena en 1887. Jim y Charlie jugaban al aire libre. Jim siempre corría más rápido que su hermano.

Cuando los hermanos tenían seis años, sus padres los enviaron a un internado. A Jim no le gustaba estar en el interior de la escuela todo el día. Charlie lo animaba para que siguiera estudiando. Al tercer año de estar en la escuela, Charlie se enfermó y murió.

Jim no quería regresar a la escuela. Su padre le dijo que tenía que ir. Jim se escapó. Su padre lo envió a otra escuela. En la nueva escuela, Jim participó en el equipo de atletismo. También aprendió a jugar fútbol americano. Más tarde fue a una universidad indígena. Él era el mejor atleta del equipo de atletismo y también jugó fútbol americano. Charlie había tenido razón. Continuar con su educación había ayudado a Jim a encontrar su camino en la vida.

Multilingual Summaries

Chinese

吉姆・索普的光明之路

　　1887 年，吉姆　索普和他的雙胞胎兄弟查理在印第安保護區出生。吉姆和查理經常在戶外玩，每次他們比賽跑步，吉姆總是跑得比查理快。

　　6 歲那一年，這對雙胞胎的父親把他們送到寄宿學校唸書。吉姆不喜歡整天都待在教室裡，不過查理一直鼓勵他要好好唸書。在寄宿學校唸書的第三年，查理生病然後就死掉了。

　　吉姆不想再回到學校了，但是他父親說他一定得回去上學。吉姆逃跑不去學校，於是他父親又把他送到另一所學校去。在新學校裡，吉姆參加了田徑隊，還學會踢足球。之後他進了印地安大學，他是學校田徑隊裡最優秀的運動員，他也會踢足球。查理是對的，吉姆　索普因為繼續唸書，所以才能找到他人生的方向和道路。

Vietnamese

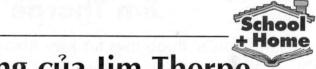

Con Đường Tươi Sáng của Jim Thorpe

　　Jim Thorpe và người anh sinh đôi của mình là Charlie sanh ra trong một khu của người Mỹ Da Đỏ vào năm 1887. Jim và Charlie chơi ở ngoài trời. Jim lúc nào cũng chạy nhanh hơn Charlie.

　　Khi hai anh em sinh đôi này được sáu tuổi, ba của họ đưa họ đi học trường nội trú. Jim ghét phải ngồi trong lớp cả ngày. Charlie khuyến khích Jim cứ tiếp tục học. Vào năm học thứ ba, Charlie ngã bệnh và qua đời.

　　Jim không muốn trở lại trường. Ba của cậu bảo cậu phải đi. Jim bỏ trốn. Ba của cậu đưa cậu đi học một trường khác. Ở trường mới, Jim được vào đội điền kinh. Cậu học chơi đá bóng bầu dục. Sau đó cậu đi học ở trường đại học của người Mỹ Da Đỏ. Cậu là vận động viên giỏi nhất trong đội điền kinh, và cậu cũng chơi đá bóng bầu dục. Charlie nói đúng. Tiếp tục việc giáo dục của mình đã giúp Jim Thorpe tìm được đường đi cho mình trong đời sống.

Multilingual Summaries

Korean

짐 토프의 밝은 미래

짐 토프와 그의 쌍둥이 형제 찰리는 1887년 인디언 보호구역에서 태어났다. 짐과 찰리는 집 밖에서 놀았고 짐은 늘 찰리보다 빨리 뛰었다.

쌍둥이 형제가 여섯 살이 되었을 때 아버지는 그들을 기숙 학교에 보냈다. 짐은 온종일 학교 안에만 있는 것이 싫었지만 찰리는 짐에게 계속 공부하도록 격려했다. 그들이 삼학년이 되었을 때 찰리는 병이 들어 죽고 말았다.

짐은 학교로 돌아가고 싶지 않았지만 아버지는 그래야만 한다고 말했다. 짐은 도망쳤고 다른 학교로 보내졌다. 새 학교에서 짐은 육상 팀에 가입했고 풋볼을 배웠다. 나중에 그는 인디언 대학에 들어갔고 육상팀의 최고 선수가 되었으며 풋볼도 했다. 찰리가 옳았다. 교육을 계속 받은 덕분에 짐 토프는 인생에서 자신의 길을 찾을 수 있었던 것이다.

Hmong

Jim Thorpe' Txoj Kev Kaj

Jim Thorpe' thiab nws tus kwv ntxaib Charlie tau yug nyob hauv cov neeg Qhab ib thaj chaw hauv xyoo 1887. Jim thiab Charlie ua siv nraum zoov. Jim yeej ib txwm dhia nrawm dua Charlie.

Thaum ob tug ntxaib tau muaj rau xyoo, nkawd txiv xa nkawd mus kawm ntawv deb. Jim tsis nyiam nyob hauv tsev ib hnub. Charlie txhawb kom Jim rau siab kawm ntawv. Thaum xyoo peb ntawm nkawd txoj kev kawm ntawv, Charlie tau muaj mob thiab taut as sim neej.

Jim tsis xav rov qab mus kawm ntawv. Nws txiv tau hais tias nws yuav tsum mus. Jim tau khiav tawm ntawm nws lub tsev mus. Nws txiv xa nws mus rau lwm lub tsev kawm ntawv. Nyob hauv nws lub tsev kawm ntawv tshiab, Jim tau nrog ib pab tub ntxhais sib xeem khiav. Nws kawm ua siv football. Tom qab ntawd, nws mus kawm ntawv hauv ib lub tsev kawm ntawv qib siab Qhab. Nws yog tus khiav nrawm tshaj hauv lawv pab, thiab nws ua siv football. Charlie yeej hais yog lawm. Txoj kev rau siab kawm ntawv pab tau Jim Thorpe' nrhiav tau nws txoj hau kev hauv lub neej no.

 ELL Handbook

Name _____

- **Read** *The Carlisle Indian School* again.
- In the Venn diagram below, **write** descriptions of the children *before* going to the Carlisle School. Then **write** how things were different *after* going to the Carlisle School. Finally, **write** your ideas about what was the *same* for the children before and after.

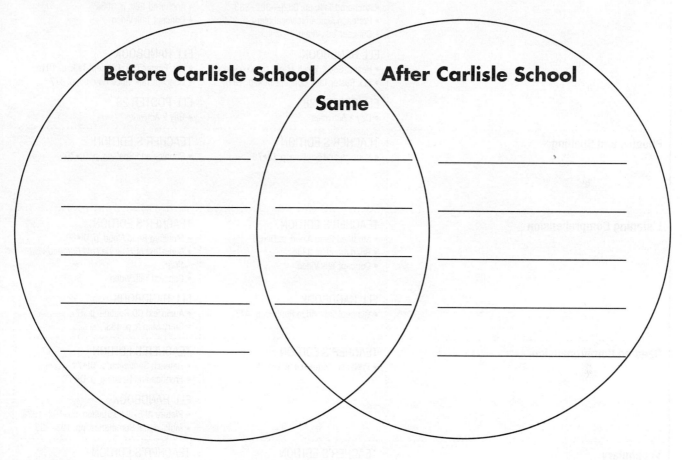

Before Carlisle School

Same

After Carlisle School

Family Link

Ask the people in your family what they think about forcing children to change the way they dress, the way they wear their hair, and the way they think. Ask them if they think sending Native American children to schools such as the Carlisle School was good or bad for the children.

For this week's content and language objectives, see p. 191e.

Instructional Strand	Day 1	Day 2
Concept Development/Academic Language	TEACHER'S EDITION • Academic Language, p. DI•66 • Concept Development, p. DI•66 • Anchored Talk, pp. 382j—382–383 • Preteach Academic Vocabulary, p. 385a • Concept Talk Video ELL HANDBOOK • Hear It, See It, Say It, Use It, pp. xxxvi–xxxvii • ELL Poster Talk, Concept Talk, p. 191c ELL POSTER 28 • Day 1 Activities	TEACHER'S EDITION • Academic Language, p. DI•66 • Concept Development, p. DI•66 • Anchored Talk, p. 386a • Concept Talk Video ELL HANDBOOK • ELL Poster Talk, Concept Talk, p. 191c • Concept Talk Video Routine, p. 477 ELL POSTER 28 • Day 2 Activities
Phonics and Spelling	TEACHER'S EDITION • Phonics and Spelling, p. DI•70	TEACHER'S EDITION • Phonics and Spelling, p. DI•70
Listening Comprehension	TEACHER'S EDITION • Modified Read Aloud, p. DI•69 • Read Aloud, p. 383b • Concept Talk Video ELL HANDBOOK • Concept Talk Video Routine, p. 477	TEACHER'S EDITION • Modified Read Aloud, p. DI•69 • AudioText of *How Tia Lola Came to ~~Visit~~ Stay* • Concept Talk Video ELL HANDBOOK • AudioText CD Routine, p. 477 • Story Map A, p. 483
Reading Comprehension	TEACHER'S EDITION • Preteach Sequence, p. DI•71	TEACHER'S EDITION • Reteach Sequence, p. DI•71 • Frontloading Reading, p. DI•72 ELL HANDBOOK • Picture It! Skill Instruction, pp. 192–192a • Multilingual Summaries, pp. 193–195
Vocabulary **Basic and Lesson Vocabulary**	TEACHER'S EDITION • Basic Vocabulary, p. DI•67 • Preteach Lesson Vocabulary, p. DI•67 ELL HANDBOOK • Word Cards, p. 191 • ELL Vocabulary Routine, p. 471 ELL POSTER 28 • Day 1 Activities	TEACHER'S EDITION • Basic Vocabulary, p. DI•67 • Reteach Lesson Vocabulary, p. DI•68 ELL HANDBOOK • Word Cards, p. 191 • Multilingual Vocabulary List, p. 431 ELL POSTER 28 • Day 2 Activities
Grammar and Conventions	TEACHER'S EDITION • Preteach Commas, p. DI•74	TEACHER'S EDITION • Reteach Commas, p. DI•74
Writing	TEACHER'S EDITION • Writing with Vivid Words, p. DI•75 • Introduce Skit, pp. 385e–385f	TEACHER'S EDITION • Writing Trait: Organization, pp. 395d–395e

This symbol indicates leveled instruction to address language proficiency levels.

Day 3	Day 4	Day 5
TEACHER'S EDITION • Academic Language, p. DI•66 • Concept Development, p. DI•66 • Anchored Talk, p. 396a • Concept Talk Video **ELL HANDBOOK** • ELL Poster Talk, Concept Talk, p. 191c **ELL POSTER 28** • Day 3 Activities	**TEACHER'S EDITION** • Academic Language, p. DI•66 • Concept Development, p. DI•66 • Anchored Talk, p. 408a • Concept Talk Video **ELL HANDBOOK** • ELL Poster Talk, Concept Talk, p. 191c **ELL POSTER 28** • Day 4 Activities	**TEACHER'S EDITION** • Academic Language, p. DI•66 • Concept Development, p. DI•66 • Concept Talk Video **ELL HANDBOOK** • ELL Poster Talk, Concept Talk, p. 191c **ELL POSTER 28** • Day 5 Activities
		TEACHER'S EDITION • Phonics and Spelling, p. DI•70
ELL HANDBOOK • Phonics Transition Lesson, pp. 287, 294	**ELL HANDBOOK** • Phonics Transition Lesson, pp. 287, 294	
TEACHER'S EDITION • AudioText of *How Tia Lola Came to ~~Visit~~ Stay* • Concept Talk Video **ELL HANDBOOK** • AudioText CD Routine, p. 477	**TEACHER'S EDITION** • Concept Talk Video	**TEACHER'S EDITION** • Concept Talk Video
TEACHER'S EDITION • Sheltered Reading, p. DI•72 **ELL HANDBOOK** • Multilingual Summaries, pp. 193–195	**TEACHER'S EDITION** • ELL/ELD Reader Guided Reading, p. DI•73 **ELL HANDBOOK** • ELL Study Guide, p. 196	**TEACHER'S EDITION** • ELL/ELD Reader Guided Reading, p. DI•73 **ELL HANDBOOK** • ELL Study Guide, p. 196
		TEACHER'S EDITION • French Word Origins, p. 413i
ELL HANDBOOK • High-Frequency Words Activity Bank, p. 446 **ELL POSTER 28** • Day 3 Activities	**ELL HANDBOOK** • High-Frequency Words Activity Bank, p. 446	**ELL HANDBOOK** • High-Frequency Words Activity Bank, p. 446
TEACHER'S EDITION • Grammar Jammer **ELL HANDBOOK** • Grammar Transition Lesson, pp. 346, 359 • Grammar Jammer Routine, p. 478	**TEACHER'S EDITION** • Grammar Jammer **ELL HANDBOOK** • Grammar Transition Lesson, pp. 346, 359	**TEACHER'S EDITION** • Grammar Jammer **ELL HANDBOOK** • Grammar Transition Lesson, pp. 346, 359
TEACHER'S EDITION • Let's Write It!, p. 406–407 • Writing Trait: Word Choice, pp. 407a–407b	**TEACHER'S EDITION** • Revising Strategy, pp. 413d–413e	**TEACHER'S EDITION** • Commas, pp. 413p–413q

Question of the Week

How can one person's view of the world affect others?

Throughout the week, use the ELL Poster to help students produce and comprehend language, understand the concept, and build English vocabulary. Use the Question of the Week and other questions to help students share ideas in pairs, small groups, or the large group. Sample questions are shown, with examples of possible responses by students.

Weekly Concept and Language Goals

• Tell how one person's actions can affect others

• Explain how art can affect people

• Describe ways people view the world

By the end of the lesson, students should be able to talk about and write sentences about people influencing one another to make changes.

ELL Poster 28

Daily Team Talk

Day 1	Day 2	Day 3	Day 4	Day 5
After Day 1 activities on Poster, ask questions such as *How do you think the artist who is painting the mural in the poster picture views the world?*	After Day 2 activity on Poster, ask questions such as *Why do you think the artist is painting a mural that shows his view of the world?*	After Day 3 activity on Poster, ask questions such as *In the poster picture, how does the mural affect the people in the subway station?*	After Day 4 activity on Poster, ask questions such as *In the story* How Tía Lola Came to ~~Visit~~ Stay, *how does Tía Lola's view of the world affect others?*	After Day 5 activity on Poster, ask questions such as *How have your actions affected another person?*
Beginning It is nice. **Intermediate** He thinks it is a nice place. People help others. **Advanced** The artist thinks people are friendly and help one another. **Advanced High** The artist views the world as a kind place where people are nice and help one another.	**Beginning** He wants to show them. **Intermediate** He wants people to see his view. **Advanced** The artist hopes his view of the world might change people. **Advanced High** The artist is painting a mural to share his view of the world with others. He hopes his mural will make the world a better place.	**Beginning** They like it. **Intermediate** They want to help people. **Advanced** The people start helping one another, like the people in the mural. **Advanced High** The people in the mural are helping one another. When the people in the subway station see the mural, they start helping one another too.	**Beginning** They like her. **Intermediate** She does things to make people happy. **Advanced** She makes the world bright and happy and brings people together. **Advanced High** Tía Lola likes to make the world bright and cheerful. Her actions help bring people closer together.	**Beginning** Helping my mom. **Intermediate** I help my mom carry bags. **Advanced** I helped my mom carry in groceries when she was tired. It made her happy. **Advanced High** My mom was tired, so I helped her carry in groceries. My help made her feel happy.

This Week's Materials

Teacher's Edition pages 382j–413q

See the support for English language learners throughout the lesson, including ELL strategies and scaffolded activities at points of use.

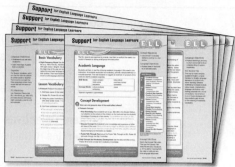

Teacher's Edition pages DI•66–DI•75

Differentiated Instruction for English language learners provides daily group activities that "frontload," or preteach, core instruction.

ELL Handbook pp. 191a–196

Find additional lesson materials that support the core lesson and the ELL instructional pages.

ELL Poster 28

ELL Reader 4.6.3

ELD Reader 4.6.3

Concept Literacy Reader

ELD, ELL Reader Teaching Guide

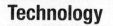

Concept Literacy Reader Teaching Guide

Technology

Online Teacher's Edition Use the digital version of the core Teacher's Edition for planning and instruction.

eReaders
This week's ELL and ELD Readers and Concept Literacy Reader are also available in digital format.

This Week's Content and Language Objectives by Strand

Concept Development/ Academic Language How can one person's view of the world affect others?	**Content Objective** • Use concept vocabulary related to coming to a new culture. **Language Objectives** • Express ideas in response to art and discussion. • Express ideas in response to new academic vocabulary.
Phonics and Spelling Suffixes –less, -ness	**Content Objectives** • Learn the relationship between the /k/ sound and the letters k, ck, cr, and c. • Identify suffixes in words. **Language Objectives** • Apply phonics and decoding skills to vocabulary. • Recognize the relationship between the sound /k/ and the letters k, ck, cr, and c.
Listening Comprehension Modified Read Aloud: "My Tío Juan"	**Content Objective** • Monitor and adjust oral comprehension. **Language Objectives** • Discuss oral passages. • Use a graphic organizer to take notes.
Reading Comprehension Sequence	**Content Objectives** • Order the sequence of events in a text. • Monitor and adjust comprehension. **Language Objectives** • Retell sequence from a reading. • Discuss following directions in a text. • Discuss evidence for sequence in a text. • Read grade-level text with expression.
Vocabulary Basic and Lesson Vocabulary	**Language Objectives** • Understand and use basic vocabulary. • Learn meanings of grade-level vocabulary. • Produce drawings, phrases, and short sentences to show understanding of Lesson Vocabulary.
Grammar and Conventions Commas	**Content Objective** • Correctly use commas in a series, in direct address, and after introductory phrases. **Language Objectives** • Speak using commas correctly. • Write phrases and sentences using commas correctly.
Writing Writing with Vivid words	**Content Objective** • Identify vivid words in a text. **Language Objectives** • Write paragraphs using vivid words and details to describe. • Share feedback for editing and revising.

Word Cards for Vocabulary Activities

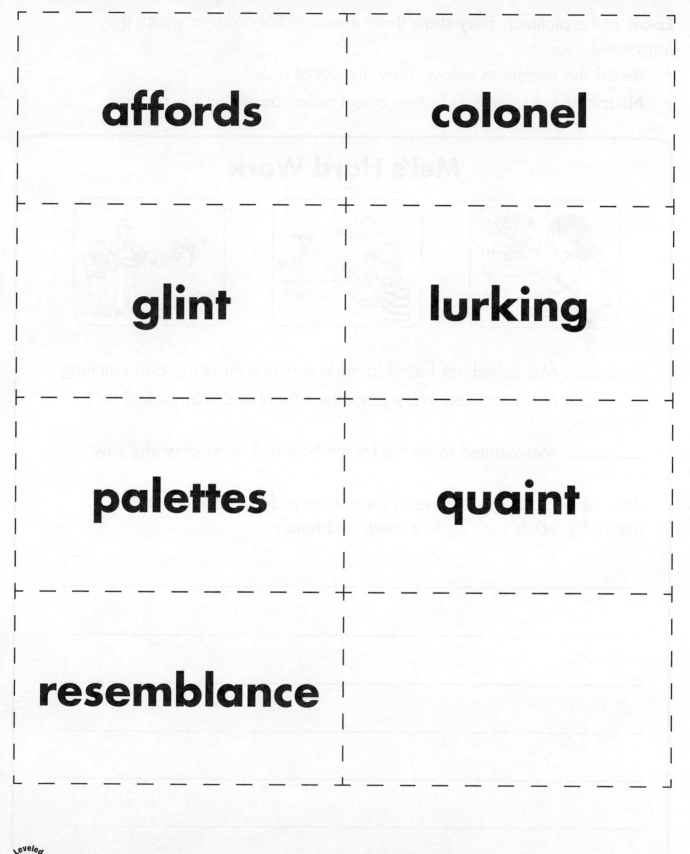

affords

colonel

glint

lurking

palettes

quaint

resemblance

Teacher Note: Beginning Teach three to four words. **Intermediate** Teach four to six words. **Advanced** Teach six to seven words. **Advanced High** Teach all words.

Look at the pictures. They show three events in the order in which they happened.

- **Read** the sentences below. They are out of order.
- **Number** the sentences in the correct order, based on the pictures.

Mei's Hard Work

_____ Mei asked her friend Jared to practice throwing and catching.

_____ Mei practiced every day after school and was picked for the team.

_____ Mei wanted to try out for the baseball team after she saw the flyer.

Rewrite the sentences above in the correct order, using time-order transition words such as *first, next,* and *finally.*

_____

_____

_____

_____

_____

_____

Sequence

Use this lesson to supplement or replace the skill lesson on page 383c of the Teacher's Edition. Display the Skill Points (at right) and share them with students.

Teach/Model

Write these sentences: *She swings her bat. Greta grabs her bat and walks to the plate. After she hits the ball, Greta runs to first base. The pitcher throws the ball. Greta is safe.*

Beginning Read the sentences aloud. Say: *These sentences are out of order.* Have students tell how to rearrange the sentences. Together reread the sentences in the correct sequence.

Intermediate Read the sentences aloud. Ask: *Are these sentences in the right order?* (no) Ask students to write the sentences in the correct sequence. Then have them reread the sentences aloud.

Advanced Ask volunteers to read the sentences. Have students write the sentences in the correct order using clue words. Then have them exchange sentences with a partner to check the sequence.

Advanced High Ask students to think of a sequence of at least four events that happened that morning at home or school. Have them write sentences using clue words to tell the sequence of events.

Then distribute copies of Picture It! page 192.

- Have students look at the pictures and tell what is happening.
- Read the paragraph aloud. Ask: *What happens first in the story?* (Mei wants to try out for the baseball team after she sees the flyer.)
- Review the Skill Points with students.
- Have students discuss the sequence of events in the story.

Practice

Read aloud the directions on page 192. Have volunteers reread each of the sentences aloud. Then have students use the pictures and the story as they identify the sequence of events.

Beginning Students can point to each picture as you describe what is happening and then number the sentences in the correct sequence before writing them on the lines in that order. Remind students to begin their sentences with the words *first, next,* and *finally*.

Intermediate Students can number the sentences in the correct sequence and then write them on the lines in that order. Remind students to use the words *first, next,* and *finally*.

Advanced Students can number the sentences and then write them on the lines in the correct sequence. Students can check their answers by comparing them to the numbered sentences and making sure they used time-order words correctly.

Advanced High Students can number the sentences, write them on the lines in the correct order, and then orally explain how they recognized the sequence of events.

Answers for page 192: 2, 3, 1

Skill Points

✔ The **sequence** is the order in which events happen in a story.

✔ Sometimes the sequence is shown by clue words such as *first, next, after,* and *finally*.

Multilingual Summaries

How Tía Lola Came to ~~Visit~~ Stay

Miguel and Juanita have moved to Vermont with Mami, their mother. Mami's aunt, Tía Lola, comes to visit. She tells stories. Some nights they all explore the old house they live in.

Miguel wants his baseball team to practice in the field behind the house. Their landlord agrees. They name Tía Lola as the team manager.

One day Tía Lola paints the house purple. Mami is worried that the landlord will make them leave. He tells them to repaint the house or leave in three weeks.

Tía Lola has a plan. She makes uniforms for the baseball team. She also makes a flag with the team's name. The team is named for the landlord. When he sees the flag, he smiles and plays ball with the team.

Cómo tía Lola llega para quedarse

Miguel y Juanita se han mudado para Vermont con Mami. La tía de Mami, tía Lola, llega de visita. Ella cuenta cuentos. Algunas noches todos exploran la vieja casa donde viven.

Miguel quiere que su equipo de béisbol practique en el campo detrás de la casa. El dueño de la casa les da permiso. Ellos nombran a la tía Lola como representante del equipo.

Un día, tía Lola pinta la casa de morado. Mami está preocupada de que el dueño los vaya a echar de la casa. Él les dice que tienen que volver a pintar la casa o abandonarla en tres semanas.

Tía Lola tiene un plan. Hace uniformes para el equipo de béisbol. También hace una bandera con el nombre el equipo. El equipo lleva el nombre del dueño de la casa. Cuando él ve la bandera, sonríe y juega pelota con el equipo.

Multilingual Summaries

蒂亞‧洛拉的妙計

馬吉爾和嘉妮塔跟著媽咪搬到佛蒙特，媽咪是他們的母親。媽咪的姑母蒂亞‧洛拉來探望他們。蒂亞‧洛拉會講故事給他們聽，有時晚上大家還會在自己居住的舊房子裡探險。

馬吉爾想帶他的棒球隊到房子後面的空地練習，房東同意了。於是球隊就請蒂亞‧洛拉來當棒球隊領隊。

有一天，蒂亞‧洛拉突然把房子漆成紫色。媽咪擔心房東會生氣，把他們趕出去。結果房東叫他們把房子漆回原來的顏色，否則三個禮拜以後就得搬家。

蒂亞‧洛拉想到一個好辦法。她幫棒球隊隊員做制服，又做了一面旗子上面有棒球隊的隊名，這個隊名是用房東名字取的。當房東看到這面旗子的時候，他笑了，後來還和大家一起打棒球。

Làm Thế Nào mà Tia Lola Đã Đến Ở

Miguel và Juanita dọn đến Vermont với Mami, mẹ của chúng. Cô của Mami, Tia Lola, đến thăm. Bà kể chuyện. Có nhiều đêm họ đi thám hiểm căn nhà cổ xưa là nơi họ đang sống.

Miguel muốn đội bóng chày của cậu tập dợt ở sân phía sau nhà. Chủ nhà đồng ý. Chúng gọi Tia Lola là người quản lý đội.

Ngày kia Tia Lola sơn ngôi nhà màu tím. Mami lo sợ là chủ nhà sẽ bắt họ dọn đi. Ông ấy bảo họ phải sơn lại ngôi nhà bằng không thì phải dọn ra trong 3 tuần lễ.

Tia Lola có một kế. Bà may các bộ đồng phục cho đội bóng chày. Bà cũng may một lá cờ có tên của đội. Đội mang tên ông chủ nhà. Khi ông ấy thấy lá cờ, ông mỉm cười và đi chơi bóng với đội.

Multilingual Summaries

Korean

티아 롤라가 머무는 법

미구엘과 주아니타는 그들의 어머니인 마미와 함께 버몬트로 이사한다. 어머니의 고모인 티아 롤라 가 놀러 와서 이야기를 들려준다. 밤이 되면 그들은 지금 살고 있는 낡은 집을 탐사하기도 했다.

미구엘은 그의 야구팀이 집 뒤뜰에서 연습하길 바라는데 집주인도 이를 허락한다. 그들은 곧 티아 롤라를 팀의 관리인으로 임명한다.

어느 날 티아 롤라는 집을 자주색으로 칠한다. 마미는 집주인이 그들을 내보내지 않을까 걱정한다. 집주인은 그들에게 집을 새로 칠하거나 아니면 3주 내로 집에서 나가라고 말한다.

티아 롤라에겐 계획이 있다. 그녀는 야구 팀의 유니폼과 팀의 이름을 새긴 깃발을 만들고 집주인의 이름을 따서 팀의 이름을 짓는다. 집주인은 깃발을 보고 미소를 짓더니 이들과 함께 야구를 한다.

Hmong

Ua Li Cas Tía Lola tau Los Nyob

Miguel thiab Juanita tau tsiv mus nyob hauv Vermont nrog Mami, nkawd niam. Mami tus viv ncaus, Tía Lola, tuaj saib lawv. Nws qhia dab neeg. Tej hmo lawv sawv daws mus ncig lub tsev qub uas nyob hauv.

Miguel xav kom nws pab ntaus pob xyaum hauv thaj chaw nyob ntawm lawv qaum tsev. Lawv tus tswv tsev kam lawv xyaum. Lawv hais kom Tía Lola ua tus coj lawv pab ntau pob.

Muaj ib hnub Tía Lola tau muab lub tsev thas xim paj yeeb. Mami tau txhawj nyob tsam tus tswv tsev hais kom lawv tawm tsev. Nws hais kom lawv rov qab thas lub tsev los sis tawm tsev ntawm peb lub lim tiam tom ntej.

Tía Lola muaj ib lub tswv yim. Nws tau ua kom pab ntau pob muaj ib cev khaub ncaw zoo li yam. Nws kuj ua ib tug chij uas muaj pab ntau pob lub npe. Pab ntau pob lub npe hu ua tus tswv tsev. Thaum nws pom tus chij, nws luag thiab ua siv nrog pab ntau pob.

Name _____

- **Read** *From Thailand to California* again.
- Use the information in the book to **answer** the questions.

---

pages 2–5

1. Where does the story take place?

_____

2. Why does Nongnoot decide to keep a picture journal?

_____

---

page 6

3. How is eating lunch at school in San José different from eating lunch in Koh Lanta?

_____

_____

---

pages 8–9

4. What is Heather's favorite place in San José? What is it like?

_____

_____

---

pages 10–12

5. How does Nongnoot feel when she writes poems about Koh Lanta?

_____

Family Link

What foods do people eat in your family's home country? Are meal times there the same as in the United States? Do students there eat in a cafeteria or go home for lunch? Ask family members to describe how their eating customs are different from those in the United States.

Weekly Resources Guide for English Language Learner Support

For this week's content and language objectives, see p. 197e.

Instructional Strand	Day 1	Day 2
Concept Development/Academic Language	**TEACHER'S EDITION** • Academic Language, p. DI•91 • Concept Development, p. DI•91 • Anchored Talk, pp. 414j—414–415 • Preteach Academic Vocabulary, p. 417a • Concept Talk Video **ELL HANDBOOK** • Hear It, See It, Say It, Use It, pp. xxxvi–xxxvii • ELL Poster Talk, Concept Talk, p. 197c **ELL POSTER 29** • Day 1 Activities	**TEACHER'S EDITION** • Academic Language, p. DI•91 • Concept Development, p. DI•91 • Anchored Talk, p. 418a • Concept Talk Video **ELL HANDBOOK** • ELL Poster Talk, Concept Talk, p. 197c • Concept Talk Video Routine, p. 477 **ELL POSTER 29** • Day 2 Activities
Phonics and Spelling	**TEACHER'S EDITION** • Phonics and Spelling, p. DI•95	**TEACHER'S EDITION** • Phonics and Spelling, p. DI•95
Listening Comprehension	**TEACHER'S EDITION** • Modified Read Aloud, p. DI•94 • Read Aloud, p. 415b • Concept Talk Video **ELL HANDBOOK** • Concept Talk Video Routine, p. 477	**TEACHER'S EDITION** • Modified Read Aloud, p. DI•94 • AudioText of *A Gift from the Heart* • Concept Talk Video **ELL HANDBOOK** • AudioText CD Routine, p. 477 • Main Idea, p. 487
Reading Comprehension	**TEACHER'S EDITION** • Preteach Generalize, p. DI•96	**TEACHER'S EDITION** • Reteach Generalize, p. DI•96 • Frontloading Reading, p. DI•97 **ELL HANDBOOK** • Picture It! Skill Instruction, pp. 198–198a • Multilingual Summaries, pp. 199–201
Vocabulary **Basic and Lesson Vocabulary** **Word Analysis: Related Words**	**TEACHER'S EDITION** • Basic Vocabulary, p. DI•92 • Preteach Lesson Vocabulary, p. DI•92 • Related Words, p. DI•95 **ELL HANDBOOK** • Word Cards, p. 197 • ELL Vocabulary Routine, p. 471 **ELL POSTER 29** • Day 1 Activities	**TEACHER'S EDITION** • Basic Vocabulary, p. DI•92 • Reteach Lesson Vocabulary, p. DI•93 • Related Words, p. DI•95 **ELL HANDBOOK** • Word Cards, p. 197 • Multilingual Vocabulary List, p. 431 **ELL POSTER 29** • Day 2 Activities
Grammar and Conventions	**TEACHER'S EDITION** • Preteach Quotations and Quotation Marks, p. DI•99	**TEACHER'S EDITION** • Teach/Model Quotations and Quotation Marks, p. DI•99
Writing	**TEACHER'S EDITION** • Word Choice, p. DI•100 • Introduce Play/Drama Scene, pp. 417e–417f	**TEACHER'S EDITION** • Writing Trait: Organization, pp. 427d–427e

197a *A Gift from the Heart* Unit 6, Week 4

ELL Handbook

This symbol indicates leveled instruction to address language proficiency levels.

Day 3	Day 4	Day 5
TEACHER'S EDITION • Academic Language, p. DI•91 • Concept Development, p. DI•91 • Anchored Talk, p. 428a • Concept Talk Video **ELL HANDBOOK** • ELL Poster Talk, Concept Talk, p. 197c **ELL POSTER 29** • Day 3 Activities	**TEACHER'S EDITION** • Academic Language, p. DI•91 • Concept Development, p. DI•91 • Anchored Talk, p. 440a • Concept Talk Video **ELL HANDBOOK** • ELL Poster Talk, Concept Talk, p. 197c **ELL POSTER 29** • Day 4 Activities	**TEACHER'S EDITION** • Academic Language, p. DI•91 • Concept Development, p. DI•91 • Concept Talk Video **ELL HANDBOOK** • ELL Poster Talk, Concept Talk, p. 197c **ELL POSTER 29** • Day 5 Activities
		TEACHER'S EDITION • Phonics and Spelling, p. DI•95
ELL HANDBOOK • Phonics Transition Lesson, pp. 287, 294	**ELL HANDBOOK** • Phonics Transition Lesson, pp. 287, 294	
TEACHER'S EDITION • AudioText of *A Gift from the Heart* • Concept Talk Video **ELL HANDBOOK** • AudioText CD Routine, p. 477	**TEACHER'S EDITION** • Concept Talk Video	**TEACHER'S EDITION** • Concept Talk Video
TEACHER'S EDITION • Sheltered Reading, p. DI•97 **ELL HANDBOOK** • Multilingual Summaries, pp. 199–201	**TEACHER'S EDITION** • ELL/ELD Reader Guided Reading, p. DI•98 **ELL HANDBOOK** • ELL Study Guide, p. 202	**TEACHER'S EDITION** • ELL/ELD Reader Guided Reading, p. DI•98 **ELL HANDBOOK** • ELL Study Guide, p. 202
		TEACHER'S EDITION • Related Words, p. 443i
ELL HANDBOOK • High-Frequency Words Activity Bank, p. 446 **ELL POSTER 29** • Day 3 Activities	**ELL HANDBOOK** • High-Frequency Words Activity Bank, p. 446	**ELL HANDBOOK** • High-Frequency Words Activity Bank, p. 446
TEACHER'S EDITION • Grammar Jammer **ELL HANDBOOK** • Grammar Transition Lesson, pp. 347, 360 • Grammar Jammer Routine, p. 478	**TEACHER'S EDITION** • Grammar Jammer **ELL HANDBOOK** • Grammar Transition Lesson, pp. 347, 360	**TEACHER'S EDITION** • Grammar Jammer **ELL HANDBOOK** • Grammar Transition Lesson, pp. 347, 360
TEACHER'S EDITION • Let's Write It!, p. 438–439 • Writing Trait: Word Choice, pp. 439a–439b	**TEACHER'S EDITION** • Revising Strategy, pp. 443d–443e	**TEACHER'S EDITION** • Quotations and Quotation Marks, pp. 443p–443q

Question of the Week
When do people choose to make sacrifices?

Throughout the week, use the ELL Poster to help students produce and comprehend language, understand the concept, and build English vocabulary. Use the Question of the Week and other questions to help students share ideas in pairs, small groups, or the large group. Sample questions are shown, with examples of possible responses by students.

Weekly Concept and Language Goals

• Indentify sacrifices people make to achieve a goal

• Name ways people can work together to achieve goals

• Discuss the steps it takes to achieve a goal

By the end of the lesson, students should be able to talk about and write sentences about achieving goals and making sacrifices.

ELL Poster 29

Daily Team Talk

Day 1	Day 2	Day 3	Day 4	Day 5
After Day 1 activities on Poster, ask questions such as *What goal do you think the family in the poster picture had for the summer?*	After Day 2 activity on Poster, ask questions such as *What did the family do during the summer to achieve the goal of growing vegetables to eat?*	After Day 3 activity on Poster, ask questions such as *What sacrifice did the boy in the poster picture make to help his family achieve their goal?*	After Day 4 activity on Poster, ask questions such as *Do you think the family in the poster picture achieved their goal of growing vegetables? Why or why not?*	After Day 5 activity on Poster, ask questions such as *How have you worked to achieve a goal you chose?*
Beginning To grow things. **Intermediate** They wanted to grow food to eat. **Advanced** The family wanted to grow vegetables in their garden to eat. **Advanced High** The family's goal was to grow plenty of potatoes, tomatoes, corn, and other vegetables to eat.	**Beginning** They worked. **Intermediate** They planted seeds and worked. **Advanced** They planted seeds and then worked hard to help the plants grow. **Advanced High** The family planted seeds in the garden. They worked hard all summer to help the plants grow.	**Beginning** No baseball. **Intermediate** He did not play baseball. **Advanced** He did not play baseball so he could help plant a garden. **Advanced High** The boy likes playing baseball, but he sacrificed playing baseball that summer so he could help his family plant and take care of the garden.	**Beginning** Yes. I see food. **Intermediate** Yes. They have a lot of food. **Advanced** Yes. The family has enough vegetables to share with many other people. **Advanced High** Yes, the family achieved their goal. They grew enough vegetables to eat and to share with all their friends and neighbors at a special dinner.	**Beginning** Read a lot. **Intermediate** I read a lot of books. **Advanced** I read many books this summer. I wanted to win a reading contest. **Advanced High** The library had a reading contest. I wanted to win it, so I spent most of my summer reading all kinds of books. I won a medal!

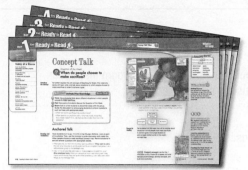

Teacher's Edition pages 414j–443q

See the support for English language learners throughout the lesson, including ELL strategies and scaffolded activities at points of use.

Teacher's Edition pages DI•91–DI•100

Differentiated Instruction for English language learners provides daily group activities that "frontload," or preteach, core instruction.

ELL Handbook pp. 197a–202

Find additional lesson materials that support the core lesson and the ELL instructional pages.

Poster 29

ELL Reader 4.6.4

ELD Reader 4.6.4

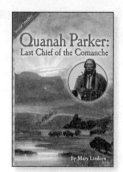

Concept Literacy Reader

ELD, ELL Reader
Teaching Guide

Concept Literacy Reader
Teaching Guide

Technology

Online Teacher's Edition Use the digital version of the core Teacher's Edition for planning and instruction.

eReaders
This week's ELL and ELD Readers and Concept Literacy Reader are also available in digital format.

This Week's Content and Language Objectives by Strand

Concept Development/ Academic Language When do people choose to make sacrifices?	**Content Objective** • Use concept vocabulary related to making personal sacrifices. **Language Objectives** • Learn new basic vocabulary heard during classroom instruction. • Express ideas in response to art and discussion.
Phonics and Spelling Suffixes –ful, -ly	**Content Objective** • Identify suffixes in words. **Language Objective** • Apply phonics and decoding skills to vocabulary.
Listening Comprehension Modified Read Aloud: "Starting a University"	**Content Objective** • Monitor and adjust oral comprehension. **Language Objectives** • Discuss oral passages. • Understand the main points and important details of spoken language.
Reading Comprehension Generalize	**Content Objectives** • Identify generalizations. • Identify information needed to support a generalization. **Language Objectives** • Discuss evidence for generalizing. • Generalize based on information in a text. • Express feelings using generalizations. • Summarize text using visual support.
Vocabulary Basic and Lesson Vocabulary	**Language Objectives** • Understand and use basic vocabulary. • Learn meanings of grade-level vocabulary. • Produce drawings, phrases, and short sentences to show understanding of Lesson Vocabulary.
Word Analysis Related Words	**Content Objective** • Identify and define related words. **Language Objective** • Discuss meanings of related words.
Grammar and Conventions Quotations and Quotation Marks	**Content Objective** • Correctly use quotation marks for quoted speech and titles. **Language Objectives** • Speak using quotations correctly. • Write sentences that include quotations.
Writing Word Choice	**Content Objective** • Recognize dull words in writing. **Language Objectives** • Revise writing to add words that are more descriptive. • Share feedback for editing and revising.

Word Cards for Vocabulary Activities

abundance	**backdrop**
ceremonial	**drought**
graze	**shock**

Teacher Note: Beginning Teach two to three words. **Intermediate** Teach three to four words. **Advanced** Teach four to five words. **Advanced High** Teach all words.

Name _____

Look at the pictures. **Read** the story.

• Use what you **read** to answer the questions below.

Four Horses

Lucia is taking horseback riding lessons. She has a lesson at the Pine Ridge Stable every Wednesday afternoon.

The stable has four horses that students ride during their lessons. Lucia has had four lessons, and she rode each of the four horses.

Spike is slow and gentle. He is easy to ride. Sparkle always seems to be in a happy mood. She makes her rider feel happy too.

Red is patient with new riders. He seems to know they are nervous. Rosie wants to gallop, but she always obeys her rider.

Lucia likes all the horses. She can't decide which horse she wants to ride during her lesson this week.

1. What generalization can you make about the horses at the stable?

_____

_____

2. What examples in the story support your generalization?

_____

_____

Generalize

Use this lesson to supplement or replace the skill lesson on page 415c of the Teacher's Edition. Display the Skill Points (at right) and share them with students.

Teach/Model

Beginning Say: *Most school libraries have magazines. Students can check out books. Which sentence tells a way that most school libraries are alike?* (the first sentence) *Which sentence is a generalization?* (the first one) Point out that the word *most* is a clue word for recognizing a generalization.

Intermediate Write and read aloud: *All students visit the school library each week.* Ask: *What makes this sentence a generalization?* (It tells a way all students are alike. It uses the word *all*.) Have students think of another generalization about students.

Advanced Write a generalization on the board. For example: *Many students ride the bus to school.* Ask students why this is a generalization. Have them write a fact that supports the generalization. Explain that telling how many students ride the bus supports the generalization: *Out of 250 students, 175 ride the bus to school.*

Advanced High Pair students. Have partners write a generalization about a topic such as school life. Say: *Remember to use a clue word such as* all, many, most, usually, *or* always *in your generalization.* Have partners write a fact that supports their generalization.

Then distribute copies of Picture It! page 198.

- Have students look at and describe the picture. Then read the story aloud.
- Ask: *What is a way that all four horses are alike?* (Possible answer: All four horses are good for beginning riders.)
- Review the Skill Points with students.
- Have students find support for their generalization.

Practice

Read aloud the directions on page 198. Have students reread the story with a partner. Then have them use the picture and the story as they answer the questions.

Beginning Students can say their generalization and supporting examples before writing their answers on the lines. Provide help with English words and writing.

Intermediate Students can first orally answer the questions and then write their answers on the lines. Provide help with writing.

Advanced Students can write their answers on the lines and then check them by discussing the story and their answers with a partner.

Advanced High Students can write their answers on the lines and then orally explain how their generalization is supported by details in the story.

Answers for page 198: 1. All the horses at the Pine Ridge Stable are suitable for student riders. 2. Spike is easy to ride. Sparkle makes her rider feel happy. Red is patient with new riders. Rosie always obeys her rider.

Skill Points

- ✔ Look for ideas about people or things in the text. A statement about how the ideas are alike is called a **generalization.**
- ✔ Clue words such as *all, most, many, always,* and *usually* show that an author is making a generalization.
- ✔ A good generalization explains and is supported by many examples.

Multilingual Summaries

A Gift from the Heart

The Comanche Indians lived on the prairie. One year, there was no rain. With no rain, there was not enough food. Wise Eagle, the Comanche shaman, prayed to the Great Spirit. He said each person must give an important possession to the Great Spirit. The gifts must be thrown into a fire. Wise Eagle said if they gave their gifts, the Great Spirit would send rain.

No one wanted to throw their possessions into the fire. A little girl threw her doll into the fire. The Great Spirit made it rain. Blue flowers grew on the prairie. Wise Eagle named these flowers "bluebonnets."

Spanish

Un regalo del corazón

Los indios Comanche vivían en la pradera. Un año no hubo lluvia. Sin la lluvia, no había suficiente alimento. Águila Sabia, el chamán Comanche, oró al Gran Espíritu. Él dijo que cada persona debía dar una posesión importante al Gran Espíritu. Debían lanzar los regalos a una hoguera. Águila Sabia les dijo que si daban sus regalos, el Gran Espíritu enviaría la lluvia.

Nadie quería lanzar sus posesiones al fuego. Una niña pequeña lanzó su muñeca. El Gran Espíritu mandó lluvia. Flores azules crecieron en la pradera. Águila Sabia llamó a esas flores "boinas azules".

Multilingual Summaries

Chinese

最诚挚的礼物

科曼奇印第安人住在大草原上。有一年特别干旱，一滴雨都没有；因为没雨，所以粮食不足。智鹰是族里的萨满祭司，他向大魔神祷告，然后说每一个人都要把一件贵重的东西奉献给大魔神，并把这件礼物抛向烈火；智鹰说如果每一个人都送出礼物，大魔神就会降雨。

没有人想自己的贵重东西在烈火中毁掉。有一个小女孩把她的洋娃娃抛向烈火，大魔神就赐雨，而且蓝色的花开满大草原；智鹰把这种花叫做蓝帽花。

Vietnamese

Một Món Quà Từ Trái Tim

Người da đỏ Comanche sống trên đồng cỏ. Có một năm, trời không mưa. Không có mưa thì không có đủ thực phẩm. Pháp sư Comanche là Wise Eagle cầu khẩn Thần Linh. Ông ta bảo mỗi người phải dâng lên Thần Linh một món của cải sở hữu quan trọng. Những món đó phải được ném vào lửa. Wise Eagle nói nếu mọi người dâng lện lễ vật, Thần Linh sẽ làm mưa.

Không một ai muốn ném vào lửa của cải sở hữu của mình. Một bé gái ném con búp bê của mình vào lửa. Thần Linh làm mưa. Hoa xanh mọc trên đồng cỏ. Wise Eagle đặt tên cho những hoa đó là "mũ xanh".

Multilingual Summaries

Korean

마음에서 우러나온 선물

코만치 인디언들은 대초원에 살았다. 어느 해 비가 오지 않았다. 비가 오지 않자, 먹을 것이 충분하지 않았다. 코만치의 주술사인 '현명한 독수리'는 대영혼에게 기도를 드렸다. 그는 모든 사람들이 귀중품 한 개씩을 대영혼에게 바쳐야 한다고 말했다. 그 선물들은 불 속으로 던져져야 한다는 것이었다. '현명한 독수리'는 만약 사람들이 선물을 바치면, 대영혼께서 비를 내려준다고 말했다.

아무도 자신의 귀중품을 불 속으로 던지고 싶어하지 않았다. 어린 소녀가 불 속으로 자기 인형을 던졌다. 대영혼은 비를 내렸다. 파란 꽃들이 초원에 자라났다. '현명한 독수리'는 그 꽃을 "달구지 국화"라고 이름지었다.

Hmong

Khoomplig tawm ntawm lub Siab

Cov khab Comanche ua neej nyob nrag hav nyom. Muaj ib xyoo, nwg tsi muaj nag los. Thaus tsi muaj nag los, lawv tsi muaj mov txaus noj. Wise Eagle, uas yog Comanche tus txivneeb, thov rau tus Dab Loj. Nwg hais tias ib tus tibneeg yuav tsum muab ib yam khoom tseemceeb uas nwg muaj pub rua tus Dab Loj. Yuav tsum muab cov khoomplig pov rau hauv lub hluavtaws. Wise Eagle hais tias yog lawv muab lawv cov khoomplig rau, tus Dab Loj mam xa nag los.

Tsi muaj leejtwg xav muab lawv cov khoom pov rau hauv lub hluavtaws. Ib tus me ntxhais muab nwg tus menyuam rojhmab pov rau hauv hluavtaws. Tus Dab Loj ua rau lug nag. Ib cov paj xiav xiav ciali tuaj rau thaj hav nyom. Wise Eagle tis cov paj lub npe hu ua "bluebonnets."

Name _____

- **Read** *Harriet Tubman* again.
- **Write** a brief summary of each group of pages in the boxes below.

pages 2–4

_____

_____

_____

pages 5–8

_____

_____

_____

pages 9–12

_____

_____

_____

Family Link

Summarize Harriet Tubman's life for your family. Ask them if they know someone who spent their life helping others. Share their story with the class.

Question of the Week

How do the achievements of others influence our dreams?

Throughout the week, use the ELL Poster to help students produce and comprehend language, understand the concept, and build English vocabulary. Use the Question of the Week and other questions to help students share ideas in pairs, small groups, or the large group. Sample questions are shown, with examples of possible responses by students.

ELL Poster 30

Weekly Concept and Language Goals

• Understand the concept of space exploration

• Discuss the inspiring achievements of astronauts

• Name ways others' achievements influence us

By the end of the lesson, students should be able to talk about and write sentences about achievements and space exploration.

Daily Team Talk

Day 1	Day 2	Day 3	Day 4	Day 5
After Day 1 activities on Poster, ask questions such as	After Day 2 activity on Poster, ask questions such as	After Day 3 activity on Poster, ask questions such as	After Day 4 activity on Poster, ask questions such as	After Day 5 activity on Poster, ask questions such as
What are the students in the poster picture making?	*Do you think the students in the poster picture believe people will land on Mars someday? Why?*	*How have the achievements of astronauts influenced the students in the poster picture?*	*According to the selection Far Side of the Moon, what did the Apollo astronauts achieve in space?*	*Whose achievements have inspired and influenced you?*
Beginning A model. **Intermediate** They are making a model. **Advanced** The students are making a model of people on Mars. **Advanced High** The students are making a model of people from Earth landing on Mars.	**Beginning** Because of others. **Intermediate** Others have done things in space. **Advanced** They believe it because people have done other things in space. **Advanced High** I think the students believe people will land on Mars someday because astronauts keep exploring places they have never been before.	**Beginning** They want to go. **Intermediate** They want to go into space too. **Advanced** The astronauts have made the students interested in space exploration. **Advanced High** The astronauts' achievements have influenced the students to learn more about space exploration and other planets.	**Beginning** Go to the moon. **Intermediate** They landed on the moon. **Advanced** The astronauts walked on the moon. Nobody had done that before. **Advanced High** The Apollo astronauts were the first men to walk on the moon. They brought back moon rocks and dust for people to see.	**Beginning** Baseball players. **Intermediate** People who play baseball make me want to play. **Advanced** Watching my favorite baseball team makes me want to practice harder. **Advanced High** My favorite baseball team won the World Series. Watching them play baseball makes me want to practice hard so I can play on the team someday.

Teacher's Edition pages 444j–477a

See the support for English language learners throughout the lesson, including ELL strategies and scaffolded activities at points of use.

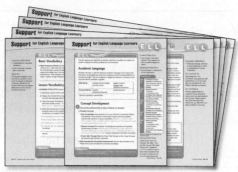

Teacher's Edition pages DI•116–DI•125

Differentiated Instruction for English language learners provides daily group activities that "frontload," or preteach, core instruction.

ELL Handbook pp. 203a–208

Find additional lesson materials that support the core lesson and the ELL instructional pages.

 Poster 30

ELL Reader 4.6.5

ELD Reader 4.6.5

Concept Literacy Reader

ELD, ELL Reader Teaching Guide

Concept Literacy Reader Teaching Guide

Technology

Online Teacher's Edition Use the digital version of the core Teacher's Edition for planning and instruction.

eReaders
This week's ELL and ELD Readers and Concept Literacy Reader are also available in digital format.

This Week's Content and Language Objectives by Strand

Concept Development/ Academic Language How do the achievements of others influence our dreams?	**Content Objective** • Use concept vocabulary related to how people can have a positive impact on others. **Language Objectives** • Express ideas in response to art and discussion. • Express ideas in response to new academic vocabulary.
Phonics and Spelling Silent Consonants	**Content Objectives** • Identify words using silent consonants. • Review word structure. **Language Objective** • Apply phonics and decoding skills to vocabulary.
Listening Comprehension Modified Read Aloud: "Weightless Worries"	**Content Objective** • Monitor and adjust oral comprehension. **Language Objectives** • Discuss oral passages. • Use a graphic organizer to take notes.
Reading Comprehension Graphic Sources	**Content Objectives** • Allow students to use graphics to aid in comprehension. • Make and adjust predictions. **Language Objectives** • Discuss importance of graphic sources. • Predict and infer content based on graphic sources. • Summarize text using visual support. • Read grade-level text accuracy.
Vocabulary Basic and Lesson Vocabulary	**Language Objectives** • Understand and use basic vocabulary. • Learn meanings of grade-level vocabulary • Produce drawings, phrases, and short sentences to show understanding of Lesson Vocabulary.
Word Analysis Prefix *astro-*	**Content Objective** • Understand use of prefix *astro-*. **Language Objective** • Discuss how use of prefix *astro-* affects meaning.
Grammar and Conventions Titles	**Content Objectives** • Decode and use titles. • Correctly form titles. **Language Objectives** • Speak using titles. • Write titles correctly.
Writing Commas	**Content Objective** • Understand the use of commas in writing. **Language Objective** • Write sentences using commas correctly to combine phrases and clauses.

Word Cards for Vocabulary Activities

astronauts

capsule

hatch

horizon

lunar

module

quarantine

Teacher Note: Beginning Teach three to four words. **Intermediate** Teach four to six words. **Advanced** Teach six to seven words. **Advanced High** Teach all words.

Name _____

Look at the pictures. **Read** the paragraph.
• **Use** the information in the paragraph to add labels to the picture.

Phases of the Moon

Every few nights, the shape of the Moon seems to change. One night, the Moon cannot be seen. This is called a New Moon. Then the Moon looks like a crescent that gets bigger, until half a circle is seen. This is called a Half Moon or Quarter Moon. A week later, a full circle, or Full Moon, is seen. This circle gets smaller, and a week later only half a circle is seen. After another week, it is a New Moon again. The Moon revolves around the Earth, and the Earth revolves around the Sun. We see different Moon shapes depending on where the Sun, Moon, and Earth are in relation to each other.

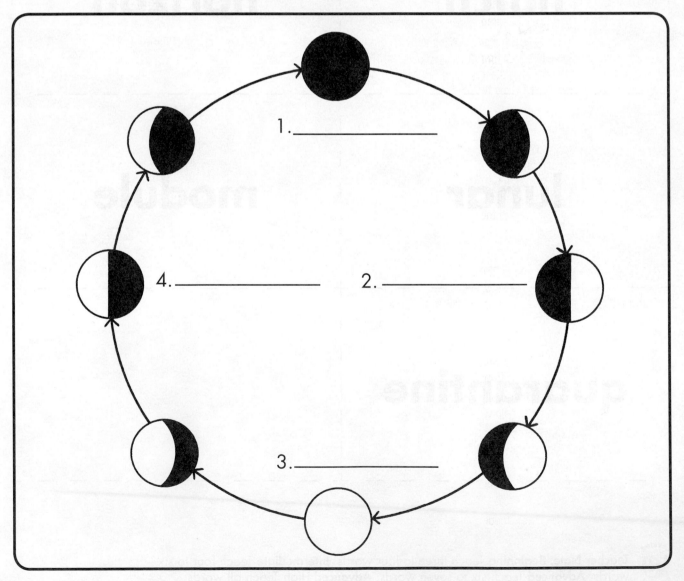

1._____

2._____

4._____

3._____

Graphic Sources

Use this lesson to supplement or replace the skill lesson on page 445c of the Teacher's Edition. Display the Skill Points (at right) and share them with students.

Teach/Model

Beginning Display a diagram of our solar system. Say: *This shows the Sun and the planets in our solar system. What can you learn from this graphic source?* (Possible responses: The Sun is in the center. Mars is next to Earth. Jupiter is the biggest planet.)

Intermediate Display a picture of an asteroid from a children's encyclopedia. Read the description of the asteroid. Ask: *How does the picture help you understand the text?* Discuss how the picture helps readers understand what an asteroid looks like.

Advanced Display and identify a star chart. Discuss with students the kind of information the star chart can tell them. Have them write a sentence that tells something they learned from this graphic source.

Advanced High Read aloud each planet's number of moons from a children's encyclopedia. Ask students how a graphic source can better show the information. Write the information on the board. Pair students and have partners make an appropriate graphic source to show the information.

Then distribute copies of Picture It! page 204.

- Have students read the title and look at the diagram. Then read the paragraph aloud.
- Ask: *What does the diagram show?* (phases of the moon)
- Review the Skill Points with students.
- Have students tell which parts of the diagram show which phases of the moon.

Practice

Read aloud the directions on page 204. Reread the paragraph aloud, explaining the words *phases, crescent, revolves,* and *relation.* Then have students use the paragraph as they label the parts of the diagram.

Beginning Students can first say what they want to write on each line before writing the words. Provide help with writing English words.

Intermediate Students can first orally say the phases of the moon and then write the words on the lines. Provide help with spelling English words.

Advanced Students can write the labels on the lines and then check them by comparing them with a partner's.

Advanced High Students can write the labels on the lines and then orally explain how a labeled diagram makes the information in the paragraph easier to understand.

Answers for page 204: 1. new moon; 2. half or quarter moon; 3. full moon; 4. half or quarter moon

---

Skill Points

✔ **Graphic sources** show information in a visual way. Maps, charts, tables, graphs, diagrams, photographs, and illustrations are examples of graphic sources.

✔ Before you read, look at the graphic sources to help you figure out the topic of the text.

✔ As you read, look at the graphic sources to help you understand the text.

Multilingual Summaries

The Man Who Went
to the Far Side of the Moon

Michael Collins, Neil Armstrong, and Buzz Aldrin are astronauts. They fly the Apollo 11 mission to the moon. Neil and Buzz land the lunar module on the moon. While Neil and Buzz do experiments on the moon, Michael is alone.

Michael flies the command module around the moon for almost thirty hours. When the command module is on the far side of the moon, the radio cannot reach the Earth. Michael has a lot of work to do. While orbiting the moon, Michael eats meals from special packages.

The three men land back on Earth. Doctors don't know if they may have caught any germs on the moon. They have to stay in a special trailer for seventeen days.

Michael decides not to travel anymore. This trip was special, but he doesn't want to go back.

Spanish

El hombre que fue al lado oscuro
de la Luna

Michael Collins, Neil Armstrong y Buzz Aldrin son astronautas. Ellos van a la Luna en la misión del Apollo 11. Neil y Buzz alunizan el módulo lunar. Mientras Neil y Buzz hacen experimentos en la Luna, Michael está solo.

Durante casi treinta horas, Michael dirige el módulo de mando alrededor de la Luna. Cuando el módulo de mando está en el lado oscuro de la Luna, la señal de radio no puede llegar a la Tierra. Michael tiene mucho trabajo que hacer. Mientras está en la órbita de la Luna, Michael come comidas de paquetes especiales.

Los tres hombres regresan a la Tierra. Los médicos no saben si los astronautas han traído algún germen de la Luna. Ellos tienen que estar en una cámara especial durante diecisiete días.

Michael decide no viajar más. Ese viaje fue especial, pero él no quiere regresar.

Multilingual Summaries

Chinese

到過月球另一端的人

麥克 科林斯、尼爾 阿姆斯壯和巴茲 歐德林是太空人。他們搭乘太空穿梭機阿波羅 11 號到月球上要完成任務。尼爾和巴茲開著登月小艇在月球上登陸，然後忙著在上面做實驗，麥克自己一人，沒和他們一起。

麥克駕著指揮艙繞月球飛了快要 30 個小時。當飛到月球另一端的時候，他的無線電突然沒辦法和地球聯絡了。麥克還有很多工作要做，所以他又駕著指揮艙沿著月球軌道飛回去，途中，麥克要是肚子餓，就從特製的包包裡拿東西出來吃。

三個人完成任務，返回地球。醫生幫他們檢查身體，看看他們有沒有在月球上感染細菌。三個人都必須在一輛特製的拖車上待 17 天。

麥克決定以後不再去外太空了。這次繞月球飛的經驗雖然很特別，但是他一點都不想再去一次。

Vietnamese

Người Đã Đi Đến Phía Bên Kia Mặt Trăng

Michael Collins, Neil Armstrong, và Buzz Aldrin là các phi hành gia vũ trụ. Họ bay chuyến bay Apollo 11 lên mặt trăng. Neil và Buzz đáp khoang hạ xuống mặt trăng. Khi Neil và Buzz làm các thí nghiệm trên mặt trăng, Michael chỉ có một mình.

Michael bay khoang chỉ huy vòng quanh mặt trăng gần đến ba mươi tiếng đồng hồ. Khi khoang chỉ huy qua phía bên kia của mặt trăng, sóng rađiô không thể truyền đến Trái Đất. Michael có nhiều việc phải làm. Trong khi bay quanh quỹ đạo mặt trăng, Michael ăn những bữa ăn từ các gói đặc biệt.

Ba người trở về Trái Đất. Các bác sĩ không biết các phi hành gia vũ trụ có thể nhiễm các vi trùng trên mặt trăng hay không. Họ phải ở trong một nhà đặc biệt đến mười bảy ngày.

Michael quyết định không du hành nữa. Chuyến đi này đặc biệt, nhưng ông ấy không muốn đi nữa.

Multilingual Summaries

달의 저편으로 간 사나이

우주 비행사인 마이클 콜린스, 닐 암스트롱, 그리고 버즈 올드린은 아폴로 11호를 타고 달에 간다. 닐과 버즈는 달에 달 착륙선을 착륙시킨다. 닐과 부즈가 달에서 실험하는 동안 마이클은 홀로 있다.

마이클은 사령선을 타고 거의 30시간 동안 달 주위를 돈다. 사령선이 달의 저 건너편에 있는 동안 지구와의 무선 수신은 할 수 없다. 마이클은 할 일이 많다. 달의 궤도를 도는 동안 마이클은 특수 제작된 주머니에 담긴 음식을 먹는다.

세 사람이 지구로 돌아온다. 의사들은 그들이 달에서 어떤 병균에 감염되었을지도 모른다고 생각한다. 그리하여 그들은 17일 동안 특수 트레일러에서 지내게 된다.

마이클은 더 이상 우주 여행을 하지 않기로 결정한다. 이번 여행은 특별했지만 그는 우주로 돌아가고 싶지 않다.

Tus Txiv Neej Uas Tau Mus Sab Deb Ntawm Lub Hli

Michael Collins, Neil Armstrong, thiab Buzz Aldrin yog cov neeg mus saum qaum ntuj. Lawv tau ya lub Apollo 11 mus saum lub hli. Neil thiab Buzz tsaws lub dav hlau mus saum qaum ntuj rau saum lub hli. Thaum Neil thiab Buzz ua ntau yam kev soj ntsuas saum lub hli, Michael nyob ib leeg.

Michael tsav lub dav hlau loj ncig lub hli siv li peb caug teev. Thaum lub dav hlau loj nyob sab deb ntawm lub hli, lub xov tooj cua txais tsis tau lus los hauv ntiaj teb los. Michael muaj ntau txoj hauj lwm ua. Thaum nws tseem ncig lub hli, Michael noj mov uas nyob hauv tej hnab.

Peb tug txiv neej tsaws rov lost saws rau hauv lub ntiaj teb. Cov kws tshuaj tsis paub xyuas lawv puas yuav kis tau tej kab mob nyob saum lub hli. Lawv tau nyob hauv ib qhov chaw tau kaum xyav hnub.

Michael txiav txim tsis rov qab mus dua lawm. Txoj kev mus saum lub hli yeej tseem ceeb, tiam sis nws tsis xav rov qab mus saum lub hli.

Name _____

- **Read** *Welcome to Space Camp* again.
- Use the information in the book to **answer** the questions.

---

pages 2–5

1. Who were the first men to walk on the Moon?

_____

2. What is a simulator?

_____

_____

---

page 6

3. Why do astronauts need to learn how to walk, work, sleep, and eat in space?

_____

_____

---

pages 8–9

4. What is one of the jobs of the team at the control center?

_____

---

page 10

5. Who were Sir Isaac Newton and Galileo Galilei?

_____

_____

Family Link

Would anyone in your family like to travel into space? Where would they like to go? What would they like to see? What would they like to do in space? How would they feel about you becoming an astronaut?

Answer Key

page 30, Picture It!
First: Ayako and Julie decide to share lunches.
Next: Ayako gives Julie a rice ball.
Next: Julie gives Ayako a cheese sandwich.
Last: The girls praise each other's lunches.

page 34, ELL Reader Study Guide
Possible responses:
1. They want to play for an audience, and they want to do a good job.
2. Sylvie: France; Pedro: Mexico; Hamisi: Kenya
3. He means he is nervous.
4. They want to play well.
5. The audience stands up, claps, and cheers.

page 36, Picture It!
1. b; 2. c

page 40, ELL Reader Study Guide
France; English, sign language; translators; a Native American woman who traveled with Lewis and Clark and translated for them

page 42, Picture It!
on a bus; Raymond and Oliver; Raymond is lonely; He makes friends with Oliver

page 46, ELL Reader Study Guide
Chicago: Abuelita arrives from Mexico. The family begins its trip in the station wagon.
Flemington: The family rents a farmhouse. The girls explore the farmlands. The family spends a day in New York City.
Chicago: The family returns to Chicago. Abuelita returns to Mexico. The family later takes more trips.

page 48, Picture It!
1. b
2. The author provides information and a definition.

page 52, ELL Reader Study Guide
Possible responses:
1. They share thoughts and feelings through art.
2. He tells stories of the people and land of the Southwest.
3. cowboys, pioneers, ranchers
4. Native Americans, Europeans, Mexicans of Hispanic background
5. to inform people about the work of artist Norton Williams and about life in the American Southwest

page 54, Picture It!
The main idea is: *Some national parks in the U.S. are historical places that teach visitors about America's past.* Details should be the historical sites and what they teach visitors.

page 58, ELL Reader Study Guide
The Coastal Range mountains are not tall.
Mt. McKinley is the tallest peak in North America.
The Sierra Nevada runs through most of the length of California.
Mountains in the Brooks Range are covered with snow and ice most of the year.

page 60, Picture It!
Causes: running on the court, jumping high
Effect: strong legs
Causes: passing and shooting, holding hands up
Effect: strong arms

page 64, ELL Reader Study Guide
Cause: Boys' basketball seemed too rough for girls.
Effects: Clara Gregory Baer had girls wear bloomers; The rules of the game today are similar for boys and girls; Dress is identical.

page 66, Picture It!
Conclusion: Being a ranch hand is hard work.
Supporting facts: digs holes for fences; repairs machines and barns; takes care of horses

page 70, ELL Reader Study Guide
The drawing should contain vaqueros, cowboys, cattle, horses, and clothing worn by vaqueros, and so on. Writing should describe the items.

page 72, Picture It!
Conclusion: They work together to make the VCR work.
Details: Alisha suggests pressing a button on the VCR. Facts: Jamal suggests plugging in the VCR.

page 76, ELL Reader Study Guide
1. Because he stopped and put the ball down.
2. Yes. Because he wants his team to work together, and he gives good advice.
3. Because John Buck stole the ball.
4. He is a team player and does not think only of himself.
5. He is glad to be part of a great team.

page 78, Picture It!
1. fact 2. opinion 3. fact 4. fact 5. opinion

page 82, ELL Reader Study Guide
Facts: Dogs have an amazing sense of smell; People use dogs to find and rescue people; Dogs can herd animals. Opinions will vary.

page 84, Picture It!
Topic: Presidents' Homes
Main Idea: Most Presidents have their own houses.
Supporting Details: President Roosevelt had a house in New York State. George H.W. Bush has a home on the coast of Maine. Thomas Jefferson had a house in Virginia.

page 88, ELL Reader Study Guide
Supporting details should prove that being class president is an important job.

page 90, Picture It!
1. the parts of trees
2. Roots are not illustrated. They are underground, so they are not shown in the diagram.
3. Drawing would show roots, trunk, branch, twig, and leaves, all drawn and labeled.

page 94, ELL Reader Study Guide
1. orange, red, or brown
2. in the spring and summer
3. Not everything that plants need for photosynthesis is present.
4. They fall off the trees.
5. They open so that new leaves can grow.

page 96, Picture It!
1. O 2. O 3. F 4. F 5. O

page 100, ELL Reader Study Guide
Facts:
2. They eat tiny creatures that live near the bottom of the ocean.
3. They have one calf every two years. The calves nurse for seven months.
4. They travel from Alaska to Baja, California, a distance of 14,000 miles round trip.
Opinions: Opinions will vary.

page 102, Picture It!
Clue words: generally, most
Generalizations: Children generally like the summer because the weather is warm and the days are longer. Most children don't like the short days of winter.

page 106, ELL Reader Study Guide
Answers may include: Night and day happen because Earth spins; It is night in some places when it is day here; A day on Venus is eight months; Some planets have short days.

page 108, Picture It!
Effect: Many schools and businesses are closed; The snow may knock down power lines.
Effect: It can cover anything in its path with piles of deep snow.

page 112, ELL Reader Study Guide
1951 The United States developed a system to name hurricanes using the letters of the alphabet.
1969 Herbert Saffir and Bob Simpson developed a hurricane scale.
2004 The East Coast of the United States had some rough weather.
2007–2009 The table in the book shows the possible hurricane names for these years.

page 114, Picture It!
Generalization: The animals in the rain forest are generally friendly.
Details: Students should write the animals and the friendly actions they showed.

page 118, ELL Reader Study Guide
Answers will vary, but should include migration, hibernation, adaptation, and/or flowering and leaf dropping.

page 120, Picture It!
Both: most famous magicians of their times; became interested in magic very young
Houdini: born in Hungary in 1874, escape artist, starred in movies, died in 1926
Copperfield: born in New Jersey in 1956, illusionist, starred in TV shows, still alive

page 124, ELL Reader Study Guide
Sample responses: Similarities: Both studied magic at a young age; Both popular with audiences.
Differences: birth places; birth years; favorite types of magic; one still alive, and one not

page 126, Picture It!
Both are home to plants, trees, and animals. Softwood forests grow in colder areas. Tropical

rain forests grow in hot, wet areas. Students can also list the different animals and plants in each type.

page 130, ELL Reader Study Guide
Students should list plants and animals in each layer.

page 132, Picture It!
First, a peasant brought the king and princess some books.
Then the king laughed, but his daughter learned to read.
Next, the peasant brought the king and princess a pen and paper.
Next, the king fell asleep, but the daughter learned how to write.
Last, the princess later became a wise queen.
The peasant became a rich man.

page 136, ELL Reader Study Guide
The best way to secure personal information is through a code.
Secret codes can be letters, words, phrases, numbers, or answers to personal questions.
Secret codes have existed thousands of years.
On a computer, a secret code is called a password.
There are rules to follow when creating a password.

page 138, Picture It!
1. pictures used for writing
2. their lives, their gods, their kings
3. It illustrates what hieroglyphics are.

page 142, ELL Reader Study Guide
1. Damien lives in Switzerland. Carol lives in the United States. Trung lives in Vietnam.
2. Damien
3. It is spoken in China, Malaysia, and Taiwan.
4. France, Germany, Italy, Austria
5. Mexico

page 144, Picture It!
1. Katie can't find her pet lizard, Leo.
2. Katie is upset and worried.
3. Katie's brother finds Leo sleeping under his log inside the cage.
4. Katie is happy and grateful to her brother.

page 148, ELL Reader Study Guide
1. because he forgot to add sugar
2. He cut the lemons.
3. He was going to be late to the game.
4. Because he did not take three full gallons of lemonade
5. It seemed to disappear.

page 150, Picture It!
1. You should know your full name and address. Call from a safe place. Do not hang up until the operator tells you.
2. to tell how to use 9-1-1 to give information about an emergency

page 154, ELL Reader Study Guide
1. Category 5 is the strongest; Category 1 is the weakest.
2. Students should name items in the kit.
3. A tornado is over land. A hurricane comes from the ocean.
4. In the basement and away from windows.
5. They have an emergency kit. They know the warning signs.

page 156, Picture It!
Pompeii: busy, important city; buried by ash and rock
Both: ancient cities in what is now Italy, located at bottom of a mountain, buried by eruption of volcano, dug up in 1700s; tourists visit today
Herculaneum: small, rich town; buried by mud

page 160, ELL Reader Study Guide
1. When she was on a vacation at the shore, a wave knocked her off her feet.
2. Both let a person breathe underwater. They use different ways of breathing.
3. Both are hard. Coral are alive; rocks are not.
4. She studied the coral reef to learn why the corals were sick or dying.
5. Sylvia's was clear.
6. Trash; people taking fish from the ocean

page 162, Picture It!
1. They are brave pilots.
2. They need to save firefighters in danger.
3. They used water to clear a path so that the firefighters could escape.
4. Brave people overcome danger to help others.

page 166, ELL Reader Study Guide
China, United States; Eileen Collins;
Space, 2003

page 168, Picture It!
Main Idea: Life was different when glaciers
covered the Earth in the Ice Age.
Details: Students should include details about the
Ice Age.

page 172, ELL Reader Study Guide
1. They didn't have enough clothing, food, or
water for the cold.
2. They studied how people live in cold places
and brought enough clothes, food, and water.
3. glaciers, rocks, volcanoes, climate, icebergs,
wildlife
4. 4,000
5. They wanted to protect the land and animals.

page 174, Picture It!
1. b 2. d 3. c

page 178, ELL Reader Study Guide
1. safe temperature, water and food, oxygen
2. Both are too hot.
3. Both have oxygen. Mars once had water.
4. It has a deadly atmosphere. People cannot
breathe in it.
5. It has rings made of ice.
6. They are far away from the sun.

page 180, Picture It!
Clue words: so, because
Cause: She wasn't allowed to go to the school
closest to her home.
Effect: Separate schools for people of different
skin colors are illegal.

page 184, ELL Reader Study Guide
Cause: He helped organize the United Nations.
Effect: This is how he won the Nobel Peace Prize.

page 186, Picture It!
Facts: Greeks invented many sports; Greek men
ran 26 miles from Athens to Olympia; Today, men
and women run marathons all over the world.
Opinions: Most of these sports would seem silly to
us today; The marathon is a long, exciting race;
The best marathon is at the Olympics.

page 190, ELL Reader Study Guide
Answers will vary but should include information
before, after, and what was the same at the school.

page 192, Picture It!
2, 3, 1

page 196, ELL Reader Study Guide
1. Koh Lanta Yai, Thailand, and San Jose,
California
2. to remember Koh Lanta
3. Students eat prepared foods in a cafeteria in
San Jose, but go home to eat fresh food in
Thailand.
4. Japanese Friendship Garden; It is beautiful,
with ponds, trees, birds, fish, and shrines.
5. She feels closer to her village.

page 198, Picture It!
1. All the horses at Pine Ridge Stable are suitable
for student riders.
2. Spike is easy to ride. Sparkle makes her rider
feel happy. Red is patient with new riders.
Rosie always obeys her rider.

page 202, ELL Reader Study Guide
1. Harriet Tubman was an enslaved person. She
escaped in 1849.
2. She came back to help her family and others
escape. She joined the Underground Railroad.
3. Harriet Tubman helped the Union Army. She
helped former slaves in many ways.

page 204, Picture It!
1. new moon 2. half or quarter moon
3. full moon 4. half moon or quarter moon

page 208, ELL Reader Study Guide
1. Neil Armstrong, Buzz Aldrin
2. a piece of equipment that lets astronauts
practice being in space
3. There is no gravity, so doing these things is
very different in space.
4. getting the shuttle safely back to Earth
5. scientists who observed space hundreds of
years ago

Part 3
Phonics Instruction for English Language Learners

Contents

Four by Four

Make and distribute copies of page 217. Work with students to generate a class list of twenty or more words that reflect the target phonics or word study skills that students have recently studied—for example, words that begin with the prefixes *im-* and *in-*. Write each word on a card. Have students choose sixteen words from the list and write them in random order in the squares on page 217. Have students cut out the star markers at the

Use with page 217.

bottom of the page. Shuffle the cards, and read aloud one card at a time. Students should look for each word on their paper and cover it with a star marker. The first one to have four marked words in a row (horizontally, vertically, or diagonally) calls out "Four by Four!" Note: For students in early stages of literacy, write consonants in the squares, and have students listen for words that begin with the consonants.

Word Hunt

Use with page 218.

Choose a target phonics or word study skill, such as "Words with long *a*" or "Words with the suffix *-ly*," and list it at the top of page 218. Make and distribute copies to individuals, partners, or small groups. Have students look around the classroom and school, in books and magazines, and perhaps at home, for

words that have the particular phonics feature. They can list the words in the chart on page 218, and either draw or attach (with glue or tape) pictures that illustrate the words. Conclude by having students share the words they find.

Name _____

Four by Four

- **Write** the words that your teacher gives you. Write one word in each square.
- **Listen** to the words. When you hear a word that is in a square, **cover** it with a star marker.
- When you have four covered words in a row, **say** "Four by Four!"

- **Cut out** the star markers. **Use** them in the game.

Name _____

Word Hunt: Words with _____

- **Find** words that share a sound or a spelling pattern.
- **Write** the words. **Add** pictures or definitions for the words.
- **Tell** your words to a friend.

Word	Picture or Definition

Transfer Skills

Many factors can influence students' understanding of print conventions. The students may be emergent readers of non-alphabetic languages or languages with alphabets similar to or different from the English alphabet. Some English learners may be familiar with reading left to right and top to bottom, as in English. Others may be accustomed to reading text from right to left, or from the bottom to the top of the page. Some have little experience with printed text. For students who are unfamiliar with English print conventions, activities such as these will help develop print awareness and strengthen literacy skills.

Print Awareness Activities

Parts of a Book Show students how to hold a book. Point out and explain the title, author byline, and illustrator's name. Turn to the selection pages and read a sentence or two. Discuss how the illustrations go with the text. Page through the book, and show how the narrative continues. Point to the text on each page. Then have students practice holding the book correctly, finding the title and author's name, turning the pages, and pointing to the text on each page.

Words, Sentences, Paragraphs Display a few paragraphs of printed text in a large format or on an overhead transparency. Frame one word with your fingers, and read it aloud. Explain that it is a word, and point out the spacing before and after the word. Then read aloud a sentence, running your finger under each word as you read. Point out the sentence boundaries: a capital letter at the beginning of the sentence and the end punctuation. Then circle a paragraph with your finger, and explain that a paragraph is a group of related sentences. Point out the indent at the beginning of the paragraph. Have students practice finding words, sentences, and paragraphs in other texts.

Directionality As you read a book aloud, put your finger on the starting point in the text on each page. Show that you read from left to right and from top to bottom by moving your finger along lines of text. Use your finger to show how to sweep back from the end of a line to the beginning of another, and how to move to the next page. Then have students use their fingers to show the correct movement as you read the text aloud again.

Writing the Alphabet Students should be introduced systematically to all the letters of the English alphabet, in manuscript and cursive writing. Students can practice writing letters, punctuation marks, and numbers, using pages 220, 221, and 222 as handwriting guides.

Name _____

The Alphabet

- **Practice** writing the letters of the alphabet.
- **Write** more of the letters on other paper.

Name _____

The D'Nealian™ Alphabet

- **Practice** writing the letters of the alphabet.
- **Write** more of the letters on other paper.

a b c d e f g h i j k

l m n o p q r s t

u v w x y z

A B C D E F G H I J K

L M N O P Q R S T

U V W X Y Z

1 2 3 4 5 6 7 8 9 10

Name _____

The D'Nealian™ Cursive Alphabet

- **Practice** writing the letters of the alphabet in cursive.
- **Write** more of the letters on other paper.

a b c d e f g h i j k

l m n o p q r s t

u v w x y z

A B C D E F G H I J K

L M N O P Q R S T

U V W X Y Z

1 2 3 4 5 6 7 8 9 10

Transfer Skills

The phonemes of certain English consonants may be unfamiliar to English language learners or easily confused with other phonemes. For example, consonant digraphs such as /th/, /sh/, and /ch/ may sound alike to some English language learners. Spanish speakers may hear and write /n/ at the end of words ending with /m/. The following lessons provide practice with certain consonant pairs that English language learners may find troublesome. You can develop similar lessons for other consonant sounds that are difficult for your students. This model lesson gives you a pattern for teaching.

☆ Model Lesson: Words with *b* and *v*   Use with page 226.

Preteach Copy and distribute page 226. Have students point to the picture of the box at the top of the page. Say: *This is a box. The word* box *begins with /b/. Say it with me: /b/, /b/, /b/, box.* Repeat the procedure with the word *van,* using the other picture at the top of the page.

Teach/Model Guide students to distinguish between /b/ and /v/, using the Pronunciation Tip. Then, direct students' attention to Row 1. Name each of the items shown, one by one: *boat, vest, bat, vase.* Continue: *I'll say each word one more time. If the word starts with the letter* b, *circle* b *under the picture. If the word starts with the letter* v, *circle* v. Read the words aloud once more, giving students enough time to circle the corresponding letter.

Repeat the process for Row 2, omitting the directions: *violin, vine, basketball, bike.*

Practice Have students look at the pictures in Row 3. Ask them to tell what the pictures show *(box, van)* and then write those words on the appropriate blank line.

Read the practice sentence aloud and have students find the words with *b* and *v (Val, Billy, dove, wave).* After they've had a chance to repeat the sentence several times, challenge students to say it as quickly as they can.

Assess Make letter cards for *b* and *v,* and give one of each to each student. Tell students: *I will say some words. Hold up the card that matches the sound you hear at the beginning of each word:* boat, vote, bolt, volt, vanilla, basket, very, berry, bent, vent, best, vest, vane. Then have students repeat the contrasting word pairs after you, striving for the correct pronunciation of /b/ and /v/. Keep in mind that students who have difficulty distinguishing /b/ and /v/ may still be able to comprehend words they hear or read that start with these consonants.

Adapting the ☆ **Model Lesson**

Use the same lesson format above to teach the following consonants and digraphs: /ch/, /sh/, /d/, /th/, /l/, /r/, /m/, /n/, and /s/. The following information will help you to customize each lesson.

Pronunciation Tip
b and v *When you say /b/, your lips start out together. Then they open and a tiny puff of air comes out of your mouth. If you touch your throat, you can feel it move because your voice box is on. Can you hold the sound /b/? Try it: /b/, /b/. No, you can't hold it. When you say /v/, you can hold it: /vvvv/. Your voice box is still on. Your top teeth touch your bottom lip. Say /v/ and feel your teeth touch your bottom lip. Hold the sound. Try it: /vvvv/, /vvvv/. Try both sounds: /b/, /vvvv/.*

Notes for Additional Lessons

Words with *ch* and *sh*

Use with page 227.

Teach/Model Use these words: *child, shop.*
Row 1 of page 227: *shoe, cherry, chair, sheep.*

Practice Row 2: *shark, shell, chicken, chalk.*
Row 3: *child, shop.* Practice sentence: *Sherry the Shark chewed and chewed on a shiny shoe.*

Assess Use these words: *chew, shoe, chin, shin, chomp, cherry, Sherry, shell, chain, chair, share.*

Pronunciation Tip
ch* and *sh When you say /ch/, your lips are open and your teeth are close together. Your tongue moves as you make the sound. Can you hold the sound /ch/? Try it: /ch/, /ch/. No, you can't hold it. When you say /sh/, your lips are also open and your teeth are close together. But your tongue doesn't move, and you can hold the sound: /shhhhh/. Try it: /shhhhh/, /shhhhh/. Try both sounds: /ch/, /shhhhh/.

Words with *d* and *th*

Use with page 228.

Teach/Model Use these words: *desk, third.*
Row 1 of page 228: *door, thorn, thirty, dinosaur.*

Practice Row 2: *thermos, thumb, dish, dog.*
Row 3: *third, desk.* Practice sentence: *Think a thought about a daring dog walking through thick grass.*

Assess Use these words: *thigh, dye, think, thirty, dirty, duck, though, dough, there, dare.*

Pronunciation Tip
d* and *th When you say /d/, the tip of your tongue touches above your top teeth. Say /d/ and feel the tip of your tongue touch above your top teeth: /d/. Is your voice box on? Yes, you can feel your throat move when you say /d/. Can you hold the sound /d/? Try it: /d/, /d/. No, you can't hold it. When you say /ŦH/ in a word like this, your voice box is also on: /ŦH/. But your tongue is between your teeth, and you can hold the sound. Try it: /ŦHHHHH/, /ŦHHHHH/. Try both sounds: /d/, /ŦHHHHH/. When you say /th/ in a word like thin, your voice box is off, and you can hold the sound: /thhhhh/. The tip of your tongue comes out between your teeth and air comes out, but no sound. Try it: /thhhhh/, /thhhhh/. Try both th sounds: /ŦHHHHH/, /thhhhh/.

Notes for Additional Lessons

Words with *l* and *r*
Use with page 229.

Teach/Model Use these words: *leg, ring*. Row 1 of page 229: *radio, lake, light, ruler.*

Practice Row 2: *rose, lizard, leaf, river.* Row 3: *leg, ring.* Practice sentence: *The red river runs into a little lake.*

Assess Use these words: *rake, lake, rip, lip, red, rice, late, rate, load, road, loud, lean.*

> **Pronunciation Tip**
> *l* and *r* When you say /l/, the tip of your tongue touches above your top teeth and stays there. Say /l/ and feel your throat move. Your voice box is on when you say /l/. Try it: /l/, /l/. When you say /r/, your voice box is on again. The tip of your tongue goes toward the roof of your mouth, but doesn't touch it. Try it: /r/, /r/. Try both sounds: /l/, /r/.

Words with *m* and *n*
Use with page 230.

Teach/Model Use these words: *mask, nest*. Row 1 of page 230: *nose, net, mouse, match.*

Practice Focus on ending sounds for Row 2: *jam, pen, stem, fan.* Row 3: *mask, nest.* Practice sentence: *The man in the moon eats ice cream with a spoon.*

Assess Use these words: *meat, neat, mole, next, moat, note, Pam, pan, tone, time, some, sun.*

> **Pronunciation Tip**
> *m* and *n* When you say /m/, your lips come together and a little air comes out of your nose. Can you hold the sound /m/? Try it: /mmmm/, /mmmm/. Yes, you can hold the sound. You can also hold the sound /n/. Try it: /nnnn/. But when you say /n/, your lips are open. Your tongue is behind your top teeth. Say it again: /n/, /n/. Try both sounds: /m/, /n/.

Words with *s* and *th*
Use with page 231.

Teach/Model Use these words: *sun, thorn*. Row 1 of page 231: *saw, thumb, thermos, soap.*

Practice Row 2: *sandwich, soup, thigh, thirteen.* Row 3: *sun, thorn.* Practice sentence: *Sara sipped thick soup.*

Assess Use these words: *some, thumb, so, think, sink, sock, thin, thing, sing, thank.*

> **Pronunciation Tip**
> *s* and *th* When you say /s/, the tip of your tongue touches above your top teeth. It makes a snake sound, and you can hold the sound. Try it: /ssss/, /ssss/. When you say /th/ in a word like thick, the tip of your tongue comes out between your teeth. You can feel air come out of your mouth. Try it: /thhhh/, /thhhh/. Try both sounds: /ssss/, /thhhh/.

Name _____

Words with *d* and *th*

- If the word begins with the sound of *d* in *desk*, **circle** the *d*.
- If the word begins with the sound of *th* in *third*, **circle** the *th*.

ROW 1

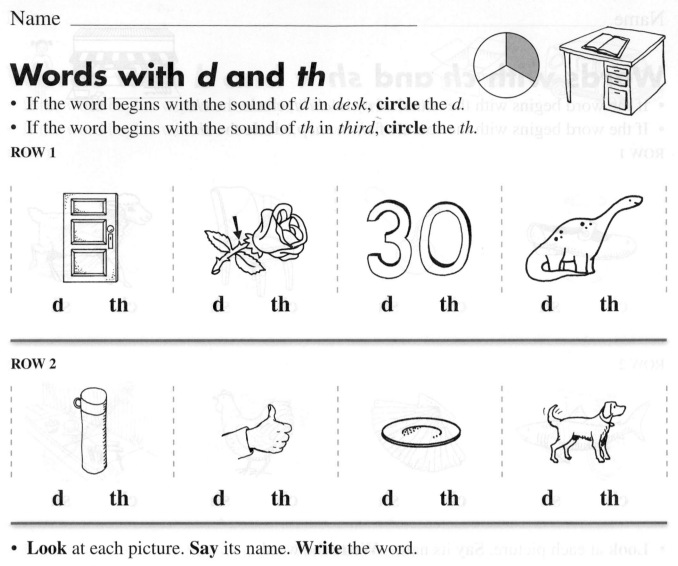

| d   th | d   th | d   th | d   th |

ROW 2

| d   th | d   th | d   th | d   th |

- **Look** at each picture. **Say** its name. **Write** the word.

ROW 3

_____   _____

Find *th* and *d* in this sentence. Then **practice** chanting or singing the sentence.

Think a thought about a daring dog walking through thick grass.

Words with *l* and *r*

- If the word begins with the sound of *l* in *leg*, **circle** the *l*.
- If the word begins with the sound of *r* in *ring*, **circle** the *r*.

ROW 1

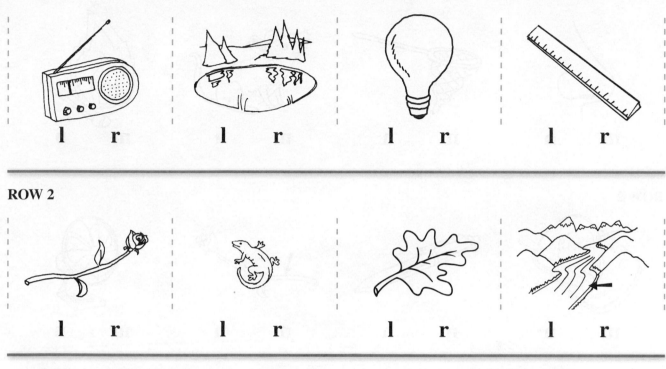

l   r   l   r   l   r   l   r

ROW 2

l   r   l   r   l   r   l   r

- **Look** at each picture. **Say** its name. **Write** the word.

ROW 3

_____   _____

Find *l* and *r* in this sentence. Then **practice** chanting or singing the sentence.
The red river runs into a little lake.

Words with *m* and *n*

- If the word has the sound of *m* in *mask*, **circle** the *m*.
- If the word has the sound of *n* in *nest*, **circle** the *n*.

ROW 1

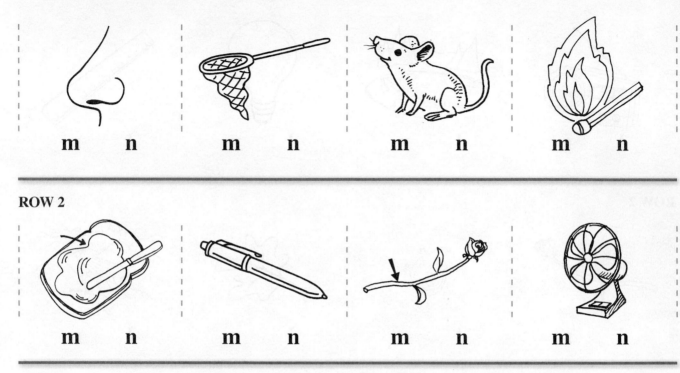

m   n   m   n   m   n   m   n

ROW 2

m   n   m   n   m   n   m   n

- **Look** at each picture. **Say** its name. **Write** the word.

ROW 3

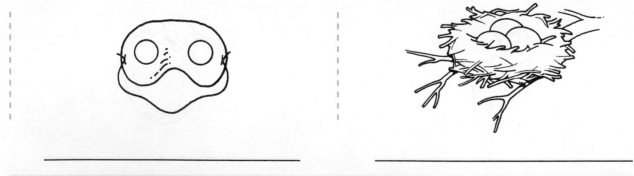

_____   _____

Find *m* and *n* in this sentence. Then **practice** chanting or singing the sentence.

The man in the moon eats ice cream with a spoon.

Words with *s* and *th*

- If the word begins with the sound of *s* in *sun*, **circle** the *s*.
- If the word begins with the sound of *th* in *thorn*, **circle** the *th*.

ROW 1

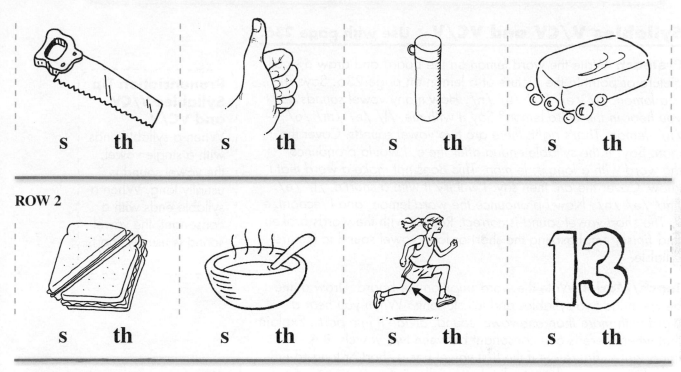

| s   th | s   th | s   th | s   th |

ROW 2

| s   th | s   th | s   th | s   th |

- **Look** at each picture. **Say** its name. **Write** the word.

ROW 3

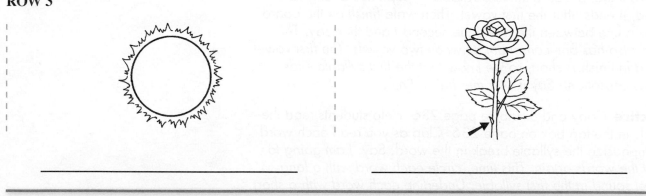

_____   _____

Find *s* and *th* in this sentence. Then **practice** chanting or singing the sentence.

Sara sipped thick soup.

Transfer Skills

The writing systems of languages such as Arabic and Hebrew focus on consonant sounds and long vowels. Short vowels are indicated with separate marks that are often optional. Speakers of these languages may need extra help in spelling words with short vowels or multiple vowel sounds.

Syllables V/CV and VC/V   Use with page 236.

Preteach Write the word *lemon* on the board and draw a small picture or point to the picture of a lemon on page 236. Say: *This is a lemon, /l/ /e/ /m/ /ə/ /n/. How many vowel sounds do you hear in the word* lemon? *Say it with me, /l/ /e/ /m/ /ə/ /n/, lemon. That's right, there are two vowel sounds.* Cover the *mon.* Say: *If the syllable ended after the* e, *I would pronounce the word with a long* e: lē mon. *This does not make a word that I know.* Cover the *on,* then say: *I will try it with a short* e, /l/ /e/ /m/ /ə/ /n/. *Now I pronounce the word* lemon, *and I recognize it. The short vowel sound is correct.* Repeat with the words *broken* and *finish,* emphasizing the short or long vowel sound in the first syllable.

Teach/Model Write the word *pupil* on the board. Draw a line between the two syllables and tell students: *When you hear a word with more than one vowel sound, divide it into parts.* Explain that when there is one consonant between two vowels, it is important to figure out if the first vowel has a short or long sound in order to know where to divide the syllable.

Point out that because the first syllable in *pupil* has a long vowel sound, it ends after the first vowel. Then write *finish* on the board. Draw a line between the *n* and the second *i* and then say: *This word also has one consonant between two vowels. The first vowel sound in* finish *is short, so we know that the first syllable ends with a consonant. Say it with me:* finish, fin/ish.

Practice Copy and distribute page 236. Help students read the words in the top box on page 236. Clap as you read each word to emphasize the syllable break in the word. Say: *I am going to read the words again. This time, circle each word with a long vowel sound in the first syllable. Underline each word with a short vowel sound in the first syllable.* Review the answers as a class (Circle: *broken, frozen, music, tulip;* Underline: *salad, lemon*).

Assess Make word cards with these word parts: *bro, ken, si, lent, sev, en, fe, male, rap, id.* In pairs, give students the pile of word cards. Have students put the various word parts together to create complete words. If necessary, list the words *broken, silent, seven, female,* and *rapid* on the board.

> **Pronunciation Tip**
> **Syllables V/CV and VC/V**
> When a syllable ends with a single vowel, the vowel sound is usually long. When a syllable ends with a consonant, the vowel sound is usually short.

Transfer Skills

Speakers of monosyllabic languages such as Cantonese, Hmong, Khmer, Korean, and Vietnamese may pronounce a two-syllable word as two separate words. Have students practice saying multi-syllabic words.

Syllables CV/VC   **Use with page 237.**

Preteach Write the word *violin* on the board and draw a small picture or point to the picture of a violin on page 237. Say: *This is a violin, /v/ /ī/ /ə/ /l/ /i/ /n/. How many vowel sounds do you hear in the word* violin? *Say it with me, /v/ /ī/ /ə/ /l/ /i/ /n/,* violin. *That's right, there are three vowel sounds.* Explain that if a word in English has three vowel sounds, it must also have three syllables. Repeat with the words *computer* and *calendar,* emphasizing vowel sounds and reviewing what students have learned about breaking words into syllables.

Teach/Model Write the word *create* on the board. Draw a line between the first *e* and *a* and tell students: *When you hear a word with more than one vowel sound, divide it into parts.* Explain that when there are two vowels side by side, you must put a syllable break between the two vowels.

   Practice breaking multi-syllabic words with the CV/VC syllable pattern into meaningful parts. Write the word *reorganize.* Point out the prefix *re-* and say: *We know that the prefix* re- *is its own syllable and means "again."* Then cover up the prefix so that only *organize* is visible. Say: Organize *means "to put in order." We know that* organize *has three vowel sounds, so it has three syllables.* Uncover the prefix, draw lines between the syllables, and blend the word. Have students repeat the word after you. Have them explain the meaning of *reorganize.* Repeat this exercise with the words *reunite, deactivate,* and *scientists.*

Practice Copy and distribute page 237. Read the directions aloud, and help students read the words if necessary. After students complete the activities, practice saying the multi-syllabic words aloud. (See answers on page 308.)

Assess Make word cards with the word parts in Part 2 of page 237. Put students in pairs. Give one student the word parts from column 1. Give the second student word parts from column 2. Once students have pieced the words together, have them write out the words and draw lines between each syllable.

> **Pronunciation Tip Syllables CV/VC**
> Remind students that a word has as many syllables as it has vowel sounds.

Syllables

Speakers of monosyllabic languages such as Cantonese, Hmong, Khmer, Korean, and Vietnamese may pronounce a two-syllable word as two separate words. Have students practice saying multisyllabic words.

Syllables VCCCV
Use with page 238.

Preteach Write *dolphin* on the board and draw a small picture. Say: *This is a dolphin, /d/ /o/ /l/ /f/ /ə/ /n/.* Point out that there are two vowel sounds in *dolphin,* and therefore two syllables. Say: *How many consonants do you see between the vowels* o *and* i *in the word* dolphin? Point to the l, p, and h as you say: *That's right, there are three consonants between the vowels.* Remind students that when two consonants, such as the *ph* in *dolphin* make one sound, those letters stay together when you divide the word into syllables. Say: *Now let's break the word* dolphin *into syllables: dol/phin, dolphin.* Repeat with the words *huddle* and *contract,* emphasizing vowel sounds and reviewing what students have learned about breaking words into syllables.

Teach/Model Write *surprise* on the board. Underline the three consonants between the vowels *u* and *i* and tell students: *There are three consonants between two vowels in this word. Each vowel means that there is a syllable, so we know that there are two syllables in this pattern.* Since it is hard to generalize where the syllable break comes in a word with the VCCCV syllable pattern, help students understand that they must look at each word separately to find its syllable breaks.

Practice breaking words with the VCCCV syllable pattern. Distribute several copies of a dictionary and point out how each word is divided into syllables. Write the word *complain* on the board. Ask: *How many syllables does this word have?* (2) *What is the first syllable?* (com) *What's the second syllable?* (plain) Repeat this exercise with the words *explore, sample, enclose,* and *hundred.*

Practice Copy and distribute page 238. Read the directions aloud, and have students look at the sample answer to help them get started. After students complete the activity, have them break each of the words into syllables. (See answers on page 308.)

Assess Write the following words on the board: *address, district, substance, complete,* and *control.* Have students write the words on a piece of paper, showing the syllable divisions. Students should use what they know about dividing words into syllables. If they have difficulty with a word, they may use a dictionary to see how a word is divided into syllables.

> **Pronunciation Tip**
> **Syllables VCCCV**
> Remind students that a word has as many syllables as it has vowel sounds.

Transfer Skills

Many languages do not have the schwa sound /ə/, so English learners may have difficulty pronouncing and spelling the unstressed syllable in words such as *table* and *apple*. Provide additional practice pronouncing these words.

C + *-le*   Use with page 239.

Preteach Say the word *candle* and draw a small picture of it or point to the picture of a candle on page 239. Say: *This is a candle, /k/ /a/ /n/ /d/ /əl/. How many syllables do you hear in the word* candle? *That's right, there are two syllables.* Sound out and blend the following words with *-le: bubble, puddle, table.* Point out that the first syllable in each word carries more stress than the second syllable.

Teach/Model Write *candle* on the board. Draw a line between the two syllables and tell students: *When you hear a word with more than one vowel sound, divide it into parts.* Cover *can.* Say: *If a word ends with* -le, *then the consonant before the* -le *is part of the last syllable.* Show that in the word *candle,* the letter *d* comes right before the *-le* and is part of the second syllable. Now write *double* on the board. Draw a line between the *u* and the *b* and say: *In the word* double, *the letter* b *comes before the* -le *and is part of the second syllable. Say it with me: double, dou/ble.*

Practice Copy and distribute page 239. Help students name the words that are pictured on the top half of page 239. Then read the words in the box. Clap as you read each word to emphasize the syllable break in the word. Say: *I am going to read the words again. This time write the word below the correct picture.* Review the answers as a class (*bubble, puddle, eagle, candle*) and then tell students to break the words into syllables.

Assess Tell students: *I will say some words. Put your thumb up if you hear a consonant with* -le *at the end of the word. Put your thumb down if you do not: purple, bubble, puppy, people, softball, broken, noodle.* Then have students repeat the C + *-le* words back to you.

> **Pronunciation Tip**
> **C + *-le***
> When a word ends in *-le*, the consonant that comes before the *-le* must be part of the last syllable.

Name _____

Syllables V/CV and VC/V

- **Read** the words in the box. **Circle** each word with a **long vowel sound** in the first syllable. **Underline** each word with a **short vowel sound** in the first syllable.
- **Write** a word on the line by each picture.

music	tulip
lemon	broken
frozen	salad

_____

_____

_____

_____

Name _____

Syllables CV/VC

PART 1
* **Read** the words.
* **Find** the syllables in each word. **Draw** a line between each syllable.

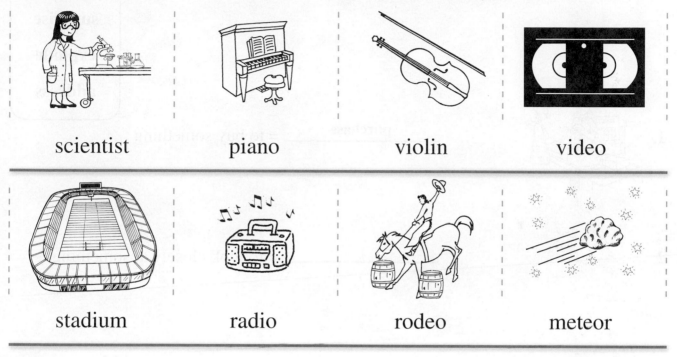

scientist	piano	violin	video
stadium	radio	rodeo	meteor

PART 2
* **Read** the two lists of words.
* **Connect** word parts from each list to make words.

studi-	-neer
cre-	-onic
ide-	-o
me-	-ate
pio-	-dium
immedi-	-ance
bi-	-a
reli-	-ate

Name _____

Syllables **VCCCV**

- **Read** the words in the box.
- **Look** at the pictures. **Read** the meanings.
- **Write** the correct word on each blank line.

inspect
children
purchase
surprise
explode
address

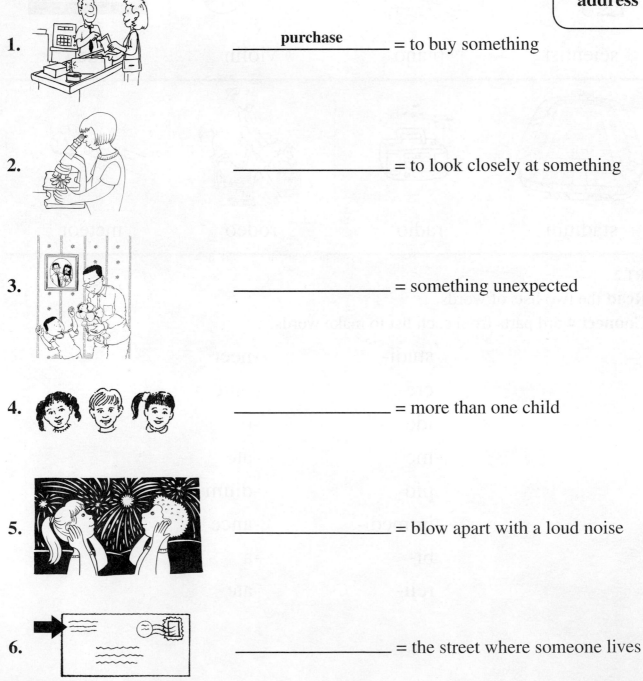

1. _____**purchase**_____ = to buy something

2. _____ = to look closely at something

3. _____ = something unexpected

4. _____ = more than one child

5. _____ = blow apart with a loud noise

6. _____ = the street where someone lives

ELL Handbook

Name _____

C + -le

PART 1

- **Look** at the pictures.
- **Read** the words in the box.
- **Write** the word on the line.

_____ _____ _____ _____

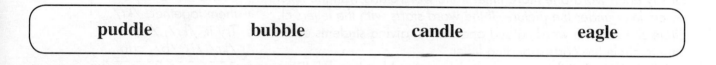

| puddle | bubble | candle | eagle |

PART 2

- **Read** the word.
- **Write** the two syllable parts that make up the word.

_____ + _____ = marble

_____ + _____ = middle

_____ + _____ = double

_____ + _____ = little

_____ + _____ = title

_____ + _____ = handle

Consonant Blends

Consonant blends in English words often are challenging for English language learners because their home languages may not combine consonant phonemes in similar ways at the beginnings and ends of words. For example, consonant blends with *l* and *r* can be particularly difficult for speakers of Asian languages such as Chinese, Korean, and Vietnamese. Speakers of Arabic may insert vowel sounds between the consonants within a blend. The following lessons provide practice with consonant blends. If your students are struggling with particular blends, you can develop similar lessons targeted to those blends.

Initial Consonant Blends   Use with page 242.

Preteach Copy and distribute page 242. Have students point to the picture of the crib at the top of the page. Say: *This is a crib. The word* crib *begins with /kr/.* Write *crib* on the board. Say: *Usually, when two letters come before a vowel* (underline the *cr*), *we blend the sounds of the letters: /k/ /r/... /kr/ /i/ /b/. Say it with me: /kr/ /i/ /b/,* crib. Repeat for *clap.*

Teach/Model Direct students' attention to Row 1. Name each of the items shown, one by one: *crab, crown, clock, cloth.* Continue: *I'll say each word one more time. If the word starts with the letters* cr, *circle* cr *under the picture. If the word starts with the letters* cl, *circle* cl. Read the words aloud once more, giving students enough time to circle the corresponding letter.

Tell students that there are many beginning blends in English. Write a 10-column chart on the board with the headings: *br, cr, cl, fl, gr, pr, pl, sn, sp, st.* List the words *crib* and *clap* in the columns where they belong. Add the words from Row 1 to the chart. Give several more examples. Invite children to suggest other words that begin with these blends that can be added to the chart.

Practice Have students look at the pictures in Row 2. Name the items shown (*princess, plant, price, plug*), and pause to let students circle their answer choices. Repeat the procedure for Row 3 (*straw, string, steak, starfish*).

Read the practice sentence aloud, and have students find the words with beginning blends (*clock, struck, students, snapped*). After they've had a chance to repeat the sentence several times, challenge students to say it as quickly as they can.

Assess Prepare sets of cards with a blend written on each one: *cr, cl, pr, pl, tr, dr, st, str.* Give each student a set of cards. Say a list of words, and have students display the correct initial blends: *crawl, please, claw, preen, tree, street, draw, stall.* Then have students repeat the words after you, striving for the correct pronunciation of the initial blends. Keep in mind that students who have difficulty pronouncing the initial blends may still be able to comprehend words they hear or read that start with these consonants.

> **Pronunciation Tip**
> **Initial Consonant Blends** *When a word begins with two consonants such as c and r, you blend the sounds of the two consonants together. In the word* crib, *take the sound /k/ and sound /r/ and put them together: /kr/. Try it: /kr/, /kr/, /kr/ /i/ /b/,* crib.

Final Consonant Blends — Use with page 243.

Preteach Copy and distribute page 243. Have students point to the picture of the pond at the top of the page. Say: *This is a pond. The word* pond *ends with /nd/. Usually, when two letters come after a vowel* (underline the nd), *we blend the sounds of the letters: /n/ /d/…/p/ /o/ /nd/. Say it with me:* pond, /p/ /o/ /nd/. Repeat for *sink*.

Teach/Model Direct students' attention to Row 1. Name each of the items shown, one by one: *(band, trunk, hand, bank)*. Continue: *I'll say each word one more time. If the word ends with the letters* nd, *circle* nd *under the picture. If the word ends with the letters* nk, *circle* nk. Read the words aloud once more, giving students enough time to circle the corresponding letter.

Tell students that there are many ending blends in English. Write a 9-column chart on the board with the headings *lt, mp, nch, nd, nk, nt, sk, sp, st*. List the words *pond* and *sink* in the columns where they belong. Add the words from Row 1 to the chart. Give several more examples. Invite children to suggest other words that end with these blends that can be added to the chart.

Practice Have students look at the pictures in Row 2. Name the items shown *(ant, paint, branch, inch)*, and pause to let students circle their answer choices. Repeat the procedure for Row 3 *(desk, vest, cast, mask)*.

Read the practice sentence aloud, and have students find the words with ending blends *(must, ask, band, paint, bench)*. After they've had a chance to read the sentence several times, challenge students to say it from memory.

Assess Prepare sets of cards with a blend written on each one: *nd, nk, nt, nch, sk, st*. Give each student a set of cards. Say a list of words, and have students display the correct final blends: *sink, cinch, bank, band, inch, ink, dusk, dust, ant, and, paint, pond*. Then have students repeat the words after you, striving for the correct pronunciation of the final blends. Keep in mind that students who have difficulty pronouncing the final blends may still be able to comprehend words they hear or read that end with these consonants.

> **Pronunciation Tip Final Consonant Blends** *When a word ends with two consonants such as* s *and* k, *you blend the sounds of the two consonants together. In the word* desk, *take the sound /s/ and sound /k/ and put them together: /sk/. Try it: /sk/, /sk/,* desk.

Name _____

Initial Consonant Blends

- If the word begins with the sound of *cr* in *crib*, **circle** the *cr*.
- If the word begins with the sound of *cl* in *clap*, **circle** the *cl*.

ROW 1

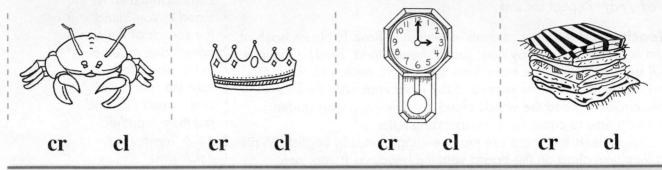

| cr cl | cr cl | cr cl | cr cl |

- If the word begins with the sound of *pl* in *plum*, **circle** the *pl*.
- If the word begins with the sound of *pr* in *prize*, **circle** the *pr*.

ROW 2

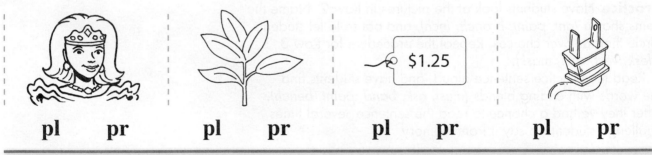

| pl pr | pl pr | pl pr | pl pr |

- If the word begins with the sound of *str* in *stripe*, **circle** the *str*.
- If the word begins with the sound of *st* in *stick*, **circle** the *st*.

ROW 3

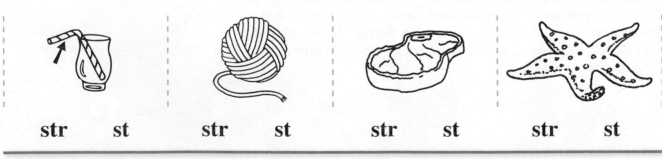

| str st | str st | str st | str st |

Find the beginning blends in this sentence. Then **practice** chanting or singing the sentence.

When the clock struck one, the students snapped their fingers.

Name _____

Final Consonant Blends

- If the word ends with the sound of *nd* in *pond*, **circle** the *nd*.
- If the word ends with the sound of *nk* in *sink*, **circle** the *nk*.

ROW 1

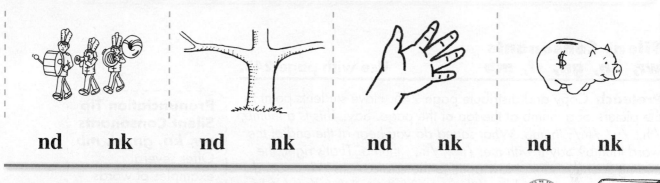

| nd | nk | nd | nk | nd | nk | nd | nk |

- If the word ends with the sound of *nt* in *cent*, **circle** the *nt*.
- If the word ends with the sound of *nch* in *bench*, **circle** the *nch*.

ROW 2

| nt | nch | nt | nch | nt | nch | nt | nch |

- If the word ends with the sound of *st* in *nest*, **circle** the *st*.
- If the word ends with the sound of *sk* in *tusk*, **circle** the *sk*.

ROW 3

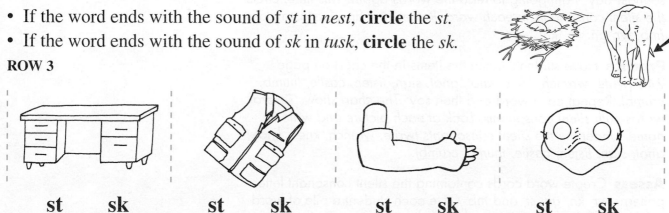

| st | sk | st | sk | st | sk | st | sk |

Find the ending blends in this sentence. Then **practice** chanting or singing the sentence.

You must ask the band to paint the bench.

Silent Consonants

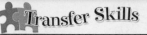

Students who are literate in their home language(s) may be familiar with the concept of silent letters. In Spanish, the letter *h* is always silent, and the letter *u* is silent when it follows a *q*. In French, the letter *s* at the end of a word is often silent. Discuss students' awareness of silent letters in their home languages before introducing *wr*, *kn*, *gn*, *st*, and *mb*.

Silent Consonants
wr, kn, gn, st, mb   Use with page 245.

Preteach Copy and distribute page 245. Have students point to the picture of a thumb at the top of the page. Say: *This is a thumb, /th/ /u/ /m/, thumb. What sound do you hear at the end of the word* thumb? *Say it with me: /m/, /m/, thumb. That's right, the ending sound is /m/.* Now point to the *castle.* Ask: *What sound do you hear in the middle of the word? Listen: /k/ /a/ /s/ /əl/. Yes, the middle sound is /s/.*

Teach/Model Write the word *thumb* on the board. Underline the *mb* in the word and tell students: *The sound /m/ in* thumb *is spelled* mb. *Say it with me: thumb, /th/ /u/ /m/. The letters* mb *make the sound /m/ in* thumb. *The letter* b *is not pronounced.* Now write *castle* on the board. Underline the *st* in the word and say: *The sound /s/ is in the middle of the word* castle. *Say it with me:* castle. *The letters* st *make the sound /s/ in* castle. *The letter* t *is not pronounced.*

Help students name the items in Row 1 on page 245 *(climb, wrist, gnat, knot, knit).* Repeat each word, stretching out the sounds. Say: *I am going to read the words again. This time, circle the silent consonants in each word.* Review the answers as a class *(mb, wr, gn, kn, kn).*

Practice Have students name the items in the chart on page 245 *(write, wrench, knee, knot, gnat, sign, listen, castle, thumb, crumb).* Repeat each word and then say: *The chart shows several words with silent consonants. Look at each picture and write its name. Underline the silent consonants (write, wrench, knee, knot, gnat, sign, listen, castle, thumb, crumb).*

Assess Create word cards containing the silent consonant letter patterns *wr*, *kn*, *gn*, *st*, and *mb*. Give each student a pile of word cards. Read the following words aloud to the class: *knob, knock, knit, write, wrist, wreath, sign, gnat, design, listen, hustle, bustle, lamb, comb,* and *numb.* Pause after each word so students can find and hold up the card that contains the silent consonant letter pattern that corresponds to each word.

Pronunciation Tip
Silent Consonants
wr, kn, gn, st, mb
Offer several examples of words containing letter patterns with silent consonants *(knee, knob, wrist, sign, castle, lamb).* See if students can point out the silent letter as they look at and listen to each word.

Silent Consonants *wr, kn, gn, st, mb*

- **Listen** for the beginning and ending sounds.
- **Circle** the correct letters.

ROW 1

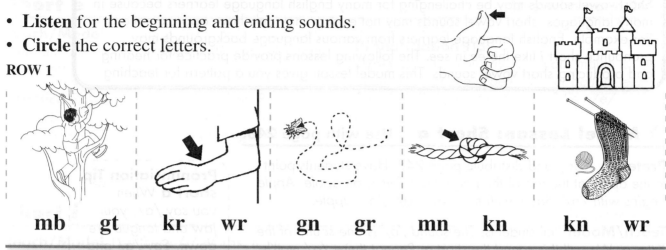

| mb | gt | kr | wr | gn | gr | mn | kn | kn | wr |

- **Look** at the pictures in each column. **Write** the word for each picture.

Silent Consonants				
wr	kn	gn	st	mb

Words with Short *i*

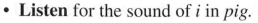

- **Listen** for the sound of *i* in *pig*.
- **Circle** the pictures of words that have this sound.

ROW 1

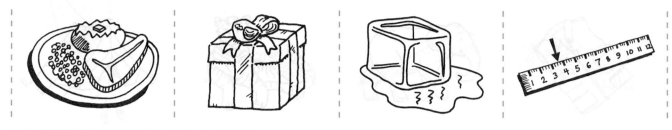

- **Look** at each picture. **Say** its name.
- **Circle** the word that names each picture.

ROW 2

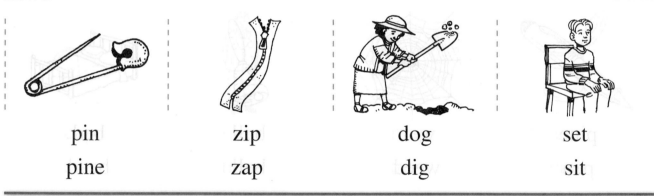

| pin | zip | dog | set |
| pine | zap | dig | sit |

- **Look** at each picture. **Say** its name.
- **Write** the name of the picture.

ROW 3

_____ _____ _____ _____

Find short *i* in this sentence. Then **practice** chanting or singing the sentence.

Six pigs with bibs grinned and did a jig in a minute.

Name _____

Words with Short o

- **Listen** for the sound of *o* in *ox*.
- **Circle** the pictures of words that have this sound.

ROW 1

- **Look** at each picture. **Say** its name.
- **Circle** the word that names each picture.

ROW 2

lick	rock	fox	hop
lock	rack	fix	hope

- **Look** at each picture. **Say** its name.
- **Write** the name of the picture.

ROW 3

_____   _____   _____   _____

Find short *o* in this sentence. Then **practice** chanting or singing the sentence.

I opened the lock and a fox jumped out of the box.

Words with Short *u*

- **Listen** for the sound of *u* in *sun*.
- **Circle** the pictures of words that have this sound.

ROW 1

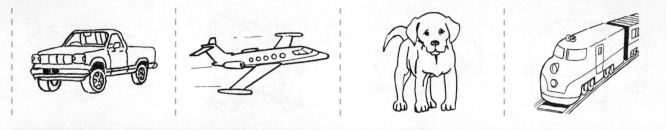

- **Look** at each picture. **Say** its name.
- **Circle** the word that names each picture.

ROW 2

| bus | dock | tub | rug |
| boss | duck | tube | rag |

- **Look** at each picture. **Say** its name.
- **Write** the name of the picture.

ROW 3

_____   _____   _____   _____

Find short *u* in this sentence. Then **practice** chanting or singing the sentence.

A bug on a rug jumped up and landed on a pup.

Transfer Skills

Long vowels and the vowel digraphs that produce long vowel sounds can be confusing for English language learners. For example, some long vowel sounds in English are similar to the sounds made by different vowels or vowel combinations in Spanish. As a result, Spanish speakers may spell long *a* words with an *e*, or long *i* words with *ai*. The following lessons provide practice for hearing, producing, and spelling long vowel sounds. This model lesson gives you a pattern for teaching.

☆ Model Lesson: Long *a*   Use with page 255.

Preteach Copy and distribute page 255. Have students point to the bunch of grapes at the top of the page. Say: *These are grapes. Grapes has the sound of /ā/. Say it with me: /ā/, /ā/, grapes.* Repeat for *rain* and *tray*.

Teach/Model Tell students: *The sound /ā/ is one sound of the letter* a. *We call this sound the long a. Repeat these /ā/ words after me: age, name, make, place, state.*

Ask students to name the items in Row 1 on page 255 *(rake, cat, train, plate)*. Repeat each word, clearly pronouncing the vowel each time. Then say: *I'll say these words again. If you hear the sound /ā/, circle the picture: rake, cat, train, plate.* Students should circle the *rake, train,* and *plate* pictures—but not the *cat.*

Point out that there are different ways of spelling long *a* words. Write a 3-column chart on the board with the headings *a_e, ai,* and *ay.* List the words *grapes, rain,* and *tray* in the columns where they belong. Add the long *a* words from Row 1 to the chart. Invite students to suggest other long *a* words they know that can be added to the chart.

Practice Have students look at the pictures in Row 2 on page 255. Have them read the words below each picture and circle the word that names it *(snake, chain, plane, hay)*. Then have them look at the pictures in Row 3, say the name of each picture, and write the names *(grapes, tray, rake, rain)*.

Read the practice sentence aloud, and have students find the long *a* words *(came, gate, cave, waited, Dave)*. Invite students to chant the sentence together, clapping each time they hear long *a.*

Assess Tell students: *I will say some word pairs. Raise your hand if both words have the sound /ā/:* sell, sale; cage, rage; ate, late; gate, get; rack, rake. Then have students repeat the word pairs after you, striving for the correct pronunciation of /ā/. Keep in mind that students who have difficulty pronouncing /ā/ may still be able to comprehend long *a* words that they hear or read.

Adapting the ☆ **Model Lesson**

Use the same lesson format above to teach the long vowels /ē/, /ī/, /ō/, and /ū/. The following information will help you to customize each lesson.

> **Pronunciation Tip**
> **long *a*** *When you start to say /ā/, your mouth is open. Your tongue is in the middle of your mouth. To finish the sound /ā/, your tongue and your jaw move up a little. Try it: /ā/, /ā/, ape. The long a sound is similar to the Spanish digraph* ei. *Example: rain/reina* (queen).

Long Vowels

Notes for Additional Lessons

Long *e*

Use with page 256.

Teach/Model Use these /ē/ words: *bee, beaver, me, team.* Row 1 of page 256: *eagle, teeth, eye, feet.* Make a 4-column chart for long e words.

Practice Row 2: *he, wheel, thirty, leaf.* Row 3: *tree, leaf, me, bee.* Practice sentence: See the leaves on the trees on our street.

Assess Use these word pairs: *team, Tim; meat, met; leaf, lean; seen, seat; wheat, wet.*

> **Pronunciation Tip**
> **long e** *When you say /ē/, your lips are stretched wide. Your mouth has a little smile when you say /ē/. Try it: /ē/, /ē/, /ē/. The long e sound is similar to the sound of i in Spanish. Examples: need/nido* (nest); *see/sí* (yes).

Long *i*

Use with page 257.

Teach/Model Use these /ī/ words: *kite, five, sky, why.* Row 1 of page 257: *bike, night, mice, fish.* Make a 5-column chart for long i words.

Practice Row 2: *ice, child, tie, light.* Row 3: *five, kite, light, sky.* Practice sentence: Five kites in the sky are flying high.

Assess Use these word pairs: *fight, fit; sky, sly; mice, miss; rice, price; light, lit.*

> **Pronunciation Tip**
> **long i** *When you say /ī/, your mouth is open and your jaw drops. Your tongue is down. To finish the sound /ī/, your tongue and your jaw move up. Try it: /ī/, /ī/, /ī/. The long i sound is similar to the Spanish digraphs ai and ay. Examples: I/hay* (there is/are); *bike/baile* (dance).

Long *o*

Use with page 258.

Teach/Model Use these /ō/ words: *rose, goat, pillow, smoke.* Row 1 of page 258: *rope, lock, nose, bone.* Make a 4-column chart for long o words.

Practice Row 2: *robe, gold, bow, boat.* Row 3: *goat, rose, snow(man), gold.* Practice sentence: Joan wrote a note and rode on a boat.

Assess Use these word pairs: *boat, bought; globe, lobe; low, blow; hose, toes; coat, cot.*

> **Pronunciation Tip**
> **long o** *When you say /ō/, your mouth is round. Try it: /ō/, /ō/, /ō/. The long o sound is similar to the sound of o in Spanish. Example: no/no.*

Long *u*

Use with page 259.

Teach/Model Use these /ū/ words: *flute, balloon, cube, use, news, true, blue.* Row 1 of page 259: *boat, boot, suitcase, foot.* Make a 5-column chart for long u words.

Practice Row 2: *glue, stool, fruit, mule.* Row 3: *fruit, flute, moon, cube.* Practice sentence: Sue used blue when she drew the moon.

Assess Use these word pairs: *tune, ton; rule, tool; soon, son; glue, blue; too, toe.*

> **Pronunciation Tip**
> **long u** *When you say /ū/ in a word like rule, your mouth is round and the opening is small. Try it: /ū/, /ū/. When you say /ū/ in a word like use, your lips start out in a line. Then they move into a circle. Try it: /ū/, /ū/. The long u sound in tube is similar to the sound of u in Spanish: tube/tubo. The long u sound in unit is similar to the sound of iu or yu in Spanish: unit/yugo.*

Words with Long *a*

- **Listen** for the sound of *a* in *grapes*.
- **Circle** the pictures of words that have this sound.

ROW 1

- **Look** at each picture. **Say** its name.
- **Circle** the word that names each picture.

ROW 2

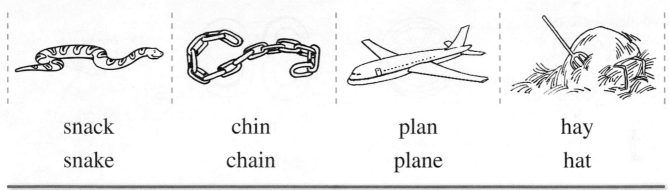

snack	chin	plan	hay
snake	chain	plane	hat

- **Look** at each picture. **Say** its name.
- **Write** the name of the picture.

ROW 3

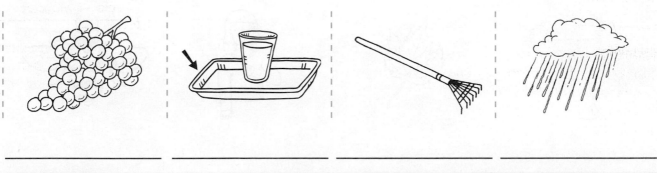

_____ _____ _____ _____

Find long *a* in this sentence. Then **practice** chanting or singing the sentence.

We came to a gate by the cave and waited for Dave.

Name _____

Words with Long e

- **Listen** for the sound of *e* in *bee*.
- **Circle** the pictures of words that have this sound.

ROW 1

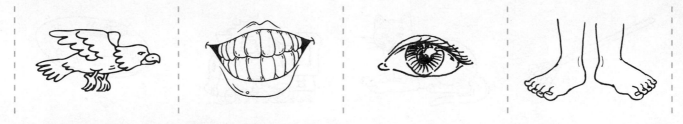

- **Look** at each picture. **Say** its name.
- **Circle** the word that names each picture.

ROW 2

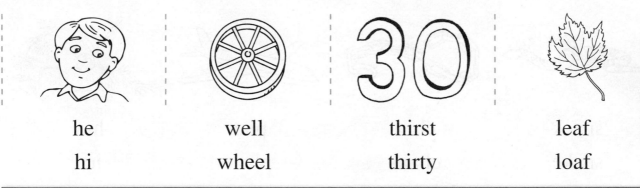

he	well	thirst	leaf
hi	wheel	thirty	loaf

- **Look** at each picture. **Say** its name.
- **Write** the name of the picture.

ROW 3

_____ _____ _____ _____

Find long *e* in this sentence. Then **practice** chanting or singing the sentence.

See the leaves on the trees on our street.

ELL Handbook

Words with Long *i*

- **Listen** for the sound of *i* in *kite*.
- **Circle** the pictures of words that have this sound.

ROW 1

- **Look** at each picture. **Say** its name.
- **Circle** the word that names each picture.

ROW 2

ice	child	tie	lit
ace	chill	tea	light

- **Look** at each picture. **Say** its name.
- **Write** the name of the picture.

ROW 3

_____ _____ _____ _____

Find long *i* in this sentence. Then **practice** chanting or singing the sentence.

Five kites in the sky are flying high.

Name _____

Words with Long o

- **Listen** for the sound of *o* in *goat*.
- **Circle** the pictures of words that have this sound.

ROW 1

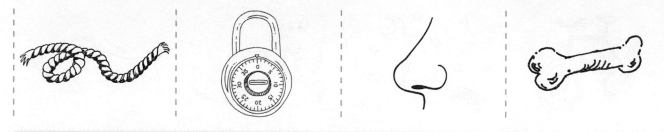

- **Look** at each picture. **Say** its name.
- **Circle** the word that names each picture.

ROW 2

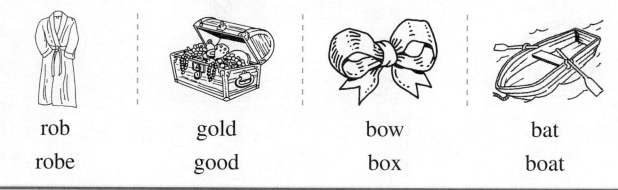

| rob | gold | bow | bat |
| robe | good | box | boat |

- **Look** at each picture. **Say** its name.
- **Write** the name of the picture.

ROW 3

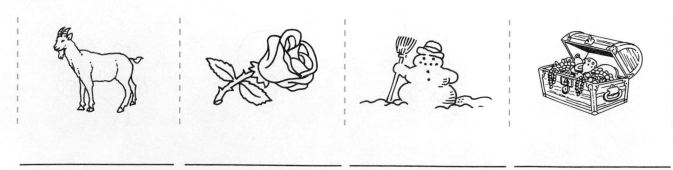

_____ _____ _____ _____

Find long *o* in this sentence. Then **practice** chanting or singing the sentence.

Joan wrote a note and rode on a boat.

Name _____

Words with Long *u*

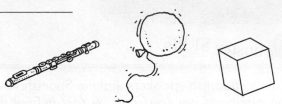

- **Listen** for the sound of *u* in *flute*.
- **Circle** the pictures of words that have this sound.

ROW 1

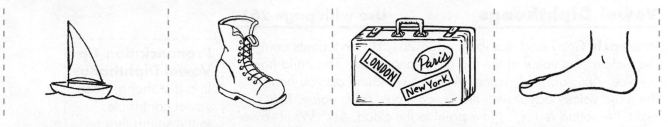

- **Look** at each picture. **Say** its name.
- **Circle** the word that names each picture.

ROW 2

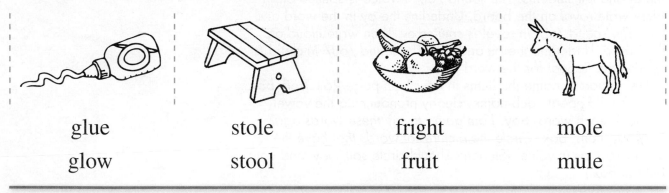

glue	stole	fright	mole
glow	stool	fruit	mule

- **Look** at each picture. **Say** its name.
- **Write** the name of the picture.

ROW 3

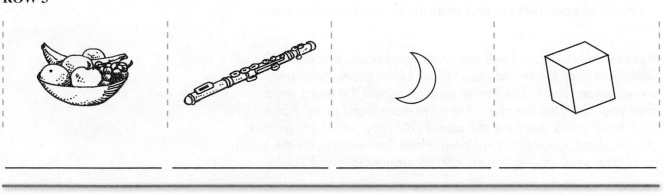

_____ _____ _____ _____

Find long *u* in this sentence. Then **practice** chanting or singing the sentence.

Sue used blue when she drew the moon.

Transfer Skills

Explain to Spanish speakers that the Spanish vowel sounds *au* and *oy* are similar in pronunciation to *ow* /ou/ and *oy* /oi/ in English. Display and discuss the examples *jaula (birdcage), flauta (flute), hoy (today),* and *soy (I am).*

Vowel Diphthongs   Use with page 261.

Preteach Copy and distribute page 261. Have students point to the picture of a *voice* at the top of the page. Say: *This child has a voice, /v/ /oi/ /s/, voice. What vowel sound do you hear in the word* voice? *Say it with me: voice, /oi/, /oi/, voice. That's right, the sound is /oi/.* Now point to the *cloud.* Ask: *What vowel sound do you hear in the word* cloud? *Listen: /k/ /l/ /ou/ /d/. Yes, the sound is /ou/.* Repeat this drill for the words *royal* and *plow.*

Teach/Model Write the word *voice* on the board. Underline the *oi* and tell students: *The sound /oi/ in* voice *is spelled* oi. Now write *royal* on the board. Underline the *oy* in the word and say: *The sound /oi/ in* royal *is spelled* oy. Then write *cloud* on the board. Underline the *ou* and say: *The sound /ou/ in* cloud *is spelled* ou. Repeat for the word *plow.*

Help students name the items in Row 1 on page 261 *(soil, boy, coin, box).* Repeat each name, clearly pronouncing the vowel sound in each word. Say: *I am going to say these words again:* soil, boy, coin, box. *Circle the pictures of words that have the sound /oi/ as in* voice. (Students should circle *soil, boy,* and *coin,* but not *box.*)

Practice Have students look at the pictures in Row 2 on page 261. Help students name each picture *(crowd, count, towel, plow).* Have them choose and circle the word that correctly names each picture. Have students look at the pictures in Row 3, say the name of each picture, and write the names *(cow, toy, voice, cloud).*

Assess Tell students: *I will say some word pairs. Raise your hand when you hear the sound /ou/:* plow, blow; grow, how; owl, snow; goose, south. Then have students repeat the word pairs after you. Then tell the class: *Here are more word pairs. Raise your hand when you hear the sound /oi/:* soy, soon; enjoy, rock; choice, short; toil, coat; join, born. Have the class repeat the word pairs after you, striving for the correct pronunciation of /oi/.

Pronunciation Tip
Vowel Diphthongs
In a diphthong, each vowel contributes to the sound that is produced or heard.

Name _____

Vowel Diphthongs

- **Listen** to the sound of *oi* in *voice* and *oy* in *royal*.
- **Circle** the pictures of words that have this sound.

ROW 1

- **Look** at each picture. **Say** its name.
- **Circle** the word that names the picture.

ROW 2

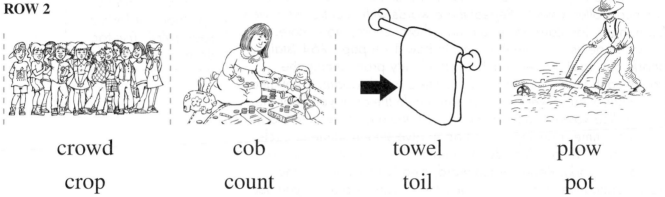

| crowd | cob | towel | plow |
| crop | count | toil | pot |

- **Look** at each picture. **Say** its name.
- **Write** the name of the picture.

ROW 3

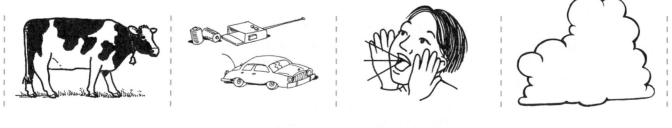

_____   _____   _____   _____

Find the vowel diphthongs in this sentence. Then **practice** chanting or singing the sentence.

The boy will count his toy cows.

Transfer Skills

> English learners may benefit from extra practice distinguishing between sounds /j/ and /ch/. Have students pronounce the sounds while placing their hands on their throats. Have them feel how the sound /j/ is voiced from their throats and the sound /ch/ is unvoiced and originates in their mouth.

Spellings of /j/, /s/, /k/ Use with page 275.

Preteach Copy and distribute page 275. Have students point to the picture of a bridge at the top of the page. Say: *This is a bridge, /b/ /r/ /i/ /j/. Where do you hear the sound /j/ in the word? Say it with me: /j/, /j/, bridge. That's right, the sound /j/ comes at the end of the word.* Now point to the *sailboat.* Ask: *Do you hear the sound /s/ in this word? Where? Listen: /s/ /ā/ /l/ /b/ /ō/ /t/. Yes, the sound /s/ is at the beginning of the word.* Repeat this drill for the word *kick.*

> **Pronunciation Tip**
> **Spellings of /j/, /s/, /k/** The sound /j/ can be spelled *g, j,* or *dge.* The sound /s/ can be spelled *s* or *c.* The sound /k/ can be spelled *c, k, ck,* or *ch.*

Teach/Model Write *bridge, jump,* and *judge* on the board. Say the words aloud, and point to the letters that make the sound /j/ in each. Write *bus* and *mice* on the board. Say the words aloud, and point to the letters that make the sound /s/ in each. Then write *care, back, kite,* and *chrome.* Say the words aloud, and point to the letters that make the sound /k/. Review each set of words. Have students repeat the words after you.

Practice Help students name the items in Row 1 on page 275 (*jet, cage, tree, jam*). Say: *I will say the words again. This time, circle the picture if the word has the sound of j, as in* bridge. Repeat each name, stretching out the sound of each letter so students can hear the sound /j/ in each word. Students should circle *jet, cage, jam,* but not *tree.* Repeat the process for Rows 2 and 3.

Read the practice sentence aloud and have students find the words with sounds /j/, /s/, and /k/ (*Jessica, checks, crossing, bridge*). After they have repeated the sentence several times, challenge students to say it as quickly as they can.

Assess Make another copy of page 275 and cut out all of the pictures. Prepare a sheet of paper with three columns that are labeled with the letters *j, k,* and *s.* Give each student the pile of pictures. Have students say the names of the pictures and place each one under the sound that the word contains.

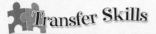
Transfer Skills

In Spanish, each vowel has only one sound. Spanish speakers may benefit from extra practice pronouncing and spelling words with variant vowel sounds in English. Let students practice saying and writing groups of words that have the sound /ȯ/ in *ball* and *walk: all, fault, awe, scald.*

Spellings of /ȯ/ (Vowel Sound in *ball*): *a, au, aw, al*   Use with page 276.

Preteach Copy and distribute page 276. Have students point to the picture of a ball at the top of the page. Say: *This is a ball, /b/ /ȯ/ /l/. What vowel sound do you hear in the word* ball? *Say it with me: /ȯ/, /ȯ/,* ball.

Teach/Model Write *call, sauce, yawn,* and *talk* on the board. Underline the *a, au, aw,* and *al* sound spellings in the words. Tell students: *The sound /ȯ/ can be spelled* a, au, aw, *and* al. *When* a *is followed by* u, l, *or* w, *it usually stands for the sound you hear in* ball. Point out the sound spellings for /ȯ/ in the words *call, sauce, yawn,* and *talk.* Segment and blend each of the words as a class.

Help students name the items in Row 1 on page 276 *(saw, sausage, fence, straw).* Repeat each name, stretching out the sound of each letter so students can hear the vowel sound in each word. Read the words again. This time, tell students to circle the pictures for words that contain the sound /ȯ/. Review the answers as a class *(saw, sausage, straw).*

Practice Have students look at the pictures in Row 2 on page 276. Help them read the words in the box. Have them write the word that names each picture *(applause, lawn, walnut, salt).* Then, *students can work with a partner to fill in the chart at the bottom of the page. When they are finished, share answers, and teach any new words students do not know.*

Assess Have students write the /ȯ/ sound spellings *a, au, aw,* and *al* on index cards. Then read the following words aloud to the class: *all, fault, raw, bald, talk, sauce, yawn, saw, crawl, call.* Pause after each word so students can find and hold up the card that contains the sound-spelling pattern that corresponds to the word.

> **Pronunciation Tip**
> **Spellings of /ȯ/ in**
> ***a, au, aw, al***
> When words end in the sound /ȯ/, the sound /ȯ/ is usually spelled *aw.*

Transfer Skills

Students may need assistance with words spelled *augh* and *ough* as in *caught* and *fought*, in which the *gh* is silent. Practice the words along with words containing the vowel patterns *aw*, *au*, and *al* as in *claw*, *jaunt*, and *call*. Display the words on the board as you practice.

Spellings of /ȯ/ as in *thought:* *augh, ough*   Use with page 277.

Preteach Display and say the word *thought*. Ask: *What vowel sound do you hear in the word* thought? *Say it with me: /ȯ/, /ȯ/,* thought. Display and say the word *caught*. Ask: *What vowel sound do you hear in the word* caught? *Say it with me: /ȯ/, /ȯ/,* caught. *In the words* thought *and* caught, *the vowel sound is /ȯ/.*

Teach/Model Write *thought* and *caught* on the board. Underline the *ough* and *augh* sound spellings in the words. Tell students: *The sound /ȯ/ can be spelled* ough *and* augh. *When you see the spellings* ough *and* augh, *you know the word will have the /ȯ/ vowel sound.* Point out the sound spellings for /ȯ/ in the words *thought* and *caught*. Segment and blend each of the words as a class.

   Write two columns on the board, labeled *ough* and *augh*. As a class, brainstorm a list of words with *ough* and *augh* sound spellings such as *sought, ought, brought, taught, daughter,* and *fraught*. Have students repeat the words after you, and then have them practice saying the words with a partner.

Practice Copy and distribute page 277. Read the directions aloud, and discuss the meanings of the words in the box. Then do the first example together. Have students choose and write a logical word in the blank. Then have students read the sentences aloud with a partner. (See answers on page 310.)

Assess Have students write the /ȯ/ sound spellings *ough* and *augh* on index cards. Then read the following words aloud to the class: *brought, caught, daughter, fraught, taught, thought, fought.* Pause after each word so students can hold up the card that contains the sound-spelling pattern that corresponds to the word.

Name _____

Sounds of j, s, k

• If the word has the sound of *j* as in *bridge*, **circle** it.

ROW 1

• If the word has the sound of *s* as in *sail*, **circle** it.

ROW 2

• If the word has the sound of *k* as in *kick*, **circle** it.

ROW 3

Find the sounds of *j*, *s*, and *k* in this sentence. Then **practice** chanting it.

Jessica checks both ways before crossing the bridge.

Name _____

Vowel Sound in *ball*

- **Listen** for the vowel sound in *ball*. This sound can be spelled *a, au, aw,* or *al*.
- **Circle** the pictures of words that have this sound.

ROW 1

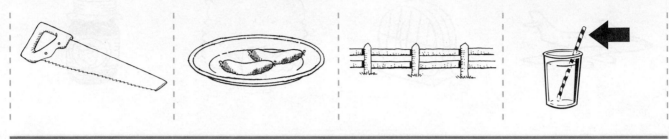

- **Look** at each picture. **Read** the words in the box.
- **Write** the word that names each picture.

| lawn | walnut | salt | applause |

ROW 2

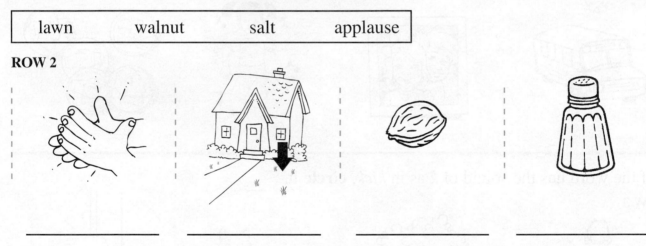

_____ _____ _____ _____

- **Write** the words with the same vowel sound as in *ball* spelled *a, au, aw,* and *al* in the chart below. **Use** a dictionary to **find** more words.

a	au	aw	al

Name _____

Vowel Sound in *thought*: *augh, ough*

- **Read** the sentences.
- **Choose** the correct word from the box to complete each sentence.
- **Write** the word on the blank line.

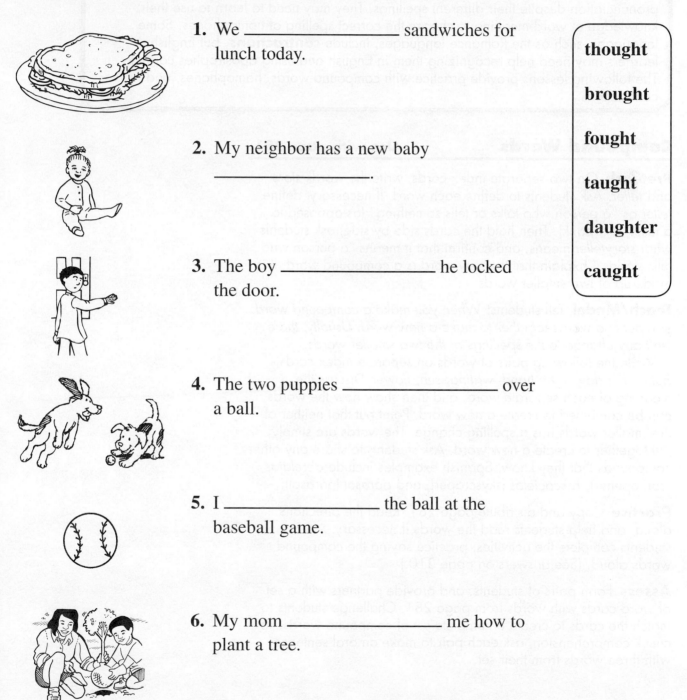

1. We _____ sandwiches for lunch today.

2. My neighbor has a new baby _____ .

3. The boy _____ he locked the door.

4. The two puppies _____ over a ball.

5. I _____ the ball at the baseball game.

6. My mom _____ me how to plant a tree.

| thought |
| brought |
| fought |
| taught |
| daughter |
| caught |

Compound Words, Homophones, and Contractions

Transfer Skills

Compound words exist in many languages, including Spanish, Vietnamese, Haitian Creole, German, and Russian. Children may readily understand the concept of compound words, but may need additional help with decoding to break English compound words into their parts. **Homophones** are also common in other languages, but English learners may not recognize that English homophone pairs have the same pronunciation despite their different spellings. They may need to learn to use their knowledge of word meaning to choose the correct spelling of homophones. Some languages, such as the Romance languages, include **contractions**, but English learners may need help recognizing them in English and using apostrophes correctly. The following lessons provide practice with compound words, homophones, and contractions.

Compound Words   Use with page 281.

Preteach On two separate index cards, write the words *story* and *teller*. Ask students to define each word. If necessary, define *teller* as "a person who talks or tells something" (as opposed to a teller at a bank). Then hold the cards side by side, ask students what *storyteller* means, and confirm that it means "a person who tells stories." Explain that the new word is a compound word. It is made up of two smaller words.

Teach/Model Tell students: *When you make a compound word, you put two words together to make a new word. Usually, there isn't any change to the spellings of the two smaller words.*

Write the following pairs of words on separate index cards: *butter, fly; day, light; hand, writing; sun, flower.* Discuss the meaning of each separate word, and then show how the words can be combined to create a new word. Point out that neither of the smaller words has a spelling change. The words are simply put together to create a new word. Ask students to share any other compounds that they know. Spanish examples include *abrelatas* (can opener), *rascacielos* (skyscraper), and *parasol* (parasol).

Practice Copy and distribute page 281. Read the directions aloud, and help students read the words if necessary. After students complete the activities, practice saying the compound words aloud. (See answers on page 310.)

Assess Form pairs of students, and provide partners with a set of word cards with words from page 281. Challenge students to match the cards to create a complete set of compound words. To check comprehension, ask each pair to make an oral sentence with three words from their set.

Homophones   **Use with page 282.**

Preteach Tell students this joke in the form of a question and answer: *What is black and white and read all over? A newspaper!* Explain to students that the question seems to be asking about colors (black, white, and red), but there is a play on the word *red*. The color red sounds the same as *read,* a past tense form of the verb *read.* Explain that this joke is based on a pair of homophones *(red* and *read),* two words that sound the same but are spelled differently and mean completely different things.

Teach/Model Write the following homophone pairs on the board: *pair, pear; flour, flower; ceiling, sealing; week, weak.* Explain the meaning of each word and point out the two different spellings. Model the pronunciation, emphasizing that the two words in each pair are pronounced in exactly the same way. Invite students to share any other homophones that they know. Spanish examples include *casa/caza* (house/hunt), *hola/ola* (hello/wave), and *ciento/siento* (one hundred/I feel).

Practice Copy and distribute page 282. Read the directions aloud, and help students answer the first item in each exercise. Help students read the words if necessary. When they are finished, invite volunteers to write their answers on the board. Review the meanings of the words. Make corrections as necessary, and tell students to correct their own work as well. (See answers on page 310.)

Assess Ask students to write three sentences that include a pair of homophones, such as: *Our English class is an hour long.* Encourage students to make simple jokes with the homophones; they can also write sentences that are fanciful or silly, as in: *On Monday, I was too weak to make it through the whole week.* Alternatively, you can dictate pairs of sentences using homophones from page 282; for example: *Mo threw the ball. The ball went through the window.* Check students' work to make sure that they used the correct homophone in each sentence.

Contractions   Use with page 283.

Preteach Write the following sentences on the board, and ask students to tell you how they are different:

I am sorry for being late to class. → *I'm sorry for being late to class.*

Confirm that *I am* has been shortened to *I'm* in the second sentence. Tell students that this is a contraction. Summarize: *The pronoun I and the verb am are put together with an apostrophe to form one word, I'm. The letter a is dropped from the word am, and the apostrophe takes its place.*

Teach/Model Write the following chart on the board, asking students to tell you how to write each contraction as you go:

The Verb "be"	The Verb "have"	Negatives
I am → I'm	I have → I've	has not → hasn't
You are → You're	You have → You've	have not → haven't
He is → He's	He has → He's	are not → aren't
She is → She's	She has → She's	is not → isn't
It is → It's	It has → It's	should not → shouldn't
We are → We're	We have → We've	can not → can't
They are → They're	They have → They've	will not → won't
		do not → don't
		did not → didn't

Conclude by showing how the future tense marker *will* can be shortened and connected to a pronoun using *'ll: I'll, you'll, she'll,* etc.

Practice Copy and distribute page 283. Read the directions aloud, and complete the first line together. Help students read the dialogue if necessary. After students complete the activities, have them practice the dialogue. (See answers on page 310.)

Assess Form pairs of students, and have partners create their own dialogue between a parent and child. Tell them to include a contraction in each line of dialogue. Circulate as they work to provide assistance. When they are finished, invite students to read their dialogues aloud for the class.

Compound Words

PART 1
- **Read** the compound words.
- **Draw** a line between the two words in each compound.

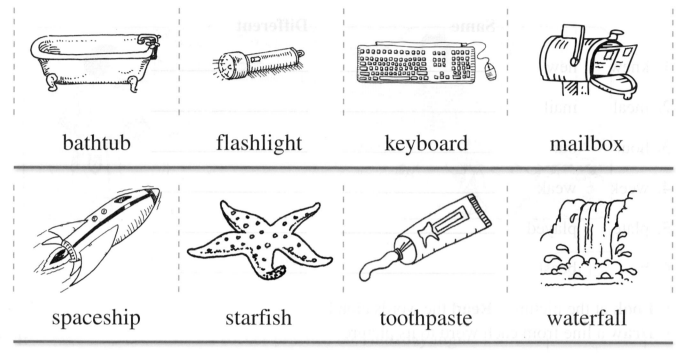

| bathtub | flashlight | keyboard | mailbox |

| spaceship | starfish | toothpaste | waterfall |

PART 2
- **Read** the two lists of words.
- **Connect** words from each list to make compounds.

back	boat
book	bow
class	brush
finger	mark
hair	nail
rain	pack
sail	room
side	walk

Prefixes and Suffixes

Transfer Skills

Some English prefixes and suffixes have equivalent forms in the Romance languages. For example, the prefix *dis-* in English *(disapprove)* corresponds to the Spanish *des- (desaprobar)*, the French *des- (desapprouver)*, and the Haitian Creole *dis-* or *dez- (dezaprouve)*. Students who are literate in these languages may be able to transfer their understanding of prefixes and suffixes by using parallel examples in the home language and in English. Some suggestions for Spanish are provided below. The following lessons provide additional practice with prefixes and suffixes.

Prefixes *un-* and *re-*   Use with page 291.

Preteach Write these word pairs on the board: *happy, unhappy; safe, unsafe; lucky, unlucky.* Read the words aloud with students, and discuss their meanings. Ask: *What do you notice about these words?* Guide students to see that each word pair is a set of opposites, and that one word in each pair begins with *un-.* Circle the prefix *un-* in each word and say: *This syllable, un-, is a prefix. A prefix is a word part that is added to the beginning of a word. Adding a prefix changes the meaning of a word. A new word is made.*

Teach/Model Present the prefixes *un-* and *re-*. Use these examples to explain how the prefixes can change the meanings of words.

Prefix	Meaning	Examples	Spanish Examples
un-	not	happy → unhappy safe → unsafe locked → unlocked	*feliz → infeliz* *seguro → inseguro*
re-	again	tell → retell do → redo write → rewrite	*contar → recontar* *hacer → rehacer*

Practice Copy and distribute page 291. Read the directions aloud, and read the first example together. Have volunteers say the words they wrote in each column of the chart. (See answers on page 310.)

Assess Have students write these prefixes and base words on cards: *un-, re-, afraid, lock, run, unite.* Have students use the cards in different combinations to make words that have prefixes. Have students show you a base word without a prefix, add a prefix, say the new word, and tell what it means.

Prefixes *im-, in-, mis-, over-*
Use with page 292.

Preteach Write these word pairs on the board: *patient, impatient; polite, impolite; proper, improper; pure, impure.* Read the words aloud with students, and discuss their meanings. Ask students what they notice about these words. Guide students to see that each word pair is a set of opposites, and that one word in each pair begins with *im-*. Circle the prefix *im-* in each word and explain: *This word part,* im-, *is a prefix. It usually changes the meaning of a word to its opposite.*

Teach/Model Present the prefixes *im-, in-, mis-,* and *over-*. Use these examples to explain how the prefixes can change the meanings of words. Tell Spanish speakers that the Spanish prefixes *im-* and *in-* have similar meanings *(impaciente, intolerante).* The Spanish prefix *sobre-* is sometimes used like the English prefix *over- (sobrecarga).*

Prefix	Meaning	Examples
im-	not	impatient, imperfect, impossible
in-	not	insecure, intolerant, indestructible
mis-	wrong	misunderstood, misbehave, mismatch
over-	beyond, more than	overcook, overpay, overweight

Practice Copy and distribute page 292. Read the directions aloud, and help students fill in the first blank line. After students complete the activity, have pairs of students practice the dialogue. (See answers on page 311.)

Assess Have students write these prefixes and base words on index cards: *im-, in-, mis-, over-, correct, interpret, load, coat, mature, take, use.* Tell students to use the cards to make words with prefixes. Circulate as they work, asking students to show you a base word and a prefix that goes with it. Ask advanced students to tell you what the word means and to use it in an oral sentence.

Prefixes and Suffixes

Transfer Skills

Point out to Spanish speakers that the prefix *mid-* is related in meaning to the Spanish word *medio,* which means *half* or *middle.* Display cognates such as *midnight/ medianoche* and *midday/mediodía* as examples.

Prefixes *pre-, mid-, over-, out-, bi-*   Use with page 293.

Preteach Write these word pairs on the board: *test, pretest; air, midair; time, overtime; side, outside; monthly, bimonthly.* Read the words aloud with students and discuss their meanings. Ask: *What do you notice about these words?* Explain that the second word in each pair has a prefix that changes the meaning of the first word. Circle the prefix *pre-* and say: *This syllable,* pre-, *is a prefix. A prefix is a word part that is added to the beginning of a word to change its meaning. When you add a prefix, a new word is made. The prefix* pre- *means "before." So,* prepay *means "to pay before."*

Teach/Model Present the prefixes *pre-, mid-, over-,* and *bi-.* Using the chart below, explain how adding prefixes to base words changes the meaning of the word.

Prefix	Meaning	Examples
pre-	before	paid → prepaid view → preview
mid-	in the middle of	day → midday night → midnight
over-	more than normal, too much	grown → overgrown cooked → overcooked
out-	outward; or to a greater degree	side → outside run → outrun
bi-	two	cycle → bicycle

Practice Copy and distribute page 293. Read the directions aloud, and complete the first example together. Have students choose a prefix to add to the base word and write a new word that makes sense in the blank. Then have them read the story aloud with a partner. (See answers on page 311.)

Assess Have students write these prefixes and base words on index cards: *pre-, mid-, over-, out-, bi-, paid, air, time, field, weekly.* Have them use the cards in different combinations to make words with prefixes. As an additional challenge, have students show a base word without a prefix, add a prefix, say the new word, and tell what it means.

Suffixes -ly, -ful, -less, -ness
Use with page 294.

Preteach Write the following words on the board: *careful, carefully, careless, carelessness*. Ask students what these words have in common and what makes them different from each other. They will notice that they all have the same base, *care*. But each successive word also has a different word part at the end. Explain that each of these word parts is a *suffix*. Say: *A suffix is a word part that is added to the end of a word. Adding a suffix changes the meaning of a word.*

Teach/Model Present the suffixes *-ly, -ful, -less,* and *-ness*. Write the following chart on the board, asking students to provide additional examples for the last column. Tell Spanish speakers that *-ly* is similar to the Spanish suffix *-mente*. The Spanish suffix *-dad (felicidad)* is similar to *-ness*.

Suffix	How and Why to Use It	Part of Speech	Examples
-ly	Add it to an adjective to tell how an action is done.	Adverb	*quickly* *calmly* *completely*
-ful	Add it to a noun to mean "full of" the noun.	Adjective	*thoughtful* *colorful* *helpful*
-less	Add it to a noun to mean "without" the noun.	Adjective	*spotless* *joyless* *flawless*
-ness	Add it to an adjective to describe a state of being.	Noun	*darkness* *happiness* *carelessness* *peacefulness*

Practice Copy and distribute page 294. Read the directions aloud, and have students look at the sample answer to help them get started. After students complete the activity, invite volunteers to take turns reading the passage aloud. (See answers on page 311.)

Assess Have students write these suffixes and base words on index cards: *-ly, -ful, -less, -ness, slow, quiet, perfect, fear, rude*. Tell students to use the cards to make words with suffixes. Circulate as they work, asking students to show you a base word and a suffix that goes with it. Ask advanced students to tell you what the word means and to use it in an oral sentence.

Suffixes -tion, -sion, -able, -ible
Use with page 295.

Introduce Write the following words on the board: *perfection, decision, walkable, sensible.* Tell students that each of these words is made up of a base word and a suffix. Circle the suffix *-tion* in the first word and explain: *This word part, -tion, is a suffix.* Ask volunteers to find the suffixes in the other three words. Point out that the base word might need a spelling change before the suffix is added. The word *decide,* for example, drops the final *-de* before adding *-sion.* The reason for these spelling changes has to do with pronunciation, and the rules are hard to generalize, as there are many exceptions to the rules. Students will learn the different spellings with practice.

Teach/Model Present the suffixes *-tion, -sion, -able,* and *-ible.* Explain that *-tion* and *-sion* have the same meaning, as do *-able* and *-ible.* Write the following chart on the board, asking students to provide additional examples for the last column. Spanish examples of these suffixes are *-ción (reacción), -sión (decisión), -able (confortable),* and *-ible (sensible).*

Suffix	How and Why to Use It	Part of Speech	Examples
-tion, *-sion*	Add it to a verb to describe an action or a state of being.	Noun	*perfection imagination reaction decision admission confusion*
-able, *-ible*	Add it to a verb to add the meaning "can be."	Adjective	*walkable comfortable dependable sensible reversible flexible*

Practice Copy and distribute page 295. Read the directions aloud, and do the first example together. Tell students that they can use the chart on the board to check spellings. After students complete the activity, review the answers together. (See answers on page 311.)

Assess Have students write these suffixes and base words on index cards: *-tion, -sion, -able, -ible, sense, comfort, confuse, react.* Tell students to use the cards to make words with suffixes. Circulate as they work, asking students to show you a base word and a suffix that goes with it. Ask advanced students to tell you what the word means and to use it in an oral sentence.

Suffixes -er, -or, -ess, -ist Use with page 296.

Preteach Write the following words on the board: *swimmer, actor, hostess,* and *tourist.* Tell students that each of these words is made up of a base word and a suffix. Remind students that a suffix is a word part added to the end of a word to change its meaning. Circle the suffix *-er* in the first word and explain: *This word part,* -er, *is a suffix.* Ask individuals to find suffixes in the other three words. Explain that the base word may require a spelling change before a suffix is added. For example, the word *swimmer* adds an *m* before the suffix. Point out that some spelling changes are related to pronunciation. Explain to students that they will become familiar with different spellings as they practice using the words.

Teach/Model Present this chart to practice the suffixes *-er, -or, -ess,* and *-ist.* Ask students for additional examples of words with these suffixes.

Suffix	What It Means	Examples
-er -or	a person or thing that does something	*teacher* *opener* *editor* *tutor*
-ess	a female who does something as a job; a female	*actress* *lioness*
-ist	a person who has studied something or does something as a job	*artist* *dentist*

Practice Copy and distribute page 296. Read the directions to students, and complete the first example together. Tell students that they can use the chart on the board to check spellings. After students complete the activity, review the answers together. (See answers on page 311.)

Assess Have students write these suffixes and base words or word parts on index cards: *-er, -or, -ess, -ist, act, sell, host, dent, tour, teach, lion.* Have students use the cards in different combinations to make words that have suffixes. As an additional challenge, have students show a base word without a suffix, add a suffix, say the new word, and tell what it means.

Suffixes -y, -ish, -hood, -ment

Use with page 297.

Preteach Write the following words on the board: *rocky, foolish, parenthood,* and *shipment.* Tell students that each of these words is made up of a base word and a suffix. Remind students that a suffix is a word part that is added to the end of a word to change its meaning. Circle the suffix *-y* in *rocky* and explain: *This word part -y is a suffix. The base word in* rocky *is* rock. Ask students to find base words in the other three words. Have them tell you what each base word means.

Teach/Model Present this chart to practice the suffixes *-y, -ish, -hood,* and *-ment.* Have students identify each base word and suffix in the examples. Ask students for additional examples of words with these suffixes.

Suffix	What It Means	Examples
-y	having the quality of	*cloudy* *rainy* *thirsty*
-ish	describing nationality or language; somewhat	*Spanish* *brownish* *foolish*
-hood	a state or condition of	*childhood* *fatherhood*
-ment	a state, action, or quality	*excitement* *movement*

Practice Copy and distribute page 297. Read the directions aloud, and have students look at the sample answer to help them get started. After students complete the activity, have individuals take turns reading the passage aloud. (See answers on page 311.)

Assess Have students write these suffixes and base words on index cards: *-y, -ish, -hood, -ment, smell, Brit, mother, excite, wind, brown, false, ship.* Have students use the cards in different combinations to make words that have suffixes. As an additional challenge, have students show you a base word without a suffix, add a suffix, say the new word, and tell what it means.

Name _____

Prefixes *un-* and *re-*

- **Read** each group of words.
- **Use** *un-* or *re-* to make one new word.
- **Write** the new word.

1. read again   reread

2. appear again   _____

3. not believable   _____

4. not familiar   _____

5. heat again   _____

6. not interested   _____

7. not like   _____

8. start again   _____

9. use again   _____

10. not kind   _____

- **Write** all the new words in the chart.

un-	re-

Name _____

Prefixes *im-, in-, mis-, over-*

- **Read** the conversation. **Finish** the sentences with words from the box.
- Then **practice** the conversation.

Alex: This game costs too much. It is _____.
(1)

Tanya: This ball doesn't cost too much. It is _____.
(2)

Alex: The price on that sign is wrong. It is not correct.

Tanya: You're right! The price must be _____.
(3)

Alex: Let's tell someone that the sign has a _____.
Then they can fix the sign. (4)

Tanya: OK, but let's hurry. I want to go.

Alex: Why are you so _____? We have a lot of time!
(5)

| impatient |
| incorrect |
| inexpensive |
| misprint |
| overpriced |

Write one more word for each prefix. You may **use** a dictionary to **find** the words.

im-   in-   mis-   over-

_____   _____   _____   _____

Name _____

Prefixes *pre-, mid-, over-, out-, bi-*

- **Read** the story.
- **Add** *pre-, mid-, over-, out-,* or *bi-* to the beginning of each word in parentheses.

Today is the worst day ever! Yesterday I took a _____ (test) in
(1)

class. I did not do well. I have a hard time with _____ (fixes). My
(2)

teacher said that I need to study hard for the next test. She said that I should make an

_____ (line) to help me study.
(3)

Last night I studied until _____ (night). I also have a report that is
(4)

_____ (due). I am going to have to work _____ (time) to
(5) (6)

finish all of my homework.

My friends are _____ (side) having fun. But I am still in my room.
(7)

My mom and dad said that I could go outside and ride my _____ (cycle)
(8)

when I finish. I hope I can finish all my work soon!

Suffixes *-ly, -ful, -less, -ness*

- **Read** the story.
- **Add** *-ly, -ful, -less,* or *-ness* to each word in parentheses.

Yesterday I took Domingo, my dog, to my grandmother's house. As usual, her

house was _____**spotless**_____ (spot). We had milk and cookies in the kitchen while

Domingo sat _____ (quiet) in the living room. In fact, he was *too* quiet.
(1)

I went to check on him. He had _____ (complete) chewed a pillow into
(2)

bits and pieces. There were feathers everywhere!

My grandmother came in the room and said, "Oh my _____!" (good)
(3)

"I'm sorry, Grandma," I said. "I should have been more _____." (care)
(4)

_____ (lucky) for me, my grandmother laughed. She
(5)

_____ (playful) threw a pillow at me and we had a pillow fight. We had
(6)

so much fun it was easy to forget Domingo's _____. (frisky)
(7)

Name _____

Suffixes -*tion*, -*sion*, -*able*, -*ible*

- **Read** the sentences. Look at the underlined word.
- **Add** -*tion*, -*sion*, -*able*, or -*ible* to make a new word. Write the word.

1.

   Yasmin <u>imagined</u> being a princess.

   She used her _____.

2.

   We can <u>walk</u> on this path.

   The path is _____.

3.

   I can <u>depend</u> on Pablo.

   Pablo is _____.

4.

   Aisha <u>decided</u> which book to read.

   She made a _____.

5.

   I can <u>reverse</u> this shirt.

   The shirt is _____.

Name _____

Suffixes -er, -or, -ess, -ist

- **Read** the sentences. **Look** at the underlined word.
- **Add** -er, -or, -ess, or -ist to **make** a new word. **Write** the word.

1.

Olivia and her mother went to the <u>pharmacy</u>.

They spoke to the _____.

2.

It is a long <u>commute</u> to my dad's office.

My dad is a _____.

3.

I like to <u>invent</u> things.

I am an _____.

4.

We saw a male <u>lion</u> on our safari.

He was sitting next to a _____.

Name _____

Suffixes -y, -ish, -hood, -ment

- **Read** the story.
- **Add** -y, -ish, -hood, or -ment to the end of each word in parentheses.

Emma looked outside. She was happy because it was not a _____rainy_____

(1)

(rain) day. It was sunny. She liked to walk outside in her _____

(2)

(neighbor). She had a lot of energy. She did not feel _____ (sleep)

(3)

at all.

Emma skipped happily down the sidewalk. She saw _____ (move)

(4)

ahead of her. She wondered what it was. But then she felt _____ (fool).

(5)

It was just her brother, John, trying to surprise her. He can be so _____

(6)

(child) sometimes!

Cognates and Word Roots

Cognates are words that share origins and appear in similar forms in different languages. For example, the English word *school* is of Greek origin, and it is similar to the Spanish *escuela,* the French *école,* the Polish *szkoła,* and the German *Schule.* For speakers of languages that share word origins with English, the study of cognates can be a powerful vocabulary-building tool. The following lessons provide practice for working with cognates and words with Greek and Latin roots.

Cognates   Use with page 303.

Preteach Present a chart like the one below. Read the words with students, and note the similarities across various languages. Tell students that when words look similar and have a similar meaning in different languages, they are called *cognates.* Invite students to suggest other cognates they know in English and another language. Tell students that cognates can help them understand more words in English.

English	Spanish	French	Haitian Creole	Polish
telephone	teléfono	téléphone	telefonn	telefon

> Use this lesson with students who are literate in languages that have many cognates of English words, such as Spanish, Portuguese, French, and, to a lesser extent, Haitian Creole, Polish, and Russian.

Teach/Model Explain to students that cognates in different languages usually have the same origins. For example, the different words for *telephone* are all based on the Greek word parts *telē,* which means "far off," and *phōnē,* which means "sound" or "voice." Explain that because many scientific words have Greek or Latin origins, they often are cognates.

Then point out that sometimes words in different languages are "false friends"—they look almost the same, but they don't mean the same thing. For example, the Spanish word *sopa* looks and sounds similar to the English word *soap,* but it means "soup." Ask students to give other examples of "false friends," words that are not cognates.

Practice Copy and distribute page 303. Have students look for English cognates of home-language words in an English text they are currently reading. (A nonfiction science or social studies text is likely to offer more examples.) Help them decide whether or not the words really are cognates. Suggest that students consult resources such as bilingual dictionaries, other students, or the Internet (with your guidance) to find translations and word meanings. Students might make a class chart showing words for *computer* in various languages. (See answers on page 311.)

Assess Ask students to say or write five examples of cognate pairs in English and their home language, and one example of "false friends."

Words with Greek Roots   Use with page 304.

Preteach Write the following words on the board: *autograph, phonograph, photograph, paragraph*. Ask students what all these words have in common. Confirm for them that they all have the word part *graph*. Tell students that this word part comes from the Greek language. It means "written." Conclude by saying: *Many other words in English have Greek roots, too. Learning these roots can help you learn more words.*

Teach/Model Write the following chart on the board, asking students to provide additional examples for the last column.

Greek Root	Meaning	Sample Words
biblio	book	bibliography
bio	life	biography
crac, crat	rule, govern	democrat
demos	people	democracy
geo	earth	geology
graph, gram	written, drawn, describe, record	photograph
log	idea, word, speech, study	biology
meter	measure	perimeter
phono	sound	symphony
scope	to see	telescope

Show students how different word parts can be combined. The root *bio*, for example, can be combined with *graph* to form *biography*, and it can also be combined with *logy* to form *biology*. Knowing this, students can conclude that any word with the root *bio* has to do with life. Tell Spanish speakers that many Spanish words have these same Greek roots. Ask them to provide translations for the sample words in the chart *(bibliografía, biografía, demócrata, democracia, geología, fotografía, biología, perímetro, sinfonía, telescopio).*

Practice Copy and distribute page 304. Read the directions aloud, and have students look at the sample answer to help them get started. After students complete the activity, invite volunteers to take turns forming other words with the Greek roots in the word box. (See answers on page 311.)

Assess Write the following words on the board: *autobiography, phonology, geography,* and *telescope*. Ask students to copy these words and to write their definitions, based on what they've learned. When they've finished, have a volunteer write his or her answers on the board, and model corrections as necessary. You can collect students' work for later assessment.

Words with Latin Roots   Use with page 305.

Preteach Write the following words on the board: *animal, animation, animated.* Ask students what all these words have in common. Confirm for them that they all have the word part *anima.* Tell students that this word part is from Latin, an ancient language that was originally spoken in Italy. *Anima* means "living." Conclude by saying: *Many other words in English have Latin roots, too. Learning these roots can help you learn more words.*

Teach/Model Write the following chart on the board, asking students to provide additional examples for the last column. Tell Spanish speakers that Spanish comes from Latin, so these roots should be familiar.

Latin Root	Meaning	Sample Words
aqua	water	aquarium
aud	to hear	auditorium
cent	one hundred	century
cert	sure, to trust	certificate
circ	around	circle
compute	to compute	computer
dic, dict	to say, to speak	dictionary
fin	to end	finish
grad	step, degree	graduate
scrib	to write	scribble

Practice Copy and distribute page 305. Read the directions aloud, and have students look at the sample answer to help them get started. After students complete the activity, invite volunteers to take turns forming other words with the Latin roots in the answer box. (See answers on page 311.)

Assess Write the following words on the board: *certain, final, audition, gradual,* and *dictate.* Ask students to copy these words and to identify their Latin roots. To check comprehension, ask students to make a sentence with each of these words.

Related Words   Use with page 306.

Preteach On the board, write *breath, breathe,* and *breathless.* Ask students what these words have in common. Confirm for them that they all have the word *breath* as the base. The endings on the other two words change their part of speech and meaning. *Breathe* is a verb and *breathless* is an adjective. Many other words are closely related in the same way. Tell students that it will help them expand their vocabulary if they try to learn new words in groups with other related words.

Teach/Model Write the following chart on the board, asking students to provide additional examples for the last column. Spanish examples include *planeta/planetario, horizonte/horizontal,* and *salud/saludable.*

Base Word	Related Words
jewel	jeweler, jewelry
planet	planetary, planetarium
paint	painter, painting
act	action, actor, active
sign	signature
compute	computer, computation
horizon	horizontal
pot	potter, pottery
bank	banker, banking
heal	health, healthy
relate	relative, relationship
produce	product, production
please	pleasant, pleasure

Practice Copy and distribute page 306. Read the directions aloud, and have students look at the sample answer to help them get started. (See answers on page 311.)

Assess Ask students to take turns thinking of other words that are related to the words in the word box on page 306 or the words in the above chart.

Reading Multisyllabic Words

Use with page 307.

Preteach On the board, write the word *dic/tion/ar/y*, dividing it into syllables, as indicated. Sound it out, pausing between each syllable, and then blend the syllables together. Ask students how many syllables it has (4). Follow the same procedure for *en/cy/clo/pe/di/a*, which has 6 syllables. Tell students: *Pay attention to the syllables in a word. This will help you spell the word, and it will help you pronounce it, too.*

Teach/Model Distribute multiple copies of a dictionary, and point out how each entry word is divided into syllables. Ask students to find the word *brontosaur*, for example. Ask: *How many syllables does this word have?* (3) *What's the first syllable?* (bron) *What are the other syllables?* (*to* and *saur*) Repeat the procedure with the following words: *mystery, parentheses, enthusiasm, personality.*

Practice Copy and distribute page 307. Read the directions aloud, and have students look at the sample answer to help them get started. Help students read the words if necessary. (See answers on page 311.)

Assess Write the following words on the board: *relative, warrior, mathematical, magnificent, principal.* Have students use a dictionary to find out how many syllables each word has. Tell students to write the words on a piece of paper, showing the syllable divisions.

Cognates

- **Read** a few pages of a book or article. **Find** English words that look like words in another language you know.
- **Write** the words in both languages on the chart.
- **Write** the meaning of each word, using dictionaries if necessary. Then **tell** if the two similar words are cognates.

English	_____ (language)	Cognates? (yes/no)
Word: Meaning:	Word: Meaning:	
Word: Meaning:	Word: Meaning:	
Word: Meaning:	Word: Meaning:	
Word: Meaning:	Word: Meaning:	
Word: Meaning:	Word: Meaning:	

- **Find out** how to say *computer* in at least two different languages. **Use** sources such as dictionaries, the Internet, and people you know. **Write** the words.
- **Decide** which words are cognates of *computer.*

Words with Greek Roots

- **Read** the word parts in the box.
- **Look** at the pictures. **Put** one word part from each box together to make a word.
- **Write** the correct word on each blank line.

auto = self	**photo** = light	**scope** = to see
mega = large	**tele** = from a distance	**phone/phono** = sound
micro = very small		**graph** = written

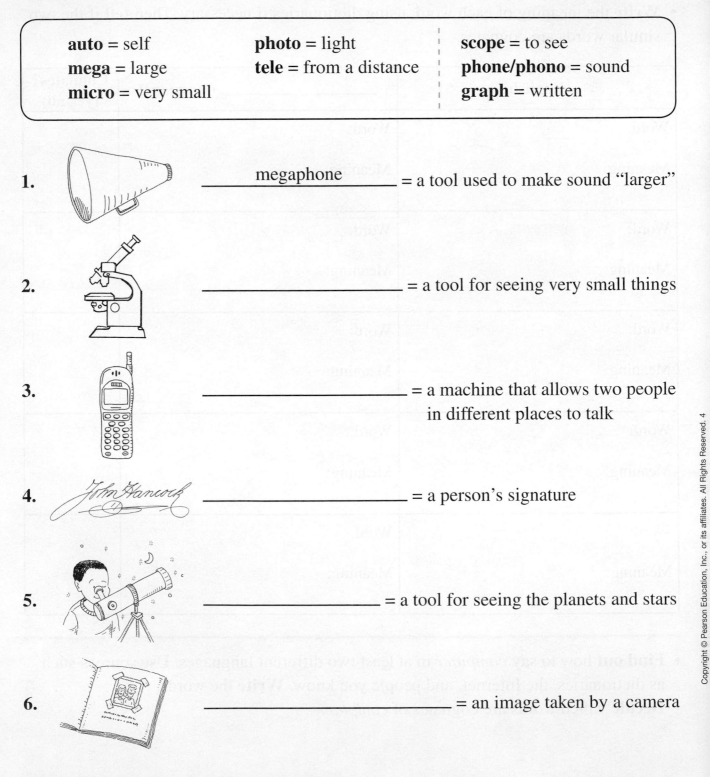

1. _____ megaphone _____ = a tool used to make sound "larger"

2. _____ = a tool for seeing very small things

3. _____ = a machine that allows two people in different places to talk

4. _____ = a person's signature

5. _____ = a tool for seeing the planets and stars

6. _____ = an image taken by a camera

Words with Latin Roots

- **Study** the word parts in the box.
- **Read** the sentences.
- **Complete** each sentence. **Write** the correct word in the blank space.

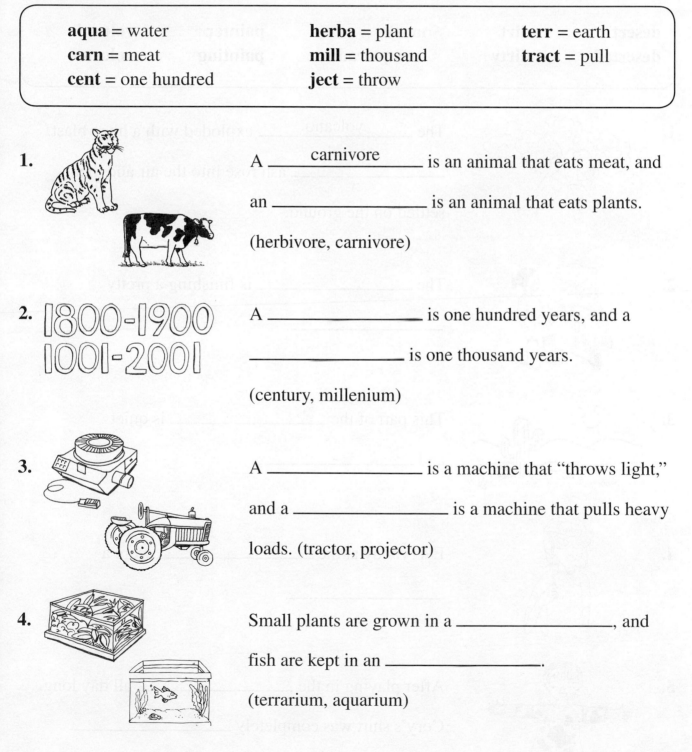

aqua = water	**herba** = plant	**terr** = earth
carn = meat	**mill** = thousand	**tract** = pull
cent = one hundred	**ject** = throw	

1. A _____carnivore_____ is an animal that eats meat, and

   an _____ is an animal that eats plants.

   (herbivore, carnivore)

2. A _____ is one hundred years, and a

   _____ is one thousand years.

   (century, millenium)

3. A _____ is a machine that "throws light,"

   and a _____ is a machine that pulls heavy

   loads. (tractor, projector)

4. Small plants are grown in a _____, and

   fish are kept in an _____.

   (terrarium, aquarium)

Related Words

- **Look** at the words in the box.
- **Read** the sentences.
- **Complete** each sentence. **Write** the correct word in the blank space.

desert	dirt	mask	painter	volcanic
deserted	dirty	masquerade	painting	volcano

1. The _____volcano_____ exploded with a huge blast.

   _____ ash rose into the air and then

   settled on the ground.

2. The _____ is finishing a pretty

   _____.

3. This part of the _____ is quiet

   and _____.

4. Everybody at the _____ wore a

   _____.

5. After playing in the _____ all day long,

   Cory's shirt was completely _____.

Reading Multisyllabic Words

- **Read** the words. **Sound out** the number of syllables.
- **Write** each word in the correct column of the chart.

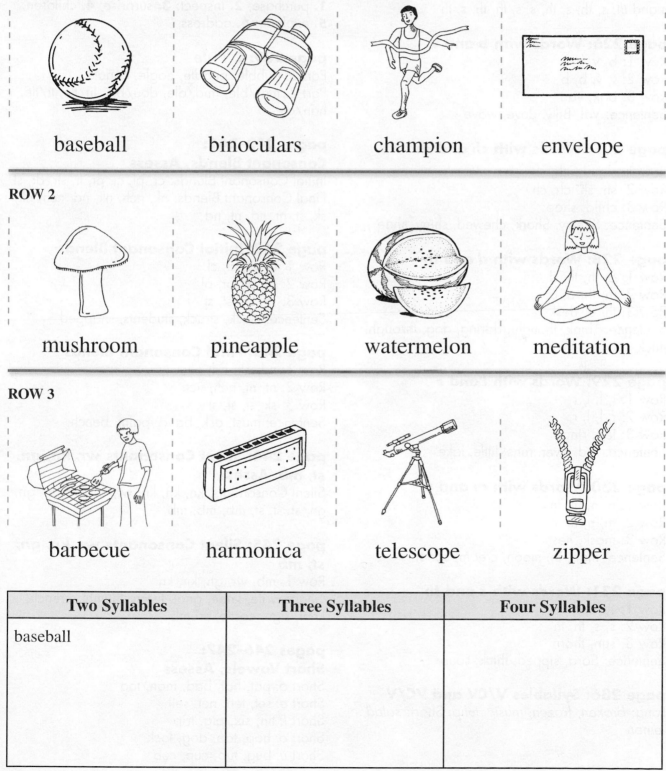

ROW 1

baseball   binoculars   champion   envelope

ROW 2

mushroom   pineapple   watermelon   meditation

ROW 3

barbecue   harmonica   telescope   zipper

Two Syllables	Three Syllables	Four Syllables
baseball		

Answer Key

pages 223–225:
Confusing Consonants, Assess
b and *v*: b, v, b, v, v, b, v, b, b, v, b, v, v
ch and *sh*: ch, sh, ch, sh, ch, ch, sh, sh, ch, ch, sh
d and *th*: th, d, th, th, d, d, th, d, th, d
l and *r*: r, l, r, l, r, r, l, r, l, r, l, l
m and *n*: m, n, m, n, m, n, m, n, n, m, m, n
s and *th*: s, th, s, th, s, s, th, th, s, th

page 226: Words with *b* and v
Row 1: b, v, b, v
Row 2: v, v, b, b
Row 3: box, van
Sentence: Val, Billy, dove, wave

page 227: Words with *ch* and *sh*
Row 1: sh, ch, ch, sh
Row 2: sh, sh, ch, ch
Row 3: child, shop
Sentence: Sherry, Shark, chewed, shiny, shoe

page 228: Words with *d* and *th*
Row 1: d, th, th, d
Row 2: th, th, d, d
Row 3: third, desk
Sentence: Think, thought, daring, dog, through, thick

page 229: Words with *l* and *r*
Row 1: r, l, l, r
Row 2: r, l, l, r
Row 3: leg, ring
Sentence: red, river, runs, little, lake

page 230: Words with *m* and *n*
Row 1: n, n, m, m
Row 2: m, n, m, n
Row 3: mask, nest
Sentence: man, in, moon, cream, spoon

page 231: Words with *s* and *th*
Row 1: s, th, th, s
Row 2: s, s, th, th
Row 3: sun, thorn
Sentence: Sara, sipped, thick, soup

page 236: Syllables V/CV and VC/V
Long: *broken, frozen, music, tulip*; Short: *salad, lemon*

page 237: Syllables CV/VC
Part 1: sci/en/tist; pi/an/o; vi/o/lin; vid/e/o; sta/di/um; ra/di/o; ro/de/o; me/te/or
Part 2: studio, create, idea, medium, pioneer, immediate, bionic, reliance

page 238: Syllables VCCCV
1. purchase; **2.** inspect; **3.** surprise; **4.** children; **5.** explode; **6.** address

page 239: C + *-le*
Part 1: bubble, puddle, eagle, candle
Part 2: mar/ble, mid/dle, dou/ble, lit/tle, ti/tle, han/dle

pages 240–241:
Consonant Blends, Assess
Initial Consonant Blends: cr, pl, cl, pr, tr, str, dr, st
Final Consonant Blends: nk, nch, nk, nd, nch, nk, sk, st, nt, nd, nt, nd

page 242: Initial Consonant Blends
Row 1: cr, cr, cl, cl
Row 2: pr, pl, pr, pl
Row 3: str, str, st, st
Sentence: clock, struck, students, snapped

page 243: Final Consonant Blends
Row 1: nd, nk, nd, nk
Row 2: nt, nt, nch, nch
Row 3: sk, st, st, sk
Sentence: must, ask, band, paint, bench

page 244: Silent Consonants *wr, kn, gn, st, mb*, Assess
Silent Consonants: kn, kn, kn, wr, wr, wr, gn, gn, gn, st, st, st, mb, mb, mb

page 245: Silent Consonants *wr, kn, gn, st, mb*
Row 1: mb, wr, gn, kn, kn
Chart: write, knee, gnat, listen, thumb; wrench, knot, sign, castle, crumb

pages 246–247:
Short Vowels, Assess
Short *a*: pat, hat, bad, man, tag
Short *e*: set, ten, net, sell
Short *i*: tin, six, pig, trip
Short *o*: hop, top, dog, lock
Short *u*: bug, tub, cup, cub

page 248: Words with Short *a*
Row 1: acrobat, bat, ant
Row 2: cap, man, map, can
Row 3: man, bat, ant, hat
Sentence: acrobat, an, apple, bat, act

page 249: Words with Short *e*
Row 1: vest, elephant, tent
Row 2: pen, web, bell, bed
Row 3: ten, bell, nest, web
Sentence: elephant, entered, tent, elegant, step

page 250: Words with Short *i*
Row 1: dinner, gift, inch
Row 2: pin, zip, dig, sit
Row 3: zip, gift, pig, six
Sentence: Six, pigs, with, bibs, grinned, did, jig, in, minute

page 251: Words with Short *o*
Row 1: dog, octopus, box
Row 2: lock, rock, fox, hop
Row 3: box, dog, lock, mop
Sentence: lock, fox, box

page 252: Words with Short *u*
Row 1: truck, puppy
Row 2: bus, duck, tub, rug
Row 3: bus, truck, duck, sun
Sentence: bug, rug, jumped, up, pup

pages 253–254:
Long Vowels, Assess
Long *a:* cage, rage; ate, late
Long *e:* leaf, lean; seen, seat
Long *i:* sky, sly; rice, price
Long *o:* globe, lobe; low, blow; hose, toes
Long *u:* rule, tool; glue, blue

page 255: Words with Long *a*
Row 1: cake, train, plate
Row 2: snake, chain, plane, hay
Row 3: grapes, tray, rake, rain
Sentence: came, (a), gate, cave, waited, Dave

page 256: Words with Long *e*
Row 1: eagle, teeth, feet
Row 2: he, wheel, thirty, leaf
Row 3: tree, leaf, me, bee
Sentence: See, leaves, trees, street

page 257: Words with Long *i*
Row 1: bike, night, mice
Row 2: ice, child, tie, light
Row 3: five, kite, light, sky
Sentence: Five, kites, sky, flying, high

page 258: Words with Long *o*
Row 1: rope, nose, bone
Row 2: robe, gold, bow, boat
Row 3: goat, rose, snow(man), gold
Sentence: Joan, wrote, note, rode, boat

page 259: Words with Long *u*
Row 1: boot, suitcase
Row 2: glue, stool, fruit, mule
Row 3: fruit, flute, moon, cube
Sentence: Sue, blue, drew, moon

page 260: Vowel Diphthongs, Assess
/ou/: plow, how, owl, south
/oi/: soy, enjoy, choice, toil, join

page 261: Vowel Diphthongs
Row 1: soil, boy, coin
Row 2: crowd, count, towel, plow
Row 3: cow, toy, voice, cloud
Sentence: boy, count, toy, cows

pages 262–263:
***r*-Controlled Vowels, Assess**
Words with *ar, are, air, or, ore*: thumbs up: chair, chore, far, stare, store, car, more; thumbs down: chew, feet, stand
Words with *er, ir, or, ur,* and *eer, ear*: cheer, steer, her, deer, fear

page 264:
Words with *ar, are, air, or, ore*
Row 1: air, ar, ar, air
Row 2: corn, horse, fork
Row 3: star, hair, store, porch
Sentence: Chairs, forks, corn, more, are, for, store

page 265:
Words with *er, ir, or, ur, eer, ear*
Row 1: ur, ear, ur, ear
Row 2: bird, butter, skirt
Row 3: worm, deer, purse, shirt
Sentence: dear, girl, tear, purse, near, here

Answer Key

page 266: The Schwa and Unstressed Syllables, Assess

asleep, final, panel, cradle, lesson, ribbon

page 267:
The Schwa and Unstressed Syllables

Row 1: circle: alarm, afraid; underline: bottle, dragon

Chart: medal, nickel, table, wagon, sandal, shovel, apple, button

Sentence: apples, bagels, alarm, (a), pretzel, table

pages 268–269:
Inflected Endings, Assess

Plurals and Possessives: Answers will vary, but will include possessives.

Verb Endings -s, -ed, -ing: Answers will vary.

page 270: Plurals and Possessives

1. pets; **2.** Martin's; **3.** birds'; **4.** Mia's;
5. Carlos's; **6.** Puppies

page 271: Verb Endings -s, -ed, -ing

Part 1: /s/: helps, writes, walks; /z/: calls, plays, runs, sees

Part 2: /d/: opened, played, rubbed; /t/: fixed, helped, walked, washed

Part 3: calling, hoping, playing, running

page 275: /j/, /s/, /k/

Row 1: jet, cage, jam
Row 2: bus, dancing
Row 3: back, cat, knock(ing)
Sentence: Jessica, checks, crossing, bridge

page 276: /ȯ/ spelled a, au, aw, al

Row 1: saw, sausage, straw
Row 2: applause, lawn, walnut, salt

page 277: /ȯ/ spelled augh, ough

1. brought; **2.** daughter; **3.** thought; **4.** fought;
5. caught; **6.** taught

pages 278–280:
Compound Words, Homophones, and Contractions, Assess

Compound Words: Answers may include any of the words on page 281.

Homophones: Answers will vary.
Contractions: Answers will vary.

page 281: Compound Words

Part 1: bath/tub; flash/light; key/board; mail/box; space/ship; star/fish; tooth/paste; water/fall

Part 2: backpack, bookmark, classroom, fingernail, hairbrush, rainbow, sailboat, sidewalk

page 282: Homophones

1. same; **2.** different; **3.** same; **4.** same;
5. different; **6.** different

Students will match pictures to words.

page 283: Contractions

I'm, Isn't, it's, we're, didn't, I've, doesn't, I'll

Answers will vary, but will be four of the following: *did not, does not, I will, I am, I have, is not, it is, we are.*

pages 284–290: Prefixes and Suffixes, Assess

Prefixes *un-* and *re-*: unafraid, not afraid; unlock, open the lock; rerun, run again; reunite, unite again

Prefixes *im-, in-, mis-, over-*: incorrect, misinterpret, overload, overcoat, intake, mistake, overtake, misuse, overuse

Prefixes *pre-, mid-, over-, out-, bi-*: prepaid, midair, overtime, outfield, biweekly

Suffixes *-ly, -ful, -less, -ness*: slowly, slowness, quietly, quietness, perfectly, fearful, fearless, rudely, rudeness

Suffixes *-tion, -sion, -able, -ible*: sensible, comfortable, confusion, reaction

Suffixes *-er, -or, -ess, -ist*: actor, seller, hostess, dentist, tourist, teacher, lioness

Suffixes *-y, -ish, -hood, -ment*: smelly, British, motherhood, excitement, windy, brownish, falsehood, shipment

page 291: Prefixes *un-* and *re-*

2. reappear; **3.** unbelievable; **4.** unfamiliar;
5. reheat; **6.** uninterested; **7.** unlike; **8.** restart;
9. reuse; **10.** unkind

un-: unbelievable, unfamiliar, uninterested, unlike, unkind; *re-*: reread, reappear, reheat, restart, reuse

page 292: Prefixes im-, in-, mis-, over-
1. overpriced; **2.** inexpensive; **3.** incorrect;
4. misprint; **5.** impatient
Additional words: Answers will vary. Words
may include *impolite, insecure, mismatch,* and
overcook.

page 293: Prefixes pre-, mid-, over-, out-, bi-
1. pretest; **2.** prefixes; **3.** outline; **4.** midnight;
5. overdue; **6.** overtime; **7.** outside; **8.** bicycle

page 294: Suffixes -ly, -ful, -less, -ness
1. quietly; **2.** completely; **3.** goodness;
4. careful; **5.** Luckily; **6.** playfully; **7.** friskiness

page 295: Suffixes -tion, -sion, -able, -ible
1. imagination; **2.** walkable; **3.** dependable;
4. decision; **5.** reversible

page 296: Suffixes -er, -or, -ess, -ist
1. pharmacist; **2.** commuter; **3.** inventor;
4. lioness

page 297: Suffixes -y, -ish, -hood, -ment
1. rainy; **2.** neighborhood; **3.** sleepy;
4. movement; **5.** foolish; **6.** childish

pages 298–302: Cognates and Word Roots, Assess
Cognates: Answers will vary.
Words with Greek Roots: autobiography: a book
about yourself; phonology: the study of sounds;
geography: description of the Earth; telescope:
something that lets you see far away
Words with Latin Roots: certain, cert; final, fin;
audition, aud; gradual, grad; dictate, dict
Related Words: Answers will vary.
Reading Multisyllabic Words: Syllabication may
vary among dictionaries. rel/a/tive; war/ri/or;
math/e/mat/i/cal; mag/ni/fi/cent; prin/ci/pal

page 303: Cognates
Chart: Answers will vary. The Spanish word for
computer, computadora, is a cognate.

page 304: Words with Greek Roots
2. microscope; **3.** telephone; **4.** autograph;
5. telescope; **6.** photograph

page 305: Words with Latin Roots
1. carnivore, herbivore; **2.** century, millennium;
3. projector, tractor; **4.** terrarium, aquarium

page 306: Related Words
1. volcano, Volcanic; **2.** painter, painting;
3. desert, deserted; **4.** masquerade, mask;
5. dirt, dirty

page 307: Reading Multisyllabic Words
Two Syllables: baseball, mushroom, zipper;
Three Syllables: champion, envelope, pineapple,
barbecue, telescope; Four Syllables: binoculars,
watermelon, meditation, harmonica

Part 4
Grammar Instruction for English Language Learners

Contents

ELL Handbook

Introduction to the Grammar Transition Lessons

English language learners may have experience mainly with their home languages, and the grammars of different languages vary widely. As these students encounter English, keep in mind that their home languages may differ in aspects such as the following:

- The languages may use different word order than English does.

- They may not use the same parts of speech as English does.

- Their tense structures may be simpler or more complex than English tense structure.

- Nouns and adjectives that are neutral in English may be masculine or feminine in a child's home language.

For teachers, it is vitally helpful to remember that grammar is much more than a set of rules for saying and writing sentences correctly. Grammar primarily consists of the ways that speakers and writers of a language communicate ideas, mainly in sentences. As students learn the meanings of new words and how English sentences work, they become able to successfully communicate their ideas. They will gradually learn rules, read and write punctuation, and eventually become proficient in standard English usage.

The core grammar and writing lessons in Scott Foresman *Reading Street* provide the systematic instruction that students need to write. The following Grammar Transition Lessons and Practice Pages will supplement the core instruction with customized lessons that meet the particular needs of English learners.

Each group of grammar lessons covers a topic, such as Nouns, Verbs, or Sentences. Each lesson is supported by a reproducible Practice Page that provides strong context for the skill. Throughout the Grammar Transition Lessons, a **Transfer Skills** feature identifies challenges faced by English learners, based on the grammar of their

home languages, as well as language knowledge that can transfer to English. Each lesson also includes a **Grammar in Action** feature to reinforce the skill through active learning.

In addition to the Grammar Transition Lessons and Practice Pages, you can further support grammar instruction with routines such as the following:

- **Emphasize sentence meaning.** Encourage children to try to understand and convey ideas rather than focusing only on separate words. Build their knowledge by presenting many examples that show how English sentences convey meaning. Include sentences that the children say or write.

- **Strengthen oral language skills.** Allow beginning English speakers to work with partners when completing grammar activities, talking about what English words and sentences mean. Encourage students to make up new phrases and sentences together.

- **Engage students as active learners.** Students who are acquiring English will make mistakes. They need encouragement rather than constant correction. Let students sing, chant, and play language games together. Allow them to communicate freely and have fun with English.

- **Relate to the home language.** Whenever possible, help students build on what they already know by making connections between a target grammar skill and the home language. Use available resources, such as bilingual staff members, language Web sites, and the students themselves, to gather information about the home language.

Nouns

Transfer Skills

Common Nouns

In languages such as Spanish and French, nouns are masculine or feminine. You can point out that while some nouns in English refer to males or females (boy, girl, uncle, aunt), English nouns do not have masculine and feminine endings.

Grammar *in Action*

Noun Hunt Have partners look through picture books and make a list of nouns they find in the pictures or texts.

Common Nouns

Preteach Point to objects in the room, and have students name them. Tell students: *We have names for the things around us. A noun is a word that names something or somebody.*

Teach/Model Present the concept and provide examples:
- A noun names a person, a place, an animal, or a thing.

person	place	animal	things
girl	yard	dog	box, music

Practice/Assess Copy and distribute page 318. Read the directions aloud, and name the items in the picture before students complete the page. (See answers on page 382.)

Transfer Skills

Proper Nouns

Students who are literate in nonalphabetic languages such as Chinese, Korean, and Japanese may not be familiar with capitalizing proper nouns.

Grammar *in Action*

Use capital letters On chart paper, have students draw pictures and write or dictate the names of people and places that are special to them. Remind them to use capital letters.

Proper Nouns

Special Names

Preteach Have students practice writing each other's names. Point out that each child's name begins with a capital letter. Tell students: *Each of us has our own special name. A proper noun is the special name of a person, place, animal, or thing. Proper nouns begin with capital letters.*

Teach/Model Present the concept and provide examples:
- A proper noun names a special person, place, animal, or thing.
- A proper noun begins with a capital letter.

special person	special place	special animal	special thing
Sandra	Africa	Fifi	Statue of Liberty

Practice/Assess Copy and distribute page 319. Read the directions aloud. Help students name the people and animals in the picture before they complete the page. (See answers on page 382.)

Titles and Abbreviations

Preteach Write the names of various school staff members on the board, including titles such as *Mr., Mrs.,* and *Dr.* Read the names aloud with students, and underline the titles as you say them. Point out the titles that are abbreviations, or shortened forms of words.

Teach/Model Present the concept and provide examples:
- Proper names may begin with a title such as *Mrs.* or *Dr.*
- A title begins with a capital letter. If a title is an abbreviation, it ends with a period.

Title	Example
Mr. *(mister)*	Mr. Garza
Ms. *(miz)*	Ms. Prince
Mrs. *(missus)*	Mrs. Dexter
Miss *(miss)*	Miss Wong
Dr. *(doctor)*	Dr. Marco

Practice/Assess Copy and distribute page 320. Read the directions aloud before students complete the page. (See answers on page 382.) Have students read their own answers aloud.

Days, Months, and Holidays

Preteach Ask students to name today's day and date. Write them on the board, and point out that the day and month begin with capital letters.

Teach/Model Present the concept and provide examples:
- The names of the days of the week, months of the year, and holidays begin with capital letters.

Days of the Week	Months of the Year		Holidays (Examples)
Sunday	January	July	Memorial Day
Monday	February	August	Labor Day
Tuesday	March	September	Thanksgiving
Wednesday	April	October	
Thursday	May	November	
Friday	June	December	
Saturday			

Practice/Assess Copy and distribute page 321. Read the directions aloud. Go through the sample calendar with students before they complete the page. (See answers on page 382.)

Transfer Skills

Titles
- Students may not realize that, in English, the title *Doctor* is used for both men and women.
- In some countries, the word *Teacher* is used as a title. Point out that in the U.S., teachers are addressed with a title such as *Mr., Ms., Mrs.,* or *Miss.*

Grammar *in Action*

Oral Language Have students practice introducing adult staff members to each other, using the correct titles.

Transfer Skills

Days and Months
- In languages including Spanish, French, Polish, and Vietnamese, the names of days and months are not usually capitalized.
- In languages such as Chinese, Vietnamese, and Portuguese, the names of the days are formed by counting from the first day of the week.

Grammar *in Action*

Word Origins Have students use dictionaries that show etymologies to find out the origins of the English names for days of the week.

Transfer Skills

Plural Nouns
- Spanish speakers use -s and -es endings for nouns.
- In some languages, including Chinese, Hmong, and Vietnamese, nouns do not have plural forms. Instead, the plural is indicated with an adjective.

Grammar *in Action*

Noun Sort Have students make a 3-column chart with the headings *"add* -s," *"add* -es," and *"change* y *to* i *and add* -es." Invite students to look through magazines to find nouns that fit each category.

Transfer Skills

Irregular Plurals
English learners may add -s to irregular nouns in sentences or to nouns for which English uses the singular for a quantity: *sheeps, mens, clothings.*

Grammar *in Action*

Concentration Have partners create "singular noun" word cards: *child, tooth, leaf, foot, man,* and "irregular plural noun" cards, including incorrect forms: *childs, children, teeth, tooths, leafs, leaves, feet, feets, men, mans.* Partners place the "singular" and "plural" cards face down in two separate groups and then take turns drawing correct pairs.

Singular and Plural Nouns

Preteach Point to one book and say: *book.* Point to two books and say: *books.* Repeat with *(lunch) box* and *(lunch) boxes.* Have students name other singular and plural nouns as you point to them. Say: *A singular noun names one thing. A plural noun names more than one thing.* Plural *means "more than one."*

Teach/Model Present the concept and provide examples:
- Add -s to most nouns to form the plural.
- If the noun ends in -ch, -sh, -s, -ss, or -x, add -es.
- If the noun ends in a consonant + y, change the y to i and add -es.

Add -s	Add -es	Change y → i and add -es
girl/girls	box/boxes	berry/berries

Practice/Assess Copy and distribute page 322 after teaching *Irregular Plural Nouns.*

Irregular Plural Nouns

Preteach Write this sentence on the board: The <u>children</u> brushed their <u>teeth.</u> Ask a volunteer to name the singular of the underlined nouns *(child, tooth).* Tell students: *Most nouns add* -s *or* -es *to form the plural. Some nouns form the plural in a special way. They are called* irregular plural nouns.

Teach/Model Present the concept and provide examples:
- Most nouns add -s or -es: *books, girls, boxes, brushes.*
- Irregular plural nouns have special forms. Here are some examples:

Irregular Plural Nouns			
child/children	foot/feet	life/lives	man/men
ox/oxen	tooth/teeth	leaf/leaves	woman/women

Practice/Assess Copy and distribute page 322. Help students name the singular and plural nouns in the picture. (See answers on page 382.) Have students name the irregular plural nouns. As an extension, have students list the singular of the plural nouns.

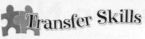

Singular Possessive Nouns

Preteach Display these sentences, gesturing as appropriate: *This is Maya. This is Maya's desk.* Explain: *The first sentence is about Maya. The second sentence says that Maya has something. To show that a person, place, or thing has or owns something, add an apostrophe* (point to apostrophe) *and the letter* s. *The word Maya's is called a singular possessive noun.*

Teach/Model Present the concept and provide examples:
- A singular possessive noun ends in 's.

Singular Nouns	Singular Possessive Nouns	Examples
Sam	Sam's	Sam's mom
friend	friend's	friend's house
class	class's	class's pet
child	child's	child's jacket

Practice/Assess Copy and distribute page 323 after teaching *Plural Possessive Nouns.*

Plural Possessive Nouns

Preteach Display these sentences: *All my students have desks. These are my students' desks.* Encourage students to discuss the meaning of the two sentences. Explain: *To show that two or more people, places, or things have or own something, use a plural possessive noun.*

Teach/Model Present the concept and provide examples:
- If the plural noun ends in *-s, -es,* or *-ies,* add an apostrophe (') to make it possessive.
- If the plural noun does **not** end in *-s, -es,* or *-ies,* add 's to make it possessive.

Plural Nouns	Plural Possessive	Examples
friends	friends'	friends' houses
classes	classes'	classes' teachers
puppies	puppies'	puppies' tails
children	children's	children's jackets

Practice/Assess Copy and distribute page 323. Make sure students understand the directions. Have students read their completed sentences aloud. (See answers on page 382.)

ELL Handbook

Transfer Skills

Possessive Nouns
In many languages, speakers show possession in phrases rather than noun endings. Show students how to change phrases such as *the tail of the cat* and *the nest of the bird* to *the cat's tail* and *the bird's nest,* in order to show possession in English.

Grammar *in Action*

Oral Language Have students place school supplies on their desks. Then have students point to and name a friend's things. For example: *This is Lin's book. This is Lin's calculator.*

Transfer Skills

Plural Possessive Nouns
An apostrophe after the letter s may seem incorrect to many students. Explain the difference between clear examples such as *a cat's tail* and *cats' tails* or *a bird's nest* and *birds' nests.* Use pictures or simple drawings to help students understand.

Grammar *in Action*

Use Plural Possessive Nouns Provide sentences such as these, and ask students to rewrite or rephrase them using plural possessive nouns: *This cake belongs to the students. (This is the students' cake.) These chairs belong to the children. (These are the children's chairs.)*

Common Nouns

Practice

- **Look** at the picture.
- **Name** the people, places, animals, and things in the picture.

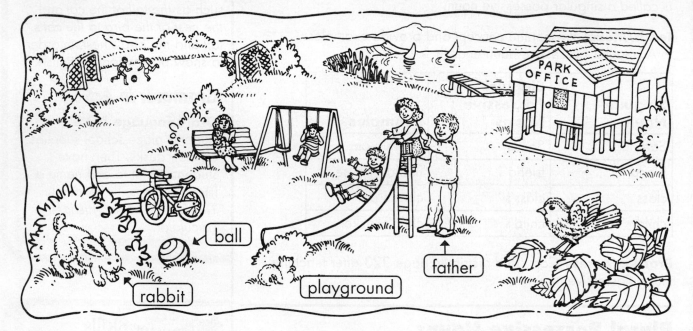

People	Places	Animals	Things
girl	pond	bird	slide

Assess

- **Look** around the room. What do you **see**?
- **Write** six nouns. **Name** things that you see.

Name _____

Special Names

Practice

- **Look** at the picture.
- **Find** the children, animals, and places that have special names.
- **Write** the names. Remember to **begin** the names with a capital letter.

Names of Children	Names of Animals	Names of Places
Maya		

Assess

- **Write** the names of two people you know.

_____

- **Write** the names of two special places you know.

_____

Name _____

Titles and Abbreviations

Practice

- **Look** at the pictures.
- **Write** the name of each person.
- **Include** a title for each person.

Title	Use with:
Mr.	a man
Ms.	a woman
Mrs.	a married woman
Miss	an unmarried girl or woman
Dr.	a doctor (male or female)

| Mark Tanaka | Mr. Turner | Eva Santos | Lisa Johnson |

1. Who is the teacher?   _____

2. Who is the doctor?   _____

3. Who is the dancer?   _____

4. Who is the carpenter?   _____

Assess

- **Write** the names of four adults you know. **Include** their titles.

_____

_____

Name _____

Days, Months, and Holidays

Practice

- Use this class calendar to **answer** the questions.
- Remember to **begin** the names of days, months, and holidays with capital letters.

November						
Sunday	**Monday**	**Tuesday**	**Wednesday**	**Thursday**	**Friday**	**Saturday**
				1	2	3
4	5	6 Election Day	7 LIBRARY VISIT	8	9	10
11 Veterans Day	12	13	14 LIBRARY VISIT	15	16	17
18	19	20	21 LIBRARY VISIT	22 Thanksgiving	23	24
25	26	27	28 LIBRARY VISIT	29	30 BOOK FAIR	

1. What holiday is on Thursday, November 22? _____

2. What holiday is on Sunday, November 11? _____

3. When is the Book Fair? _____

4. When is Election Day? _____

5. When does the class visit the library? _____

Assess

- **Write** the names of the seven days of the week.

_____

- **Write** the name of a holiday or another day that is important to you. **Tell** the date of the holiday, or when it takes place.

_____   _____
Name of the holiday   Date of the holiday

Name _____

Singular and Plural Nouns

Practice

• **Look** at the picture.
• **Write** three singular nouns. **Write** three plural nouns.

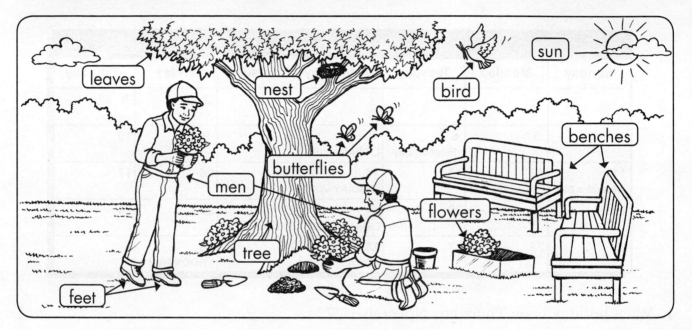

Singular Nouns	Plural Nouns
tree	flowers

Assess

• **Look** around the room. What do you **see**?
• **Write** three singular nouns and three plural nouns.

_____

_____

Singular and Plural Possessive Nouns

Practice

- **Look** at the picture. **Read** the sentences.
- **Circle** the correct possessive noun to complete each sentence.

1. (Today, Today's) date is May 19.
2. It is time for the (childrens', children's) story hour.
3. The (reader's, readers) name is Ed.
4. The (lady's, ladies') book club chooses a book.

Assess

- **Choose** a singular possessive noun from the sentences above. **Use** it in another sentence here.

_____

- **Choose** a plural possessive noun from the sentences above. **Use** it in another sentence here.

_____

Verbs

Transfer Skills

Present Tense

English verb endings differ from verb endings in languages such as Spanish and Polish, which use different endings for person and number. However, students may need practice adding -s or -es to present-tense verbs with third-person singular subjects.

Grammar *in Action*

Present Tense Practice

Write these subjects on index cards: *The baby, The girls, Sam, My brother, I.* Write these verbs on another set: *work, sleep, jump, run, play.* Have students draw a card from each set and create a sentence.

Transfer Skills

Past Tense

- Explain that regular past-tense verbs in English always have an *-ed* ending.
- In Chinese, Hmong, and Vietnamese, verbs do not change to show the tense. Adverbs or expressions of time indicate when an action has taken place.

Grammar *in Action*

Oral Language

Display a list of verbs: *walk, play, jump, call, move, push, listen, watch.* Begin to tell a story: *Yesterday I walked to the park with my friend.* Have students add to the story, using the verbs from the list in the past tense.

Verbs in Present Tense

Preteach Perform these actions as you narrate: *I walk to the front of the room. I point to the board. The words* walk *and* point *are verbs. The tense of a verb tells when something happens. A verb in present tense, like* walk *or* point, *tells what happens now. To talk about one other person or thing, add -s: He walks. She points.*

Teach/Model Present the concept and provide examples:
- Verbs in present tense tell what happens now.

	Verb	Example
I, you, we, they	see	I <u>see</u> my sister.
he, she, it	sees	She <u>sees</u> me.

Practice/Assess Copy and distribute page 330. Help students describe the picture. (See answers on page 382.)

Verbs in Past Tense

Preteach Display these sentences: *I <u>walked</u> to the front of the room. I <u>pointed</u> to the board.* Explain: *I did these things in the past. Many verbs in past tense end with* -ed. *If a verb ends in* e, *like* move, *drop the* e *and then add* -ed: moved. *If a verb has one syllable and ends with a vowel followed by a consonant, such as* shop, *double the consonant before adding* -ed: shopped.

Teach/Model Present the concept and provide examples:
- Verbs in past tense tell what happened in the past.

	Verbs in Past Tense
Add *-ed*	He <u>jumped</u> over the chair.
Drop the final *e* and add *-ed*	I <u>moved</u> the chair.
Double the consonant and add *-ed*	He <u>slipped</u> on the rug.

Practice/Assess Copy and distribute page 331 after teaching *Irregular Verbs*, page 325.

Irregular Verbs

Preteach Display these sentences: *I* _think_ *about you. I* _write_ *a note. I* _thought_ *about you. I* _wrote_ *a note.* Explain: *Usually, you add -ed to a verb to form the past tense. But here, I didn't use* thinked *or* writed. *Some verbs are not regular verbs. They are called* irregular verbs. *An irregular verb has a different spelling in the past tense.*

Teach/Model Present the concept and provide examples:
• Irregular verbs do not add *-ed* to form the past tense.
• Irregular verbs have different spellings in the past tense.

Irregular Verbs	Past Tense
write	I <u>wrote</u> a poem yesterday.
sing	I <u>sang</u> a song last night.
eat	I <u>ate</u> an apple earlier today.

Practice/Assess Copy and distribute page 331. Explain that some answers will be irregular verbs. (See answers on page 382.)

Verbs in Future Tense

Preteach Say: *What will I do after school today? I* _will go_ *home. I* _will eat_ *a snack. I* _will read_ *my e-mail.* Explain: *To talk about the future, we use verbs in future tense. The future may be later today, next week, or even next year.* Write one of the statements and point out the word *will.* Say: *Use the helping verb* will *to form the future tense.*

Teach/Model Present the concept and provide examples:
• Verbs in future tense tell what will happen in the future.

Verbs in Future Tense
I <u>will go</u> home.
I <u>will eat</u> a snack.
I <u>will do</u> my homework.

Practice/Assess Copy and distribute page 332. Help students describe the picture. Review the meanings of the verbs. (See answers on page 382.)

Transfer Skills

Irregular Verbs
Many English learners need extra practice with the variety of irregular verbs that also feature unfamiliar phonics elements, such as *catch/caught, buy/ bought,* and *can/could.*

Grammar *in Action*

Oral Language
Prepare index cards with irregular verbs. On one side, write the present tense. On the other side, write the past tense: *write/wrote; sing/sang; make/made; give/gave; eat/ ate; have/had.* Have partners dictate sentences to each other using the words on both sides.

Transfer Skills

Future Tense
Spanish, Haitian Creole, and Hmong speakers may use present tense in places where English calls for future tense. Help students practice verbs in statements such as *I will read later* and *After we hear the story, we will write a new story.*

Grammar *in Action*

Oral Language Have partners tell each other what they will do when they get home from school or at some other time. If students can pantomime the action, have them act out the verb.

Transfer Skills

Verb Tenses
Speakers of several languages, including Arabic, may find the English distinction between the past and present perfect tenses unfamiliar. Show contrasting examples, and explain how the sense of time differs.

Grammar *in Action*

Present Participle Practice
Say and display these verbs: *jump, walk, talk, wave, laugh*. Have students give the present participle of each verb, with the subjects *I, you, she*, and *they*. Have them pantomime the actions and point to the corresponding subject.

Transfer Skills

Learning Verb Forms
Spanish, like English, has irregular verbs (such as *ser*, which means "to be," and *ir*, "to go"). Challenge students who are literate in Spanish to identify irregular Spanish verbs, and see whether English verbs with the same meanings are irregular.

Grammar *in Action*

Find the Parts
Write the principal parts of *go, sing, take*, and *write* on index cards. Give each student a card. Students circulate to find others with principal parts of the same verb.

Principal Parts of Regular Verbs

Preteach Display these sentences: *I talk to you. I am talking to you. I talked to you. I have talked to you many times.* Explain: *A verb's tenses are made from four basic forms: Present, Present Participle, Past, and Past Participle. These are called the verb's principal parts. The present form is used in the first sentence. The second sentence uses the present participle form. The third sentence uses the past form, which is the -ed form of the regular verb. The fourth sentence uses the past participle.*

Teach/Model Present the concept and provide examples:
- The four basic forms are called the principal parts.
- The present participle can use *am, is,* or *are* and the *-ing* form.
- The past participle uses *has, have,* or *had* and the *-ed* form.

	Principal Parts: Regular Verbs
Present	The baby plays all day.
Present Participle	The baby is playing now.
Past	You helped me yesterday.
Past Participle	You have helped me before.

Practice/Assess Copy and distribute page 333. Have students share their sentences. (See answers on page 382.)

Principal Parts of Irregular Verbs

Preteach Display these sentences: *You grow every day. You are growing so much! You grew an inch last year. You have grown an inch every year.* Point out the past and past participle: *Irregular verbs change spelling in these forms.*

Teach/Model Present the concept and provide examples:
- The principal parts of irregular verbs are the same four kinds as the principal parts of regular verbs. The *-ing* form is made the same way, such as *growing* or *going*.
- But irregular verbs do not use the *-ed* ending for the past and the past participle. For example, we do not say "growed"; we say "grew." We do not say "have growed"; we say "have grown."

  I go. I am going. I went. I have gone.
  He sees it. He is seeing it. He saw it. He has seen it.

Practice/Assess Copy and distribute page 334. Remind students that irregular verbs have their own spellings of the past and past participle. (See answers on page 383.)

Helping Verbs

Preteach Display these sentences: *I am planting seeds. They will grow fast. I have planted seeds before.* Explain: *The underlined parts are called* verb phrases. *The main verbs*—planting, grow, *and* planted—*show action. The helping verbs*—am, will, *and* have—*tell more about the action. The helping verb* am *tells what I am doing now.* Will *tells what the seeds will do in the future.* Have *tells what I have done that started in the past.*

Teach/Model Present the concept and provide examples:
• Helping verbs can tell the time of the action.

	Helping Verbs
Present	The dog **is** wagging his tail.
Past	He **was** barking last night.
Future	He **will** stay inside tonight.
Started in the Past	You **have** helped me before.

Practice/Assess Copy and distribute page 335. Have students read their sentences aloud. (See answers on page 383.)

Linking Verbs

Preteach Display these sentences: *I am tired. I feel sick. She seems sad. He is the leader. The car was new.* Explain: *In these sentences, the underlined words are called* linking verbs. *They tell what the subject is or what the subject is like.*

Teach/Model Present the concept and provide examples:
• Linking verbs do not show actions.
• They tell what the subject is or what the subject is like.

Linking Verbs	**Examples**
is	Summer <u>is</u> here.
are	The days <u>are</u> longer.
feels	The sun <u>feels</u> warmer.

Practice/Assess Copy and distribute page 336. Help students describe what is happening in the picture. (See answers on page 383.)

Transfer Skills

Helping Verbs
The uses of *have* and *had* as helping verbs may be familiar to Spanish-speaking students once they learn the English words. The Spanish verb *haber* is used similarly.

Grammar *in Action*

Time to Listen Have each student create three index cards labeled *present, past,* and *future.* Say these sentences and have students hold up the corresponding card: *You were playing basketball yesterday. You are listening to me now. You will go to the library later.* Encourage students to say other sentences with helping verbs.

Transfer Skills

Linking Verbs
• In languages including Chinese and Korean, linking verbs often are not required: *She tired. They sad.* Help students practice English sentences with linking verbs.
• Vietnamese speakers may use the English verb *have* in place of *There are* or *is,* as in "Inside the box have a gift." Help students practice with sentences using forms of *be.*

Grammar *in Action*

Oral Language Have partners tell each other three nice things they observe about each other: *You seem happy. You are smart. You are funny.*

Verbs

Transfer Skills

Contractions

Ask students if there are contractions in their home languages. (In Spanish, *a* + *el* = *al* and *de* + *el* = *del;* in Portuguese, *de* + *as* = *das.*) Explain that an English contraction uses an apostrophe to replace the missing letters.

Grammar *in Action*

Contraction Substitution

Say these sentences, and have students rephrase them using contractions: *You are hiding. I do not see you. I am going to find you. I will not stop looking.* If necessary, help students learn *you're, don't, I'm,* and *won't.*

Contractions

Preteach Display these sentences: <u>You're</u> *calling me.* <u>I'm</u> *far away. I* <u>can't</u> *hear you.* Explain: *The underlined words are contractions. A contraction is a shortened form of two words. An apostrophe* (point to an apostrophe) *takes the place of one or more letters. Look at these contractions:* you *and* are *become* you're, I *and* am *become* I'm. Can *and* not *become* can't.

Teach/Model Present the concept and provide examples:
- A contraction is a shortened form of two words.
- An apostrophe takes the place of a letter or letters that are removed when you write a contraction.

	Contractions
I *and* **have**	<u>I've</u> eaten breakfast.
Should *and* **not**	You <u>shouldn't</u> run in the hall.
Can *and* **not**	She <u>can't</u> come to my party.

Practice/Assess Copy and distribute page 337 after teaching *Negatives.*

Transfer Skills

Negatives

In Spanish, Haitian Creole, and some other languages, double negatives (similar to *We did not do nothing*) are correct. Tell students that standard English does not use double negatives.

Grammar *in Action*

Double Negatives

Write these sentences on the board. Invite students to come up and show how they would fix the double negative. Ask them to read the new sentence. *I can't never tell you. I won't say nothing. I don't want nobody to hear.*

Negatives

Preteach Display these sentences: *I* <u>never</u> *eat fish. I* <u>don't</u> *ever eat fish.* Explain: *The underlined words are negatives. They mean "no" or "not." Contractions with* n't *are negatives. In English, we use only one negative with one verb.* I <u>don't</u> <u>never</u> *eat fish has a double negative. Take away one negative.* (See the first two examples.)

Teach/Model Present the concept and provide examples:
- Use only one negative with one verb.
- Use a positive word in a sentence with *not.*

	Examples
Negative	<u>Nothing</u> is on the table.
Positive	I don't see <u>anything</u> there.
Negative	They went <u>nowhere</u>.
Positive	We didn't go <u>anywhere</u>.

Practice/Assess Copy and distribute page 337. Remind students to watch for double negatives. (See answers on page 383.)

Troublesome Verbs, Lie/Lay, Sit/Set

Preteach Write and say: *The boy lays his book on the table. Then he lies down on his bed to take a nap.* Explain that in the first sentence, the boy puts his book down on a table. In the second sentence, he goes to bed to rest. Write and say: *Miguel sets the plates on the table. Then he sits at the table.* Show the difference between *set* and *sit* in these sentences by pantomiming the actions.

Teach/Model Present the concept and provide examples:
- Some verbs look similar or have similar meanings.
- Think of the meanings and the main parts of verbs.

Troublesome Verb	Past	Past Participle
Lie: "rest" or "recline"	lay	(has, have, had) lain
Lay: "put" or "place"	laid	(has, have, had) laid
Sit: "sit down"	sat	(has, have, had) sat
Set: "put something somewhere"	set	(has, have, had) set

Practice/Assess Copy and distribute page 338. Read the directions aloud and discuss the picture with students before they complete the activity. Then ask students to read their original sentence aloud. (See answers on page 383.)

Troublesome Verbs, Leave/Let, Rise/Raise

Preteach Write and say: *The girl will leave with her friends. Her mother let her go.* Explain that first the girl is going away. Her mother allows, or permits, her to go. Write and say: *The sun will rise every day. The children raise their hands in class.* Use pantomime or pictures to discuss the differences between *rise* and *raise* in these sentences.

Teach/Model Present the concept and provide examples:
- Some verbs look similar or have similar meanings.
- Think of the meanings and the principal parts of the verbs to use them correctly.

Practice/Assess Copy and distribute page 339. Read the directions aloud. Discuss the picture. Have students complete page 339. Then ask them to read their original sentence aloud. (See answers on page 383.)

Transfer Skills

Troublesome Verbs
Tell students that the verbs *set* and *lay* usually take a direct object. Display the sentences: *She set her keys on the counter. He lays his wallet on the table.* Use the sentences to show students that a direct object (keys, wallet) is a noun or pronoun that receives the action of a verb (set, lays) or shows the result of the action.

Grammar *in Action*

My Turn, Your Turn
In pairs, have students take turns creating sentences that include troublesome verbs. The partner accepts a correct example and offers a new example.

Transfer Skills

Troublesome Verbs
Have English learners study the meanings and principal parts of troublesome verbs. Then provide additional examples of the verbs used correctly.

Grammar *in Action*

Incomplete Sentences
Display several incomplete sentences, asking students to complete each sentence with a troublesome verb. For example, say: *The teacher _____ (let) the children go home. The children _____ (left) quickly.*

Name _____

Verbs in Present Tense

Practice

- **Look** at the picture. **Read** the sentences.
- **Write** the correct verb in present tense to complete each sentence.

bench

1. At 8:00, we _____ (wait, waits) for the bus.

2. Liz _____ (talk, talks) to her mom.

3. Adam _____ (sit, sits) on the bench.

4. I _____ (see, sees) the bus!

Assess

- **Look** at the picture. **Write** a sentence about the dog. **Use** a verb in present tense.

_____

Name _____

Verbs in Past Tense

Practice

- **Look** at the picture. **Read** the sentences.
- **Circle** the correct verb in past tense.

picnic

soccer ball

Yesterday was my little sister's first day of school. We (celebrated, celebrates) with

a picnic. I (gived, gave) her a soccer ball. She (play, played) with it all day. My mom

(maked, made) snacks. We (haved, had) a good time!

Assess

- **Look** at the picture again. **Write** another sentence about the picnic. Use the verb *ate*.

Name _____

Verbs in Future Tense

Practice

- **Look** at the picture. **Read** the story. **Read** the verbs in the box.
- **Write** the correct verb in future tense to complete each sentence.

The mother bird _____ food for the babies.

In a few days, she _____ them to fly. Soon,

the baby birds _____ big and strong. They

_____ away from the nest.

| **will find** | **will fly** | **will teach** | **will grow** |

Assess

- What do you think the mother bird will do when the baby birds fly away? **Write** a sentence about it.

_____

Principal Parts of Regular Verbs

Practice

- **Look** at the picture. **Read** the sentences.
- **Circle** the verb in each sentence. **Write** *present*, *present participle*, *past*, or *past participle* to name the principal part of the verb.

1. The concert has started. _____

2. We listen to Sofia, Ben, and Ray. _____

3. Sofia and Ben are playing violins. _____

4. Sofia has played the violin for three years. _____

5. Ray plays the flute well. _____

Assess

- **Write** a sentence about the concert. **Use** the present participle *playing*.

_____

Principal Parts of Irregular Verbs

Practice

- **Look** at the picture. **Read** the sentences.
- **Circle** the verb in each sentence. **Write** *present*, *present participle*, *past*, or *past participle* to name the principal part of each irregular verb.

1. Yesterday I went to the doctor's office. _____

2. I go every year. _____

3. I have grown two inches this year. _____

4. I am growing very fast. _____

Assess

- **Write** a sentence to say what the doctor did. Use the past tense verb *wrote*.

_____

Name _____

Helping Verbs

Practice

- **Look** at the picture. **Read** the sentences.
- **Circle** the verb phrase in each sentence. **Underline** the helping verb.

1. We are learning about dolphins in class.

2. We have seen dolphins at the zoo.

3. I am using the Internet now.

4. I will give my report tomorrow.

Assess

- **Write** a sentence about the girl's report. Use the verb phrase *will tell*.

Linking Verbs

Practice

- **Look** at the picture. **Read** the sentences.
- **Circle** the linking verb in each sentence.

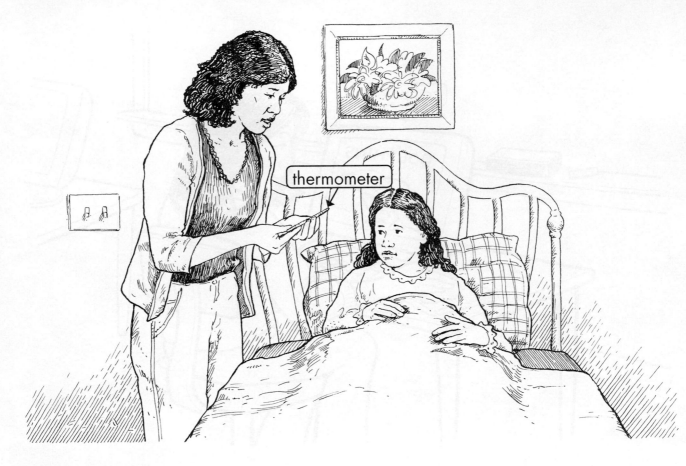

thermometer

1. I am sick today.

2. I feel tired and cold.

3. Mom seems worried.

4. My temperature is 102°F.

Assess

- **Write** a sentence about the girl. Use the linking verb *is*.

_____

Name _____

Contractions and Negatives

Practice

- **Look** at the picture. **Read** the sentences.
- **Circle** the correct word to complete each sentence.

1. Dad, (I'm, I'll) going out to play baseball.

2. (Shouldn't, Should'nt) you do your homework first?

3. Oh, (I've, I'm) already done it.

4. (You're, Your) such a good student!

5. I won't (ever, never) forget to do my schoolwork.

Assess

- **Write** a sentence about the girl's dad. Use a contraction with *not*.

Name _____

Troublesome Verbs Lie/Lay, Sit/Set

Practice

- **Look** at the picture. **Read** the sentences.
- **Circle** the correct verb in each sentence.

1. Judy (lays / lies) on the chair by the pool.

2. She likes to (set / sit) on the edge of the pool.

3. The little girl (set / sit) her goggles on the table.

4. My mom (lays / lies) her towel on the chair.

Assess

- **Look** at the picture again. **Write** and then **say** a sentence about it. Use the verbs *lie*, *lay*, *sit*, or *set*.

Name _____

Troublesome Verbs Leave/Let, Rise/Raise

Practice

- **Look** at the picture. **Read** the sentences.
- **Circle** the correct verb in each sentence.

1. Marcos, do not (let / leave) class without your music!

2. (Leave / Let) me play this song for you.

3. The teacher told us to (raise / rise) our hand when we have a question.

4. We want to (let / leave) a gift for our teacher.

5. We watched the balloons (raise / rise) into the air.

Assess

- **Look** at the picture again. **Write** and **say** a sentence about it. Use the verbs *leave, let, rise,* or *raise.*

Subjects and Predicates

Preteach Display this sentence: <u>The girl</u> walks to school. Explain that "The girl" is the subject of the sentence. The sentence is about the girl. A sentence is about its subject. Explain that "walks to school" is the predicate. What does the girl do? (walks to school) A predicate tells something about the subject.

Teach/Model Present the concept and provide examples:
- The subject of a sentence tells whom or what the sentence is about.
- The predicate of a sentence tells what the subject is or what the subject does.

Subject	Predicate
Sam	went to the store.
The students	write a paper.
The vegetables	are fresh.
My dog	had puppies.

Practice/Assess Copy and distribute page 348. Look at the picture after students complete the page. Have students contribute other sentences and identify the subjects and predicates. (See answers on page 383.)

Subject-Verb Agreement

Preteach Display these sentences: *The <u>bird</u> <u>sings</u> a song. The <u>birds</u> <u>sing</u> a song.* Encourage students to discuss the differences between the underlined parts. Explain: *The first sentence has a singular subject:* bird. *The second sentence has a plural subject:* birds. *The subject and the verb must work together, or agree. That's why the first sentence uses* sings *and the second sentence uses* sing.

Teach/Model Present the general concept and provide examples:
- If the subject is singular, add -s to the verb.
- If the subject is plural, do not add -s to the verb.

Subject	Verb
man	dances
Mom	works
friends	play
both feet	hurt

Practice/Assess Copy and distribute page 349. Help students describe the picture, emphasizing subject-verb agreement. (See answers on page 383.)

Transfer Skills

Subjects and Predicates
The typical English sequence of subject then predicate is not standard in some languages. For example, in Spanish the verb often appears before the subject, while in Korean and Hindi the verb typically appears at the end of a sentence.

Grammar *in Action*

Sentence Scramble Write these sentences onto strips: *My friend rides a bike. My dog barks at cats. The fish smells good. The clown is funny.* Cut each strip into subject and predicate. Have students scramble the sentence parts to form new sentences such as *The fish rides a bike.*

Transfer Skills

Verbs and Subjects
Students of various language backgrounds may add *-s* to both the nouns and verbs in sentences: *The robots walks.* Point out that, in English, verbs add *-s* for singular nouns *(A robot walks)*, not for verbs with plural nouns *(The robots walk)*.

Grammar *in Action*

Subject-Verb Agreement
Encourage students to scour the day's headlines for examples of subject-verb agreement. For example: *Schools Close; Teams Win; Gas Prices Rise; Dog Saves Girl.*

Word Order

Preteach Display these sentences and read them aloud, gesturing: *The bird flies. Flies the bird.* Ask: *What is the subject of the first sentence? (The bird) The second sentence does not sound right. The words are not in the right order to make a statement. In an English statement, the subject usually comes first. The predicate usually follows.*

Teach/Model Present the concept and provide examples:
- Sentences need to have words in the right order.
- In a statement, the subject usually comes first. The predicate usually follows.

In the right order:	Pablo is my friend.
Not in the right order:	Is friend my Pablo.

Practice/Assess Copy and distribute page 350. Help students describe what is happening in the picture. (See answers on page 383.)

Complete Sentences and Sentence Fragments

Preteach Write this sentence and fragment on the board: *Tom went to the library. Went to the library.* Ask: *Who went to the library? (Tom) Which sentence tells you this? The first sentence tells a complete idea. It says who did something. The second set of words (went to the library) is called a sentence fragment. It does not tell a complete idea. It does not say who went to the library. How would you make this fragment a complete sentence? (Add a subject.)*

Teach/Model Present the concept and provide examples:
- A sentence tells a complete idea.
- A fragment is a piece of a sentence. It does not tell a complete idea.

Sentence	Cheny eats her lunch.
Fragment	Her lunch in a bag.

Practice/Assess Copy and distribute page 351. As an extension, have students choose a fragment from the Practice and create a sentence from it. (See answers on page 383.)

Transfer Skills

Word Order
- Help students see that word order strongly affects meaning in English. *Lee thanked Tony* has a different meaning from *Tony thanked Lee.*
- See the Transfer note about the sequence of subjects and predicates on page 340.

Grammar *in Action*

Oral Language Say these groups of words: *The food is good. Is good the food. My friend rides a bike. Rides a bike my friend. Plays the dog. The dog plays.* Have students say which sentences are in correct word order.

Transfer Skills

Sentence Fragments
Spanish- and Chinese-speaking students may omit some pronouns as sentence subjects because in their home languages the pronoun may be unnecessary. For example, the Spanish equivalent of *Am reading* is a complete sentence.

Grammar *in Action*

Time to Listen Say these groups of words. Have students call out *sentence* or *fragment* after each one: *My brother. We walk to school. We ride on the bus. In the car. After school.* Invite students to contribute other sentences.

Sentences

Transfer Skills

Statements

Children who have begun to read in Spanish and other alphabetic languages may recognize that sentences begin with capital letters and end with periods.

Grammar *in Action*

Fix the Statements Write groups of words such as these on the board, including the mistakes: *my friends are funny. / They tell me jokes / I laugh every day* Have volunteers come up and fix the statements by adding correct punctuation and a capital letter at the beginning.

Transfer Skills

Questions

Speakers of Chinese, Vietnamese, and other Asian languages often form questions by adding words to statements, comparable to *The food is hot, no?* or *You see or not see the bird?* Provide model English questions for students to understand and to follow the patterns.

Grammar *in Action*

Oral Language Have pairs of students ask each other questions about what they did yesterday. For example, *What did we do in school yesterday? What is your favorite subject?*

Types of Sentences

Statements

Preteach Display these sentences: *I went to the library. My brother went too. We both found good books.* Say: *Let's look at these sentences. Each one starts with a capital letter and ends with a period. Each one tells something. A sentence that tells something is called a* statement.

Teach/Model Present the concept and provide examples:
* A sentence that tells something is called a *statement*.
* It begins with a capital letter and ends with a period.

Statements
I had a party yesterday.
All of my friends came to my house.
You ate pizza.

Practice/Assess Copy and distribute page 352 after teaching *Questions*.

Questions

Preteach Display these sentences: *What is your name? Where do you live? How old are you? Do you have any brothers?* Ask: *How are these sentences different from statements? They each ask something, and they end with question marks. A sentence that asks something is called a* question. Model the difference in intonation between these two sentences: *That is your dog. Is that your dog?*

Teach/Model Present the general concept and provide examples:
* A sentence that asks something is called a *question*.
* It starts with a capital letter and ends with a question mark.

Questions
How are you?
Did you go to Sam's party?
Does Ami like pizza?

Practice/Assess Copy and distribute page 352. Help students describe the picture. (See answers on page 383.)

Exclamations and Interjections

Preteach Write and say in an excited voice: *I am so happy!* Have students repeat, and then ask: *What feeling does that sentence express? (excitement; happiness) Whenever you say something with strong feeling, you are saying an exclamation. A written exclamation ends with an exclamation mark.* Next, write and say: *Hooray!* Explain: *This word also shows strong feeling and ends in an exclamation mark. However, it is not a complete sentence. It is called an* interjection.

Teach/Model Present the concept and provide examples:
- An exclamation is a sentence that shows strong feeling. It ends with an exclamation mark.
- An interjection is a word or group of words that shows strong feeling. It ends with an exclamation mark, but it is not a complete sentence.

Exclamation	I have a new baby brother!
Interjection	Wow!

Practice/Assess Copy and distribute page 353. Remind students that exclamations are complete sentences. (See answers on page 384.)

Commands

Preteach Give students various commands such as these: *Please stand up. Walk to the front of the class. Say hello. Sit down.* Ask: *How are these sentences the same? Sentences that tell someone to do something are called* commands.

Teach/Model Present the concept and provide examples:
- A command is a sentence that tells someone to do something.
- It begins with a capital letter and ends with a period.

Commands
Open the door. Turn on the light. Sweep the floor.

Practice/Assess Copy and distribute page 354. Have students use it as a model for writing another recipe. (See answers on page 384.)

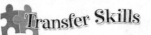
Transfer Skills

Exclamations
Speakers of Russian, Polish, and other languages may need to practice correct word order in exclamations. Have students make and use sentence strips, correcting exclamations such as *We enjoy very much movies!*

Grammar *in Action*

Interjection Charades
Write these interjections on index cards: *Ouch! Wow! Oh, no! Hooray!* Display them. Have a volunteer secretly choose an interjection and pantomime a scene that would elicit that interjection. Whoever guesses correctly takes the next turn.

Transfer Skills

Commands
Vietnamese speakers may recognize commands when they include an adverb or another clue word: *Go to school now. Take this to the office; go now.*

Grammar *in Action*

Oral Language Teach students the jump rope chant "Teddy Bear," in which the jumper obeys these commands while jumping rope: *Teddy Bear, Teddy Bear, turn around. Teddy Bear, Teddy Bear, touch the ground. Teddy Bear, Teddy Bear, stomp your feet. Teddy Bear, Teddy Bear, show your teeth.* Invite students to play.

Transfer Skills

Compound Sentences
Students may have difficulty distinguishing the clauses in a compound sentence in English. Give them additional practice finding the subject and verb within each independent clause.

Grammar *in Action*

Oral Language Say several pairs of simple sentences. Have students say compound sentences, keeping in mind the differences among *and, but,* and *or: I want to buy juice. I do not have a dollar. / I can drink water. I can borrow a dollar. / Tom is my friend. He gave me a dollar.*

Transfer Skills

Combining Sentences
Speakers of Indonesian and some other Asian languages may need practice combining sentences.

Grammar *in Action*

Form Sentences Make a set of sentence cards: *Mari wrote a poem. David sings. Rita went home.* Make a second set and distribute: *Mari read it to the class. David plays the guitar. Simón went home.* Read a sentence from the first set. The student holding a sentence with the same subject or predicate reads it. Have a volunteer form a combined sentence.

Simple and Compound Sentences

Preteach Display these sentences: *I went to Sal's house. We watched a movie.* Ask students to tell the subjects and predicates. Explain: *A simple sentence has one subject and one predicate. You can join the two simple sentences this way: I went to Sal's house, and we watched a movie. The new sentence is called a compound sentence. The two simple sentences are joined with the word* and.

Teach/Model Present the concept and provide examples:
- A simple sentence has one subject and one predicate.
- A compound sentence has two simple sentences joined by a comma and one of these words: *and, but,* or *or.*

Simple Sentences	Lena is my sister. I love her. I like peanuts. They make me sick. You can walk to school. I can drive you.
Compound Sentences	Lena is my sister, and I love her. I like peanuts, but they make me sick. You can walk to school, or I can drive you.

Practice/Assess Copy and distribute page 355. In the first compound sentence, help students see the two simple sentences. (See answers on page 384.)

Combining Sentences

Preteach Display these sentences: *I ate a sandwich. I drank some milk.* Ask: *What is the subject of both sentences? You can combine two sentences that have the same subject: I ate a sandwich and drank some milk.* Display these sentences: *Max went to the beach. I went to the beach. What is the predicate of both sentences? You can combine two sentences that have the same predicate: Max and I went to the beach.*

Teach/Model Present the concept and provide examples:
- Combine two sentences that have the same subject.
- Combine two sentences that have the same predicate.

Same Subject	Dan sat down. Dan did his homework. Dan sat down and did his homework.
Same Predicate	Miguel walked to school. I walked to school. Miguel and I walked to school.

Practice/Assess Copy and distribute page 356. Help students describe the picture. (See answers on page 384.)

Complex Sentences

Preteach Review compound sentences. Then present these complex sentences: _When I run, I feel good. I feel good when I run._ Explain: _This type of sentence is called a_ complex sentence. _It has two parts, called_ clauses. _The underlined part cannot stand alone as a sentence. If it comes first in the sentence, use a comma. The other part_ (I feel good) _can stand alone as a complete sentence._

Teach/Model Present the concept and provide examples:
* A complex sentence is made of two clauses.
* The two clauses are joined together with words such as _because, when, since, if,_ or _until._

Complex Sentences	When I grow up, I will be a teacher. I will be a teacher when I grow up.

Practice/Assess Copy and distribute page 357. Remind students that a complex sentence has two clauses. (See answers on page 384.)

Independent and Dependent Clauses

Preteach Present this complex sentence: _We cross the street when the light is green._ Explain: _The underlined part cannot stand alone as a sentence. It is a_ dependent clause. _It depends on another part. The other part_ (we cross the street) _can stand alone. It is an_ independent clause.

Teach/Model Present the concept and provide examples:
* A complex sentence is made of an independent clause and a dependent clause.
* The dependent clause cannot stand alone.
* The independent clause can stand alone.

Independent Clause	Dependent Clause
I am happy	because I passed the test.

Practice/Assess Copy and distribute page 358. Remind students that dependent clauses often start with words such as _since, although, when, if,_ or _until._ (See answers on page 384.)

Transfer Skills

Complex Sentences Functional words such as _if, that, so,_ and _because_ are often used somewhat differently in English than how their equivalents are used in other languages. Help students practice and understand usages of these words.

Grammar _in Action_

Identify Complex Sentences Have students write these sentences and tell whether they are complex or not: _My sister's name is Lupe._ (no) _Since she is little, I help her with homework._ (yes) _I also tie her shoes._ (no) _When I was little, my mom helped me._ (yes)

Transfer Skills

Dependent Clauses Provide models of dependent clauses that begin with words such as _after, although, as, because, before, if, since, then, until, when,_ and _while._ These words may have uses that are unfamiliar to students of many language backgrounds.

Grammar _in Action_

Write Complex Sentences Say these dependent clauses. Have students add independent clauses to form complex sentences: _Since I was little / When I grow up / Because it was raining / If you help me / Until my alarm clock rings._ Have students write the complex sentences.

Transfer Skills

Commas

Some students may use commas in places where periods are used in the United States, such as in decimals (*1,5* for *1.5*). Determine the intended meaning, and clarify the standard usage in American English.

Grammar *in Action*

Oral Language On the board, write menu items such as *soup, salad, sandwich, milk, tea, juice.* Have pairs play the roles of server and customer at a café. The server starts with *"May I take your order?"* The customer names three items, such as: *I want soup, salad, and milk.* The server says and writes the order: *"He wants soup, salad, and milk."* Have students switch roles.

Transfer Skills

Commas

Commas can be challenging for any student. English language learners may need help distinguishing needs for commas from uses of other kinds of punctuation.

Grammar *in Action*

Comma Practice

Brainstorm names of school staff. Write their names and job titles, such as *Mrs. Olson, the bus driver.* Have students use this information to write sentences with appositives.

Commas

In a Series and in Direct Address

Preteach Display this sentence: *My favorite colors are red, blue, and yellow.* Point out the commas. Say: *Commas help you understand a sentence. They tell you when to pause, or rest. Put commas after items in a series of words such as red, blue, and yellow.* Display these sentences: *Kim, may I use your pen? Yes, Lucas, you may.* Say: *When we write a sentence in which a person is directly addressed by name, we use a comma.*

Teach/Model Present the concept and provide examples:
• Use commas to separate items in a series.
• Use commas with direct address.

Commas in a Series	I like baseball, basketball, and soccer. I play Monday, Wednesday, and Friday.
Commas in Direct Address	Lori, would you come here? Yes, Mom, I'm coming. I need your help, Lori.

Practice/Assess Copy and distribute page 359 after the lesson on commas with appositives and introductory phrases.

With Appositives and Introductory Phrases

Preteach Display these sentences: *Mr. Hays, <u>my teacher</u>, speaks Spanish. <u>Yes</u>, I know.* Explain: *The underlined part of the first sentence is called* an appositive. *It is a noun phrase that describes another noun. Use a comma before and after an appositive. The underlined part of the second sentence is called an* introductory word. *Put a comma after an introductory word or phrase such as* well, no, oh, *and* "in other words."

Teach/Model Present the concept and provide examples:
• Use a comma before and after an appositive.
• Use a comma after an introductory word or phrase.

Appositives	Mr. Sims, <u>my neighbor</u>, has a dog. The dog, <u>a poodle</u>, barks all night.
Introductory Words or Phrases	<u>Oh</u>, I am very sorry. <u>In other words</u>, you cannot sleep.

Practice/Assess Copy and distribute page 359. Read the sentences, pausing where commas belong. (See answers on page 384.)

Quotations

Preteach Display and read the following dialogue: *"Do you have homework?" my mother asked. "Yes, I have to read a book," I said. "What is the name of the book?" my mother wanted to know.* Point out the position of the quotation marks in the dialogue.

Teach/Model Present the concept and provide examples:
- A quotation shows the exact words of a speaker.
- Quotation marks enclose a quotation.
- Use a comma to separate the speaker's exact words from the rest of the sentence when the quotation doesn't end with a question mark or exclamation mark.
- Quotation marks are also used for poetry, song titles, and story titles.

Quotation	Story Title
"Mr. Chung is my favorite teacher," said Joy.	"The Cat Has a Hat"

Practice/Assess Copy and distribute page 360. Have students add quotation marks in the sentences where appropriate. (See answers on page 384.)

Parentheses

Preteach Write and say the following sentence: *Jin has several pets (dog, bird, fish), but he is allergic to cats.* Ask: *What information is provided in the parentheses of this sentence?* Explain: *The information in the parentheses tells us more about Jin's pets.*

Teach/Model Present the concept and provide examples:
- Words in parentheses give an explanation or a comment in an already complete sentence.
- The information in parentheses is not necessary but adds detail to the sentence.

Sentence Without Parentheses	Sentence With Parentheses
Some subjects are very hard for me.	Some subjects (especially math and science) are very hard for me.

Practice/Assess Copy and distribute page 361. Have students add parentheses in the sentences where appropriate. (See answers on page 385.)

Transfer Skills

Quotation Marks
Help students use quotation marks by having them complete the following sentence frame in English: *My favorite song is "_____."* Model an answer and write it with quotation marks. Have students repeat. Ask about writing song titles in home languages.

Grammar *in Action*

Correct or Incorrect?
Display correct and incorrect examples of quotation use within a sentence. Write the sentences *"He plays soccer"* (incorrect) and *He said, "I am going to play soccer."* (correct). Offer several examples and ask students to identify correct and incorrect usage.

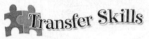

Transfer Skills

Parentheses
The writing systems of students' home languages may have different conventions for parentheses. Have students practice finding parentheses in classroom texts.

Grammar *in Action*

Oral Language Have students give extra details about a friend by completing the following sentence: *My friend likes to do many things after school (such as _____).*

Name _____

Subjects and Predicates

Practice

- **Look** at the picture. **Read** the sentences.
- **Circle** the complete subject of each sentence. **Underline** the complete predicate of each sentence.

1. The farmer's market is a busy place.

2. The sun shines brightly today.

3. A man sells big, red tomatoes.

4. A woman puts carrots into her bag.

Assess

- **Look** at the picture again. **Write** a subject to begin this sentence.

_____ sells flowers at the market.

Subject-Verb Agreement

Practice

- **Look** at the picture. **Read** the sentences.
- **Circle** the correct verb to complete each sentence.

1. Mom (give, gives) the children sandwiches.

2. The children (enjoy, enjoys) a day at the park.

3. The boys (throw, throws) a ball.

4. The girl (like, likes) to skate.

Assess

- **Write** a sentence about one person or two people doing something at the park. Make sure that the subject and the verb work together.

Word Order

Practice

- **Look** at the picture. **Read** the sentences.
- **Circle** the sentences with the words in the right order.

1. We went to the zoo.
   Went to the zoo we.

2. Elephants I saw the.
   I saw the elephants.

3. Were tall the giraffes.
   The giraffes were tall.

Assess

- **Look** at the picture again. **Write** another sentence about it.

Complete Sentences and Sentence Fragments

Practice

- **Look** at the picture. **Read** the groups of words.
- **Write** each group of words that is a complete sentence.

1. How the baker bakes.   The baker bakes bread.

_____

2. He puts the bread into the oven.   Many different breads.

_____

3. Makes delicious bread.   He makes delicious bread.

_____

Assess

- **Choose** one of the fragments. **Add** more words and **make** a complete sentence.

_____

Statements and Questions

Practice

- **Look** at the picture. **Read** the sentences.
- **Write** each sentence correctly. If it is a statement, **end** it with a period. If it is a question, **end** it with a question mark.

1. This is Raquel's party

_____

2. Do you like to dance

_____

3. Raquel's mom takes pictures

_____

4. Len eats pizza

_____

5. What time is it

_____

Assess

- **Look** at the picture again. **Write** another question about Raquel's party. **Start** with one of these words: _did, was, when, how._

_____

Name _____

Exclamations and Interjections

Practice

- **Look** at the picture. **Read** the sentences.
- **Write** the exclamation or interjection that each person says.

I am running fast!

Hooray! You will win!

I want to go home!

Assess

- What would you say if you won a contest? **Write** it here.

_____

Name _____

Commands

Practice

- **Look** at the pictures. **Read** the sentences.
- **Circle** the sentences that are commands.

1. Lemonade is easy to make.

2. Squeeze lemon juice into the pitcher.

3. Add water, sugar, and ice.

4. This lemonade is so good!

Assess

- **Write** how to make lemonade. Use only commands. Use these words: *find, cut, squeeze, add.*

_____

_____

Simple and Compound Sentences

Practice

- **Look** at the picture. **Read** the compound sentences.
- **Write** the two simple sentences in each compound sentence.

bowl of cereal

1. Mom needs to go to work, but Jon is still eating his cereal.

_____

_____

2. Jon needs to hurry, or Mom will be late for work.

_____

_____

3. Jon finishes his cereal, and they both run out the door.

_____

_____

Assess

- Do you think Jon's mom will be late for work? **Write** a compound sentence about it.

_____

_____

Combining Sentences

Practice

- **Look** at the picture. **Read** the sentences.
- **Combine** each pair of sentences. Use the underlined words only once in the new sentence.

1. Dad <u>went to the park</u>. I <u>went to the park</u>.

_____

2. <u>Dad</u> sat on a bench. <u>Dad</u> read his book.

_____

3. <u>I</u> found a stick. <u>I</u> threw it.

_____

4. <u>My dog</u> ran far. <u>My dog</u> got the stick.

_____

Assess

- **Write** another sentence using one of the underlined parts.

_____

_____

Complex Sentences

Practice

- **Look** at the picture.
- **Read** the sentences. **Check** the circle next to the ones that are complex sentences.

1. ○ I watch Tran because she is a good painter.
   ○ She is making a big, beautiful painting!

2. ○ I want a painting for my room.
   ○ Since this painting is big, Tran will put it in Mom's room.

3. ○ Tran will make a smaller painting.
   ○ She will start it when she finishes this one.

Assess

- **Write** another complex sentence about the girl who is painting.

_____

_____

Independent and Dependent Clauses

Practice

- **Look** at the picture. **Read** the sentences.
- **Circle** the dependent clause in each sentence.

basketball

1. After I do my homework, I play basketball.

2. When David is there, he plays with me.

3. We play until we are very tired.

4. David goes home because he has homework.

Assess

- **Write** a sentence that starts with *When David goes home.*

_____

_____

Commas

Practice

- **Look** at the picture.
- **Read** the sentences. **Add** commas where they are needed.

restaurant

Gino's

Gino's

menu

1. Gino's the new Italian restaurant has great food.

2. Mom thank you for buying us dinner.

3. I want soup salad pizza and lemonade.

4. Well I hope you can eat all that!

Assess

- **Write** three things you would order at your favorite restaurant. Then **read** your sentence to a partner. Remember to **pause** after each comma.

_____

_____

Quotation Marks

Practice

- **Read** the sentences.
- **Add** quotation marks.

1. I am excited about our skating lesson, said Aunt Beverly.

2. David said, I think you will be great.

3. What if I fall down on the ice? Aunt Beverly asked.

4. I fell down the first time too, David said. But you should keep trying.

5. I will feel better if you stay close to me, Aunt Beverly said.

6. Don't worry, David said, I will.

Name _____

Parentheses

Practice

- **Read** the sentences.
- **Add** parentheses.

1. Anita and her father are making dinner. They need different cooking utensils pan, spoons, cups, knife for their dish.

2. Anita put the food eggs, sausage, cheese, bread on the counter.

3. Her father showed her how to prepare cutting, pouring, stirring the dish.

4. When they were finished, Anita and her father put the rest of the meal vegetables, potatoes on the table.

5. Anita told the rest of her family mother sister brother that dinner was ready.

Assess

- **Write** another sentence with parentheses about the picture.

_____

_____

Name _____

Pronouns and Antecedents

Practice

- **Look** at the picture. **Read** the sentences.
- **Circle** the correct pronoun in each sentence. The antecedent is underlined for you.

balloons

1. Cecilia wanted to surprise <u>Ali</u> in (her, their) new home.

2. Cecilia bought <u>balloons</u> and gave (they, them) to Ali.

3. <u>Ali</u> said, "(I, We) am so surprised!"

4. <u>Balloons</u> are fun, and (them, they) make people happy.

Assess

- **Look** at the picture again. **Write** another sentence about the balloons. Use the word *they* or *them*.

_____

Indefinite and Reflexive Pronouns

Practice

- **Look** at the picture. **Read** the sentences.
- **Circle** the correct pronoun in parentheses to complete each sentence.

1. (Other, Someone) left a note on my desk.

2. I read it out loud to (myself, itself).

3. It said that (everyone, either) thinks I am a good writer.

4. (Somethings, No one) heard me read the note.

5. Maybe the writer of the note will identify (himself, ourselves).

Assess

- **Write** a sentence about yourself. Use a reflexive pronoun.

Articles, Adjectives, and Adverbs

Transfer Skills

Articles

- Spanish speakers may use the word *one* in place of the article *a* (or *an*), just as *un/una* is used in Spanish. Students may use *ones* as a plural article.
- English learners may use (or omit) the article *the* differently from native English speakers—*I like the science; my cousin is nurse.*

Grammar *in Action*

Time to Listen Copy and distribute a simple newspaper article. Read it aloud and have students follow along, highlighting the articles they encounter.

Transfer Skills

Adjectives

- Spanish adjectives have endings that match the gender and number of nouns they modify. Assure students that English adjectives do not have these endings.
- In Spanish and Vietnamese, adjectives often follow nouns.

Grammar *in Action*

Oral Language Have a student describe a classmate: *She is smart. She is quiet. She is wearing a blue sweater.* Whoever correctly guesses the classmate gives the next clues.

Articles

Preteach Say: *I need a pencil.* Hold up a pencil and say: *Here is a pencil with an eraser. The pencil is yellow.* Show some pencils: *The pencils are new.* Explain that *a*, *an*, and *the* are called *articles*: Articles are these words that come before nouns: *A pencil, the paper, an ink pen.* Use *a* or *an* before a singular noun. You can use *the* before singular nouns or plural nouns.

Teach/Model Present the concept and provide examples:
- *A*, *an*, and *the* are articles.
- Use *a* before a singular noun that begins with a consonant sound; use *an* before a singular noun that begins with a vowel sound.

Articles
I want <u>a</u> banana. Sue wants <u>an</u> apple.
<u>The</u> fruit salad was good. <u>The</u> girls ate it all.

Practice/Assess Copy and distribute page 373. Explain that *an* is used before a word beginning with silent *h*. (See answers on page 385.)

Adjectives

Size, What Kind, How Many

Preteach Say: *You know that nouns are words that name people, places, animals, or things—for example, girls and house. Adjectives are words that tell more about the nouns: small house, four girls, blue car, long hair. Which words are the adjectives?* (small, four, blue, long)

Teach/Model Present the concept and provide examples:
- An adjective tells more about a noun or pronoun.

	Adjectives
What Kind?	a <u>good</u> friend; The food is <u>spicy.</u>
How Many?	<u>two</u> men; <u>many</u> apples
Size	a <u>big</u> hat; The school was <u>small</u>.

Practice/Assess Copy and distribute page 374. Explain the chart to students. (See answers on page 385.)

Comparative and Superlative Adjectives

Preteach Draw three long lines of different lengths on the board. Point to the different lines and say: *This line is long. This line is longer. This line is the longest.* Say: Long *is an adjective.* Longer *compares two nouns, such as two lines. To compare two nouns, add* -er *to most adjectives.* Longest *compares three or more nouns. To make a superlative adjective, add* -est *to most adjectives.*

Teach/Model Present the concept and provide examples:
- Many comparative adjectives end in *-er: faster, thinner, tinier.* Change the spelling of some adjectives, such as *tiny*, when you add *-er*.
- Many longer adjectives use the word *more* instead of *-er: more exciting, more beautiful.*
- Many superlative adjectives end in *-est: brightest, loudest, tallest.* Use *most* with longer adjectives: *most beautiful.*
- Some adjectives have irregular forms, such as *good, better, best.*

Comparative	Superlative
bigger; more important	fastest; most difficult

Practice/Assess Copy and distribute page 375. Discuss the completed sentences. (See answers on page 385.)

Demonstrative Adjectives

Preteach Present three girls and three boys, with the boys farther away. Ask: *Which students are girls? These students are girls. Those students are boys. Which girl is Tina? This girl is Tina. That boy is Ben.* These, those, this, *and* that *are called* demonstrative adjectives. *They help you demonstrate, or show, which one or which ones. Use* this *and* these *when things are close. Use* that *and* those *when things are far.*

Teach/Model Present the concept and provide examples:
- Demonstrative adjectives: *this, that, these, those*

	Demonstrative Adjectives
Singular	<u>This</u> book is longer than <u>that</u> book.
Plural	<u>These</u> shoes are bigger than <u>those</u> shoes.

Practice/Assess Copy and distribute page 376. Remind students that *this* and *that* are used with singular nouns. (See answers on page 385.)

Transfer Skills

Comparative and Superlative Adjectives
Speakers of African and Asian languages may use English adjectives in patterns from their first languages: *She was the most fastest runner. My story is less longer than yours.*

Grammar *in Action*

Classroom Comparisons
Have pairs of students find pairs or sets of objects in the classroom to compare. For example, one pencil might be longer than another, while one book might be the heaviest of three. Have pairs present their findings.

Transfer Skills

This and That
In certain languages, including Korean, the relationship between expressing *this* and *that* and *here* and *there* does not correspond exactly to the way these terms are used in English. Clarify that the words *this* and *that* can modify nouns.

Grammar *in Action*

Oral Language Provide two sets of word cards for a game of Concentration. Place both sets face down, and have students find matching pairs. As they play, they should say: *I want this card, I want that card,* or *These cards match.*

Articles, Adjectives, and Adverbs

Transfer Skills

Adverbs

- English learners may use adjectives as adverbs. Help students use adverbs.
- Point out to Spanish speakers that the adverb suffix -ly is like the ending -mente in Spanish. Give examples with cognates such as *rapidly/rápidamente*.

Grammar *in Action*

Time to Listen Write adverbs on slips of paper: *slowly, quickly, loudly, sleepily.* Display them. Have a volunteer choose one. Give a command, such as *Walk to the door.* The volunteer must walk in the manner of the adverb. The student who guesses the adverb takes the next turn.

Transfer Skills

Comparative Adverbs

English phrases can be challenging for students whose home languages use different phrasing, and students may say or write: *running quickly more than you* or *studying more hard than you.* Model sentences with comparative adverbs.

Grammar *in Action*

Oral Language Display 3 pictures of athletes. Have students compare them, using *well, better, best* or *fast, faster, fastest* with verbs *run, play,* or *swim.*

Adverbs

Adverbs for When, Where, and How

Preteach Say and act out this chant: *Slowly I turn. Loudly I clap! I walk here and there. I end with a tap.* Say: Slowly, loudly, here, and there *are adverbs. They tell how, when, or where something happens.*

Teach/Model Present the concept and provide examples:
- Adverbs tell more about the actions of verbs.
- Adverbs that tell *how* something happens often end in *-ly.*

	Adverbs
When?	I <u>always</u> walk to school.
Where?	I like to walk <u>outside</u>.
How?	I walk <u>quickly</u>.

Practice/Assess Copy and distribute page 377. Explain that an adverb can come before or after the verb. (See answers on page 386.)

Comparative and Superlative Adverbs

Preteach Say each sentence: *I speak quietly. Katya speaks more quietly. Raúl speaks most quietly.* More quietly *is a comparative adverb. It compares two actions: I speak, Katya speaks.* Most quietly *is a superlative adverb. It compares three or more actions. If an adverb does not end in* -ly, *add* -er *or* -est *to compare.*

Teach/Model Present the concept and provide examples:
- A comparative adverb compares two actions.
- A superlative adverb compares three or more actions.
- Some adverbs are irregular: *well, better, best*

Comparative and Superlative Adverbs
Julia runs <u>fast</u>. Anil sings <u>beautifully</u>.
Pat runs <u>faster</u>. Kenji sings <u>more</u> <u>beautifully</u>.
Tere runs the <u>fastest</u>. Ivan sings <u>most</u> <u>beautifully</u>.

Practice/Assess Copy and distribute page 378. Remind students that *more* or *most* are not added to an adverb that already has an *-er* or *-est* ending. (See answers on page 386.)

Articles

Practice

- **Look** at the picture. **Read** the sentences.
- **Circle** the article in parentheses that completes each sentence.

1. Cali, Beth, and Lyn found (an, a) rope in their garage.

2. (An, The) rope was six feet long.

3. Beth knew (a, an) song for jumping rope.

4. (The, A) girls jumped rope for (a, an) hour.

Assess

- What can you do for an hour? **Write** about it here. Use articles.

_____

Name _____

Adjectives for Size, What Kind, How Many

Practice

- **Look** at the picture. **Read** the story.
- **Circle** the adjectives in the story.

My two brothers and I have a small garden. We have three plants. The plants have many

tomatoes that are big and red. They are delicious!

Assess

- **Write** the adjectives from the story in the chart.

Size	What Kind	How Many

Name _____

Comparative and Superlative Adjectives

Practice

- **Look** at the picture. **Read** the sentences.
- **Write** the correct adjective to complete each sentence.

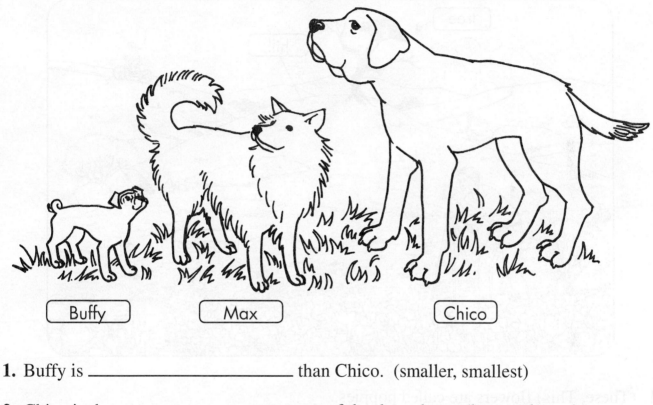

Buffy   Max   Chico

1. Buffy is _____ than Chico. (smaller, smallest)

2. Chico is the _____ of the three dogs. (largest, larger)

3. Max is _____ than Buffy. (more beautiful, beautifulest)

4. The big dog should have a _____ name. (gooder, better)

5. Buffy has the _____ name of all. (funniest, funnier)

Assess

- **Write** your own sentence that compares one of the dogs to another dog.

_____

Name _____

Demonstrative Adjectives

Practice

- **Look** at the picture. **Read** the sentences.
- **Circle** the correct adjective to complete each sentence.

1. (These, This) flowers are called poppies.

2. Each spring, (this, these) field is full of poppies.

3. (That, Those) tree on the hill looks like a person.

4. People ride their bikes in (those, this) hills.

5. Many people take pictures of (this, these) place.

Assess

- **Look** at the picture again. **Write** another sentence about the field. Use *this, that, these,* or *those.*

_____

Adverbs for When, Where, and How

Practice

- **Look** at the picture. **Read** the sentences.
- **Circle** the correct adverb for each sentence.

1. My sister sings (loudly, neatly).

2. I stand (outside, below) and listen.

3. She sings (beautifully, safely)!

4. I (always, yesterday) like listening to my sister sing.

Assess

- **Write** a sentence that tells how, when, or where you do something. Use an adverb.

Name _____

Comparative and Superlative Adverbs

Practice

• **Look** at the picture. **Read** the sentences.
• **Circle** the correct adverb to complete each sentence.

1. The stars shine (more brightly, brightly) in the country than in the city.

2. The dogs bark (louder, more louder) here.

3. I sleep (better, goodly) with the window closed.

4. People walk (more faster, faster) in the city.

5. This is the place I like to visit the (later, most).

Assess

• Do you like the city or the country better? **Write** a sentence about it.
Include an adverb.

_____

Prepositions and Prepositional Phrases

Preteach Stand behind a chair, and have students do the same. Say: *Behind the chair,* and have students repeat. Continue moving and speaking with *beside, around,* and *on* (sit). Explain: Behind, beside, around, *and* on *are prepositions.* Behind the chair *and* on it *are prepositional phrases.* Behind *is a preposition, and* chair *is a noun.* On *is a preposition, and* it *is a pronoun.*

Teach/Model Present the concept and provide examples:
- A prepositional phrase can tell where, when, how, or which one.
- A prepositional phrase begins with a preposition (*above, across, at, behind, for, from, in, near, with,* and so on).
- It ends with a noun or pronoun.

Preposition	around
Prepositional Phrase	around the chair

Practice/Assess Copy and distribute page 380. Help students describe the picture. (See answers on page 386.)

Transfer Skills

Prepositional Phrases
Prepositional phrases will be familiar to speakers of various languages, but students may choose prepositions based on home-language usage or meanings: *in Friday; on April; until there.*

Grammar *in Action*
Following Directions
Model as you give students directions to follow: *Walk to this side of the room. Walk across the room. Stand by a desk. Look under the desk.* Have volunteers take turns giving directions that include prepositional phrases.

Conjunctions

Preteach Use colored pens or markers to illustrate: *I have a red pen <u>and</u> a green pen.* The word *and* joins two similar things: two colors of pens. *Do you like red <u>or</u> green better?* The word *or* gives a choice: red or green. *You can use the green pen, <u>but</u> don't use the red pen right now.* The word *but* joins two different ideas: use and don't use. *Or, but,* and *and are called* conjunctions.

Teach/Model Present the concept and provide examples:
- A conjunction joins words, phrases, and sentences.

Related ideas: *Pak <u>and</u> I are friends.*
Different ideas: *We live far apart, <u>but</u> we talk often.*
Choice: *We talk on the phone <u>or</u> we send e-mail.*

Practice/Assess Copy and distribute page 381. Help students name the items in the picture. (See answers on page 386.)

Transfer Skills

Conjunctions
Speakers of Chinese and some other languages may build sentences using two conjunctions where English typically uses one: *Because the sun came up, so I could see the clock.* Help students practice English patterns.

Grammar *in Action*
Common Phrases Share these common phrases with conjunctions: *salt and pepper; thanks, but no thanks; stop-and-go traffic; left or right; boy or girl.* Invite students to say them while using gestures to help show the meanings.

Prepositions

Practice

- **Look** at the picture. **Read** the sentences.
- **Circle** the correct preposition to complete each sentence.

1. We are (behind, at) the lake.

2. I play a game called "catch" (with, over) my dad.

3. Jeff walks (after, near) the water.

4. Mom sits (under, on) a chair and reads.

5. Ducks swim (in, from) the water.

Assess

- **Write** a sentence about the lake. Use a prepositional phrase.

Name _____

Conjunctions

Practice

- **Look** at the picture. **Read** the sentences.
- **Circle** the correct conjunction to complete each sentence.

1. Are you ready to order, (but, or) do you want me to come back later?

2. I want a tuna sandwich, (and, or) the young lady wants soup.

3. Do you want a roll, (or, but) do you want a salad with your lunch?

4. I would like a salad, (or, but) please do not put salad dressing on it.

Assess

- What do you think the waiter said next? **Write** a sentence that has one of these words: *and, but, or.*

Answer Key

page 318: Common Nouns

Practice

People: father, boys, woman; **Places:** soccer field, playground, park office; **Animals:** rabbit; **Things:** swing, ball, bike

Assess

Answers will vary. Students should write the names of items found in the classroom.

page 319: Special Names

Practice

Names of Children: Alex, Karen, Tuan; **Names of Animals:** Spot, Lulu, Speedy, Goldie; **Names of Places:** Greenview School, Hope Garden, Barton Library

Assess

Answers will vary. Students should write the names of specific places and people, beginning each name with a capital letter.

page 320: Titles and Abbreviations

Practice

1. Mr. Turner; **2.** Dr. Lisa Johnson;
3. Miss Eva Santos; **4.** Mr. Mark Tanaka

Assess

Answers will vary. Verify that students include a title such as Mr., Ms., Mrs., Miss, and Dr. when writing each names of adults they know.

page 321: Days, Months, and Holidays

Practice

1. Thanksgiving; **2.** Veterans Day; **3.** Friday, November 30; **4.** Tuesday, November 6; **5.** on Wednesdays

Assess

Sunday, Monday, Tuesday, Wednesday, Thursday, Friday, Saturday; Answers will vary. Students should begin the name of each holiday and each month with a capital letter.

page 322: Singular and Plural Nouns

Practice

Singular Nouns: nest, bird, sun;
Plural Nouns: men, butterflies, feet, leaves, benches

Assess

Answers will vary but should include three singular and three plural nouns. Students should write the names of items found in the classroom.

page 323: Singular and Plural Possessive Nouns

Practice

1. Today's; **2.** children's; **3.** reader's; **4.** ladies'

Assess

Answers will vary. For sentences using singular possessive nouns, students may choose *reader's* or *today's*. For sentences using plural possessive nouns, students may choose *children's* or *ladies'*.

page 330: Verbs in Present Tense

Practice

1. wait; **2.** talks; **3.** sits; **4.** see

Assess

Answers will vary, but students may write a sentence such as *The dog barks.*

page 331: Verbs in Past Tense

Practice

celebrated; gave; played; made; had

Assess

Answers will vary, but students may write *We ate apples at the picnic.*

page 332: Verbs in Future Tense

Practice

The mother bird <u>will find</u> food for the babies. In a few days, she <u>will teach</u> them to fly. Soon, the baby birds <u>will grow</u> big and strong. They <u>will fly</u> away from the nest.

Assess

Answers will vary, but students may write a sentence such as *The mother bird will go too.*

page 333: Principal Parts of Regular Verbs

Practice

1. *has started*, past participle; **2.** *listen*, present; **3.** *are playing*, present participle; **4.** *has played*, past participle; **5.** *plays*, present

Assess

Answers will vary, but students may write a sentence such as *Ray is playing the flute.*

page 334: Principal Parts of Irregular Verbs

Practice

1. *went*, past; **2.** *go*, present; **3.** *have grown*, past participle; **4.** *am growing*, present participle

Assess

Answers will vary, but students may write a sentence such as *The doctor wrote on the chart.*

page 335: Helping Verbs

Practice

1. <u>are</u> learning; **2.** <u>have</u> seen; **3.** <u>am</u> using; **4.** <u>will</u> give

Assess

Answers will vary, but students may write a sentence such as *She will tell her friends about dolphins.*

page 336: Linking Verbs

Practice

1. *am*; **2.** *feel*; **3.** *seems*; **4.** *is*

Assess

Answers will vary, but students may write *The girl is sick.*

page 337: Contractions and Negatives

Practice

1. *I'm*; **2.** *Shouldn't*; **3.** *I've*; **4.** *You're*; **5.** *ever*

Assess

Answers will vary, but students may write *The dad didn't know she already did her homework.*

page 338: Troublesome Verbs Lie/Lay, Sit/Set

Practice

1. lies; **2.** sit; **3.** set; **4.** lays

Assess

Answers will vary, but students may write *The cat lies on the bed.*

page 339: Troublesome Verbs Leave/Let, Rise/Raise

Practice

1. leave; **2.** Let; **3.** raise; **4.** leave; **5.** rise

Assess

Answers will vary, but should include *leave, let, rise,* or *raise.*

page 348: Subjects and Predicates

Practice

1. The farmer's market / is a busy place;
2. The sun / shines brightly today;
3. A man / sells big, red tomatoes;
4. A woman / puts carrots into her bag.

Assess

Answers will vary, but students may begin the sentence with *A woman.*

page 349: Subject-Verb Agreement

Practice

1. gives; **2.** enjoy; **3.** throw; **4.** likes

Assess

Answers will vary. Check for subject-verb agreement.

page 350: Word Order

Practice

1. We went to the zoo. **2.** I saw the elephants. **3.** The giraffes were tall.

Assess

Answers will vary, but make sure students start sentences with the subject or use another word order that makes sense.

page 351: Complete Sentences and Sentence Fragments

Practice

1. The baker bakes bread. **2.** He puts the bread into the oven. **3.** He makes delicious bread.

Assess

Answers will vary but should be complete sentences.

page 352: Statements and Questions

Practice

1. This is Raquel's party. **2.** Do you like to dance? **3.** Raquel's mom takes pictures. **4.** Len eats pizza. **5.** What time is it?

Assess

Answers will vary; possible questions: *Did you go to Raquel's party? Was it fun? When did people dance?*

page 353: Exclamations and Interjections

Practice

Runner would think: "I am running fast!"
Friend would say: "Hooray! You will win!"
Crying boy would say: "I want to go home!"

Assess

Answers will vary. Encourage students to imagine themselves winning at a school or sports competition. Some suggestions: *Hooray! Wow! I worked so hard!*

page 354: Commands

Practice

Sentences 2 and 3 are commands.

Assess

Answers will vary, but students may write *First, find a pitcher and some lemons. Cut the lemons. Squeeze the lemons. Add water, sugar, and ice.*

page 355: Simple and Compound Sentences

Practice

1. Mom needs to go to work. Jon is still eating his cereal. **2.** Jon needs to hurry. Mom will be late for work. **3.** Jon finishes his cereal. They both run out the door.

Assess

Answers will vary, but students may write *Jon will not be late for school, and Mom will not be late for work.*

page 356: Combining Sentences

Practice

1. Dad and I went to the park. **2.** Dad sat on a bench and read his book. **3.** I found a stick and threw it. **4.** My dog ran far and got the stick.

Assess

Answers will vary, but sample answers include: *My friend and I went to the park. Dad drove us there and read his book. I played with my friend and with my dog. My dog was happy and playful.*

page 357: Complex Sentences

Practice

1. I watch Tran because she is a good painter; **2.** Since this painting is big, Tran will put it in Mom's room; **3.** She will start it when she finishes this one.

Assess

Answers will vary, but students may write sentences such as *When Tran finishes this painting, she will make another one. Since Tran's sister wants a painting, Tran will make one.*

page 358: Independent and Dependent Clauses

Practice

1. After I do my homework; **2.** When David is there; **3.** until we are very tired; **4.** because he has homework

Assess

Answers will vary, but sample answers include: *When David goes home, I go home also. When David goes home, he does his homework.*

page 359: Commas

Practice

1. Gino's, the new Italian restaurant, has great food. **2.** Mom, thank you for buying us dinner. **3.** I want soup, salad, pizza, and lemonade. **4.** Well, I hope you can eat all that!

Assess

Answers will vary, but make sure students use a comma after each menu item in the series.

page 360: Quotation Marks

Practice

1. "I am excited about our skating lesson," said Aunt Beverly. **2.** David said, "I think you will be great." **3.** "What if I fall down on the ice?" Aunt Beverly asked. **4.** "I fell down the first time too," David said. "But you should keep trying." **5.** "I will feel better if you stay close to me," Aunt Beverly said. **6.** "Don't worry," David said, "I will."

page 361: Parentheses

Practice
1. They need different cooking utensils (pan, spoons, cups, knife) for their dish. **2.** Anita put the food (eggs, sausage, cheese, bread) on the counter. **3.** Her father showed her how to prepare (cutting, pouring, stirring) the dish. **4.** When they were finished, Anita and her father put the rest of the meal (vegetables, potatoes) on the table. **5.** Anita told the rest of her family (mother, sister, brother) that dinner was ready.

Assess
Answers will vary, but make sure students use parentheses correctly.

page 365: Subject Pronouns

Practice
1. I; **2.** We; **3.** They; **4.** he

Assess
Answers will vary, but students may write a sentence such as *They were late for school.*

page 366: Object Pronouns

Practice
me; us; them; them

Assess
Answers will vary, but students may write a sentence such as *Jen gave the book to him.*

page 367: Possessive Pronouns

Practice
1. our; **2.** His, its; **3.** your; **4.** his

Assess
Answers will vary, but students may write a sentence such as *The bird will fly to its cage.*

page 368: Pronouns and Antecedents

Practice
1. her; **2.** them; **3.** I; **4.** they

Assess
Answers will vary, but students may write a sentence such as *Ali loved the balloons because they were from her friend.*

page 369: Indefinite and Reflexive Pronouns

Practice
1. Someone; **2.** myself; **3.** everyone; **4.** No one; **5.** himself

Assess
Answers will vary, but students may write a sentence such as *I like to teach myself English words.*

page 373: Articles

Practice
1. a; **2.** The; **3.** a; **4.** The, an

Assess
Answers will vary, but students may write a sentence such as *I can play baseball for an hour.*

page 374: Adjectives for Size, What Kind, How Many

Practice
two; small; three; many; big; red; delicious

Assess
Size: small, big; **What Kind:** red, delicious; **How Many:** two, three, many

page 375: Comparative and Superlative Adjectives

Practice
1. smaller; **2.** largest; **3.** more beautiful; **4.** better; **5.** funniest

Assess
Answers will vary, but students may write a sentence such as *Max is larger than Buffy.*

page 376: Demonstrative Adjectives

Practice
1. These; **2.** this; **3.** That; **4.** those; **5.** this

Assess
Answers will vary, but students may write a sentence such as *This field is beautiful.*

page 377: Adverbs for When, Where, and How

Practice

1. loudly; **2.** outside; **3.** beautifully; **4.** always

Assess

Answers will vary, but students may write a sentence such as *I run quickly.*

page 378: Comparative and Superlative Adverbs

Practice

1. more brightly; **2.** louder; **3.** better; **4.** faster; **5.** most

Assess

Answers will vary, but students may write a sentence such as *I like the city better.*

page 380: Prepositions

Practice

1. at; **2.** with; **3.** near; **4.** on; **5.** in

Assess

Answers will vary, but students may write a sentence such as *Ducks live near the lake.*

page 381: Conjunctions

Practice

1. or; **2.** and; **3.** or; **4.** but

Assess

Answers will vary, but students may write a sentence such as *Thank you for your order, and I will be back soon.*

Part 5
Workshops for English Language Learners

Contents

Introduction to Workshops for English Language Learners

To develop their skills in English, English language learners need instruction that integrates speaking, listening, reading, and writing. While core lesson content encourages the development of these skills, English language learners need targeted instruction to navigate listening and speaking in situations that, for native speakers, come naturally. Students who are first using spoken English may have difficulty in areas such as the following:

- knowing appropriate times to use formal and informal English.
- using the correct syntax patterns for sentences, including placement of nouns, verbs, adjectives, and prepositions
- expressing opinions and feelings
- using the transactional language of the classroom
- retelling or summarizing a message in English

In addition, students who are newcomers or who have not interacted with instructional materials in English may have difficulty with the following:

- interacting with environmental print and understanding what information they can get from reading the words around them
- using classroom resources
- expanding their knowledge and use of academic vocabulary words
- using graphic organizers to record ideas and organize information

Each one of these lessons covers a particular topic with a lesson for the teacher and a reproducible blackline master for students. The lessons are designed to be fluid and needs-based. Some of the lessons will correspond to your teaching with the core program, while others can be introduced when students have a need for the instruction. The workshop on group discussion, for example, can be introduced when you notice that students are struggling to use the transactional give-and-take language in group discussions. All Workshops follow the same format:

- A **Preteach** section provides simple scripted language that allows you to introduce the strategy or skill.
- The **Teach/Model** section involves students while you carefully scaffold instruction in the skill or strategy.
- In the **Practice** section, students begin to take ownership of the skill, sometimes through practice with a blackline master, and sometimes through interaction with peers.
- Each workshop includes an **Assess** section, with ideas for both assessment and corrective feedback.
- **Leveled Support** suggestions allow students to practice the skills at their individual levels of proficiency and progress from level to level.
- An accompanying **blackline master** allows for practice with the skill. The master often includes a rubric for self-assessment or a word bank to which students can add their ideas throughout the year.

Many of the blackline masters can be used multiple times. Based on students' needs, consider how to integrate the workshops into your instruction and use them multiple times to measure students' growth as users of classroom and conversational English.

In addition to the workshops, support students' development of spoken English with activities such as the following:

- **Answering questions**. Have students answer questions that you pose, first with yes/no questions and then with longer answers. Supply sentence frames and models as necessary.
- **Have dialogues**. Use various scenarios to have dialogues with students before having them pair up to have conversations of their own.
- **Picture the conversation**. Show students a photograph of people immersed in conversation in a familiar setting. Have them talk about what the people in the picture might be saying. Encourage them to role-play.

Preteach Model informal language for students and explain: *The words I use depend on who I am talking to and why I am speaking. When I am talking with my friends in casual situations, I use informal language. I might use slang words. I might speak in sentences that are not complete. I usually don't organize my ideas before I speak. It's more like having a conversation.*

Teach/Model With a volunteer, act out the scene on the right side of the page. Model using informal language, such as sentence fragments. Then model rating your knowledge using the rubric.

Practice Direct students to look at the second picture. Explain that in the picture, two teammates are talking about a soccer game. *Why would their language be informal?* (They are teammates in a game. They do not need to speak formally.) *What phrases might the friend say?* (Hey! Let's go! Good job!) For additional practice, students can draw another scenario that calls for informal English and use that drawing as the basis for role play. As students role-play, work with them to create a bank of words and phrases that they use when they speak informally with their friends or family.

Assess Assess students' conversations to clear up any misconceptions about informal English. Review students' ratings. Revisit the workshop so that students can reevaluate their progress in recognizing speaking situations in which informal language is acceptable and using appropriate language.

Beginning Have students do a simple role-play activity in which one student acts as a student in class and the other acts as a new student who is trying to find a certain room in the building. The students may use informal English.

Intermediate Ask students to work with partners to role-play a conversation with a sibling that would use informal English. Remind students that informal English is "relaxed," but it should also be appropriate.

Advanced/Advanced High Have students create new scenarios where they might use informal language and model appropriate language they might use and hear.

Name _____

Act out what is happening in the picture. **Say** what the people would be saying.

Draw a situation in which you could use informal English.

Circle the rating for each sentence. **Tell** how you use informal English.

1. I need help to do this better.

2. I do this sometimes.

3. I know how to do this.

I understand when to use informal English.	1	2	3
I am respectful of others when I use informal English.	1	2	3
I use slang that is appropriate.	1	2	3
I listen to others before I speak.	1	2	3

Use Formal English

Preteach Model formal language for students and explain: *The words I use depend on who I am talking to and why I am speaking. When I am talking with older people or to bigger groups, I use formal language. For example, I use titles for people, such as Mrs. or Mr. I don't use slang in formal language. I might say* Hello *instead of* Hey. *My speech may be slower. I might take more time to organize my thoughts before I speak.*

Teach/Model With a volunteer, act out the scene on the right side of the page. Model using formal language, such as titles. Then model rating your knowledge using the rubric. *When I speak to a teacher or other adult, I use titles such as Miss, Mr., and Mrs. I ask questions using more formal words, such as* please.

Practice Direct students to look at the second picture. Explain that in the picture, a girl is introducing a friend to her grandparents. *Why would she use formal language?* (to show respect for her grandparents) *What phrases might the friend say?* (Pleased to meet you.) For additional practice, students can draw another scenario that calls for formal English and use that drawing as the basis for role play. As students role-play, work with them to create a bank of words and phrases used in formal English for their reference.

Assess Assess students' conversations to clear up any misconceptions about formal language. Review students' ratings. Revisit the workshop so that students can reevaluate their progress in recognizing formal speaking situations and using appropriate language.

Beginning Have students do a simple role-play activity in which one student acts as a student and the other as the principal. The student should use formal language in greeting the principal.

Intermediate Ask students to work with partners to role-play introducing themselves in a formal situation, such as a club meeting. Write out the students' introductions and have them read them back to you. Identify phrases that make the speech formal, such as *It's nice to meet you.*

Advanced/Advanced High Have students create new scenarios where they might use formal language and model appropriate language they might use and hear.

Name _____

Act out what is happening in the picture. **Say** what the people would be saying.

Circle the rating for each sentence. **Tell** how you use formal language.

1. I need help to do this better.

2. I do this sometimes.

3. I know how to do this.

When speaking formally with adults:

I do not use slang.	1	2	3
I use titles and formal names such as *Mr., Mrs., Ms.,* and *Miss.*	1	2	3
I use polite words such as *please* and *thank you.*	1	2	3

When speaking formally to a big group:

I think about and organize what I will say.	1	2	3
I slow down my speech.	1	2	3

Distinguish Between Formal and Informal English

Preteach *Informal language is casual or relaxed. Formal language does not use casual language, such as slang.* Have students name differences between formal and informal language. Then write these examples of informal English on the board. Have students say the same phrases in more formal English. Examples: *Hi, teach! How are ya'? What's up?*

Teach/Model With a volunteer, act out the first scene of the child shaking hands with an adult. Ask students to identify if they would use formal or informal English. Why would they use that type of English? What words or phrases would they use? *When I speak to a teacher or other adult, I use titles such as Miss, Mr., and Mrs. If I am meeting them for the first time, I might say things like* How do you do? *or* It is nice to meet you.

Practice Direct students to look at the second picture. Have them identify if this is a formal or informal speaking situation. With partners, have them take turns telling what the friends might say to each other when skating. Model using informal language or slang, such as referring to a friend as *dude* or talking about *grinding* on their skateboards.

Assess Have students use the T-chart to record situations in which they would use formal or informal English in the correct columns. Assess their placements of the situations to see if they need more support in distinguishing between when to use formal and informal English. Have them choose situations to role-play and add other situations to the chart.

Beginning Show students magazine pictures of various settings (e.g., a business meeting, family watching television). Ask the students to indicate whether the people in the situation would use formal or informal English.

Intermediate Write an informal conversation on the board. (Sample: *Hey John. Wanna play a game?*) Have the students work with partners to repeat the conversation. Then have them role-play the conversation again, this time substituting formal language for the informal.

Advanced/Advanced High Have students work with partners to talk about a soccer game. The first conversation should be telling a friend about a game. The second conversation should be a recap of the game for the school announcements.

Name _____

Act out what is happening in the picture. **Say** what the people would be saying.

Decide if the language you used was formal or informal.

Read each situation below. **Write** each situation in the chart under Formal English or Informal English.

Write and **share** your own situations. Have others decide if they are formal or informal.

a family dinner
playing a game with friends
giving a speech at school
meeting a new teacher
asking for help at the store
helping a younger brother

Formal English	Informal English

Preteach *I am going to give you directions for making a cheese sandwich: Last, eat the sandwich. Next, put the bread slices together. Second, put the cheese on the bread. First, take out two pieces of bread and some cheese. Did those directions make sense? What was wrong? They did not make sense because they are out of order! When we give directions, we need to be sure the steps are clear. The steps need to be in order.*

Teach/Model Provide a simple scenario for students, such as *I want to give directions for getting from our classroom to the lunchroom.* Ask students to provide steps as you write them on the board. Help them to use sequence words and clear directions. Read the directions back. Can students use the directions to find the lunchroom? As students form the directions with you, write order words on the board for students' reference.

Practice Place students in groups and ask them to give directions orally for a simple task, such as sharpening a pencil or folding a sheet of paper. One student can give directions while the others complete the task. Do the directions make sense? Guide practice as needed. Have volunteers share the best examples with the class.

Assess Listen in as students give directions. Assess their ability to provide clear steps and use sequence words.

Beginning On index cards, write steps or draw simple pictures for a simple process. Write one step per card. Give the cards to groups of students and have them work together to place the cards in order. Then students can say or read the directions aloud.

Intermediate/Advanced Provide out-of-order directions without order words. Have students place the directions in order and say them aloud, inserting sequence words to add organization.

Advanced High Have students work with partners to create a list of sequence words they can use in giving directions. Then have them give directions for a simple task, using words from their list.

Name _____

Use the sentence starters to give directions for a task, such as tying your shoe.

First, you should . . .

Second, . . .

Next, . . .

After that, . . .

Finally, . . .

Ask a friend to follow your directions. Were the directions clear? How could you improve them?

Circle the rating for each sentence. **Tell** how you give directions.

1. I need help to do this better.

2. I do this sometimes.

3. I know how to do this.

I can give direction with more than one or two steps.	1	2	3
I use order words when I give directions.	1	2	3
My directions are clear. People can follow them.	1	2	3

Follow Directions

Teaching Tip
As students are able, make directions more complex. Start with simple one- or two-step directions for students to follow, both oral and written. Then gradually increase the complexity of the directions you give and have them restate the directions to clarify meaning.

Preteach *I have to follow directions every day. This morning, I followed directions for making breakfast in the microwave. I follow directions when I drive to school. I had to read the directions for using the DVD player when I showed you a video. And my teacher books have directions for teaching lessons. It is important to look at the steps in directions and read them (or listen) carefully to follow them.*

Teach/Model *Listen as I give you directions.* Give students directions for drawing things on sheets of paper, such as *First, draw a star in the upper right corner. Next, draw a circle in the middle.* After students have followed your directions, have them compare their drawings to the "answer." Point out important features of directions: time-order words that organize directions, and steps that need to be completed in order. If students had trouble following the directions, what made them difficult?

Practice Have students work in pairs to answer the questions on the student worksheet. Discuss and identify what makes the directions easy to follow (details in the steps and the numbers in order). Then have pairs read the directions for making a healthy snack to each other. One student can listen and the other student can gesture to show understanding.

Assess Assess students' oral and written work to check their ability to follow directions. Be sure that students understand they need to look for important details in directions and follow steps in order. Help them to understand that restating directions helps to clarify understanding.

Beginning Give simple one- or two-step directions for students to follow. Ask them to restate the most important details of each step before they follow it.

Intermediate Gather directions for students, such as recipes or directions for making or building simple things at home. Have them look for sequence words or other clues to order as well as the important details in the steps. Discuss in small groups, and then practice giving each other directions.

Advanced/Advanced High Provide directions for making or doing something. Have students work in small groups to discuss the directions and complete the tasks.

Name _____

Read the directions.

Answer the questions.

Make a healthy snack!

You will need: one red or green pepper, carrot sticks, celery sticks, salad dressing, a sharp knife, an adult helper

1. Have an adult cut the pepper in half across the middle.

2. Scoop out the seeds and material from inside the pepper.

3. Wash the inside and outside of each pepper. Each half of the pepper is a bowl!

4. Put salad dressing in each bowl.

5. Dip carrots and celery into the salad dressing. Eat them.

6. When you finish eating the celery and carrots, you can eat the bowl!

How many pepper bowls does this recipe make?

_____

What do you do with the salad dressing in step 5?

_____

_____

What does the adult helper do? Why do you need an adult helper? _____

_____

Draw the steps on the back of this sheet.

Teaching Tip
While some classroom language is straightforward transactional language that students need to practice in order to learn, other classroom language is idiomatic and may be confusing for students. When you tell students to "line up," for example, they may think of drawing a line or putting up a line such as a clothesline. Tell students the meanings of the idiomatic phrases used in the classroom in language they can understand.

Preteach *Every day in class, we communicate with each other. We ask questions and give directions. We work in groups. Students listen and ask for help from classmates and from the teacher. We have some words and sentences that we use often in the classroom. It's important for us to know how to use classroom language to get help, work with others, and understand what is happening around us in class.*

Teach/Model Ask several students to assist you in a role play. *Please take out your books. Open your books to page 15.* Assist students as needed to open their books to the correct page. *I used classroom language. You hear your teacher ask all the time to open your books to a certain page. That means that you can see that page in front of you.* Pairs can role-play, taking turns saying the classroom language and opening their books to the correct page.

Practice Help students gather examples of classroom language to record in the chart on the student worksheet. Some examples are already included on the chart. Have students role-play using the language. As students think of more examples of classroom language, add the examples to a large chart displayed on the wall.

Assess As students role-play and use classroom language, listen to the conversations and clear up any misconceptions. Continue to have students add examples to the worksheet and the chart in the classroom.

Beginning Give simple examples of classroom language for students to use, role-playing a scenario such as a student asking another student or the teacher to repeat what he or she said.

Intermediate/Advanced Have students role-play a scenario in which they are trying to understand a new word. They can use classroom language such as *What does _____ mean? How do you say _____ in English?*

Advanced High Have students create reference sheets or posters to use in the classroom that capture various examples of classroom language. Students can illustrate the posters to show the situations in which they use the classroom language and teach those words and phrases to others.

Name _____

Read the examples of classroom language.
Use them in conversations with classmates.

Is this right?
What are we supposed to do?
Put this in your own words.
Can you say it again, please?
How do you say it in English?
How do you spell it in English?
What does . . . . mean?
What do you think?
I agree with you.
I disagree. Here's why.
Let's ask the teacher about this.
Open your book to page . . .
Copy this into your notes.
Listen and repeat.
The homework is . . .
Work in pairs.
Work in groups.

Circle the rating for each sentence. **Tell** how you use
classroom language.

1. I need help to do this better.
2. I do this sometimes.
3. I know how to do this.

I ask for help in English.	1 2 3
I use classroom language with classmates.	1 2 3
I use classroom language with the teacher.	1 2 3
I understand the directions my teacher gives me.	1 2 3

Learn New Words

Teaching Tip
Make multiple copies of the student master. As you introduce words tied to the reading selections, as well as words from content areas, students can add to their own dictionaries of new words. Challenge students to refer to their dictionaries and use the new words twelve times in their writing and speaking to internalize meaning.

Preteach Copy the student blackline master on chart paper or display on an overhead. *When I read or hear a word I don't know, I think about what I do know about the word. Does it have a cognate I know to give a clue to meaning? Then I try to describe what the word means in a way that makes sense to me. I think about how the word relates to something in my own life. I try to remember where I've seen this word before. Sometimes I even draw a picture to help me remember what the word means. Then I use the word many times so I don't forget the meaning.*

Teach/Model Model how to use the chart with a word from a reading selection or from content-area studies, such as *weather*. Write the word on the line. Then model rating your knowledge: *A 1 means that I don't know this word at all. A 4 means I know it well enough to explain it to someone else. I understand what weather is, but I'm not sure I could define it. I'll give it a* 3. Then explain or describe weather and write a description. Be sure that your description uses simple language that all students understand.

Practice Write a word for students to copy on the chart. Pronounce the word, and then have students say it three times. Ask students to rate their knowledge of the word. Then guide students to describe the word to build understanding. Give an example of how the word relates to a class experience, tell a story that includes the word, or show a picture that defines the word. After you have defined the word, students should create their own descriptions of the word on their charts. Students can work in pairs or small groups.

Assess Assess students' word descriptions to clear up any misconceptions about the words. Look over word understanding ratings and periodically have students reevaluate their understandings of the words. Give students multiple opportunities to listen, speak, read and write with the new words, to internalize meaning.

Beginning Rather than write word meanings, students can draw and label pictures of the words.

Intermediate Have students use the words in simple spoken sentences that they share with partners. Listen in for correct word use.

Advanced/Advanced High Students can use a dictionary or glossary to reinforce their understandings of the words.

Name _____

Write the word on the line.

Rate how well you understand the word.

1. I don't know the word.
2. I think I know what the word means.
3. I know the word. I can use it in a sentence.
4. I can teach this word to someone else.

Describe the word in a way that helps you understand it.

Word: _____ My Understanding   1   2   3   4

Describe the word: _____

_____

Word: _____ My Understanding   1   2   3   4

Describe the word: _____

_____

Word: _____ My Understanding   1   2   3   4

Describe the word: _____

_____

Preteach *If I don't understand something, I need to ask the person speaking to repeat what they said. Then I can understand it. That is* called *clarifying. I ask questions to clarify, or be sure I understand. I also ask questions when I am reading. I ask questions before I read, while I read, and after I read. That helps me understand what I am reading.*

Teach/Model Work with a student to role-play a situation in which you would ask a clarifying question. Have the student give you simple directions for doing something. As the student speaks, find an opportunity to ask a question such as *What does that mean? Can you repeat that, please?* or *How do you do that?*

Practice Share the worksheet with students and talk about situations in which students would use each of the clarifying questions. Then point out the question starters. Have students use the question starters to ask questions about a selection you have recently read.

Assess As students role-play asking clarifying questions, assess their ability to ask the questions in appropriate situations. Provide multiple opportunities to practice using question starters. Assess students' ability to use those question words to form questions that make sense.

Beginning Have students role-play situations with you in which they ask for assistance for completing a math problem or other classroom task.

Intermediate/Advanced Have students work in small groups to identify questions they would ask the teacher, their parents, other students in a group, and so on to clarify their understanding.

Advanced High Have student use the "5Ws and an H" to ask and answer questions about a reading selection.

Name _____

Read the examples of clarifying questions.

Use them in conversations with classmates and your teachers.

Use the question starters to ask questions about what you read or hear.

Is this right?
Can you say it again, please?
Can you speak slower, please?
How do you say it in English?
How do you spell it in English?
What does . . . mean?
What do I need to do?
What should I do next?

Use these sentence frames to ask questions. Use the sentence frames to answer questions, too.

Who is _____? That person is _____.

What is _____? That is _____.

When did _____ happen? It happened _____.

Where is _____? The _____ is _____.

Why did _____ happen? It happened because _____.

Preteach *I was reading a story, and I found a word I didn't know. I tried to figure out what the word meant from reading the words around it, but I still needed help. I asked my friend, but she didn't know either. So I used this.* (Show a dictionary.) *A dictionary is a classroom resource. It's a tool that I can use to find out word meanings.* Model how to use a dictionary and its features: guide words, pronunciations, and so on.)

Teach/Model Draw attention to the student worksheet with the list of classroom resources. Start with the first one. *A map shows the locations of things. I'll write that in the chart. Why would I use a map? I'd use a map to find the capital of our state. I'd use a map to figure out how to get somewhere. I'd use a map to locate natural features. I'll write one of these uses in the chart.*

Practice As you use various resources with students, have students consider how and why to use the resources. The worksheet can be completed as an ongoing activity. Be sure to think aloud as you use various resources and demonstrate how and why to use them. Students can add resources that are particular to your classroom.

Assess Assess students' ability to choose appropriate resources. They would use a thesaurus, for example, to make writing more interesting. Other examples would be to use a DVD to get information in a visual way and to use a computer to find out information for presentations.

Beginning Have students work in pairs to use a picture dictionary to find a word from a reading selection. Help them restate the definition in their own words.

Intermediate/Advanced Have small groups of students use a classroom resource such as a map to locate directions, cities, and physical features.

Advanced High Ask students to add more classroom resources to the chart and explain to other students how to use those resources.

Name_____

Read the name of the resource.
Explain what the resource is like.
Tell why you would use it.
Add more resources to the chart.

Classroom Resources

Resource	What's it like?	Why would I use it?
Dictionary	a book of words and definitions; words are in alphabetical order	to find out the meaning of a word; to find out how to say a word
Map		
Thesaurus		
Almanac		
Encyclopedia		
Computer		

Retell or Summarize

Preteach *I saw a movie yesterday. When my friends asked me about it, I didn't tell every detail from the beginning to end. Instead, I told the most important things. This is called summarizing. I summarize things I see, things I read, and things I hear. When I summarize, I know that I have sorted out the most important details. A summary includes important things, not everything. Retelling is a little different. When you retell something, you listen to or read the message, and then say it in your own words to show you understand it.*

Teach/Model Ask students to listen carefully as you read a short passage aloud. After you read, ask students to contribute to a summary of the passage. Help frame their thinking as you list their ideas to create a summary. Have pairs of students read the complete summary together. Then reread the passage. Have pairs decide if the summary lists the most important details. What should be added or changed? Discuss and clarify answers.

Practice Have students use the graphic organizer on the student worksheet to list details from a written or spoken passage. In the box at the bottom, students can write their summaries. Encourage them to keep their summaries short and to the point. Ask them to read their summaries aloud and compare them with classmates' summaries.

Assess Assess students' summaries to be sure that students have included only important details. Ask questions to guide their thinking, (e.g., *Why is this detail important? Does your summary match what the author wanted us to remember?*).

Beginning Have students orally summarize a simple spoken message or a simple text, such as a comic strip. They can work in pairs to practice and then share oral summaries with the group.

Intermediate Provide a simple text and a sample summary that is missing some information and provides too many details about the text. Ask students to read and discuss the summary in pairs. *What details are missing? What details don't need to be included?*

Advanced/Advanced High Ask students to work in pairs to create directions for summarizing. Have them share their directions and sample summaries with other students.

Name _____

Use the graphic organizer to list important details.

Write a summary in the box.

Say the summary aloud.

Use the summary starters if you need to.

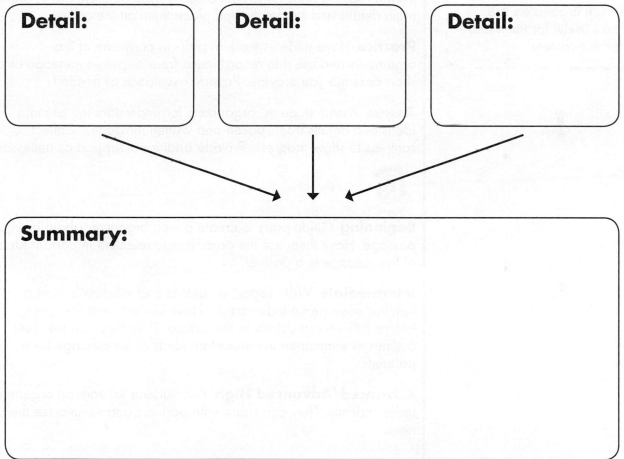

Detail:

Detail:

Detail:

Summary:

Summary language:

In summary, . . .

The most important ideas are . . .

What we need to remember is . . .

Take Notes/ Create an Outline

Preteach *When I am in a meeting, I listen for important ideas and take notes. You do the same thing in class. When you listen, you write down important ideas. When you read, you write down important ideas too. Writing down ideas, or taking notes, helps you remember them later.*

Teach/Model Model using the web graphic organizer and the outline on the student worksheet. Tell students that the web organizer is great for writing down details about one idea. Then model using the outline form to record main details and subdetails from a reading selection. Think aloud as you differentiate between main details and subdetails and place them on the outline.

Practice Have students work in pairs to copy one of the organizers and use it to record ideas from a spoken message or a short passage you provide. Provide assistance as needed.

Assess Assess students' organizers for understanding of main ideas and details from spoken and written messages. Collect samples to show progress. Provide additional support as necessary.

Beginning Guide pairs to create a web organizer about a simple passage. Have them use the organizer to retell the important ideas of the passage to a partner.

Intermediate Write important details and subdetails from a familiar passage on index cards. Have students sort the cards before they record details in the outline. Then they can use their outlines to summarize the important ideas of the passage for a partner.

Advanced/Advanced High Ask students to work on organizers independently. They can share with partners and summarize their notes.

Name_____

Choose a graphic organizer to take notes.

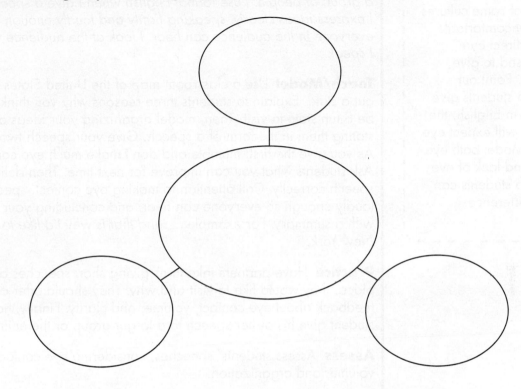

Outline

I. _____

   A. _____

   B. _____

II. _____

   A. _____

   B. _____

III. _____

   A. _____

   B. _____

Give a Speech

Preteach *A speech is a planned talk that you give in front of a group of people. I use formal English when I give a speech. I express ideas clearly, speaking firmly and loudly enough so everyone in the audience can hear. I look at the audience when I speak.*

Teach/Model Use a classroom map of the United States to pick out a state. Explain to students three reasons why you think it would be a fun state to visit. Then, model organizing your ideas and stating them in the form of a speech. Give your speech two times. As you give the first, mumble and don't make much eye contact. Ask students what you can improve for next time. Then deliver the speech correctly. Call attention to making eye contact, speaking loudly enough so everyone can hear, and concluding your speech with a summary. For example: *...and that is why I'd like to visit New York.*

Practice Have partners take turns giving short speeches about places they would like to visit and why. They should offer corrective feedback about eye contact, volume, and clarity. Finally, have each student give his or her speech to a larger group or the entire class.

Assess Assess students' speeches, considering eye contact, volume, and organization.

Beginning Have students work on delivering speeches by answering simple questions, speaking aloud. Because speeches are planned, give students a chance to plan what they will say. Tell them the questions first so they can think through their answers.

Intermediate Have students work on elaborating. Lead them by explaining that sentences that add more details include words such as *because, as a result,* etc.

Advanced/Advanced High Give students time to plan, then have them speak on a topic for two minutes. Speakers should elaborate with details and avoid using *um, uh,* and *you know.*

Name _____

Use the planner to organize ideas for your speech.

Write your topic.

Explain how you will introduce your speech.

List details to include in the speech.

End with a conclusion, or a final thought for your audience to remember.

Topic:

_____

To **introduce** my topic, I will:

_____

_____

Details I will include:

_____

_____

_____

I will **end** my speech by:

_____

Evaluate your speech.

1. I need to practice more to do this.
2. I did this sometimes.
3. I did this during my whole speech.

I spoke loudly enough for my audience to hear.	1	2	3
I looked at the audience when I spoke.	1	2	3
I spoke clearly.	1	2	3
I used formal English.	1	2	3
I organized my ideas with a clear beginning and end.	1	2	3

Teaching Tip

Students may think of facts as "true" and opinions as "false." Locate statements of opinions that are supported by facts and discuss them with students. Point out that people trust opinions when they are supported with facts.

Preteach *We express opinions to show what we think or believe. We cannot prove if an opinion is true or false. If I say,* It is raining outside, *that's a fact. I can look outside and see rain falling. If I say,* Rainy weather is the best weather, *that's an opinion. I like rainy weather because it helps my flowers grow in the garden. But some people don't like rain. They have a different opinion.*

Teach/Model Display the words and phrases from the student page. *We use these words to give our opinions. These words tell what we think or believe.* Model creating an opinion using one of the words or phrases.

Practice Have students work with partners to state opinions about sports, food, television shows, books, or movies. Have them use the words in the box on the student page. Refer them to the sentence frames as needed. Point out that these frames will help them correctly express opinions in English. For additional practice, have students write statements of opinion and then say them aloud with partners. Have students elaborate by giving reasons for their opinions.

Assess As students state opinions, assess understanding. Do students state ideas that cannot be proven true or false and express feelings or beliefs? Do students use words or phrases from the box? Correct students as necessary.

Beginning Write sentence frames on index cards and distribute them to students. Have them work in pairs to state opinions using the frames.

Intermediate When calling on students to give oral opinions, have them use phrases such as *I like* or *I do not like* rather than single words. Have pairs ask each other why they have that opinion. Report answers to the class.

Advanced/Advanced High Challenge students to add other opinion words or phrases to the box and write additional sentence frames. They can use the frames to state opinions.

Name _____

Opinion Words

I think	I believe	my opinion is	I agree
I disagree	I like	I do not like	
best	worst	good	bad

Complete opinions using these sentence frames:

I like _____.

I think _____.

I believe _____.

I do not like _____.

My opinion is _____.

Statements of opinion:

_____

_____

_____

Challenge! Add more details to your sentence.

I like _____ because _____.

Her opinion is _____ because _____.

Preteach *If you see someone with a frown on his or her face* (demonstrate for students), *you know that person might be sad or angry. Anger and sadness are feelings. We often express our feelings with our facial expressions and our actions, but we can also use words to express feelings. Finding the right words isn't always easy!*

Teach/Model Use exaggerated facial expressions and body language to express a feeling, such as happiness or confusion. Model by speaking: *I am happy. I feel happy.* Model another feeling and have students use the frames after you model:

You feel _____. You are _____.

Practice Explain a situation to students that would elicit a feeling, such as *Your favorite cousin is coming to a family party. You haven't seen your cousin in a long time. How do you feel?* (excited, happy) *You came to school without your homework. You know your teacher is going to ask for it.* (worried, guilty) Have students gesture to show the emotion and then work with partners to express that feeling in words. As students suggest more feeling words, write them on a chart for reference so that students can include them on their worksheets.

Assess As students express their feelings, assess the sentences they use as well as their ability to identify feelings. Correct any misconceptions as students use sentence frames to express feelings.

Beginning Have students draw or make faces to show a facial expression that expresses a feeling. Partners can identify the feeling and create a sentence: *He/she feels _____.*

Intermediate Have students look for pictures in magazines or newspapers that show a situation that would elicit feelings. Have them speak about the picture.

Advanced/Advanced High Challenge students to think of specific words for feelings, such as *joyful, ecstatic, lively, overjoyed, pleased, thrilled,* or *upbeat* instead of *happy.*

Name _____

Record words that express feelings in the box. A few words are already in the box. **Add** more.

Feeling Words

glad	afraid	proud	angry
lonely	confused	surprised	

Speak a sentence using one of the frames below.
Choose words from the box.

I feel _____.

I am _____.

He/She is _____.

They felt _____.

They are _____.

He/She was _____.

They were _____.

Challenge! Add more details to your sentence.

I feel _____ because _____.

They felt _____ when _____.

Discuss with Classmates

Preteach *When do we have discussions? I discuss work with students. I talk with my family at the dinner table. I discuss ideas with other teachers at school. In a discussion, we speak and we listen. We respect other people's ideas.*

Teach/Model Create a fishbowl, in which you and a few students are in the center while others are around you watching. Introduce an easy discussion topic such as a question about a selection you have just read. Model the discussion behaviors from the rubric on the next page. As you model these behaviors, pause to think aloud. You might say *I repeated back what Tommy said to me. He knows that I have understood him. He also knows I was listening. Now it is my turn to speak. It is important to take turns being a good listener and a good speaker.*

Practice Have students work in small groups. Introduce a topic such as: *What is your favorite thing to do after school?* As students discuss, monitor and encourage the positive behaviors you observe. Share these positive behaviors with the class and have students identify others they know.

Assess Use the rubric on the student page to have students assess their discussion skills. Follow up with your own observations of student discussions.

Beginning Offer students examples of nonverbal communication skills that a good listener uses: nodding, making eye contact, and making appropriate expressions. Have them mimic you as you model them.

Intermediate Offer students an example of a conversation that could occur at the lunch table. Have the students mimic you, each partner playing another role. Stress the importance of active listening and behaviors that go with it.

Advanced/Advanced High Have students model discussion scenarios and demonstrate behaviors of listening and speaking for other groups.

Name_____

Rate what you do during discussions with your classmates.

1. I need to practice this skill.
2. I do this sometimes.
3. I almost always do this.

I share my ideas with others.	1	2	3
I answer questions when classmates ask.	1	2	3
I give a lot of facts or details when I speak.	1	2	3
I respect other people in the group.	1	2	3
I listen to other people's ideas.	1	2	3
I look at the person speaking.	1	2	3
I repeat back what other people say to show I understand.	1	2	3
I support other people's ideas.	1	2	3

What topics would you like to discuss with classmates?
List them here. Then discuss!

_____

_____

_____

_____

_____

Act Out or Draw Meaning

Preteach Choose a content-area or lesson word that students recently learned. *When I learn new words, I want to remember them. Drawing a picture of a word's meaning or acting out the meaning of a word helps me remember a word, what it means, and how it is used. I just learned a new word in science: fault. A fault is a place in the earth where an earthquake takes place. I drew a picture of a circle to show the Earth and drew a line on it. I put arrows to show how the Earth shifts at the fault line. (Show picture.) I can also act out the meaning by taking two blocks and rubbing them together to show what happens at a fault to make an earthquake.*

Teach/Model Introduce words from a recent story or from content-area studies. Place students in small groups, and give each group a word. Have students work together to create a picture and/or gestures to demonstrate meanings of the words. Groups can share with other groups as you monitor for understanding.

Practice Play a guessing game with students. Distribute words on index cards that students have learned in class. Students can take turns drawing pictures or acting out word meanings for other classmates to guess. Use the student worksheet for students to create "dictionaries" of word meanings. Distribute copies of the drawing frames when students learn new words. Have students keep and add to their own personal word books.

Assess Assess students' drawings to clear up any misconceptions about the words. Discuss with students how drawing words may help them remember word meanings.

Beginning Ask students to follow up their drawings or gestures by explaining word meanings orally.

Intermediate Ask students to use each word in a sentence to describe what they drew or acted out.

Advanced/Advanced High Have students look up the definitions of words in a dictionary to supplement their understanding of the words. They can write definitions in their own words to show understanding.

Name _____

Word: _____

Drawing

This word means _____

Word: _____

Drawing

This word means _____

Read the Words Around You

Preteach Before starting, draw a stop sign on the board and ask what it means. Students may answer *stop*. *We are surrounded by words and signs that can be useful. We need to learn what these signs tell us.* Point out that the name of the school is on the front of the building. *The sign tells people what this building is. It helps people find the school.* Then, point out that the classrooms have numbers. *These help students find their way around the school.*

Teach/Model Walk around the classroom until you find an example of instructional environmental print. Model reading the word, and figuring out what it means: *A sign on this door reads P-U-L-L. I know that word is* pull. *This sign tells me how to open the door.* Then, model opening the door.

Practice Tell students that their task is to keep a log of the signs they notice and can read throughout the school day. They must keep track of the words in the table on their worksheets. At the end of the day, have students share one word they recognized in a sign, and one they did not. Discuss as a class. Help them understand the meanings of words they did not recognize. As you discuss students' examples, talk about the information they get from reading the signs or other environmental print. Students can keep a running log of environmental print they see and learn. Discuss the words regularly.

Assess Assess students' understandings of environmental print by questioning them as they share their results, for example: *Why do you think the sign "gymnasium" was placed in that spot?* (The sign tells us where the gym is.) Explain the meanings of unknown words to students.

Beginning Have beginning students only keep track of words they recognize and know.

Intermediate Have students organize their words by category, such as *foods, signs, rooms, clubs,* and so on.

Advanced/Advanced High Provide environmental print for students, such as store advertisements, posters, and additional signs. Students can discuss with partners what they learn from reading the signs and texts.

Name _____

Write the words you see around you.

Practice saying each word aloud.

Date	Words I Know	Words I Do Not Know Yet

Teaching Tip

In some languages, there is no difference between count and noncount nouns. For students who speak these languages, provide sentence frames and models to help them understand the difference.

Preteach *Nouns are words that name people, places, or things. Nouns can name one thing, or they can name more than one thing. I can count these pencils: one, two, three, four. But the word* weather *is a noun, too. I can't count weather, though: one weather, two weathers, three weathers? That doesn't make sense! There must be different kinds of nouns, with different rules for how we say them and write them.*

Teach/Model Write *desks* and *furniture* on the board and draw a quick sketch under each: three desks under *desks* and a desk, chair, and couch under *furniture. Let's make sentences with these words. I see three desks. I can count them: one, two, three. I see that furniture. I used the word* that *because I cannot count furniture and say* one furniture, two furnitures, three furnitures. *Nouns that you can count, such as* desk, *are called* count nouns. *Nouns that you cannot count, such as* furniture, weather, *or* anger, *are called* noncount nouns.

Practice Have students complete the student worksheet. Focus on the ability to count some nouns and ask questions to frame as necessary. For the first sentence, for example, you might say: *You can count the apples. One, two, three, four. Write the word* four *on the line.* For the second sentence: *When I drink the water, I can't count how many waters. So I'll complete the sentence with* the. As students complete the exercise, point out that some noncount nouns might have the word *a* or *an* in front of them.

Assess As students complete their worksheets, circulate to assess their work and clear up any misconceptions.

Beginning Say a count noun, such as *bird*. Ask students to use the word in a sentence. Then say a noncount noun, such as *music*. Have students use the word in a sentence. Check for understanding.

Intermediate Write words on index cards, one word per card. Have students work together to sort the words into count and noncount nouns. They can choose one count noun and one noncount noun to use in a sentence.

Advanced/Advanced High Challenge students to find sentences in magazines or newspapers and underline the nouns. Have them work in pairs to classify nouns as count or noncount nouns. Then have them speak using those nouns as you check for understanding.

Name _____

Look at the picture.

Read the sentence.

Complete the sentence by writing a number OR by writing the word *the*.

Say the sentences aloud.

1. We need _____ apples for our pie.

2. Hold up _____ fingers.

3. _____ weather is hot.

4. We heard _____ music.

5. There are _____ houses on this block.

6. Please put those _____ books on the shelf.

Circle the count nouns in the sentences above.

Explain the difference between a count and a noncount noun to a partner.

Listen for other count and noncount nouns you hear in conversations.

Use Prepositions and Adjectives in Your Speaking

Preteach Demonstrate as you describe prepositions. *I push the chair under the table. I put my coat on the hook. When I was describing where I put things, I used special words to tell where. These words,* on *and* under, *are called prepositions. We can use prepositions to tell locations. We can also use prepositions to tell when things happen. We eat lunch after our math class. In that sentence,* after *is a preposition that helps us tell time.*

Teach/Model Use a preposition in a sentence that shows location, such as *I walk between the rows of desks.* Demonstrate by walking between the desks. Say the sentence again and ask students to raise their hands when they hear the preposition. Then pair students. Assign each a preposition. Have students say and demonstrate a sentence using the preposition.

Practice Have students use the space on the bottom of the worksheet to draw a picture. They can write about the picture using prepositions. Model if necessary: *I drew a picture of myself riding my bicycle. I put my helmet on my head. I was careful when I rode across the street.* Students can also use this sheet to work with adjectives. Have them list adjectives in the second column. They can use adjectives to describe the picture they drew.

Assess Assess students' pictures and sentences for understanding of how to use prepositions. Provide extra support as necessary.

Beginning Write prepositions on index cards, one preposition per card. Demonstrate putting books *on* the table or putting your pencil *into* a desk. As you model and say the prepositional phrases, students can repeat the prepositions and hold up the cards with the corresponding prepositions. Then have students use gestures to demonstrate prepositions, while other students guess the prepositions they are demonstrating.

Intermediate/Advanced Share photographs from magazines. Ask students to describe locations of items in the photographs using prepositions. They can use adjectives to describe the photos as well.

Advanced High Challenge students to find prepositions and adjectives from their reading or from other sources. They can add them to the worksheet and to a chart for class reference. Have them practice using prepositions that tell time in addition to location.

Name_____

Write prepositions in the first column.

Write adjectives in the second column.

Prepositions	Adjectives

Draw a picture.

Write about it. **Use** prepositions and adjectives.

Use Verbs in Your Speaking

Teaching Tip

Phrasal verbs may prove difficult for students, because they are idiomatic expressions. Use the worksheet as a basis for a chart to which you can add phrasal verbs as students encounter them in their reading and listening. As you add phrasal verbs to the chart, have students discuss their meanings and use them in sentences.

Preteach *Verbs are words that show action. I look before I cross the street.* (Model turning your head to look both ways before crossing the street.) *The word* look *is a verb. It describes something I do. If I said, Please look up a word in the dictionary, does that mean that you would really look up?* (Model looking up toward the ceiling.) *Look up is a group of words that has a different meaning as a group of words than if you say each word individually. The phrase* Look up *is called a phrasal verb. It's a verb with a preposition or an adverb. The phrase makes a meaning different from the verb's meaning.*

Teach/Model Choose a phrasal verb from the chart for modeling. *Let's focus on the phrase* go over. *A car can* go over *a hill. But* go over *can have a different meaning. What does it mean if I say* Let's go over your homework? *That means that we are going to review and check your answers.* Guide students by choosing another phrasal verb and explaining and modeling its meaning.

Practice Have students work in pairs to complete the worksheet by choosing the correct phrase to complete each sentence.

Assess Assess students' answers on the worksheet. Correct any errors, and explain misconceptions students may have.

Beginning Assist students by reading the sentence and inserting the meaning of the correct answer. After students use the chart to choose the correct answer, they can reread the sentence to reinforce their understanding of the concept in English.

Intermediate/Advanced Ask students to choose a phrase and work in pairs to write a sentence that includes the phrase. They can illustrate their sentences to show meaning.

Advanced High Have students search for phrasal verbs in their reading selections or other printed material, share them in small groups, and discuss their meanings.

Name _____

Read each phrasal verb in the chart.

Phrasal Verb	Meaning
show up	arrive
make up	create or invent something
run into	meet
look up	find
back up	support an idea
come across	find something
come up with	think of an idea
do over	do something again
give up	stop doing something
go over	check something; review
hold on	wait for a short time
keep up	go at the same speed
make up one's mind	decide something
turn in	give something to someone

Circle the verbal phrase that fits the sentence.

1. Let's _____ the correct answers.

    go over   give up

2. I want to make a better drawing. I'll _____.

    give up   do it over

3. Did you _____ that story?

    keep up   make up

4. Please _____. I am almost ready to go.

    hold on   back up

5. I cannot _____ my mind about for lunch.

    make up   give up

Role-play conversations with phrasal verbs. Share them.

Part 6
Multilingual Vocabulary

Introduction to Multilingual Vocabulary

The lesson words are arranged by unit and week to coincide with the reading selections. Each lesson word is translated into Spanish, Chinese, Vietnamese, Korean, and Hmong. Use the translated lesson words to build students' background knowledge before reading a selection. Frontloading the vocabulary will allow students to access the content and will aid their comprehension of the text.

The multilingual thinking words, also translated into the same languages, are process words, such as *analyze, compare, describe, illustrate, list*, and *predict*. Students can use these words to discuss the strategies they use as they read various selections, including content-area texts.

Table of Contents

Multilingual Vocabulary
Unit 1

English	Spanish	Chinese	Vietnamese	Korean	Hmong
Week 1: Because of Winn-Dixie					
memorial	conmemorativo	纪念的	tưởng niệm	기념하는	nco txog
prideful	orgulloso	自大	hãnh diện	교만한, 건방진	tsaj hwjchim
recalls	recordar	记起	nhớ lại	기억하다	nco txog
peculiar	peculiar	奇特	riêng biệt	특이한	muaj ntsiv zoo li
grand	de gran importancia	宏伟	vĩ đại	웅대한	loj
positive	positivo, optimista	正面	tích cực	분명한, 명백한	xam zoo
selecting	selectionar	挑选	tuyển chọn	골라내는, 선별하는	mus xaiv
Week 2: Lewis and Clark and Me					
docks	diques	船坞	vũng tàu đậu	부두, 선착장	chaw nres nkoj
migrating	emigrando	移居	di trú	이주하는	mus ib qhov chaw rau ib qho
scan	escudriñar	细看	quét; đọc lướt	유심히 쳐다보다, 자세히 조사하다	xyuas
scent	aroma	气味	hương thơm	향기,냄새	tus ntxhiab
wharf	muelle	码头	cầu tàu	부두, 선착장	chav nres nkoj
yearned	anheló	渴望	thương mến	갈망하는	ntshaw
Week 3: On the Banks of Plum Creek					
badger	tejón	獾	con lửng	오소리	hmab
bank	orilla	河岸	bờ	둑	npoo
bristled	encrespó	毛骨耸立	có nhiều lông	털을 곤두세웠다	txhav
jointed	juntado	连接	gắn chặt	이음매(관절)가 있는	sis dhos
patched	reparado	修补	chắp vá	고쳤다	ntxiv rau

English	Spanish	Chinese	Vietnamese	Korean	Hmong
ruffled	encrespado	惹怒	bối rối	주름(장식)이 있는	ua ntxhov nyo
rushes	juncos	芦苇	loại cây cỏ	골풀	tsob hav nyom

Week 4: The Horned Toad Prince

English	Spanish	Chinese	Vietnamese	Korean	Hmong
bargain	pacto	交易	mặc cả	거래	hais nqi
favor	favor	厚待	ân huệ	친절	yam (dab tsi) thov ua
lassoed	enlazó	用套索捕捉	bắt bằng dây thòng lọng	~을 올가미 밧줄로 잡다	txoj hlua ua muaj ib voj
offended	ofendida	冒犯	bị xúc phạm	감정을 해치다, ~을 위반하다	ntxuam
prairie	pradera	大草原	đồng cỏ rộng lớn ở Mỹ	대초원	plag tiaj nyom
riverbed	lecho	河床	lòng sông	강바닥	paj dej uas tus dej ntws los rau
shrieked	chilló	尖叫	kêu thét	비명을 지르다	quaj txias siab

Week 5: Letters Home from Yosemite

English	Spanish	Chinese	Vietnamese	Korean	Hmong
glacier	glaciar	冰川	dãy băng hà	빙하	(thooj) dej khov
impressive	impresionante	印象深刻	gây ấn tượng sâu sắc	인상적인	ua tau ntxim nyiam
naturalist	naturalista	博物學家	nhà vạn vật học	동물(식물)학자	neeg tshuaj xyuas yam nyob hauv ntiaj teb
preserve	preservar	保存	bảo quản	보존하다	tseg cia
slopes	laderas	斜坡	những dốc	경사지다	toj
species	especies	種類	các loài	종	tsiaj
wilderness	zona silvestre	荒野	miền hoang dã	자연 보호 구역, 다수	hav zoo

Unit 2

English	Spanish	Chinese	Vietnamese	Korean	Hmong
Week 1: What Jo Did					
fouled	hizo una falta	弄髒	phạm luật	반칙하다	thawb
hoop	aro	箍	rổ	(농구의) 링	tawb pov basketball
jersey	camiseta	緊身運動套衫	một loại vải, đồng phục bóng rổ bằng loại vải này	(운동선수가 입는) 셔츠	cev khawb ncaws yas nyias nyias
marveled	se maravillaban	驚奇	thán phục	놀라다	xav txog
rim	canasta	外緣	vòng rổ	(농구의 골망을 달아 매는) 테	sab ntug
speechless	boquiabierto	無言	không nói nên lời	말로 표현할 수 없는, 말을 못하는	hais tsis tau lus, tsis muaj lus hais
swatted	le dio	猛擊	đập mạnh	세게 치다	npuaj
unbelievable	increíble	難以相信	không thể tin được, lạ kỳ	믿을 수 없는	ntseeg tsis tau
Week 2: Coyote School News					
bawling	berreando	大喊	la hét	크게 외치다	quaj, qw
coyote	coyote	凱奧特	sói nhỏ ở sa mạc	코요테	coyote
dudes	dandis	花花公子	(từ lóng) mấy thằng bạn	멋쟁이	ib tug txiv neej
roundup	rodeo	召集	gom lại, lùa về	총괄, 요약	sau, suaj kaum, khi cia
spurs	espuelas	踢馬刺	bộ đinh thúc ngựa	격려하다	khau ncaws thos neeg
Week 3: Scene Two					
advice	consejo	建議	khuyến nghị	충고	cob qhia
argument	discusión	爭論	tranh luận	논쟁	sib ceg
arrangements	arreglos	改編	thương lượng	정리	muab los ua ke
descendants	descendientes	後代	con cháu về sau	자손들	nws li caj ces

English	Spanish	Chinese	Vietnamese	Korean	Hmong
dishonest	deshonesto	不誠實	không thành thật	부정직한	tsis ncaj
script	libreto	劇本	kịch bản	대본	cov ntawv
snag	problema	障礙	xé toạt	뜻하지 않은 장애	tu nro

Week 4: Horse Heroes

English	Spanish	Chinese	Vietnamese	Korean	Hmong
ambition	ambición	野心	khát vọng	야망	muaj siab
infested	infestado	受侵擾的	bị nhiễm	몰려드는	kis taus
landslide	movimiento de tierra	山崩	đất lở	산사태	toj pob
quicksand	arenas movedizas	流沙	cát lún	위험한 상태	qhov xyuab zeb
resistance	resistencia	抵抗	sức kháng cự	저항	tsis kam
rickety	en ruinas	搖搖晃晃的	yếu đuối	흔들흔들하는	roob hav
roamed	vagaban	漫遊	có khắp nơi	돌아다녔다	mus thoob
vast	vasta	寬廣的	khoảng trống	광대한	Loj

Week 5: So You Want to Be President?

English	Spanish	Chinese	Vietnamese	Korean	Hmong
Constitution	Constitución	憲法	Hiến Pháp	헌법	Mis kas txoj cai
howling	rotundo	嗥叫	hú lên	쓸쓸한	quaj qw
humble	humildes	謙卑	khiêm nhường	겸손한	tus paub siab paub qis, hwm niam hwm txiv
politics	política	政治	chính trị	정치	kev ua nom
responsibility	responsabilidad	責任	trách nhiệm	책임감	saib xyus txoj dej num
solemnly	solemnemente	莊嚴地	nghiêm trang	엄숙하게	tus coj tiag tiag tsis dag
vain	vano	自負	vô vọng	우쭐대는, 공허한	muaj phlus

Unit 3

English	Spanish	Chinese	Vietnamese	Korean	Hmong
Week 1: The Man Who Named the Clouds					
apprentice	aprendiz	学徒	học nghề	견습	tus neeg xyaum ua haujlwm
atmosphere	atmósfera	大气	khí quyển	대기	cua nyob ib ncig ntiajteb
chemical	sustancia química	化学	hóa chất	화학의, 화학적인	tshuaj
club	club	俱乐部	hội	클럽, 모임	koom haum
essay	ensayo	文章	luận văn	수필, 에세이	rab ntawv
manufacturing	manufactura	生产	chế tạo	제조의	tsim khoom
pressure	presión	压力	sức ép	압력	txhawb ntxhov siab
scales	escamas	鳞	vỏ ngoài	비늘	txheej tawv sab nrau
Week 2: Adelina's Whales					
biologist	bióloga	生物學家	nhà sinh vật học	생물학자	tus kawm txog txua yaj muaj sia
bluff	despeñadero	懸崖	lừa phỉnh	(해안, 곶 따위가) 깎아세운 듯한, 절벽	tso ya, tso hem
lagoon	laguna	礁湖	hồ nước biển	초호 (환초로 둘러싸인 얕은 바다)	av suav puam uas kem tus dej me thiab tus dej loj
massive	inmensas	巨大	khổng lồ	육중한	ntau ntau
rumbling	retumbante	隆隆響	kêu ầm ầm	우르르 하는 소리	suab ua zog
tropical	tropical	熱帶	về vùng nhiệt đới	열대의	chaw sov
Week 3: How Night Came from the Sea					
brilliant	brillante	明亮	ngời sáng	훌륭한	tsw yim zoo heev
chorus	coro	合唱	dàn hợp xướng, dàn đồng ca	합창	nqi xab
coward	cobarde	懦夫	người hèn nhát	겁쟁이	tais caus

English	Spanish	Chinese	Vietnamese	Korean	Hmong
gleamed	relucía	閃爍	lấp lánh	빛나는	duab ci
shimmering	centelleante	閃閃發光	lung linh	아른아른 빛나는	ci nplas

Week 4: Eye of the Storm

destruction	destrucción	破壞	sự phá hủy	파괴	tsoo pov tseg
expected	esperaba	期望	được mong đợi	예상하다	vam tias
forecasts	pronósticos	預報	tiên đoán	일기예보	huab cua
inland	tierra adentro	內陸	trong đất liền	내륙의	saum qhuab
shatter	hace añicos	震裂	làm vỡ tan	산산이 부서지다	ntsoog
surge	oleada	浪湧	sự dấy lên	큰 파도	txav ze

Week 5: Paul Bunyan

announcement	anuncio	宣告	tuyên bố	발표	tshaj tawm
feature	características	特色	đặc điểm	특징	muaj feem
harness	arnés	馬具	yên ngựa	마구	khi
lumberjacks	leñadores	伐木工	người đốn củi	벌목하는 사람들	yav cav
requirements	requisitos	條件	đòi hỏi	조건	yuav tsum ua li
thaw	descongelarán	解凍	làm tan	녹다	yaj
unnatural	extraño	不自然的	quái lạ	부자연스러운	ib txwm tsis muaj
untamed	en estado natural	未馴服的	chưa thuần thục	야생의	qus qus

Unit 4

English	Spanish	Chinese	Vietnamese	Korean	Hmong
Week 1: The Case of the Gasping Garbage					
analysis	análisis	分析	phân tích	분석	kev tshuaj ntsuam
beakers	vasos de laboratorio	烧杯	chén nước	유리컵, 비이커	khob
hollow	hueco	空洞	trống rỗng	구멍, 우묵한 (곳)	khoob lug
identify	identidad	辨认	nhận diện	구분하다, 식별하다	txheeb xyuas
lecture	presentar	发表	diễn thuyết	강의하다	lus qhuab qhia
microscope	microscopio	显微镜	kính hiển vi	현미경	koobxoom tsom khoom me
precise	preciso	准确	chính xác	정확한, 정밀한	raug kiag
relentless	implacable	枚枚不倦	không nao núng	잔인한	tsi tso tseg
Week 2: Encantado					
aquarium	acuario	水族館	bồn hoặc tòa nhà nuôi cá	수족관	tsev rau tsiaj deg
dolphins	delfines	海豚	cá heo	돌고래	dolphins
enchanted	encantado	迷惑	bị mê hoặc	매혹되다, 황홀해지다	zoo nkauj
flexible	flexibles	靈活	uyển chuyển	유연한, 다루기 쉬운	yooj yim
glimpses	vistazos fugaces	瞥見	nhìn thoáng	힐끗 보기	pom ib muag
pulses	impulsos	脈衝	nhịp tim	맥박	plawv nrhia
surface	superficie	表面	bề mặt, hiện lên bề mặt	표면	saum daim tawv
Week 3: Navajo Code Talkers					
advance	por anticipado	前進	tiến tới trước	앞서의	tshiab tshaj
developed	desarrollaron	發展	phát triển	개발했다	ua tswm sim
exhausting	agotadoras	疲累的	mệt mõi	소모적인	nkee kawg lawm
headquarters	cuartel general	總部	trụ sở chánh	본부	tom hauv paus loj

English	Spanish	Chinese	Vietnamese	Korean	Hmong
impossible	imposible	不可能的	không thể	불가능한	ua tsis tau kiag
intense	intenso	強烈的	nồng nhiệt	격렬한	ua heev
messages	mensajes	訊息	thông điệp	전언	muaj lus faj tseg
reveal	revelaron	揭露	phơi bày ra	드러내다	qhia tawm

Week 4: Seeker of Knowledge

English	Spanish	Chinese	Vietnamese	Korean	Hmong
ancient	antiguo	古老	cổ xưa	고대의	qub qub
link	conexión	連接	nối	연결 고리	kev mus rau lwm qhov
scholars	eruditos	學者	các học giả	학자	tub kawm ntawv
seeker	buscador	尋找者	người tìm tòi	탐구자	tus nrhiav
temple	templo	寺廟	đền thờ	사찰	tsev teev hawm
translate	traducir	翻譯	phiên dịch	번역하다	txhais (lus)
triumph	triunfo	勝利	đắc thắng	승리	yeej
uncover	descubrir	揭露	phát hiện	노출하다	qhib tau, nrhiav tau

Week 5: Encyclopedia Brown

English	Spanish	Chinese	Vietnamese	Korean	Hmong
amphibians	anfibios	兩棲類動物	động vật lưỡng cư	양서 동물	cov tsiaj muaj peev xwm nyob hauv dej thiab ntawm av
crime	crimen	罪行	tội	범죄	ib qhov kev phem yuam cai
exhibit	exposición	展覽	trưng bày, biểu lộ	전시하다	qhib saib, nthuav ntawm
lizards	lagartos	蜥蜴	thằn lằn	도마뱀	nab qa
reference	referencia	參考	việc tham khảo	참조	txheeb ze
reptiles	reptiles	爬行動物	loài bò sát	파충류	tsiaj muaj nplai thiab yug qe
salamanders	salamandras	火蜥蜴	kỳ nhông	도롱뇽	nab qa salamander
stumped	perplejo	連根挖去	bị bí lối	난처하게 하다	pob ntoos

Unit 5

English	Spanish	Chinese	Vietnamese	Korean	Hmong
Week 1: Smokejumpers					
concentrating	concentrándose	專心	chú ý	집중하는	npaj ua kiag li
dedication	dedicación	奉獻	cống hiến	헌신	ua rau
essential	esencial	重要的	bản chất	필수적인	tseem ceeb heev
method	método	方法	phương pháp	방법	ua licas
parachute	paracaídas	降落傘	cây dù	낙하산	lub kaus
steer	dirigirse	操控	bẻ lái	조종하다	muab tig
underbrush	pequeñas plantas	矮樹叢	dưới bụi cây	덤불	hauv tej qab nplooj
wind	viento	風	gió	바람	Cua
Week 2: Lost City					
curiosity	curiosidad	好奇心	trí tò mò	호기심	xav paub
glorious	gloriosa	光榮的	vinh quang	영예로운	zoo nkauj
granite	granito	花崗岩	đá hoa cương	화강암	pob zeb granite
ruins	ruinas	殘留的廢墟	các tàn tích	폐허	yam khoom puas ntsoog tag
terraced	en terrazas	臺階形的	làm thành bậc thang	계단식 땅을 만들다	qab tsib taug, chaw ua si
thickets	matorrales	叢林	các bụi cây	덤불	tsob nyom
torrent	torrente	洪流	dòng nước chảy mạnh	급류	ntws
Week 3: Cliff Hanger					
coil	rollo	盤繞	cuộn dây	고리	kauj hlaus
descent	descenso	下降	đi xuống	하강	nqis mus
foresaw	previó	預見	thấy trước	예견했다	pom li lawm

English	Spanish	Chinese	Vietnamese	Korean	Hmong
rappel	descender	垂直下降	tuột bằng dây	매달려서 내려오다	maj mas nqis
ridge	cresta	山脊	cái mép	봉우리	ntxuj zeb
shaft	pasadizo vertical	手柄	trục	기둥	raw li
trekked	caminaron	緩慢行進	khó khăn	힘들게 전진하다	raw qab
void	vacío	空的	chỗ trống	허공	zam

Week 4: Antarctic Journal

English	Spanish	Chinese	Vietnamese	Korean	Hmong
anticipation	anticipación	預期	sự trông đợi	예상	tos tos, cia siab
continent	continente	大陸	lục địa	대륙	teb chaws
convergence	convergencia	匯合	sự hội tụ	집합점	sib sau
depart	salir	分離	khởi hành	떠나다	sib ncaim
forbidding	inhóspita	禁止	cấm đoán	금지하다	txwv tsis pub
heaves	sube	隆起	ráng sức nâng lên	들어올리다, 물결치다	tsaws
icebergs	icebergs	冰山	các tảng băng	빙하	thooj dej pob zeb khov tshwm sau dej

Week 5: Moonwalk

English	Spanish	Chinese	Vietnamese	Korean	Hmong
loomed	surgía	隱約地出現	đã hiện ra lờ mờ	어렴풋이 나타나다	ua ntos
rille	valle lunar	溝	đường rãnh trên mặt trăng	골짜기	ib lub hav nyob rau saum hli
runt	pequeño	矮子	nhóc tì	작은 동물(식물)	tus tsiaj me me
staggered	se tambaleó	搖擺	đi loạng choạng	비틀거리다	nyob tsis ntseg
summoning	armándose	召喚	kêu gọi	호출하는, 요구하는	hu tuaj ua kev
taunted	burló	嘲笑	đã khiêu khích	비웃다	thuam
trench	zanja	溝槽	mương, hào	깊은 도랑	tsev qhov av
trudged	caminaron fatigosamente	費勁地走	đã lê bước	터덜터덜 걷다	mus kev li pob tw nyav nyav

Unit 6

English	Spanish	Chinese	Vietnamese	Korean	Hmong
Week 1: My Brother Martin					
ancestors	ancestros	祖先	tổ tiên	조상	poj koob yawg koob
avoided	evitaba	避免	đã tránh	피하다	ua txuj tsis pom, nkaum
generations	generaciones	世代	các thế hệ	세대	tiam
minister	ministro	部長	mục sư	목사	xib hwb
numerous	numerosos	眾多	rất nhiều	매우 많은	ntau ntau (leej, tus)
pulpit	púlpito	講壇	bục giảng	설교	qhov chaw sawv (qhia lus ntseeg)
shielding	protegiéndonos	防護	che chở	보호하는	thaiv
Week 2: Jim Thorpe's Bright Path					
boarding school	internado	寄宿學校	trường nội trú	기숙 학교	tsev nkawm ntawv them nyiaj
dormitory	dormitorio	宿舍	ký túc xá	기숙사	tsev pw rau cov tub ntxhais nkawm ntawv
endurance	resistencia	忍耐	sức bền bỉ	참을성, 시련	nyiaj, uv
manual	manual	手工的	bằng tay	수동의, 육체를 쓰는	yam ua los ntawm tes
reservation	reserva	保護區	sự dè dặt	보류, 조건, 제한	chaw tseg cia
society	sociedad	社會	xã hội	사회	zej zog
Week 3: How Tía Lola Came to ~~Visit~~ Stay					
affords	ofrece	負擔得起	có tiền để mua	할 수 있다, 여유가 있다	yuav tau, khwv tau
colonel	coronel	上校	đại tá	대령	thawj coj
glint	destello	閃閃發光	sáng lấp lánh	반짝 빛나다	ci
lurking	acechando	潛伏	ẩn núp chờ đợi	숨은	nkag los, nyiag los
palettes	paletas	調色板	tấm nâng hàng; giường hẹp và cứng	팔레트	daim rau xim uas tus neeg thas xim, tuav rau ntawm tes

English	Spanish	Chinese	Vietnamese	Korean	Hmong
quaint	pintoresco	古雅	kỳ lạ	진기한, 별난	txawv
resemblance	semejanza	相似	sự giống nhau	닮음	zoo li

Week 4: A Gift from the Heart

English	Spanish	Chinese	Vietnamese	Korean	Hmong
backdrop	telón de fondo	背景	hậu trường	배경	daim duab nyob tom qab
graze	pastar	放牧	găm cỏ	목초	noj nyom
drought	sequía	旱灾	hạn hán	가뭄	qhuav qhawv
ceremonial	ceremonial	正式的	theo nghi lễ	의식의	ua kevcai
shock	chocante	震惊	sửng sốt	충격, 쇼크	tauj tej plhaws
abundance	abundancia	大量	dồi dào	풍부	muaj seem muaj so

Week 5: The Man Who Went to the Far Side of the Moon

English	Spanish	Chinese	Vietnamese	Korean	Hmong
astronauts	astronautas	太空人	phi hành gia	우주 비행사	tus neeg mus saum qaum ntuj
capsule	cápsula	密封艙	khoang có thể tách ra trên tàu vũ trụ	캡슐	lub nkoj mus saum qaum ntuj
hatch	escotilla	艙口蓋	cửa ra vào trên tàu vũ trụ	(항공기, 우주선의) 출입문	kab pleb nyob rau hauv lub dav hlau
horizon	horizonte	地平線	chân trời	수평선	npoo ntuj
lunar	lunar	登月	về mặt trăng	달의	lub hli
module	módulo	小艇	khoang có thể tách ra trên tàu vũ trụ	착륙선	xws li lub tsheb
quarantine	cuarentena	檢疫	cô lập	격리하다, 검역하다	lub sij hawm raug kaw cia (vim tej zaum yus muaj kab mob kis tau)

Multilingual Thinking Words

English	Spanish	Chinese	Vietnamese	Korean	Hmong
Analyze	Analizar	分析	Phân tích	분석하다	Xam pom
Apply	Aplicar	应用	Áp dụng	응용하다	Tso rau
Assess	Calcular	估值	Lượng định	평가하다, 감정하다	Ntsuam xyuas
Categorize	Categorizar	分类	Phân loại	분류하다	Teev uake tej pawg
Clarify Information	Clarificar la información	阐明信息	Nói rõ thông tin	정보를 분명히 하다	Ntaub ntawv meej zog ntxiv
Classify	Clasificar	分类	Xếp loại	분류하다	Xaiv uake tej pawg
Combine Information	Combinar la información	拼合信息	Kết hợp thông tin	정보를 합치다	Ntaub ntawv sis dhos
Compare	Comparar	比较	So sánh	비교하다	Sis piv
Conclude	Concluir	归纳	Kết luận	마무리짓다	Xaus
Connect	Conectar	联系	Kết nối	연결하다	Txuas
Construct	Construir	建构	Xây dựng	건축하다, 구성하다	Ua txuas
Contrast	Contrastar	对比	Đối chiếu	대조하다	Tsi sib thooj
Define	Definir	限定	Định nghĩa	정의하다	Txhais
Demonstrate	Demostrar	示范	Chứng minh	증명하다	Nthauv tawm
Describe	Describir	描述	Mô tả	묘사하다	Piav
Determine Importance	Determinar la importancia	判断重要性	Thẩm định tầm quan trọng	중요성을 결정하다	Xam tseem ceeb
Determine Main Idea	Determinar la idea principal	判断要旨	Thẩm định Ý Chính	주제를 정하다	Xam ntsiab lus
Diagram	Diagrama	图表	Lập biểu đồ	그림, 도표	Kos duab
Differentiate	Diferenciar	辨别	Phân biệt	구별하다	Qhia qhov txawv
Elaborate	Abundar	阐述	Tạo lập	상세히 말하다	Piav meej zog
Evaluate	Evaluar	评估	Lượng giá	평가하다	Soj ntsuam
Examine	Examinar	核查	Khảo sát	조사하다	Tshuaj xyuas

English	Spanish	Chinese	Vietnamese	Korean	Hmong
Explain	Explicar	辩解	Giải thích	설명하다	Piav
Generalize	Generalizar	概括	Tổng quát hóa	일반화하다	Hais dav dav
Identify Characteristics	Identificar características	辨认特征	Nhận diện các Đặc tính	특징을 밝히다	Qhia yam ntxwv
Identify Pattern	Identificar patrones	辨认规律	Nhận diện Khuôn mẫu	형태를 밝히다	Qhia tus qauv
Identify Relationships	Identificar relaciones	辨认关系	Nhận diện Tương quan	관계를 밝히다	Qhia kev txheeb ze
Illustrate	Ilustrar	说明	Minh họa	설명하다	Taw qhia
Infer	Inferir	推论	Luận ra	추론하다	Txhais
Judge	Juzgar	判定	Xét thấy	판단하다	Txiav txim
Label	Etiquetar	命名	Dán nhãn	(-라는) 딱지를 붙이다	Lo ntawv
List	Hacer una lista	列表	Liệt kê	열거하다	Teev
Match	Igualar	相配	Tương xứng	-에 어울리다, 필적하다, 대등하다	Sib phim
Observe	Observar	观察	Quan sát	관찰하다	Saib
Organize	Organizar	组织	Tổ chức	정리, 조직구성하다	Sis sau
Outline	Esbozar	概述	Phác thảo	윤곽을 그리다	Teev cov ntsiab
Predict	Predecir	预计	Đoán trước	예측하다	Kwv yees
Recall	Recordar	回想	Nhớ lại	기억하다	Xam txog
Record	Grabar	纪录	Ghi lại	기록, 녹음하다	Teev tseg
Restructure	Reestructurar	重构	Tái cấu trúc	재구성, 구조조정하다	Teeb dua
Sequence	Secuenciar	次序	Xếp thứ tự	순서대로 나열하다	Teev cov ntsiab sis dhos
Show	Mostrar	展示	Chỉ ra	보여주다	Qhia
Solve a Problem	Resolver un problema	解决一个问题	Giải quyết	문제를 풀다, 해결하다	Kho teeb meem
Summarize	Resumir	概括	Tóm tắt	요점정리하다	Piav zuaj zog uake
Verify	Verificar	查证	Kiểm lại	확인하다, 입증하다	Kuaj kos meej

Part 7
High-Frequency Words, Linguistic Contrastive Analysis, ELL Teaching Routines, and Graphic Organizers

Contents

High-Frequency Words

The high-frequency words section includes activities and word cards that allow students to use these words in speaking and writing to build their competency and fluency.

Linguistic Contrastive Analysis

Use these pages to find out more about challenges in pronunciation and grammar that your English language learners may face as they produce spoken English. The linguistic contrastive analysis chart equates sounds in English with sounds in Spanish, Vietnamese, Cantonese, Hmong, Filipino, Korean, and Mandarin.

English Language Learner Teaching Routines

These routines support systematic and scaffolded instruction in using core lesson materials.

Graphic Organizers

Graphic organizers provide visual support important to English language learners' comprehension.

High-Frequency Words

The high-frequency words are words that appear most often in written English, words of the greatest general service to English language learners. Many of the words are part of word families that are useful for students to know as they learn English.

Each week, provide the list of high-frequency words for students' reference for speaking and writing. Choose strategies from this bank of activities to ensure students' mastery.

Cloze Activity

Create a passage that includes high-frequency words. Display the passage covering high-frequency words with sticky notes. Ask students to read the passage with you, substituting the missing words. Have them explain how they figured out which words to use.

Play Bingo

After students have learned at least 25 words, provide a 5 x 5 grid with a high-frequency word written in each square. Read aloud high-frequency words as you draw them randomly. Students cover words they hear with markers to create a row. When a student has created a row, have him or her read the words aloud.

Semantic Map

For words with richer meanings, create semantic maps. Place the word in the middle of a web and ask students to supply related words for the "arms." Discuss word relationships.

High-Frequency Scavenger Hunt

Have students keep the word lists on their desks for the week. Ask them to tally how many times they see each word in their reading selections, science or social studies books, magazine articles, and so on. They can tally how often they say the word.

Realia and Visuals

Use both hands-on experiences and visuals to reinforce meanings of the words.

- Provide realia that evokes meanings of high-frequency words. For *year,* for example, you might show a calendar. For *see,* you might show a pair of eyeglasses. Discuss the items, using the high-frequency words.
- Use visuals to teach abstract high-frequency words. For *of,* for example, you could show pictures: a basket of laundry, a slice of bread, a glass of water.

Word Sorts

Have students sort the words. Provide index cards with words, one word per card. Students can sort them into categories you provide (*words that show action, words that name things, words in the same family,* and so on) or sort them and explain the rationale behind their categories.

Flashcard Activities

- Post high-frequency words on a word wall as you introduce them. From time to time, hand students flashcards with the words on them, one word per card. Students match the card to the word on the wall and then use the word in a sentence.
- Hand out flashcards, one word to each pair of students. Students work together to create two sentences using the word.
- Make up simple sentences using the high-frequency words. Write the sentences on cards, one word per card. Hand the cards out to students. Have them unscramble the words to make a sentence and read it aloud chorally.
- Pair students and give one student in each pair a card. The student with the card gives clues about the word for the other student to guess.

Unit 1 Week 1	Unit 1 Week 2	Unit 1 Week 3
1 the	11 that	21 by
2 be	12 for	22 this
3 of	13 they	23 we
4 and	14 I	24 you
5 a	15 with	25 do
6 to	16 as	26 but
7 in	17 not	27 from
8 he	18 on	28 or
9 have	19 she	29 which
10 it	20 at	30 one

Unit 1 Week 4	Unit 1 Week 5	Unit 2 Week 1
31 would	41 if	51 about
32 all	42 no	52 than
33 will	43 man	53 into
34 there	44 out	54 could
35 say	45 other	55 state
36 who	46 so	56 only
37 make	47 what	57 new
38 when	48 time	58 year
39 can	49 up	59 some
40 more	50 go	60 take

Unit 2 Week 2	Unit 2 Week 3	Unit 2 Week 4
61 come	71 work	81 day
62 these	72 now	82 also
63 know	73 may	83 after
64 see	74 such	84 way
65 use	75 give	85 many
66 get	76 over	86 must
67 like	77 think	87 look
68 then	78 most	88 before
69 first	79 even	89 great
70 any	80 find	90 back

Unit 2 Week 5	Unit 3 Week 1	Unit 3 Week 2
91 through	101 because	111 little
92 long	102 good	112 world
93 where	103 each	113 very
94 much	104 those	114 still
95 should	105 feel	115 nation
96 well	106 seem	116 hand
97 people	107 how	117 old
98 down	108 high	118 life
99 own	109 too	119 tell
100 just	110 place	120 write

Unit 3 Week 3

121	become
122	here
123	show
124	house
125	both
126	between
127	need
128	mean
129	call
130	develop

Unit 3 Week 4

131	under
132	last
133	right
134	move
135	thing
136	general
137	school
138	never
139	same
140	another

Unit 3 Week 5

141	begin
142	while
143	number
144	part
145	turn
146	real
147	leave
148	might
149	want
150	point

Unit 4 Week 1	Unit 4 Week 2	Unit 4 Week 3
151 form	161 interest	171 again
152 off	162 large	172 hold
153 child	163 person	173 govern
154 few	164 end	174 around
155 small	165 open	175 possible
156 since	166 public	176 head
157 against	167 follow	177 consider
158 ask	168 during	178 word
159 late	169 present	179 program
160 home	170 without	180 problem

Unit 4 Week 4	Unit 4 Week 5	Unit 5 Week 1
181 however	191 fact	201 city
182 lead	192 group	202 put
183 system	193 play	203 close
184 set	194 stand	204 case
185 order	195 increase	205 force
186 eye	196 early	206 meet
187 plan	197 course	207 once
188 run	198 change	208 water
189 keep	199 help	209 upon
190 face	200 line	210 war

Unit 5 Week 2	Unit 5 Week 3	Unit 5 Week 4
211 build	221 side	231 study
212 hear	222 try	232 woman
213 light	223 provide	233 member
214 unite	224 continue	234 until
215 live	225 name	235 far
216 every	226 certain	236 night
217 country	227 power	237 always
218 bring	228 pay	238 service
219 center	229 result	239 away
220 let	230 question	240 report

Unit 5 Week 5	Unit 6 Week 1	Unit 6 Week 2
241 something	251 though	261 better
242 company	252 young	262 big
243 week	253 less	263 boy
244 church	254 enough	264 cost
245 toward	255 almost	265 business
246 start	256 read	266 value
247 social	257 include	267 second
248 room	258 president	268 why
249 figure	259 nothing	269 clear
250 nature	260 yet	270 expect

Unit 6 Week 3

271 family

272 complete

273 act

274 sense

275 mind

276 experience

277 art

278 next

279 near

280 direct

Unit 6 Week 4

281 car

282 law

283 industry

284 important

285 girl

286 food

287 several

288 matter

289 usual

290 rather

Unit 6 Week 5

291 per

292 often

293 kind

294 among

295 white

296 reason

297 action

298 return

299 foot

300 care

How People Speak

All languages have consonant and vowel sounds. Consonants are made with some obstruction of the vocal tract, either a complete stoppage of air or enough constriction to create friction. Vowels are produced with a more open vocal tract; there is no constriction that might cause friction.

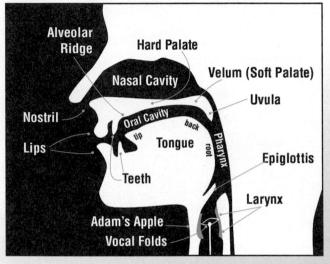

Figure 1: The human vocal tract makes the sounds of speech.

Consonants

Every consonant can be described by noting three characteristics: voicing, place of articulation, and manner of articulation.

Voicing
Many sounds of language, including all vowels, employ vibration of the vocal folds in the larynx. This creates more resonance and energy for the sound. All speech sounds are characterized as either voiced (with vocal fold vibration) or voiceless (with no vocal fold vibration). Feeling the vibration around the Adam's apple can help you understand this difference. If you say "sssss" and then "zzzzz," you can feel the distinction: /s/ is voiceless and /z/ is voiced.

Place of Articulation
This is the location in the vocal tract where the air stream may be constricted. The /s/ sound, for example, is made with the tongue tip close to the alveolar ridge (see Figure 1).

Place of Articulation Terms

Alveolar: tongue tip and ridge behind teeth
Bilabial: using both lips
Glottal: produced at the larynx
Interdental: tongue tip between upper and lower teeth
Labio-dental: upper teeth and lower lip
Labio-velar: rounding of lips; tongue body raised toward velum
Palatal: body of tongue and high part of palate
Palato-alveolar: tongue tip and palate behind alveolar ridge
Velar: body of tongue and velum (soft palate)

Manner of Articulation
This is the type or degree of constriction that occurs in an articulation. For example, the /t/ sound completely stops the airflow with the tongue tip at the alveolar ridge, but /s/ allows air to pass noisily through a small opening.

Manner of Articulation Terms

Affricate: complete constriction followed by slow separation of the articulators resulting in friction
Approximant: close constriction, but not enough for friction
Fricative: narrow constriction; turbulent airflow causing friction
Glottal: produced at the larynx
Lateral: air passes over sides of tongue
Nasal: lowered velum to let air escape through the nose
Stop: complete constriction, closure so that air cannot escape through the oral cavity
Tap: brief contact between tongue tip and alveolar ridge

Vowels

Vowels are open, sonorous sounds. Each vowel can be uniquely described by noting the position of the tongue, the tension of the vocal tract, and the position of the lips. Vowels are described by **height,** where the tongue is relative to the roof of the mouth. They can be high, mid, or low. Tongue backness tells if the tongue articulation is in the front or back of the mouth.

Tense vowels are more common around the world. In English, they are longer and include an expansion of the throat at the pharynx. Lax vowels are shorter with a more neutral pharynx. An example is the tense long *e* as in *meet*

Speaking English

versus the lax short *i* as in *mitt*. The lips either can be in a spread or neutral position, or they can be rounded and protrude slightly.

English is the third most widely spoken native language in the world, after Mandarin and Spanish. There are about 330 million native speakers of English and 600 million who speak it as a foreign language.

English Consonant Sounds

The following chart gives the International Phonetic Alphabet (IPA) symbol for each English consonant along with its voicing, place, and manner of articulation. This information can be used to understand and help identify problems that non-native speakers may encounter when learning to speak English.

CONSONANTS OF ENGLISH		
IPA	Articulation	Example
p	voiceless bilabial stop	**p**it
b	voiced bilabial stop	**b**it
m	voiced bilabial nasal stop	**m**an
w	voiced labio-velar approximant	**w**in
f	voiceless labio-dental fricative	**f**un
v	voiced labio-dental fricative	**v**ery
θ	voiceless interdental fricative	**th**ing
ð	voiced interdental fricative	**th**ere
t	voiceless alveolar stop	**t**ime
d	voiced alveolar stop	**d**ime
n	voiced alveolar nasal stop	**n**ame
s	voiceless alveolar fricative	**s**oy
z	voiced alveolar fricative	**z**eal
ɾ	voiced alveolar tap	bu**tt**er
l	voiced alveolar central approximant	**l**oop
ɹ	voiced palato-alveolar affricate	**r**ed
ʃ	voiceless palato-alveolar fricative	**sh**allow
ʒ	voiced palato-alveolar affricate	vi**s**ion
tʃ	voiceless palato-alveolar affricate	**ch**irp
dʒ	voiced palato-alveolar affricate	**j**oy
j	voiced palatal approximant	**y**ou
k	voiceless velar stop	**k**ite
g	voiced velar stop	**g**oat
ŋ	voiced velar nasal stop	ki**ng**
h	voiceless glottal fricative	**h**ope

English Vowel Sounds

Most languages in the world have around five vowel sounds. English has 13 common vowel sounds, which means that many students of English must learn more vowel distinctions than there are in their native language. The lax vowels are most difficult. Some vowels are diphthongs, meaning the tongue is in one position at the beginning of the sound, and it moves to another position by the end of it.

VOWELS OF ENGLISH		
IPA	Sound	Example
i	ē	b**ea**t
ɪ	ĭ	b**i**t
e	ā	b**ai**t
ɛ	ĕ	b**e**t
æ	ă	b**a**t
u	ōō	b**oo**t
ʊ	ŏŏ	c**ou**ld
o	ō	b**oa**t
ɔ	aw	l**aw**
ɑ	ŏ	h**o**t
ə	ə	**a**bout
ʌ	ŭ	c**u**t
ɝ	er	b**ir**d
ɑ ʊ	ow	h**ou**se
ɔ ɪ	oy	b**oy**
ɑ ɪ	ī	b**i**te

Figure 2 is a schematic of the mouth. The left is the front of the mouth; the right is the back. The top is the roof of the mouth and the bottom is the floor. Placement of the vowel shows where the tongue reaches its maximum in the English articulation.

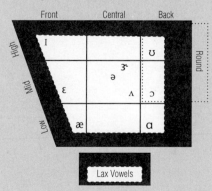

Figure 2: English vowel sounds

Transference

Pronunciation

All languages build on the same fundamentals. All languages contrast voiced and voiceless sound and have stops and fricatives. Many languages use the same places of articulation for consonants as well. The majority of sounds will easily transfer from another language to English.

However, there will always be some sounds that are not found in a person's native language that can pose a challenge to the English language learner. English has a few relatively rare sounds, such as the interdental sounds spelled with *th, /ə/* and */ð/*. The /r/ sound in English is also a very rare type of sound. Most other languages use a tap or trill articulation for an /r/ sound.

In some languages, the /l/ and /r/ sounds belong to one psychological category. This means that they count as the same sound in that language. In this case, it is not the articulation that is difficult, but the perception of the difference and consistent use of one versus the other in any word context. This type of psychological category is called a *phoneme,* and multiple speech sounds all can be categorized as the same phoneme in that language.

This is true for English as well, where, for example, the alveolar lateral /l/ as in *lob* and the velarized lateral /ɫ/ as in *ball* are both counted as the same sound—an *l*—to native speakers of English. It is important to keep in mind that both the phonetic articulation of a sound and its psychological, phonemic category factor into the learning of a new language.

Grammar

Pronouncing English is not the only stumbling block for English learners. The grammar and usage, or syntax, of English may present distinctions that are unique to the language. For example, English syntax requires adjectives to precede the nouns they modify, as in *the tall girl.* In other languages, such as Spanish, Hmong, and Vietnamese, adjectives follow nouns, as in *la chica alta* (literally *the girl tall* in Spanish). This may cause word-order problems, particularly for less advanced English learners.

Other syntactic differences are less obvious and may cause problems even for advanced learners. For example, many East Asian languages (such as Mandarin, Cantonese, and Korean) do not mark agreement between subject and verb. Speakers of these languages may therefore leave out agreement markers, such as the *-s* in *The girl like cats.*

The use of articles varies across languages. For instance, Spanish uses the definite article more often than English, while Mandarin and Cantonese do not have articles. A Spanish-speaking English learner might say *The girl likes the cats* instead of *The girl likes cats,* and a Mandarin or Cantonese speaker might say *Girl like cat.*

Plural marking is another potential trouble spot: Vietnamese, Filipino, Cantonese, and Mandarin do not add plural markers to nouns. Learners speaking these languages may have difficulty with English plurals, saying *cat* instead of *cats.*

> ### Grammar Hot Spots
>
> **Look for Grammar Hot Spots** on the following pages for tips on the most common syntax errors by speakers of languages other than English.

Common First Languages

In the Common First Languages section, you will find details of some common non-English languages spoken in the United States. They are:

- Spanish
- Vietnamese
- Cantonese
- Hmong
- Filipino
- Korean
- Mandarin

You can use the fundamentals of speech articulation already covered to help you understand where the languages differ from English. Differences in the spoken language and in the writing systems are explored as well. These sections pinpoint common trouble spots specific to learners of English.

Culture Clues

Look to Culture Clues for insights into the cultural differences of each language learner as well as ideas for ways to embrace students' diversity.

Linguistic Contrastive Analysis

The Linguistic Contrastive Analysis Charts provide a quick reference for comparing English sounds with those of other languages. The charts allow you to check at a glance which sounds have equivalents in other languages. For those sounds that don't have equivalents, you can find the closest sound used as a substitute and suggestions for helping someone gain a native English articulation.

In these charts, the sounds are notated using the International Phonetic Alphabet (IPA). This is the most widely recognized and used standard for representing speech sounds in any language. A guiding principle of the IPA across all languages is that each sound is uniquely represented by one symbol, and each symbol represents only one sound.

The chart has columns for each native language with rows corresponding to each English phoneme. Each cell in the chart gives an example word using that sound in the native language, a definition in parenthesis, and transference tips below. If there is no sound equivalent to English, a common substitution used by speakers of that language may be provided.

Transference Tips

Transference tips give you ideas of how the sound will be produced by the learner. Cells in bold print indicate where the English learner may have particular difficulty with the English sound.

Spanish

Background

Spanish is the second most widely spoken language in the world. There are more than 400 million native Spanish speakers in 20-plus countries on three continents. Spanish vocabulary and pronunciation differ from country to country. While most dialect differences in English are in vowel sounds, Spanish dialects differ in their consonants.

Spoken

Spanish sounds are similar to those found in English, so there is a strong foundation for the native Spanish speaker learning English. However, there are three key differences between English and Spanish consonants:

1. Most of the alveolar sounds in English, such as /t/, /d/, and /n/ are produced farther forward in the mouth in Spanish. Instead of the tongue touching the alveolar ridge as in English, in Spanish it touches the back of the teeth.

2. Another difference is that the /r/ sound in English is not found in Spanish. There are two /r/ sounds in Spanish. One is the tap /ɾ/, which occurs in English as the quick sound in the middle of the name *Betty*. Psychologically, this tap sound is a kind of /t/ or /d/ sound in English, while in Spanish it is perceived as an /r/. The other /r/ sound in Spanish is a trill, or series of tongue taps on the alveolar ridge. This does not occur in English.

3. The third key difference between English and Spanish can be found in the English production of the voiceless stops /p/, /t/, and /k/. In English these sounds are aspirated, with an extra puff of air at the end, when the sound occurs at the beginning of a word or stressed syllable. So, /p/ is aspirated in *pit.* Learners can add a puff of air to such sounds to sound more like native English speakers.

Culture Clues

The Spanish language covers many countries, dialects, and cultures. Always encourage students to share special things about their culture, such as foods, festivals, or social customs.

There are five vowels in Spanish, which are a subset of the English vowels. Spanish vowels include tense vowel sounds a, e, i, o, u. Lax vowel sounds in English are the problematic ones for native Spanish speakers.

Written

Like English, written Spanish uses the Roman alphabet, so both writing systems are similar. There are a few orthographic differences to note, however:

- The letter *h* in Spanish is silent, but the sound /h/ is written as *j* or *g*.

- A single letter *r* in Spanish represents a tap, while the double *rr* represents a trill.

- Accents are used to show the stress on a syllable when the stress is different from the usual rules. In some cases, words change meaning according to the accents. For example, *el* means *the* while *él* means *he.*

Written Spanish vowels are pronounced like the symbols in the IPA. So, the Spanish "i" is pronounced with the long *e* as in the word *beat*. The IPA and Spanish symbol for this letter is the same: i.

Grammar Hot Spots

- Double negatives are part of standard grammar in Spanish. Stress the single negative construction in English.

- English prepositions are a common stumbling point for Spanish speakers.

Vietnamese

Background
Approximately 80 million people in Vietnam speak Vietnamese. The northern dialect is the standard, though central and southern dialects also exist. Most Vietnamese speakers in the United States are from southern Vietnam and speak the southern dialect.

Spoken
Vietnamese is a tonal language, so each syllable is pronounced with a distinctive tone that affects meaning. Vietnamese has a complex vowel system of 12 vowels and 26 diphthongs. Its consonants are simpler, but Vietnamese syllable structure allows few possibilities for final consonants.

Students may need help noticing and learning to reproduce final consonant sounds in English words and syllables. Vietnamese syllable structure allows for limited combinations of initial consonants. Students also may need help with the more complex initial consonant clusters of English words and syllables.

Culture Clues

In traditional Vietnamese education, there is a strict division between the roles of student and teacher. Students may be confused if asked to direct a part of their own study, so encourage group work.

Written
Since the 1600s, Vietnamese has used a Romanized alphabet. Many characters written in Vietnamese have sounds different from their English counterparts, such as *d, x, ch, nh, kh, g, tr, r,* and *e.*

Grammar Hot Spots

- Like English, Vietnamese uses Subject-Verb-Object (SVO) syntax, or word order.
- Vietnamese does not use affixes; instead, syntax expresses number, case, and tense.

Cantonese

Background
Cantonese is one of the seven major Chinese languages, not all of which are mutually intelligible. Cantonese is mostly spoken in China's southern provinces, Hong Kong, and Macau by about 66 million people. It is a tonal language, and the same sequence of letters can have different meanings depending on their pitch.

Spoken
Cantonese has six stops, aspirated and non-aspirated /p/, /t/, /k/; three fricatives /f/, /s/, /h/, and two affricates /ts/, /tsʰ/. Some that do not exist in Cantonese can be difficult for the English language learner. The /v/ often gets pronounced as /f/ or /w/; the /z/ is often said as /s/; the sounds spelled with *th* are often said as /t/, /d/, or /f/. Cantonese speakers have difficulty distinguishing between /l/ and /r/, since /r/ is not present in their language. They tend to produce an /l/-like sound for both English sounds in words such as *ride* and *lied.*

Cantonese has 11 vowels and 10 diphthongs. One of the major problems for Cantonese speakers is distinguishing between English tense and lax vowels because the distribution of Cantonese short and long vowels is determined by the sound context.

Syllables in Cantonese don't have consonant clusters. English consonant clusters are often deleted or broken up by vowel insertion (e.g., *list* becomes *lis*). This may be especially problematic when producing English past tense (e.g., *baked*).

Written
Cantonese is written with standard Chinese characters known as *Hànzi* where each character represents a syllable and has a meaning. Additional Cantonese-specific characters were also added. Cantonese speakers may have difficulty with sound-letter correspondences in English.

Grammar Hot Spots

- English articles and prepositions are difficult for Cantonese speakers. *In, on,* and *at,* for instance, can be translated as the same preposition in Cantonese.
- Plurals, tenses, and gerund endings are difficult for Cantonese speakers to transfer to English.

Common First Languages

Hmong

Background
Hmong is a group of approximately 18 languages within the Hmong-Mien family. There are roughly four million speakers of Hmong, including 200,000 in the United States. They are mainly from two groups with mutually intelligible dialects—Hmong Daw and Mong Leng.

Spoken
Hmong vowels are few and simple, but its consonants are complex and differ from those of English. Notable features of Hmong phonology absent from English include consonantal pre-nasalization (the /m/n/ŋ/ sound before a consonant) and the contrast between nasalized and non-nasalized vowels. Hmong is tonal. Each syllable is pronounced with a distinctive pitch.

Culture Clues
In traditional Hmong culture, learning takes place through hands-on experience. Students may find it difficult to adjust to the use of graphics or print media. Competition, personal achievement, and self-directed instruction may be unfamiliar concepts, so students may prefer group work.

Written
The Romanized Popular Alphabet (RPA), developed in the 1950s, is the usual way of transcribing Hmong. Syllable-final consonants are absent in pronunciation but are used to orthographically represent the tonal value of a given syllable. Students may need particular help in identifying and learning to reproduce the final consonant sounds of English words and syllables.

Grammar Hot Spots
- Like English, Hmong is an SVO language. Personal pronouns are marked for number, including inflection for singular, dual, and plural, though they are not marked for case.
- Because Hmong and English prepositions often have different semantic qualities, students may need help mastering uses of English prepositions. For example, it is correct to say "think about [something]" rather than "think on [something]."

Filipino

Background
Filipino and English are the official languages of the Philippines, where 175 languages are spoken. There are about 24 million native speakers of Filipino, and more than 50 million people speak Filipino as a second language. You may hear the terms Filipino and Tagalog being used interchangeably. Another term is Pilipino.

Spoken
Filipino has many similar speech sounds to English. The notable exceptions are the lack of the consonant sounds /f/, /v/, and those spelled with *th.* Of these, the English /f/ and /v/ cause the most difficulty for learners. For /f/, they may substitute /p/. The distinction between long *e* (as in *beat*) and short *i* (as in *bit*) is also a trouble spot. Filipino does not allow consonant clusters at the end of syllables, so *detect* may be simplified to just one final consonant (*detec*).

Culture Clues
Most people from the Philippines can speak Filipino, but for many it is not their first language. Ask Filipino students about other languages they speak. Because English is used alongside Filipino as the language of instruction in the Philippines, most Filipinos are familiar with English.

Written
The Filipino alphabet has 28 letters and is based on the Spanish alphabet, so the English writing system poses little problem.

Grammar Hot Spots
- Filipino word order is Verb-Subject-Object (VSO), which does not transfer well to English.
- Inflectional verb endings, such as *-s, -en, -ed,* and *-ing* do not exist in Filipino, so it is common to leave out the third person singular verb marker (*"He walk,"* not *"He walks"*).

Korean

Background
Korean is spoken by 71 million people in North and South Korea. Standard Korean is based on the speech in and around Seoul.

Spoken
Korean does not have corresponding sounds for English /f/, /v/, /θ/, /ð/, and /dʒ/. In word-initial position, all Korean stops are voiceless. Voiced stops /b/, /d/, and /g/ are only produced between two vowels. Korean speakers may have difficulty producing /s/, /ʃ/, and /z/ in some contexts, in addition to English /r/ and /l/ sounds (e.g., *rock* and *lock*). They may have problems in producing English consonant clusters (e.g., *str-, sk-*). These problems can often be eliminated by vowel insertion or consonant deletion. In addition, the distinction between English tense and lax vowels (e.g., long *e* as in *beat* vs. /ɪ/ as in *bit*) may be problematic for Korean speakers.

Culture Clues

Korean uses a complex system of honorifics, so it is unusual for Korean students to use the pronoun *you* or call their teachers by their first name.

Written
Modern Korean uses the Korean alphabet *(Hangul)* or a mixed script of *Hangul* and Chinese. *Hangul* is an alphabetic script organized into syllabic blocks.

Grammar Hot Spots

- In contrast to English, Korean word order is Subject-Object-Verb (SOV). The verb always comes at the end of a sentence.

- Korean syllable stress is different, so learners may have difficulties with the rhythm of English.

Mandarin

Background
Mandarin Chinese encompasses a wide range of dialects and is the native language of two-thirds of China. There are approximately 870 million Mandarin speakers worldwide. North Mandarin, as found in Beijing, is the basis of the modern standard language.

Spoken
Mandarin Chinese and English differ substantially in their sound structure. Mandarin lacks voiced obstruent consonants (/b/, /d/, /g/, /dʒ/), causing difficulty for speakers in perceiving and producing English voiced consonants (e.g., *buy* may be pronounced and perceived as *pie*). The sounds spelled with *th* are not present in Mandarin, so they are often substituted with /s/ or /t/ causing, for example, *fourth* to be pronounced as *fours.* Mandarin Chinese has five vowels. Due to the relatively small vowel inventory and contextual effects on vowels in Mandarin, many English vowels and tense/lax distinctions present problems for speakers of Mandarin Chinese. Mandarin allows only a very simple syllable structure, causing problems in producing consonant clusters in English. Speakers may drop consonants or insert vowels between them (e.g., *film* may become /filəm/). The use of tones in Mandarin may result in the rising and falling of pitch when speaking English.

Written
Chinese is written with characters known as *Hànzi.* Each character represents a syllable and also has a meaning. A Romanized alphabet called *Pinyin* marks pronunciation of characters. Chinese speakers may have problems mastering letter-sound correspondences in written English, especially for sounds that are not present in Mandarin.

Grammar Hot Spots

- The non-inflected nature of Chinese causes Mandarin speakers to have problems with plurals, past tense markers, and gerund forms *(-s, -ed, -ing)*.

- Mastering English tenses and passive voice is difficult. Students should be familiarized with correct lexical and syntactic features as well as appropriate situations for the use of various tenses and passives.

The Consonants of English

IPA	ENGLISH	SPANISH	VIETNAMESE	CANTONESE
p	*pit* Aspirated at the start of a word or stressed syllable	*pato* (duck) Never aspirated	*pin* (battery)	*pʰa (to lie prone)* Always aspirated
b	*bit*	*barco* (boat) Substitute voiced bilabial fricative/ɞ/ in between vowels	*ba* (three) Implosive (air moves into the mouth during articulation)	**NO EQUIVALENT** Substitute /p/
m	*man*	*mundo* (world)	*mot* (one)	*ma* (mother)
w	*win*	*agua* (water)	**NO EQUIVALENT** Substitute word-initial /u/	*wa* (frog)
f	*fun*	*flor* (flower)	*phưʼơng* (phoenix) Substitute sound made with both lips, rather than with the lower lip and the teeth like English /f/	*fa* (flower) Only occurs at the beginning of syllables
v	*very*	**NO EQUIVALENT** Learners can use correct sound	*Việt Nam* (Vietnam)	**NO EQUIVALENT** Substitute /f/
θ	*thing* Rare in other languages. When done correctly, the tongue will stick out between the teeth.	**NO EQUIVALENT** Learners can use correct sound	**NO EQUIVALENT** Substitute /th/ or /f/	**NO EQUIVALENT** Substitute /th/ or /f/
ð	*there* Rare in other languages. When done correctly, the tongue will stick out between the teeth.	*cada* (every) Sound exists in Spanish only between vowels; sometimes substitute voiceless θ.	**NO EQUIVALENT** Substitute /d/	**NO EQUIVALENT** Substitute /t/ or /f/
t	*time* Aspirated at the start of a word or stressed syllable English tongue-touch. Is a little farther back in the mouth than the other languages.	*tocar* (touch) Never aspirated	*tám* (eight) Distinguishes aspirated and non-aspirated	*tʰa (he/she)* Distinguishes aspirated and non-aspirated
d	*dime* English tongue-touch is a little farther back in the mouth than the other languages.	*dos* (two)	*Đong* (Dong = unit of currency) Vietnamese /d/ is implosive (air moves into the mouth during articulation)	**NO EQUIVALENT** Substitute /t/
n	*name* English tongue-touch is a little farther back in the mouth than the other languages.	*nube* (cloud)	*nam* (south)	*na* (take)
s	*soy*	*seco* (dry)	*xem* (to see)	*sa* (sand) Substitute *sh*– sound before /u/ Difficult at ends of syllables and words
z	*zeal*	**NO EQUIVALENT** Learners can use correct sound	*ròi* (already) In northern dialect only Southern dialect, substitute /y/	**NO EQUIVALENT** Substitute /s/
ɾ	*butter* Written 't' and 'd' are pronounced with a quick tongue-tip tap.	*rana* (toad) Written as single *r* and thought of as a /r/ sound.	**NO EQUIVALENT** Substitute /t/	**NO EQUIVALENT** Substitute /t/
l	*loop* English tongue-touch is a little farther back in the mouth than the other languages. At the ends of syllables, the /l/ bunches up the back of the tongue, becoming velarized /ɫ/ or dark-l as in the word *ball*.	*libro* (book)	*cú lao* (island) /l/ does not occur at the ends of syllables	*lau* (angry) /l/ does not occur at the ends of syllables

HMONG	FILIPINO	KOREAN	MANDARIN
peb (we/us/our) — Distinguishes aspirated and non-aspirated	*paalam* (goodbye) — Never aspirated	*pal* (sucking)	*pʰei* (cape) — Always aspirated
NO EQUIVALENT — Substitute /p/	*baka* (beef)	NO EQUIVALENT — /b/ said between vowels Substitute /p/ elsewhere	NO EQUIVALENT
mus (to go)	*mabuti* (good)	*mal* (horse)	*mei* (rose)
NO EQUIVALENT — Substitute word-initial /u/	*walo* (eight)	*gwe* (box)	*wen* (mosquito)
faib (to divide)	NO EQUIVALENT — Substitute /p/	NO EQUIVALENT — Substitute /p/	*fa* (issue)
Vaj ('Vang' clan name)	NO EQUIVALENT — Substitute /b/	NO EQUIVALENT — Substitute /b/	NO EQUIVALENT — Substitute /w/ or /f/
NO EQUIVALENT — Substitute /th/ or /f/	NO EQUIVALENT — Learners can use correct sound, but sometimes mispronounce voiced /ð/.	NO EQUIVALENT — Substitute /t/	NO EQUIVALENT — Substitute /t/ or /s/
NO EQUIVALENT — Substitute /d/	NO EQUIVALENT — Learners can use correct sound	NO EQUIVALENT — Substitute /d/	NO EQUIVALENT — Substitute /t/ or /s/
them (to pay) — Distinguishes aspirated and non-aspirated	*takbo* (run) — Never aspirated	*tal* (daughter)	*ta* (wet) — Distinguishes aspirated and non-aspirated
dev (dog)	*deretso* (straight)	NO EQUIVALENT — Substitute /d/ when said between vowels and /t/ elsewhere.	NO EQUIVALENT — Substitute /t/
noj (to eat)	*naman* (too)	*nal* (day)	*ni* (you) — May be confused with /l/
xa (to send)	*sila* (they)	*sal* (rice) — Substitute *shi*– sound before /i/ and /z/ after a nasal consonant	*san* (three)
NO EQUIVALENT — Learners can use correct sound	NO EQUIVALENT — Learners can use correct sound	NO EQUIVALENT — Learners can use correct sound	NO EQUIVALENT — Substitute /ts/ or /tsʰ/
NO EQUIVALENT — Substitute /t/	*rin/din* (too) — Variant of the /d/ sound	Only occurs between two vowels — Considered a /l/ sound	NO EQUIVALENT
los (to come) — /l/ does not occur at the ends of syllables	*salamat* (thank you)	*balam* (wind)	*lan* (blue) — Can be confused and substituted with /r/

The Consonants of English (continued)

IPA	ENGLISH	SPANISH	VIETNAMESE	CANTONESE
ɹ	*red* Rare sound in the world Includes lip-rounding	NO EQUIVALENT Substitute /r/ sound such as the tap /ɾ/ or the trilled /r/	NO EQUIVALENT Substitute /l/	NO EQUIVALENT Substitute /l/
ʃ	*shallow* Often said with lip-rounding	NO EQUIVALENT Substitute /s/ or /tʃ/	*sieu thị* (supermarket) southern dialect only	NO EQUIVALENT Substitute /s/
ʒ	*vision* Rare sound in English	NO EQUIVALENT Substitute /z/ or /dʒ/	NO EQUIVALENT Substitute /s/	NO EQUIVALENT Substitute /ts/
tʃ	*chirp*	*chico* (boy)	*chính phủ* (government) Pronounced harder than English *ch*	NO EQUIVALENT Substitute /ts/
dʒ	*joy*	NO EQUIVALENT Sometimes substituted with /ʃ/ sound Some dialects have this sound for the ll spelling as in llamar	NO EQUIVALENT Substitute /ch/, the equivalent sound, but voiceless	NO EQUIVALENT Substitute /ts/ Only occurs at beginnings of syllables
j	*you*	*cielo* (sky) Often substitute /dʒ/	*yeu* (to love)	*jau* (worry)
k	*kite* Aspirated at the start of a word or stressed syllable	*casa* (house) Never aspirated	*com* (rice) Never aspirated	*kʰa* (family) Distinguishes aspirated and non-aspirated
g	*goat*	*gato* (cat)	NO EQUIVALENT Substitute /k/	NO EQUIVALENT Substitute /k/
ŋ	*king*	*mango* (mango)	*Ngūyen* (proper last name)	*phaŋ* (to cook)
h	*hope*	*gente* (people) Sometimes substitute sound with friction higher in the vocal tract as velar /x/ or uvular /χ/	*hoa* (flower)	*ha* (shrimp)

HMONG	FILIPINO	KOREAN	MANDARIN
NO EQUIVALENT **Substitute /l/**	**NO EQUIVALENT** **Substitute the tap /ɾ/**	**NO EQUIVALENT** **Substitute the tap or /ɾ/** **confused with /l/**	*ran* (caterpillar) Tongue tip curled farther backward than for English /r/
sau (to write)	*siya* (s/he)	Only occurs before /i/; Considered a /s/ sound	*shi* (wet)
zos (village)	**NO EQUIVALENT** Learners can use correct sound	**NO EQUIVALENT**	**NO EQUIVALENT** **Substitute palatal affricate /tɕ/**
cheb (to sweep)	*tsa* (tea)	*cʰal* (kicking)	*cheng* (red)
NO EQUIVALENT **Substitute *ch* sound**	*Dios* (God)	**NO EQUIVALENT** **Substitute *ch* sound**	**NO EQUIVALENT** **Substitute /ts/**
Yaj (Yang, clan name)	*tayo* (we)	*je:zan* (budget)	*yan* (eye)
Koo (Kong, clan name) Distinguishes aspirated and non-aspirated	*kalian* (when) Never aspirated	*kal* (spreading)	*ke* (nest) Distinguishes aspirated and non-aspirated
NO EQUIVALENT **Substitute /k/**	*gulay* (vegetable)	**NO EQUIVALENT** **Substitute /k/** **Learners use correct sound between two vowels**	**NO EQUIVALENT** **Substitute /k/**
gus (goose)	*angaw* (one million)	*baŋ* (room)	*tang* (gong) Sometimes add /k/ sound to the end
hais (to speak)	*hindi* (no)	*hal* (doing)	**NO EQUIVALENT** **Substitute velar fricative /x/**

The Vowels of English

IPA	ENGLISH	SPANISH	VIETNAMESE	CANTONESE
i	*beat*	*hijo* (son)	*di* (to go)	*si* (silk)
ɪ	*bit* Rare in other languages Usually confused with /i/ (*meat* vs. *mitt*)	NO EQUIVALENT Substitute /ē/	NO EQUIVALENT Substitute /ē/	*sik* (color) Only occurs before velars Substitute /ē/
e	*bait* End of vowel diphthongized—tongue moves up to /ē/ or short *e* postions	*eco* (echo)	*kê* (millet)	*se* (to lend)
ɛ	*bet* Rare in other languages. Learners may have difficulty distinguishing /ā/ and /e/ (short e): *pain* vs. *pen*	NO EQUIVALENT Substitute /ā/	NO EQUIVALENT Substitute /ā/	*seŋ* (sound) Only occurs before velars; difficult to distinguish from /ā/ in all positions
æ	*bat* Rare in other languages Learners may have trouble getting the tongue farther forward in the mouth	NO EQUIVALENT Substitute short *o* or short *u*	*ghe* (boat)	NO EQUIVALENT Hard to distinguish between /ā/ and /æ/
u	*boot*	*uva* (grape)	*mua* (to buy)	*fu* (husband)
ʊ	*could* Rare in other languages. Learners may have difficulty distinguishing the vowel sounds in *wooed* vs. *wood*	NO EQUIVALENT Substitute long *u*	NO EQUIVALENT Substitute long *u* (high back unrounded)	*suk* (uncle) Only occurs before velars Difficult to distinguish from long *u* in all positions
o	*boat* End of vowel diphthongized – tongue moves up to long *u* or ʊ position	*ojo* (eye)	*cô* (aunt)	*so* (comb)
ɔ	*law*	NO EQUIVALENT Substitute long *o* or short *o* Substituting long *o* will cause confusion (*low* vs. *law*); substituting short *o* will not	*cá* (fish)	*hok* (shell) Only occurs before velars Difficult to distinguish from long *o* in all positions
ɑ	*hot*	*mal* (bad)	*con* (child)	*sa* (sand)
ɑ ʊ	*house* Diphthong	*pauta*	*dao* (knife)	*sau* (basket)
ɔ ɪ	*boy* Diphthong	*hoy* (today)	*ròi* (already)	*soi* (grill)
ɑ ɪ	*bite* Diphthong	*baile* (dance)	*hai* (two)	*sai* (to waste)
ə	*about* Most common vowel in English; only in unstressed syllables. Learners may have difficulty keeping it very short	NO EQUIVALENT Substitute short *u* or the full vowel from the word's spelling	*mua* (to buy)	NO EQUIVALENT
ʌ	*cut* Similar to schwa /ə/	NO EQUIVALENT Substitute short *o*	*giờ* (time)	*san* (new)
ɝ	*bird* Difficult articulation, unusual in the world but common in American English Learners must bunch the tongue and constrict the throat	NO EQUIVALENT Substitute short *u* or /er/ with trill	NO EQUIVALENT Substitute /ɨ/	*hæ* (boot)

HMONG	FILIPINO	KOREAN	MANDARIN
ib (one)	*ikaw* (you) This vowel is interchangeable with /ɪ/; hard for speakers to distinguish these	zɩːʃaŋ (market)	*ti* (ladder) Sometimes English /i/ can be produced shorter
NO EQUIVALENT **Substitute /ē/**	*limampu* (fifty) This vowel is interchangeable with /ē/; hard for speakers to distinguish these	NO EQUIVALENT **Substitute long *e***	NO EQUIVALENT
tes (hand)	*sero* (zero)	*beːda* (to cut)	*te* (nervous) Sometimes substitute English schwa /ə/
NO EQUIVALENT **Substitute /ā/**	*sero* (zero) This vowel interchanges with /ā/ like *bait*; not difficult for speakers to learn	*thɛːdo* (attitude)	NO EQUIVALENT
NO EQUIVALENT **Substitute short *e***	NO EQUIVALENT **Substitute short *o* as in *hot***	NO EQUIVALENT	NO EQUIVALENT **Substitute /ə/ or short *u***
kub (hot or gold)	*tunay* (actual) This vowel interchanges with vowel in *could*; not difficult for speakers to learn	*zuːbag* (watermelon)	*lu* (hut) Sometimes English long *u* can be produced shorter
NO EQUIVALENT **Substitute a sound like long *e* (mid central with lips slightly rounded)**	*gumawa* (act) This vowel interchanges with long *u* like *boot*; not difficult for speakers to learn	NO EQUIVALENT	NO EQUIVALENT
NO EQUIVALENT	*ubo* (cough)	*boːzu* (salary)	*mo* (sword) This vowel is a little lower than English vowel
Yaj (Yang, clan name)	NO EQUIVALENT **Spoken as short *o*, as in *hot***	NO EQUIVALENT	NO EQUIVALENT **Substitute long *o***
mov (cooked rice)	*talim* (blade)	*maːl* (speech)	*ta* (he/she) Sometimes substitute back long *o* or *u*
plaub (four)	*ikaw* (you)	NO EQUIVALENT	NO EQUIVALENT
NO EQUIVALENT	*apoy* (fire)	NO EQUIVALENT	NO EQUIVALENT
qaib (chicken)	*himatay* (faint)	NO EQUIVALENT	NO EQUIVALENT
NO EQUIVALENT	NO EQUIVALENT **Spoken as short *o*, as in *hot***	NO EQUIVALENT **Difficult sound for learners**	NO EQUIVALENT
NO EQUIVALENT	NO EQUIVALENT **Spoken as short *o*; as in *hot***	NO EQUIVALENT	NO EQUIVALENT
NO EQUIVALENT **Substitute diphthong /əɪ/**	NO EQUIVALENT **Spoken as many different vowels (depending on English spelling) plus tongue tap /ɾ/**	NO EQUIVALENT	NO EQUIVALENT

1 Introduce the Word Point to the word and say it slowly. Supply a student-friendly definition and relate the word to students' prior knowledge and experience. When possible, also relate the word to the weekly concept. Have students say the word.

Example: A place is an area. Your home is a place. Your school is a place. Today we will learn about other places. Say place.

2 Demonstrate Provide examples to show meaning. When possible, use gestures, pictures, realia, or other visuals to help convey the meaning.

Example: Look at the picture. This is a park. A park is a place. This is a building. A building is a place too.

3 Apply Have students demonstrate understanding of the word. Include opportunities for both verbal and nonverbal responses, such as using the word in a sentence, drawing, or physical gestures to show understanding.

Example: Draw a place you know. What is this place, a house or a park?

4 Display the Word Display the word in the classroom. Use a word wall or a graphic organizer to show meaning.

Example: Write the word place *at the top of a chart. Have students write or draw examples below. When possible, have students include examples from the weekly concept.*

1 Introduce Whole-Word Blending Write the word. When possible, use visuals or gestures to help convey the meaning.

2 Connect Sounds to Spelling

MODEL Point to each spelling and say its sound. Remind students to watch how you move your mouth and emphasize any letter combinations.

Example: Show how the letters s *and* h *make one sound, /sh/. Say /f/ /i/ /sh/ as you touch under* f, i, *and* sh.

GUIDE PRACTICE Have students say the sounds as you touch under the letter(s). *When I touch under the letter(s), you say the sound.*

CORRECTIVE FEEDBACK If students say an incorrect sound, refer them to the appropriate Sound-Spelling Card. Provide examples of other words with this sound spelling and have them pronounce the words. Point out any sounds that may be different or new to students' native languages.

3 Blend Sounds

MODEL Blend the word by saying the sound for each spelling, with no pause between sounds, as you move your hand in a continuous motion from one letter to the next. Stretch continuous sounds.

Example: Blend /f/ /i/ /sh/.

GUIDE PRACTICE Run your hand below the word as students blend the sound with you and without you.

Example: Students blend /f/ /i/ /sh/ as you run your hand under the word fish.

CORRECTIVE FEEDBACK If students stop between sounds, then model how to say the sound without stopping between them.

4 Read the Word Display the word.

MODEL Blend the word by pronouncing it normally as you smoothly, but quickly, run your hand beneath it.

GUIDE PRACTICE Have students say the sounds quickly to read the word.

CORRECTIVE FEEDBACK If students have difficulty saying the sound quickly, then model how to say the words first slowly and then quickly.

ROUTINE 3 • SOUND-BY-SOUND BLENDING

❶ Introduce Blending Write and say the word and use visuals and gestures to convey its meaning.

❷ Connect Sounds to Spelling

MODEL Say the first sound in the word and write the letter(s) that spell that sound. Tell students to watch your mouth and emphasize any letter combinations. Touch under the letter(s) as you say the sounds.

GUIDE PRACTICE Have students say the sound as you touch under the letter(s).

CORRECTIVE FEEDBACK If students say an incorrect sound, refer them to the appropriate Sound-Spelling Card.

❸ Add a Sound-Spelling

MODEL Say the next sound in the word and add the letter(s) for that sound. Touch under the letter(s) as you say the sound.

GUIDE PRACTICE Have students say the sound as you touch under the letter(s).

CORRECTIVE FEEDBACK Use corrective feedback as shown above.

❹ Blend Sounds

MODEL Run your hand from letter to letter as you say the sounds without pausing. Repeat until all sounds have been blended.

Example: Blend /sssaaaa/, /sssaaannn/, and /sssaaannnd/.

GUIDE PRACTICE Have students repeat each sound. Then have students blend the sounds with you and then without you.

CORRECTIVE FEEDBACK If students stop between sounds, then model how to say the sounds without stopping between them.

❺ Read the Word

MODEL Blend the whole word. Run your hand under the letters as you say the sounds quickly to read the word.

GUIDE PRACTICE Have students blend the sound quickly to read the word.

CORRECTIVE FEEDBACK If students have difficulty saying the sound quickly, then model how to say the sounds first slowly and then quickly.

ROUTINE 4 • NONDECODABLE WORDS

❶ Introduce Nondecodable Words
Some English words do not sound like their spellings. We learn how to say them by remembering the letters. We will say and spell the words together.

Example: Write we.

❷ Connect Letters to Words

MODEL Point to and say the word. Use visuals, gestures, or examples to demonstrate the meaning of the word. Identify the letters in the word and indicate the number of letters in the word.

Example:
This is the word we.
It has two letters.
The letters are w and e.

GUIDE PRACTICE Have students repeat with you the word, the letters of the word, and the number of letters in the word. Then have the students do this with a partner and then on their own.

CORRECTIVE FEEDBACK If students pronounce the word incorrectly, model again the sounds in the word. Remind students to watch how you move your mouth. Point out any letters that do not follow the standard rules or may be different from their native language patterns.

❸ Demonstrate Usage

MODEL Use the nondecodable word in a sentence to demonstrate usage of the word. Provide an example that relates to their experience and uses the word in the same context as the text.

Example: Listen to this sentence: We go to school together.

GUIDE PRACTICE Have students use the word in a sentence. Provide a sentence frame if necessary.

CORRECTIVE FEEDBACK If students are not using the word correctly, model the correct usage again.

Use this routine for multisyllabic words that do not have prefixes, suffixes, or roots.

1 Introduce the Strategy *We can break some words into parts. Word parts, or chunks, help us read longer words.*

Example: Write *rabbit.*

When possible, use visuals or gestures to demonstrate the meaning of the word.

2 Connect to Sound-Spellings Explain that the parts of a word are called *syllables.* Break the word into syllables.

Example: Rabbit *has two syllables:* rab *and* bit.

MODEL *The syllables help me say the word.* Say each syllable as you run your hand from one syllable to the next. Then read the syllables together as you say the word.

GUIDE PRACTICE Have students say each syllable as you run your hand underneath the letters in that syllable. Point out any letters or syllables that may be different from the students' native language.

CORRECTIVE FEEDBACK If students have difficulty understanding syllables, have them place their hands underneath their chin. Then have the students repeat the word. Explain that each time their chin touches their hands, it indicates a syllable. Then write the words to show them how the words are divided into syllables.

3 Read the Word

MODEL Read the syllables as you run your hand beneath them, and then read the syllables together as you say the word.

Example: This is how I read this word. First I read each syllable, and then I read the syllables together: rab/bit—rabbit.

GUIDE PRACTICE Have students read the syllables, and then read the word as you run your hand beneath the parts.

CORRECTIVE FEEDBACK If students have difficulty using sound-spellings and syllabication to read word parts, then read one part at a time as you cover the remaining parts.

Use this routine to teach word structure skills: base words and inflected endings, prefixes, suffixes, contractions, compound words, syllables.

1 Introduce the Strategy *We will break longer words into smaller parts. Some word parts help us understand what a word means.*

Example: Write *shorten.*

When possible, use visuals, gestures, or examples to demonstrate the meaning of the word.

2 Introduce the Word Parts Discuss the word part that is the focus of the lesson, and, if appropriate, describe its relationship to the base word. Help students make any connections between suffixes or prefixes in English and their native language.

Example: A word part added at the end of a word is called a suffix. *This word has two parts—*short *and* -en. Short *is the base word, and* -en *is the suffix.*

3 Use Word Parts for Meaning Explain the meaning of prefixes, suffixes, and inflected endings when introducing them. For compound words, demonstrate how you can sometimes, but not always, tell the meaning from its parts. Provide examples. Then check students' understanding.

Example: The suffix -en *means "to make." When you add* -en *to the end of* short, *it changes the word. What does* shorten *mean?*

4 Read the Word

MODEL Read the word parts as you run your hand beneath them, and then read the parts together to say the word.

Example: First, I read the base word, short; *next, I read the suffix,* -en. *Then I read the two parts together:* short, en—shorten.

GUIDE PRACTICE Have students identify the word parts and then read the word as you run you hand beneath the parts.

CORRECTIVE FEEDBACK If students have difficulty reading word parts, then have them identify one part at a time as you cover the remaining parts. It may be necessary to have them blend the base word or individual syllables before reading the whole word.

1 **Select the Text** Select a text or passage that is at students' reading level. If possible, pair the ELL with a student who reads fluently.

2 **First Reading** Students read the selected text, switching readers at a logical breaking place—for example, at the end of a sentence, paragraph, or page. Choose a smaller segment of text for students needing more support. Reader 1 begins while Reader 2 follows along, tracking the print with his or her fingers or eyes when the partner is reading.

3 **Second Reading** Partners reread, but Reader 2 begins so that each child is reading different text.

4 **Reread** For optimal fluency, students should reread the text three or four times.

5 **Provide Corrective Feedback** Listen to students read and provide corrective feedback regarding their oral reading (stress, rhythm, and intonation) and use of blending strategies. Keep in mind that ELLs can read fluently in English with an accent.

1 **Select a Passage** Select a grade-level passage.

2 **Model** Have students track the print as you read. While you read, pay attention to the elements of fluency. Read at an appropriate rate and rhythm. Emphasize the correct stress and intonation for each sentence, such as phrasing a question and stressing the important words in the sentence.

3 **Guide Practice** Have students read along with you.

4 **On Their Own**
- Have the class read aloud with you.
- For optimal fluency, students should reread three or four times.

1 Select a Passage
- Select a passage at the student's reading level.
- Have two copies of the passage. Allow the student to read the text to him or herself before beginning.

2 Timed Reading
- Have the student read the text aloud.
- On your copy, mark any errors the student makes.
- Mark where the student is after one minute.

3 Figure Words Correct per Minute (WCPM) To figure WCPM, subtract the number of mistakes from the number of words the student read in one minute. Tell the student his or her WCPM, and explain that by practicing, he or she will try to exceed it.

4 Review Review with the student mistakes he or she made. Help the student reread unknown words until he or she can do so without errors.

5 Timed Reading
- Have the student reread the passage now that he or she is comfortable with the difficult words.
- Figure out his or her WCPM during the second round. Let the student know how much he or she has improved. Point out the importance of practicing.

6 Provide Corrective Feedback Remind students that the goal is not to read as quickly as possible, but to read accurately and quickly.

7 Extra Time Invite students to set their own WCPM goal for another section. Help them to reach that goal.

1 Introduce Retelling *When we retell a story, we tell the story in our own words. Before we can retell a story, we need to know the parts of the story.*

2 Identify Setting and Character

MODEL *First, I think about the setting and characters. The setting is where the story takes place. The characters are the people or animals in the story.* Give an example from a familiar story. You may choose a story the student knows from his or her native culture.

Example: In this story, there is a little girl named Goldilocks and three bears. The three bears live in the forest.

GUIDE PRACTICE Help students list the characters and setting of the story. *The three bears live in the forest. What is the setting? The three bears are characters. Who is another character in the story?*

CORRECTIVE FEEDBACK If students have difficulty identifying the setting and characters, have them use the illustrations or Retelling Cards as clues.

3 Identify Plot Help students create a three-part story map to list what happens at the beginning, middle, and end of the story. *When I retell a story, I think about the plot. The plot is what happens in a story. A plot has a beginning, middle, and an end.*

MODEL *In the first part of the story, Goldilocks was walking in the forest when she saw an empty house.*

GUIDE PRACTICE *What happens at the middle of the story? What happens at the end?* Help students draw or write their answers in each section.

4 Retell the Story

MODEL *My story map will help me retell the story.* Model retelling the story, emphasizing the characters, setting, and the plot.

GUIDE PRACTICE Have partners take turns retelling the story using their own story map.

CORRECTIVE FEEDBACK If a student has difficulty retelling the story, have him or her reread the story or use the illustrations in their retelling.

1 Introduce Summarizing Explain to students that summarizing a passage means telling what it was about. Summarizing does not include details. It just includes the most important parts.

2 What Happened?

MODEL *When I summarize, I ask myself, what is the passage mostly about? Sometimes, I use pictures or graphic sources to remind me.*

Example: This selection is mostly about wild animals, because most of the selection tells about animals that can be found in the wild. I also see a picture of a bear in a forest.

GUIDE PRACTICE Help students make a concept web. In the center, write a few words about the selection. Then have students write or draw the most important parts in the outer circles.

CORRECTIVE FEEDBACK If students have difficulty telling the important parts, model how to find them by pointing to pictures and talking about what you see.

3 When Did It Happen?

MODEL *I can also summarize important events that happen over a period of time. I tell what happened first, next, and last. Knowing when the events happened helps me understand what I read.*

Example: First, the bird collects twigs. Next, it builds a nest. Last, the bird lays its eggs.

GUIDE PRACTICE Help students fill out a sequence chart. Write the words *first, next,* and *last* and fill in the first event. Have students write or draw to fill in the chart.

CORRECTIVE FEEDBACK If students have difficulty tracking the sequence, have them use the pictures and point to what happens first, next, and last.

1 Introduce Spelling *We will use the sounds and letters we know to spell words. First, listen to the word. Then say its sounds and write the letters.*

2 Dictate the Word Say the word, use it in a sentence, and then repeat the word.

Example: clog. The sink has a clog. clog.

3 Segment the Sounds

MODEL Sound out the word. The word is clog. The sounds in clog are /kl/ /o/ /g/. Have students echo each sound.

GUIDE PRACTICE Repeat the word and have students segment the sounds.

CORRECTIVE FEEDBACK If students are having difficulty, drag each sound out: /kl/ /o/ /g/. Remind students to watch how you move your mouth. Emphasize any sounds that may be different or new to the students' native languages.

4 Spell the Sounds

MODEL Say the first sound and write its spelling. Continue with each sound and spelling until the entire word has been written.

GUIDE PRACTICE Ask a volunteer what letter or letters make the first sound. Write the letter or letters. Repeat with the other sounds. Have students say each sound with you, and then write its spelling after you.

CORRECTIVE FEEDBACK If students have difficulty spelling a sound, have them refer to the Sound-Spelling Card to identify the spelling.

5 Proofread Spelling Continue the dictation until all words have been spelled. Then display the correct spelling for each word. Help students proofread their work, circle any misspelled words, and write them correctly. Help them understand any common errors by asking their reasoning for the mistake. Point out any spelling patterns that do not follow the standard rules or may be different from their native language.

1 **Introduce Talk Video** Explain to students that they will be watching a video. Explain that the video will introduce the Question of the Week.

2 **Assess Understanding** Once the video ends, ask students, "What is the Question of the Week?" Have students write the answer. Then replay the section of the video that answers this question. Pause it when done. Ask students if everyone got the answer right.

3 **Access Prior Knowledge** Invite students to discuss any prior knowledge they have about the weekly question or concept. Encourage them to share their experiences. Invite struggling speakers to draw a picture that illustrates their experience.

4 **Summarize** Begin the video again. Pause it at critical points, such as when new information is taught. Confirm that students understand what they have seen by asking them to summarize the section they just watched.

CORRECTIVE FEEDBACK If students are unable to summarize sections, rewind and watch that section again. Before they attempt to summarize, ask questions that will guide them to understand the main idea of the section.

5 **Graphic Organizer** Draw a two-columned graphic organizer. Title one column *What I Knew* and the next *What I Learned*. Have students fill in the columns using information about the weekly question that they already knew and information they learned while watching the video.

CORRECTIVE FEEDBACK If students struggle when filling in the second column, allow them to watch the video again.

1 **Before Listening** Have students open their Student Edition to the selection. Explain to students that they are going to read along while listening to the selection on a CD.

2 **During Listening** Ask students to keep pace with the CD by moving their finger along the text of their Student Edition. Encourage students to raise their hand if they get lost or hear a phrase or word they do not understand. Pause the CD and write the problem words and phrases. Allow the selection to finish.

3 **Model** Replay the CD, allowing students to watch you choral read along with it. Make sure you imitate not only the words but the expression with which they are read.

4 **After Listening** Review any misunderstood words or phrases. For words, sound each out, calling special attention to blends before putting them all together. Have students choral read the words with you. If a phrase is an idiom, explain its meaning.

5 **On Their Own** Place students in pairs. Instruct them to practice reading sections of the text until they are comfortable reading them at the same pace as the CD. Encourage partners to help each other through passages they may find difficult.

CORRECTIVE FEEDBACK Make sure students do not sacrifice accuracy for speed. If there is a difficult section in the reading, replay it so students can practice.

1 **Introduce Grammar Jammer** Tell students that you will play a song about the weekly convention. Describe what the song is about and how it relates to the lesson.

Example: The song is about adjectives. It tells how to use adjectives to compare people, places, or things.

2 **Display the Concept** Review the concept before playing the song. Write one or more key parts from the song that is supported by the text on the screen.

Example: You can use an adjective to compare two people. Just add an -er.

short + er = short<u>er</u>

tall + er = tall<u>er</u>

loud + er = loud<u>er</u>

quiet + er = quiet<u>er</u>

MODEL Play the song for students. Pause the song at key points to review concepts. Write the text on screen and point to the visuals that support the concept. Replay these parts and model using them to understand the concept.

GUIDE PRACTICE Have students read aloud the text on screen. Prompt students to apply the grammar concepts. Ask questions, provide sentence frames, or have students give more examples.

Example: Shorter, taller, louder, quieter. These are comparative adjectives. Can you give another example?

CORRECTIVE FEEDBACK Replay any parts that students do not understand. Pause to review the text on screen and visuals. Have a volunteer explain how the song relates to the concept. As appropriate, have students use the Journal function to write, using the conventions skill.

1 **Before Listening** Tell students that they will be listening to a CD to help with sound pronunciation. Advise them to keep their Sound-Spelling Cards ready.

2 **During Listening** After each pronunciation, hit Pause. Repeat the sound, exaggerating your mouth movements. Then have students repeat the sound after you. Rewind and play the sound again. Write the letters that make the sound. Repeat it and have students do the same.

Example: The sound is /mp/. The letters that make the sound are m and p. Listen as I say the sound again: /mp/.

3 **After Listening** Guide students to look at the letters you wrote. Then have them match their Sound-Spelling Cards to the sounds they learned. Once again, go through each sound, this time allowing the student to look at his or her card as you do so.

4 **Guided Practice** Hold up a Sound-Spelling Card and call on a volunteer to pronounce the sound. Continue to do so until they have all been pronounced in the order they were learned. Finally, challenge students by rearranging the cards and have them repeat the exercise.

5 **On Their Own** Pair students with partners. Challenge them to pronounce the sound on each card without referring to the CD.

CORRECTIVE FEEDBACK If students have difficulty recalling the sound, replay the CD and point out each example as it plays.

Graphic Organizers

Table of Contents

K-W-L Chart

Topic _____

What Do I **K** now?	What Do I **W** ant to Learn?	What Did I **L** earn?

Word Rating Chart

Word	Know	Have Seen	Don't Know

Story Predictions Chart

Title _____

What might happen?	What clues do I have?	What did happen?

Story Map A

Title _____

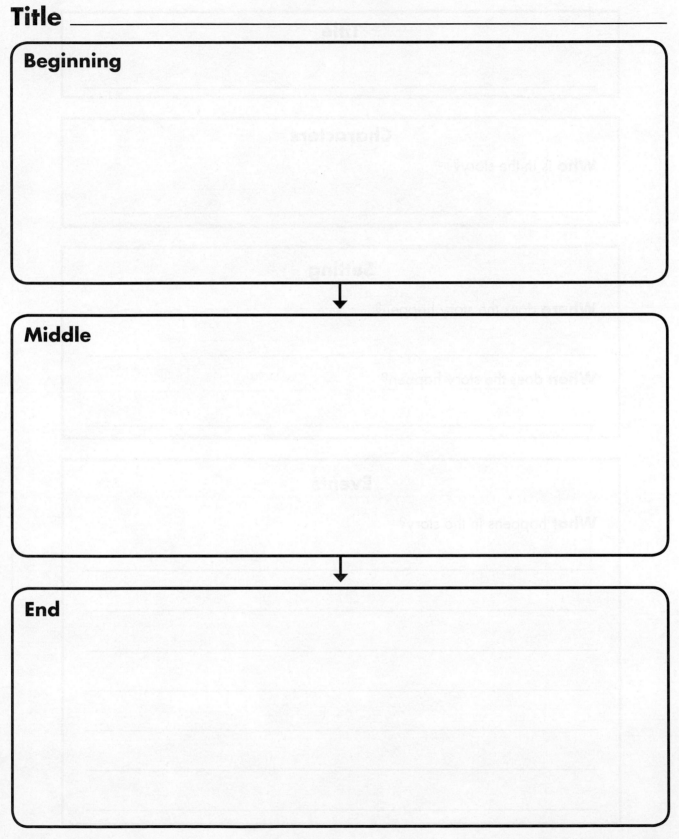

Beginning

Middle

End

Story Map B

Title

_____

Characters

Who is in the story?

_____

Setting

Where does the story happen?

_____

When does the story happen?

_____

Events

What happens in the story?

_____

_____

_____

_____

_____

_____

_____

Story Comparison

Title A _____   **Title B** _____

_____   _____

Characters

Who is in the story?

Setting

Where and **when** does it happen?

Events

What happens in the story?

Characters

Who is in the story?

Setting

Where and **when** does it happen?

Events

What happens in the story?

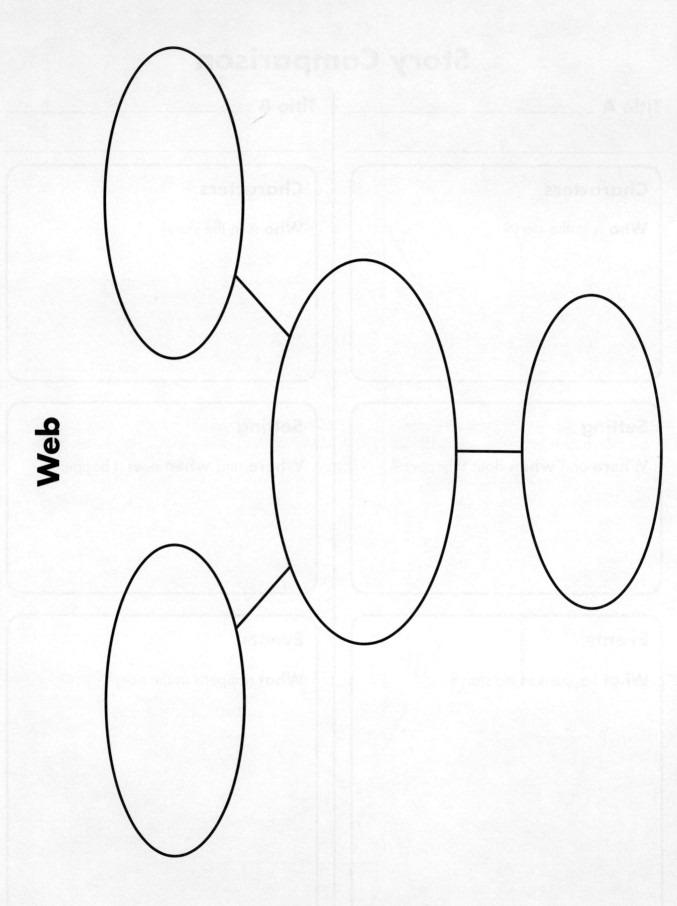

Web

Main Idea

Main Idea

Details

Venn Diagram

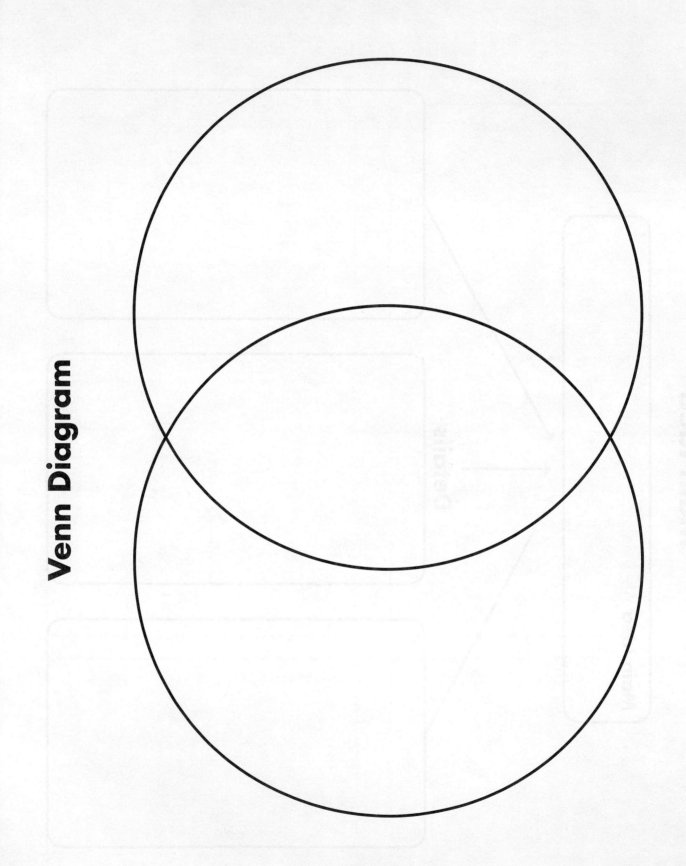

Cause and Effect

Causes

Effects

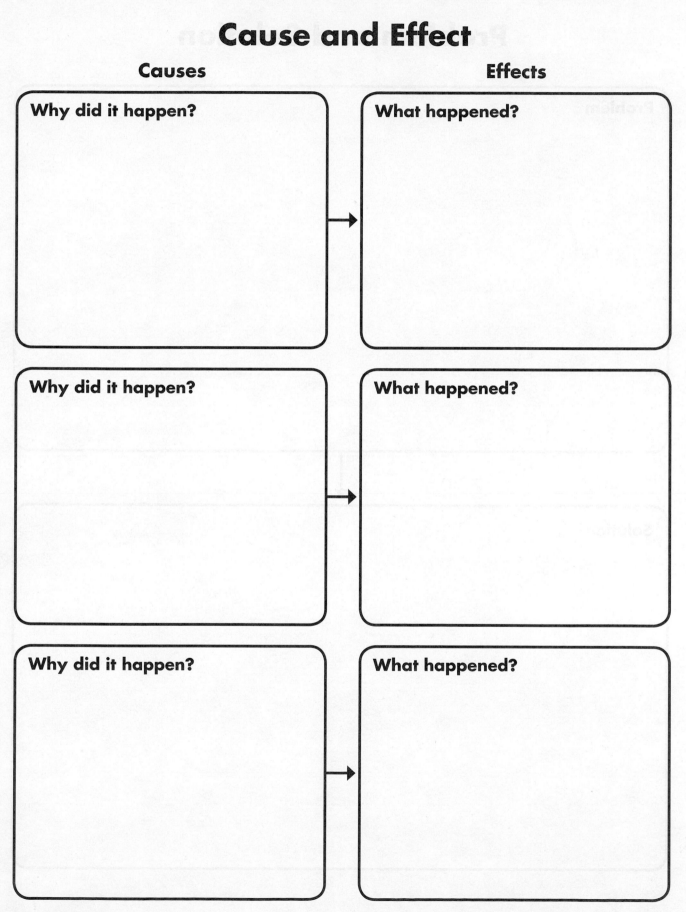

Why did it happen?

What happened?

Why did it happen?

What happened?

Why did it happen?

What happened?

Problem and Solution

Problem

Solution

Time Line

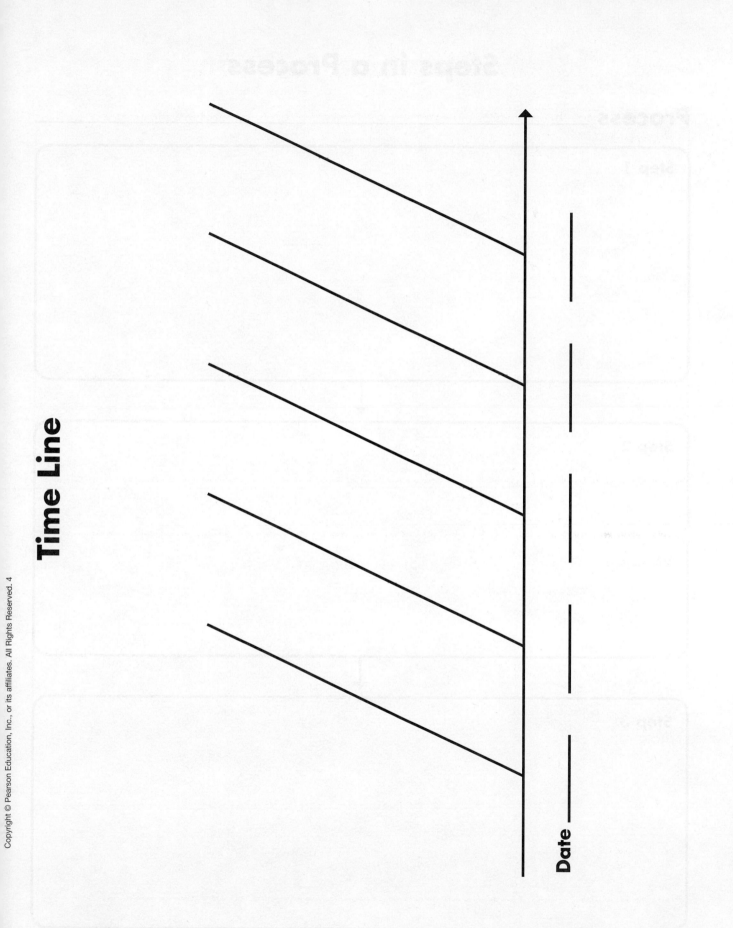

Date _____

Steps in a Process

Process _____

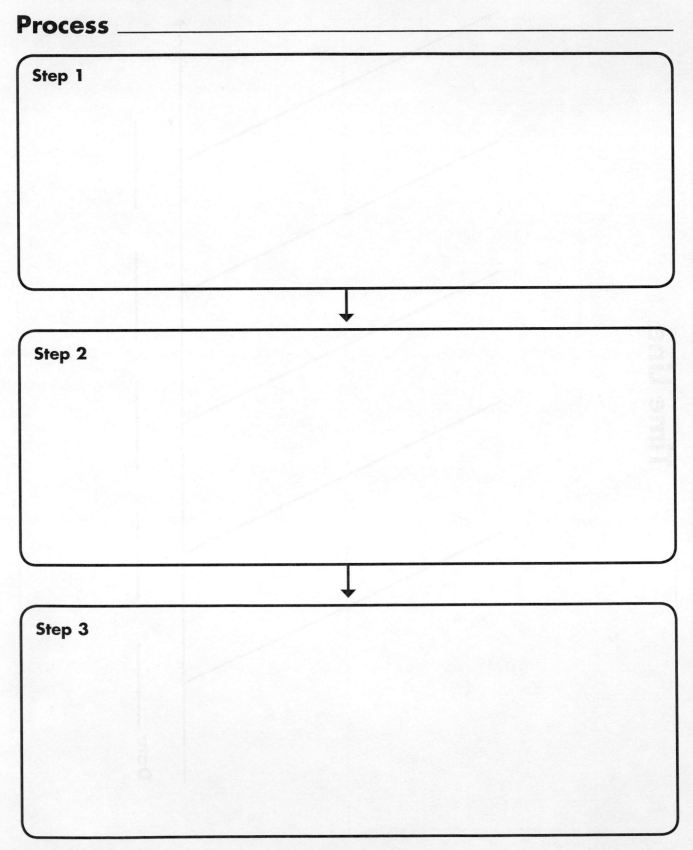

Step 1

Step 2

Step 3

T-Chart

Three-Column Chart

Outline Form

Title _____

A _____

  1. _____

  2. _____

  3. _____

B _____

  1. _____

  2. _____

  3. _____

C _____

  1. _____

  2. _____

  3. _____

K-W-L CHART

About the Graphic Organizer

Students use what they know to explore prior knowledge about a selection, set purposes for reading, and record what they learn as they read.

Instructional Routine

The K-W-L chart works well with expository text. Display the chart for students.

○ Write the word *Know* on the board. Underline the *K*. Tell students that the *K* stands for "What Do I Know?" Ask students what they know about the topic and model, recording their responses.

○ Write *Want* on the board and underline *W*. Tell students that the *W* stands for "What Do I Want to Learn?" Ask students what they want to know about the topic. Model recording their responses in the form of questions.

○ Write *Learn* on the board. Underline the *L*. Tell students that the *L* stands for "What Did I Learn?" As you read, ask students what they are learning. Model recording their responses on the chart.

Teaching Tips

• After modeling, students can complete the K-W-L chart in pairs or small groups.

• Suggest that, if students are unclear about a topic they have recorded in the *K* column, they can turn it into a question for the *L* column.

• Modify the chart if necessary by changing the headings into sentence frames: *I know* _____. *I want to know* _____. *I learned* _____.

Extensions

• Create K-W-L charts that you can post in the room as you learn about different topics in content areas, such as social studies and science. Students can add to the charts as they learn more.

• Have students work in pairs to read an article at their reading level. They can use K-W-L charts to organize their thinking.

Skill and Strategies

• Activate Prior Knowledge

• Set Purpose

• Summarize

WORD RATING CHART

About the Graphic Organizer

The word rating chart helps students explore what words they already know and what words are new to them.

Instructional Routine

You can use this chart with any list of words that students are studying.

○ Display the chart for students and list words on the chart. Have students copy the chart.

○ Explain that the word *Know* means that students know and can use the word. Model placing a check in the second column for words that students know.

○ Explain that column 3, *Have Seen*, means that students have seen or heard the word, but they aren't sure what it means. Model placing a check in the third column.

○ Explain that column 4, *Don't Know*, means that students don't know the word at all. Model placing a check in the fourth column.

Teaching Tips

• After modeling, students can complete a word rating chart on their own. You might write the words in the chart and copy before distributing.

• Use the chart as a diagnostic tool to determine which words you'll focus on in classroom studies.

Extensions

• Have students revisit their chart after they have read a selection or studied the words. They can adjust their ratings.

• Consider adding a column to the chart in which students can write sentences with words they know.

• Encourage students to state meanings of words in their own words. Explain what it means to tell a meaning in your own words.

Skill and Strategies

• Activate Prior Knowledge

• Recall and Retell

• Context Clues

STORY PREDICTIONS CHART

About the Graphic Organizer

Students preview the selection title and illustrations and then predict what might happen in the selection.

Instructional Routine

This graphic organizer works well with any selection in which the title and/or pictures suggest predictions about the events in a story. Consider using it for content-area selections as well.

- Preview the selection with students. Read the title and lead a picture walk. Ask students to predict what they think will happen in the selection. Remind them to use what they know about the topic of the story. Record their predictions in the chart.

- Ask students how they figured out what would happen. Tell them that they used *clues*. Ask what clues they used and record those clues in the chart.

- After reading, look back at the predictions. Write what actually happened in the third column. Ask students how their predictions were different. Why do they think their predictions were different from what really happened?

Teaching Tips

- Focus on clues in illustrations. What details in the illustrations help students make predictions?

- Provide sentence frames for predicting. *I think _____ will happen. I think this will happen because _____.*

Extensions

- After completing this activity as a class exercise, have students use the chart in pairs, small groups, or independently.

- Use the chart with content-area selections. Focus on the content, giving students a sentence frame to use: *I think I will learn about _____ because _____.*

Skill and Strategies

- Predict
- Activate Prior Knowledge
- Draw Conclusions

STORY MAP A

About the Graphic Organizer

Students use this chart to record the sequence of events in a selection.

Instructional Routine

This organizer works well with any selection with a clear sequence of events.

- Display the organizer. Write the title of the selection.

- Start reading. Ask students to tell you what events in the beginning of the story are important. Write them on the chart.

- Focus on events in the middle of the story, recording them in the chart.

- As you finish the selection, record important events from the end.

Teaching Tips

- Make a list of words that tell time order, such as *after, later, first,* or *next.* Provide sentences frames to help students use them.

- Encourage students to use story maps to retell the events to partners.

Extensions

- Have students draw pictures of events in the organizer. They can label the pictures.

- Use the story map with events in social studies or with steps in a sequence in other content-area reading.

Skill and Strategies

- Sequence/Plot
- Recall and Retell
- Text Structure
- Summarize

STORY MAP B

About the Graphic Organizer

Students record the characters and setting of a story and track a sequence of events.

Instructional Routine

This graphic organizer works well with any selection that has a clear series of events. It can help students understand the relationship between the sequence of events and the outcome of the story.

○ Display the organizer. Write the title of the selection on the organizer.

○ Read the selection. Ask students where and when the story takes place. Record those details in the *setting* section.

○ As you read, record information about characters on the organizer.

○ As you read, pause to record information about the sequence of events.

Teaching Tips

• Model sentences frames for talking about characters and setting: _____ *is a person/animal in this story. This story takes place in (the future/the past/today).*

• Help students look for clue words for sequence. Make a list of clue words to display for students' reference.

• Students may not need all the boxes, or they may need more. Help them modify the organizer depending on the story.

Extensions

• After completing this activity as a class exercise, have students use the chart in pairs, small groups, or independently.

• Students can draw events in the organizer and label those events.

• Help students think of words to use to describe characters. Make a list and have students add to it.

Skill and Strategies

• Story Elements: Character, Setting, Plot

• Recall and Retell

• Summarize

STORY COMPARISON

About the Graphic Organizer

Students use this chart to record how two selections are similar and different.

Instructional Routine

This organizer works well with selections that have something in common. It's a great tool for comparing texts by the same author or about the same topic.

○ Choose two stories to compare. Write their titles on the organizer.

○ Ask questions to elicit characters, setting, and plot events. Record details on the chart.

Teaching Tips

• After modeling how to use the organizer, students can work on the organizer with partners or in small groups.

• Provide sentence frames for comparison and model how to use them, such as: *The characters in this story are _____, but the characters in that story are _____.*

• Invite students to use the chart to retell stories.

Extensions

• Students can use the chart to compare a story and a nonfiction text about the same topic.

• Have students use one half the chart to plan the writing of their own story.

Skill and Strategies

• Story Elements: Character, Setting, Plot

• Text Structure

• Summarize

• Compare and Contrast

WEB

About the Graphic Organizer

Students explore their prior knowledge as they brainstorm related ideas, recognize concept relationships, and/or organize information. They can highlight a central concept and connect it to related words, ideas, or details.

Instructional Routine

This graphic organizer has multiple uses and is appropriate for all levels of learners. Use different approaches to the web as you develop the organizer with students.

○ Display the organizer. Write a central idea or topic in the middle of the web.

○ Ask students for ideas that are related to the central idea. Record those ideas in the circles attached to the middle circle.

○ You can add ideas related to the "sub ideas" in additional ovals.

Teaching Tips

• Once you have modeled how to use the organizer, have students complete the organizer independently, in pairs, or in small groups.

• Encourage students to explain how the ideas on the web are related to the central ideas. Provide sentence frames to help students talk about the web. *The main idea is* _____. *One related idea is* _____.

• Use this web to explore main ideas and details, character names along with their traits, vocabulary words and their synonyms, and so on.

Extensions

• Students can use the organizer to record ideas about a theme or about a topic in content-area reading.

• Have students use the web to record background knowledge about a topic. Use the webs to assess gaps in understanding as you plan instruction.

• Enlarge the graphic organizer so that students can draw in the circles. They can label or write sentences about their drawings.

Skill and Strategies

• Classify

• Summarize

• Main Idea and Details

MAIN IDEA

About the Graphic Organizer

Students recognize a main idea and distinguish between the main idea and the details.

Instructional Routine

This organizer works especially well with nonfiction selections that are organized around main ideas and details.

○ Record a main idea in the top box. Define *main idea* as the most important idea.

○ Model by recording a detail that supports, or tells more about, the main idea. Then have students supply additional supporting details as you record them.

Teaching Tips

• Supply a sentence frame about main ideas: *The most important idea is* _____. Supply a sentence frame about supporting details. *One detail about this idea is* _____.

• Model how to tell a supporting detail from a detail that is not a supporting detail. Let students know that some ideas are important to know and other ideas are interesting to know. Display part of a selection and model highlighting important ideas.

• Extend or add additional boxes if necessary to add more details.

Extensions

• Have students use the organizer to record ideas for writing pieces of their own.

• Have students use the chart in pairs or small groups to record important ideas from content-area reading, such as in social studies or science.

Skill and Strategies

• Main Idea and Details

• Summarize

VENN DIAGRAM

About the Graphic Organizer

Students use this organizer to record similarities and differences between places, ideas, characters, or other elements of fiction or nonfiction.

Instructional Routine

A Venn diagram works well in any situation that lends itself to comparing and contrasting.

○ Start by comparing and contrasting something simple and familiar, such as cats and dogs. Write the subjects you are comparing over the circles of the Venn diagram.

○ Point to where the circles overlap. Let students know that in this section, you'll write similarities, or how the two things are alike. Ask how the two subjects are alike. Record students' responses.

○ Point to an individual circle and let students know that, in this section, you'll write details that describe only what is labeled at the top of the circle. Ask students to list details as you record them.

Teaching Tips

• It might help students if you ask questions that lead to details to write in the diagram, such as *Are both of these objects blue? Do both of them have four legs?* and so on.

• Help students with sentence frames: *These two things are alike because _____. These two things are different because _____.*

• List words that signal comparing and contrasting, such as *alike, different, but,* and so on. Students can point to those words in the text.

Extensions

• Students can create Venn diagrams to compare themselves to characters in fictional texts.

• Students can use Venn diagrams to compare topics in content areas, such as comparing two types of rock, two types of volcanoes, or two animals or plants.

Skill and Strategies

• Compare and Contrast

• Summarize

CAUSE AND EFFECT

About the Graphic Organizer

Students identify cause-and-effect relationships in either fiction or nonfiction.

Instructional Routine

This graphic organizer works well with any selection that has clear cause-and-effect relationships.

○ Tell students that something that happens is an effect. Record an effect on the graphic organizer.

○ Then ask students "Why did it happen?" Tell them the reason something happens is a cause. Record the cause on the graphic organizer.

Teaching Tips

• Remind students to ask themselves *What happened?* and *Why did it happen?* to identify effects and causes. It is usually easier to identify effects first, before the causes.

• List clue words that signal causes and effects, such as *because* and *so.* Look over the clue words with students, but remind them that not all causes and effects in selections have clue words.

Extensions

• Students can write causes and effects in their content-area classes. They could record, for example, causes of thunderstorms or of events in history.

• Once students are able to use this organizer, point out that, in some cases, there are many causes for one effect or many effects for one cause. Alter the organizer with students so they can use it with multiple causes and effects.

• If students need extra assistance, fill in either causes or effects before distributing the organizer. Ask students to work in pairs to find the corresponding causes or effects.

Skill and Strategies

• Cause and Effect

• Summarize

• Text Structure

PROBLEM AND SOLUTION

About the Graphic Organizer

Students identify problems and solutions presented in fiction or nonfiction.

Instructional Routine

This graphic organizer works well with any selection with clear problems and solutions.

○ Tell students that a problem is something that needs to be solved. Give an example of a simple classroom problem. Record it in the organizer.

○ Ask students what they might do to "fix" the problem. Tell students that fixing a problem is solving a problem. Ask students how they might solve the problem. Record their ideas in the solution section.

Teaching Tips

• Once students understand how to use the organizer, focus on a problem and solution from a piece of text.

• Point out that not all solutions are "good." Sometimes the way a character solves a problem might result in an unhappy ending for the story.

• Provide sentence frames to help students discuss problems and solutions. *One problem in the text is _____. One way to solve it is _____.*

Extensions

• Write a problem in the school, classroom, or community in the first box and distribute organizers to pairs or small groups. Students can brainstorm solutions.

• Students can draw problems and solutions in the organizer and then label them with words or phrases.

Skill and Strategies

• Plot

• Summarize

• Text Structure

TIME LINE

About the Graphic Organizer

Students organize events from fiction or nonfiction in sequential order along a continuum.

Instructional Routine

This organizer works well with any selection that presents events in sequential order. It can also help students organize events in order.

○ After reading a short text, ask students what happened first. Record the first event on the chart.

○ Continue asking students to name events in order, placing them on the continuum.

Teaching Tips

• Remind students to look for clues in the text to the order in which things happen. They might find dates or clue words such as *first, next, then,* and *last.*

• If students need extra support, write events from the text on sentence strips. Have students work in pairs or small groups to place the strips in order and then write the events on the time line.

Extensions

• Students can create time lines about events in history or even things that have happened in their school or community.

• Have students interview partners and create time lines based on important events in their partners' lives.

• Share time lines from social studies texts with students. Have them discuss what the time lines have in common and identify their features.

Skill and Strategies

• Summarize

• Text Structure

• Sequence/Plot

STEPS IN A PROCESS

About the Graphic Organizer

Students break down a process into simple steps or directions.

Instructional Routine

This graphic organizer works well with any procedure that has relatively few steps. If students need more or smaller steps, help students redesign the organizer.

○ Display the organizer. Write the title on the organizer, such as *Making a Peanut Butter Sandwich*.

○ Ask students what the first step is. Record the first step in the organizer.

○ Write the remaining steps in the organizer in order as students supply them.

Teaching Tips

• Once students can contribute to a steps in a process chart, have them work in pairs or small groups to write the steps of a simple process.

• Tell students to look for clue words such as *first, next,* and *later* to help them sequence the steps.

Extensions

• Students may draw the steps in the organizer and label them with words or phrases.

• Have students use the organizer to show steps in a recipe, a science project, or in another content area.

Skill and Strategies

• Steps in a Process

• Sequence

• Visualize

T-CHART

About the Graphic Organizer

Students can explore and compare ideas, story elements, or vocabulary words. They can also chart ideas within and across texts, or between prior knowledge and new ideas.

Instructional Routine

This is a multipurpose graphic organizer that is helpful when exploring two concepts. It works well with all types of selections.

○ Model using the chart. Display the chart and write two topics being studied on the chart, one topic per column.

○ Elicit responses from students based on the topics chosen. Record responses in the chart.

Teaching Tips

• Students can write in the chart, but they can also draw and list or label.

• Students can use the T-chart to compare story elements, such as the traits of two characters.

• Use a T-chart to organize ideas gathered in a class brainstorming session.

• Use a T-chart to explore two vocabulary words. Write the words at the tops of the columns. Then under each word, list part of speech, a simple definition, and a sentence using the word in context.

Extensions

• Students can work with partners, each partner completing one half of the chart.

• Students can use T-charts to write the pros and cons of a topic for a debate or discussion.

Skill and Strategies

• Compare and Contrast

• Main Idea and Details

• Summarize

• Activate Prior Knowledge

THREE-COLUMN CHART

About the Graphic Organizer

The chart can be used to explore or classify ideas, story elements, genres, or vocabulary features. It can also help students recognize comparisons and contrasts, or chart ideas within and across texts.

Instructional Routine

This is a multi-purpose organizer that works well for exploring and organizing ideas for three concepts, words, or ideas. It works well with many selections.

○ Display the organizer. Choose three simple headings and write them on the chart, such as three different vocabulary words.

○ Ask students for details for each heading and record them on the chart. Point out that this chart helps organize information.

Teaching Tips

• Once you have modeled how to use the organizer, students can complete organizers independently or in pairs or small groups.

• Students can draw in the charts as well as list ideas.

• Students can use the three-column chart to explore story characteristics or characteristics of genre.

• Students can use the chart to organize ideas they generate during brainstorming.

• Students can use the chart to organize synonyms, antonyms, and multiple meanings of words. Create a class chart to model using the chart for vocabulary study.

Extensions

• Students can use the organizer to record ideas that follow the idea of *before, during,* and *after.*

• Students can use the chart to organize ideas in any curricular area. For example, students could organize odd numbers, even numbers, and prime numbers in math. In science, they could record details about categories of animals, such as birds, reptiles, and mammals.

Skill and Strategies

• Classify

• Summarize

• Main Idea and Details

• Activate Prior Knowledge

OUTLINE FORM

About the Graphic Organizer

Students use a simplified outline form to take notes on the organization of print materials or to organize their own thoughts before writing.

Instructional Routine

Writers can change the outline form to suit their own purposes, but this form gets students started with the basic outline organization.

○ Model using the outline form by outlining a simple text. Place the title on the top line.

○ Show students how to record the main ideas. You might display the text to point out where to find the main ideas in the text. Reread the main ideas as you record them on the form.

○ Break down the main ideas into smaller details on the secondary lines.

○ Model the same form as the basis for a class writing about something that you are currently studying.

Teaching Tips

• Depending on their English proficiency, students can use words, phrases, or sentences in their outlines. Encourage them to be consistent throughout the entire outline.

• If students use outlines for writing, point out that the outlines are tools that can be revised before and during writing if the organization will make more sense.

Extensions

• Create an outline by doing a class outline on a piece of content-area text, such as an article from a science book.

• Show students text features in a content-area book, such as titles, heads, subheads, labels, and captions. Ask how these features might help them create an outline.

Skill and Strategies

• Text Structure

• Summarize

• Main Idea and Details